Economics

Economics

Michael Bradley

University of Maryland, Baltimore County

Scott, Foresman and Company

Glenview, Illinois
Dallas, Tex.   Oakland, N.J.   Palo Alto, Cal.
Tucker, Ga.   London, England

To my family,
with love and thanks

Library of Congress Cataloging in Publication Data

Bradley, Michael, 1939-
   Economics.

   Includes index.
   1. Economics. I. Title.
HB171.5.B6946   1980   330   79-22968
ISBN 0-673-15231-6

Copyright © 1980 Scott, Foresman and Company.
All Rights Reserved.
Printed in the United States of America.

2345678910-KPF-858483828180

Preface

In the preface to the first edition of his *Principles of Political Economy* in 1848, John Stuart Mill wrote, "The appearance of a treatise like the present, on a subject on which so many works of merit already exist, may be thought to require some explanation." There are far more "works of merit" on economic principles available today than there were in 1848. Why, then, produce yet another?

Economics offers a much-needed alternative to the other principles texts currently on the market. It fills a gap between the massive encyclopedic texts that attempt to include every conceivable institutional detail and the shorter books that skimp on explanations and applications. The book also fills a widening gap between the increasingly simplified principles texts and the increasingly sophisticated and rigorous texts at the intermediate level. For students who don't go beyond the principles course, *Economics* provides a solid foundation in economic thinking that will enable them to evaluate issues logically and analytically and remain skeptical of seemingly simple solutions to complex problems. For students who pursue further study in economics, the text provides a sound preparation for intermediate and upper-level courses.

Economics isn't a particularly easy subject to learn, but it isn't made any easier by oversimplifications or shallow explanations. *Economics* reflects my own experience in teaching principles courses and my basic optimism concerning students' motivation to learn and instructors' motivation to teach. Nothing is made unnecessarily difficult, but I haven't shied away from the fact that some important concepts are difficult and that solutions to complex problems aren't to be found in simplistic bromides. All topics are presented clearly, in terms that can be easily understood by undergraduate students and with maximum use of real-world illustrations and applications.

Controversy is a vital part of modern economics which cannot and should not be ignored. *Economics* examines several areas of current economic debate, giving fair treatment to opposing arguments and alternative solutions to problems. I have been careful throughout the book to distinguish between positive and normative questions, pointing out the limitations as well as the strengths of economic analysis in resolving issues that are partly positive and partly normative.

Organization

Economics is intended to serve as the text in one-year introductory courses at the university level. The text is written in a micro-macro-international sequence. However, the chapters are designed to give instructors maximum flexibility in the order in which they present the material. Suggested outlines for alternative course formats are included in the *Instructor's Manual* that accompanies the text. For instructors who teach only half of the sequence, *Economics* is also available in split paperback volumes.

The introductory section on demand, supply, markets, and equilibrium provides an important foundation for both microeconomics and macroeconomics and should serve as a starting point for any course in economics. This compact (3-chapter) overview therefore appears in both paperback volumes, *Microeconomics* and *Macroeconomics*.

The microeconomic analysis proceeds logically from the rational, maximizing actions of households and firms to equilibrium price and output in markets. The sections on markets and market structures are organized differently than in most other texts, presenting perfectly competitive product and resource markets in sequence, followed by monopolistic and imperfectly competitive markets. However, these chapters are written so that instructors can present the material in the more traditional order if they wish.

The macroeconomics portion of the text reflects many recent developments in macroeconomic analysis. The basic Keynesian income determination model and the chapters on money present aggregate demand in an economy with a constant price level. This sets the stage for a comprehensive treatment of contemporary unemployment and inflation, utilizing a fully developed model of aggregate supply and aggregate demand. An analysis of policy strategies to deal with unemployment and inflation through demand and supply management concludes the macro section.

The chapters on international economics stress basic principles of trade and exchange and apply those principles to a number of current trade policy issues. The final section of the text, on economic growth and development and alternative economic systems, provides students with a sense of the kinds of important economic choices that must be made in coming years.

Special Features

This book contains a number of special features to make it more useful to students and instructors.

Previews at the beginning of each chapter and each part provide an overview of the material that will be covered and show how it fits into the overall structure of the text. These previews give students a sense of continuity as they study.

Definitions and key points are set off from the text and highlighted. This calls students' attention to important concepts and makes subsequent review of the material much easier.

Applications are used frequently to reinforce the relevance of the analysis and enhance student interest by breaking up the analytical discussions. Two types of applications appear throughout the text. Relatively brief **Close-ups** demonstrate the real-world basis of many theoretical concepts. Longer **Applying the Tools** provide detailed applications of analytical techniques to important problems and issues of yesterday and today.

Questions and Problems at the end of every chapter require the student to apply the concepts that he or she has learned. Some of the questions are straightforward and analytical with clear-cut answers; others are more subtle "discussion" questions that point out not only the ways that analysis can be applied, but also some of its limitations. The problems at the end of nearly every chapter are designed to make students more comfortable with analytical tools and concepts by working with them.

Appendices are used to increase instructors' flexibility in teaching from *Economics*. A mathematical appendix to Chapter 1 concisely reviews virtually all of the mathematical concepts used in principles of economics courses. In addition to providing a review, it can help make students less anxious about the difficulty of the math required. Appendices at the end of other chapters treat special topics—the *IS-LM* model and benefit-cost analysis, for example —in more depth and more analytical detail than would be expected in most principles courses.

Supplementary materials serve as important aids to instructors and students. Accompanying *Economics* is an **Instructor's Manual** that provides helpful teaching tips and suggested answers to chapter questions and problems, as well as nearly two thousand test questions. For those who adopt the text, **Transparency Masters** of the most important figures and tables will also be available. For students, excellent **Study Guides** by Bruce Allen of Michigan State University and Bruce Mann of the University of Puget Sound provide ample opportunity for further applying the analytical tools studied in *Economics*.

Acknowledgments

In this book's seemingly endless gestation period, I have received a great deal of help from many colleagues and friends. I have deluged my colleagues in the economics department at UMBC with questions and manuscript pages for comments and suggestions. I would, of course, be remiss if I didn't also acknowledge the contributions of the several thousands of students who have taken principles of economics with me—their hard questions and unwillingness to accept inadequate explanations have contributed greatly to this work.

Like many authors, I consider criticism of my work a bad-tasting medicine that is good for me. My book has benefitted greatly from the comments of the following excellent (but tough) reviewers of the manuscript:

Elizabeth Allison, Harvard University
William J. Barber, Wesleyan University
John Chizmar, Illinois State University
Ward S. Curran, Trinity College (Conn.)
Thomas Dalton, Northern Illinois University
Richard W. Douglas, Bowling Green State University
Lawrence Haverkamp, Northwestern University
James Johannes, Michigan State University
Steven Klepper, SUNY, Buffalo
Prem Laumas, Northern Illinois University
Bruce Mann, University of Puget Sound
Jeffrey Miller, University of Delaware

W. Douglas Morgan, University of California, Santa Barbara
Richard Rosenberg, Pennsylvania State University
Michael Salemi, University of North Carolina
Richard T. Selden, University of Virginia
Rosalind Seneca, Columbia University
George Tauchen, Duke University
Barbara White, SUNY, Buffalo
Roberton Williams, Williams College

My special thanks go to Professor Bruce T. Allen of Michigan State University, who remains my toughest critic and one of my closest friends. The people at Scott, Foresman have also been extremely helpful. I want to thank in particular Bruce Borland and George Lobell for signing the project and managing it to completion, and Dane Tyson, who is without peer as an editor. My appreciation goes as well to the many designers, artists, typesetters, and others who contributed so much to the book.

Finally, I must thank my wife, Ann, and my children, Sarah and Jim, for their support and understanding through an experience from which most families are spared.

Columbia, Maryland   Michael Bradley

Contents

Part One

An Introduction to Economics 1

1 The Art and Science of Economics 2

THEORIES, MODELS, AND FACTS 3
  Building and Testing Economic Theories   Marginal Analysis   Ex Ante and Ex Post   Why Bother with Theory at All?
POSITIVE AND NORMATIVE ARGUMENTS 8
A CONCLUDING REMARK 9

APPENDIX: A BRIEF MATHEMATICAL REVIEW 11
  Hypotheses, Functions, and Equations   Graphs   The Elements of Statistical Estimation

2 Scarcity and Choice: The Economic Problem 24

THE LIMITS ON PRODUCTION 24
  Limited Resources   Technology
THE ECONOMIC PROBLEM 25
THREE BASIC ECONOMIC QUESTIONS 26
  What?   How?   For Whom?
PRODUCTION POSSIBILITIES 28
  The Production Possibilities Curve   Opportunity Cost   Technology and Production   Close-up: Technological Change in Agriculture   Growth vs. Consumption   Close-up: The Soviet Forced Industrialization Drive

APPLYING THE TOOLS: THE COST AND ECONOMIC IMPACT OF WORLD WAR II 35

THE ECONOMIC SYSTEM 36

3 Demand, Supply, and Price: An Overview 39

HOUSEHOLDS, FIRMS, AND MARKETS 39
  Consumer Sovereignty   Markets and Democracy
PRICES IN THE MARKET ECONOMY 41
DEMAND AND PRICE 42
  The Demand Schedule and the Demand Curve   Changes in Quantity Demanded vs. Changes in Demand
SUPPLY AND PRICE 45
  The Supply Schedule and the Supply Curve   Changes in Quantity Supplied vs. Changes in Supply
EQUILIBRIUM PRICE 48
  Changes in Equilibrium Price

APPLYING THE TOOLS: THE BASIC ECONOMICS OF PRICE CONTROLS 53
  Rent Controls and Housing Shortages   Farm Price Supports and Minimum Wages

PARTIAL AND GENERAL EQUILIBRIUM 56

4 Elasticity of Demand and Supply 62

SLOPE AS A MEASURE OF RESPONSIVENESS 62
ELASTICITY OF DEMAND 66
  Determinants of Elasticity of Demand   Elasticity Along the Demand Curve   Elasticity and Total Revenue   Some Constant Elasticity Demand Curves

APPLYING THE TOOLS: THE ECONOMICS OF BUSTING PUSHERS 73

ELASTICITY OF SUPPLY 75
  Elasticity and the Supply Curve   Time and the Elasticity of Supply

APPLYING THE TOOLS: WHO PAYS EXCISE TAXES? 78

Part Two

Demand in the Product Market   83

5 Product Demand: The Household 84

THE CONCEPT OF UTILITY 84
  Cardinal vs. Ordinal Utility   Total Utility   Marginal Utility   Diminishing Marginal Utility
THE HOUSEHOLD'S PREFERENCE 87
  Indifference Curves   The Household's Indifference Map
THE HOUSEHOLD'S INCOME CONSTRAINT 90
THE HOUSEHOLD'S PREFERENCE 92
  Maximizing Utility: Marginal Utility Approach   Maximizing Utility: Indifference Curve Approach

APPLYING THE TOOLS: INDIFFERENCE ANALYSIS AND HOUSEHOLD BUDGETING 95

THE HOUSEHOLD'S DEMAND CURVE 96
  Marginal Utility and Demand   Indifference Curves and the Household's Demand Curve
CHANGES IN THE HOUSEHOLD'S DEMAND 98
  Changes in Money Income   "Normal" and "Inferior" Goods   Changes in Prices of Other Goods   Changes in Tastes

APPLYING THE TOOLS: FOOD STAMPS VS. INCOME SUBSIDIES 102

6 Product Demand: The Market 107

HOUSEHOLD AND MARKET DEMAND CURVES 107
CHANGES IN MARKET DEMAND 109
    Close-up: Advertising, Tastes, and Demand   Close-up: Population and Demand in Urban Housing Markets
ELASTICITIES OF MARKET DEMAND 111
    Price Elasticity of Demand   Income Elasticity of Demand   Close-up: The Incidence of Sales Tax   Cross-Elasticity of Demand

APPLYING THE TOOLS: THE DEMAND FOR AUTOMOBILE TRAVEL 114
    Dealing with the Problem: "More Freeways"   Dealing with the Problem: Raising the Price   Dealing with the Problem: Improving Substitutes   Some Conclusions

Part Three

Supply in the Product Market   121

7 Production In the Short Run 122

WHY THE FIRM PRODUCES 122
    Behavioral Theories of the Firm   Close-up: Why the Firm Produces: A Simple Behavioral Analysis   Marginalist Theories of the Firm   Close-up: Why the Firm Produces: A Simple Marginalist Analysis   Which Approach Is Best?
HOW THE FIRM PRODUCES 125
    The Firm's Production Function   Total Product (TP)   Marginal Product (MP)   Average Product (AP)   Close-up: Productivity
THE PRINCIPLE OF DIMINISHING RETURNS 131
CHANGES IN THE PRODUCTION FUNCTION 133

APPLYING THE TOOLS: POPULATION GROWTH AND HUNGER IN THE THIRD WORLD 134

8 Output and Cost in the Short Run 138

ECONOMIC COST AND PROFIT 138
    Close-up: Economic Cost vs. Accounting Cost   Close-up: "How Ya Gonna Keep 'em Down on the Farm (After They Pay Their Property Taxes)?"
THE FIRM'S COST OF PRODUCTION 142
    Total Cost (TC)   Marginal Cost (MC)   Average Cost (AC)   Close-up: "We Never (or Nearly Never) Close"   Short-Run Cost Relationships
CHANGES IN SHORT-RUN COST 150
    Change in Fixed Cost   Change in Variable Cost

9 Production and Cost in the Long Run 155

THE SUBSTITUTION OPTION 156
    Isoquants   Marginal Rate of Technical Substitution ($MRTS$)   The Isoquant Map   Isocost Lines   Economic Efficiency: The Isocost-Isoquant Model

APPLYING THE TOOLS: COAL MINING AND "LEWIS' LAW" 163

THE SIZE OPTION 164
    Returns to Scale   The Firm's Expansion Path   Long-Run Total Cost ($LRTC$)   Long-Run Average Cost ($LRAC$) and Returns to Scale   The Shape of the $LRAC$ Curve
BEYOND THE LONG RUN: TECHNOLOGICAL CHANGE 171
    Close-up: Economies of Scale, Technological Change, and the Cost of Electric Power   Types of Technological Change   Is Technological Change "Good for the Community"?   Close-up: Man vs. Machine

Part Four

Perfect Competition

10 The Perfectly Competitive Product Market 180

CHARACTERISTICS OF PERFECTLY COMPETITIVE PRODUCT MARKETS 180
  Price Takers   Identical Products   Atomistic Competition   Market Information   Freedom of Entry and Exit   Close-up: Price Takers in the Stock Market

THE FIRM IN PERFECT COMPETITION 182
  Demand for the Firm's Output   Revenue   Equilibrium Output   Profit or Loss   The Shut-Down Point   The Short-Run Supply Curve

THE INDUSTRY IN THE SHORT RUN 191
  Market Period Supply   Short-Run Supply   Short-Run Equilibrium

THE INDUSTRY IN THE LONG RUN 193
  Long-Run Supply   Changes in Long-Run Supply

APPLYING THE TOOLS: COMPETITION AND POLICY IN U.S. AGRICULTURE 200
  Unstable Prices and Incomes   "Crime Doesn't Pay (Neither Does Farming)"   Government Price Supports   Who Gains Most from Price Supports?

11 The Perfectly Competitive Resource Market 208

CHARACTERISTICS OF PERFECTLY COMPETITIVE RESOURCE MARKETS 209
  Price Takers   Atomistic Competition   Market Information and Resource Mobility   Homogeneous Resources

EQUILIBRIUM RESOURCE PRICES 210

RESOURCE DEMAND: A CLOSER LOOK 210
  Marginal Factor Cost (*MFC*)   Marginal Revenue Product (*MRP*)   Increasing and Diminishing Returns Again   The Firm's Demand   Market Demand   Elasticity of Resource Demand

APPLYING THE TOOLS: THE ECONOMICS OF MINIMUM WAGES 218

RESOURCE SUPPLY: A CLOSER LOOK 219
  Wages, Leisure, and the Household's Supply of Labor   Interest and the Supply of Capital   Rent and the Supply of Land   Close-up: The Single Tax Movement in the United States   Rent on Special Abilities and Talents   Close-up: Two "Big E's": Elvin and Evert   Changes in Resource Supply

PERFECT COMPETITION AND INCOME DISTRIBUTION 227
  Functional Distribution of Income   Size Distribution of Income   Wage Differences

12 Perfect Competition: The Best of All Worlds? 233

THE MEANING OF EFFICIENCY 234
  Minimizing the Cost of a Given Output   Optimum Firm Size and Output   Marginal Cost Pricing   Efficiency of Resource Allocation

THE EFFICIENCY OF PERFECT COMPETITION 237
  Efficiency in Pricing and Output   Zero Profit, Optimum Firm Size, and Optimum Output   Efficiency in Resource Allocation   Efficiency of Information

MARKET FAILURES 241
    Public Goods   Close-up: "Please Help Us Stay on the Air"
    Externalities   External Social Costs   Close-up: Smoking Grass or: "How Green Was My Valley"   External Social Benefits and Efficiency   Externalities and Government Policy

APPLYING THE TOOLS: MAKING POLLUTERS PAY 247

PERFECT COMPETITION AND WELFARE: EQUITY 248
DOES COMPETITION DESTROY ITSELF?

APPENDIX: BENEFIT-COST ANALYSIS 253
    Defining Objectives   Identifying Benefits and Costs   Quantifying Benefits and Costs   Benefit-Cost Ratios   The Usefulness of Benefit-Cost Analysis

Part Five

Monopoly and Imperfect Competition   259

13 Monopoly 260

WHAT IS MONOPOLY? 260
    Close-up: 28 Varieties of Ice Cream, One Variety of Restaurant
THE MONOPOLIST'S DEMAND AND REVENUE 261
    Close-up: "We're the Only Phone Company in Town"   The Monopolist's Marginal Revenue   Marginal Revenue and Elasticity of Demand
THE MONOPOLIST'S EQUILIBRIUM 264
MONOPOLY, COMPETITION, AND THE COMMUNITY 266
    Price and Marginal Cost   Efficiency and Economic Profit   Consumer Surplus and "Deadweight Loss"
PRICE DISCRIMINATION 271
    Market Splitting and Peak Load Pricing   Close-up: Peak-Load Pricing: Water Rates   Block Pricing

APPLYING THE TOOLS: NATURAL MONOPOLY AND PUBLIC UTILITIES 274
    Finding the Right Price   Unprofitable Public Utilities

IMPACT OF MONOPOLY ON THE LABOR MARKET 278
    VMP and MRP for a Monopolist   Employment and Exploitation of Labor
THE MONOPOLY MODEL: A FINAL NOTE 280

14 Imperfect Competition in the Product Market 284

WHAT IS "IMPERFECT" COMPETITION? 284
THE FIRM AND THE INDUSTRY 285
    Interdependence of Firms' Demand   The Firm's Equilibrium   Short-Run Industry Equilibrium   Close-up: NOW Accounts and Price Wars in Banking   Long-Run Industry Equilibrium
OLIGOPOLY: COMPETITION AMONG THE FEW 292
    Interdependence and Strategic Decision Making   The *Kinked* Demand Curve   The Cost of Changing Prices   Formal Collusion and Cartels   Close-up: Cartels: The Shakiest of Marriages   Informal Collusion: Gentlemen's Agreements and Price Leadership   Close-up: How "Kinky" Is Oligopoly Demand?

HOW IMPERFECT COMPETITORS "COMPETE" 300
    Quality and Service Competition   Advertising and Product Differentiation   Close-up: An Aspirin Is an Aspirin Is an Aspirin   Deception and Consumerism   Innovation and Competition

15 Market Power and the Role of Government 308

ANTITRUST POLICY 310
    Antitrust Laws   "Workable Competition"   Problems of Antitrust   Close-up: The Wheels of Antitrust Justice Grind Exceedingly Slow   Close-up: A Case of Mistaken Identity?
PUBLIC REGULATION 315
    Health and Safety Regulations   Regulations and Externalities   Regulation of Markets, Industries, and Firms   Close-up: "Who's in Charge Here?" (Regulating the Safety of Kitty Litter Miners)   How Much and What Kinds of Regulation? Close-up: The Dismantling of the C.A.B., 1976–1985
NATIONALIZATION AND PUBLIC OWNERSHIP 321

16 Imperfections in Labor Markets 326

MONOPOLY IN THE SALE OF LABOR: THE ECONOMICS OF LABOR UNIONS 326
    Legal Status of Trade Unions   What Do Unions Maximize?   Unions and Wages: Craft Unions   Unions and Wages: Industrial Unions   Bargaining Power
MONOPSONY IN THE PURCHASE OF LABOR 332
    Monopsony and Employment   Monopsony and "Exploitation"   Close-up: Monopsony and Professional Sports
INSTITUTIONAL IMPERFECTIONS 335
    Lack of Market Information   Geographic Immobility   Occupational Immobility   Immobility, Transfer Price, and Rent
DISCRIMINATION 338
    Discrimination: What Is It?   Equal Pay for Equal Work   Education, Productivity, and Mobility

APPLYING THE TOOLS: DISCRIMINATION AND WOMEN'S WAGES 341
    Hours Worked   Industry and Occupation   Experience and Labor Force Participation Patterns   Education and Training   Broadly Defined Occupation   Last, But Not Least, Discrimination   Improving the Economic Status of Women

Part Six

Economic Challenges for the Eighties 349

17 Energy and the Economy 350

CHEAP ENERGY AND THE DEPLETION OF RESERVES 351
DEALING WITH THE PROBLEM 352
    Price Deregulation   Reducing Demand   Relaxing Environmental Standards   Alternative Energy Sources   Close-up: The Three-Mile Island "Incident" and the Costs of Nuclear Power   Won't Anything Work?
A VERY SHORT CONCLUSION 363

18 Poverty
366

HOW POOR IS POOR? 367
    "Relative" Poverty   "Absolute" Poverty
THE POOR: WHO AND HOW MANY? 371
    Poverty, Race, and National Origin   Poverty and Sex   Education and Poverty   Unemployment and Poverty
THE ECONOMIC ROOTS OF POVERTY 373
SEARCHING FOR SOLUTIONS 374
    Full Employment and Economic Growth   Investing in Human Capital   Geographic Mobility   Equal Employment Opportunity
PUBLIC ASSISTANCE AND TRANSFERS 378
    Transfers in Kind vs. Cash Transfers   The Negative Income Tax (NIT)   **Close-up: Welfare, Negative Income Taxes, and Incentive**   The Level of Transfer Benefits   Welfare Fraud
THE ROAD AHEAD 382

Part Seven

Understanding the Aggregate Economy   385

19 Introduction to Macroeconomics
386

THE VILLAINS: UNEMPLOYMENT AND INFLATION 387
    The Aggregate Demand-Aggregate Supply Model: A Sneak Preview   Inflation and Unemployment in the YD-YS Model
VARIETIES OF MACROECONOMIC THINKING 392
    Classical Macroeconomics: The Old Orthodoxy   Keynesian Macroeconomics: The "New" Orthodoxy   Monetarism: The Classical Resurgence   Macroeconomics in the 1980s: Sound and Fury Signifying Much

20 Measuring Aggregate Output, Income, and Prices
398

THE FLOW OF NATIONAL INCOME AND OUTPUT: AN OVERVIEW 399
MEASURING NATIONAL INCOME AND OUTPUT 400
    Gross National Product (GNP)   **Close-up: The *Value Added* Tax**   Measuring GNP: The Expenditure Approach   Measuring GNP: The Factor Payments Approach   **Close-up: Are the National Income Accounts *Sexist*?**   Net National Product (NNP)   National Income (NI)   Personal Income (PI)   Disposable Personal Income (DI)
MEASURING CHANGES IN PRICES AND OUTPUT 409
    Real and Nominal Income   Consumer Price Index (CPI)   Implicit Price Deflator (IPD) and Real GNP
GNP AS A MEASURE OF ECONOMIC WELFARE 413
    Per Capita Income   Pattern of Income Distribution   Composition of GNP   GNP and Gross National Cost

APPENDIX: HOW NOT TO BE FOOLED BY GROWTH INDEXES 418
    Real and Nominal Growth   Look at the Base Year   Price Weights and the "Index Number Problem"

Part Eight

Aggregate Demand: The Goods Market   421

21 Aggregate Demand and Income Determination: The Private Sector 422

AGGREGATE DEMAND AND OUTPUT IN THE CIRCULAR FLOW   423
    Unintended Investment   Equilibrium Output
CONSUMPTION   430
    Marginal Propensity to Consume   Autonomous Consumption
    Estimates of the Consumption Function, 1929–1978   Consumption and Saving
INVESTMENT   437
THE SIMPLE KEYNESIAN MODEL   440
    Equilibrium in the Simple Keynesian Model   Calculating Equilibrium GNP in the Simple Model   Aggregate Demand, Unemployment, and Inflation

22 Aggregate Demand and Income Determination: Completing the Model 448

THE PUBLIC SECTOR   448
    Government Spending   Net Taxes
THE INTERNATIONAL SECTOR   449
EQUILIBRIUM IN THE COMPLETE MODEL   449
    Aggregate Demand in the Complete Model   Aggregate Demand and Equilibrium GNP
CHANGES IN EQUILIBRIUM INCOME   454

APPLYING THE TOOLS: AGGREGATE DEMAND AND WORLD WAR II   455

    Changes in Savings and the Paradox of Thrift
THE MULTIPLIER EFFECT   458
    How It Works   The Multiplier in the Keynesian Model   The Size of the Multiplier
THE KEYNESIAN MODEL: SOME PRECAUTIONS   462

23 Fluctuations of Aggregate Demand and GNP 465

BUSINESS CYCLES   466
    Measuring and Defining Business Cycles   Are There Business Cycles?
CONSUMPTION AND INSTABILITY   470
    The Relative Income Hypothesis   The Permanent Income Hypothesis   The Life-Cycle Hypothesis
INVESTMENT AND INSTABILITY   474
    Induced Investment   The Accelerator and the Stability of Investment   Expectations, Uncertainty, and Investment
GOVERNMENT SPENDING AND INSTABILITY   479
BUILT-IN STABILIZERS   480
    Induced Taxes   Unemployment Insurance
ECONOMIC FLUCTUATIONS: WHAT CAN THE GOVERNMENT DO?   483

24 Fiscal Policy: Mechanics, Problems, and Issues 486

GOVERNMENT SPENDING VS. TAXES   488
    Taxes, Government Spending, and Ideology   Close-up: The Democrats' Free Lunch: The Humphrey-Hawkins Bill   Close-up: The Republicans' Free Lunch: The Kemp-Roth Bill   The Multiplier Effect of Government Spending and Taxes
DISCRETIONARY FISCAL POLICY AND BALANCED BUDGETS   492
    Close-up: Should an Unbalanced Budget Be Unconstitutional?   The Balanced-Budget Multiplier   Close-up: The Vietnam Tax Surcharge

FISCAL POLICY AND THE NATIONAL DEBT 497
"The National Debt Will Bankrupt the Country"   "The National Debt Is a Burden on the Community and on Future Generations"
SOME NORMATIVE ASPECTS OF FISCAL POLICY 500
Spending Priorities   Distributing the Tax Burden: Who Pays?
Close-up: The 101 Percent Tax   Loopholes and Tax Reform
PRACTICAL AND POLITICAL PROBLEMS 505
Political Appeal   Time Lags and Information

APPLYING THE TOOLS: THE 1964 TAX CUT 507

Part Nine

Aggregate Demand: The Money Market 511

25 Money: What It Is and What It Does
512

A BRIEF HISTORY OF MONEY 512
Commodity Money   Close-up: The Price Revolution in Europe   The Gold Standard   Fiat Money
THE BASIC FUNCTIONS OF MONEY 516
Unit of Account and Exchange   Store of Value
DEFINING MONEY AGGREGATES 516
The Strict Definition   Broader Definitions of Money   Near Monies
Close-up: Are Credit Cards Money?
BASIC MOTIVES FOR HOLDING MONEY 520
CHOICE OF ASSETS AND THE DEMAND FOR MONEY 521
Liquidity, Risk, and Rate of Return   Money as an Asset   Changes in the Demand for Money
EQUILIBRIUM IN THE MONEY MARKET 526
The Supply of Money   The Equilibrium Interest Rate   Money, Interest, Investment, and GNP: The "Keynesian Connection"

26 The Supply of Money
532

THE SUPPLY OF MONEY AND AGGREGATE OUTPUT 532
MONEY SUPPLY, OUTPUT, AND PRICES: THE QUANTITY THEORY OF MONEY 534
The Velocity of Money   The Equation of Exchange   **Close-up: The Free Silver Movement**   The Equation of Exchange and Equilibrium in the Money Market
COMMERCIAL BANKS AND THE MONEY SUPPLY 541
Goldsmiths and the Origins of Commercial Banking   The Commercial Bank's Balance Sheet   Creation of Money by the Banks   The Banking System Multiplier   The Banking System Multiplier: Some Qualifications   But Is It Really Money?
THE FEDERAL RESERVE AND THE MONEY SUPPLY 547
The Structure of the Federal Reserve   How Does the Fed Control the Money Supply?

27 Monetary Policy: Mechanics, Problems, and Issues
559

DISCRETIONARY MONETARY POLICY: THE MECHANICS 560
Unemployment and Expansionary Monetary Policy   Inflation and Restrictive Monetary Policy   Close-up: Political Business Cycles?   Choice of Monetary Policy Objectives   Close-up: The "Credit Crunch" of 1966

THE EFFECTIVENESS OF MONETARY POLICY 564
    Money and Depression: The Liquidity Trap   Weak Effects of Monetary Policy   Strong Effects of Monetary Policy   Information Problems   Expectations   Leads and Lags
RELATIONSHIP BETWEEN MONETARY AND FISCAL POLICIES 572
    Unsupported Fiscal Expansion   Unsupported Fiscal Restraint   Consolidation of Monetary and Fiscal Policy: Pro   Consolidation of Monetary and Fiscal Policy: Con   Close-up: Carter and the Chairmen
THE MONETARIST PRESCRIPTION 577
    No Discretionary Monetary Policy   Fiscal Policy   Employment   Critique of the Monetarist Program   The Monetarist Controversy: Who's Right?
APPENDIX: MONEY, INTEREST, AND GNP: THE IS-LM APPROACH 583
    The Goods Sector and Real GNP   The Monetary Sector   Equilibrium in Goods and Money Markets   Effects of Fiscal and Monetary Policies   Unsupported Fiscal Policy   Supported Fiscal Policy

Part Ten

Inflation and Unemployment   593

28 Inflation and Unemployment: Defining the Problem 594

THE MEANING AND SIGNIFICANCE OF INFLATION 594
    Inflation: Winners and Losers   Inflation and Savings   Inflation and Taxation

APPLYING THE TOOLS: THE GRANDDADDY OF INFLATIONS 598
    What Caused the Inflation?   Effects of the Hyperinflation   The End of the Inflation

THE MEANING AND SIGNIFICANCE OF UNEMPLOYMENT 600
    How Unemployment Is Measured   The Duration of Unemployment   Kinds of Unemployment   What the Unemployment Rate Hides
THE COSTS OF UNEMPLOYMENT 606
SETTING AN EMPLOYMENT GOAL 608

29 Aggregate Demand and Aggregate Supply 612

ANOTHER VIEW OF AGGREGATE DEMAND 613
    Aggregate Demand and the Price Level   The Slope of the Aggregate Demand Curve   Shifts of the Aggregate Demand Curve
AGGREGATE SUPPLY: OUTPUT AND THE PRICE LEVEL 618
    Employment and Output: The Aggregate Production Function   Equilibrium in the Labor Market   Prices, Employment, and Output   The Shape of the Aggregate Supply Curve   Shifts of the Aggregate Supply Curve
EQUILIBRIUM OUTPUT, EMPLOYMENT, AND PRICE LEVEL 626
    Demand Shifts   Supply Shifts

30 Inflation and Unemployment: Is There a Trade-off? 633

AGGREGATE DEMAND, AGGREGATE SUPPLY, INFLATION, AND UNEMPLOYMENT 633
    Aggregate Supply and the Inflation Rate   Aggregate Demand and the Inflation Rate   Aggregate Output and the Inflation Rate   Inflation, Output, and Unemployment

THE PHILLIPS CURVE 638
    Unemployment and Inflation in the 1960s   The Breakdown of the Trade-off in the 1970s
IS THERE A LONG-RUN TRADE-OFF? 641
    Expectations, Aggregate Supply, and the Natural Unemployment Rate   Long-Run Aggregate Supply and the Long-Run Phillips Curve
APPLYING THE TOOLS: RATIONAL EXPECTATIONS 648

31 Inflation and Unemployment: Attacking the Problem 652

MONETARISM AND THE MARKET SOLUTION 652
MANAGING AGGREGATE DEMAND: FINE TUNING 654
MANAGING AGGREGATE SUPPLY: INCOMES POLICIES 656
    Voluntary Guideposts and Guidelines   Close-up: The Carter Wage-Price Guidelines   Mandatory Wage and Price Controls   Can Incomes Policies Work?
MANAGING AGGREGATE SUPPLY: INDEXING 659
    Escalator Clauses   Indexing Taxes   Indexing Interest Rates   Control of Inflation or Surrender to It?   Close-up: TIPs
WON'T ANYTHING WORK? 662
    Monetary and Fiscal Policy   The Unemployment Target   Reducing the Natural Unemployment Rate   Wage and Price Standards   Reducing Inflationary Expectations

Part Eleven

The World Economy 667

32 The Gains from Trade 668

SPECIALIZATION, TRADE, AND EFFICIENCY 668
COMPARATIVE ADVANTAGE 669
    Comparative Advantage and Specialization   Comparative Advantage and International Trade
TERMS OF TRADE 672
    Terms of Trade and the Gains from Trade   Terms of Trade and Trade Between Countries
TRADE AND WELFARE 674
    Production Possibilities in a Closed Economy   The Impact of Trade
APPLYING THE TOOLS: "THE IMPORTANCE OF BEING UNIMPORTANT" 676

33 International Exchange 680

EXCHANGE RATES AND INTERNATIONAL CURRENCY 680
    Exchange Rates and the Price of Exports and Imports   Currency Appreciation and Depreciation   How Exchange Rates Are Determined
THE BALANCE OF INTERNATIONAL PAYMENTS 683
    The Merchandise Account   The Capital Account   The International Settlements Account
EXCHANGE RATES AND THE BALANCE OF PAYMENTS 686
    Pegged Exchange Rates

APPLYING THE TOOLS: PEGGED EXCHANGE RATES AND THE U.S. BALANCE OF PAYMENTS, 1946–1972   689
    Floating Exchange Rates
A NEW MONETARY SYSTEM?   692
    Special Drawing Rights (SDRs)   The European Monetary System   What Next?

APPENDIX: U.S. INTERNATIONAL TRANSACTIONS, 1977   696
    The Current Account   The Capital Account   International Settlements

34 Trade Policy: Mechanics, Problems, and Issues   699

TARIFFS AND IMPORT QUOTAS   700
    Tariffs and Efficiency   Tariffs and Gains from Trade   Import Quotas
THE CASE FOR IMPORT RESTRICTION   705
    Protecting American Workers from Cheap Foreign Labor   Fair Competition   Tariffs and Full Employment: "Beggar-My-Neighbor"   Tariffs as a Source of Tax Revenue   Infant Industries   National Security
EXPORT POLICIES   709
    Export Subsidies   Restricting Exports
TRADE POLICY PROBLEMS AND ISSUES OF THE 1980s   712
    Dealing with OPEC   Dumping   Trade Policy and International Politics   The Tokyo Round and Future Trade Policy
HOW FREE FOREIGN TRADE?   715
    Adjusting to Freer Trade   Close-up: "On Sudden Changes in the Channels of Trade"   The Future of Free Trade

Part Twelve

The Economic Future   721

35 Economic Growth: Boon or Bane?   722

WHAT IS ECONOMIC GROWTH?   722
    Output and Capacity   Changes in Potential and Real GNP
SOURCES OF GROWTH   724
    Quantity and Quality of Resources   Technology Investment and Capital Formation   Education and Human Capital   Close-up: Resources, Productivity, and U.S. Economic Growth
GROWTH AND WELFARE   727
    Growth and Living Standards   Growth, Employment, and Inflation   Growth, the Environment, and Social Costs   Distribution of Benefits and Costs
CAN GROWTH CONTINUE?   729
    The Classical Prognosis: The Stationary State   The Marxian Prognosis: "Fetters on Production"   Technological Change   Investment Opportunities
MUST GROWTH CONTINUE?   733
    The Pressure to Continue Growth   Zero Economic Growth (ZEG)   Close-up: "Bigger and Better" vs. "Small Is Beautiful"
DEALING WITH POVERTY: GROWTH OR REDISTRIBUTION?   736

36 Economic Development and World Poverty 738

THE ROOTS OF WORLD POVERTY 739
    Resources   Imperialism   Tradition and Institutions   Population
WORLD POVERTY: IS THERE A WAY OUT? 744
    Investment and Capital Formation   Social Overhead   Land Reform and Agricultural Investment   Foreign Assistance   Specialization and Trade   Limiting Population Growth
ECONOMIC DEVELOPMENT: MISSION IMPOSSIBLE? 749

37 Alternative Economic Systems 751

SOCIALISM 751
    Socialism and Democracy   Market Socialism   The Lange-Lerner Model of Market Socialism
CENTRAL ECONOMIC PLANNING 754
    Planning and Economic Welfare   The Planners' Task: Feasibility   The Planners' Task: Consistency   The Planners' Task: Optimality   Indicative Planning
SOME LONG-RANGE CONSIDERATIONS: THE CONVERGENCE HYPOTHESIS 760
    The "New Industrial State"   The Participatory Economy
WHAT IS THE BEST ECONOMIC SYSTEM? 762

Index 765

PART ONE
An Introduction to Economics

Throughout history, every individual and every society has been forced to choose among alternative uses of scarce resources, money, and time. In choosing to take this course, you were forced to give up the opportunity of taking a course in physics or French, or perhaps just sleeping an hour later in the morning. In buying this textbook, you were forced to give up the opportunity of treating yourself to a meal at a good restaurant or buying a new shirt. Understanding how and why such choices as these are made is what economics is all about.

In this first section, we'll look closely at how economics approaches the dual problem of scarcity and choice. The **production possibilities model**, introduced in Chapter 2, illustrates the problem graphically and suggests some ways in which it can be alleviated. The remainder of the section presents a general overview of how a market economy—an economy not unlike our own—uses free market forces to make key economic decisions.

1

The Art and Science of Economics

Preview: In this first chapter, we'll take a general look at the subject matter and methods of economics. Since much of this text deals with economic theory, we'll focus particular attention on how economists go about building and testing their theories. We'll also explore some of the limitations of economic theory and the questions that even the best course in economics can't answer.

Most students in introductory college economics courses are being exposed to economics for the first time and don't know exactly what to expect—except that the subject must be very hard or else it would have been taught in high school. They may even have heard economics referred to as the *dismal science*—hardly a reassuring description.

In fact, economics is an exciting and vital subject. It deals with problems and issues that are critical to us as members of society. Perhaps more importantly, it deals with nearly every aspect of our individual daily lives—from buying a car to taking a vacation to getting married and having children. In fact, it could be argued without much exaggeration that there is *no* human activity which does not fall within the realm of economics.

Economics can, however, be an exasperating subject for students and professional economists alike. Dramatic economic events since the late 1960s have raised serious doubts about many things we economists thought we already understood. Economics has never been a field noted for consensus among its practitioners, but seldom has there been more economic controversy than there is today. Lay all the economists in the world end to end, goes one old saying, and they won't reach an agreement.

Perhaps the most valuable lesson of economics is that every course of action has a cost. If we spend more on income maintenance programs for the poor, we'll have to spend less on other public programs or raise taxes. If we follow the Proposition 13 approach of the late 1970s and cut taxes drastically, we may have to give up the public services our taxes paid for. If we want cleaner air, we may have to pay higher prices for some of the goods we consume and do without others altogether. The goal of economics isn't to find universal bliss, but to find the best way of allocating our scarce resources among alternative uses to achieve competing goals—to balance the costs borne by society with the benefits received.

A basic understanding of economics won't provide you with a set of "correct" answers to the unresolved questions and continuing controversies over economic problems and issues. It will, however, give you something much more valuable—the basic tools to approach problems logically and analytically. Many economic problems are so complex that recognizing the relevant questions (let alone finding answers) is difficult or impossible without a logical and analytical approach. We live in a constantly changing world, and even if we did have correct answers to all of today's economic problems, those answers might not be relevant to future problems. But the ability to deal with issues in a logical manner never becomes obsolete.

Theories, Models, and Facts

Much of what we study in economics involves the use of theories.

- **Economic theories** are logical explanations of cause-and-effect relationships among economic variables.

The goal of almost all economic theories is to explain what *has* happened and predict what *will* happen in an economy. Many students find theory the hardest part of economics to learn or accept. Economists themselves don't agree on the validity of all theories, and some even reject theorizing as an approach to understanding economic relationships and problems. Such disagreement isn't all bad: skepticism about the validity or relevance of established theories has been an important force for progress throughout the history of economic thought.

Economic theories present and analyze economic relationships in unrealistic abstract settings or *models*.

- A **model** is a simplified picture of the real world.

Economic models allow economists to present their theories in a way that is easy to see and understand. Frequently, the model itself is part of the economist's theory, and if we accept the model, we accept the theory. The lack of realism in many economic models is a necessary evil, because economic relationships may be impossible to identify or analyze in the very complicated real world. Many of the laws of the physical sciences are also stated for highly unrealistic conditions: the *law of falling bodies*, for example, is stated for a vacuum; this "vacuum model" of the real world is necessary in order to isolate the force of gravity on falling bodies from the effects of the atmosphere.

Building and Testing Economic Theories

The first step in constructing a theory is to isolate the things we're interested in from other things. If we want to analyze the effect of higher gasoline prices on the consumption of gasoline, for example, we'd have to eliminate all of the other variables that may affect gasoline consumption—population, tastes, income, housing patterns, etc. Since we can't isolate variables physically in a laboratory, we have to isolate them by making **assumptions**. To isolate the effect of changes in the price of gasoline from all of the other variables that affect sales and consumption of gasoline, we have to assume that all of those other variables remain unchanged. This particular assumption is made so frequently in economics that it even has a name.

- The **ceteris paribus** assumption states that all variables except those under investigation remain constant.

Human behavior is extremely complex, of course, so before we can make many predictions about the way households or firms will respond to economic variables, we also have to make some simplifying assumptions about the general pattern of economic behavior. Economics makes two very basic assumptions about behavior that are usually lumped together into one:

- Economics assumes that economic behavior is **rational** and aimed at **maximizing** something.

Rationality doesn't necessarily mean moral, ethical, or desirable behavior, nor does the assumption of rationality mean that people don't make mistakes.

- **Rationality** means that behavior is consistent with reaching a known goal or objective.

We don't have to assume that every single individual behaves rationally all of the time. This is an assumption of a *general* pattern of behavior, and it's more reasonable than the alternatives. **Irrational behavior** is deliberate behavior that is inconsistent with reaching a known goal, and **random behavior** is behavior that isn't directed at any goal or objective.

Economics assumes that the *goal* of rational economic behavior is to *maximize* something. We assume that households try to maximize their satisfaction or **utility**. In the theory of a private, market economy, firms are assumed to seek maximum **profits** (sales revenue minus costs of production). These simplified assumptions about behavior aren't always valid empirically, but they aren't unreasonable as simplified approximations of behavior. The crucial test of a theory isn't the empirical accuracy of its assumptions, but the ability to make general predictions that are generally supported by the evidence. Of course, in societies where these assumptions about economic behavior aren't reasonable approximations of actual motives, the predictions from the theory probably won't be supported by the facts, and theories based on other assumptions may well be needed.

In addition to these basic general assumptions, most models will contain a number of specific assumptions as well. It is important to realize how vital the assumptions of a model are, since we arrive at an economic theory by applying simple logic to the assumptions. For example, let us make the following assumptions about the shoppers at a local grocery:

1. The shoppers are *rational*.
2. The shoppers try to maximize their satisfaction from their weekly food budgets, and will buy a quantity of each good where the *last unit* bought is just worth its price.
3. Successive loaves of bread are worth less to the shoppers.
4. Everything else that might affect the amount of bread people will buy remains the same *(ceteris paribus)*.

Applying simple logic to these assumptions, we'd reach a conclusion that a reduction in the price of bread, other things equal, would cause shoppers to buy more bread per week. This *conclusion*—also called a *prediction*, a *hypothesis*, or a *theory*—follows logically from the assumptions.

Our next step is to test the predictions of our theory against the facts, or *empirical evidence*.

- **Empirical evidence** is factual data based on observation and experience and not on theory.

Empirical evidence provides the real acid test of any theory. If an empirical study showed that consumers generally bought less bread at low prices than at high prices, we'd have cause to reexamine the theory and the empirical methods used. If the logic and the empirical methods are sound, and the theory still continues to give us wrong predictions, we must reject it.

"Good in theory, wrong in practice" is one of the most commonly held views of economic theory, but it's not a valid criticism. If a theory fails to give predictions that are generally consistent with the empirical evidence, the theory is rejected—in spite of any logical or mathematical beauty and rigor it may possess. Theories that consistently give the wrong predictions are "wrong in practice," but they are not "good" theories.

To be valid, however, a theory doesn't have to give accurate predictions in every conceivable case—in fact, if it does, it's probably an *identity* (something that's always true, such as 2 = 2). A theory is a *generalization*, and there may be exceptions that don't invalidate it. For example, the general prediction that auto traffic will tend to move more slowly on dark rainy nights than on bright sunny days isn't invalidated if a normally safe and sane driver gets drunk at a party and is ticketed for driving 90 miles an hour during a midnight downpour.

Marginal Analysis

Much of the attention of economic theory focuses upon *marginal units*.

- A **marginal unit** is the change in one variable that results from a given change in another variable.

People make decisions involving marginal units all the time. Whether or not you will have one more beer (in addition to the previous six) at your local tavern, for example, is a marginal decision. In this case, you would have to decide whether the additional (marginal) enjoyment you would get out of drinking the beer outweighs the additional (marginal) costs of 75¢ and a more serious hangover tomorrow. Similarly, in deciding whether or not to hire additional police officers or fire fighters, a community must decide whether the marginal protection is worth the marginal cost.

Ex Ante and Ex Post

Economic analysis deals mainly with *ex ante* relationships. **Ex ante** simply means *intended* or *before the fact*. In analyzing demand, for example, we're interested in the *ex ante* quantities of a good that consumers are willing and able to buy at a given price. The actual measured quantities are called **ex post** (after the fact) quantities.

The distinction is important. *Ex post* data may yield important information from which theory can be forged, but that theory must focus upon *ex ante* relationships if it is to have much value. We want our analysis to make predictions and not merely to record what has happened in the past.

Why Bother with Theory at All?

It's very easy to become impatient with economic theorizing and to question the value of all of this mental effort as a means of understanding economic relationships and making economic predictions. There are some alternatives to theory but they are less satisfactory.

"Common Sense" and Logical Fallacies. Common sense, or intuition, is a valuable gift. Many breakthroughs in economics and other fields began with an intuitive notion that something was wrong with accepted ideas. However, relying on one's common sense alone can lead to two rather common logical fallacies.

The *fallacy of composition* is perhaps the most common logical fallacy in common-sense economic arguments.

- The **fallacy of composition** asserts that something true of the part must be true of the whole.

In projecting our own common sense to broad economic relationships, we tend to generalize our own reactions and experience to the economy as a whole. For example, if I have more money to spend, this is good for me. Therefore, if everybody had more money to spend, everybody would be better off. The fallacy here is obvious. If I have more money, my increased spending won't have any effect on prices, but if everybody had more money, increased spending by all of us could raise prices enough that nobody would be better off. Something that's valid for an individual economically won't necessarily be valid for the economy as a whole. "What's good for General Motors" is not necessarily good for the country.

The *fallacy of division* isn't as common as the fallacy of composition, but it does appear from time to time.

- The **fallacy of division** asserts that something true of the whole must be true of the part.

For example, lower foreign trade barriers tend to be good for the economy as a whole in the sense that resources are used more efficiently and more goods are available at lower prices. It does not follow, however, that lower trade barriers must be good for every individual or industry—workers in industries that are forced to contract or shut down as a result of import competition, for example, will be worse off as a result of lower trade barriers.

"Let's Just Look at the Facts." Since the facts are essential for testing the predictions of theories, why not just dispense with the theory altogether and look at the facts alone? The problem is that facts alone have no logical structure and offer no logical explanation of cause and effect—even if we use sophisticated statistical techniques to show that different facts are related. Looking at the facts alone leads to a common logical fallacy with an uncommon name—the *post hoc, ergo propter hoc*, or simply the *post hoc fallacy*.

- The **post hoc fallacy** argues that because one event follows another, there is a cause-and-effect relationship between the two events—"after this, therefore because of this."

If your neighbor's dog always barks at rush hour, you can't avoid rush hour by having your neighbor get rid of the dog. If the national unemployment rate generally rises after birth rates rise in Topeka, Kansas, a massive contraception drive in Topeka would be a questionable full-employment policy.

To identify cause and effect, and even to identify the relevant facts to look at, we have to have some form of logical theory—even if we don't recognize the theory as such. Facts are essential to knowledge, but facts alone don't tell us very much.

Prejudice and Scapegoats. The third alternative to logical theorizing as an approach to economic problems is to blame those problems on persons or groups that we don't like or don't trust—blacks, whites, Republicans, Democrats, industrialists, labor unions, short people, or just about any group will do. If we don't like or trust more than one group, we can combine them into a conspiracy—Republicans and industrialists, Democrats and unions, Arabs and Russians, to name only a few of the infinite possibilities. This approach has a distinct advantage in that it requires virtually no mental effort, but there's generally no logical relationship between our prejudices and the roots of economic problems.

Positive and Normative Arguments

As we've seen in the preceding pages, economic analysis can be a powerful tool in understanding and dealing with a variety of complex issues. It does have some serious limitations, however. Many economists like to think of their field as a set of logical principles or arguments that are free of value judgments.

- A **positive argument** involves no value judgment and can be tested by logic or fact.

It's probably impossible for economics to be completely free of value judgments, however, because economics deals with too many issues that touch our basic social, philosophical, and ethical beliefs. Thus, nearly all controversies over economic issues and policies contain *normative* as well as positive arguments.

- A **normative argument** rests on some value judgment and thus cannot be tested by logic or facts.

Sometimes positive and normative arguments *sound* quite similar. The following, for example, is a positive statement that can be tested logically or empirically.

- Taxing high incomes at a higher rate than low incomes will redistribute income between high-income households and low-income households.

Here is a similar-sounding normative statement that *can't* be proven valid or invalid without a value judgment.

- Taxing high incomes at a higher rate than low incomes is unjust because it redistributes income between high-income households and low-income households.

One of the greatest lasting benefits of a basic understanding of economics is the ability to recognize and separate the positive aspects of economic issues and arguments from the normative aspects. Economic analysis alone can't answer normative questions, but to the extent that it *can* identify the costs and benefits, gains and losses, winners and losers, from alternative economic policies, economic theory allows us to make *informed* and *intelligent* value judgments in determining proper courses of action.

A Concluding Remark

If you like unsettled questions and controversy, you'll probably like economics. If you like simple and straightforward answers to difficult and complex problems, however, you may be disappointed. You may find that economic problems are more complex than they appear on the surface, that there is generally more than one way to deal with any given problem, and that any policy has some advantages and disadvantages compared with alternative policies. You may in the end even find yourself in agreement with the late American humorist Will Rogers, who once confessed publicly that he didn't know any more about economic problems than an economist, and ". . . Lord knows, he don't know anything."

Summary

1. **Economics** is a logical and analytical approach to economic problems and issues.
2. **Economic theory** is a set of logical explanations of cause-and-effect relationships between economic variables. These variables are typically identified analytically in an abstract, oversimplified setting or **model**. Theories are typically stated as conclusions or hypotheses that follow logically from assumptions.
3. Economic theory assumes that the general pattern of economic behavior is **rational** and **maximizing**.
4. The most important test of a theory is its ability to make predictions that are generally supported by the evidence.
5. Arguments that aren't based on theory or logical reasoning typically contain logical fallacies—the fallacies of composition and division and the post hoc fallacy are quite common.

Concepts for Review

positive argument
model
rational behavior
empirical evidence
ex post
post hoc fallacy

normative argument
assumption
maximizing behavior
marginal analysis
fallacy of composition

theory
ceteris paribus
utility
ex ante
fallacy of division

Questions

1. Consider the following hypotheses:
   "Other things remaining the same, more baseball tickets will be sold at a lower price than at a higher price."
   "In a vacuum, all falling objects will fall at the same rate."
   a. Which hypothesis is stated under more realistic conditions?
   b. Why is it necessary to specify "other things equal" and "in a vacuum"?
   c. Which hypothesis would be easier to test?
2. How many times do you make the *ceteris paribus* assumption (whether you recognize it or not) in your everyday life?
3. Which of the following are examples of rational behavior? If not rational, what kind of behavior is it?
   a. Stanley Fern is 5'3" tall (in his elevator shoes), weighs 110 lbs., and wants to play center on a professional basketball team. Every day, Stanley goes to the gym to work on his hook shot and rebounding.
   b. George Sloth wants to spend his life doing nothing, so he seldom gets out of bed in the morning.
   c. Kathy Kinetic is serious and energetic. Every morning she rises at 6 A.M. and works hard all day flitting from one thing to another without finishing anything.
   d. Steve Slick wants to get from Cleveland to New York, and deliberately takes the westbound lanes on the Ohio Turnpike.
   e. Steve Slick still wants to get from Cleveland to New York, but gets lost in Newark, N.J.
4. Uncle Joe runs a candy store, and gives away a lot of candy to make children happy.
   a. Could Uncle Joe be considered rational?
   b. Does Uncle Joe's behavior invalidate the assumption that firms (sellers) generally seek to maximize their profits?
5. Suppose that you're given the following facts on the price and sales of women's slacks in 1946 and 1976.

Year	Price per pair	Pairs sold (millions)
1946	$10	10
1976	$35	30

   a. What do these facts *alone* tell you about the relationship between the price of women's slacks and the sales of women's slacks?
   b. Do you accept the relationship in part (a)? If you don't accept it, how do you explain it? What are you doing in rejecting (a)?
6. Sort out the positive and normative aspects of this argument, "Taxes on liquor are a good thing, because they discourage the consumption of demon rum."
7. Pick any economic issue or policy dispute from your daily paper or television news. What are the positive aspects and the normative aspects of the dispute?

APPENDIX

A Brief Mathematical Review

Economics uses mathematics to state and test abstract propositions clearly and conveniently. There is no reason to be intimidated by this, since the mathematics used in the book does not go beyond the ninth or tenth grade level. This appendix will help you review the basic mathematical tools used in the book. For some students, this review may not be necessary. However, if your recollection of high-school mathematics is shaky, it would be worthwhile to review these concepts and tools. The appendix can also be used as a reference when unfamiliar mathematical techniques are used in the text.

Hypotheses, Functions, and Equations

Economic analysis consists of a number of hypotheses.

- A **hypothesis** states or predicts a relationship between variables.

Hypotheses can be expressed verbally, mathematically by function or equation, or geometrically by a graph.

Functions, equations, and graphs are not inherently more difficult to understand and interpret than verbal statements, and in most cases they make the analysis easier to follow than complicated verbal statements alone. Mathematics and graphs are a kind of shorthand to make explanations *easier*—not to make an easy explanation unnecessarily difficult.

Variables and Functions

Variables are the things we study—prices, output, consumption, cost, etc. Consider any two variables x and y. A relationship between x and y could be stated verbally as follows:

- The value of y depends on the value of x.

This simple statement tells us:

1. x and y are related;
2. x is the **independent variable** (the value of x determines the value of y); and
3. y is the **dependent variable** (the value of y is determined by the value of x).

Identifying dependent and independent variables is essential in trying to identify cause and effect.

The same relationship can be expressed by the **function**

$$y = f(x),$$

which is read as "y is a function of x," or simply "y depends on x." It says exactly the same thing as the verbal statement. When a larger number of variables is involved, shorthand functions are often more convenient than verbal statements. For example, the verbal statement "The value of y depends on the values of $a, b, c, d, e, x,$ and z" can be expressed by the function

$$y = f(a, b, c, d, e, x, z).$$

Direct and Inverse Relationships

A simple function tells us that one variable depends on the other but does not tell us the nature of the relationship. The function $y = f(x)$, for example, does not indicate whether greater values of x will cause y to rise or fall.

- If variables are **directly related**, they will vary in the *same direction*. The larger x is, the larger y will be.
- If variables are **inversely related**, they vary in *opposite directions*. The larger x is, the smaller y will be.

Equations

One specific form of function is called an equation.

- An **equation** is a function that expresses a specific relationship between variables.

Equations can state fairly complicated relationships much more clearly than verbal statements alone. For example, consider this statement.

- The value of y is a when x is zero, and every change in x causes y to change in the same direction and by some proportion (b) of the change in x.

Exactly the same thing is said in the equation

$$y = a + bx.$$

Which is harder to understand and interpret?

Solving Equations

An equation can tell us the value of y for any given value of x, or the value of x that would determine a given or desired value of y. This involves *solving* the equation for the missing variable. There is a simple, but very important, rule to remember in solving equations:

- Anything can be done to an equation without changing it, as long as the same thing is done to both sides of the equation.

For example, if $x = y$, $x + 75 \neq y$ (the sign $\neq$ means *does not equal*), but $x + 75 = y + 75$.

Consider the equation

$$y = 20 + \tfrac{1}{2}x.$$

To solve for y when $x = 50$, substitute 50 for x, and perform the operations instructed by the equation.

$$y = 20 + \tfrac{1}{2}x = 20 + \tfrac{1}{2}(50) = 20 + 25 = 45.$$

In other words, given $x = 50$, the equation defines $y = 45$.

To find the value of x that will define a given value of y, the equation is solved for x with the given value of y. Suppose we want $y = 100$. To solve for x, substitute 100 for y in the equation.

$$y = 20 + \tfrac{1}{2}x$$
$$100 = 20 + \tfrac{1}{2}x, \text{ or}$$
$$20 + \tfrac{1}{2}x = 100.$$

Isolate the terms with x on one side of the equation by subtracting 20 from both sides, and

$$20 + \tfrac{1}{2}x - 20 = 100 - 20$$
$$\tfrac{1}{2}x = 80.$$

Multiplying both sides of this by 2,

$$x = 160.$$

To verify this, see if $y = 100$ when $x = 160$ in the equation $y = 20 + \tfrac{1}{2}x$.

Graphs

Graphs, like functions and equations, express relationships between variables. Like functions and equations, the purpose of graphs is to make the analysis *easier* than it would be without them.

Graphs of Equations

Table A–1 shows values of y determined by values of x from 0 to 100 at 10-unit intervals from the equation $y = 20 + \tfrac{1}{2}x$. In Figure A–1, values of x are represented by distances along the horizontal (x) axis, and values of y are represented by distances along the vertical (y) axis. Each of the pairs of x and y in the table is represented by a point in Figure A–1. Point A shows the value of y when $x = 0$ in the equation $y = 20 + \tfrac{1}{2}x$. It has an **x-coordinate** of 0 and a **y-coordinate** of 20. Point B has an x-coordinate of 10 and a y-coordi-

Table A–1 Paired Values of x and y

x	y
0	20
10	25
20	30
30	35
40	40
50	45
60	50
70	55
80	60
90	65
100	70

nate of 25. The other points in Figure A–1 represent other pairs of x and y from Table A–1.

Figure A–1 Graph of Table A–1

The straight line connecting the points in Figure A–1 show all possible pairs of x and y for the equation $y = 20 + \frac{1}{2}x$ for values of x between 0 and 100. This would be impossible to show with a table, because the table would be infinitely long even before $x = 1$! The straight line in Figure A–1 is a picture of the equation $y = 20 + \frac{1}{2}x$.

Figure A–2 is a graph representing an *inverse relationship* between x and y. Specifically, it is a picture of the equation $y = 100 - \frac{1}{2}x$. Like the equation, the graph makes it possible to find the value of y for a given value of x, or the value of x that would determine a given value of y.

Change and Slope

Economics frequently deals with changes in variables, and the effect of changes in one variable on changes in another.

- Change in a variable is expressed by the symbol Δ—the Greek letter *delta*.

Slope shows the degree to which one variable responds to changes in another.

- The **slope** is the ratio of the change in the dependent variable over the change in the independent variable.

Algebraically,

$$\text{slope} = \frac{\text{change in } y}{\text{change in } x} = \frac{\Delta y}{\Delta x}.$$

In an equation of the form $y = a + bx$, the slope is the term b. In the equation $y = 20 + \frac{1}{2}x$, the slope is $\frac{1}{2}$, which means that every change in x by one unit will cause y to change in the same direction by $\frac{1}{2}$ unit, or $\Delta y / \Delta x = \frac{1}{2}$. For example, let x change from $x_1 = 20$ to $x_2 = 40$. The change in x is

$$\Delta x = x_2 - x_1 = 40 - 20 = 20.$$

With $x_1 = 20$,

$$y_1 = 20 + \tfrac{1}{2} x_1 = 20 + \tfrac{1}{2}(20) = 30.$$

With $x_2 = 40$,

$$y_2 = 20 + \tfrac{1}{2} x_2 = 20 + \tfrac{1}{2}(40) = 40.$$

The change in y is

$$\Delta y = y_2 - y_1 = 40 - 30 = 10.$$

The slope is

$$\frac{\Delta y}{\Delta x} = \frac{y_2 - y_1}{x_2 - x_1} = \frac{40 - 30}{40 - 20} = \frac{10}{20} = \frac{1}{2}.$$

In Figure A–1, the slope of the line $y = 20 + \frac{1}{2}x$ is the slope of the equation. In the graph, x *runs* along the horizontal axis, and changes in x are called the **run**. Changes in y are called the **rise** since y changes vertically as x changes. If x changes from 20 to 40 in Figure A–1, the *run* is 20. Since y increases from 30 to 40 with this change in x, the *rise* is 10. The slope of the line in Figure A–1 is the same as the slope of the equation—

$$\text{slope} = \frac{\text{rise}}{\text{run}} = \frac{\Delta y}{\Delta x} = \frac{10}{20} = \frac{1}{2}.$$

In the equation $y = 20 + \frac{1}{2}x$ and in the graph of the equation in Figure A–1, there is a direct relationship between x and y, as shown by the positive (*uphill*, left to right) slope.

- **Positive slopes** indicate *direct relationships* between variables.

The equation

$$y = a - bx$$

represents an inverse relationship between x and y, and has a negative (*downhill*, left to right) slope.

- **Negative slopes** indicate *inverse relationships* between variables.

Go back to the equation $y = 100 - \frac{1}{2}x$ and the graph of the equation in Figure A–2. Let x increase from $x_1 = 20$ to $x_2 = 40$. The change in x is

$$\Delta x = x_2 - x_1 = 40 - 20 = 20.$$

With x_1, the value of y is

$$y_1 = 100 - x_1 = 100 - \tfrac{1}{2}(20) = 90.$$

When x increases to x_2, y falls to

$$y_2 = 100 - x_2 = 100 - \tfrac{1}{2}(40) = 80.$$

The change in y is

$$\Delta y = y_2 - y_1 = 80 - 90 = -10,$$

and the slope is

$$\frac{\Delta y}{\Delta x} = \frac{-10}{20} = -\frac{1}{2}.$$

In Figure A–2, y falls toward the horizontal axis as x runs out horizontally, or the *rise* is negative with inverse relationships.

Figure A–2 Inverse Relationship Between x and y

The Value of the Slope

The value of the slope indicates the degree to which one variable responds to changes in the other. Compare two equations representing direct relationships,

$$y = 20 + \tfrac{1}{2}x$$

and

$$y = 20 + x.$$

The equation with the greater slope indicates that y is more responsive to changes in x. Turning this around, it will take smaller changes in x to achieve a given change in y in the equation with the greater slope. Figure A–3 shows the two equations graphically. The steeper line indicates that y is more responsive to changes in x. As an exercise, draw lines representing the equations $y = 20 + \tfrac{1}{4}x$ and $y = 20 + 2x$.

Figure A-3 Positive Slopes

With inverse relationships, the *absolute* value of the slope (ignoring its negative sign) indicates how responsive one variable is to changes in the other. Compare the equations below representing inverse relationships between x and y.

$$y = 100 - \tfrac{1}{2}x$$

and

$$y = 100 - x.$$

The two equations are shown graphically in Figure A-4. The steeper line represents the equation with the greater absolute slope and the one in which y is more responsive to changes in x. Again, as an exercise, draw lines in Figure A-4 representing the equations $y = 100 - \tfrac{1}{4}x$ and $y = 100 - 2x$.

Linear Relationships

All of the relationships in the above examples are *linear relationships* between x and y.

- In **linear relationships,** y is equally responsive to all changes in x, and the slope is constant for all changes in x and y.

Linear relationships are shown graphically by straight lines.

Curves

Most economical relationships are *nonlinear*. Equal changes in one variable do not always produce the same change in the other. For example, food output on a 100-acre plot of land would be zero with no labor and no capital. Adding labor and capital would change output, but every additional unit of labor and capital will not add the same amount of output—if it did, the world could be fed from the single 100-acre plot of land. Eventually, the entire 100 acres would be taken up with workers and equipment, and output would be zero again. This is an example of a nonlinear relationship.

- In **nonlinear relationships,** equal changes in x will not cause equal changes in y.

Nonlinear equations involve powers of x, and will not be used in the text. However, nonlinear equations are easy to deal with graphically. Nonlinear relationships are represented graphically by *curves*.

Figure A–4 Negative Slopes

Slopes of Curves

Slopes of curves are expressed in two ways—*arc approximations* and *slopes at points* on the curve.

- The **arc approximation** of the slope of a curve is the average value of the slope of the curve between two points on the curve, or the slope of a line between the points.

Moving from point A to point B on the curve in Figure A–5 involves moving from x_1 and y_1 to x_2 and y_2. The arc approximation of the slope is

$$\frac{\Delta y}{\Delta x} = \frac{y_2 - y_1}{x_2 - x_1},$$

or the slope of the broken line between A and B. The smaller the arc—i.e., the smaller the changes in x and y—the closer the slope of the line between the points approximates the slope of the curve itself.

A straight line that touches only a single point on a curve is **tangent** to the curve at that point.

- The *slope of a curve at a point* is the slope of a straight line tangent to the curve at that point.

The slope of the curve in Figure A–5 at point A is the same as the slope of the line tangent to the curve at point A.

Figure A–5 Determining the Slope of a Curve

Interpreting Curves

Interpreting curves is not very difficult. As in linear relations, negatively sloped curves indicate inverse relationships and positively sloped curves indicate direct relationships.

The curve in Figure A–6a shows a direct relationship between x and y, and y moves in the same direction as changes in x along the curve. However, as x increases, the slope of the curve increases.

- The curve in Figure A–6a shows y *increasing at an increasing rate* as x increases.

The curve in Figure A–6b is positively sloped, indicating a direct relationship between x and y. However, the slope of this curve gets smaller as x increases.

- The curve in Figure A–6b shows y *increasing at a decreasing rate* as x increases.

The curve in Figure A–6c is negatively sloped, indicating an inverse relationship between x and y. As x increases, the curve gets steeper. Ignoring the minus sign of the slope, the slope increases as x increases.

- The curve in Figure A–6c shows y *decreasing at an increasing rate* as x increases.

Figure A–6 Interpreting Curves

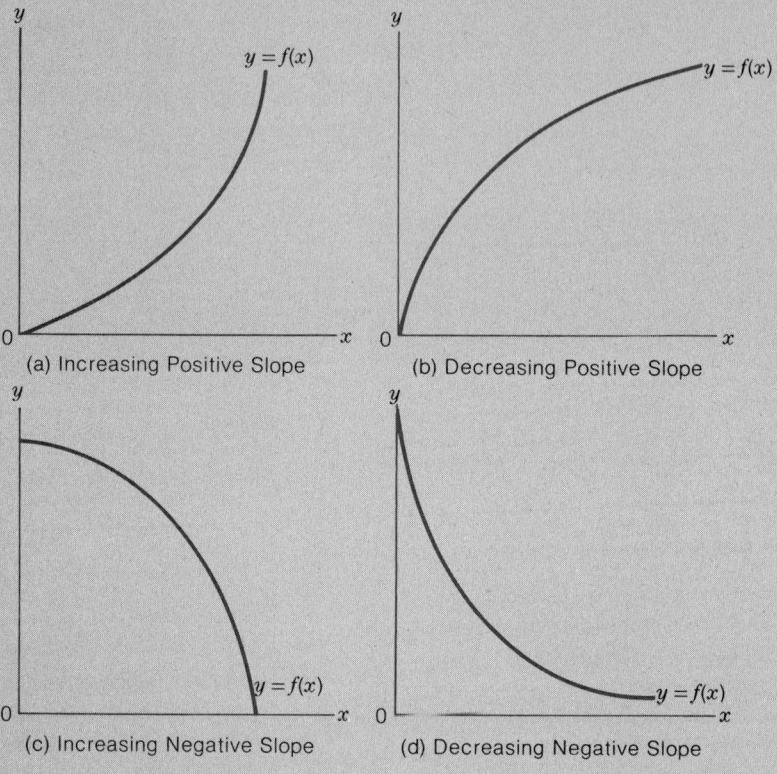

In Figure A–6d, the curve is negatively sloped, indicating an inverse relationship, and the slope of the curve (ignoring the minus sign) gets smaller as x increases and the curve "flattens out."

- The curve in Figure A–6d shows *y decreasing at a decreasing rate* as x increases.

In some instances, y may increase at an increasing rate for some changes in x, at a constant rate for other changes in x, and may even change from a direct relationship to an inverse relationship. Figure A–7 shows what probably would happen as labor is added to a fixed amount of land and capital. Initially, output (q) increases at an increasing rate (labor inputs between 0 and ℓ_1) and the curve resembles that in Figure A–6a. Between ℓ_1 and ℓ_2, output increases at a diminishing rate as the labor input increases and the curve resembles that in Figure A–6b. Output reaches its maximum with ℓ_2 units of labor employed—the slope of the curve is zero at this point. Beyond labor inputs of ℓ_2, increasing the labor input actually causes output to fall, and the relationship between labor input and the level of output shifts from a direct to an inverse relationship like the one shown in Figure A–6c.

Figure A–7 Productivity of Labor Curve

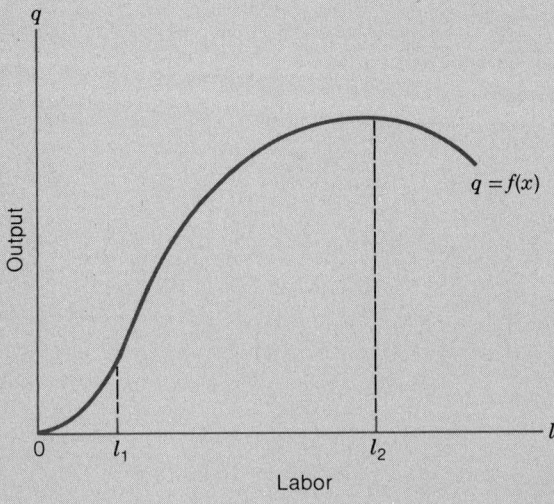

Graphic Solution of Equations	Graphs of equations make it easy to solve for one variable with a given value of the other. But what if we are dealing with more than one relationship between variables and want to find values of the variables that are consistent with both relationships? One approach is simultaneous solution of the equations representing the relationships. This is not especially difficult with two linear equations, but graphs make the solution much easier.

For example, in Figure A–8a, one positively sloped line represents one relationship—$y = 20 + \tfrac{1}{2}x$—and the other represents the equation $y = x$. At point A, where the two lines intersect, $y = 20 + \tfrac{1}{2}x$ and $y = x$. This is the same result we would get by simultaneous solution of the equations $y = 20 + \tfrac{1}{2}x$ and $y = x$.

Simultaneous solution of nonlinear equations is more difficult, but finding solutions graphically is quite easy. For example, in Figure A–8b, $y = f(x)$ and $y = x$ at the points where the curve is cut by the line $y = x$, at 0 and at A. In Figure A–8c, we have two nonlinear relationships—$y = f(x)$ and $y = g(x)$—and both are met at the point where the two curves intersect.

The Elements of Statistical Estimation	Many economic relationships can be estimated statistically from actual data with a technique called **regression analysis**. Regression analysis simply tries to find the function or equation that *fits* the data. For example, suppose that we have found statistical data for x (the independent variable) and y (the dependent variable).

Figure A–8 Graphical Solutions of Equations

x	y
0	100
100	200
300	270
400	340
500	510
600	570
700	670
800	760
900	840
1000	920

Each of the pairs in the above table is represented by a point in Figure A–9a, which is called a *scatter diagram*. A look at the scatter diagram indicates a direct relationship between x and y.

To estimate the specific relationship between x and y, we try to find a line that comes as close as possible to all of the points in the scatter. This can be done visually by moving a line around until it apparently comes as close as possible to all of the points, or more reliably with a statistical technique called **least squares**. In Figure A–9a, the line

$$y = 82 + 0.86x$$

is the *estimated* relationship between x and y. This estimate indicates that $y = 82$ is autonomous, or can't be explained by the value of x. Every change in x by 1 unit causes y to change in the same direction by 0.86. Since the points are tightly bunched around the estimated line, we have a stable and predictable relationship between x and y.

In Figure A–9b, the scatter indicates an inverse relationship between x and y. Also, the points are more widely scattered around the estimated line, indicating a somewhat less stable and predictable relationship between x and y than in Figure A–9a.

Scatter diagrams that resemble Figure A–9c indicate that there is no relationship between x and y.

Figure A–9   Scatter Diagrams for Regression Analysis

2

Scarcity and Choice: The Economic Problem

Preview: Faced with limited resources and unlimited wants, society is forced to make certain economic choices. Specifically, society must decide what it will produce, how it will produce, and how it will distribute that production to its members. The **production-possibilities model** introduced in this chapter serves as a useful tool in analyzing and understanding these kinds of choices.

Although we use theory to understand many economic questions and issues, economics isn't really *about* theory. Economics is primarily concerned with a basic fact of life—**scarcity**. Since the fall of Adam, the human race has been faced with a conflict between unlimited wants and limited resources. As individuals, we have to choose among our wants to make ourselves as well off as possible with limited amounts of income, time, and stamina. As communities, we have to choose among the needs of the community to make the community as well off as possible with its limited resources.

The Limits on Production

Society's basic economic problem is to find the best combination of goods and services that can be produced with its limited capacity to produce. The capacity to produce, in turn, is limited by society's *resources*, the state of *technology*, and a number of noneconomic and institutional factors—such as religious tradition, social and economic class structures, etc.

Limited Resources

Producing goods and services is impossible without land, labor, machinery, raw materials, time, and other resources. In reality, there are millions of different resources, but for simplicity, we can classify all resources as *land*, *labor*, and *capital*.

- **Land** refers to resources that are permanently fixed in supply.
- **Labor** refers to the human strength and talent used in production.
- **Capital** refers to a class of resources that are produced by the economic system—for example, machinery and buildings.

Obviously, if the *quantities of resources* available are limited, there will be a limit on the number of possible combinations of goods and services that can be produced and consumed. The *quality of resources* also affects society's capacity to produce. Even with vast expanses of land, a country may have a very small capacity to produce agricultural crops if the land is of poor quality for agricultural production (mountains, swamps, and deserts, for example), or if the climate is too harsh for most crops. A well-fed, well-trained, and stable labor force will be more productive than a labor force made up of untrained, poorly educated, transient workers. A stock of modern machinery and equipment will be more productive than obsolete machinery and equipment.

Technology

Technology also limits the capacity to produce.

- **Technology** is the "state of the art" in production, or the known applications of scientific and technical knowledge to production.

A given state of technology defines the relationship between resource inputs and the level of output. In other words, technology tells us how much we can produce with a given quantity and quality of resources. Unfortunately, no known technology allows the production of goods and services without using scarce resources in the process.

The Economic Problem

Most societies share a common economic goal of making the members of the society as well off as possible economically. This goal, however, isn't as clearly defined as it appears, and in fact a society's definition of what is *best* economically isn't a strictly economic problem.

A given society's definition of a best economic result is affected by the dominant ideology in the society and the prevailing social and political philosophy. The definition of the best economic result may even involve religious considerations—for example, not producing or consuming goods prohibited by religious tradition or conducting business according to religious standards. The religious government of Iran, for example, attempted upon taking power to force banks to conform to Islamic laws against *usury* (charging interest on loans).

Defining the best economic outcome for society is complicated further by the fact that a result that is *best* by some generally accepted definition—for example, the *best* result for the majority of the population—usually isn't the best possible result for every person or group within society. Producing goods more efficiently by mechanization, for example, isn't best for workers who will have to be retrained or relocated or who will become unemployed as a result. In other words, the very definition of what is best economically is in part a *normative* definition resting on value judgements.

Economic analysis emphasizes *economic efficiency*, or getting the greatest possible output out of a given capacity. This emphasis simplifies reality by excluding many noneconomic considerations. For example, if making the most efficient use of productive capacity required extensive restrictions of political and economic freedom of choice, a society might well opt for more freedom, even at the expense of some efficiency.

Three Basic Economic Questions

The millions of specific economic choices that society must make boil down to three basic questions that are common to all societies and economies—*what* goods to produce, *how* to produce, and *for whom* to produce.

What?

The capacity to produce goods and services, or *productive capacity*, defines society's "menu" of possible choices of goods and services. If this capacity is fully employed, the decision to produce more of one thing requires reduced output of something else. More concisely, in economics, "there ain't no such thing as a free lunch."

Choosing *what* goods to produce requires a determination of what is best for society. In some cases, this determination is made by consumer demand as expressed in the markets for goods and services. In other instances, the decision on what goods to produce is made by a central authority. Sometimes, society's needs and priorities are determined by external considerations—for example, the demands of a major war or the real or perceived external threats to national security that dictate the output of goods for military purposes.

The *what* question also involves the choice between goods now and goods in the future. If all resources are used to produce goods for current consumption, for example, no machinery or equipment will be produced. Over time, as machines wear out and aren't replaced with new ones, our "menu" of choices shrinks. On the other hand, if we produce large outputs of machines now in order to produce more consumption goods in the future, we have to give up some current consumption.

In market economies, the decision of *what* to produce depends largely on the distribution of wealth and income. It is seldom, if ever, decided by a simple majority of the population in a one-person-one-vote election. Also the choice of *what* to produce involves normative considerations concerning the importance of various groups in determining society's economic welfare.

How?

If the object is to make society as well off as possible economically with a limited capacity, it follows that this capacity should be used as efficiently as possible. The question of *how* to produce goods and services concerns the efficient utilization of society's resources and technology.

If there are idle resources—unemployed labor, idle machines, empty factories, etc.—society loses the goods and services that could have been produced by these resources. Efficiency also involves the most efficient combinations of resources. For example, in countries where labor is very scarce relative to land and capital, it wouldn't be very efficient to produce wheat with methods that required large amounts of labor and little machinery. If a machine in a factory can be operated efficiently by one worker, it isn't efficient to put two workers on the machine.

Efficiency, or full employment of capacity, is hard to achieve for a number of reasons. Resources generally aren't sufficiently mobile among geographic areas or occupations. Lack of information, inadequate education, emotional attachments, geographical and family ties, discrimination, and other factors, for example, contribute to immobility of labor into industries, occupations, or geographic areas in which they would be most productive. Work rules to preserve individuals' jobs, managerial bureaucracies, and some governmental regulations also may contribute to inefficiency.

Deciding *how* to produce, like most economic questions, involves normative issues and value judgements as well as positive analytical questions. For example, elimination of work rules that protect individual jobs at the expense of efficiency benefits producers and possibly consumers of the affected goods and services, but a disproportionate share of the cost of such a move is borne by the affected workers. To say that elimination of the work rules is a *good* thing requires some normative argument that the benefits to producers and consumers are more important than the costs borne by the affected workers.

For Whom?

Finally, society has to decide *for whom* to produce—the distribution of output among members of the community. Should everybody get an equal share of the output? Should output and income be distributed on the basis of effort and contribution or on the basis of an individual's initial wealth? What role should tradition play in the distribution of output and income?

These questions involve many normative and positive issues. For example, rewarding persons on the basis of their individual effort and resources may be efficient but may lead to a normatively unacceptable degree of inequality of income. To say that one pattern of income distribution is *better* or *worse* than another involves normative value judgements on the importance of *equity* and *efficiency*.

Production Possibilities

To see the problem of scarcity in very simplified terms, imagine a country that produces only two goods—food (F) and clothing (C). Assume further that the country has limited resources with which to produce food and clothing, and that these resources can be used in both food and clothing production. Finally, assume a given state of *technology*—i.e., a set relationship between resource inputs and the level of output.

Table 1 Efficient Combinations of Food and Clothing

C	F
500	0
475	100
425	200
325	300
200	400
0	500

Table 1 shows some of the combinations of food and clothing that fully employ the economy's productive capacity. If all resources were used to produce food, food production would be at its maximum, $F^* = 500$, and clothing production would be zero. If all resources were used to produce clothing, clothing production would be at its maximum, $C^* = 500$, and food output would be zero.

The Production-Possibilities Curve

If our imaginary economy were to produce some food and some clothing, it would have to produce less than 500 units of each. This is shown clearly in Table 1. The possible combinations of goods in Table 1 define points on the economy's *production-possibilities curve* in Figure 1.

- The **production-possibilities curve** shows all the combinations of goods that can be produced with full and efficient employment of an economy's capacity to produce.

In Figure 1, the combination of 100 units of food and 475 units of clothing determines point B on the production-possibilities curve. The combination of 300 units of food and 325 units of clothing determines point D on the curve. All combinations of outputs on the production-possibilities curve require full employment of all resources, combined as efficiently as possible. At all points on the production-possibilities curve, there will be no idle or inefficiently used resources (such as two workers doing a job that requires only one).

Notice in Table 1 and Figure 1 that successive 100-unit increases in the production of food require successively larger reductions of clothing production, and that the production-possibilities curve gets steeper as we move from $C^* = 500$ toward $F^* = 500$. This is because all resources aren't equally suited for producing both goods. If the maximum clothing output were produced, clothing production would employ all of the economy's resources—even those least suitable for clothing production. Likewise, producing the maximum output of food requires the employment of all resources in food production—again including those not well-suited for this task.

To raise food output from 0 to 100 in Figure 1, we'd expect the land, labor, and capital least suited to clothing production and most suited to food production to be taken out of clothing production to produce food. In this case, little clothing would have to be given up for the first 100 units of food produced.

However, increasing food production to 200, 300, 400, and 500 would require the use of resources less and less suitable for food production.

Figure 1 Production Possibilities Curve

As clothing production is cut back, resources more suitable for clothing production must be removed, increasing the clothing reductions for each additional 100 units of food. Since more and more clothing must be given up for equal increases in food, clothing output falls at an increasing rate, and the production-possibilities curve *bows away* from the origin (or is *concave*).

An economy can only produce combinations of goods that lie *on* or *inside* its production-possibilities curve. Combinations of goods that define points outside the production-possibilities curve—such as 300 units of food and 475 units of clothing (point E) in Figure 1—cannot be produced with the economy's resources and technology.

Combinations of goods that define points inside the production-possibilities curve—such as point A in Figure 1—can be produced, but they don't employ the economy's capacity fully. If productive capacity isn't fully employed, the community cannot be as well off as possible economically. The unemployed capacity at point A could be used to increase food output from 100 to 300 without reducing clothing output, to increase clothing production from 325 to 475 without reducing food output, or to produce more of both goods along the segment BD. With unemployed capacity, increasing the output of a good doesn't require a reduction of output of other goods.

Opportunity Cost

In a fully employed economy, the cost of producing more of one good is the amount of other goods that must be given up. For example, suppose that the economy in Figure 1 is at point B and increases its food output from 100 to 300. This would require a reduction of clothing production from 475 to 325. The 150 units of clothing given up represent the *opportunity cost* of the additional 200 units of food.

- **Opportunity cost** is the cost of foregone alternatives.

Economics is about *choice*, and opportunity cost tells the cost of any choice we make. It is thus one of the most important concepts in economics. If the economy moved from point D to point B in Figure 1, the opportunity cost of the additional 150 units of clothing would be the 200 units of food that would have to be given up.

Points on the production-possibilities model answer the fundamental question of *how* goods should be produced. If the economy wishes to get the maximum output from its resources, it *must* produce a combination of goods that lies along the production-possibilities curve, since it would be impossible to produce a combination outside the curve and inefficient to produce one inside the curve.

Deciding *what* the economy should produce involves finding the combination of goods that makes the community as well off as possible. Not all combinations on the curve will make the community equally well off. Consider the points $C^* = 500$ and $F^* = 500$. At C^*, the economy would produce clothing, but no food. While it's nice to be well dressed, starving to death is very painful. A well-fed, naked community producing $F^* = 500$ may seem to be more interesting, but it would be uncomfortable except in tropical climates, and the undraped overfed human form has only limited appeal. The task of the economic system is to find the combination of goods on the production-possibilities curve that is best for the community, and the production-possibilities model alone can't make that judgment.

After deciding *how* and *what* goods to produce, the community must decide *for whom* the goods are to be produced, or how the goods are to be distributed among members of the community. This may be easier said than done. Deciding that one segment of the community deserves a greater share of the output than another involves a value judgment, and arguments involving value judgments are difficult to resolve with analytical tools.

Technology and Production

Technological change—change in the way that things are produced—has been a dominant theme in economic history for several centuries, and technological change is one of the main sources of modern economic growth. We can analyze one of the effects of technological change, expansion of productive capacity, by returning to a simple food-and-clothing economy.

Suppose that a technological change—say, the discovery of a new type of fertilizer—makes it possible to produce more food with the resources available. The maximum food output goes from F^* to F^{**} in Figure 2. Nothing happens to clothing technology, but the technological change in food production changes the production-possibilities curve to C^*F^{**}. The shaded area represents additional combinations

Figure 2 Technological Change in Production

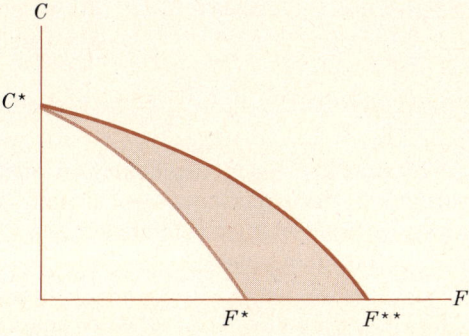

of food and clothing that can be produced as a result of the technological change in food production.

You should work out for yourself the effect of a technological change in clothing production and a technological change in both industries on the economy's production possibilities. Many other things can alter an economy's production-possibilities curve—for example, discovery of new or superior resources and depletion of resources.

Close-up

Technological Change in Agriculture

In the United States, technological change has been especially dramatic in the agricultural sector. The invention of new machinery (from the cotton gin and the reaper to modern self-propelled grain combines), the development of new strains of seed, and the application of chemistry to agriculture have created what many have termed a *Green Revolution*.

These technological advances have raised the output per worker and the output per acre of land dramatically. In the table below, notice the large increases in the production of corn and soybeans over the period 1940–1969, despite a drop in total farm population of nearly two-thirds and an even more impressive decline in the proportion of the total population involved in agriculture. One clue as to how these production increases have been possible lies in the rapid increases in the use of agricultural technology—tractors and fertilizer.

	Total Farm Population (1000's)	% of Total Population	Tractors Used (1000's)	Fertilizer Used (1000 tons)	Value of Products ($ Millions)	Corn (Millions of bushels)	Soybeans (Millions of bushels)
1940	30,547	23.2	1,597	9,360	6,682	2,457	78
1945	24,420	17.5	2,354	15,128	16,231	2,869	193
1950	23,048	15.3	3,394	18,343	22,217	3,075	299.2
1954	19,019	11.8	4,243	22,773	24,645	3,058	324.1
1959	16,592	9.4	4,673	25,313	30,493	3,697	515.6
1964	12,954	6.8	4,755	30,681	35,292	3,361	669.7
1969	10,307	5.1	4,810	38,948	45,609	4,357	1041.5

Source: U.S. Bureau of the Census, *Historical Statistics of the United States: Colonial Times to 1970, Bicentennial Edition.* Washington, D.C., 1975.

Technological change and rising productivity in agriculture freed labor from the agricultural sector for nonagricultural employment. The additional labor available in the nonagricultural sector contributed to an increased capacity of the economy to produce industrial goods.

Figure 3 Growth vs. Consumption

(a) Country A

(b) Country B

Growth vs. Consumption

Another major economic choice which can be analyzed using the production-possibilities model is the choice between growth and consumption. The choice of goods produced today may affect a country's productive capacity in the future. If, for example, we produced no industrial machinery this year, our productive capacity would shrink in the future as existing machines wore out. For a more general example, we can classify all goods as **consumer goods** (goods for current consumption) and **capital goods** (goods, such as industrial machinery, to be used for further production). Now, consider two imaginary economies with identical production possibilities, as shown in Figure 3.

Initially, Country B produces more consumer goods (C_B) than does Country A (C_A), but Country A produces more capital goods (K_A) than does Country B (K_B). Living standards would be higher in Country B initially, because Country B produces more consumer goods. The additional capital goods in Country A add little to the living standards of the people.

However, in the future, Country A will have a larger capacity to produce consumer goods and capital goods than will Country B because of its greater output of capital goods now. The expansion of productive capacities in the two countries is shown by the shift of their production-possibilities curves outward in Figure 3. Country A's additional capacity in the future would allow it to produce more capital goods *and* more consumer goods than Country B.

This simple example illustrates a very important and sometimes very painful choice that societies must make—the choice between current consumption and future economic growth. This is one of the basic choices facing the economically underdeveloped countries of the Third World, and the alternatives are unattractive—maintaining current living standards and allowing capacity and output to stagnate, or promoting economic growth by worsening living standards that already border on biological survival.

Close-up

The Soviet Forced Industrialization Drive

Nowhere has the choice between restricting current consumption and promoting future economic growth been more dramatic than in the Soviet Union. In 1928, the first year of the first Five Year Plan, capital goods accounted for 39.5 percent of Soviet industrial output, and consumer goods accounted for 60.5 percent. By 1940, Soviet planners had turned these proportions around—capital goods accounted for 61.2 percent of industrial output and consumer goods accounted for 38.8 percent of industrial output.

In the table below, notice the tremendous increases in the production of industrial goods in the U.S.S.R. between 1928 and 1940, compared to the much more modest increases—and, in the case of cows, decrease—in the production of consumer goods. Note also that between 1928 and 1933, production of *all* the consumer and agricultural goods in the table actually declined.

	1928	1933	1940
Industrial Goods			
Electric Power (millions of KW)	5	16	48
Coal (millions of tons)	36	76	166
Steel (millions of tons)	4	7	18
Machine Tools (1000 units)	2	21	58
Trucks (1000 units)	0.7	39	136
Consumer and Agricultural Goods			
Cotton Fabrics (billions of meters)	3	3	4
Sugar (millions of tons)	2	1	3
Grain (millions of tons)	73	69	96
Cows (millions)	29	19	28

Based on statistics from *Narodnoe khozyaystvo SSR v 1958 godu* (Moscow, 1959).

The squeezing of the consumer goods industries was an integral part of the Soviet strategy to generate rapid economic growth. The transformation of the Soviet economy from a backward, largely agricultural economy to a major industrial power owes much to the sacrifices of Soviet consumers in the 1930s, 1940s, 1950s, and 1960s.

The production-possibilities model is a very simple picture of the choices available to society. All modern economies produce thousands of goods and services, not just two. Nonetheless, the model does illustrate some important concepts—scarcity, choice, opportunity cost—and we can apply it to problems of choice in more complex economies.

Applying the Tools

The Cost and Economic Impact of World War II

The impact of World War II on the United States was much different from the impact of the war on the other belligerent nations. The opportunity cost of prosecuting the war (in terms of the kinds of other things that had to be given up) was much lower for the United States than it was for other countries. We can see why if we look at the cost and impact of the war in terms of production possibilities of three countries involved in the war—the United States, Germany, and the Soviet Union.

The productive capacity of the United States was grossly underemployed in the 1930s. During the Great Depression, 25 percent of the labor force was out of work, and many factories and machines lay idle. In contrast, by 1939 Germany had taken up much of the slack in its economy with public works projects (like the Autobahn) and military production. Between 1928 and 1939, the Soviet Union had pushed its modest production potential to the limit in a ruthless industrialization drive (see *Close-up*, p. 34). During the course of the war, the increased demand for military goods affected these countries quite differently, as shown in Figure A. In Figure A, all goods are classified as *military (M)* or *civilian (C)* goods, and productive capacity is expressed as the capacity to produce these broad categories of goods.

The high unemployment in the United States in 1939 meant that the economy was operating inside its production-possibilities curve, as shown by the outputs C_{1939} and M_{1939} in Figure A (i). Between 1939 and 1945, the United States was able to increase military production dramatically from M_{1939} to M_{1945} without a drastic reduction of the output of civilian goods. There was some reduction of output of civilian goods in the United States during the war, but the effect on most American households was more of an inconvenience than a drastic deterioration in the quality of life.

Figure A

(i) United States (ii) Germany (iii) The Soviet Union

In Germany and the Soviet Union, the costs of prosecuting the war (in terms of civilian goods) was much greater than in the United States. Both countries had less slack in their economies at the outset of the war. Germany was producing very close to its production-possibilities curve, as shown by C_{1939} and M_{1939} in Figure A(ii). The Soviet Union was probably producing *on* its production-possibilities curve in 1939, as shown in Figure A(iii). In these countries, the increased military production during the war required substantial reductions of the output of civilian goods. In addition, both countries were invaded during the war, and their productive capacities were partially destroyed. This pushed the production-possibilities curves of Germany and the Soviet Union inward to the darker curves in Figures A(ii) and (iii). Civilian goods production was so low in these countries in 1945 that biological survival was a very real problem for many German and Soviet households.

This doesn't mean that World War II was *free* for the United States. Although the war required no drastic reductions in the output of civilian goods or in living standards, the resources used to produce military goods during the war could have been employed in the production of civilian goods. The prosecution of the war and the support of allied countries during the war meant that the United States had to forego the alternative of employing its capacity to produce more civilian goods.

The Economic System

Every society has a set of economic arrangements and economic institutions that make up its **economic system.** The economic system is the end product of a variety of economic and noneconomic forces in the society—prevailing social philosophy and ideology, historical experience, traditional relationships among social classes, as well as political goals and the adequacy of resources to meet those goals. Societies deal with the problem of scarcity and choice through their economic systems, and there are about as many different economic systems in the world as there are societies.

Despite their diversity, however, the economic systems of the world do have a common goal: to make the society as well off as possible. Of course, it is in the process of trying to define and achieve this goal that systems differ. The very definition of what is *best* for the society depends on who makes the decision—buyers and sellers in the market place, governmental economic policymakers, or central economic planners. The means by which economic welfare (once the term has been defined) is to be maximized also leads to important differences among the world's economic systems.

We'll take a closer look at various economic systems in Chapter 19. For the time being, however, we'll focus our attention upon economic problems and relationships in a basically private market economy, since this is the closest approximation to our own economy.

Summary

1. All human societies face the problem of **scarcity**—unlimited wants in the face of limited resources and limited capacity to produce.
2. All societies have to make three basic economic choices—**what** to produce, **how** to produce it, and **for whom** to produce.
3. A society's feasible combinations of goods—given its resources and technology—is defined by its **production-possibilities curve**, which shows combinations of goods that require full efficient employment of the economy's capacity to produce.
4. In a fully employed economy, producing more of something means that the output of something else must be reduced.
5. The cost of foregone alternatives is called **opportunity cost**.
6. The production-possibilities curve may shift as a result of technological change, changes in resource quality, or as a result of a change in the proportion of the economy's capacity devoted to the production of capital goods.

Concepts for Review

scarcity
choice
land
labor
capital
technology
efficiency

productive capacity
production-possibilities curve
opportunity cost
technological change
capital goods
consumer goods
economic system

Questions

1. Sarah and Jim's parents have told the children that they "can't get everything they want."
   a. What economic lesson are the parents teaching the children?
   b. If the parents were the world's richest couple, would their argument be valid?
2. In the early years of the Vietnam War, President Johnson assured the nation that the war wouldn't reduce our output of consumer goods, nor would it lead to cuts in government spending on nonmilitary programs. Under what circumstances would this be plausible?
3. Petroleum is an important raw material used in producing many goods in our economy. Explain the effect of the following developments on our production possibilities.
   a. The discovery of new sources of petroleum.
   b. The depletion of petroleum reserves.
   c. The discovery of a substitute for petroleum in automobile transportation.
4. Some people argue that the United States has gone "beyond the problem of scarcity," and that scarcity would not be a problem in our society if we changed the economic system and the pattern of distribution of goods and services among members of the community. Do you think that this is a valid argument?

Problems

1. The following combinations of steel and wheat outputs require full employment of Neverland's productive capacity.

Combination	Steel, million tons/yr.	Wheat, million tons/yr.
A	12	0
B	11	3
C	9	6
D	6	9
E	0	12

   a. Construct Neverland's production-possibilities curve from the above information.
   b. Could the economy produce 9 million tons of steel and 9 million tons of wheat per year? Explain.
   c. Could the economy produce 9 million tons of steel and 3 million tons of wheat per year? Could it be maximizing the society's economic welfare if it produced this combination of goods? Explain.
   d. Do all combinations of goods that employ productive capacity fully make society equally well off economically?
   e. What is opportunity cost? What is the opportunity cost of moving from combination B to combination C above?
   f. Does it require a value judgement to argue that combinations inside the production-possibility curve aren't the best possible combinations for the community? Does it require a value judgement to argue that moving from one point on the production-possibility curve to another point on the production-possibility curve is good or bad?

3

Demand, Supply, and Price: An Overview

Preview: In a market economy, society's necessary economic choices are made through the interaction of individual buyers and sellers behaving in their own best interests in the free market. The **partial equilibrium model of supply and demand** introduced in this chapter demonstrates how the prices generated by these market activities ensure that the quantities of goods and services supplied by producers will exactly equal the quantities demanded by consumers.

Households, Firms, and Markets

What do we mean when we speak of a market? What determines the boundaries of a market?

- A **market** is a setting in which buyers and sellers can deal with each other conveniently.

The U.S. economy is made up of many markets, and different markets have different characteristics, or **market structures**. Some markets are very small geographically, such as the markets served by neighborhood grocers. Others, such as commodities markets and markets for financial securities, are national or even worldwide markets. Some markets have many small buyers and sellers that compete vigorously with each other. Others have only a few buyers or sellers. In fact, some markets have only one buyer or one seller.

Economic analysis of the market economy assumes two basic economic units—households and firms.

- The **household** is the basic buyer of products and the basic seller of resources.
- The **firm** is the basic seller of products and the basic buyer of resources.

Consumer Sovereignty

In a market economy, the actions of these buyers and sellers in product and resource markets are translated into economic choices for the community.

Economic theory typically assumes that a market economy is directed by **consumer sovereignty** (*rule by the consumer*). Every household tries to spend its income on the combination of goods and services that it believes will give it maximum satisfaction. In economic terms, the household wants to maximize *utility* (*utility* is the economist's term for *satisfaction*) through its choice of goods and services. By purchasing the combination of goods and services that maximizes utility, the household casts *dollar votes* in the product market.

Firms in a market economy are assumed to want to produce the combination of goods and services that will maximize *profit*, and will thus try to produce the goods and services that households want. In other words, firms try to produce in direct response to the dollar votes cast by consumers. In order to do this, firms must purchase resources (land, labor, and capital) from households, and provide income to the households in return. Each household's income depends on the scarcity of the resources it sells relative to the demand for them: scarce resources in great demand will command higher prices than abundant resources that few firms want. Firms, in turn, will economize in their use of the scarcest and highest-priced sources and will try to produce any output as efficiently as possible. In this way, the market economy decides how the total number of dollar votes will be distributed to households.

In short, economic theory assumes that in a consumer-sovereignty economy, the free interaction of buyers and sellers in product and resource markets ultimately determines the answers to the three fundamental economic questions.

- **What** the economy produces is determined by the way households cast their dollar votes (i.e., spend their incomes) and the way firms respond to those votes.
- **How** the economy produces is determined by the scarcity and prices of resources and by firms' efforts to produce efficiently and at the lowest possible cost.
- **For whom** the economy produces is determined by the distribution of dollar votes (i.e., income) to households, based on the kinds and amounts of resources households own and the need for those resources in production.

Markets and Democracy

Laissez-faire is an economic philosophy that opposes government interference in the operation of the market system. Many advocates of laissez-faire argue that the market system is an efficient and democratic means of making the community's economic choices and that it provides the greatest good for the greatest number of people. But while the market system may encourage efficiency, it does not guarantee equity. Consumer sovereignty is a *one-dollar-one-vote* system, not *one-person-one-vote*. Individuals with large incomes will cast more dollar votes than individuals with smaller incomes. If a tiny minority controls the bulk of the income in an economy, markets will respond to the preferences of this minority. There is thus no assurance that the answers provided by the market system to the fundamental economic questions will be defensible on any normative grounds.

It is possible, as many critics of the market system argue, to replace markets with some other means of economic decision-making, such as a central economic authority. But simply replacing the market system with some other mechanism wouldn't resolve all potential questions of equity and fairness. Whose view of economic welfare, social justice, and equity should prevail? To whose needs would the economic authority most likely respond? These are questions you should ask yourself as we look more closely at the market system.

Prices in the Market Economy

Everybody is familiar with prices. However, not many people are aware of the economic significance of prices in the market system—what they do and what would happen if they didn't exist.

Contrary to some rather optimistic views, there simply aren't enough raw materials, labor, land, and capital to produce enough of everything for everybody. Economics is concerned with *scarce* goods and resources.

- **Scarce goods and resources** are those that don't exist in sufficient quantities that all users can have as much as they want.

Since there isn't enough of a scarce good or resource to go around, there must be some means of deciding which of the potential users will be able to get the good. In a market economy, *prices ration scarce goods and resources* by excluding users who are unwilling or unable to pay the price. A price of $10 on a bleacher seat at the World Series rations the seats to those who are willing and able to pay $10 to see the game. It excludes baseball fans who don't have the $10, as well as persons with only passing interest in the World Series who wouldn't get $10 worth of enjoyment out of attending a game.

Goods and resources that *are* so abundant that all users can have as much as they want are *free* goods and resources. Things may be free because they exist in very large quantities relative to the demand for them (e.g., sunlight) or simply because nobody wants them (e.g., garbage). There is no need to ration a free good or resource, so free goods and resources don't have prices (actually, the price is zero).

Simply setting the price of a good at zero, however, doesn't make it free in the strict economic sense. A law setting the price of World Series tickets at zero wouldn't make the tickets a free good, except in the unlikely event that the number of persons interested in seeing a game was equal to or smaller than the number of seats available. When the price of a scarce good is set so low that consumers demand more of the good than is made available by sellers, some non-price means of rationing will have to be devised. The "free" Series tickets might be rationed first-come-first-served, through a lottery, or in some other way. The long lines at gas pumps during the gasoline crunch of 1979 provided a vivid example of first-come-first-served rationing.

Common sense suggests that the prices of scarce goods are determined by demand and supply. If the supply of World Series seats were infinite, their price would be very low (zero, in fact); if only a hundred tickets were available, their price would be very high (as ticket scalpers well know). In the winter, when fresh vegetables are scarce, their prices are so high that many consumers can't afford them; in late summer, when supplies are plentiful, many grocers barely find it worthwhile to stock fresh vegetables because the prices are so low. Gasoline frequently costs more in summer, when people are taking long automobile trips and demand for gas is high, than in winter, when many people leave their cars at home and take public transportation to work. All these examples illustrate the importance of demand and supply in determining prices. A fuller understanding of price determination, however, requires a closer look at these relationships.

Demand and Price

The quantity of a good that consumers would be willing and able to buy (*ex ante*) depends upon a number of things—the price of the good, the prices of other goods, consumers' incomes, tastes, custom and tradition, and legal regulations, among others. The *law of demand* states a general relationship between the price of a good and the quantity demanded by consumers:

- The **law of demand:** Assuming everything else remains constant (*ceteris paribus*), the quantity of a good demanded by buyers tends to vary inversely with the price of the good. In other words, the quantity of a good demanded will be greater at low prices than at high prices.

Like all economic laws, the law of demand can only tell us what *usually* happens. There may be some owners of Jaguars who would no longer buy them if the price of Jaguars fell enough that members of the middle-class could afford them. But the decrease in quantity of Jaguars demanded by such snobs would be overwhelmed by the increase in quantity demanded by the middle class. Thus the law of demand holds true as a generalization, if not for every buyer of every

DEMAND, SUPPLY, AND PRICE: AN OVERVIEW   43

good. One way to test the law of demand is to try to sell one of your textbooks (not this one, of course) at a high price and at a low price; see how many potential customers you have at each price.

The Demand Schedule and the Demand Curve

The law of demand is illustrated in the hypothetical *demand schedule* in Table 1.

- A **demand schedule** shows the quantity of a good demanded at various prices, *ceteris paribus*.

Table 1 shows the hypothetical quantity of coffee demanded at various prices ranging from $1 to $8 a pound.

In real commodities markets, the price of coffee changes by very small amounts. What if the price fell from $4 to $3.90, $3.99, or even $3.9999 a pound? A demand schedule showing such small changes in prices would be extremely long and cumbersome. Fortunately, there is a way to avoid such long demand schedules. We can graph the quantity demanded at each price (from Table 1) on axes labeled **price** and **quantity**. Points A through I in Figure 1 are the result. Connecting these points with a line then shows all the possible combinations of price and quantity demanded, and defines the *demand curve* for coffee.

- A **demand curve**, or **demand function**, illustrates the relationship between the price of a good and the quantity demanded, *ceteris paribus*.

Table 1 Demand Schedule for Coffee

Price per pound of coffee	Quantity of coffee demanded (billions of pounds per year)
$8.00	20
7.00	40
6.00	60
5.00	80
4.00	100
3.00	120
2.00	140
1.00	160

Changes in Quantity Demanded vs. Changes in Demand

In order to isolate the relationship between the price of a good and the quantity demanded, the demand curve D in Figure 1 assumes that all other variables (e.g., taste, income, prices of other goods, numbers of buyers) that would affect the amount consumers would be willing and able to buy remain constant.

A drop in the price of coffee in Figure 1 from $6 to $5 a pound would cause a movement along D from point C to point E. The increase on

Figure 1 Demand Curve for Coffee

the quantity axis from 60 billion to 80 billion pounds a year is a response to a change in the price of coffee and is called an increase in the *quantity demanded*.

- **Changes in quantity demanded** are due to changes in the price of the good and are shown as *movements along the demand curve*.

An increase in coffee sales from 120 million to 160 million pounds a year at a constant price of $3.00 reflects a change in some other variable. If consumers developed a stronger preference for coffee over other drinks, or if their incomes rose, or if the number of coffee drinkers increased, more coffee would be demanded at any price. Changes in variables other than price alter the entire relationship between price and quantity demanded and cause *changes in demand*, as illustrated in Figure 2. There will be a new quantity demanded at every price and a different price that consumers would be willing and able to pay for any quantity.

Figure 2 Change in Demand

- **Changes in demand** are due to changes in variables other than the price of the good and are shown as *shifts of the demand curve*.

If more coffee is demanded at every price, the demand curve will shift to the right—as shown by the shift of the demand curve from D to D' in Figure 2.

In the demand curve graph, the variables price and quantity are called *endogenous* variables. **Endogenous** means literally *originating from within*. All other variables besides price and quantity are called **exogenous** variables. Exogenous, you won't be surprised to learn, means *originating from outside*.

Figure 3 illustrates changes in demand and changes in quantity demanded that result from changes in a number of significant variables. Study this figure carefully until you understand why each change occurs as it does.

Supply and Price

Making something as a hobby and giving it away isn't economic activity. Rational, profit-maximizing firms will produce and sell a good or service only if they can receive a price for it. In a competitive market, the quantity of a good which firms will be willing and able to produce and sell tends to vary directly with the price of the good. Higher prices encourage producers to offer larger quantities of products for sale. Unfortunately, there isn't a *law of supply* equivalent to the law of demand—the exceptions are more numerous and important than the rare exceptions to the law of demand.

The Supply Schedule and the Supply Curve

The quantity of a good supplied by sellers depends on a number of things—the price they can get for the good, the prices of resources used to produce it, and the state of production technology. To isolate the relationship between the price of a good and the quantity supplied, it is necessary to assume that all the other variables remain constant.

The **supply schedule** in Table 2 shows a hypothetical relationship

Table 2 Supply Schedule for Coffee

Price per pound of coffee	Quantity of coffee supplied (billions of pounds per year)
$8.00	170
7.00	160
6.00	150
5.00	140
4.00	130
3.00	120
2.00	110
1.00	100

Figure 3 Changes in Quantity Demanded vs. Changes in Demand

Changes in Quantity Demanded
a) Airlines lower New York–Los Angeles fare from $500 to $350, increasing passengers per flight from 150 to 250.
b) Increase in price of gasoline from 60¢ to $1.00 a gallon reduces quantity demanded from 60 billion to 40 billion gallons a year.

Changes in Demand
c) Rising income increases demand for recreational land.
d) Imports of low-priced shoes reduces demand for American-made shoes.
e) Increasing population increases demand for wheat.
f) Rising beef prices increase demand for chicken.

between the price of coffee and the quantity supplied. The prices and quantities supplied in Table 2 define points on the **supply curve** S in Figure 4. Notice the general relationship between price and quantity

DEMAND, SUPPLY, AND PRICE: AN OVERVIEW 47

supplied that is suggested by the shape of the supply curve: as price goes up, quantity supplied also goes up.

Figure 4 Supply Curve for Coffee

Changes in Quantity Supplied vs. Changes in Supply

Producers will adjust the quantity of a good they are willing and able to produce and sell in response to a change in the price of the good. This is called a *change in quantity supplied*. In Table 2, an increase in the price of coffee from $6 to $7 a pound would cause the *quantity supplied* to increase from 150 billion pounds a year to 160 billion pounds a year. In Figure 4, this change in quantity supplied would be shown as a movement along the supply curve S from A to B.

- **Changes in quantity supplied** are due to changes in the price of the good and are shown as *movement along the supply curve*.

Changes in any exogenous variables that affect supply—e.g., technology, costs of labor and materials, weather—alter the relationship between price and quantity supplied and cause *changes in supply*.

- **Changes in supply** are due to changes in variables other than the price of the good and are shown as *shifts of the supply curve*.

For example, the United States experienced unusually good weather for growing corn in 1978 and harvested a record corn crop. This change in weather was an exogenous change that increased the amount of corn

Figure 5 Change in Supply

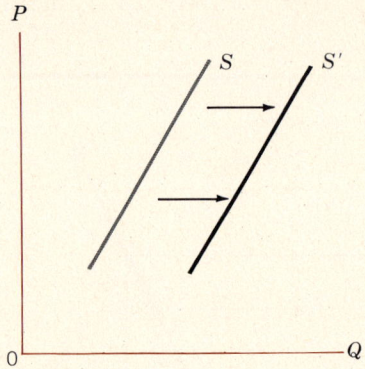

available at all prices. This *change in supply* is shown in Figure 5 as a shift of the supply curve to the right from S to S'.

Figure 6 illustrates changes in supply and changes in quantity supplied resulting from changes in various important endogenous and exogenous variables. Study the figure carefully until you understand the changes that take place.

Equilibrium Price

The interaction among buyers and sellers of a scarce good or resource determines the *equilibrium price* in the market.

- **Equilibrium price** is the price at which the quantity demanded by buyers equals the quantity supplied by sellers.

If the price is at the equilibrium level, it will tend to stay there unless something disturbs demand or supply. If the price isn't at its equilibrium level, it will tend to move toward it. The equilibrium price *clears the mar-*

Table 3 Demand and Supply Schedules

Price per pound of coffee	Quantity demanded (billions of pounds per year)	Quantity supplied (billions of pounds per year)
$8.00	20	170
7.00	40	160
6.00	60	150
5.00	80	140
4.00	100	130
3.00	120	120
2.00	140	110
1.00	160	100

DEMAND, SUPPLY, AND PRICE: AN OVERVIEW   49

ket: at this price, there will be no unsold goods or resources left in the hands of sellers and no unsatisfied buyers waiting in line.

Equilibrium price can be analyzed easily with the demand and supply schedules and curves already introduced. Table 3 combines the demand

Figure 6 Change in Quantity Supplied vs. Changes in Supply

Changes in Quantity Supplied
a) Increase in price of beef from $1.20 to $1.80 a pound increases quantity supplied from 240 to 360 million pounds a week.
b) Falling wheat prices cause annual production of wheat to drop.

Changes in Supply
c) Revolutionary leaders in Iran decide to reduce oil output regardless of price.
d) a 15¢-per-pack tax on producers of cigarettes causes a reduction in supply.
e) A technological advance in the manufacture of computer chips allows production of calculators at a lower cost, increasing supply at every price.
f) Liberalization of restrictions on imported shoes leads to an increase in supply of imported shoes at every price.

Figure 7 Equilibrium Price and Quantity

schedule from Table 1 and the supply schedule from Table 2. Figure 7 combines the demand curve (D) from Figure 1 and the supply curve (S) from Figure 4.

In Table 3 and Figure 7, the quantity of coffee demanded is greater than the quantity supplied at all prices below $3.00 a pound. At all of these prices, there is *excess demand* for coffee.

- **Excess demand** occurs when the quantity demanded by buyers exceeds the quantity supplied by sellers at a certain price.

With *excess demand*, competition among buyers should bid the price upward. As a result, more sellers are willing to sell more coffee at the higher price, increasing the quantity supplied and reducing the quantity demanded until price and quantity reach the equilibrium level.

At all prices *above* $3 a pound, the quantity supplied is greater than the quantity demanded, and there is *excess supply* of coffee.

- **Excess supply** occurs when the quantity supplied by sellers exceeds the quantity demanded by buyers at a certain price.

With *excess supply*, sellers will try to get rid of unsold coffee by offering it at lower prices. As the price falls, more consumers are willing to buy coffee. The quantity demanded will thus increase and the quantity supplied decrease until price and quantity reach the equilibrium level.

Shortages occur when the price of a good is below the equilibrium price because the quantity supplied isn't sufficient to clear the market of unsatisfied demand. As the price rises, the quantity supplied tends to increase and the quantity demanded falls. When the equilibrium price is reached, the "shortage" disappears. The opposite occurs if there is a **surplus** of a good on the market: the price is too high to clear the market

Figure 8 Changes in Equilibrium Price and Quantity

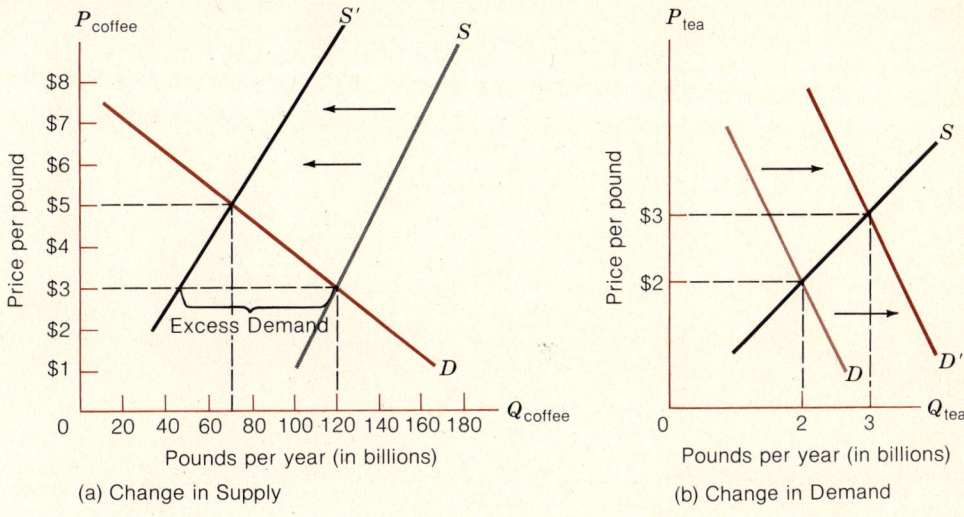

(a) Change in Supply

(b) Change in Demand

of unsold goods. As the price falls, the quantity of the good demanded increases and the quantity supplied falls until equilibrium is reached and the "surplus" disappears.

The equilibrium price, $3.00 in our example, is reached where the quantity demanded equals the quantity supplied. This price *clears the market* of unsold goods and of unsatisfied buyers. Prices above equilibrium fail to clear the market of unsold goods, and excess supply drives the price downward. Prices below equilibrium clear the market of unsold goods, but not of unsatisfied buyers, and excess demand will drive the price upward.[1]

Changes in Equilibrium Price

Equilibrium price can be disturbed by changes in demand or supply. Once the equilibrium is disturbed, the price will move toward a new equilibrium where quantity demanded again equals quantity supplied.

What would happen, for example, if the governments of some coffee-exporting countries tried to raise the price of coffee by withholding part of the crop from market? The situation is shown graphically in Figure 8a. The reduction in the supply of coffee is shown by the shift of the supply curve to the left from S to S'. At the original equilibrium price of

---

1. Throughout this text, equilibrium price will usually be represented by the symbol $\bar{P}$ and equilibrium quantity by the symbol $\bar{Q}$. The horizontal bar over the variable letters means *equilibrium*. Also, *industry* or *market* variables will generally be represented by capital letters, *individual household* or *firm* variables by lower-case letters.

Figure 9 Changes in Equilibrium

Disturbances from the Demand Side
a) Increase in demand for coal increases equilibrium price and quantity of coal.
b) Liberalization of Catholic dietary rules reduces the demand for fish, decreasing equilibrium price and quantity of fish.

Disturbances from the Supply Side
c) Favorable weather increases supply of corn, lowering equilibrium price and increasing equilibrium quantity of corn.
d) Acreage reduction lowers supply of hay, raising equilibrium price and reducing equilibrium quantity of hay.

$3.00, there is now excess demand because the quantity demanded on D is more than the quantity supplied on S'. The excess demand bids the price upward to its new equilibrium at $5.00, where the quantity demanded again equals the quantity supplied.

Equilibrium price and quantity may be disturbed by changes in other exogenous variables as well. As coffee prices rise, many people may turn to substitutes for coffee—such as cocoa and tea. This would create an increase in demand for cocoa and tea and would result in higher prices for those goods. The situation is shown graphically in Figure 8b. As more people substitute tea for coffee, the demand curve for tea shifts to the right from D to D', creating excess demand for tea at the original equilibrium price of $2. The excess demand for tea at $2 will drive the price upward until the new equilibrium price is reached at $3.

Figure 9 summarizes our discussion of equilibrium price by showing changes in equilibrium price which would result from changes in important supply and demand variables. Study this figure until you feel confident that you could predict the effect of a change in any endogenous or exogenous variable upon the equilibrium price of a good or service.

Applying the Tools

The Basic Economics of Price Controls

Even a basic understanding of prices and markets is useful in getting beyond simplistic and shallow arguments on some important economic issues. What should a community do, for example, if markets determine equilibrium prices that many of its members feel are too high or too low? The seemingly simple answer is to enact policies that keep price from rising above some desired maximum or from falling below some desired minimum. Unfortunately, as we shall see, life isn't quite so simple.

Rent Controls and Housing Shortages

In many cities, increases in the demand for rental housing have pushed equilibrium rents to levels higher than many tenants are able to pay. To deal with this problem, some city governments have enacted rent-control laws that establish maximum rents below the equilibrium level. Rent-control does keep rents from rising, but its effects go beyond this.

As Figure A illustrates, the equilibrium rent, $\overline{R}$, is reached where the quantity demanded equals the quantity supplied. The controlled rent, R^*, is an *effective maximum price*.

- An **effective maximum price** is a set maximum price which is lower than the equilibrium price.

Setting the maximum rent at R^* results in excess demand for housing at that price, or a *housing shortage*, since the rent can't rise to the level that would clear the market of potential renters. The available housing at R^* must be allocated through some non-price means—position on a waiting list, family size, income, age, need, or simply first-come-first-served. In addition, a government bureaucracy will be needed to enforce the rent controls. Unable to increase rent, many landlords will try to maintain the rate of return on their investments by reducing services to tenants, maintaining properties poorly, and ultimately abandoning the dilapidated buildings altogether when they become uninhabitable.[2] Other owners of rental properties may avoid rent controls and earn handsome returns on their investments by converting rental units to condominiums. Those renters unable to buy condos are displaced.

Figure A

Decay and conversion have a common effect. They reduce the supply of rental housing units, as shown by the shift of the supply curve from S to S' in Figure A. This puts greater upward pressure on rents and increases the excess demand at the controlled rent (R^*). Thus, economic analysis suggests that simple rent controls are an inadequate means of providing adequate housing at reasonable costs.

Advocates of free markets argue that simply allowing rents to rise eliminates the need for enforcement machinery and will eventually increase the supply of rental housing available. Higher rents will encourage owners to maintain units and will attract resources for the construction of more units. This in turn will increase the supply of rental housing and dampen the initial rise in rents. In the short run, however, the higher rents may have a devastating effect upon those at the bottom of the income scale.

---

2. A most dramatic example of this was the rash of arsons that raged in the Bronx section of New York City in the late 1970s, as decayed units were burned by owners seeking to collect insurance or by enraged tenants who could no longer tolerate their living conditions.

Another alternative, the construction of publicly owned housing units, would increase the supply of rental housing and drive the equilibrium rent downward. But such construction is not free. With a fixed government budget, funds for public housing will have to come from reductions in other programs. If the government budget is increased to finance additional housing, members of the community will have to pay through higher taxes.

The ultimate choice among alternative plans for dealing with high rents and housing shortages depends largely upon one's values, ideology, and view of economic reality. One thing is clear from our analysis, however: rent control programs alone cannot eliminate high rents without creating a serious housing shortage.

Farm Price Supports and Minimum Wages

Sometimes price controls take the form of minimum prices set *above* the equilibrium price. In the United States, government farm price supports are a good example of **effective minimum prices**. Price supports are promoted as a way to stabilize agricultural prices and incomes and preserve the family farm. But they have had other effects as well.

Figure B

In Figure B, the support price of wheat, P^*, is set above the equilibrium price, $\overline{P}$. The higher price encourages farmers to produce more wheat (W') than the amount that can be sold at that price (W^*), resulting in excess supply. The government is forced to find some way of dealing with the excess supply. A number of alternative strategies for handling this problem will be examined in detail in a later chapter.

A *minimum wage* for employed workers is another kind of effective minimum price. In Figure C, the equilibrium market wage is $2.00 an hour. At this wage, employees are willing to supply $\overline{Q}$ hours of labor to firms, and firms in turn wish to purchase exactly $\overline{Q}$ hours. There are no workers unable to find work at the market wage, and no firms unable to find labor.

Now suppose the Congress passes legislation establishing a minimum wage of $4.00 an hour, in order to aid the lowest paid workers in the economy. At this wage,

Figure C

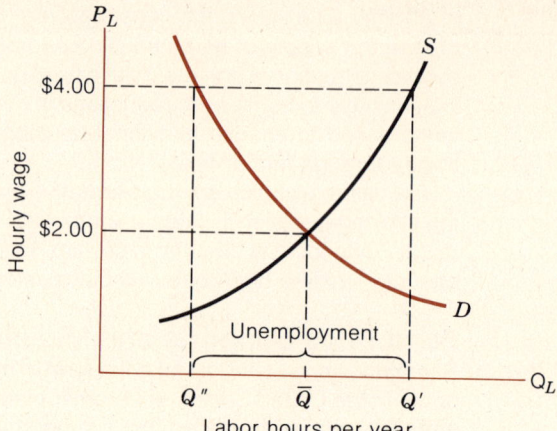

many more workers than before are willing to supply labor, so Q' hours of labor are now made available. Firms, on the other hand, are now less willing to hire labor, demanding only Q'' hours of labor. The difference between the quantity of labor supplied by households and the quantity demanded by firms represents *unemployment*.

The admirable intention behind most minimum-wage laws is to raise the wages of the lowest-paid workers in the economy; economic analysis suggests that one additional result may be a loss of employment for the very workers the laws are meant to help. Minimum wage laws and their effects on employment will be discussed in more detail in a later chapter. Our present analysis of minimum wages, like our analysis of rent controls, does demonstrate a sad truth of economics: that good intentions do not always bring about good economic results.

Interfering with markets to establish maximum or minimum prices requires some means of dealing with resulting surpluses and shortages. This doesn't necessarily mean that price controls are always bad, however. Sometimes price controls are implemented for good normative or practical reasons, and they may be fairly effective for short periods of time. Clearly, though, this seemingly simple approach to complex problems isn't sufficient by itself, and the difficulties created by price controls will be greater the longer they are maintained in the face of growing surpluses or shortages.

Partial and General Equilibrium

So far, we have looked at prices and quantities only in a single market or a couple of related markets. This approach is called **partial equilibrium analysis**. In the real world, of course, markets aren't isolated from one another and disturbances in one market may have far-reaching effects in others.

- **General equilibrium analysis** analyzes the interrelationships among all markets in the economy.

Figure 10 General Equilibrium

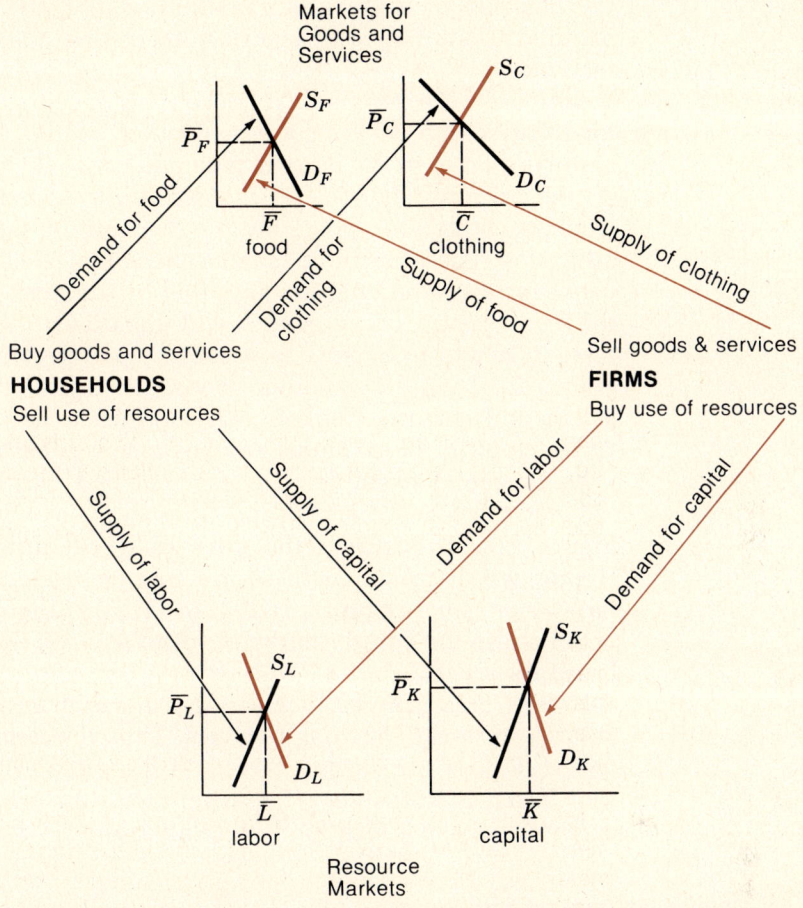

Because general equilibrium analysis is quite complex, virtually all the analysis of equilibrium in this text is partial analysis. But it is important to look for a moment at a more general picture of the market economy.

Figure 10 is a very simple sketch of a private market economy. Households own the resources (land, labor, and capital) and earn income by selling the use of their resources in resource markets. Each household decides for itself how much of its resources to sell in the resource market and how much of each good to purchase in the goods market in order to maximize utility. In other words, households exert supply pressure in resource markets and demand pressure in product markets.

Similarly, each firm chooses for itself the quantity of goods to produce in order to maximize profits. To produce the goods, the firm must purchase resources in the resource market. Thus firms exert supply pressure in product markets and demand pressure in resource markets.

Product markets will adjust to an equilibrium level of prices and quantities where the quantity of each good demanded is equal to the quantity supplied. Resource markets will adjust to equilibrium where the quantity of each resource supplied is equal to the quantity demanded. Disturbance of equilibrium in one market will affect other markets.

Suppose, for example, that households develop a stronger preference for leisure time over income and other goods. This will reduce the supply of labor in the labor market and cause the price of labor to rise. As the price of labor rises, firms will try to substitute other resources (such as capital) for labor, and the demand for capital will increase at all prices. These resource market changes will affect the relationship between price and quantity supplied by the firms (that is, it will shift the firms' supply curve), which will disturb equilibrium in the product market. In addition, since households have developed a stronger preference for leisure over other goods, the demand for goods will fall. Goods and resource markets will continue to adjust to the initial disturbance until the economy reaches a new **general equilibrium**.

As a second example, suppose that bad weather in the Midwest reduces the wheat harvest and the supply of wheat from S to S' in Figure 11a. This drives the price of wheat upward from $\bar{P}_w$ to $\bar{P}'_w$. Higher wheat prices increase the cost of producing goods that contain wheat, such as bread. In Figure 11b, this higher cost of producing bread shifts the supply curve of bread from S_b to S'_b, and the price of bread rises to $\bar{P}'_b$.

Higher bread prices increase the demand for goods that are substitutes for bread, such as potatoes. Thus the demand curve for potatoes in Figure 11c shifts to D'_p, and the price of potatoes rises to $\bar{P}'_p$. The initial disturbance of equilibrium in the wheat market has now spread to the markets for two related goods—and the story doesn't

Figure 11 Changes in General Equilibrium

(a) Fall in Supply of Wheat
(b) Fall in Supply of Bread
(c) Increase in Demand for Potatoes

end here. Higher prices for potatoes will increase the demand for substitutes for potatoes, such as stuffing, which is made from bread, which contains wheat....

Higher wheat prices also affect the allocation of resources. As the price of wheat rises, farmers are encouraged to use more of their land, labor, and capital in wheat production. This increases the supply of wheat and reduces the supplies of crops that had been produced with the reallocated resources. Thus, for example, a shortage of wheat and high wheat prices in 1973 eventually led to a popcorn shortage!

Summary

1. The basic units in economic models are **households** (which buy goods and supply the use of resources) and **firms** (which sell goods and buy the use of resources).
2. With **consumer sovereignty**, the basic decisions for the economy are made by the utility-maximizing actions of households and the profit-maximizing actions of firms in markets. Firms respond to consumer preferences as expressed by *dollar votes* in the markets for goods and services.
3. The basic function of prices is to ration and allocate scarce goods and resources among potential buyers. *Free* goods and resources are so abundant relative to the demand for them that they command no price.
4. The **demand function**, or **demand curve**, shows the relationship between price and quantity of a good demanded, other things equal. In all relevant circumstances, there is an inverse relationship between price and quantity demanded.
5. Movements along a demand curve in response to a change in the price of the good are called **changes in quantity demanded**. Changes in the quantity people are willing and able to buy due to changes other than changes in price are called **changes in demand**.
6. A **supply function**, or **supply curve**, shows the relationship between the price of a good and the quantity supplied, other things equal. Movements along a supply curve due to a change in price are called **changes in quantity supplied**, and changes in the amount supplied due to changes other than changes in price are called **changes in supply**.
7. **Equilibrium price and quantity** are reached when there is no tendency for price to change. This occurs where the quantity demanded equals the quantity supplied. Price tends to move toward or remain at its equilibrium level.
8. If the price is below equilibrium, quantity demanded exceeds quantity supplied and **excess demand** causes the price to rise. If the price is above equilibrium, the quantity supplied exceeds quantity demanded, and **excess supply** drives the price downward.
9. An **effective maximum price** set below equilibrium price keeps price from rising to its equilibrium level, and results in excess demand. An **effective minimum price** set above equilibrium price keeps price from falling to equilibrium, and results in excess supply.
10. **Partial equilibrium** analyzes equilibrium in a single market independently of other related markets. **General equilibrium** analyzes equilibrium in all markets and the interrelationships among markets.

Concepts for Review

market
market structure
household
firm
consumer sovereignty
laissez-faire
price
scarce goods
free goods

law of demand
demand schedule
demand curve or function
endogenous
exogenous
supply schedule
supply curve
equilibrium price
cleared market

excess demand
excess supply
shortage
surplus
price controls
effective maximum price
effective minimum price
partial equilibrium
general equilibrium

Questions

1. Nostalgia buffs and older students may recall a popular song entitled "The Best Things in Life Are Free."
   a. How many things in your life are free, in the sense that economics defines the term *free*?
   b. Can you think of any things that were free to your parents, grandparents, or great-grandparents that aren't free to you? What happened to the things that used to be free?
2. The energy crisis has produced a controversy over whether higher gasoline prices or gasoline rationing is the more effective means of allocating gasoline.
   a. Are higher prices and rationing really different? How should the alternatives be stated to be more accurate economically?
   b. Would there be any rationing of gasoline if we simply "froze" gasoline prices?
3. Why is the law of demand stated with a *ceteris paribus* assumption?
4. Would it be correct to define *equilibrium price* as the price at which the quantity bought equals the quantity sold?
5. Does *consumer sovereignty* mean the same thing as *majority rule*?
6. In each of the following, will the effect be an increase or decrease in demand, an increase or decrease in quantity demanded, an increase or decrease in supply, or an increase or decrease in quantity supplied?
   a. Higher oil prices encourage the production of more oil.
   b. An international cartel of oil producers decides to withhold oil from the market at prevailing prices.
   c. Higher retail prices of gasoline reduce gasoline consumption.
   d. Higher gasoline prices cause more people to travel by train and bus.
   e. A massive antismoking advertising and public information program causes the sales of cigarettes to fall.
7. Suppose that all the product and resource markets in the economy are in equilibrium, and suddenly the price of coal rises. We know from the law of demand that the quantity of coal demanded will fall. Can you think of several other markets which might be affected (directly or indirectly) by the coal price increase? What would be the nature of those effects?

Problems

1. If electronic gizmos cost $300 each, consumers wouldn't be able or willing to buy any gizmos at all, while producers would be willing and able to supply 500 gizmos. Every $20 reduction in the price of gizmos would increase the quantity of gizmos demanded by 10. Every $20 reduction in the price would decrease the quantity of gizmos supplied by 40.
   a. From the above information, fill out a demand schedule showing the quantity of gizmos demanded at prices of 300, 280, 260, 240, 220, 200, 180, 160, 140, 120, 100, and 80. On a graph, construct the demand curve for gizmos from this information.
   b. Fill out a supply schedule showing the quantity supplied at the prices in part (a), and construct the supply curve for gizmos from this information on the same graph you used for the demand curve.
   c. Find the equilibrium price and quantity of gizmos from the information, and explain how you know that you have found equilibrium price and quantity.
   d. Suppose that the government froze the price of gizmos at $P^* = \$100$ because it was felt that this is the fair price to pay for them. What would be the results of this action?
   e. Suppose that, as a result of improvements in gizmo technology, sellers are now willing and able to offer an additional 20 gizmos for sale at every price. Explain the effects of this (if any) on demand, supply, equilibrium price, and equilibrium quantity.

4

Elasticity of Demand and Supply

Preview: The equilibrium model of the last chapter illustrated that quantities of goods and services demanded and supplied will change in response to changes in price, and that prices will change in response to changes in supply and demand. But for many policy decisions—from those of a small retailer to those of the federal government—the central question is how large those changes will be. The concept of **elasticity** introduced in this chapter can provide an answer to that question.

Would excise taxes and higher prices on gasoline have a significant effect on gasoline consumption? Would gasoline buyers spend more or less on gasoline at higher prices than at lower prices? Would a decline in the supply of wheat have its greatest effect on the price of wheat or the quantity of wheat demanded? These, obviously, are important questions, and answers to them involve the responsiveness of quantity demanded or supplied to changes in price.

Slope as a Measure of Responsiveness

The appearance of a demand or supply curve may give us some clue about the responsiveness of quantity to changes in price. A *steep demand curve*, such as that in Figure 1a, seems to indicate that quantity demanded is not very responsive to changes in price. Notice that a large drop in price from P to P' in Figure 1a results in only a small increase in quantity demanded from Q to Q'. A *flat demand curve*, such as that in Figure 1b, seems to show quantity demanded much more responsive to the same change in price. The same general observations hold true for supply curves: for *steep supply curves*, such as that in Figure 1c, quantity supplied seems relatively unresponsive to changes in price; for *flat supply curves*, such as that in Figure 1d, quantity supplied seems much more responsive.

Figure 1 Slopes and Responsiveness

(a) "Steep" Demand Curve (b) "Flat" Demand Curve (c) "Steep" Supply Curve (d) "Flat" Supply Curve

These general observations can be made more precise by looking at the *slopes* of demand and supply curves.

- The **slope** of a demand or supply curve is the ratio of the change in price over the change in quantity demanded or supplied.

Algebraically, the slopes of these curves are expressed as

$$\text{slope} = \frac{\Delta P}{\Delta Q} \tag{1}$$

where ΔP is the change in price and ΔQ is the change in quantity demanded or supplied.[1]

The slope of a demand curve shows in absolute terms how responsive quantity demanded is to changes in price. This is a useful piece of information for certain types of questions. Suppose, for example, that we want to reduce daily gasoline consumption by ten million gallons, i.e., $\Delta Q_d = -10$ million gallons. If we know that the slope of the demand curve for gasoline is -2, we can set $\Delta P / \Delta Q_d$ equal to -2 and solve for ΔP:

$$\frac{\Delta P}{\Delta Q_d} = \frac{\Delta P}{-10 \text{ mill. gal.}} = -2$$

$$\Delta P = -2 \times -10 = 20¢ \text{ a gallon.}$$

Thus we must increase the price of a gallon of gasoline by 20¢ in order to bring about a 10 million gallon decrease in quantity of gasoline demanded. Figure 2 illustrates this situation.

The slope of a supply curve shows in absolute terms the responsiveness of quantity supplied to changes in price—again, useful informa-

---

1. The Greek letter delta (Δ) means *a change in*. See appendix to Chapter 1.

Figure 2 Slope of a Demand Curve

tion for some purposes. For example, the advocates of natural gas price deregulation in the middle and late 1970s argued that higher gas prices would increase the quantity of gas supplied by producers. Suppose that we know that the supply curve for natural gas looks like the curve in Figure 3, with a slope of 2. Suppose further that govern-

Figure 3 Slope of a Supply Curve

ment forecasters predict a price increase of 20¢ per cubic foot of gas if the price of gas is deregulated. We can find the increase in quantity of gas supplied that will result from this price increase by setting $\Delta P / \Delta Q_s$ equal to 2 and solving for ΔQ_s:

$$\frac{\Delta P}{\Delta Q_s} = \frac{20¢}{\Delta Q_s} = 2$$

$$\Delta Q_s = \frac{20}{2} = 10 \text{ million cu. ft.}$$

Despite their usefulness for certain kinds of questions, however, slopes of demand and supply curves have serious limitations as measures of responsiveness of quantity demanded or quantity supplied to changes in price. In the first place, associating slope with the steepness of demand and supply curves can be misleading. Both demand curves in Figure 4 show exactly the same relationship between price and quantity demanded. The demand curve in Figure 4b is steeper because the scales are different on the axes. The vertical axis in Figure 4b has been stretched out, and the horizontal axis has been compressed.

Even the numerical value of the slope can be misleading because the value of the slope depends on the units used to express price and quantity. For example, suppose that a $1 reduction in the price of a good causes quantity demanded to increase by 20 units. Calculating the value of the slope, we have

Figure 4 The Illusion of Slope

$$\frac{\Delta P}{\Delta Q_d} = \frac{-\$1}{20} = -0.05.$$

If we stated exactly the same relationship using cents instead of dollars for price units, every 100¢ reduction in price causes quantity demanded to increase by 20, and the slope is

$$\frac{\Delta P}{\Delta Q_d} = \frac{-100¢}{20} = \frac{-10}{2} = -5.$$

In order to get around these problems with slopes, economists measure the responsiveness of demand and supply in terms of *elasticity*.

- **Elasticity of demand or supply** is the ratio of *percentage* change in quantity over the *percentage* change in some other variable.

Although there are many different elasticities, probably the most important is *price elasticity*.

- **Price elasticity** is the ratio of the percentage change in quantity over the percentage change in price.

Because changes are expressed in percentage terms, elasticity isn't affected by the choice of units or by the apparent steepness of demand and supply curves. In this chapter, all references to *elasticity* refer to price elasticity.

Elasticity of Demand

Elasticity of demand tells us how responsive quantity demanded is to changes in price. It is expressed numerically by the **elasticity coefficient**, which can be written as

$$e_d = -\frac{\% \text{ change in quantity demanded}}{\% \text{ change in price}} = -\frac{\% \Delta Q_d}{\% \Delta P}. \quad (2)$$

The minus sign in the equation is placed there simply to give the coefficient a positive value.

Many students confuse the elasticity of demand with the slope of the demand curve. Actually, the two are quite different. Elasticity measures the ratio of percentage changes in quantity demanded over price, while the slope measures the ratio of absolute change in price over absolute change in quantity demanded. Percentage changes are proportional changes—the change in price or quantity as a proportion of the total price or quantity. Thus, $\%\Delta Q$ can be written $\Delta Q/Q$ and $\%\Delta P$ can be written $\Delta P/P$. With these changes, the *elasticity coefficient* becomes

$$e_d = -\frac{(\Delta Q_d/Q_d)}{(\Delta P/P)}. \quad (3)$$

This expression can be written in a way that expresses the relationship between e_d and slope clearly and allows convenient calculation of the value of the coefficient.

$$e_d = -\frac{P}{Q_d} \times \frac{\Delta Q_d}{\Delta P} = -\frac{P}{Q_d} \times \frac{1}{\text{Slope}}. \tag{4}$$

For example, if we are given $P = \$50$, $Q_d = 20$, and the slope of the demand curve $= -2$, e_d is

$$e_d = -\frac{P}{Q_d} \times \frac{1}{\text{Slope}} = -\frac{50}{20} \times \frac{1}{-2} = \frac{5}{4}.$$

This tells us that the elasticity of demand at the given price and quantity is 5/4.

Many times, the relevant question is the elasticity for a given change in prices, or the elasticity between two prices. This is called an *arc approximation* of elasticity.

- An **arc approximation** of elasticity shows the average elasticity between two prices.

To be meaningful approximations, arc approximations are taken for relatively small changes in price and quantity.

To calculate the arc approximation of elasticity of demand between two prices and quantities, we have to rewrite equation 3 slightly. If price changes by $\Delta P = P_1 - P_0$ and quantity demanded changes (in the opposite direction) by $\Delta Q = Q_1 - Q_0$, the average price is $(P_1 + P_2)/2$ and the average quantity is $(Q_1 + Q_0)/2$. To calculate the arc approximation of elasticity of demand, we simply take the changes in quantity and price as percentages of the average quantity and price. Substituting the average price for P and the average quantity for Q in equation 3 above, we get.

$$e_d = -\frac{\frac{\Delta Q}{Q}}{\frac{\Delta P}{P}} = -\frac{\frac{Q_1 - Q_0}{\left(\frac{Q_1 + Q_0}{2}\right)}}{\frac{P_1 - P_0}{\left(\frac{P_1 + P_0}{2}\right)}} = -\frac{\left(\frac{Q_1 - Q_0}{Q_1 + Q_0}\right)}{\left(\frac{P_1 - P_0}{P_1 + P_0}\right)}. \tag{5}$$

The value of the elasticity coefficient yields important information on elasticity of demand.

- If the percentage change in quantity demanded is greater than the percentage change in price, the value of the elasticity coefficient is greater than 1, and demand is **elastic**.
- If the percentage change in quantity demanded is less than the percentage change in price, the value of the elasticity coefficient is less than one, and demand is **inelastic**.

- If the percentage change in quantity demanded equals the percentage change in price, the value of the elasticity coefficient is 1, and demand is **unitarily elastic.**

Determinants of Elasticity of Demand

Demand is *more elastic* the larger the percentage change in quantity as a result of a given percentage change in price. What factors determine the elasticity of demand for a particular good?

Perhaps the single most important determinant of elasticity of demand is the availability and attractiveness of substitutes for the good.

- Demand is *more elastic* the greater the availability and attractiveness of substitutes for a good.

At prevailing prices, the elasticity of demand for such things as telephone calls, insulin for diabetics, and heroin for addicts is low because there are very few close or attractive substitutes. The demand for a single farmer's wheat or for different brands of the same product is much more elastic because it's easier to find close substitutes for them.

Elasticity also depends on the percentage of a household's income spent on the good.

- Demand is *more elastic* the greater the percentage of the household's income spent on the good.

Some items, such as water and salt, account for such a small part of the typical household's budget that large percentage changes in price won't be noticed, and quantity demanded will fall very little. If a household consumed 6 pounds of table salt a year at a price of 25¢ per pound, and the price doubled to 50¢ per pound, the household's annual expenditure on salt would rise by a mere $1.50 if it didn't reduce its salt consumption at all—a trivial increase for most households. On the other hand, if the price of automobiles, housing, or some other large expenditure increased, the effect would be much more obvious, and households would be likely to respond with substantial reductions in quantity demanded.

Generally, the elasticity of demand for a good isn't the same at all prices (some exceptions will be discussed later). If the price of telephone calls rises sharply, for example, substitutes (letters, telegrams, etc.) for telephone calls become more attractive than they were when telephone calls were cheaper, and demand becomes more elastic at the higher price.

- Generally, demand for a good is *more elastic* at higher prices than at lower prices.

Time also affects the elasticity of demand.

- Demand for a good tends to be *more elastic* the longer the time period considered.

For example, empirical studies of the demand for gasoline have estimated very low elasticities for short periods and greater elasticities for longer periods. The reason is quite simple. For short periods of time, most households must use their existing (and usually fuel-inefficient) cars. It takes time for habits to change (for example, driving habits and preference for large cars). It also takes time to design more fuel-efficient cars and retool to produce them. As the price of gasoline remains high for a longer period of time, however, quantity demanded becomes more responsive to the change in price. Over long periods of time, consumers will tend to substitute smaller, more fuel-efficient cars, and alter driving habits to save on the more expensive gasoline.

Elasticity Along the Demand Curve

Since elasticity is affected by the price of a good, elasticity generally isn't constant at all points on the demand curve. To see why, let's look at a short example.

The demand schedule and demand curve for the Rocky Road Bus Company are given in Table 1 and Figure 5. The slope of the demand curve in this example is constant—every 10-cent change in the fare changes the number of passengers per run by 10—but price elasticity of demand is quite different for different ranges of prices.

Reducing the fare from 90¢ to 80¢, for example, would increase the number of passengers per run from 10 to 20. The elasticity of demand between prices of 90¢ and 80¢ is

$$e_d = -\frac{\frac{10-20}{10+20}}{\frac{.90-.80}{.90+.80}} = -\frac{\frac{-10}{30}}{\frac{.10}{1.70}} = -\frac{-\frac{1}{3}}{\frac{1}{17}} = \frac{1}{3} \times \frac{17}{1} = \frac{17}{3}.$$

Demand is elastic (e_d is greater than 1) between these two prices.

Table 1 Demand Schedule for Rocky Road Bus Company

Bus fare	Passengers per run	Total revenue per run
$1.00	0	$ 0.00
0.90	10	9.00
0.80	20	16.00
0.70	30	21.00
0.60	40	24.00
0.50	50	25.00
0.40	60	24.00
0.30	70	21.00
0.20	80	16.00
0.10	90	9.00
0.00	100	0.00

Figure 5 Demand Curve for Rocky Road

Now consider the same absolute change in price from 20¢ to 10¢. Since the slope is constant, the change in passengers per run will be the same as it was in the previous example. However, compared with the previous example, we have a smaller *percentage* change in quantity and a larger *percentage* change in price. Thus, we should expect a less elastic demand over this range of prices than when price changed from 90¢ to 80¢. In fact, the elasticity coefficient is

$$e_d = -\frac{\dfrac{80-90}{80+90}}{\dfrac{.20-.10}{.20+.10}} = -\frac{\dfrac{-10}{170}}{\dfrac{.10}{.30}} = -\frac{-\dfrac{1}{17}}{\dfrac{1}{3}} = \frac{1}{17} \times \frac{3}{1} = \frac{3}{17}.$$

Even though the slope is constant everywhere on the demand curve in Figure 5, elasticity of demand isn't. Demand is elastic for all prices above 50¢ and inelastic for all prices below 50¢. You should verify this by calculating elasticities of demand for the various changes in price shown in Table 1.

Elasticity and Total Revenue

If Rocky Road wants to raise its *total revenue* per run, should it raise its price or lower it? The answer depends on two things—the original price, and the elasticity of demand at that price.

- **Total revenue** (*TR*) is the price per unit of a good, multiplied by the quantity demanded at that price, or $TR = P \times Q_d$.

From the consumers' viewpoint, this represents **total expenditure**. The bus company's TR for various prices and quantities is shown in the third column of Table 1. The TR at a price of $.40 and 60 passengers per run is shown graphically as the shaded area in Figure 5.

Starting at a fare of $1.00 and TR = $0, lowering the fare increases TR until the fare reaches 50¢. Over this range of prices, demand is elastic (verify this by calculating the elasticity coefficient for price changes in this range).

- If demand is *elastic*, changing the price causes TR to change in the opposite direction.

Reducing price when demand is elastic increases quantity demanded by a larger percentage than the percentage reduction in price, and TR rises. If the price is increased with elastic demand, the percentage reduction in quantity demanded is larger than the percentage increase in price, and TR falls.

Below prices of 50¢, Rocky Road's TR would fall if it lowered the fare, and would rise as it raised the fare (up to a fare of 50¢). Over this range of prices, demand is *inelastic* (verify the elasticity by calculating the value of the coefficients for several price changes over this range).

- If demand is *inelastic*, changing the price causes TR to change in the same direction.

Reducing the price with inelastic demand increases quantity by a smaller percentage than the percentage reduction of price, so TR falls. If price is increased with inelastic demand, the percentage reduction in quantity demanded is less than the percentage in price, and TR rises.

At a fare of 50¢, demand changes from elastic (above 50¢) to inelastic (below 50¢). At this point, demand is *unitarily elastic*, and TR is at its maximum.

- If demand is *unitarily elastic*, TR is constant or at its maximum.

These results are summarized graphically in Figure 6. All three parts of the figure show the same demand curve, and in each part, the grey areas represent losses of TR as a result of selling the original quantity at a lower price, and the brown areas represent gains in TR as a result of the additional units sold at the lower price. Lowering the price from $16 to $14 in Figure 6a results in a loss of revenue of $40 (the grey area) on the first 20 units, and a gain of $280 from selling 20 more units at the lower price. Demand is *elastic* in this range, as shown by the fact that TR rises (the brown area is larger than the grey area) as price falls.

If the price falls from $10 to $8, as in Figure 6b, the loss in revenue (the grey area) equals the gain in revenue (the brown area), and TR is unchanged. Thus, demand is *unitarily elastic* between prices of $10 and $8. Finally, lowering the price from $4 to $2, as in Figure 6c, leads to a larger loss in revenue (the grey area) than is gained by the additional

Figure 6 Elasticity and Total Revenue

(a) Elastic Demand   (b) Unitarily Elastic Demand   (c) Inelastic Demand

Some Constant Elasticity Demand Curves

units sold (the brown area), and TR falls because demand is *inelastic*.

With the correct mathematical form, a demand curve may have constant elasticity over its entire range of prices and quantities, but constant-elasticity demand curves are the exception rather than the rule. Figure 7 shows three constant-elasticity demand curves.

Figures 7a and 7b are the extreme cases. In Figure 7a, demand is *completely inelastic*—quantity demanded is the same at all prices, and e_d is zero at all prices or for any change in prices. Figure 7b shows the opposite extreme—*completely elastic* demand. If the price that buyers are willing and able to pay is the same for all quantities, $e_d = \infty$ for all quantities or changes in quantity.

Other demand functions of the proper mathematical form will exhibit constant elasticity. Figure 7c is the simplest of these—a demand curve

Figure 7 Constant Elasticity Demand Curves

(a) Complete Inelasticity   (b) Complete elasticity   (c) Rectangular Hyperbola that is *unitarily elastic* for all prices and quantities. This type of demand curve is called a *rectangular hyperbola*—all prices and quantities yield the same *TR*.

Although it's possible for demand to be completely elastic or inelastic at a point or over a segment of the demand curve, it's most unlikely that it would be completely elastic or inelastic for all prices and quantities. With limited incomes, there must be an upper limit on the price buyers would offer for a given quantity of a good, or at least some price at which the quantity demanded would fall as the price rose. Similarly, with limited incomes, there must be some maximum quantity demanded at a given price. *All* demand curves are somewhat unrealistic, of course, but demand curves conforming to the strict mathematical requirements of constant elasticity would be most rare. In short, while constant elasticity is possible, in virtually all practical cases, elasticity of demand won't be constant at all prices and quantities.

Applying the Tools

The Economics of Busting Pushers

To alleviate the serious problem of drug addiction in our country, law enforcement officials have directed most of their efforts at arresting narcotics pushers and thus shutting off the supply. This approach has had some undesirable side effects, however, and an understanding of elasticity of demand helps explain some of the unforeseen and undesirable results of dealing with such a problem from the supply side.

At prevailing prices in illegal street markets, the price elasticity of demand for heroin is probably very low, as shown at the equilibrium price $\bar{P}$ in Figure A. In the eyes of the addict, there simply aren't many good substitutes for heroin. Furthermore, demand probably is price inelastic over a wide range of prices. Heroin prices would have to rise to astronomical levels to induce the addicts to seek substitutes or a cure for their habits.

Now suppose that a major campaign against sellers is effective in reducing the supply from S to S'. Because of the inelasticity of demand, the most dramatic effect of reducing the supply is to raise the price from $\bar{P}$ to $\bar{P}'$. Since *demand is price inelastic*, this *increases total expenditures on heroin* and the total revenues of the surviving sellers—a result hardly consistent with the intent of the policy.

To increase their expenditures on heroin, addicts must intensify their fund-raising activities. We would thus predict worsening problems of burglary, street crime, prostitution, and violence as a result of the campaign. One of the worst periods of street crime and even murder in recent years in Baltimore, for example, occurred during a dock strike that effectively shut off the supply of illegal heroin.

The problem of addiction can be also attacked from the demand side. Effective public education programs and more effective and attractive cures could reduce the growth of demand. A good substitute (such as Methodone) might

Figure A

Quantity of heroin

reduce the demand for heroin.[2] Government-sponsored heroin maintenance programs could depress the demand in illegal street markets. All these strategies would tend to shift the demand curve for heroin in Figure B to the left (from D to D'), thus lowering the price from $\overline{P}$ to $\overline{P}^*$ and lessening the incentive to sell illegal drugs.

Unfortunately, the results of efforts to deal with the problem of drug addiction from the demand side are hard to measure. Furthermore, some such programs conflict with community standards and values. We cannot go into the medical, social, and ethical controversies involved here, but our analysis does make one point very clear: "busting pushers" alone is an inadequate and ineffective means of dealing with the tragic problems of drug addiction.

Figure B

Quantity of heroin

---

2. The substitute may be addictive, however; heroin itself was originally hailed as a substitute for morphine addiction.

Elasticity of Supply

The concept of elasticity and the mechanics of calculating elasticity are the same for elasticity of supply as for elasticity of demand.

- **Elasticity of supply** is the ratio of the percentage change in quantity supplied over the percentage change in price.

Elasticity of supply is measured by the **coefficient of elasticity of supply** (e_s). Algebraically, the coefficient is

$$e_s = \frac{\%\,\Delta Q_s}{\%\,\Delta P} = \frac{P}{Q_s} \times \frac{\Delta Q_s}{\Delta P} = \frac{P}{Q_s} \times \frac{1}{\text{Slope}}$$

where ΔQ_s is the change in quantity supplied. To calculate the elasticity of supply for given changes in price and quantity supplied, use the *arc approximation* technique described for calculating elasticity of demand.

- If the percentage change in quantity supplied is greater than the percentage change in price, the elasticity coefficient is greater than one, and supply is *elastic*.
- If the percentage change in quantity supplied is less than the percentage change in price, the elasticity coefficient is less than one, and supply is *inelastic*.
- If the percentage change in quantity supplied equals the percentage change in price, the value of the elasticity coefficient is one, and supply is *unitarily elastic*.

Basically, the elasticity of supply depends upon the difficulty and cost of changing the quantity supplied. If it is easy to vary quantity supplied, relatively small percentage changes in price will yield relatively large percentage changes in quantity supplied. The more difficult it is to vary quantity supplied, the less responsive quantity supplied will be to changes in price.

- Supply is *more elastic* the easier it is to vary quantity supplied.

Elasticity and the Supply Curve

Generally, supply curves tell us more about elasticity of supply than demand curves tell us about elasticity of demand. The two extremes are easy to show graphically. In Figure 8a, supply is *completely inelastic*. Since quantity supplied doesn't vary with price in Figure 8a, the elasticity coefficient is zero for all prices. Figure 8b shows the other extreme, *completely elastic supply*. In Figure 8b, the price is the same for all quantities, and the coefficient of elasticity is ∞ for all quantities supplied.

In Figure 8c, *all* of the supply curves are *unitarily elastic* for all prices and quantities supplied.

- All straight line supply curves from the origin are unitarily elastic for all prices and quantities.

In Figure 8d, supply curve S_1 is elastic for all prices and quantities. The value of the elasticity coefficient isn't constant, but its value is greater than one for all meaningful prices and quantities.

- Straight-line supply curves that start from the price axis are elastic for all prices and quantities.

Supply curve S_2 in Figure 8d is inelastic for all meaningful prices and quantities. Again, the value of the elasticity coefficient isn't constant along the curve, but its value is always less than one.

- Straight-line supply curves that start from the quantity axis are inelastic for all prices and quantities.

Straight-line supply curves are useful in estimating empirically the relationship between the price and quantity of a good supplied. Generally, a straight-line supply function is "fitted" statistically to price and quantity data.[3]

In the real world, however, supply is unlikely to remain either inelastic or elastic at all levels of output. At very low levels, it is usually possible to increase quantity supplied easily, and supply thus tends to be relatively elastic. As output increases, however, the capacity of firms to produce is more fully employed and resources may not be as readily available. When the firms' capacities are fully employed or additional resources aren't available, it becomes impossible for them to increase output further, and supply becomes completely inelastic. Figure 9 is a more realistic picture of the typical relationship between price and quantity supplied. At any point on the supply curve in Figure 9, we can tell whether supply is elastic, unitarily elastic, or inelastic by constructing straight lines tangent to the supply curve—the

Figure 8 Elasticity and the Supply Curve

(a) Complete Inelasticity   (b) Complete Elasticity   (c) Unitary Elasticity   (d) Straight-Line Supply Curves

---

3. For more on this subject, see the appendix to Chapter 1.

Figure 9 Realistic Supply Curve

elasticity on the curve will be the same as the elasticity on the line tangent to it. For example, at point A on the supply curve, we can tell that supply is elastic because a line tangent to the curve at A hits the price axis. Similarly, we can tell that supply is unitarily elastic at point B and inelastic at point C.

Time and the Elasticity of Supply

Except where quantity supplied is permanently fixed—original Rembrandt paintings, antiques, acre lots on the Malibu coast, etc.—quantity supplied is more responsive to changes in price over longer periods of time than over shorter periods. Consider the effects of the dramatic increase in foreign demand for U.S. wheat in the early 1970s, illustrated by the shift in the demand curve for wheat from D to D' in Figure 10. The immediate effect was an increase in the price of the wheat that had already been produced from $\overline{P}$ to P_1. Because the harvest was already in, the supply of wheat was fixed at $\overline{Q}$ until the next planting and harvest.

- The period of time in which output is fixed is called the *market period*.

During the market period, supply of wheat is completely inelastic, as shown by the vertical supply curve S_1 in Figure 10.

After enough time had passed, farmers were able to respond to the higher price and increased the quantity of wheat supplied, shifting the supply curve from S_1 to S_2. This increase caused the price of wheat to fall to P_2, where D' intersects S_2. As the time period lengthened further, allowing for more reallocation of land and resources to wheat production, the supply of wheat became even more elastic, and the price continued to fall. In Figure 10, the supply curves S_1, S_2, and S_3 reflect longer and longer periods of time and greater ability of producers to change the quantity supplied.

Figure 10 Time and Elasticity of Supply

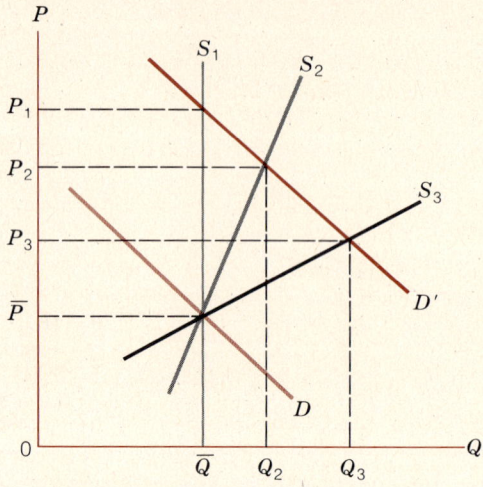

Applying the Tools

Who Pays Excise Taxes?

Excise taxes are taxes levied on products rather than directly on households. Technically, excise taxes are levied on the sellers of products, but the seller tries to pass the tax on to the consumer in the form of a higher price. The ability of the

Figure A

seller to pass the tax on to buyers depends on the elasticity of demand and the elasticity of supply over the relevant range of prices.

In Figure A, demand for cigarettes is inelastic at the initial price, $\overline{P} = \$.40$; supply is elastic. Now, suppose that an excise tax of $.30 per unit is levied on sellers. This will raise the sellers' supply price by the amount of the tax at every quantity supplied, or it will shift the supply curve upward by the amount of the tax to $S + t$. This causes the equilibrium price to rise to $\overline{P}' = \$.65$ and the equilibrium quantity to fall from 60 to 48. At the new price and quantity, however, the sellers actually receive $(\overline{P}' - t) = \$.35$ after the tax is paid. In other words, the sellers "passed on" $(\overline{P}' - \overline{P}) = \$.25$ to buyers, and absorbed $\overline{P} - (\overline{P}' - t) = \$.05$.

In Figure B, demand is elastic at the initial equilibrium price $(\overline{P} = \$.40)$, and supply is inelastic. Suppose that the same excise tax $(t = \$.30)$ per unit is levied, shifting the supply curve to $S + t$. In this case, much less of the tax $(\overline{P}' - \overline{P}) = \$.10$ is passed on to buyers, and more of it, $\overline{P} - (\overline{P}' - t) = \$.20$ is absorbed by sellers.

- The amount of an excise tax that is passed on to buyers is greater the smaller the elasticity of demand relative to the elasticity of supply.

Figure B

At one extreme, if supply is completely elastic or demand is completely inelastic, the entire tax is passed on, as in Figure C(i). At the other extreme, if supply is completely inelastic, the market won't clear if the seller tries to raise the price above $\overline{P}$, and sellers will absorb the entire tax, as in Figure C(ii).

Figure C

Summary

1. The **slope** of a demand or supply curve shows the responsiveness of quantity demanded or quantity supplied to changes in price in absolute terms. Slope can be a misleading measure of responsiveness because the value of the slope is affected by the units used. The apparent steepness or flatness of demand or supply curves is affected by the scales on the price and quantity axes.
2. **Elasticity** measures the responsiveness of quantity to changes in price in percentage terms. As a measure of responsiveness, elasticity is not affected by the choice of units or scales on price and quantity axes.
3. **Elasticity of demand** is the ratio of the percentage change in quantity demanded over the percentage change in price. It may be expressed as an average over a range of prices and quantities **(arc elasticity)** or for a given price and quantity **(point elasticity)**.
4. The most important determinant of the elasticity of demand for a good is the availability and attractiveness of substitutes. Demand is less elastic at any price the greater the difficulty of finding an attractive substitute for the good.
5. Elasticity of demand determines the relationship between changes in the price of a good and changes in total expenditure on the good (or **total revenue**).
6. **Elasticity of supply** is the ratio of percentage change in quantity supplied over percentage change in price.
7. The most important determinant of elasticity of supply is the ability to vary quantity supplied. If quantity is fixed—as, for example, the quantity of land or rare works of art—supply is completely inelastic. If quantity can be increased or decreased easily without increasing price, supply is completely elastic. Supply is more elastic the easier it is to vary quantity supplied.
8. Elasticity of demand and supply determine the reaction of price and quantity to changes in demand or supply, and the proportion of changes in cost that will be passed on to consumers as changes in price and the proportion that will be absorbed by sellers.

Concepts for Review

elasticity of demand
elastic demand
inelastic demand
unitary elasticity
arc approximation

elasticity coefficient
constant elasticity
   demand curves
total revenue
elasticity of supply

elastic supply
inelastic supply
unitarily elastic
   supply
market period

Questions

1. Consider the following pairs of goods. At prevailing prices, which good in each pair is likely to show the greater elasticity of demand? Explain each answer.
   a. A single brand of cigarettes, or all brands of cigarettes considered as a single good?
   b. Gasoline consumed by high-income persons or gasoline consumed by low-income households?
   c. Single-family houses or beer?
   d. Soda pop or water?
2. The Rocky Road Bus Co. is running at a loss because its revenue per run does not cover its cost per run. The cost per run is about the same whether the bus runs empty or full. At a public utility hearing concerning a fare increase, the following arguments are made:
   ROCKY ROAD BUS CO.: We need to raise the fare to increase the revenue per run and cover our costs.
   BUS RIDERS' INTEREST GROUP: More people would ride the bus at lower fares, and the bus company would earn enough additional revenue from the new customers to cover its costs.
   What determines which argument is correct and why?
3. Estimates of the elasticity of demand for gasoline range from 0.1 for very short periods of time to 0.7 for longer periods.
   a. In what ways would the length of time covered affect the elasticity of demand?
   b. Would the estimates of elasticity of demand for gasoline be a reasonable estimate of the demand for gasoline sold by a single station? Explain.
4. Suppose that a 2 percent sales tax, or excise tax, is levied on all goods and services.
   a. Will this cause total spending on every good and service to increase?
   b. Will all prices rise by 2 percent as a result of the tax?
   c. Will every household's total expenditure on any given good or service increase as a result of the tax?
   d. Will the burden of the tax be shared equally by all buyers and all sellers of every good and service?
   Explain your answers, using elasticity of demand and elasticity of supply.
5. One of the determinants of the rental value of land is its *site value*, or the value that is determined by the quality and location of the land. In the nineteenth century, an American journalist and economist named Henry George advocated a "single tax" on the site value of land, and argued that the entire tax would be borne by landlords.
   Under what circumstances (if any) would George's argument be valid? Explain.

Problems

1. The following figures show the quantity of shoes demanded per week for the Hop, Skip & Jump Shoe Co. at various prices.

PRICE	QUANTITY DEMANDED
$50	0
45	10
40	20
35	30
30	40
25	50
20	60
15	70
10	80
5	90
0	100

   a. Plot the data graphically and draw the demand curve for Hop, Skip & Jump Shoes.
   b. Calculate the value of the slope of the demand curve. What does the slope tell you? For what types of questions is the value of the slope relevant information? Are there any difficulties in using the slope as a measure of responsiveness of quantity demanded to changes in price?
   c. Calculate the seller's total revenue (TR) at each price.
   d. Without calculating the coefficient of elasticity of demand, identify the range of prices over which demand is elastic and the range of prices over which it is inelastic. Find the price where demand is unitarily elastic.
   e. Using the arc approximation technique, calculate the elasticity of demand between prices of $15 and $20 and between prices of $40 and $45.

PART TWO
Demand in the Product Market

Chapter 3 introduced the two basic kinds of markets—**product markets** and **resource markets**—and the two sides of *any* market—the buyer's side (**demand**) and the seller's side (**supply**). In the next two chapters, we'll take a more detailed look at the behavior of households as **buyers** in the **produce** market.

We begin by asking *why* an individual household chooses to consume any particular combination of goods. A technique known as **indifference analysis** can be used to analyze the household's buying decisions and to show how those decisions will change in response to a variety of exogenous events. In Chapter 6, we move beyond the individual household to the collection of *all* buyers of a specific good—the **market demand** for that good. To see the kinds of factors that influence market demand, we'll look in some detail at an issue of particular interest in recent years: the demand for automobile travel.

5

Product Demand: The Household

Preview: Like society as a whole, the individual *household* is faced with unlimited wants and limited resources and thus must make economic choices. The major difference, however, between a society and an individual household is that the household is not faced with the impossible task of satisfying the conflicting wants of its many members; rather, it will make the choice which will result in the maximum possible satisfaction or *utility*. The **indifference analysis model** introduced in this chapter allows us to examine how individual households attain the greatest utility from their economic choices.

To appreciate the problem of choice at the household level, suppose you had to make a list of all the things you want or need, regardless of your ability to purchase or consume them. Even if you stayed within the boundaries set by laws, morality, and good taste, your list would probably be so long that you couldn't purchase and consume everything on it. Most of us find that our possible choices of goods are constrained by our incomes, but even persons or households with enormous incomes are constrained by time, energy, and stamina.

Households try to choose the combinations of goods that will make them as well off as possible, given their incomes, tastes, and the prices of the goods they consume. In the markets for goods and services, these choices by households are translated into demands for goods and services.

The Concept of Utility

Utility, we saw in Chapter 3, is the economist's term for "satisfaction." Economics assumes that households behave rationally and that they seek to *maximize utility* through their purchases of goods and services.

But can satisfaction be measured? If not, how do we know when it is maximized?

Cardinal vs. Ordinal Utility

Early writers on utility treated it in *cardinal* (i.e., numerical) terms. They asserted that utility was something that could be observed, measured in units (which they called *utils*), and added together.

- **Cardinal utility** can be measured numerically, and utilities of different persons and households can be compared and added.

If utility could, in fact, be measured numerically and compared, some very important and difficult normative economic questions could be easily answered. The economic welfare of a society, for example, could be measured simply as the sum of the utilities of its members. If the last $1,000 of your income gives you 40 utils, but an additional $1,000 would give me an additional 60 utils, our community's economic welfare could be raised by redistributing $1,000 income from you to me.

Obviously, life is not as simple as this. Most modern economists feel it's much more reasonable to treat utility in *ordinal* terms.

- **Ordinal utility** assumes that the household can only tell whether a change in consumption makes it better or worse off. Ordinal utilities of different households cannot be compared or added together.

With ordinal utility, it isn't necessary to assume that a person can express his utility from drinking a beer numerically, and it would be impossible to find the total utility of a group of people who shared in the consumption of a case of beer. More significantly, ordinal utility makes it impossible to say anything about the effect on the community's economic welfare of changes that make some people better off and others worse off.

Total Utility

In analyzing the household, **total utility** is simply the satisfaction that the household experiences as a result of consuming a combination of goods. Obviously, the utility of a good to a specific household depends on the household's *tastes* or *preferences*. A person with a highly developed taste for opera, for example, would get much more utility from a performance by La Scala than would a person whose musical tastes ran toward bluegrass or hard rock.

In the theory of demand, we assume that *tastes are given*. Tastes or preferences determine the relationship between goods consumed and the household's total utility.

Marginal Utility

Households make *marginal decisions* in reaching their highest level of utility. They change the quantities of goods they consume until they are as well off as possible. This makes *marginal utility* an important variable for the household.

- **Marginal utility** is the rate at which total utility changes as the quantity of a good consumed changes. If consumption changes by one unit, marginal utility is the change in total utility which results from that one-unit change.

Algebraically, marginal utility (*MU*) is the ratio

$$MU = \frac{\Delta U}{\Delta q}, \qquad (1)$$

where ΔU is the change in utility and Δq is the change in the quantity of the good consumed by the household.

Diminishing Marginal Utility

As long as additional units of a good make the household better off, the marginal utility of the good is positive. However, as more and more of the good is consumed, the marginal utility of additional units declines. A pint of water would add a lot to the utility of a person suffering from thirst, but additional pints of water would add less and less utility.

- The **principle of diminishing marginal utility** states that the marginal utility of a good declines as more of it is consumed.

To illustrate the relationship between total and marginal utility, assume that the houshold can assign an index to the utility it receives from various quantities of water, other things constant, as shown in Table 1. The value of the utility index simply shows the household's subjective level of satisfaction, not units or quantities of utility.

The relationship between water consumed and the total utility index is shown graphically in Figure 1a. Notice that the utility index increases less and less as more water is consumed between 0 and 7 gallons. This reflects diminishing marginal utility. The rate at which the utility index changes as water consumption changes, or the slope of the total utility curve in Figure 1b, is $\Delta U/\Delta q_w$—the marginal utility of water. In Figure 1b, this is shown by the negatively sloped marginal utility curve (*MU*).

Table 1 Diminishing Marginal Utility

Gallons of water per day	Utility index	Marginal Utility index
0	0	—
1	30	30
2	55	25
3	75	20
4	90	15
5	100	10
6	105	5

Figure 1 Total and Marginal Utility Curves

(a) Total Utility

(b) Marginal Utility

The Household's Preference

Modern demand theory utilizes an analytical approach called **indifference analysis** to understand how the household makes the economic choices it must make. Indifference analysis makes a few basic assumptions about the household:

1. The household can identify its utility with any combination of goods and can tell whether or not another combination of goods would change its level of utility.
2. The household will be better off if it consumes more of one good without reducing its consumption of other goods.
3. The household will be worse off if it consumes less of one good without increasing its consumption of other goods.
4. The household can identify different combinations of goods that yield the same utility.

Because this approach is built on *ordinal utility*, the household can choose among combinations without assigning numerical values to utility.

Suppose that a household has 15 units of food and 35 units of clothing, defining combination A in Figure 2. This combination of goods gives the household a level of utility which we can call U_1. According to our assumptions, if the household had at least 15 units of food and more than 35 units of clothing, it would be better off than at A, and its utility would be greater than U_1. Likewise, more than 15 units of food and at least 35 units of clothing would be better than A. All of the combinations in the area labeled *Better than* A in Figure 2 yield utility greater than U_1.

The household would be worse off than at A if had less than 15 units of food and no more than 35 units of clothing, or less than 35 units of cloth-

Figure 2 Household's Indifference Curve

ing and no more than 15 units of food. All combinations of food and clothing in the area labeled *Worse than A* yield a lower level of utility than U_1.

Combinations of food and clothing which lie *northwest* and *southeast* of A contain more of one good and less of the other. Some of these are better than A, others are worse than A, and still others yield the same utility as A. Suppose that combinations B, C, and D yield the same utility as A—the additional utility from having more of one good just offsets the loss of utility from having less of the other. If all three combinations yield the same level of satisfaction, there is no reason for the household to prefer one to another.

- The household is *indifferent* among combinations of goods that yield the same level of utility.

In other words, this household is just as happy with 30 units of food and 20 units of clothing (point C), or with 10 units of food and 50 units of clothing (point B), or with 35 units of food and 18 units of clothing (point D), as it was with the original 15 units of food and 35 units of clothing.

Indifference Curves

If all combinations on the curve U_1 in Figure 2 give the household the same utility, the household will be indifferent among them.

- All the combinations of goods that yield the same level of utility define a household's **indifference curve**.

The *slope* of an indifference curve is called the *marginal rate of substitution*.

- The **marginal rate of substitution (MRS)** is the rate at which the household can substitute one good for another without changing the level of utility.

The MRS between two goods depends on the marginal utilities of the goods. If the household moves from B to A on U_1 in Figure 2, for example, the loss of utility from the reduction in clothing depends on the marginal utility of clothing, and the additional utility from the additional food depends on the marginal utility of food. The MRS can thus be expressed as the ratio of the marginal utilities, or

$$MRS = \frac{\Delta c}{\Delta f} = -\frac{MU_f}{MU_c}, \qquad (2)$$

where MU_f is the marginal utility of food and MU_c is the marginal utility of clothing.[1]

In Figure 2, the slope of a line between A and C would be the average MRS between these two points. The MRS at a particular point on U_1 is the slope of a line tangent to U_1 at that point. The MRS at point A, for example, is the slope of the short line tangent to U_1 at A.

As the household moves along an indifference curve, consuming more of one good and less of the other, the marginal utilities of the goods and the MRS will change. In Figure 2, for example, the household could give up 15 units of clothing to increase food consumption from 10 to 15 without changing its utility because the marginal utility of clothing is relatively low and the marginal utility of additional food is relatively high. However, for an equal increase in food consumption from 30 to 35 in Figure 2, the household could give up much less clothing (2 units) to maintain the same level of utility because the marginal utility of food is relatively low and the marginal utility of clothing is relatively high. In other words, the absolute value of the MRS falls as the household has more food and less clothing. This means that indifference curves will generally bend toward the origin, making them *convex* curves.

The Household's Indifference Map

All combinations of goods don't yield the same level of satisfaction, and therefore don't lie on the same indifference curve. Different levels of

---

[1]. Giving up Δc units of clothing for an additional Δf units of food on the indifference curve, Δc causes utility to fall by $\Delta c \cdot MU_c$ and Δf causes utility to rise by $\Delta f \cdot MU_f$. By definition,

$$\Delta c \cdot MU_c = -\Delta f \cdot MU_f$$

Dividing both sides by $\Delta f \cdot MU_c$ gives

$$\frac{\Delta c}{\Delta f} = -\frac{MU_f}{MU_c}.$$

utility are represented by different indifference curves in the **indifference map** in Figure 3.

- Utility is constant along any given indifference curve, and indifference curves indicate higher levels of utility the farther they lie from the origin.

Figure 3 Household's Indifference Map

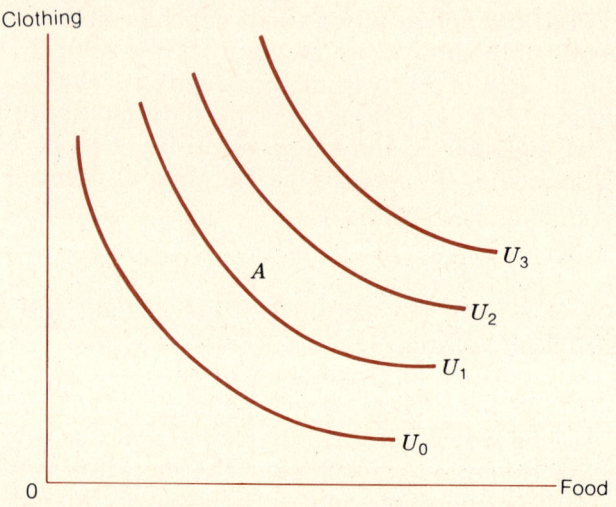

There is an infinite number of indifference curves representing a household's tastes, and the indifference map in Figure 3 shows only a few of the household's possible indifference curves.

The Household's Income Constraint

The indifference map represents the household's preferences. The household's ability to purchase goods is limited by its *real income*. Real income, in turn, depends on the household's money income and the prices of the goods it consumes.

In our simple food-and-clothing example, suppose that the household's money income (y_m) and the prices of food (P_f) and clothing (P_c) are given. The maximum amount of clothing that the household can purchase with its money income is c^*, and

$$c^* = \frac{y_m}{P_c}. \tag{3}$$

This point lies directly on the clothing axis in Figure 4. At this point, the household is spending *all* its income on clothing and none on food.

The maximum amount of food it can buy with its income is f^*, and

$$f^* = \frac{y_m}{P_f}. \qquad (4)$$

This point lies directly on the food axis in Figure 4. At this point, the household is spending *all* its income on food and none on clothing.

These two combinations *exhaust* the household's income—both require the entire money income. Other combinations that exhaust the household's income lie on the line c^*f^* in Figure 4. For any combination of food and clothing on this line,

$$P_f f + P_c c = y_m. \qquad (5)$$

This line is called the household's *income constraint*.

- The **income constraint** shows combinations of goods that exhaust the household's income.

Suppose that the household's money income is $200 per week, and that it spends this income to buy food and clothing. Given a price of $10 per unit of food, the maximum possible purchase of food is

$$f^* = \frac{y_m}{P_f} = \frac{\$200 \text{ per week}}{\$10 \text{ per unit of food}} = 20 \text{ units of food per week.}$$

If the price of clothing is $20, the maximum possible purchase of clothing is

$$c^* = \frac{y_m}{P_c} = \frac{\$200 \text{ per week}}{\$20 \text{ per unit of clothing}} = 10 \text{ units of clothing per week.}$$

Figure 4 Household's Income Constraint

Both of these combinations exhaust the household's money income. Other combinations of food and clothing that exhaust a money income of $200 at these prices lie on the *income constraint* in Figure 4.

The **relative prices** of the goods the household consumes (i.e. the price of one good compared to the price of another) determine the *slope* of its income constraint.

- The **slope of the income constraint** is the rate at which a household can substitute one good for another, given the prices of the two goods.

Algebraically, the slope of the income constraint can be expressed as

$$\frac{\Delta c}{\Delta f} = -\frac{P_f}{P_c}. \tag{6}$$

The slope of the income constraint tells us the amount of one good that a household must give up in order to buy an additional unit of the other good, or the *opportunity cost* of consuming more of one good in terms of the amount of the other good that must be given up. In our food and clothing example, if the price of food (P_f) is $10 a unit and the price of clothing (P_c) is $20, the slope of the income constraint will be $-(P_f/P_c) = -(\$10/\$20) = -½$. This means that the household has to give up half a unit of clothing in order to consume one additional unit of food.[2]

The Household's Choice

Given tastes, income, and the prices of the goods it consumes, the household will try to choose the combination of goods that makes it as well off as possible. The first requirement for maximizing utility is fairly obvious.

- To maximize its utility from its income, the household must exhaust its income.

If this isn't so obvious, go back to Figure 4. If the household were at point D inside the income constraint, it could make itself better off by moving to A (more clothing, no less food), B (more food, no less clothing) or any combination between A and B (more of both).

However, all combinations that exhaust income don't maximize satisfaction—consider being starving and well clothed at c^* or naked and well fed at f^* in Figure 4. The household must find the particular combination that makes it as well off as possible with its income.

---

2. The income constraint is a straight line, and its slope is constant. Suppose that the household goes from one extreme to the other—from c^* units of clothing and no food to f^* units of food and no clothing. The change in clothing is $\Delta c = 0 - c^* = -c^*$, and the change in food is $\Delta f = f^* - 0 = f^*$. The slope of the income constraint, then, is

$$\frac{\Delta c}{\Delta f} = \frac{-c^*}{f^*} = \frac{-(y_m/P_c)}{(y_m/P_f)} = -\frac{y_m}{P_c} \cdot \frac{P_f}{y_m} = -\frac{P_f}{P_c}.$$

Maximizing Utility: Marginal Utility Approach

Households allocate income among goods and services until they reach the highest possible level of utility.

- Utility is maximized when the household exhausts its income, and when the last dollar spent on each good yields the same additional satisfaction.

If the last dollar spent on clothing gave less additional satisfaction than the last dollar spent on food, the household could raise its total utility by spending a dollar less on clothing and a dollar more on food. The loss in utility from the reduction in clothing consumption is more than offset by the added utility from a dollar's worth of additional food.

The additional satisfaction from the last dollar spent on a good is the ratio of its marginal utility over its price (MU/P). If the household exhausts its income on food and clothing, then the condition for maximum utility is

$$\frac{MU_f}{P_f} = \frac{MU_c}{P_c}. \tag{7}$$

Let's look at a situation in which this condition is not met. Suppose that a household exhausts its income on food and clothing. The prices of food and clothing are $10 and $20 respectively, the household's marginal utility index for the amount of food it consumes (MU_f) is 50, and its marginal utility index for the amount of clothing it consumes (MU_c) is 60. This household isn't getting the maximum satisfaction from its income because its additional satisfaction per dollar spent on food ($MU_f/P_f = 50/10 = 5$) is greater than its additional satisfaction per dollar spent on clothing ($MU_c/P_c = 60/20 = 3$). Spending $1 less on clothing would lower the household's utility index by 3, but spending that dollar to buy more food would increase the index by 5. The net effect of substituting a dollar's worth of food for a dollar's worth of clothing, then, is to raise the utility index by 2.

As the household consumes more food and less clothing, MU_f (and therefore MU_f/P_f) falls, and MU_c (and therefore MU_c/P_c) rises. The household will continue to substitute food for clothing until its utility is maximized with $MU_f/P_f = MU_c/P_c$. The condition for maximizing utility can be rewritten[3] as

$$\frac{MU_f}{MU_c} = \frac{P_f}{P_c} \tag{8}$$

The significance of this simple rearrangement will become clear after we look at an alternative method of analyzing utility maximization.

---

3. Both sides of the equation

$$\frac{MU_f}{P_f} = \frac{MU_c}{P_c}$$

can be multiplied by P_f/MU_c, giving us

$$\frac{MU_f}{P_f}\left(\frac{P_f}{MU_c}\right) = \frac{MU_c}{P_c}\left(\frac{P_f}{MU_c}\right); \text{ or } \frac{MU_f}{MU_c} = \frac{P_f}{P_c}.$$

Maximizing Utility: Indifference Curve Approach

The household's choice of goods to maximize utility is analyzed graphically in Figure 5, which simply combines Figures 3 and 4. The highest level of utility available to the household in Figure 5 is U_2, which lies tangent to the household's income constraint c^*f^*, touching it only at point X. With combination X, the household exhausts its income by consuming $\bar{f}$ units of food and $\bar{c}$ units of clothing. Other combinations on the income constraint—such as A and B—lie on lower indifference curves and thus yield a lower level of satisfaction than X. Other combinations on U_2—such as Y and Z—are impossible because they lie outside the household's income constraint. All combinations on U_3 would be preferable to X, but none is possible because they all lie outside the income constraint. Thus X must be the combination of food and clothing that maximizes utility.

- The household will be as well off as possible with its income by consuming the combination of goods where its *income constraint is tangent to an indifference curve*.

At the tangency of U_2 and the income constraint, the condition for maximum utility is fulfilled. At the tangency, the slopes of U_2 and the income constraint are equal. The slope of U_2 is $MRS = -MU_f/MU_c$. The slope of the income constraint is $-P_f/P_c$. At the tangency, these slopes are equal, or

$$\frac{MU_f}{MU_c} = \frac{P_f}{P_c}. \tag{8}$$

This, you will notice, is precisely the same equation (8) we derived for utility maximization using the marginal utility approach.

Figure 5 Maximizing Utility

Applying the Tools

Indifference Analysis and Household Budgeting

The simple examples in which the household consumes only two goods reduce the household's choice to very simplified terms. However, the income constraint can also be applied to more realistic examples of household choice. Consider a specific good that the household consumes—beef, for example. If the entire money income of $200 per week were spent on beef and the price of beef (P_b) were $1 per pound, the maximum possible purchase of beef would be $b^* = y_m/P_b$ = $200 per week/$1 per pound = 200 pounds per week. Of course, no money would be available for other goods.

If the household purchased no beef, its entire money income (y_m) would be available for other goods. The household's income constraint in Figure A shows possible combinations of beef and money for other goods.

Figure A

The household can substitute money to buy other goods for beef at a rate of $1 per pound of beef.[4] In other words, the slope of the income constraint in Figure A is

$$\frac{\Delta y_m}{\Delta b} = -\frac{\$1}{1 \text{ pound of beef}} = -P_b.$$

---

4. The "price" of money for other goods is 1—i.e., the price of $1 is $1—and the slope of the income constraint is

$$\frac{\Delta y_m}{\Delta b} = -\frac{P_b}{P_{y_m}} = -\frac{P_b}{1} = -P_b.$$

The household's indifference curve U shows its preferences between beef and money to spend on other goods. This household will maximize its utility from beef by buying 3 pounds of beef a week and spending the remaining $197 of income on other goods. By constructing a graph such as this for each of its weekly expenditures, the household can budget its weekly income in such a way as to maximize utility from the income.

The Household's Demand Curve

The quantity of a good demanded by a household at any given price, other things equal, is shown by its demand curve for the good. This quantity is also amount consistent with maximizing the household's utility. As the price of the good changes, the household must adjust the quantity it demands in order to maximize utility at the new price.

Marginal Utility and Demand

Suppose that a household is maximizing the utility of its $500 income with 10 units of food and 20 units of clothing, ($P_f = 10 and $P_c = 20). For sake of illustration only, suppose that the household's marginal utility index for food is $MU_f = 40$ and that its marginal utility index for clothing is $MU_c = 80$ at these quantities, so we have

$$\frac{MU_f}{P_f} = \frac{40}{10} = \frac{MU_c}{P_c} = \frac{80}{20}; \quad \text{or} \quad \frac{MU_f}{MU_c} = \frac{40}{80} = \frac{P_f}{P_c} = \frac{10}{20}.$$

Now, suppose that the price of a unit of food falls to $5, while income, tastes, and the price of clothing remain constant. With the initial quantities of food and clothing,

Figure 6 Household's Demand Curve for Food

$$\frac{MU_f}{P_f'} = \frac{40}{5} > \frac{MU_c}{P_c} = \frac{80}{20}; \quad \text{or} \quad \frac{MU_f}{MU_c} = \frac{40}{80} > \frac{P_f'}{P_c} = \frac{5}{20}.$$

The household will substitute the relatively cheaper food for the relatively more expensive clothing until its utility is maximized again; that is, until

$$\frac{MU_f}{MU_c} = \frac{P_f'}{P_c} = \frac{5}{20} = \frac{1}{4}.$$

In other words, the lower price of food caused an increase in the quantity of food demanded by the household, as shown in Figure 6. Since the price of food is the only thing that changes, points A and B in Figure 6 lie on the household's demand curve for food (d_f), and the change in consumption from A to B is a change in quantity demanded.

Indifference Curves and the Household's Demand Curve

The relationship between the household's utility-maximizing decisions and its demand curve for a good is easily shown with indifference analysis. Given its income of $500, preferences, and prices of food and clothing (P_f = $10 and P_c = $20), the household in Figure 7a maximizes

Figure 7 Indifference Curves and the Household's Demand Curve

its utility by consuming 10 units of food and 20 units of clothing—i.e., at point x where the income constraint c^*f^* is tangent to the indifference curve U_1. At this point the slope of the indifference curve (MRS) equals the slope of the income constraint ($-P_f/P_c = -10/20 = -\frac{1}{2}$). If the price of food falls to \$5, other things equal, the household's income constraint rotates outward, and the slope of the new income constraint c^*f^* is $-P_f'/P_c = -\$5/\$20 = -\frac{1}{4}$. The household will now maximize its utility by consuming at point y, where the new income constraint is tangent to indifference curve U_2. Here the household consumes 30 units of food and 17.5 units of clothing. Since the only variable that changed is the price, this represents a change in the quantity of food demanded, or a movement along the household's demand curve for food (d_f) in Figure 7b.

Changes in the Household's Demand

Changes in demand are caused by changes in variables other than the price of the good. If income, prices of other goods, or tastes change, this causes the household's demand curve for a good to shift.

Changes in Money Income

Changes in money income shift the household's income constraint, but don't affect relative prices or the slope of the income constraint. In Figure 8a, an increase in money income is shown by the shift of the income constraint from y_m to y_m'. A reduction in income is shown by the shift from y_m to y_m''.

The changes in food consumption from $\bar{f}$ to $\bar{f}'$ and from $\bar{f}$ to $\bar{f}''$ in Figure 8b are *changes in the household's demand* for food in response to changes in the household's money income. In Figure 8b, the points A, B, and E lie on different demand curves for food. The changes in clothing consumption in Figure 8a are also changes in demand and will shift the demand curve for clothing.

"Normal" and "Inferior" Goods

In the above example, food and clothing are what economists call *normal goods*.

- The demand for **normal goods** is greater at high levels of income than at low levels of income. As income rises, the demand for normal goods also rises.

All goods aren't normal goods for a household, however. Some goods are referred to as *inferior goods*. The term *inferior* doesn't necessarily mean low quality, but refers to the response of demand to changes in income.

- The demand for **inferior goods** is lower at high levels of income than at low levels of income. As income rises, the demand for inferior goods falls.

Figure 8 Changes in Money Income

A poor household may consume some goods—for example, flour and "fatback"—simply because it can't afford a more balanced diet. If the household's income increased, it could consume more meat, milk, fresh produce, and other foods it couldn't afford at the low income, and less of the inferior goods that it had to consume to survive at the low level of income. Some studies have shown that local public transportation is an inferior good. As households' incomes rise they tend to demand more automobile travel (because they can afford it, or because they move to suburbs that don't have access to mass transit for commuting) and demand less public transit.

Changes in Prices of Other Goods

A change in the price of one good may cause a change in the household's demand for another. Suppose that the household in Figure 9a initially maximizes its utility by consuming $\bar{c}$ units of clothing and $\bar{f}$ units of food —given its tastes, income, and prices of food and clothing. If the price of clothing falls from P_c to P_c', the household will consume $\bar{f}'$ units of food

Figure 9 Changes in Prices of Other Goods

and $\bar{c}'$ units of clothing—where the new income constraint ($c^{**}f^*$) is tangent to indifference curve U_2.

In Figure 9b, the amount of food consumed by the household decreases from $\bar{f}$ to $\bar{f}'$, even though the price of food remained constant at P_f. This indicates a change in the household's demand for food in response to a change in the price of clothing, and a shift of the demand curve from d_f to d_f'.

In fact, it is not always easy to predict the effect of a change in the price of one good on the demand for other goods. Often, there will be no effect: a change in the price of tomatoes will probably not influence the demand for erasers. However, we can make some general predictions.

Substitute goods are goods that play roughly the same role in consumption and thus can be substituted for one another. Butter and margarine, for example, would be substitute goods for most households, as would be private auto travel and mass transit, or ball-point and felt-tipped pens. In general, if the price of a good goes up, people will demand less of that good and more of available substitutes. Higher beef prices generally lead to increased demand for such substitutes as pork, chicken, and fish.

- A rise in the price of a good will generally increase the demand for substitutes; a fall in the price of a good will generally decrease the demand for substitutes.

Complementary goods are goods that are normally consumed together—coffee and cream, cars and gasoline, and even left and right shoes. If the price of a good goes up, people will demand less of that good, and so will also demand less of goods they consume with it. A higher price of potato chips will cause people to buy fewer potato chips and less onion dip as well.

- A rise in the price of a good will generally decrease the demand for complements; a fall in the price of a good will generally increase the demand for complements.

Sometimes, however, unexpected changes in demand result from changes in the price of other goods. This is because a change in the price of one good, other things equal, changes both the relative prices of goods *and* the household's real income. Households always tend to substitute the relatively cheaper good for the more expensive, but changes in real income affect its demand for all goods.

For example, higher gasoline prices will raise the relative price of auto travel and reduce a household's real income—especially if expenditures on auto travel represent a large part of the household's income. This reduction of real income, or *income effect*, of higher gasoline prices may lead to reduced consumption of some goods—clothing, for example—that are neither complements with nor substitutes for auto travel.

Changes in Tastes

The choice of goods that maximizes utility depends in part on the household's tastes. If tastes change, the household will alter its choice of goods, even if the prices of goods and money income remain constant.

In Figure 10a, the household maximizes its utility by consuming combination A, where its income constraint is tangent to the most distant indifference curve in its current indifference map, U_1. Here the household consumes $\bar{f}$ units of food and $\bar{c}$ units of clothing. A change in the household's tastes is represented graphically by a change in its entire indifference map. A stronger preference for food over clothing, for example, is reflected in the new indifference curves U_0', U_1', U_2', etc. Money income and prices remain constant, so the income constraint does not change.

To maximize utility with its new tastes, the household will consume combination B, where its income constraint is tangent to the highest indifference curve of its new indifference map, U_1'. The household increases its food consumption to $\bar{f}'$ and reduces its clothing consumption to $\bar{c}'$. In Figure 10b, the movement from $\bar{f}$ to $\bar{f}'$ at the same price of

Figure 10 Changes in Tastes

food represents a change in demand in response to the change in tastes. Thus, the demand curve shifts from d_f to d_f'. The change in clothing consumption from $\bar{c}$ to $\bar{c}'$ also represents a change in demand and a shift in the demand curve for clothing as a result of the change in tastes.

Applying the Tools

Food Stamps vs. Income Subsidies

Our traditional method of giving public assistance to low-income households has been to provide *aid-in-kind*—housing subsidies, food stamps, Medicaid, etc. By lowering the prices of large items in the households' budgets, these programs have raised the households' real income. In recent years, traditional welfare programs have been attacked by those who would eliminate such programs altogether and from others who advocate a new approach to welfare. The most interesting and controversial proposal has been to replace aid-in-kind with direct income subsidies (such as a *negative income tax*). The impact of such a change on a household can be analyzed easily with indifference curve analysis.

Suppose a household has a money income of $200 per month which it spends on food and non-food items. In Figure A, the vertical axis represents dollars to spend on non-food items and the horizontal axis represents "units" or "baskets" of food worth $1 apiece (we'll call these *dollar-units*). The household's income constraint is represented by the line GF: the household may spend all $200 on non-food items (point G), or it may buy 200 dollar-units of food (point F), or it may purchase any combination of food and non-food items that lies along the constraint line. The household maximizes its utility at point A, where its indifference curve U_1 is tangent to the income constraint. At this point, the household consumes 100 dollar-units of food and spends $100 on non-food items each month.

Figure A

Now suppose that the household receives from the government food stamps which allow it to buy all the food it wants for one-half the market price. In other words, the price of a dollar-unit of food for the household will now be 50¢. This means that the household can buy as many as 400 dollar-units of food with its $200 income. The household's income constraint rotates outward to GF', and the household will now maximize its utility at point B, where the new income constraint is tangent to a new indifference curve U_2. Here the household consumes 180 dollar-units of food and spends $110 on non-food items each month.

The cost of this food-stamp program to the government is the difference between the value of the goods the household was able to consume and the household's actual money income. Since the household consumed $180 worth of food and $110 worth of other goods and received an income of only $200, the cost to the government is ($180 + $110) − $200 = $290 − $200 = $90 per month.

Clearly the household is better off and more satisfied now than it was before the food-stamp program: indifference curve U_2 is farther from the origin than was U_1. But is the household as satisfied as it could be? Suppose that the government took the $90 the program costs and instead gave the money to the household outright as a cash subsidy. The household could now spend as much as $290 on non-food items or purchase up to 290 dollar-units of food. The household's entire income constraint shifts outward from GF to $G''F''$. Notice that the new constraint intersects indifference curve U_2 at two points (one of which is B). This means that U_2 is not tangent to the income constraint, and more importantly, that *it is not the highest possible indifference curve*. The household will now maximize utility at point C, where the new income constraint is tangent to a new indifference curve U_3. Here the household consumes 150 dollar-units of food and $140 worth of other goods per month. The household is clearly more satisfied with the cash subsidy than with the food stamps: U_3 is farther from the origin than U_2. The extra utility from the subsidy program stems from the household's freedom to allocate its increased income between food and non-food items.

Advocates of cash subsidies cite the result shown in Figure A as an advantage of this approach over aid-in-kind. Critics of cash subsidies argue that low-income households need guidance in spending their incomes, and that their needs are better met by aid-in-kind or subsidies on specific goods than by cash subsidies. The resolution of this issue, then, depends in part on the question of who knows what is best for low income households—welfare personnel or the households themselves.

Summary

1. Every household makes choices to maximize its utility, given its tastes and income and the prices of goods. The household will choose quantities of goods that make it as well off as possible.
2. **Utility** is the satisfaction that the household experiences from consuming a given combination of goods.
3. **Marginal utility** is the change in utility as a result of changing the quantity of a good consumed, other things constant. Marginal utility generally declines as more of a good is consumed.
4. The **cardinal utility** assumption assumes that utility can be expressed in numerical values that can be added together for different households.
5. Since utility is subjective with each individual, modern demand theory treats it in *ordinal* terms—a household can tell whether changes in combinations of goods make it better off, worse off, or leave its level of satisfaction unchanged. It isn't necessary to express **ordinal utility** in numerical values, and utilities of different households can't be added together.
6. The household's **utility function** defines the level of utility associated with various combinations of goods, and is represented graphically by the household's **indifference map**.

7. The household's choices of goods are limited by its **income constraint**, which is determined by its *real income*. The household will choose the combination of goods on its income constraint that is tangent to a curve on its indifference map. With this combination, the household maximizes its utility.
8. The **household's demand curve** for a good is defined for given tastes, income, and prices of other goods.
9. Changes in income, tastes, and prices of other goods will cause the household's demand for a given good to shift.

Concepts for Review

utility
cardinal utility
ordinal utility
marginal utility
principle of diminishing marginal utility
indifference curve

indifference map
marginal rate of substitution
relative prices
income constraint
complementary goods
substitute goods
household demand curve

Questions

1. Imagine a community made up of two classes of people—the affluent and the downtrodden. The affluent constitute a small minority of the population, but control nearly all of the community's wealth and income.
   a. What (if anything) could you say about the effect on the economic welfare (or utility) of the community as a result of redistributing wealth and income from the affluent to the downtrodden, if we looked at utility in *cardinal* terms?
   b. How would your answer differ (if at all) if we looked at utility in *ordinal* terms?
2. For many years, economists were puzzled because some luxury goods (like diamonds) command very high prices, while other goods which are necessary to sustain life (like water) command very low prices. How would you explain this apparent paradox?
3. Make a list of some of the goods that you consume that are complementary with each other. Make a list of some of the goods that you consume that are substitutes for each other. How might a higher price for one good that you consume alter your demand for other goods that are not related to it in consumption?
4. During the Great Depression of the 1930s, some firms actually experienced increases in sales as households' incomes fell. Can you think of any firms that might have experienced this? Can you explain it?
5. In some societies, relatively affluent people are better fed than the poor and are relatively plump. However, in our country, a number of poor people are obese, while many persons with higher incomes are relatively thin. How could you explain this?

Problems

1. The Fern household has a monthly meat budget of $60, which it allocates between beef and chicken. Shown below are various combinations of beef and chicken that yield levels of utility U_1 and U_2 to the household.

U_1		U_2	
lb. chicken/mo.	lb. beef/mo.	lb. chicken/mo.	lb. beef/mo.
55	5	60	13
30	10	40	16
20	15	30	20
17	20	24	24
15	30	22	30
14	40	20	40

   a. Do all of the above combinations of chicken and beef lie on the same indifference curve?
   b. Plot the combinations of chicken and beef graphically and draw appropriate indifference curves.
   c. What is the marginal rate of substitution (MRS)? What is the relationship between MRS and the marginal utility (MU) of chicken and beef? Calculate MRS for the given combinations of chicken and beef. How do you explain the behavior of MRS as the household moves to different combinations of beef and chicken?
   d. If the price of beef is $2.00 and the price of chicken is $1.50, find the combination of beef and chicken that gives the household the highest level of utility possible with its meat budget.
   e. Suppose that the price of beef falls to $1.00. How will this affect the household's utility and the amounts of chicken and beef it consumes? Show this graphically. For which good is there a change in demand, and for which is there a change in quantity demanded?
   f. Draw the household's demand curve for beef, based on the quantities of beef demanded at prices of $2.00 and $1.00.

2. Draw a diagram representing the income constraint for a household that consumes food and clothing. Show how each of the following would affect the income constraint, and draw diagrams to show the changes:
   a. an increase in money income;
   b. a decrease in money income;
   c. food stamps, which subsidize the household's food purchases;
   d. an excise tax on clothing;
   e. a 10 percent reduction in the prices of food and clothing.

6

Product Demand: The Market

Preview: Many policy issues and "real world" problems concerned with demand focus upon the entire market and not the individual household. Since markets are made up of a number of households, however, those households' individual utility-maximizing decisions will ultimately determine the **market demand** for goods and services. In this chapter, we will look more closely at the properties and behavior of market demand.

The effect of higher gasoline prices on gasoline consumption and on the demand for public transportation, the impact of a high excise tax on cigarette consumption, the effect of higher beef prices on the demand for pork and chicken, and the effect of changing income on the demand for various goods and services are questions that involve the *market demand* for goods and services. Of course, since markets include a number of individual households that buy goods and services, the actions of the households (analyzed in Chapter 5) will affect market demand.

Household and Market Demand Curves

Households are buyers in the product market, and the quantity of a good demanded by the entire market is simply the sum of the quantities demanded by the individual households. Consider a simplified market in which there are only three households—Adams (A), Brown (B), and Clark (C). The individual households' demand curves are d_A, d_B, and d_C in Figure 1. The total quantity of gasoline demanded at any price by these buyers is the sum of the quantities demanded by the individual households. At a price of $.75, for example, the quantity demanded for the market is the sum of 10 gallons per week (by Adams)

Figure 1 Household Demand Curves

+ 18 gallons per week (by Brown) + 32 gallons (by Clark) = 60 gallons per week.

In Figure 2, the *market demand curve D* shows the total quantity of gasoline demanded at various prices.

- The *quantity demanded in the market* at any price is the sum of the quantities demanded by the households in the market. The

Figure 2 Market Demand Curve

market demand curve is the sum of the individual households' demand curves.

Individual households' demand curves are "added" horizontally to get the market demand curve—i.e., quantities demanded are added at various prices.

Peculiar responses to changes in price by a single household or a small number of households are generally overshadowed by the actions of other households whose behavior is consistent with the law of demand.

- The **law of large numbers** argues that the effects of exceptional behavior by a few households will be offset by the *normal* or *typical* behavior of the vast majority of households.

Changes in Market Demand

Anything that changes households' demand curves will change the market demand as well. (Of course, if only a small number of individual households' demands change, the effect on market demand may not be noticeable.) For example, a rise in households' income might increase the households' demand for gasoline, and this would increase the market demand for gasoline as well, shifting the demand curve to the right, as in Figure 3a. Changes in tastes, changes in the price of other goods, and in other exogenous variables that affect the household's demand curve will also shift the market demand curve.

Close-Up

Advertising, Tastes, and Demand

The primary objectives of most advertising is to increase the demand for the advertised brand of toothpaste, deodorant, hamburger, automobile, or political candidate. Some advertising does this by providing information to consumers on the availability and characteristics of the product. But many modern mass advertising and marketing methods go beyond this information function and try to increase demand by altering the tastes of households through such familiar devices as endorsements, slogans, appeals to our fantasies.

In 1957, for example, Proctor & Gamble acquired the Clorox Bleach Company, and launched a major advertising campaign. Over $5 million was spent promoting Clorox that year, and the demand for Clorox increased while the demand for Purex (its only serious competitor in the industry) fell. Clorox increased its share of the market from 48.8 percent to 52 percent. Apparently, the advertising campaigns increased the demand for Clorox by changing tastes, since all liquid bleach is chemically identical (5 percent solution of sodium hypochlorite). Purex later regained some of its lost market by its own advertising campaign aimed at changing household tastes.

Figure 3 Changes in Market Demand

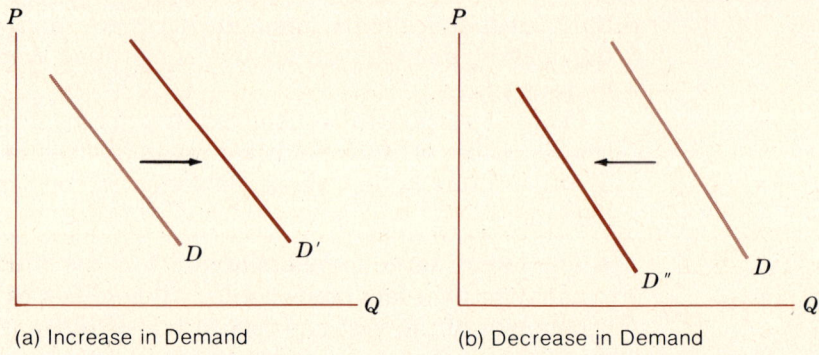

(a) Increase in Demand

(b) Decrease in Demand

Changes in the number of households in the market also changes the market demand for a good. An increase in the number of households in the market means that the quantity demanded by the additional households has to be added to quantity demanded by the original households. This increases market demand, shifting the market demand curve to the right—as shown by the shift from D to D' in Figure 3a. If the number of households in the market declines, the quantity demanded by the households who leave the market must be subtracted from the original quantity demanded at each price, so market demand will fall. The market demand curve shifts to the left—as shown by the shift from D to D'' in Figure 3b.

Close-up

Population and Demand in Urban Housing Markets

Shifts of the population from rural to urban metropolitan areas and between cities and suburbs have affected urban housing prices by changing the demand for housing. A boom in demand for suburban housing through the 1970s resulted from a preference among new families in metropolitan areas for suburban over urban housing and a subsequent shift of families from central cities to the suburbs. Although the population of metropolitan areas rose in the 1950s, 1960s, and 1970s, the population of some of our major cities (Detroit, Baltimore, and Washington, for example) fell. The demand for suburban housing pushed suburban housing prices up sharply, while the decline in demand for housing in the cities brought prices down in city housing markets.

Since the mid 1970s, however, the demand for housing in the cities has risen.

High prices in the suburbs have driven a number of people to the cities to find housing at reasonable prices. The energy crunch increased the cost of commuting and thus made city housing more attractive. Many cities undertook major redevelopment campaigns. As more potential home buyers have returned to the city housing markets, a number of cities (Washington, D.C., being a dramatic example) have experienced rapid increases in housing prices.

Elasticities of Market Demand

Many policy questions require relatively accurate information concerning market demand behavior. In some cases, market demand can be estimated from available empirical data. In others, it is possible to make reasonable inferences about the characteristics of market demand. In the absence of either accurate empirical information or realistic inferences, some economic policies turn out to be little more than "hit-or-miss" attempts to deal with economic problems or simply wishful thinking at odds with reality.

The most important pieces of information concerning market demand are *elasticities*. Specifically, we need to know the responsiveness of quantity demanded to changes in price *(price elasticity)*, changes in income *(income elasticity)*, and changes in the prices of other goods *(cross elasticity)*.

Price Elasticity of Demand

Price elasticity of demand, you will recall from Chapter 4, is the ratio between the percentage change in the quantity of a good demanded and the percentage change in its price. Price elasticity is relevant for a number of policy questions. If excise taxes are placed on gasoline, will consumers' total expenditures on gasoline rise or fall? Can the losses incurred by a public transit system be reduced by raising or lowering fares? If excise taxes are imposed on goods, how much of the tax will be passed on to consumers, and how much will be absorbed by sellers? The answers to these and similar questions depend, at least in part, on price elasticity of demand.

Income Elasticity of Demand

Recall that a change in income will cause a shift in the demand curve for a good; this shift, in turn, will cause a change in the quantity of the good demanded at any price. *Income elasticity of demand* measures the responsiveness of demand for a good to changes in income.

- **Income elasticity of demand** is the ratio of the percentage change in the quantity of a good demanded over the percentage change in income.

Income elasticity of demand is measured by the *income elasticity, coefficient* (e_I):

$$e_I = \frac{\text{percentage change in quantity demanded}}{\text{percentage change in income}} = \frac{\%\,\Delta Q_d}{\%\,\Delta I}. \quad (1)$$

To calculate income elasticity for a given change in income and a given change in quantity demanded, you can use the arc approximation technique introduced in Chapter 4.

All goods can be classified into three broad categories, based on the value of their income elasticity coefficients:

- If quantity demanded changes by a greater percentage than income, e_I will be greater than one, and demand is said to be **income elastic**.

- If quantity demanded changes by a smaller percentage than income, e_I will be less than one, and demand is said to be **income inelastic**.

- If quantity demanded and income change in opposite directions, e_I will be negative, and the good is an **inferior good**.

For most households, the first priority in consumption is to meet its requirements for necessities. But as its income rises, the typical household's consumption of necessities doesn't rise as rapidly. Having met its needs for food, for example, households don't increase food consumption proportionally to increases in income. Thus, food has become a smaller proportion of the typical American household's budget over the past thirty years as incomes have risen. In short, the demand for necessities tends to have a relatively low income elasticity.

Low-income households typically don't buy luxuries or nonessentials because they can't afford them and because necessities have a higher priority—food is more important than jewelry for most poor households. As income rises and basic needs are met, expenditures on luxuries generally rise more than proportionally. Of course, when income falls, luxuries are the first items given up, and the consumption of luxuries falls more than proportionally to the decline in income. In other words, the demand for luxuries tends to be relatively income elastic.

Close-up

The Incidence of Sales Tax

State and local sales taxes are paid by consumers as a percentage of the value of their purchases. Most of these taxes are *regressive*—i.e., they tax a higher proportion of low incomes than high incomes. In many states and localities, "necessities" are exempt from sales tax in order to reduce the burden of the tax on low-income households. To reduce the burden of sales taxes on the poor, goods with the lowest income elasticities of demand should be exempt from the tax.

Unfortunately, many exemptions to sales taxes reflect the subjective notions of legislators concerning the "necessity" of various goods, and not their income elasticities. Food is typically exempt, but soap may be taxed as a nonfood item or even as a cosmetic. In some states, all clothing is exempt from sales tax, even though some types of clothing (furs, formal attire, expensive suits, etc.) are luxuries consumed only by high-income households.

Cross-Elasticity of Demand

Recall from Chapter 3 that a change in the price of coffee caused a shift in the demand curve for tea, and hence a change in the quantity of tea demanded at any given price. *Cross-elasticity of demand* measures the responsiveness of demand for one good to changes in the price of another.

- **Cross-elasticity of demand** is the ratio of the percentage change in the quantity demanded of one good over the percentage change in the price of another good.

For two goods, x and y, the *cross-elasticity coefficient* (e_{xy}) is the ratio

$$e_{xy} = \frac{\text{percentage change in quantity of } x \text{ demanded}}{\text{percentage change in price of } y} = \frac{\% \Delta Q_{d_x}}{\% \Delta P_y}. \quad (2)$$

You can calculate the value of the cross-elasticity coefficient for given changes in quantity and price using the arc approximation approach. The more responsive the demand for x is to changes in the price of y, the higher will be the cross-elasticity of demand.

The coefficient of cross-elasticity of demand may be a positive or negative number, depending on the relationship between the goods. If two goods are substitutes for each other in consumption—beef and chicken, for example—a fall in the price of one would encourage households to reduce consumption of the other. If the price of chicken fell, this would reduce the demand for beef as households substitute the cheaper chicken for the relatively more expensive beef. Since the price of chicken and the demand for beef change in the same direction, the coefficient of cross-elasticity of demand (e_{bc}) is positive.

- The cross-elasticity of demand between substitutes is generally positive.

The value of the cross-elasticity coefficient will be greater for close substitutes than for weak ones. The cross-elasticity of demand is greater between different cuts of beef, for example, than between beef and chicken.

A decrease in the price of one good generally causes an increase in the demand for *complementary* goods. Lower gasoline prices will tend to increase the quantity of gasoline demanded and the volume of automobile travel; this will increase the demand for oil, tires, automobile service, and other goods and services that are complementary with gasoline. In this case, the price of gasoline and the demand for complementary goods change in opposite directions, so the cross-elasticity coefficient is negative.

- The cross-elasticity of demand between complements is generally negative.

Applying the Tools

The Demand for Automobile Travel

In the United States there is approximately one automobile for every two persons. In most communities, the household that does not own at least one car is unusual. The volume of automobile traffic continues to increase in spite of higher prices for gasoline, insurance, parts, and repairs that have raised the overall price of automobile travel. This growing demand has attracted considerable attention in recent years because of two major problems associated with automobile use: pollution and the energy shortage. The basic tools of demand theory can provide some insight into the causes of rising demand for automobile travel and the probable effectiveness of alternative policies to reduce it.

For most individual households, there simply aren't many good substitutes for the private automobile as a means of transportation. The automobile allows greater flexibility than mass transit, taking travelers *where* they want to go *when* they want to go there. For many households, walking and bicycling are unacceptable alternatives for reasons of health, personal safety, and distance.

Given a transportation budget, then, the typical household will allocate most of it to automobile travel, as in Figure A(i). The household's transportation budget and the current prices of mass transit and auto travel define the income constraint or budget line m^*a^*. Preferences for mass transit and auto travel are reflected in the household's indifference curves (U_0 and U_1). The household will maximize its satisfaction with its transportation budget with relatively little use of mass transit ($\overline{m}$) and rather heavier reliance on automobile travel ($\overline{a}$). In Figure A(ii), the quantity of automobile travel demanded at P_a is thus $\overline{a}$, given P_m.

Since the household sees mass transit as a poor substitute for auto travel, a large rise in the price of auto travel from P_a to P_a' (which shifts the budget line to m^*a^{**}) causes the household to reduce its auto travel only from $\overline{a}$ to $\overline{a}'$. The household's demand for auto travel in Figure A(ii), then, is price inelastic over a wide range of prices. If this household is typical, the market demand for auto travel will also be price inelastic at prevailing prices, as in Figure B, and increases

Figure A

in the cost of auto use will have relatively little effect in reducing the total volume of automobile travel.

Compounding this problem of price inelasticity, the demand for automobile travel has been rising in recent years, overwhelming the mild dampening effects of higher prices. Population growth has contributed to the increased demand, as

Figure B

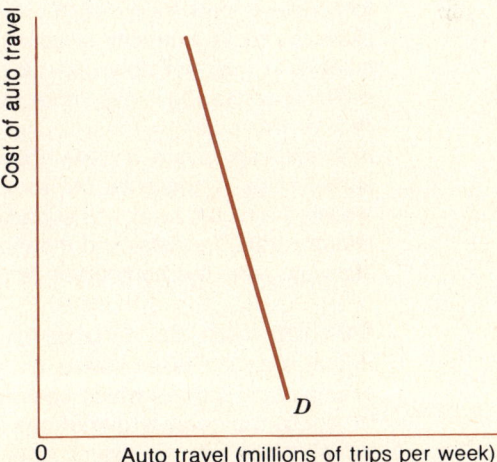

have changing housing patterns and changing preferences for the automobile and alternative means of transportation. Furthermore, auto travel is highly income elastic: as incomes rise, some people can afford cars that previously couldn't, while others can afford to move to the suburbs and use their cars to commute to the city. Finally, rising fares and deteriorating quality of public transit have weakened it as a substitute for the private automobile; the cross-elasticity of demand between automobile travel and public transportation is generally very low.

The situation in many urban areas is depicted in Figure C. In spite of an increase in the price of automobile travel from P_a in 1965 to P_a' in 1980, the volume of auto travel increased substantially. The effect of the higher price (a move along the demand curve to the left) has been overwhelmed by the increased demand (a shift in the demand curve to the right). As a result, pollution has increased and scarce energy resources have been further depleted.

Figure C

Dealing with the Problem: "More Freeways"

The traditional response to the growing demand for automobile travel has been to construct new freeways. For a given flow of traffic, this isn't unreasonable, since the move from city streets to freeways reduces congestion and noise pollution and may cut down on air pollution and fuel use if that given volume of traffic is allowed to move more rapidly. But this approach doesn't deal with the root of the problem—increasing demand for automobile travel—and may, in fact, only aggravate it. New freeways may accelerate the migration from the center cities to the suburbs; as new suburbs develop further and further from the city ("minutes away" on superhighways), more people drive greater distances. Intercity travel is faster and more convenient (if not very interesting) on interstate highways, and this contributes to the high demand for intercity auto travel.

Dealing with the Problem: Raising the Price

Higher gasoline taxes, taxes on automobiles, and higher registration fees are examples of policies which seek to raise the price of automobile travel in order to reduce the quantity demanded. All things equal, such policies might succeed, but all things are not equal. Low price elasticity of demand combined with increasing demand mean that taxes and fees would have to be much higher than those discussed publicly by policymakers if they are to have any significant effect. To appreciate this, find the price for 1980 which would have stabilized automobile travel at the 1965 level in Figure C.

Dealing with the Problem: Improving Substitutes

High speed express lanes and preferred parking for buses and car pools, improvements in the quality, reliability, and cost of public transit, and even safer bike and pedestrian routes are examples of policies which seek to reduce the demand for automobile travel by making substitute goods more attractive. So far, such attempts have met with limited success. Reducing mass transit fares, for example, won't cause the use of mass transit to increase proportionately because the price elasticity of demand for mass transit is relatively low. Furthermore, it would take drastic changes in the relative prices of mass transit and auto travel to reduce the demand for auto travel significantly because the cross-elasticity of demand between the two is low. Finally, most studies show a very low income elasticity of demand for mass transit—some studies even estimate it to be negative; thus, as incomes rise, the demand for auto travel will rise much more rapidly than the demand for mass transit.

Some Conclusions

None of the policies we have examined to reduce the demand for automobile travel has promised much success. Our market demand analysis highlights the peculiar characteristics of the demand for automobile travel (high income elasticity, low price and cross-elasticities) which make it a difficult problem to solve. One possible conclusion that could be reached is that it is hopeless to attempt to reduce the demand for automobile travel and to get people to substitute modes of transportation that are less harmful to the environment and more fuel efficient than the private car. This seems a bit too pessimistic, however. What the analysis does show is the hopelessness of simplistic and half-hearted policies to deal with the problem; only policies too drastic to be popular politically stand much chance of effectively reducing automobile use.

Summary

1. The **market demand** for a product is the sum of the households' demand curves for the product; it shows the quantity of a good demanded by all households at various prices, other things constant.
2. The market demand may change in response to any exogenous changes that change households' demand and as a result of changes in the number of households in the market.
3. The **price elasticity of market demand** is the percentage change in quantity demanded per percentage unit change in price. It defines the relationship between changes in the price of the product and changes in total expenditure by all households.
4. **Income elasticity of demand** is the percentage change in demand for a good per percentage point change in income. *Luxuries* generally have high

income elasticities, and *necessities* have low income elasticities.
5. **Cross-elasticity of demand** measures the effect of changes in the price of one good on the demand for another good. Cross elasticities tend to be relatively high between close *substitutes*, low between weak substitutes, and negative between *complements*.

Concepts for Review

market demand curve
the *law of large numbers*
income elasticity of demand

cross elasticity of demand
substitute goods
complementary goods

Questions

1. Much of the emphasis in the discussion of world hunger has been on technological and organizational changes, or *green revolutions*, which would increase food output and attack the problem from the supply side.
   Would it be possible to attack the problem from the demand side?
2. Excise taxes on tobacco and liquor have been promoted as effective measures for raising public tax revenue and as a means of reducing alcohol and tobacco consumption.
   a. Could these excise taxes be effective in raising tax revenue and reducing alcohol and tobacco consumption? Explain in the context of the market demand for these products.
   b. Empirical evidence suggests that these taxes have been more effective in raising tax revenue than in discouraging consumption of the products. What does this suggest about the market demand for these products?
   c. What information on market demand would you need to tell whether the burden of alcohol and tobacco taxes is greater on low-income households or high-income households?
3. Suppose that you have been appointed to a committee to study the need for health care facilities in your community for the next decade. The community wants to provide adequate facilities to meet the demand, but doesn't want to overbuild and end up with unused facilities.
   What kinds of information would you look for? What characteristics of market demand would affect the future demand for health care? Explain.
4. Because of your prowess in economic analysis, you have been asked to evaluate a proposed program to reduce traffic congestion in your community. The program includes taxes on gasoline, parking, and other items that determine the price of automobile travel. The tax revenues would be used to subsidize mass transit to make it more available and attractive to consumers.
   a. What information would you need to make your evaluation?
   b. Under what circumstances would you predict a high degree of success for the proposed program?
   c. Under what circumstances would you predict a low degree of success for the program?

Problems

1. Suppose that the market for aphrodisiacs is made up of three households—A, B, and C (who wish to remain anonymous because of the nature of the product). The following table shows the quantity demanded by each household at prices between $1 and $10.

	QUANTITY DEMANDED BY		
PRICE	A	B	C
$10	20	16	10
9	24	18	11
8	28	20	12
7	32	22	13
6	36	24	14
5	40	26	15
4	44	28	16
3	48	30	17
2	52	32	18
1	56	34	19

    a. Find the quantity demanded for the market at each price, and construct a market demand schedule.
    b. Draw demand curves for each consumer and for the market over this range of prices and quantities.
    c. How could you explain the differences in the demand functions of these consumers? Does the market demand reflect the demand of the typical consumer in this market? What does it represent?
    d. A new consumer (E) enters the market whose demand for aphrodisiacs is identical to B's. Repeat parts a and b to show how this affects market demand.
    e. Consumer A dies because of his heavy consumption of aphrodisiacs. How does this affect the market demand relationship you found in part d?

2. Between 1965 and 1975, Mr. Hy Pothetical's income rose from $10,000 per year to $15,000 per year. During this period, the price of gasoline in Mr. Pothetical's community remained at 50¢ per gallon, and his consumption increased from 10 gallons per week to 30 gallons per week. In 1975, his income remained at $15,000, the price of gasoline rose to 75¢ per gallon, and he reduced his gasoline consumption from 30 gallons per week to 27 gallons per week.
    a. If this person is typical of consumers of gasoline, is gasoline a "luxury" or a "necessity"? How do you know?
    b. If this person is typical of consumers of gasoline, how effective would the imposition of an excise tax of 15¢ per gallon be in reducing gasoline consumption during a period of rising incomes? Explain.

PART THREE

Supply in the Product Market

The last two chapters looked in considerable detail at the **demand side** of the product market. In the next three chapters, we turn our attention to the **supply side** and examine how firms behave in their role as sellers in the product market.

Modern economic theory assumes that firms, like households, always try to act in their own best interest. Just as the household's goal is to get the most satisfaction from what it consumes, so the firm's goal is to get the greatest profit from what it produces. It achieves this goal by producing its output as efficiently as possible and at the lowest possible cost. In the first two chapters of this section, we look at how the firm achieves efficiency in the **short run**, a period in which at least one of the resource inputs used in production is fixed. In Chapter 9, we see how relaxing this assumption can lead to even further efficiency in the long run, and then explore the possibility of even further increases in efficiency through technological change.

7

Production in the Short Run

Preview: Economic theory typically portrays the firm as a sort of profit-maximizing machine. Resource inputs go in one end of the machine and product output comes out the other. The relationship between the level of input and the level of output is defined by the quality of inputs, the state of technology, and the firm's **production function**. In this chapter, we'll examine some key production relationships to see how the firm goes about choosing the most efficient level of output to produce.

Why the Firm Produces

The analysis of demand began with a question: what is the household's goal in consumption? As an answer to that question, we assumed that households behave rationally to maximize utility, and the theory of demand is built on that basic assumption. Similarly, in analyzing the behavior of the firm, we begin by asking the same question: what is the firm's goal in production? Is there a fundamental economic goal underlying the firm's decisions? Contemporary theories of the firm differ in their assumptions about such a purpose. These theories can be lumped into two broad categories—*behavioral* or *organizational* theories, and *marginalist* or *maximizing* theories.

Behavioral Theories of the Firm

Most of the nonagricultural goods we buy are produced by large corporations. The typical corporation is a complex organization in which a variety of economic, political, sociological, psychological, and institutional forces shape decisions. In fact, the firm as an organization may have its own organizational goals which shape and control the decisions of managers of the firm.

- **Behavioral theories of the firm** analyze the economic and noneconomic forces that determine the decisions of managers of firms.

Behavioral analyses of the firm—such as those of Nobel laureate Herbert A. Simon—provide comprehensive and realistic pictures of the firm's actions. Such analyses take into account the effects of the organizational features of the firm—ownership, control, division of managerial responsibility, features of the managerial bureaucracy, etc.

Based on their analyses, behavioral theorists conclude that managers of firms may simply engage in what is called **satisficing behavior**. They perform tasks and responsibilities just sufficiently to please superiors, to maintain or improve a place in the managerial hierarchy, to please stockholders, etc. The following hypothetical case is a highly simplified example of the variables considered in a behavioral approach to the firm.

Close-up

Why the Firm Produces: A Simple Behavioral Analysis

Gordon Stein is in charge of production for the Hi-Collar Brewery. Gordon decides to hire an additional plant worker, based on the following considerations:

1. Hi-Collar advertises itself as the fastest growing brewery in Iowa, and Gordon sees this as an incentive to increase employment and output.
2. By increasing the production of beer, Gordon's superiors in the managerial bureaucracy will look favorably on his performance in his position.
3. Gordon's immediate predecessors were fired for low levels of production.
4. Gordon thinks of himself as an important manager, and enjoys having an additional employee responsible to him.

In this simple behavioral analysis, Gordon's decision is explained in terms of the firm's *organizational objectives*, and Gordon's view of what constitutes satisfactory managerial performance within the organization.

Marginalist Theories of the Firm

In economics, we make a much simpler assumption that firms, like households, are *rational maximizers*. This approach is called *marginalist* because it portrays the firm as making marginal decisions—changing resource inputs, production output, or price—until something (profit, sales, growth, market share, etc.) reaches a maximum.

- **Marginalist theories of the firm** are based on the assumption that the firm behaves rationally to maximize something.

Marginal analysis provides a simplified, abstract sketch of firm behavior in order to identify general patterns and make statistically testable predictions.

Traditionally, economics has assumed that the objective of the firm is to maximize *profit*.

- **Profit** is the difference between the money a firm receives for the goods it sells (revenue) and the money it had to pay to produce those goods (costs).

Firms will change their output as long as such change causes profit to rise and will stop changing when profit starts to fall. When the final marginal change in output doesn't change profit at all, the firm has reached the point where profits are maximized.

Close-up

Why the Firm Produces: A Simple Marginalist Analysis

Bruce Sudds has taken over as the new owner and president of the Hi-Collar Brewery, and his primary interest is in the firm's profit. In reviewing Gordon's decision to hire the additional worker, Mr. Sudds finds the following:

1. The additional worker increased output by thirty cases per week. At a price of $5 per case, this adds $150 to the firm's weekly revenue.
2. The new worker receives a weekly wage of $200, adding $200 to the firm's weekly costs.
3. The new worker's contribution to the firm's weekly profit is the difference between the added revenue and the added cost, or $150 − $200 = −$50 per week.

Sudds decides to fire the new worker, thus reducing the firm's revenue by $150 and its cost by $200 per week. In other words, firing the new worker raises weekly profit by $50 a week. This tells Sudds to keep firing workers as long as profit rises. Unfortunately, his next choice for the ax is Gordon. By firing Gordon, the firm loses weekly revenue of $250 but it also reduces cost by $275 a week (Gordon's weekly wage)—i.e., its profit rises by an additional $25 as Gordon joins the ranks of the jobless.

Which Approach Is Best?

Neither the behavioral nor the marginalist approach can answer all questions about firm behavior. The behavioral approach helps us understand all the forces that go into a specific decision by a specific firm, but the analysis is typically so complex that it won't allow us to draw any general conclusions about the behavior of firms. Some behavioral models of firms contain so many variables that complex computer simulations of situations are used to predict the firm's behavior.

The marginalist, profit-maximizing model is highly simplified and abstract, and doesn't even begin to portray all the complexities of modern corporate decision-making. The predictions of firm behavior that follow from the profit-maximizing model (which we will explore in this chapter) remain valid as generalizations, however, and the true test of any theory is its ability to make empirically valid predictions. Since we are more interested in predicting firm behavior *ex ante* than in analyzing it *ex post*, we will make the assumption for the remainder of this text that firms are indeed rational profit-maximizers.

How the Firm Produces

By assuming that profit-maximization is *why* the firm produces, we are able to make two fundamental predictions about *how* the firm produces:

- A profit-maximizing firm will not use more than the minimum amount of resources required to produce a given level of output.
- A profit-maximizing firm will not produce a given level of output at more than the minimum necessary cost.

We will explore the first of these two predictions for the remainder of this chapter, and will look more closely at the second in Chapter 8.

The actual decisions of firms in the real world are quite complex. The typical firm produces a number of products, and uses a large number of things in production that could be defined as separate resource inputs —different types of labor, machinery, raw materials, entrepreneurial skill, etc. To analyze the firm's decisions in the simplest possible terms, we'll make a number of assumptions that simplify reality.

1. **Resource inputs.** We'll start by assuming that our hypothetical firm uses only *two resources* in production—**labor** (ℓ) and **capital** (k). Capital includes all nonlabor resource inputs—machinery, buildings, materials, etc.
2. **Quality of resources.** In the real world, there are hard workers and lazy workers, efficient and inefficient machines, good land and bad land, etc. However, our analysis will simplify this by assuming that the *quality of resources* is given, and that each resource is **homogeneous**. In the analysis, there are no differences among units of labor or among units of capital.
3. **Technology.** Technology defines the relationship between

resource inputs and the level of output, and is discussed in detail in a later chapter. A change in technology—for example, a new scientific discovery that can be applied to production or a major innovation in production methods—alters the relationship between resource inputs and the level of output. For now, we'll assume that the state of technology used by our hypothetical firm is constant.

The Firm's Production Function

For resources of given quality and a given state of technology, the output that a firm can produce from a given combination of resource inputs, or the resources required to produce a given level of output are defined by the firm's *production function*.

- The **production function** is the relationship between resource inputs and the level of output.

The production function is defined by the quality of resources and the state of technology. We can express the production function in mathematical shorthand as

$$q = f(\ell, k), \qquad (1)$$

where q is output, ℓ is the input of labor, and k is the input of capital.

Initially, we'll focus our attention on the firm's production in the *short run*. The short run in economics isn't any particular period of calendar time, but is defined in terms of the firm's ability to vary resource inputs.

- In the **short run,** the firm operates with at least one *fixed resource* whose input doesn't change.

In some cases, the short run is a brief period of time—a small contractor, for example, could hire more workers, buy more tools, and rent an additional truck in a matter of days (or even hours). For large firms, the short run may be a long period of time—it would take years or even decades for General Motors or most large corporations to change all of the resources they use.

To illustrate some important short-run production relationships, assume that our hypothetical firm—the Hi-Collar Brewery—varies its output in the short run by varying the input of labor with its capital input fixed at k^*. Hi-Collar's short-run production function, then, is

$$q_b = f(\ell, k^*). \qquad (2)$$

This simply says that the output of beer (q_b) in the short run depends on the input of labor (ℓ) combined with the fixed input of capital (k^*). Table 1 shows the output that Hi-Collar can produce with its fixed capital input and various inputs of labor, and illustrates three important variables—*total product*, *marginal product*, and *average product*.

Total Product (TP)

Columns 1 and 2 in Table 1 show the relationship between Hi-Collar's labor input (ℓ) and the total output of beer (q_b) produced. This total output for a given input of labor is called the firm's *total product* of labor.

- The **total product** (*TP*) of a variable resource is the maximum possible output produced by combining a given input of that resource with the fixed resource.

We can plot the labor inputs and corresponding outputs from Table 1 on a graph in order to draw Hi-Collar's **total product curve**,[1] labeled TP_ℓ in Figure 1. For any given level of output, Hi-Collar will want to operate on the TP curve. To produce an output of 56 cases of beer a week, for example, it will employ 4 workers. Fixed levels of technology and resource quality prevent Hi-Collar from producing *more* than 56 cases using only 4 workers, so the company can't operate above the curve. It could operate below the curve, producing fewer than 56 cases with its 4 workers or using more than 4 workers to produce the 56 cases, but if it did so it wouldn't be maximizing profit.

Table 1 Production Figures for Hi-Collar Brewery

Labor input (ℓ)	Output (q)	$MP = \Delta q / \Delta \ell$	$AP = q/\ell$
0	0		—
		8	
1	8		8
		26	
2	34		17
		14	
3	48		16
		8	
4	56		14
		4	
5	60		12
		0	
6	60		10
		−4	
7	56		8

Marginal Product (MP)

Firms make marginal decisions in order to reach an output that maximizes profit. Thus the *change* in output which results from a *change* in a variable resource input is an important piece of information for the firm.

- The **marginal product** (*MP*) of a variable resource is the change

---

1. Since the total product curve shows the relationship between inputs of a variable resource and the level of output with a fixed resource, it is sometimes also referred to as the firm's *short-run production function*.

in total product that results from a given change in the variable resource input. If the variable resource input increases by one unit, MP tells how much TP changes as a result of that one-unit increase. In other words, marginal product measures the rate at which output changes as a resource input changes.

For the Hi-Collar Brewery, the marginal product of labor is the ratio of the change in its total product (ΔTP) divided by the change in the number of workers employed ($\Delta \ell$), or

$$MP_\ell = \frac{\Delta TP}{\Delta \ell} \tag{3}$$

Notice that this algebraic formula for the marginal product is written in such a way that we can use it to find the MP of changes in the resource input that are larger or smaller than one unit. Applying this MP formula to the figures for the Hi-Collar Brewery in Table 1, we find that the MP of the first worker is $(8 - 0)/1 = 8$, the MP of the second is $(30 - 8)/1 = 22$, etc.

Graphically, the MP of a variable resource at any input is the slope of the TP curve at that input. If the TP curve becomes steeper as more labor is added, the MP of labor is rising. In Figure 1, this occurs as Hi-Collar increases the number of workers it employs from 0 to 2. If the slope of the TP curve gets flatter as more labor is added, the MP of labor is falling—as it does for all labor inputs greater than 2 in Table 1 and Figure 1.

To find the value of the MP of labor at any point along the TP curve, we have to find the value of the curve's slope at that point. In Figure 1,

Figure 1 Total Product Curve

Figure 2 Marginal and Average Product Curves

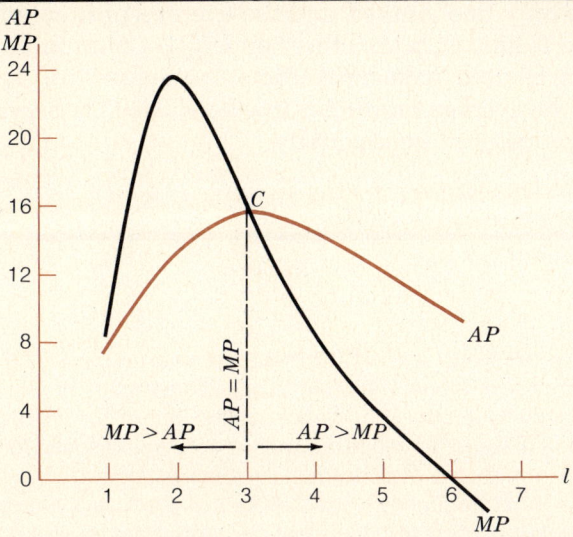

the slope of the TP curve at point C is the same as the slope of line T, which is tangent to TP at point C. Note, however, that the slope of tangent line T gives us the MP of an infinitely small change in the labor input. The MP of a full additional unit of labor at point C will be the slope of the broken line connecting points C and D.

Plotting the MP, or the value of the slope of the TP curve, at each labor input graphically defines the marginal product curve, labeled MP in Figure 2. Note the relationship between the shapes of the TP curve in Figure 1 and the MP curve in Figure 2.

Average Product (AP)

A third variable of particular importance to firms is the *average product*.

- The **average product** (AP) of a variable resource is simply the total product of the resource divided by the total input of the resource. It measures the average output per unit of input.

For the Hi-Collar Brewery, labor is the variable resource, so the firm's *average product of labor* (AP_ℓ) will be

$$AP_\ell = \frac{TP}{\ell} \qquad (4)$$

In Table 1, we can divide the figures in the TP column by the figures in the labor input (ℓ) column to get the *average product of labor* for each level of labor input. The relationship between AP and ℓ is plotted in Figure 2 to form the **average product curve**, labeled AP.

Average product is one measure of a firm's efficiency in production in the short run. If Hi-Collar employed only one worker, that worker would have to run all of the machines and perform all the operations in brewing. The firm would be using its fixed plant and equipment inefficiently with only one worker, and the average product of labor would be low (note Table 1). On the other hand, if Hi-Collar hired 6 workers, this is too much labor to make most efficient use of the firm's plant and equipment, and the average product is low here also. Thus, *average product of labor* is an indicator of **productivity**.

Close-up

Productivity

Nearly everyone has heard the term *productivity* in discussions of economic performance. Managers of firms are interested in *productivity* as an indicator of efficiency in production. Labor unions often cite increases in *productivity* in support of wage demands. Economic policymakers and forecasters use *productivity* as a measure of performance of the economy.

The most frequently used indicator of productivity is output per unit of labor—sometimes expressed as output per labor-hour, output per employee-hour, or (in the sexist "old days") output per man-hour. Output per unit of labor is, of course, simply the average product (AP) of labor. The following table shows output per hour of labor in the private sector of the U.S. economy between 1967 and 1977 as a percentage of output per hour in the base year 1967.

Notice in the table that productivity falls during serious recessions—such as the one in 1974—and rises during periods of economic recovery and expansion. When output falls in a recession, firms underutilize their capacities and average product falls. In periods of rising output, firms use their capacities more efficiently, and average product rises. Thus, employment falls more slowly than output during recessions and increases more slowly than output during recoveries. This is particularly important in predicting how quickly employment will return to previous levels after a recession.

OUTPUT PER HOUR, 1967–1977 (1967 = 100)

Year	Output per hour
1967	100.0
1968	102.7
1969	102.7
1970	103.9
1971	107.7
1972	111.1
1973	113.7
1974	110.8
1975	112.2
1976	116.5
1977	119.5

Source: U.S. Dept. of Labor, B.L.S., *Handbook of Labor Statistics 1977.* (Washington: Government Printing Office, 1977). U.S. Department of Commerce, Bureau of the Census, *Statistical Abstract of the United States, 1978.* (Washington: Government Printing Office, 1978), p. 419.

In Figure 2, the marginal product curve (*MP*) and the average product curve (*AP*) are plotted on the same pair of axes in order to illustrate the important relationship between the two variables. If a firm employs one additional unit of a variable resource, its *MP* will affect the firm's *AP* as follows:

- If the *MP* of the last unit is greater than the firm's *AP*, *AP* will rise.
- If the *MP* of the last unit is less than the firm's *AP*, *AP* will fall.
- If the *MP* of the last unit = the firm's *AP*, *AP* is at its maximum.

The first two of these statements can be illustrated easily using a noneconomic example. Suppose that a baseball team has a team batting average of .250 and signs a new player with a batting average of .375. The addition of the new player will raise the team average because he's a better hitter than the average player already on the team. If the new player were a good pitcher or outstanding fielder with a modest batting average of .190, he would lower the team average because his batting average is below the average of the players already on the team.

Looking at the data for the Hi-Collar Brewery in Table 1 and Figure 2, we can see that the *MP* for the first and second workers hired is higher than the firm's *AP*, so the *MP* curve lies above the *AP* curve. The *MP* for units of labor above 2 is less than the *AP*, so the *AP* curve lies above the *MP* curve. At a labor input somewhere between 2 and 3, the *AP* curve and the *MP* curve intersect: at this point, *MP* = *AP*, and the *AP* curve has reached its maximum.

The Principle of Diminishing Returns

As Hi-Collar adds more units of its variable resource (labor) to its fixed input (capital) in Table 1 and Figures 1 and 2, a number of things happen. At first, the additional units of labor enable Hi-Collar to make better use of its fixed capital. The increased number of workers are able to make better use of the machinery and to improve their efficiency through specialization. As it adds the first two workers to the brewery, Hi-Collar experiences *increasing returns*.

- With **increasing returns**, each additional unit of the variable resource adds more to the firm's output, and the *marginal product of the variable resource rises as more of it is used*.

As the number of workers employed increases, however, there is less capital per worker, and eventually this will cause each additional worker to add less output than the last. As a third, fourth, fifth, and sixth worker are added to the brewery's work force, Hi-Collar experiences *diminishing returns*.

- With **diminishing returns**, each additional unit of the variable resource adds less to the firm's output, and the *marginal product of the variable resource falls as more of it is used*.

If Hi-Collar hires a seventh worker, there will be little for him to do, and he may end up getting in the other workers' way. As a result, the firm's output is actually less than it was with only six workers, and the firm is experiencing *negative returns*.

- With **negative returns**, each additional unit of the variable resource subtracts from the firm's output, and the *marginal product of the variable resource is negative*.

Of course, no rational profit-making firm would hire more labor if it knew output would fall as a result.

Hi-Collar employs a small work force, and can vary its labor input by small amounts, so that the firm goes from increasing returns to diminishing returns at a point—point C in Figure 3—which is called the **point of diminishing returns**. At this point, the firm experiences *constant returns*.

- With **constant returns**, additional units of a variable resource add the same amount to the firm's output, and the *marginal product of the variable resource is either constant or at its maximum*.

Figure 3 Increasing and Diminishing Returns

Some larger firms may experience constant returns over a range of labor inputs and outputs in which each additional worker adds the same amount of output.

Figure 3 illustrates graphically the relationships between *TP*, *MP*, and *AP*, and shows the returns a firm will experience with various levels of resource inputs. Increasing returns are dominant and *MP* rises over the range of labor inputs from zero through ℓ_1 and outputs from zero through q_1. Diminishing returns and falling MP_ℓ occur between labor inputs of ℓ_1 and ℓ_3 and outputs of q_1 and q_3. Output reaches its maximum and MP_ℓ reaches zero at ℓ_3 and q_3. Beyond ℓ_3, the firm experiences negative returns. *MP* is negative and output falls as labor is added.

Every production function will have a point of diminishing returns, and this fact is the basis of perhaps the most universally valid proposition in economics—the *principle of diminishing returns*.

- The **principle of diminishing returns** states that with at least one fixed resource input, goods must eventually be produced under conditions of diminishing returns.

If diminishing returns never became dominant, there would be some interesting (if peculiar) results. For example, if food production on fixed land never reached a point of diminishing returns, the world could be fed from a backyard garden (or even a flower box) simply by adding enough labor and capital to the fixed land. While this example may seem trivial at first glance, it has tragic implications for many of the poorest people on earth, as illustrated on pp. 134–36.

Changes in the Production Function

Recall that in order to simplify our analysis of the firm's production function, we assumed that a number of potentially significant variables —technology, resource quality, and the level of the fixed resource— would remain constant. It is important to keep that fact in mind, because a change in any one of those variables could alter the entire relationship between inputs of a variable resource and the level of output.

Suppose that Hi-Collar purchases an additional pot still. Capital is now at a higher level, k^{**}, and the short-run production function with capital fixed at k^{**} is

$$q_b = f(\ell, k^{**}). \qquad (5)$$

The effect of this change would be to increase the amount of beer that Hi-Collar could produce with each input of labor. This would shift the *TP* curve upward to *TP'*, as in Figure 4a. With greater output at every labor input (except zero), *MP* and *AP* will also rise at every level of labor input; the *AP* and *MP* curves in Figure 4b shift upward to *AP'* and *MP'*.

Changes in resource quality and technological innovations in production will also cause *TP*, *MP*, and *AP* to change. Improvements in resource quality or production technology will have basically the same effect on the variables as did the increase in fixed resource, shifting

Figure 4 Changes in the Production Function

TP, MP, and AP in Figure 4 upward to TP', MP', and AP'. Deterioration in the quality of resources pulls TP, MP, and AP downward to TP'', MP'', and AP'''.

Applying the Tools

Population Growth and Hunger in the Third World

In countries such as Egypt, India, much of sub-Saharan Africa, and parts of Latin America, one of the greatest economic challenges is to produce enough food to support the growing population. We can analyze one of the roots of the problem of world hunger as well as future prospects for improvements by considering the food production in these countries as a short-run production problem.

Most underdeveloped countries have fixed amounts of usable agricultural land. Capital is limited because capital investment requires saving and most households live very near the biological subsistence level. In addition, the structure of the agricultural sector and the small size of land holdings in many cases preclude the use of modern agricultural technology.

As the population and labor force grow in these countries, more and more labor is being added to these fixed inputs of land and capital. Because of diminishing returns, additional labor adds less and less to food output because so much labor is being combined with so little land and capital. Food output grows more and more slowly as the amount of labor increases, and the MP of labor is very low, as illustrated in Figure A. In some areas, the situation has become so severe that production has been pushed into the region of negative returns.

Figure A

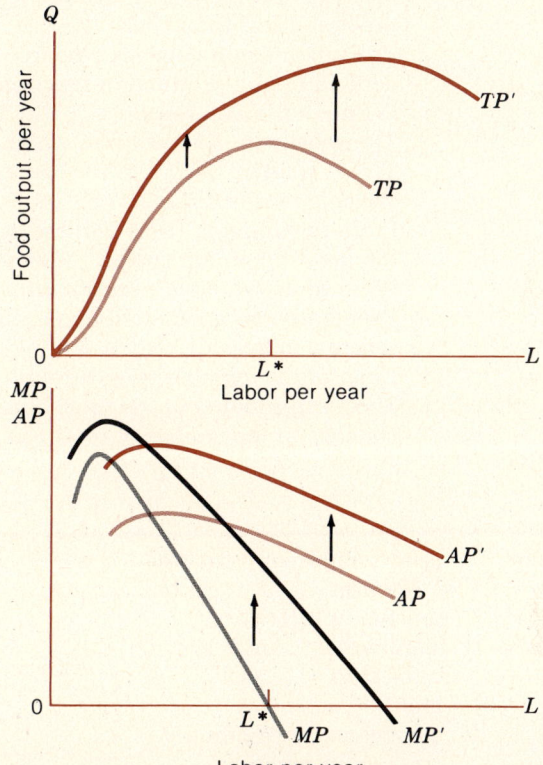

Pessimistic assessments of the problem of food production and hunger in the underdeveloped world see population and labor increasing to the point where food output will cease to rise at all ($MP_\ell = 0$), or toward L^* in Figure A. More optimistic prognoses are based on the ability of countries to limit population growth, which would slow the movement toward $MP_\ell = 0$, and on so-called *Green Revolutions* that would raise the productivity of agricultural labor. Green Revolutions consist of such things as technological innovations, new types of crops, etc. Green Revolutions would shift the TP, MP, and AP curves upward, as in Figure A, increasing both the productivity of labor and the total output from the land.

Green Revolutions have not been unqualified successes, and they are not a panacea to solve the population-food problems in the Third World. Investing in agricultural research and development, like any other investment, requires saving, and this is difficult with average incomes at the subsistence level. The gains in output haven't been as great as originally hoped for because some of the land isn't conducive to intensive cultivation, and because traditional agriculture in some areas has been resistant to changes.

Summary

1. The assumption that firms are **rational profit-maximizers** is a useful and necessary abstraction from reality that enables us to make general predictions of firms' behavior.
2. The relationship between resource inputs and the level of output is defined by the **production function**. The production function, in turn, is defined for given resource quality and technology.
3. The **short run** is a period in which at least one resource input is fixed. The firm alters output in the short run by changing the input of the variable resource.
4. Profit-maximizing firms will try to produce any given level of output at the lowest possible cost in the short run by using the smallest possible input of the variable resource with its fixed resource.
5. Eventually, all goods will be produced under conditions of **diminishing returns**. Increasing output will require larger and larger increases in the input of the variable resource with diminishing returns.
6. Short-run production relationships may change as a result of exogenous changes in the quality of resources or the state of technology.

Concepts for Review

behavioral theories of the firm
satisficing behavior
marginalist theories of the firm
profit
homogeneous resources
production function
short run
fixed resource
total product
total product curve
marginal product
marginal product curve
average product
average product curve
productivity
increasing returns
constant returns
diminishing returns
point of diminishing returns
principle of diminishing returns
Green Revolutions

Questions

1. Most economists readily admit that the goals of firms in the US in 1977 are more complex than simply maximizing profit, yet most continue to work with a basic theory of the firm in which it is assumed that the firm seeks to maximize its profit.
   a. How could such strange behavior possibly be justified analytically? Explain. (The fact that economists are a peculiar lot is not a sufficient explanation.)
   b. What would induce the majority of economists to give up the profit maximizing model of the firm?
2. Can you think of any situations in which the short-run production period is a long period of calendar time? How about situations in which the long-run production period is a short period of calendar time?
3. "Further efforts will be fruitless because we've passed the point of diminishing returns." Is this fairly common use of diminishing returns accurate? Explain.
4. In some areas in underdeveloped countries, experts argue that removing people from the countryside and labor from the land will raise agricultural production. How could this be possible? Explain.

Problems

1. The Drop-Kick Delivery Co. operates in the short run with a fixed capital input, and varies its output by varying its labor input.

labor ℓ	output q	MP_ℓ	AP_ℓ
0	___	___	. . .
1	___	___	10
2	30	___	___
3	___	12	___
4	___	10	___
5	___	___	12
6	66	___	___
7	___	4	___
8	___	___	9
9	72	___	___
10	___	___	7

   a. Fill in the missing numbers to complete the above table.
   b. Plot the figures graphically to show the firm's TP, MP, and AP curves. Explain what each means.
   c. Identify the ranges of labor inputs and output which exhibit increasing returns, diminishing returns, zero returns, and negative returns. Why doesn't every additional unit of labor add the same amount of output?
   d. Which labor input and output combination(s)—if any—wouldn't be used by a profit-maximizing firm, regardless of the price of labor?

8

Output and Cost in the Short Run

Preview: Profit, you will recall, is the difference between a firm's revenue and its costs. Our assumption in Chapter 7 that firms are rational profit-maximizers led us to predict that firms will produce any level of output at the minimum necessary cost. In order to understand how firms go about doing that, we must translate the *basic production relationships* of Chapter 7 into a series of *basic cost relationships*.

Economic Cost and Profit

Before we can even begin to understand the firm's cost of production, we must take a close look at exactly what economists mean by *cost*. Most of us think of cost as monetary outlay, or **accounting cost**. But to an economist, accounting cost is only part of any total cost. In economic analysis, **economic cost** includes both accounting costs and **opportunity costs**. *Opportunity costs*, you will recall from Chapter 2, are the costs of foregone alternatives.

Close-up

Economic Cost vs. Accounting Cost

By camping out for 24 hours, Mr. Fred E. Fan was able to purchase a ticket to the Super Bowl at the regular price of $15. On the day of the game, he was shocked to find that scalpers were able to sell tickets in the parking lot for $150. He thought it shocking that anyone would pay so much to see a football game (even the Super Bowl), and felt lucky he could see the game at a cost of $15.

If we defined costs as monetary outlays (accounting costs), the cost of seeing the game was the $15 Mr. Fan paid for his ticket. However, the economic cost he incurred in seeing the game is much greater. Fred had the alternatives of using his ticket himself or selling it at its market value of $150. By using the ticket himself, he gave up the alternative of selling his ticket, and his *economic cost* is thus the $15 he spent on the ticket (accounting cost) plus the $135 profit he lost by not selling the ticket (opportunity cost) = $150. In addition, if by camping out 24 hours to buy his ticket, Mr. Fan gave up the opportunity of working, the opportunity cost of his lost wage income would also be included in the economic cost of his ticket.

As a second example, consider the economic cost of a year's college education. Tuition, room and board, and other expenses might come to $6,000 for the year. The accounting cost for that year is thus $6,000. But the economic cost includes the monetary outlay, plus the foregone income from alternative uses of the student's time and money. Had she been employed for the year instead of attending college, the student could have earned $7,000 (for simplicity assume that none of this would have been saved). The $6,000 which was paid to cover her expenses in college could have been deposited in a savings account at 5% interest, in which case it would have earned $300 for the year. Thus, the economic cost of a year in college (monetary outlays, foregone wages, and foregone interest) is, in this example, $13,300.

Since profit is the difference between total revenue and total cost, different definitions of cost will yield different levels of profit at any given level of output.

- **Accounting profit** is the difference between total revenue and *accounting costs*.
- **Economic profit** is the difference between total revenue and *economic costs*.

Accounting profit tells us whether or not a firm is covering its monetary outlays, while economic profit tells us whether or not a firm is covering all of its opportunity costs as well.

- **Positive economic profit** indicates that the firm is more than compensated for its opportunity costs.
- **Negative economic profit** indicates that the firm is less than compensated for all of its opportunity costs, and that it would gain income by moving its resources to an alternative employment.
- **Zero economic profit** indicates that the firm is just compensated for its opportunity costs, and that it would neither gain nor lose income if it moved its resources to an alternative employment.

Since economic cost is a more inclusive definition than accounting cost, a firm's economic profit at any given level of output generally will be less than its accounting profit.

Consider, for example, a Mom & Pop Grocery (owned and operated by

Mom and Pop), whose assets are shown in Table 1a. In Table 1b, Mom & Pop show an accounting profit after all monetary outlays of $20,000 for the year.

However, in operating their grocery, Mom and Pop have sacrificed the income they could have earned in other employment of their time and financial assets. They could have rented out the store building, found other employment, and sold their equipment and inventory, and purchased securities with the proceeds. This foregone income represents an opportunity cost to Mom and Pop that is not included in the accountant's definition of cost.

Table 1c is an income statement which defines costs as economic costs. Thus, the cost figures include (along with those already covered by accounting cost): normal wages Mom & Pop could have earned in other employment, $500 per month rent on their building, and the income they could earn by liquidating their equipment and inventory and using the funds in an alternative undertaking with risks similar to those in the grocery (assuming that such an undertaking would yield an

Table 1 Mom & Pop Grocery

(a) Assets

Assets		Current Market Value
Building		$50,000
Equipment		10,000
Inventory (12/31/80)		20,000
		$80,000

(b) Accounting Profit

Sales (1/1/80–12/31/80)		$80,000
Less: Costs		
Stock purchased	$40,000	
Operating expense	10,000	
Employees' wages	10,000	60,000
Profit		$20,000

(c) Economic Profit

Sales (1/1/80–12/31/80)		$80,000
Less: Economic costs		
Stock purchased	$40,000	
Operating expenses	10,000	
Employees' wages	10,000	
Foregone wages (Pop)	8,000	
Foregone wages (Mom)	6,000	
Foregone interest	3,000	
Foregone rent	6,000	$83,000
Economic Profit		−$ 3,000

interest rate of 10 percent per year). When all economic costs are included, Mom and Pop realize an *economic loss* (negative economic profit) for the year, even though the store's revenue more than covered its accounting costs.

Economic losses are fairly common in some types of firms. Family-owned retail stores—service stations, grocery stores, restaurants—frequently incur economic losses. Many small farms operate with economic losses, especially in areas where the market value of land is high.

Sometimes economic losses persist because the owners of the firms don't identify the foregone returns from alternative uses of their resources. If a firm is making a sufficient accounting profit, the owners may not seek out alternative uses for their resources, or the owners may not consider such things as foregone wages, rent, or interest. Many family enterprises which employ family members typically hide part of their economic losses by paying low wages to family members.

Close-up

"How Ya Gonna Keep 'em Down on the Farm (After They Pay Their Property Taxes)?"

Many family farms incur large economic losses because the owners don't take the value of their land and the income that could be earned on the proceeds from selling it into account. Some people who are committed to farming as an occupation and as a life-style may not be interested in the market value of their land for nonfarming uses, except possibly as a means of financing retirement or as an estate to heirs.

Whether the farmer cares about it or not, however, local tax authorities are very interested in the value of land. If land is worth $20,000 per acre for real estate development, and is assessed at this value, the farmer will be hit with a big tax bill that may cause him to earn an accounting loss as well as an economic loss.

Sometimes, land that has always been assessed as *farm land* is reassessed at its market value (for farming or other uses) for inheritance taxes, and heirs frequently have to sell the farm to pay the inheritance taxes on it.

Thus the taxing authorities have, among other things, made the value of the land and the economic costs of farming more obvious by reassessing land at its highest market value.

Economic losses also may reflect **psychic income** and **psychic costs** which are not quantifiable in meaningful monetary terms because of their subjectivity. A self-employed butcher may gain personal satisfaction (psychic income) from the responsibility and independence of being his own boss, while the alternative of working as a journeyman butcher under a foreman's direction in a large supermarket would involve for him an unquantifiable psychic cost. Many small farmers incur economic losses, but also gain psychic income from the life-style associated with farming that isn't included in the farm's revenue.

The analysis of cost in this text expresses cost as economic cost and profit as economic profit, unless otherwise noted. The prices of resources are assumed to reflect the opportunity costs to the owners of resources, and all psychic income and psychic costs are assumed to be reflected in the firm's revenue and cost.

The Firm's Cost of Production

In order to understand *how* the firm produces in the short run, we looked closely in Chapter 7 at the relationships between three basic production variables: *total product*, *marginal product*, and *average product*. To understand the short-run relationship between the firm's output and cost, we will look at three important cost variables: *total cost*, *marginal cost*, and *average cost*.

Total Cost (TC)

The total cost to the firm of producing a particular level of output depends upon the amounts of fixed and variable resources required and the prices of those resources. In the short run, the firm operates with at least one fixed resource; thus part of its cost is fixed and doesn't vary with output. In addition to this fixed cost, the firm must pay for the variable resources required. In other words, **cost** in the short run is made up of two components—*fixed cost* and *variable cost*.

Fixed cost, or *overhead*, is the part of the firm's cost that does not vary in the short run, regardless of output.

- **Fixed cost** (FC) is cost of the firm's fixed resources.

Even if the firm produces no output, it will incur a fixed cost in the short run and this cost doesn't change as the firm increases or reduces its output.

Depreciation is a good example of a fixed cost. Capital equipment depreciates in value over time, whether it produces any output or not. If the firm shuts down, it will incur a depreciation cost as long as its capital is fixed. If the firm produces its maximum short-run output, depreciation will be the same.

Any resource—raw materials, land, labor, capital—can be fixed in the short run. Fixed cost is always simply the amount of the fixed resource multiplied by its price. We have assumed, for example, that the Hi-Collar Brewery's capital input is fixed at k^*. If the price of capital is P_k, the fixed cost is simply

$$FC = P_k k^*. \tag{1}$$

OUTPUT AND COST IN THE SHORT RUN 143

In Table 2, Hi-Collar's capital input is fixed at $k^* = 1$, and the price of capital is $P_k = \$100$, so the figure in the FC column is $100 at all levels of output.

Graphically, FC is a horizontal line. In Figure 1a, Hi-Collar's fixed cost is plotted at $100 for all levels of output, including zero. *Even if Hi-Collar shuts down and ceases production in the short run, it must still pay its fixed costs.*

Variable cost is, by definition, the part of short-run cost that varies with output.

- **Variable cost** (VC) is the cost of the variable resource(s) required to produce any given level of output.

For Hi-Collar, labor is the variable resource. If the price of labor is P_ℓ the variable cost at any level of output is

$$VC = P_\ell \ell. \tag{2}$$

In Table 2, the price per unit of labor is $50. Thus the variable cost at any level of output is simply $50 times the number of labor units required to produce that output. The VC column in Table 2 shows the variable costs Hi-Collar must pay at different levels of output. Plotting those figures on a graph, we can construct Hi-Collar's **variable cost curve**, labeled VC in Figure 1b. Notice that the labor input of 7 and output of 56 from Table 2 isn't included in the curve: if Hi-Collar is a rational profit-maximizing firm, it won't increase its labor input to 7, raise its VC to $350, and allow its production to fall from 60 to 56 units.

The combination of fixed cost and variable cost is called total cost.

- **Total cost** (TC) is the sum of fixed and variable cost at any level of output: $TC = FC + VC$.

Table 2 Cost Figures for Hi-Collar Brewery

q	k	P_k	FC	ℓ	P	VC	TC	AFC	AVC	AC	MC
0	1	$100	$100	0	$50	$ 0	$100	$ inf.	$ inf.	$ inf.	
											$ 6.25
8	1	100	100	1	50	50	150	12.50	6.25	18.75	
											1.92
34	1	100	100	2	50	100	200	2.94	3.33	5.88	
											3.57
48	1	100	100	3	50	150	250	2.08	3.13	5.21	
											6.25
56	1	100	100	4	50	200	300	1.79	3.57	5.36	
											12.50
60	1	100	100	5	50	250	350	1.67	4.17	5.84	
											inf.
60	1	100	100	6	50	300	400	1.67	5.00	6.67	
56	1	100	100	7	50	350	450	1.79	6.25	8.04	

Since capital is fixed at $k^* = 1$ and labor is variable for the Hi-Collar Brewery, Hi-Collar's total cost will be

$$\begin{aligned} TC &= P_k k^* + P_\ell \ell \\ &= \$100 \times 1 + \$50 \times \ell. \end{aligned} \quad (3)$$

In Table 2, the figures in the TC column are simply the sums of the figures in the FC and VC columns at each level of output. Remember, the behavior of TC as output varies depends *only* on the behavior of VC, since FC (by definition) will remain constant.

Figure 1c combines the horizontal FC line from Figure 1a and the VC curve from Figure 1b to form the **total cost curve**, labeled TC. An important point should be repeated here: profit-maximizing firms will use the minimum amount of the variable resource required to produce any level of output, so the *TC curve shows the minimum cost of producing any given level of output*.

Figure 1 Short-Run Cost Curves

(a) Fixed Cost   (b) Variable Cost   (c) Total Cost

Marginal Cost (MC)

In seeking to minimize costs, a profit-maximizing firm will want to know how much cost will change when output is increased or decreased. The *marginal cost* measures the rate at which TC changes as output changes.

- **Marginal cost** (MC) is that change in total cost (TC) that results from a given change in output. If output increases by one unit, MC tells how much TC will change as a result. In other words, MC measures the rate at which TC changes as output changes.

Algebraically, MC can be expressed as the change in TC divided by the change in output, or

$$MC = \frac{\Delta TC}{\Delta q} = \frac{\Delta FC}{\Delta q} + \frac{\Delta VC}{\Delta q}. \tag{4}$$

By definition, FC does not change with output, so $\Delta FC/\Delta q$ is always equal to 0. Thus a firm's marginal cost is not affected by its fixed cost. Note that the above formula is sufficiently general to be used to find the MC of changes in output larger or smaller than one unit.

The marginal cost of a unit of additional output depends on the additional amount and price of the variable resource required to produce that unit. The additional amount of the variable resource required for a given increase in output, in turn, depends on the *marginal product* of the variable resource (MP).[1] Thus, MC can be written as

$$MC = \frac{\text{Price of variable resource}}{\text{MP of variable resource}}.$$

For Hi-Collar, labor is the variable resource, so

$$MC = \frac{P_\ell}{MP_\ell}. \tag{5}$$

This relationship between marginal cost and marginal product gives us some important information about how MC will behave under conditions of increasing and diminishing returns:

- With *increasing returns*, MP *rises* as more of the variable resource is employed, so MC *falls* as output increases.
- With *diminishing returns*, MP *falls* as more of the variable resource is employed, so MC *rises* as output increases.
- At the *point of diminishing returns*, the MP of the variable resource is at its *maximum* so MC is at its *minimum*.

Graphically, MC is the slope of the TC and VC curves (FC doesn't affect MC). Plotting the values of Hi-Collar's MC at every level of output defines the firm's **marginal cost curve** (MC) in Figure 2. Increasing returns are indicated by falling MC as output increases from 0 to 34. At

---

1. Some simple algebra will show this result. Start with the definition

$$MC = \frac{\Delta VC}{\Delta q} = \frac{\Delta P_\ell \ell}{\Delta q} = \frac{P_\ell \Delta \ell}{\Delta q} = P_\ell \frac{\Delta \ell}{\Delta q}.$$

Recall that $MP_\ell = \Delta q/\Delta \ell$, so

$$\frac{\Delta \ell}{\Delta q} = \frac{1}{MP_\ell}.$$

Therefore,

$$MC = P_\ell \frac{1}{MP_\ell} = \frac{P_\ell}{MP_\ell}.$$

Figure 2 Marginal Cost Curve

the point of diminishing returns, MC reaches its minimum—at an output of 34 in Figure 2. If Hi-Collar operates with diminishing returns dominant—at all outputs greater than 34 in Figure 2—MC rises as output increases.

Average Cost (AC)

Cost per unit of output, or *average cost*, is important in analyzing the actions of the firm and understanding certain issues concerning the firm. For example, the difference between the unit price and the average cost per unit of the firm's output determines whether the firm will earn a profit, incur a loss, or produce at all.

Average cost also indicates how well the firm is using its capacity. Outputs that seriously underutilize or overutilize a firm's plant and equipment will be inefficient; this inefficiency will be reflected in higher average costs than the firm would incur by producing outputs that made better use of its capacity.

- **Average cost** (AC) is simply the cost per unit produced, or the ratio of total cost over output.

Algebraically, average cost can be written

$$AC = \frac{TC}{q}.$$

(6)

Since TC is the sum of fixed and variable costs, AC is the sum of *average fixed cost per unit of output* (AFC) and *average variable cost per unit of output* (AVC), and can be written as

$$AC = \frac{FC + VC}{q} = \frac{FC}{q} + \frac{VC}{q} = AFC + AVC. \qquad (7)$$

Since fixed cost doesn't vary with output, the **average fixed cost** ($AFC = FC/q$) *must fall as output increases*. Note that AFC falls as long as output increases in Table 2, defining a negatively sloped **average fixed cost curve** (AFC in Figure 3a). As a firm increases its output in the short run, it spreads its fixed costs or overhead over more units of output, so the tendency for AFC to fall as output increases is sometimes called *spreading the overhead*.

Figure 3 Average Cost Curves

(a) Average Fixed Cost

(b) Average Variable Cost

Close-up

"We Never (or Nearly Never) Close"

A generation ago, the food stores with the longest hours of operation were small family operations. To compete against the buying power and advertising economies of large chain stores, small "convenience" stores stayed open when the supermarkets were closed. Today, all of that has changed. There are fewer "Mom and Pop" stores, for one thing, and the largest supermarkets in many communities are open for 16 to 24 hours per day.

How can large supermarkets stay open at hours when there are very few customers? The reason is simple. The additional variable cost of staying open for business is negligible. Most large supermarkets do their shelf stocking at night; lights are generally left on for security reasons even if the store is closed; rent, depreciation, and other fixed costs go on whether the store is open or not. The only variable cost of serving customers during the night hours is the cost of a checker, and this can be done by one of the persons (perhaps a night supervisor) who are there anyway. By attracting even a few customers, the stores are spreading their large fixed costs (or overhead) over more customers and sales.

This example illustrates an important point about spreading the overhead: the larger the percentage of a firm's total costs that is fixed, the greater the incentive for the firm to increase output and sales in order to reduce *AFC*.

The **average variable cost** per unit of output (AVC) depends on the amount of the variable resource required per unit of output and the price of the variable resource. The amount of the variable resource needed per unit of output, in turn, depends on its average product (AP). Algebraically, AVC can be written[2] as

$$\text{AVC} = \frac{\text{VC}}{q} = \frac{\text{price of variable resource}}{\text{AP of variable resource}}. \tag{8}$$

For the Hi-Collar Brewery, the average variable cost per unit is thus

$$\text{AVC} = \frac{P_\ell \ell}{q} = \frac{P_\ell}{\text{AP}_\ell}.$$

From this expression of AVC, the following relationship between the AP of the variable resource and the AVC per unit of output is fairly obvious.

- When the *AP of the variable resource rises* as more of it is employed, AVC *falls* as output increases.
- When the *AP of the variable resource falls* as more of it is employed, AVC *rises* as output increases.

---

2. A formal verification is quite easy. First, the definition of AVC is

$$\text{AVC} = \frac{\text{VC}}{q} = \frac{P_\ell \ell}{q} = P_\ell \left(\frac{\ell}{q}\right).$$

Recalling that $\text{AP}_\ell = q/\ell$,

$$\frac{\ell}{q} = \frac{1}{\text{AP}_\ell}$$

and

$$\text{AVC} = P_\ell \frac{1}{\text{AP}_\ell} = \frac{P_\ell}{\text{AP}_\ell}.$$

- When the *AP of the variable resource is at its maximum*, AVC is at its minimum.

In Table 2 and Figure 3b, rising AP between labor inputs of zero and 3 and outputs between zero and 48 causes AVC to fall as output increases. Beyond a labor input of 3 and output of 48, falling AP_ℓ causes AVC to rise as output is increased.

The firm's AVC determines whether the firm will produce or shut down in the short run. In the short run, if a firm shuts down, it incurs a loss equal to its fixed cost. If it receives a price that covers AVC, it may be able to reduce its short-run losses by staying in operation. If the price it receives doesn't cover AVC, the firm won't cover its variable costs, and would do better by shutting down. This point is discussed in more detail in Chapter 10.

Short-Run Cost Relationships

The change in cost as output changes (MC) affects the average cost per unit. The general relationship between MC, AVC, and AC is shown graphically in Figure 4.

- If MC is less than AVC or AC, AVC or AC falls as output is increased.
- If MC is greater than AVC or AC, AVC or AC rises as output is increased.
- MC = AVC at the minimum AVC, and MC = AC at the minimum AC.

Figure 4 Short-Run Cost Relationships

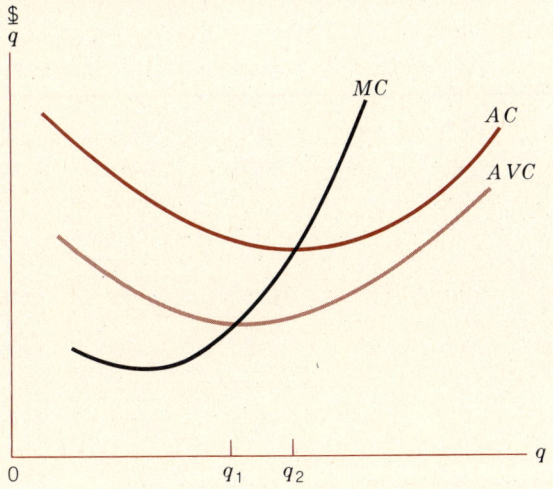

In Figure 4, MC must cut through the minimum points on the AVC and AC curves. As output increases from zero to q_1, AFC falls as the firm's overhead is spread over a larger output, and AVC falls as a result of rising AP over this range. If AFC and AVC both fall as output increases, obviously AC = AFC + AVC must fall also. AC continues to fall between q_1 and q_2 because MC is less than AC, and because the effect of spreading the overhead on AFC is stronger than the effect of rising AVC. As output increases, however, AFC gets smaller and is a smaller proportion of AC. Beyond q_2, the effect of falling AFC as output increases is too weak to offset the effect of rising AVC, and AC rises. At the point where MC = AC, q_2 in Figure 4, AC is at its minimum, and this is the firm's most efficient output in the short run.

Changes in Short-Run Cost

The relationship between output and cost in the short run may change as a result of changes that affect fixed cost or variable cost. However, changes in fixed cost and changes in variable cost have quite different effects on the actions of the firm.

In order to see these effects more easily, we will turn our attention now from the small Hi-Collar Brewery to its much larger competitor, the Schmitz Brewing Company of Detroit. We will make the same basic assumptions about Schmitz as we made about Hi-Collar on pp. 125–26.

Let us assume that Schmitz operates in the short run with a fixed capital input of $k^* = 10$ and with labor as the variable resource. The price of capital is $P_k = \$50$, and the price of labor is $P_\ell = \$20$. Table 3a shows the firm's short-run costs at outputs of 100 and 110 units.

Table 3 Changes in Costs

	q	k^*	ℓ	FC	VC	TC	AC	MC
a)	100	10	20	$500	$400	$ 900	$ 9	
								$20
	110	10	30	$500	$600	$1100	$11	
b)	100	10	20	$750	$400	$1150	$11.50	
								$20
	110	10	30	$750	$600	$1350	$12.27	
c)	100	10	20	$500	$600	$1100	$11	
								$30
	110	10	30	$500	$900	$1400	$12.73	

Change in Fixed Cost

Suppose that the price of capital (the fixed resource) rises from $50 to $75 (Table 3b) while everything else is unchanged. This raises Schmitz's fixed cost (FC) from $500 to $750, and the firm's TC is $250 higher at every level of output because of the higher FC. Higher TC at every output, of course, means that AC is higher also. However, higher FC does not affect VC, AVC or MC.

The effect of the higher fixed cost is shown graphically in Figure 5a. TC moves upward by the increase in FC at every level of output. However, since the VC curve isn't affected, TC' has the same slope at every level of output as TC. In Figure 5b, the effect of higher FC is to move AC upward to AC', while MC and AVC aren't affected. MC still cuts AC' at the minimum point on AC'.

Figure 5 Change in Fixed Cost

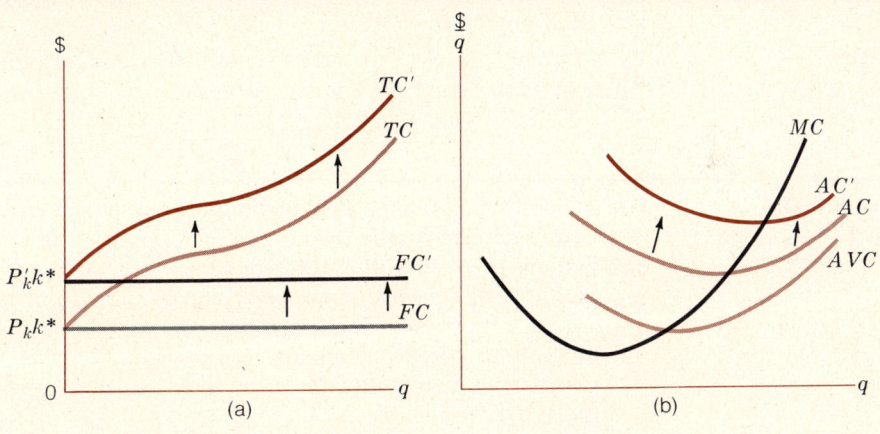

Change in Variable Cost

Instead of an increase in the price of capital and FC, suppose that a new union contract raises the price of labor (the variable input) from $20 to $30. In Table 3c, FC is unaffected, but the higher price of labor increases Schmitz's VC, TC, AC, AVC, and MC at every output. The result is shown graphically in Figures 6a and b.

The distinction between the effects of changes in fixed and variable costs is important. Profit-maximizing firms arrive at their equilibrium output by making marginal decisions—changing output until the last unit produced and sold adds the same amount to the firm's cost (MC) that it adds to the firm's revenue. The firm's decision whether to produce or shut down in the short run depends on its ability to cover at least its variable costs. Raising VC, then, affects the firm's output and may

Figure 6 Increase in Variable Cost

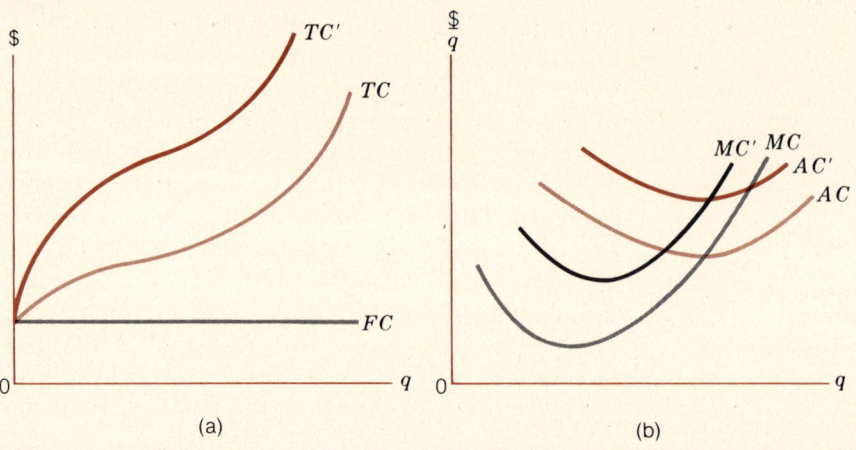

even cause it to shut down in the short run. Changes in *FC* would have no short-run effect on the firm's output or shut-down decisions.

Summary

1. Economists define cost as **economic cost**, which includes all opportunity costs incurred by the firm.
2. **Economic profit** is the difference between the firm's revenue and its economic cost. A *zero economic profit* means that the firm is just compensated for its opportunity cost. A *positive economic profit* means that the firm is more than compensated for its opportunity costs, while a *negative economic profit* means that the firm is not fully compensated for its opportunity costs.
3. In the short run, the firm's **total cost** at any level of output is the sum of its **fixed cost** and **variable cost**. *Fixed cost*, or *overhead*, is the cost of the firm's fixed resource inputs. *Variable cost* is the cost of the variable resource inputs used by the firm.
4. **Marginal cost** is the rate at which total cost varies with output, or the ratio of the change in cost over the change in output. Marginal cost is a key determinant of the firm's output. Marginal cost falls with increasing returns, reaches a minimum at the point of diminishing returns, and rises with diminishing returns.
5. **Average cost** is the cost per unit of output. It is the sum of the fixed cost per unit of output (**average fixed cost**) and the variable cost per unit of output (**average variable cost**).
6. Marginal cost equals average variable cost when average variable cost is at its minimum, and it equals average cost when average cost is at its minimum.
7. Changes in the price of the variable resource will affect variable cost, total cost, average variable cost, and marginal cost. Changes in the price of fixed resource input affect fixed cost, total cost, average fixed cost, and average cost, but not marginal cost.

Concepts for Review

accounting cost
economic cost
accounting profit
economic profit
zero economic profit
total cost
fixed cost
variable cost
variable cost curve

total cost curve
marginal cost
marginal cost curve
average cost
average fixed cost
average fixed cost curve
average variable cost
average variable cost curve
average cost curve

Questions

1. Ted Williams played for the Boston Red Sox from 1939 through 1960. His career was interrupted for military service twice—1943–45 and 1950–53. In his autobiography, he argued that the military draft placed a much greater cost on professional athletes than on other draftees. Is this argument correct, if we use the economic definition of cost? Explain.
2. The Froozomat XB286 is a specialized machine that can produce *only* froozes. What is the opportunity cost of employing a Froozomat XB286 in the production of froozes? Explain.
3. Would firms be more likely to remain in operation at an economic loss or at an accounting loss? Explain.
4. If firms are earning an accounting loss, does this mean that they also earn an economic loss? Does an accounting profit necessarily mean an economic profit? Explain your answers.
5. Bumpes & Jarrs is a profit-maximizing trucking firm. The state highway department is concerned with the noise and air pollution generated by trucks, and is considering two alternative ways of dealing with the problem—increasing the annual registration fee for trucks, and increasing the tax per gallon of truck fuel.

    How would each of these alternatives affect the firm's TC, FC, VC, AC, AVC, AFC, and MC?

Problems

1. The Chris Columbus Globe Co. produces revolutionary globes that are supposed to represent the earth (when we know it's really flat). The relationship between output and cost is given below.

output q	FC	VC	TC	AFC	AVC	AC	MC
0	___	___	$200	inf.	...	inf.	...
2	___	___	300	___	___	___	___
4	___	160	___	___	___	___	___
6	___	___	___	33.33	___	___	10
8	___	___	___	___	___	60	___
10	___	___	___	___	40	___	___
12	___	___	___	16.67	___	___	70
14	___	___	900	14.29	___	___	___
16	___	___	1080	___	___	___	___
18	___	___	___	11.11	___	___	100
20	___	1300	___	___	___	___	___

a. Fill in the missing numbers in the table. (HINT: Note that the changes in output are two-unit changes.)
b. At what level of output is the marginal physical product (*MP*) of the variable resource at its maximum? What is this point called?
c. Over what range of outputs (if any) does the firm experience increasing returns? Over what range of outputs does it experience diminishing returns? Explain.
d. At what level of output is the output per unit of the variable resource maximized? Explain.
e. What is this firm's most efficient output in the short run? Explain how you know.

9

Production and Cost in the Long Run

Preview: In the *long run*, no resource is fixed and the firm is able to vary its inputs of all resources. This greater flexibility allows the firm to substitute one resource for another or to increase or decrease the use of all inputs and thus alter the total size of the firm. In this chapter, we will use the **isocost-isoquant model** to analyze how the firm will utilize its increased capabilities to maximize profit. We will then look *beyond* the long run to the period when even the state of production technology is no longer fixed, and see how the firm behaves under those conditions.

In the analysis of the firm and of markets, the long run isn't something that never arrives, nor is it (as John Maynard Keynes once asserted) a period in which "we all are dead." Like the short run, economics defines the *long run* in terms of the ability to vary resource inputs.

- The **long run** is a period of time sufficiently long that the firm can vary all resource inputs.

The firm has two options in the long run that it doesn't have in the short run—we can call them the *substitution option* and the *size option*.

- The **substitution option** refers to the firm's ability to substitute resources for each other in production in the long run.
- The **size option** refers to the firm's ability to vary its size and the scale of its operations by varying *all* resource inputs in the long run.

In the long run, the firm can respond to changing resource prices by substituting relatively cheaper resources for relatively more expensive ones. It can contract or expand the size of its operations by reducing or increasing all resource inputs. New firms can start up in the long run by purchasing all necessary resource inputs to produce, and can shut down by reducing all resource inputs to zero. Clearly, the firm is more flexible in the long run than in the short run.

The Substitution Option

The ability of the firm in the long run to substitute one resource for another allows the firm to lower its costs without lowering its output. In order to use this ability, the firm must have a clear understanding of the effects of such substitutions upon production.

Isoquants

In the analysis of the household, the household's set of preferences—its utility function—was presented graphically as an *indifference map*. The indifference map indicated the household's level of utility with various combinations of goods. A similar technique can be used to analyze how firms will produce in the long run.

The production function facing the Schmitz Brewing Company in the long run is

$$q = f(\ell, k) \tag{1}$$

where k is no longer fixed at k^*. This function will define a level of output for each of an infinite number of possible resource combinations. Some of these combinations are *technologically inefficient*, however, and Schmitz won't consider such combinations if it is a rational, profit-maximizing firm.

- A resource combination is **technologically inefficient** if it is possible to produce the same level of output with less of one resource and no more of other resources.

Suppose that 15 units of labor and 10 units of capital would allow Schmitz to produce an output of 200 barrels per day. In Figure 1, the point with coordinates $\ell = 15$ and $k = 10$ is labeled $q = 200$ to indicate the level of output.

Changing one resource input without changing the other or changing both resource inputs in the same direction will change the level of output. If more than 15 units of labor were combined with 10 or more units of capital, or more than 10 units of capital were combined with 15 or more units of labor, output would be greater than 200 barrels per day, as shown in the area labeled "more than 200." If fewer than 15 units of labor were combined with 10 or fewer units of capital, or fewer than 10 units of capital were combined with 15 units of labor or less, output would fall, as shown in the area labeled "less than 200" in Figure 1.

Suppose, however, that labor is *substituted* for capital—the firm uses more labor and less capital. If the increased labor input causes output to rise more than the reduced capital input causes it to fall, output will rise. If the increased labor input causes output to rise less than the reduced capital input causes it to fall, output will fall. If the increased labor input causes output to rise by the same amount that the reduced capital input causes it to fall, output won't change.

In order to find the particular combination of resources that will allow

Figure 1 Isoquant

it to maximize profit, Schmitz must first find the various combinations that will produce any particular level of output.

- Different combinations of resources which produce the *same level of output* lie along the same **isoquant**.

Table 1 shows some combinations of labor and capital that produce 200 barrels of beer per day. These combinations lie on the isoquant $q = 200$ in Figure 1. Isoquants are similar to indifference curves, except that isoquants indicate equal output by the firm while indifference curves show equal satisfaction or utility for the household. Also, unlike indifference curves, actual quantities can be assigned to isoquants,

Table 1 Resource Combinations on Isoquant $q = 200$

Capital (k)	Labor (ℓ)	MRTS ($\Delta k / \Delta \ell$)
30	5	
		−3/1
15	10	
		−1/1
10	15	
		−3/5
7	20	
		−2/5
5	25	

since it is easier to measure output than it is to measure subjective utility.

Marginal Rate of Technical Substitution (MRTS)

The slope of an isoquant is called the *marginal rate of technical substitution*.

- The **marginal rate of technical substitution** (*MRTS*) is the rate at which one resource can be substituted for another without changing the level of output. If the input of one resource is *decreased* by a unit, *MRTS* tells how much the input of the other must be *increased* in order to maintain the same level of output.

For any movement along the isoquant $q = 200$ in Figure 1, for example, the *MRTS* is

$$\text{MRTS} = \frac{\Delta k}{\Delta \ell}. \tag{2}$$

At any point on an isoquant, *MRTS* is defined by the marginal products (*MP*) of the resources used in production.[1] Specifically,

$$\text{MRTS} = -\frac{MP_\ell}{MP_k}. \tag{3}$$

Isoquants generally are "*convex*"—i.e., the slope (ignoring its negative sign) gets smaller as labor is substituted for capital along the isoquant. This is due to *diminishing returns*. As more and more labor is used, MP_ℓ generally falls because of diminishing returns. As more and more capital is given up, MP_k rises for the same reason.

The Isoquant Map

Resource combinations that produce different levels of output lie on different isoquants. Figure 2 is an **isoquant map** which includes a few of the infinite number of isoquants defined by the **production function**. The isoquant map can be interpreted basically the same as an indifference map, except that it indicates output and not utility.

---

1. Reducing the capital input by some Δk would cause output to *fall* by

$$\Delta q = \frac{\Delta q}{\Delta k} \Delta k = MP_k \Delta_k$$

Increasing the labor input by $\Delta \ell$ causes output to *rise* by

$$\Delta q = \frac{\Delta q}{\Delta \ell} \Delta \ell = MP_\ell \Delta \ell$$

The level of output is unchanged along an isoquant, so

$$\Delta k \, MP_k = -\Delta \ell MP_\ell$$

Dividing both sides of this equation by $\Delta \ell MP_k$ gives us

$$\frac{\Delta k}{\Delta \ell} = -\frac{MP_\ell}{MP_k}.$$

Figure 2 Isoquant Map

- Resource combinations that produce the *same level of output* lie on the *same isoquant*.
- Isoquants indicate *higher levels of output* the *further they lie from the origin*.

Isocost Lines

As we saw in the last chapter, whenever a firm increases or reduces its use of a resource, costs will change. However, with all resources variable, it is possible to find different combinations of resources that will result in the same level of total cost. For example, in Table 2, the price of labor (P_ℓ) is $50, the price of capital (P_k) is $75, and the total cost for all the resource combinations is $300. These combinations define points on the *isocost line*, C = $300, in Figure 3.

- Combinations of resources that cost the same define an **isocost line**.

Table 2 Resource Combinations on Isocost Line C = 300

Capital (k)	×	Price of capital (P_k)	+	Labor (ℓ)	×	Price of labor (P_ℓ)	=	C
4		$75		0		$50		$300
2		75		3		50		300
0		75		6		50		300

Figure 3 Isocost Lines

The *slope of an isocost line* indicates the rate at which one resource can be substituted for another without changing cost. This slope is defined by the prices of the resources. Specifically, the slope of an isocost line is

$$\frac{\Delta k}{\Delta \ell} = -\frac{P_\ell}{P_k}. \qquad (4)$$

For example, in Table 2 and Figure 3, the slope of the isocost line is

$$\frac{\Delta k}{\Delta \ell} = \frac{0 - 4}{6 - 0} = \frac{-4}{6} = -\frac{2}{3}.$$

for any change along the isocost line. This slope is also equal to the ratio of resource prices.[2]

$$-\frac{P_\ell}{P_k} = -\frac{\$50}{\$75} = -\frac{2}{3}.$$

---

2. For a more formal proof of this, consider the slope of an entire isocost line along which the total cost is C_1. At one extreme, using all capital and no labor, the amount of capital used is

$$\frac{C_1}{P_k}$$

At the other extreme, with all labor and no capital, the amount of labor is

$$\frac{C_1}{P_\ell}$$

Moving from one extreme to the other, the slope of the isocost line is

$$\frac{\Delta k}{\Delta \ell} = \frac{0 - C_1/P_k}{C_1/P_\ell - 0} = \frac{-C_1/P_k}{C_1/P_\ell} = -\frac{C_1}{P_k} \frac{P_\ell}{C_1} = -\frac{P_\ell}{P_k}.$$

There is an isocost line for every level of cost, and every combination of resources will define a point on some isocost line. A family of isocost lines, as in Figure 3, should be interpreted as follows.

- Resource combinations on the same isocost line indicate the same level of cost.
- Isocost lines indicate higher levels of cost the further they lie from the origin.

All of the isocost lines in Figure 3 are parallel (have the same slope) because the slope is defined by given resource prices.

Economic Efficiency: The Isocost-Isoquant Model

In the long run, profit-maximizing firms will produce any given level of output with an *economically efficient* combination of resources.

- **Economic efficiency** requires that a given output be produced at the lowest possible cost, given the production function and the prices of resources.

If it is possible to produce the same level of output at a lower cost by substituting resources for each other, the original combination of resources was **economically inefficient.**

Economic efficiency requires that the additional output from the last dollar spent be the same for all resources. The additional output per dollar spent on a resource is the ratio of its marginal physical product (*MP*) over its price. The additional output per additional dollar spent on labor is MP_ℓ/P_ℓ, and the additional output per additional dollar spent on capital is MP_k/P_k. The formal condition for economic efficiency, then, is

$$\frac{MP_\ell}{P_\ell} = \frac{MP_k}{P_k}. \tag{5}$$

Suppose that $P_\ell = \$50$, $P_k = \$75$, and that Schmitz is producing a given output with $MP_\ell = MP_k = 100$. If the firm substitutes one unit of labor for one unit of capital, the change in output is

$$MP_\ell \Delta \ell + MP_k \Delta k = 100 + (-100) = 0.$$

However, the change in cost as a result of this substitution is

$$P_\ell \Delta \ell + P_k \Delta k = \$50 + (-\$75) = -\$25.$$

The original combination of labor and capital must have been economically inefficient, because the cost of producing the same level of output fell by substituting labor for capital.

Suppose that the firm were producing with $MP_\ell = 100$ and $MP_k = 200$, with $P_\ell = \$50$ and $P_k = \$75$. In this case, the firm should substitute capital for labor. The firm could substitute one unit of capital for two units of labor without changing its output. Reducing the labor input by 2 units reduces cost by $P_\ell \Delta \ell = -\$100$, while an additional unit of capital adds only $P_k = \$75$ to cost.

These examples illustrate the *principle of substitution*.

- The **principle of substitution** predicts that firms will substitute one resource for another until the cost of producing a given output is minimized.

The principle of substitution and the condition for economic efficiency lead to the following predictions.

- If MP_ℓ/P_ℓ is *greater than* MP_k/P_k, the firm will *substitute labor for capital*.
- If MP_ℓ/P_ℓ is *less than* MP_k/P_k, the firm will *substitute capital for labor*.
- If $MP_\ell/P_\ell = MP_k/P_k$, there will be no tendency to substitute one resource for another.

Figure 4 illustrates economic efficiency and cost minimization graphically for the Schmitz Brewing Company. The diagram combines several isoquants and isocost lines. In this example, the *economically efficient* combination of resources to produce 200 barrels of beer is combination A, 15 units of labor and 10 units of capital, *where the isoquant $q = 200$ is tangent to isocost line $C = \$1500$*. None of the isocost lines below $C = \$1500$ touches the isoquant, which means that this output

Figure 4 Minimizing Cost

can't be produced at a lower cost. All other combinations of resources on the isoquant $q = 200$ lie on higher isocost lines.

- Economic efficiency is attained where an isoquant is *tangent* to an isocost line.[4]

What does this result mean in plain English? For a given output, represented by a given isoquant, the point of tangency of the isoquant with an isocost line shows the least expensive combination of resources to produce the given output. Alternatively, for a given cost (represented by a given isocost line), the tangent isoquant is the highest level of output that can be produced at the given cost. In short, tangencies of isoquants and isocost lines indicate economically efficient combinations of resources.

To test your understanding of the isoquant-isocost model, look closely at the graph of the model in Figure 4. Point B is on the same isocost line as tangency point A. If Schmitz's level of cost is given at $1500, why will the firm use that $1500 to purchase resource-combination A rather than combination B? Point C is on the same isoquant as tangency point A. If Schmitz wants to produce 200 barrels of beer a day, why will it use resource-combination A rather than combination C?

Applying the Tools

Coal Mining and "Lewis' Law"

Coal production today uses more capital and less labor per ton produced than was the case in the 1930s and before. In modern underground mines, miners use elaborate and sophisticated equipment which allows each miner to produce far more coal than his counterpart in the 1930s. Strip mining, which digs coal out of shallow seams from the surface, is more common today than it was a few decades ago, and this technique uses much more capital relative to labor than underground mining.

One of the causes of the substitution of capital for labor was a rise in the price of labor relative to the price of capital, due in large part to the bargaining of the United Mineworkers' Union (UMW) under the charismatic leadership of the late

---

4. This can be verified more formally. At the tangency of an isoquant and an isocost line, the slope of the isoquant ($MRTS = -MP_\ell/MP_k$) equals the slope of the isocost line ($-P_\ell/P_k$), or

$$\frac{MP_\ell}{MP_k} = \frac{P_\ell}{P_k}.$$

With some algebraic manipulation, this expression is another way of expressing

$$\frac{MP_\ell}{P_\ell} = \frac{MP_k}{P_k}.$$

John L. Lewis. The UMW gained numerous wage increases which made labor more expensive relative to capital.

Figure A is a very simple sketch of what happened in coal mining in this period. For simplicity, assume that P_k didn't change as P_ℓ rose to P_ℓ'. In Figure A, the broken isocost line reflects the original prices of labor and capital, and the slope of this isocost line is $-(P_\ell/P_k)$. The solid isocost lines reflect the higher price of labor, and the slope of these isocost lines is $-(P_\ell'/P_k)$.

Figure A

Originally, it was economically efficient to produce 100 tons of coal with resource-combination A, $\bar{\ell}$ units of labor and $\bar{k}$ units of capital—where the isoquant $q = 100$ is tangent to $C = \$100$. At the higher price of labor, it became impossible to produce this output at a cost of $100 (the new isocost line $C' = \$100$ no longer touches the isoquant $q = 100$), and the lowest cost of producing 100 tons of coal rose to $125. Also, the higher price of labor encouraged mineowners to substitute capital for labor until the isoquant $q = 100$ is tangent to the isocost line $C' = \$125$ at resource-combination B, using ℓ' units of labor and $\bar{k}'$ units of capital.

Some of Lewis' critics argued that Lewis and the UMW failed to see that one of the effects of higher wages for miners would be a displacement of some miners from their jobs. However, Lewis was explicit in his goal of having fewer but better paid coal miners.

The Size Option

Thus far, we have assumed that Schmitz wishes to produce 200 barrels of beer per day, and we have used isoquant-isocost analysis to find the combination of resource inputs which would produce those 200 barrels at a minimum cost. What if the company decided to adjust its output in the long run to 300 barrels instead of 200? Since more labor and more capital would be used, this would increase the firm's size and its total cost. Decisions of this kind are **firm size decisions** since changing all resource inputs changes the size or scale of the firm's operations. Note that firm size decisions apply to entry and exit decisions—analysis may show a currently operating firm should shut down in the long run, or that market conditions would justify the entry of a new firm into the industry.

Analysis of firm size decisions also deals with the effect of firm size on the efficiency of the firm as a producer. If Schmitz increases its size and total cost to increase its output, what effect will this have on efficiency and the cost per barrel of beer produced? Will Schmitz be more efficient, less efficient, or neither more nor less efficient as a producer of beer as it gets larger?

Returns to Scale

In most industries, the average size of firms is larger than it was a generation ago. Even the family farm of today is larger than its counterparts in the past. Does this mean that large firms are inherently more efficient producers than smaller ones?

If a firm increases or decreases all of its resource inputs, the *size* or *scale* of the firm changes as well as its output. The effect of such changes on efficiency depends on *returns to scale*.

- **Returns to scale** is the relationship between changes in the firm's inputs of all resources (i.e., changes in the firm's size or *scale*) and changes in output.

Say, for example, that the Schmitz Brewing Company doubles its inputs of labor and capital. We know that total output of the firm will increase, but we don't know by how much. There are three possibilities. The doubling of inputs might cause output to *more* than double.

- If output changes by a greater proportion than changes in resource inputs, the firm is experiencing **economies of scale,** or **increasing returns to scale.**

With economies of scale, the firm gets more efficient as it gets bigger and less efficient as it gets smaller. Economies of scale may occur for a number of reasons. A large firm may be better suited to sophisticated production techniques or better able to organize production efficiently and train workers in specialized production tasks than a small firm.

Alternatively, Schmitz may find that doubling all resource inputs causes output to *less* than double.

- If output changes by a smaller proportion than changes in resource inputs, the firm is experiencing **diseconomies of scale,** or **diminishing returns to scale.**

With diseconomies, large firms are less efficient producers than small firms. One of the common causes of diseconomies of scale is the difficulty of supervising and coordinating many operations, large numbers of workers, and physically large firms. The problem of supervision is more serious the greater the number of workers employed, and the greater the physical size of the plant.

There is one final possible result of changes in the size of the firm.

- If output changes by the same proportion as changes in resource inputs, the firm is experiencing **constant returns to scale.**

With constant returns to scale, firm size doesn't affect the firm's efficiency as a producer.

Generally, firms experience economies of scale, constant returns to scale, and diseconomies of scale in production as they grow larger. When the forces which yield economies of scale are dominant (better organization, more sophisticated techniques, etc.), the firm will become more efficient as it gets larger. When the tendency for diseconomies of scale are dominant, the firm will become less efficient as it gets larger.

The Firm's Expansion Path

The different returns to scale for the Schmitz Brewing Company are illustrated in Figure 5. Initially, doubling its use of resources from $1000 to $2000 results in a more than double increase in output, from

Figure 5 Expansion Path

100 to 400 barrels. This is clearly an example of economies of scale. When the firm again doubles its resource input, from $2000 to $4000, however, total output less than doubles, from 400 barrels to 750 barrels—diseconomies of scale.

Figure 6 Long-Run Total Cost Curve

The tangencies of isoquants and isocost lines in Figure 5 trace out the firm's **expansion path.** The expansion path shows the combinations of resources that the firm will use to vary its output in the long run. All combinations of resources on the expansion path are economically efficient.

Long-Run Total Cost (LRTC)

In the long run, as in the short run, the firm will try to produce any output at the lowest possible cost.

- **Long-run total cost** (LRTC) is the cost of the economically efficient combination of resources to produce a given output. It is the lowest possible cost of producing a given output.

Schmitz's **long-run total cost curve** shows the relationship between output and LRTC and is easily derived from the expansion path introduced in Figure 5. In Table 3 and Figure 6, the outputs are from the isoquants in Figure 5: LRTC at any level of output is taken from the tangent isocost lines.

Table 3 Long-Run Cost Figures

Output (q)	LRTC	LRAC
0	$ 0	$ 0
100	1000	10.00
200	1500	7.50
300	1800	6.00
400	2000	5.00
500	2300	4.60
600	2800	4.67
700	3500	5.00
750	4000	5.33

Long-Run Average Cost (LRAC) and Returns to Scale

Long-run average cost (LRAC) is the average cost per unit of output in the long run. Algebraically, LRAC is the ratio

$$LRAC = \frac{LRTC}{q}. \qquad (6)$$

Since LRTC is the lowest possible total cost of producing any level of output, it follows that

- **Long-run average cost** is the lowest possible cost per unit at any level of output with a given production function and given resource prices.

The LRAC curve is, in fact, an "envelope" made up of portions of SRAC (short-run average cost) curves. The firm in Figure 7a has three alternative sizes, each of which is indicated by a SRAC curve. At its smallest size, the firm would operate in the short run along $SRAC_1$; at a "middle" size, the firm would operate in the short run along $SRAC_2$;

Figure 7 Long-Run Average Cost Curve

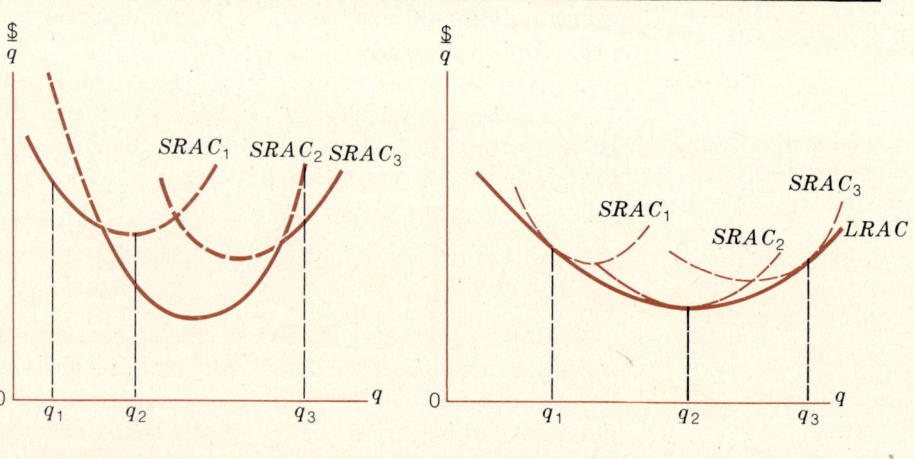

(a) Three Firm Sizes

(b) Many Firm Sizes

and at its largest size, the firm would operate in the long run along $SRAC_3$. Suppose that the firm initially produces output q_1 in Figure 7a. In the long run, the firm would produce this output with the smallest firm size (along $SRAC_1$), because this is the most efficient size for this output. The larger firm sizes produce q_1 at a higher cost per unit than the smallest firm. (To find the average cost of producing q_1 at these larger sizes, trace the vertical line at q_1 up to where it intersects $SRAC_1$ and $SRAC_2$.)

Now, suppose that the firm increases its output to q_2 in Figure 7a. In the short run, it would move along $SRAC_1$ to q_2, and it would be using the smallest firm more efficiently than it did at q_1 (it would be at a lower point on $SRAC_1$). In the long run, however, the firm would expand to a larger size because it could produce q_2 at a lower cost per unit along $SRAC_2$. Similarly, in the long run the firm would expand still further to produce q_3.

If the firm could choose only three possible sizes, its *LRAC* curve would be the solid segments of $SRAC_1$, $SRAC_2$, and $SRAC_3$ in Figure 7a. If the firm had many choices of size and thus more alternative *SRAC* curves, the *LRAC* would be smooth, as in Figure 7b, with each *SRAC* curve tangent to it at a point, indicating the best size of firm for each level of output.

If *LRAC* is falling as output and the size of the firm increase, the firm is becoming more efficient as it gets larger, and is experiencing *economies of scale*. In Figure 7b, economies of scale are indicated along the negatively sloped portion of the *LRAC* curve. Note in Figures 7a and 7b that if the firm is operating with economies of scale along the negatively sloped portion of its *LRAC* curve, it is also operating on the negatively sloped portion of an *SRAC* curve. This means that the firm operating under economies of scale in the long run is *underutilizing* its capacity. In Figure 7b, for example, $SRAC_1$ indicates the best size of firm to produce q_1, but q_1 is less than the output that minimizes $SRAC_1$.

Diseconomies of scale as firm size and output increase are indicated by the rising, positively sloped portion of the *LRAC* curve. As the firm grows and becomes a less efficient producer, the cost per unit rises—as for all outputs greater than q_2 in Figure 7b. If the firm is operating in the long run with diseconomies of scale, it will *overutilize* its capacity. In Figure 7b, $SRAC_3$ indicates the best size of firm to produce q_3, but q_3 is greater than the output that minimizes $SRAC_3$.

The most efficient size of firm, given the production function and resource prices, is called the *optimum size of firm*. In Figure 7b, the optimum size of firm is indicated by $SRAC_2$. The optimum size of firm can't produce all outputs at a lower average cost than larger or smaller firms, but it can produce the output that minimizes *LRAC*—q_2 is the *optimum output* in Figure 7b. The *optimum output* is produced by using the most efficient size of firm as efficiently as possible—i.e., by operating at minimum *SRAC* and minimum *LRAC*.

The Shape of the LRAC Curve

The shape of the *LRAC* curve has some important implications. If *LRAC* always falls as output increases, as in Figure 8a, the firm experiences *unlimited economies of scale*. In this situation, competition among firms would lead to the survival of one large and efficient firm, called a **natural monopoly**. The subject of natural monopoly will be dealt with in Chapter 13.

In Figure 8b, the *LRAC* is horizontal, indicating constant *LRAC* for all sizes of firm and all levels of output. In this case, there is no unique optimum size of firm because all are equally efficient. The firm experiences constant returns to scale.

The traditional "U-shaped" *LRAC* curve in Figure 7 indicates a unique optimum size of firm and a unique optimum output. This shape gives nice neat results in analysis of firms and markets, and it isn't an unreasonable shape to infer for the firm. However, most empirical estimates of actual *LRAC* curves indicate a somewhat different shape, an "L-shaped" curve similar to the one in Figure 8c. The shape of this curve indicates that economies of scale are realized up to a point, but beyond that point constant returns dominate and diseconomies of scale don't occur until output gets very large.

The apparent conflict between the normal shape assumed for the

Figure 8 The Shape of the LRAC Curve

(a) Natural Monopoly

(b) Constant Returns to Scale

(c) "L-shaped" Curve

LRAC curve and the results of empirical estimates may be explained in part by the differences between actual accounting-cost data and economic cost or opportunity cost. In addition, savings realized by large firms in the average cost of advertising and marketing may offset diseconomies of scale in production.

Beyond the Long Run: Technological Change

Thus far, we have looked at short- and long-run production and cost relationships under the assumption that the state of *technology* does not change.

- **Technology** refers to scientific and technical knowledge that is relevant for production and known applications of this knowledge to production.

Technological change alters the relationships between resource inputs and the level of output and between output and cost. Technological change makes it possible to produce a given level of output with smaller resource inputs, and therefore at lower cost.

The effect of technological change on long-run total cost (LRTC) is shown in Figure 9. The new technology lowers the LRTC curve to LRTC' in Figure 9a. A lower LRTC at every level of output means, of course, that LRAC will be lower as well. The effect of technological change on LRAC is shown by the shift from LRAC to LRAC' in Figure 9b. Because technological change lowers LRAC, it can sometimes be difficult to tell whether or not an expanding firm which is also subject to technological change is experiencing genuine economies of scale as it grows larger.

Figure 9 Technological Change and Long-Run Costs

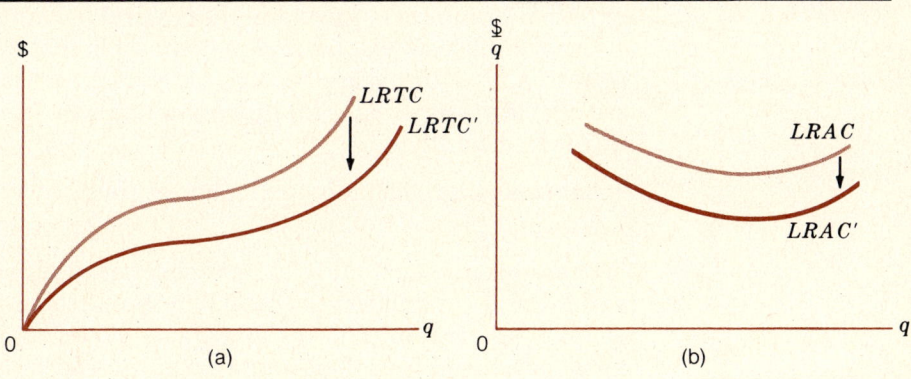

Close-up

Economies of Scale, Technological Change, and the Cost of Electric Power

The electric power industry is the economist's favorite example to illustrate economies of scale. If we include generation of electric power and transmission of electric power as a single industry, the economies of scale are indeed enormous because of the high cost of transmission facilities. In just the generation of electric power, however, the picture isn't as clear.

The cost of generating electricity, or producing anything else, is affected both by returns to scale and by technological change. If we ignore the effect of technological change and attribute all cost savings over time to economies of scale, we may end up with inefficiently large generating plants in an attempt to produce electricity more efficiently.

In a study of 114 electric generating plants, Laurits R. Christensen and William H. Greene attributed most of the reduction in the average cost per thousand kilowatt hours between 1955 and 1970 to technological change. Their data show that beyond an initial range of economies of scale, electric power plants can operate over a very broad range of outputs with no significant economies or diseconomies of scale. However, they also found that almost half of the combined power generated by the plants in their study was produced with economies of scale, and that the combined output of the 114 firms could have been produced by 33 optimum sized firms.[1]

---

1. Laurits R. Christensen and William H. Greene, "Economies of Scale in U.S. Electric Power Generation," *Journal of Political Economy*, vol. 84, no. 4 (Pt. I), August 1976, pp. 655–676.

Types of Technological Change

Technological change may lower cost by reducing the amount of labor required per unit of output, the amount of capital per unit of output, or both the amount of labor and the amount of capital per unit of output.

Labor-saving technological change is the type that has received the most attention over the years because its social and political implications are obvious—especially for those workers whose jobs and earnings are threatened by it.

- **Labor-saving technological change** reduces the amount of labor required per unit of output.

Labor-saving technological change has had a profound effect on agricultural production in the U.S. Sophisticated farm technology has enabled single-family farms to produce large outputs with little or no hired labor, and for a declining agricultural labor force to produce ever larger outputs.

The effects of labor-saving technological change are illustrated graphically in Figure 10a. Technological change alters the production function and the isoquant map. In Figure 10a, the combinations of labor and capital that would produce 100 bushels of wheat before the technological change are represented by the lighter isoquant $q = 100$. The isoquants that would produce the same output after the technological change are on the darker isoquant $q' = 100$.

Given prices of labor and capital, the economically efficient combination of factors to produce 100 bushels of wheat with the old technology is $\bar{\ell}$ units of labor and $\bar{k}$ units of capital, where the isocost line $C = \$200$ is tangent to the isoquant $q = 100$. With the new technology, the economically efficient combination of resources to produce 100 bushels of wheat is ℓ' units of labor and $\bar{k}'$ units of capital, where the isocost line $C = \$160$ is tangent to the new isoquant $q' = 100$. The technological change allows the production of 100 bushels of wheat at a lower $LRTC$ than was possible with the old technology ($\$160$ vs. $\$200$). By lowering the $LRTC$ of this output it also lowers the $LRAC$ from $\$2$ per bu. with the old technology to $\$1.60$ with the new. The technological change in Figure 10a is called *labor-saving* because the economically efficient combination of factors to produce an output of 100 bushels uses less labor. This particular change is also *capital-using*; the economically efficient combination of factors uses more capital with the new technology.

The computer revolution since the end of World War II, and especially since the early 1960s, is a dramatic example of labor-saving technological change. Computers have replaced many clerical workers. Even the time-honored position of legal clerk, which gives many fledgling attorneys their starts, makes increasing use of computers. In medicine,

Figure 10 Types of Technological Change

(a) Labor-Saving
(b) Capital-Saving
(c) Labor- and Capital-Saving

"sonic pictures" which can be interpreted by computers are replacing some of the functions of radiologists.

In education, the development of instructional television technology—particularly progress in videotaping and replay—has made instruction less labor-intensive by substituting capital (cameras, playback equipment, etc.) for labor ("live" classroom instructors) in some courses. Computer-assisted instruction substitutes capital (the computer) for a tutor as well as an instructor.

Not all technological changes are labor-saving, however. Some technological changes are *capital-saving*.

- **Capital-saving technological change** reduces the amount of capital per unit of output.

Figure 10b illustrates a capital-saving technological change. The change in technology shifts the isoquant for $q = 50$ to $q' = 50$. Given resource prices, the firm would produce this output with less capital ($\bar{k}'$) and more labor ($\bar{\ell}'$) than with the original technology. Since more labor is used per unit of output, this is also a *labor-using technological change*.

Some technological changes are both labor-saving and capital-saving, as in Figure 10c. Revolutionary developments in electronics and solid-state technology in the past decade, for example, have produced a "new breed" of small computers and calculators. Modern hand-held calculators do some work that previously required tedious hours of manual calculations on larger and more expensive machines. This "new breed" of solid-state electronic calculators are labor-saving because they reduce the amount of labor required to perform many operations. They are also capital-saving because they're generally much less expensive and require smaller expenditures for capital than the "old breed" of calculators and computers.

Is Technological Change "Good for the Community"?

Improvements in technology have made it possible to produce larger outputs with our resources and have thus been the major source of U.S. economic growth in the twentieth century. By expanding the capacity to produce, technological change has made it possible to produce more of just about everything, as the advertising campaigns of many large corporations constantly remind us.

The costs of technological change, however, are as real, if not as obvious, as the benefits. Much of the technological change in production either introduces or extends economies of scale. This, coupled with the expense of implementing modern technology, has forced some small producers out of business. Some jobs have been decimated or eliminated by technological change, and the displaced workers have borne a heavy cost—as any former railroad fireman or wet plasterer will testify. In some cases, however, workers have taken direct action against the machines that threaten their livelihoods.

Close-up

Man vs. Machine

Man against machines is one of the themes that has emerged from industrialization and labor-saving technological change. It's even part of our folklore—recall, for example, Paul Bunyan's unsuccessful duel with machines in logging or John Henry's ill-starred race with a steam drill. Sometimes, however, the reaction against machines and technological change has been both real and dramatic.

In the eighteenth century, a series of technological changes revolutionized English textile production and eliminated a number of skilled textile trades. The *stocking frame* was a mechanized loom that virtually eliminated the demand for skilled hand-loom weavers. The displaced weavers, under the leadership of one Ned Lud, reacted by forming gangs and wrecking the new machines. Early in the nineteenth century, similar gangs, calling themselves *Luddites*, engaged in systematic attacks on machines. This kind of reaction to labor-saving innovations is still called *luddism*.

Fortunately, luddism isn't a very common reaction against technology, but it isn't dead either. During a strike against the *Washington Post* in October, 1975, in which new printing equipment and job security were issues, a number of the *Post*'s new printing presses were destroyed or damaged.

Some technological changes impose other kinds of costs on large segments of society. Technological advances in the production and processing of food, for example, have made it possible to grow more food and have reduced the problems associated with spoilage (such as botulism). However, some of these advances have imposed costs by creating health hazards for the community. Some chemical food preservatives may be carcinogenic, and pesticides and chemicals that have entered our environment pose other health hazards.

Recognizing that technological change involves costs as well as benefits, of course, doesn't mean that technological change has been a "bad" thing for society. Only the most hopeless romantic would argue that we would be better off in a society in which economic activity consisted of subsistence agriculture and cottage industries.

It *is* important, however, to recognize that technological change isn't good for everybody, and that the persons who bear the brunt of the costs may not be the persons who reap the greatest benefits from technological change. In evaluating the effects of new technology, it's necessary to consider the costs as well as the benefits and to make informed value judgements on the effects of technological change on society's economic welfare. Recognition of some of the costs should lead to greater efforts to minimize these costs—for example, retraining programs for technologically displaced workers.

Summary

1. The **long run** is a period of time in which all resource inputs are variable.
2. In the long run, the firm can substitute one resource for another to lower costs, or it can vary all resource inputs to vary output.
3. The firm's production function in the long run can be represented graphically by the **isoquant map**.
4. The relationship between resource inputs and cost in the long run can be represented graphically by **isocost lines**.
5. The firm will produce any output in the long run using an economically efficient combination of resources. Such combinations are defined by points of tangency between isoquants and isocost lines, and represent the lowest possible cost of producing any level of output.
6. If the relative prices of resource change, the firm will substitute the relatively cheaper resource for the relatively more expensive resource in the long run.
7. If firms experience **economies of scale,** they become more efficient as they get larger. With **diseconomies of scale**, firms become less efficient as they get larger. The optimum size of firm is the one that can produce at the lowest possible cost per unit.
8. Changes in technology due to new scientific discoveries that can be applied to production or discovery of new applications of existing scientific knowledge change the production function and tend to lower the $LRTC$ and $LRAC$ curves at every level of output.

Concepts for Review

long run
technological inefficiency
isoquant
marginal rate of technical substitution ($MRTS$)
isocost lines
economic efficiency
principle of substitution
"Lewis' law"
expansion path
returns to scale
constant returns to scale

economies of scale
diseconomies of scale
long-run total cost
long-run average cost
natural monopoly
technology
technological change
labor-saving technological change
capital-saving technological change
substitution option
size option

Questions

1. If the price of labor increases with the price of capital constant, is the effect on the firm's employment of labor likely to be greater in the short run or in the long run? Why? Can you think of any examples to support your answer?
2. If average cost falls as output increases, is the firm necessarily experiencing economies of scale? Explain.
3. Some people argue that competition will eliminate small firms because firms always tend to become more efficient as they get larger. Is this always a valid argument? Is it ever a valid argument? Explain your answers.
4. A firm is operating in the long run, producing an output of 1000 gizmos per day. It must pay $50 per worker day for labor and $100 per unit of capital per day. It has combined labor and capital so that the marginal products of labor and capital are equal—i.e., $MP_\ell = MP_k$ for the last units of labor and capital employed. Is this economically efficient? Why?
5. The *Albion Evening Recorder* is a small-town daily newspaper published in Albion, Michigan. Recently, the paper employed modern computerized composition and typesetting equipment. The editor of the paper claimed that the decision to computerize its operation was made easier by a state tax levied on payrolls.

    Is this an example of a long-run or short-run adjustment? How could the imposition of a payroll tax influence the paper's decision to computerize its operations?

Problems

1. The following table shows the inputs of labor (ℓ) and capital (k) that will produce outputs of 100, 200, and 300 barrels of beer per day.

q = 100		q = 200		q = 300	
ℓ	k	ℓ	k	ℓ	k
1	17	4	18	8	24
2	9	6	10	10	15
4	5	8	7	12	11
6	3	10	5	14	9
10	2	14	4	16	8
16	1	20	3	20	7
18	1	28	2	26	6

    a. One of the above combinations of labor and capital wouldn't be used by the firm, regardless of the prices of labor and capital. Which one? Why?
    b. Construct isoquants from the above information.
    c. Calculate the marginal rates of technical substitution *(MRTS)* for all changes in labor and capital for all levels of output.
    d. If the price of labor is $P_\ell = \$50$ and the price of capital is $P_k = \$100$, find the economically efficient combination of resources, long-run total cost *(LRTC)*, and long-run average cost *(LRAC)*, at each level of output.
    e. Does this firm ever experience economies of scale? Does it ever experience diseconomies of scale? Explain.

2. The following table shows the short-run total cost *(TC)* of producing various outputs of mechanical egg scramblers for three sizes of firm—I (smallest), II (medium), and III (largest).

q	I TC	II TC	III TC
0	50	75	100
5	100	125	200
10	150	180	270
15	195	195	330
20	240	200	340
25	325	225	375
30	450	255	405
35	630	315	455
40	920	400	560
45	1350	540	720
50	2000	950	950
55	2750	1650	1210
60	3600	2400	1800

a. Calculate short-run average cost *(AC)* for each level of output in each size of firm. Plot the *AC* curves for each size of firm, and the firm's long-run average cost *(LRAC)* curve.
b. Identify economies of scale, diseconomies of scale, the optimum size of firm, and the optimum output for the firm.
c. In the long run, what size of firm would be used to produce an output of 10? Why?
d. If the firm increased its output temporarily from 10 to 20 to meet what it saw as a temporary increase in demand, what size of firm would it use, and what would its *AC* be? Does this output use the firm's capacity efficiently?
e. If the firm foresaw a permanent, or long-run, increase in its output from 10 to 20, would the long-run adjustment be the same as the adjustment in part (d)? After its long-run adjustment, would it be using its capacity efficiently? Why?
f. If the firm increased its output from 20 to 45 in the long run, would it adjust its size? What if it increased output from 45 to 55 in the long run?

PART FOUR
Perfect Competition

By now, you should have a pretty fair understanding of the kinds of behavior by households and firms that underlie the demand and supply curves introduced in Chapter 3. In this section, we want to put the two together again to examine how the interaction of supply and demand determine society's basic economic choices in a market economy. Our first step, ironically, will be to construct a model of an economy that has no real-world counterpart—a **perfectly competitive economy**. No modern economy is perfectly competitive, and it is doubtful that such an economy has *ever* existed or ever will exist. Nonetheless, the model is valuable because it shows how competitive market forces would operate in the absence of a variety of real-world "imperfections." In other words, perfect competition is to economics what "zero friction" is to physics.

Chapter 10 builds on the material presented in the last two sections of the text, examining the interaction between households as buyers and firms as sellers in a perfectly competitive product market. Chapter 11 looks at the other side of the economy—the resource markets—where firms are buyers and households are sellers of resources. Finally, in Chapter 12, we will try to reach some positive and normative conclusions by exploring the implications of perfect competition for society's economic welfare.

10

The Perfectly Competitive Product Market

Preview: In a world in which competitive market forces were free to operate without restrictions, how would the prices and outputs of goods be determined? This chapter explores the answer to that question. We'll also look at the sector of our own economy that most closely resembles the perfectly competitive model: the agricultural sector.

Characteristics of Perfectly Competitive Product Markets

The first step in understanding perfect competition is to recognize some of the important characteristics that are assumed for perfectly competitive markets.

Price Takers

Perhaps the most fundamental assumption of perfect competition is that individual buyers and sellers are *price takers*.

- **Price takers** are unable to affect the prices of the things they buy or sell, and must "take" the price determined for the market as a whole.

The price-taking firm is so small relative to the market as a whole that its individual output decisions have no significant effect on market supply or price and are thus unnoticed by other firms. This doesn't mean that price-taking firms must be small in terms of value of assets, output, sales, etc. Wheat farms in the United States, for example, are often large units in terms of land area cultivated, value of capital equipment, and annual output. But even the largest wheat farm in the country produces a very small part of the total wheat crop. If the largest farm decided to double its output, this action by itself wouldn't affect the price of wheat.

Identical Products

A second major assumption we will make about perfectly competitive markets is that firms' products are identical in all respects, including conditions of sale. One farm's no. 2 red winter wheat is a *perfect* substitute for another farm's. If one farm tried to raise the price of its wheat above the market price, it would thus lose all of its sales to other farms selling their wheat at the market price.

Atomistic Competition

Individual buyers and sellers in perfect competition are also assumed to be *atomistic competitors*. This means that each firm makes its decisions without considering the effects of these decisions on other firms, and there is no *collusion* or agreement among firms which affects their output decisions or the price at which they sell their products. Likewise, we assume that individual buyers act independently of each other.

Market Information

Buyers and sellers in competitive markets are assumed to have *market information*. This simply means that buyers have enough market information that they won't pay a price higher than the price dictated by the market, and that sellers have enough information that they won't sell at a price below that dictated by the market.

Freedom of Entry and Exit

Finally, we assume that in perfect competitive markets, firms are free to enter or leave the market. There are no significant legal or economic barriers that keep firms out of the market.

Close-up

Price Takers in the Stock Market

The firm in a perfectly competitive product market is in a position very similar to that of most individual buyers and sellers of common stock. In fact, there are a number of points of similarity between financial securities markets and perfectly competitive product markets. Individual buyers and sellers are small relative to the market, the products of individual buyers and sellers are identical, and complete market information is readily available and transmitted almost simultaneously to all parts of the country.

If a single stockholder decides to buy or sell 100 shares of common stock in a large company such as General Motors, this action will have no effect on the market. On December 6, 1978—not an unusual day on the stock market—nearly 1.5 million shares of GM stock were traded, so one person's purchase or sale would have little or no noticeable effect on the price of GM stock. The individual has to take the price determined by demand and supply in the market. Of course, if large numbers of individual stockholders decided to buy or sell a stock at the same time—or if a very large institutional investor made a very large transaction—this would affect the market price.

The Firm in Perfect Competition

The perfectly competitive firm is a price taker, but what price does it "take"? The equilibrium price in perfect competition is the price at which the quantity demanded by all buyers in the market is equal to the quantity supplied by all sellers in the market—where the market demand curve intersects the market supply curve. In Figure 1, the equilibrium price is $\overline{P} = \$10$. The individual firm *must* take this price as given; in maximizing profit, therefore, it can make only a decision about how much it will produce at that price.

Demand for the Firm's Output

Because the firm can't affect price and can sell any meaningful output at the equilibrium price for the market, the firm faces a *completely elastic demand curve* for its product. In Table 1, the firm can sell any output for a price of $10. Plotting the figures from the price (P) and output (q) columns in Table 1 on a graph, we get a horizontal line

Figure 1 Demand in the Perfectly Competitive Product Market

at a price of $10. This horizontal line, d_w in Figure 1b is the demand for the individual firm's output.

This does not mean that the *market demand* for a product in a perfectly competitive market is completely price elastic. The market demand, D_w in Figure 1a is the sum of the quantities demanded by all households. The horizontal demand curve for the individual firm's

Table 1 Revenue, Cost, and Profit in the Perfectly Competitive Product Market

Output (q)	Price (p)	TR	MR	TC	MC	Profit
0	$10	$ 0		$ 50		−$50
			$10		$ 6	
1	10	10		56		− 46
			10		4	
2	10	20		60		− 40
			10		2	
3	10	30		62		− 32
			10		1	
4	10	40		63		− 23
			10		1	
5	10	50		64		− 14
			10		2	
6	10	60		66		− 6
			10		3	
7	10	70		69		1
			10		4	
8	10	80		73		7
			10		5	
9	10	90		78		12
			10		6	
10	10	100		84		16
			10		7	
11	10	110		91		19
			10		8	
12	10	120		99		21
			10		9	
13	10	130		108		22
			10		10	
14	10	140		118		22
			10		11	
15	10	150		129		21
			10		12	
16	10	160		141		19
			10		13	
17	10	170		154		16
			10		14	
18	10	180		168		12
			10		15	
19	10	190		183		7
			10		16	
20	10	200		199		1

output, d_w, simply indicates that the firm is too small relative to the market to have any impact on the price of its product. If the firm in Figure 1b tried to sell its output at a price above $10, it would sell nothing because competitors are offering identical products at $10. Of course, since the firm can sell any output it could produce at a price of $10, it has no reason to offer its output for sale at a price below $10.

Revenue

Total revenue that the firm receives from selling any given output at a given price, you will recall from Chapter 4, is simply the price per unit (P) multiplied by the quantity sold (q), or

$$TR = P \cdot q. \tag{1}$$

The TR column in Table 1 shows the firm's total revenue at various levels of output. Since the firm is a price taker, every additional unit it produces adds the same amount to total revenue, or *TR increases at a constant rate as output increases*. Combinations of output and total revenue in Table 1 will define points on the TR curve in Figure 2. Since price is constant for all outputs in Table 1, the TR curve in Figure 2 is a straight line.

Average revenue (AR) is the revenue per unit of output, or the ratio of total revenue over output. If a firm sells its product at a uniform price, average revenue is simply another term for price. Algebraically,

$$AR = \frac{TR}{q} = \frac{Pq}{q} = P. \tag{2}$$

This can be verified easily from the figures in Table 1.

Marginal revenue (MR) is a very important variable, since firms

Figure 2 The Total Revenue Curve

make marginal decisions in reaching their profit-maximizing output. In deciding whether to increase or decrease its output, the firm has to consider the change in revenue that results from a change in output, and this is determined by marginal revenue.

- **Marginal revenue** (*MR*) is the change in total revenue that results from a given change in output. If the firm increases its output by one unit, *MR* tells how much *TR* changes as a result of that one-unit increase. In other words, *MR* shows the *rate* at which *TR* changes as output changes.

$$MR = \frac{\Delta TR}{\Delta q}. \tag{3}$$

A one-unit change in quantity from 8 to 9 units in Table 1 yields a *MR* of

$$MR = \frac{(\$10 \times 9) - (\$10 \times 8)}{9 - 8} = \frac{\$90 - \$80}{1} = \$10.$$

The price and marginal revenue columns in Table 1 illustrate a special relationship between *P* and *MR* for price-taking firms in perfectly competitive markets.

- *For a price taker*, price and marginal revenue will be identical, or $MR \equiv P$.

Every time a price-taking firm raises its output by one unit, it increases its total revenue by $1 \times P$. Since marginal revenue is the change in *TR* due to this change in output, *MR* must equal $1 \times P = P$.

Graphically, marginal revenue is the slope of the *TR* curve. In Figure 2, the firm's *TR* curve is a straight line with a constant slope. The marginal revenue curve is thus the same as the horizontal demand curve for the firm's output, illustrated in Figure 1.

Equilibrium Output

The goal of any perfectly competitive firm is to maximize its profit. Economic profit, you will recall from Chapter 8, is the difference between *total revenue* (*TR*) and *total cost* (*TC*), including all opportunity costs. Algebraically, total profit (π) can be written

$$\pi = TR - TC. \tag{4}$$

Because a perfectly competitive firm cannot affect the market price it receives for its output, it can only decide *how much* output to produce in order to maximize profit. The firm knows that increasing output increases revenue, but also increases cost. Reducing output reduces cost, but also reduces revenue. The net effect on profit of a one-unit change in output depends on the difference between the marginal revenue received by selling the unit and the marginal cost of producing it.

In Table 1, the firm's profit rises as output increases from zero to 13 units because the marginal revenue from selling each additional unit exceeds the marginal cost of producing it. If the firm increases output from 13 to 14 units, it experiences no change in profit because the MR of the 14th unit is equal to its MC (MC = MR = $10). If the firm increases its output beyond 14 units, profit will decrease because MR is less than MC for all these outputs—it costs the firm more to produce the output than it can get from selling it.

The relationship between MR and MC is thus extremely important in determining how much output the firm will want to produce in order to maximize profit.

- If MR is greater than MC (and MC is rising), the firm will increase its output.
- If MR is smaller than MC (and MC is rising), the firm will decrease its output.
- If MR = MC (and MC is rising), the firm has reached its *equilibrium output* and has maximized its profit.

Figure 3 shows the MR (demand) curve, the MC curve, and the AC curve for the firm in Table 1. The firm's equilibrium occurs at the

Figure 3 Equilibrium with Profit

point labeled B, where the rising portion of the MC curve cuts the MR curve. The equilibrium output corresponding to this point is 14 units.

The firm's total revenue, you will recall from Chapter 4, is represented by the area of the large rectangle beneath the demand curve, labeled $ABDO$. That area is

$$TR = P \times q = \$10 \times 14 \text{ units} = \$140.$$

The firm's average cost can be found at the point along the average cost curve (AC) corresponding to an output of 14 units (point C). Here the average cost per unit of output is $8.43. Since average cost is simply total cost divided by quantity, the firm's total cost can be found by multiplying the average cost times the quantity,

$$TC = AC \times q = \$8.43 \times 14 \text{ units} = \$118.$$

In graphic terms, the total cost of producing 14 units is thus the unshaded portion of the TR rectangle, labeled $ECDO$ in Figure 3.

The shaded rectangle ($ABCE$) in Figure 3 represents the difference between total revenue and total cost. Since $TR - TC =$ total profit (π), we can conclude that the area of the shaded rectangle represents the total profit the firm receives by producing 14 units of output,

$$\pi = TR - TC = \$140 - \$118 = \$22.$$

Profit or Loss

Whether or not the firm will actually earn an economic profit depends on the relationship between price and average cost at the firm's equilibrium output.

- If the price per unit (P) is greater than the average cost of producing each unit (AC), total profit will be positive. Total revenue (TR) will be greater than total cost (TC), so the firm is more than compensated for its opportunity costs.
- If P is less than AC, total profit will be negative. TR will be less than TC, so the firm isn't fully compensated for its opportunity costs and incurs an economic loss.
- If $P = AC$, total profit is zero. TR will be equal to TC, so the firm is just compensated for its opportunity costs.

Graphically, this relationship is easy to understand because the height of the dark shaded profit rectangle in Figure 3 is simply the difference between P and AC. Since the area of a rectangle can be found by multiplying its height times its length, we can find the area of the profit rectangle, and hence the profit,

$$\pi = (P - AC) \times q = (\$10 - \$8.43) \times 14 \text{ units} = \$1.57 \times 14 = \$22.$$

Since the price per unit exceeds the average cost at equilibrium output, the firm earns a positive economic profit.

The smaller the difference between P and AC, the smaller will be the area of the rectangle and hence the smaller the economic profit earned by the firm. When $P = AC$, $(P - AC) = 0$, so the rectangle disappears and the firm is earning zero economic profit. If AC is greater than P, $(P - AC)$ will be negative and the firm is earning a negative economic profit or *economic loss*.

If a firm can't earn a positive profit, it may produce where $MR = MC$ to minimize its losses in the short run. If the price of wheat fell to $6, the farm in Table 1 would adjust its output unit $MR' = \$6 = MC$. Its new equilibrium output would be 10 units. This price is below the farm's average cost if it produces where $MR = MC$, so the best the farm can do is to minimize its loss. This result is shown graphically in Figure 4. Since P is now below AC, $(P - AC)$ is negative, and the shaded area in Figure 4 represents the firm's economic loss.

Figure 4 Equilibrium with Economic Loss

The Shut-Down Point

If the best the firm can do is to minimize its loss by producing where $MR = MC$, why bother to produce at all? Why doesn't the firm simply shut down?

In the short run, the firm will incur a loss even if it shuts down, because part of its costs are fixed. The firm's short-run profit is

$$\pi = TR - TC = TR - VC - FC. \tag{5}$$

If the firm shuts down, output, TR, and VC all fall to zero, but FC remains constant, so the firm's loss from shutting down in the short run is

$$\pi = TR - VC - FC = 0 - 0 - FC = -FC. \tag{6}$$

If the firm in Table 1 shuts down, for example, its short-run loss would be

$$\pi = TR - VC - FC = 0 - 0 - 50 = -\$50.$$

Suppose that a firm produces where $MR = MC$, and that its total revenue at that output just covers its variable cost ($TR = VC$). In this case, its loss from producing would be the same as its loss from shutting down, since

$$\pi = (TR - VC) - FC = 0 - FC = -FC.$$

This firm is at its *short-run shut-down point*, since its loss from producing where $MR = MC$ is the same as its loss from shutting down. If $TR = VC$, then

$$\frac{TR}{q} = \frac{VC}{q} \text{ or } P = AVC. \tag{7}$$

Thus, we have two ways of finding the firm's *short-run shut-down point*.

- The **shut-down point** is reached in the short run if $TR = VC$ or $P = AVC$ at the firm's equilibrium output.

Graphically, the short-run shut-down point is reached if the market price falls below the minimum point on the AVC curve, where $MC = AVC$ in Figure 5. This same situation would occur if the AVC curve were to rise until its minimum point was above the market price.

As long as it can earn enough revenue to cover at least its variable cost (VC), the firm will produce in the short run, even if it incurs a loss. When the price fell to $6 in the previous example, the firm's output fell to 10 units. From Table 1 and Figure 4, the firm's profit (loss) at 10 units of output is

$$\pi = TR - TC = \$60 - \$84 = -\$24.$$

If it had shut down, its loss would have been greater than this (−$50), so the firm will remain in production in the short run. With some simple arithmetic, you should be able to verify that the firm more than covers its VC and that price is greater than AVC at an output of 10 units.

Suppose that the price of wheat in Table 1 fell to $2. From Table 1 or Figure 5, $P \equiv MR = MC = \$2$ at an output of 6. At this output,

$$\pi = TR - TC = \$12 - \$66 = -\$54,$$

so the firm will minimize its loss by shutting down.

The Short-Run Supply Curve

We have seen that the firm can maximize its profit (or minimize its loss) by producing an output where $MR = MC$. Since $P \equiv MR$ for a price taker, we can conclude that the firm will maximize profit at a given price by producing where $P = MC$. At a price of $16, the firm in Figure 5 will supply 20 units of output, corresponding to the point where a horizontal line at $P = \$16$ cuts the firm's MC curve. At $10, the firm supplies 14 units; at $6, 10 units. If the price falls to AVC, the firm will shut down and its quantity supplied will fall to zero.

In short, since the firm makes output decisions in response to prices called out in the market, MC determines the quantity supplied at each price. As long as P exceeds AVC, a perfectly competitive firm will adjust its output so that $P = MC$. Thus we can easily find the firm's *short-run supply curve*.

- The perfectly competitive firm's **short-run supply curve** (srs) is the portion of its MC curve that lies above AVC.

Figure 5 Short-Run Supply Curve

The short-run supply curve is illustrated in Figure 5. Remember, however, that this relationship between price and quantity supplied exists only in perfect competition, and only because the individual firms are price takers.

The Industry in the Short Run

An industry or market reaches equilibrium when there is no incentive for firms in the industry to make adjustments of output. In perfectly competitive industries, equilibrium is reached at a price where the quantity supplied by the firms equals the quantity demanded by buyers. Equilibrium can be disturbed by disturbances in demand or supply, and the industry's adjustment to a new equilibrium depends on the period of time considered and the ability of firms in the industry to make short-run or long-run adjustments.

- The **market period** is a period in which the firms cannot change their output.
- The **short run** is a period in which firms can make short-run adjustments of output along their short-run supply curves.
- The **long run** is a period in which firms can make long-run adjustments—including entry and exit.

These periods don't refer to any particular periods of calendar time, but to the ability of firms in the industry to vary output and resource inputs.

Market Period Supply

Once this year's wheat crop is in, no more wheat can be produced until the next crop is harvested. Thus, the market period for wheat is the period between harvests. In other cases, such as many manufactured products, output can be changed almost instantly, so the market period in these industries would be a brief period.

In the market period, the industry supply curve is vertical, or supply is *completely inelastic*, as in Figure 6. Changes in demand will affect only price in the market period. An increase in demand in Figure 6 from D to D', for example, raises the price from $\bar{P}_m$ to $\bar{P}_m'$ in the market period, but output remains at Q_m.

Short-Run Supply

At a given price, the quantities of a good supplied by the firms in a perfectly competitive market are determined by the firms' short-run supply curves. For the perfectly competitive industry, the quantity supplied at a given price is simply the sum of the quantities supplied by firms in the industry.

Figure 6 Industry Supply in the Market Period

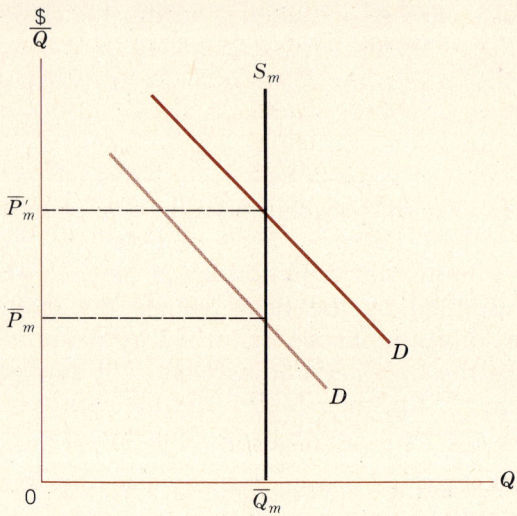

- The **short-run supply curve** (SRS) for a perfectly competitive industry shows the total quantity supplied by all firms at various prices in the short run.

Suppose that the firm in Figure 7 is typical of firms in the industry. At any price above the firm's short-run *shut-down point* (P = AVC),

Figure 7 Industry Supply in the Short-Run

the firm produces where $P = MR = MC$ to maximize its profit or minimize its losses. The sums of the quantities supplied by all firms at various prices define points on the industry's short-run supply curve (*SRS*). At $8, for example, the firm would produce 12 units of wheat, and the sum of the wheat supplied by all firms would be 40 million units on the industry's short-run supply curve (*SRS*). At a price of $14, the firms would adjust their quantities supplied—the firm in the diagram moves to 18—and the sum of the quantities supplied by the firms at this price would give us a quantity supplied of 80 million for the industry.

Since firms operate with at least one fixed resource input in the short run, a new firm cannot purchase all necessary resource inputs and enter the industry, nor can a firm already in the industry sell off all its resource inputs and leave the industry (though it can shut down operations if P is less than minimum AVC).

- In the *short run*, the *number of firms in the industry is fixed*.

The short-run supply curve for the industry (*SRS*), then, is defined for a given number of firms, and it reflects the short-run adjustments of those firms to changes in price.

Short-Run Equilibrium

A perfectly competitive industry is in **short-run equilibrium** when the quantity supplied by firms is equal to the quantity demanded by households, or where the industry SRS intersects the market demand curve (D) in Figure 7. At $\bar{P} = \$10$, the market is *cleared* of unsold goods and unsatisfied buyers. There is no incentive for firms to alter their output because the typical firm in the industry produces $\bar{q} = 14$ where $MR = MC$.

Depending upon the *fixed* number of firms in the industry, a perfectly competitive industry can reach *short-run* equilibrium with firms earning *economic profits* (more than compensated for opportunity costs), *economic losses* (not fully compensated for opportunity costs), or *zero economic profit* (just compensated for all opportunity costs).

The Industry in the Long Run

Since all resources are variable in the long run, firms are able to enter or leave an industry at will. New firms can enter an industry by purchasing all the necessary resource inputs. Firms can shut down and leave an industry without incurring economic losses, because all costs are variable in the long run.

This assumption of free entry and exit in the perfectly competitive model is critical to the adjustment of the industry to long-run equilibrium. Economic profit will attract new firms to an industry, since economic profit indicates that the firms presently in the industry are more than compensated for their opportunity costs. As new firms enter, supply increases, price falls, and economic profits fall. Losses by firms will cause the number of firms in an industry to decline as firms shut down and leave the industry. As the number of firms declines, supply falls, price rises, and profit rises (losses decline).

Entry and exit of firms will cease when the firms in the industry are earning *zero economic profit*. At this point, the industry has reached its *long-run equilibrium*.

- **Long-run equilibrium** is reached in a perfectly competitive industry only when economic profits of the firms in the industry are zero.

An industry's adjustment to long-run equilibrium is illustrated in Figure 8. In Figure 8a, the industry is in a short-run equilibrium at $\overline{P} = \$14$. The typical firm is producing where $\overline{P} = MR = MC$ at \$18 and is earning a profit of \$84, as indicated by the shaded area. In the long run, these economic profits will attract new firms, and as new firms enter the industry's SRS curve will shift to the right. As *SRS* shifts, *P* falls, and the typical firm's profit will fall.

What if so many firms entered this industry that a new short-run equilibrium was reached at $\overline{P}' = \$6$, as in Figure 8b? At this price the typical firm is making an economic *loss* of \$25, as shown by the shaded area. In the long run, firms will now leave the industry, causing the *SRS* for the industry to shift to the left. As *SRS* shifts to the left, price rises, and the typical firm's economic profit rises—or, more accurately, its loss is reduced.

In Figure 8c, the industry has again reached a short-run equilibrium: there is no tendency for price to change because the quantity demanded equals the quantity supplied for the industry, and there is no incentive for firms to change output, since $MR = MC$. In addition, there are no economic profits to attract new firms, and firms in the industry would gain nothing by leaving since they are fully compensated for opportunity costs. Thus the industry has achieved *long-run equilibrium*.

In a long-run equilibrium, the firms in a perfectly competitive industry earn the same *economic* profit (zero), but not necessarily the same *accounting* profit. Suppose that the Jones' dairy farm earns \$10,000 more accounting profit per year than similar farms in the area, and that this is due solely to the superior managerial talents of Mrs. Jones. Market information and competition will place a value on this managerial talent because firms would be willing to pay for the use of Mrs. Jones' managerial ability. The Jones' farm, then, has an additional opportunity cost (foregone salary) that the more typical farm doesn't have.

Figure 8 Adjustment to Long-Run Industry Equilibrium

Long-Run Supply

Equilibrium can be upset by disturbances in either demand or supply. As firms make long-run adjustments, the industry moves to a new long-run equilibrium output or price. To analyze these long-run adjustments in perfect competition, we need to know something about *long-run supply*.

- Long-run equilibrium prices and quantities in a perfectly competitive industry define the industry's **long-run supply curve.**

Every point on the long-run supply curve represents a long-run equilibrium for the industry. The industry's long-run supply curve may be horizontal, positively sloped, or even negatively sloped, depending on the effect of expansion or contraction of the industry on the firms' costs.

Constant Cost Industries. In some industries, expansion or contraction has no effect on the costs of production. These are called **constant-cost industries**. Generally, constant-cost industries have little or no impact on the prices of the resource inputs they use for production because the amounts of those inputs they require are small relative to the total demand for them.

- Expansion or contraction of a *constant-cost industry* causes no change in the costs of production for firms in the industry.

In Figure 9, the initial long-run equilibrium at $\overline{P}_L$ and $\overline{Q}_L$ is disturbed by an increase in demand from D to D'. The immediate ef-

Figure 9 Long-Run Supply Curve: Constant-Cost Industry

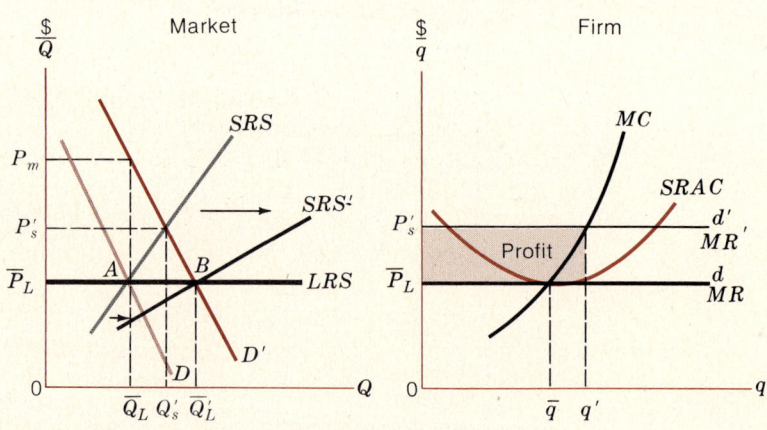

fect, in the *market period*, is to raise the price of $\overline{Q}_L$ to P_m. As firms respond to the higher price, the industry moves to a new short-run equilibrium at a price of P'_s and an output of Q'_s. The profits earned by the firms in the industry at this new price will attract new firms in the long run, expanding the industry and shifting SRS to the right, to SRS'.

Since this is a *constant-cost industry*, nothing happens to the firms' cost curves as the industry expands, and new firms will enter until the price falls back to the original equilibrium price, $\overline{P}_L$. At that point, the typical firm produces the same output as it did before the increase in demand, but there are more firms in the industry and the industry's new long-run equilibrium output is $\overline{Q}_L'$. The different combinations of price and quantity supplied in equilibrium define a *long-run supply curve* that is completely elastic for a constant-cost industry.

- The **long-run supply curve** (LRS) in *constant-cost industries* is *horizontal*, with a slope of zero.

To be sure you understand this, work out the effects in the market, short-run, and long-run periods of a fall in demand from D to D'.

Increasing-Cost Industries. If an industry is a large enough user of inputs, expansion or contraction can influence input prices and the costs of production for firms in the industry. For example, suppose a rise in the demand for wheat attracts new producers to wheat production. This would lead to a noticeable increase in demand for the inputs used in wheat production—fertilizer, seed, farm machinery, fuel, etc.—and would probably result in higher prices for these inputs. Higher input prices would increase the cost of producing wheat as the industry expands.

- Expansion of an *increasing-cost industry* causes an increase in the costs of production for firms in the industry.

In Figure 10, an increase in demand from D to D' disturbs the initial long-run equilibrium at $\overline{P}_L$ and $\overline{Q}_L$. The adjustments in the market period and short-run period are the same as in the previous example. As the industry expands through the entry of new firms, supply increases and SRS shifts to the right. Because this is an increasing cost industry, the entry of new firms also causes firms' AC and MC curves to rise to AC' and MC'. When the industry finally reaches a new long-run equilibrium, the new equilibrium price $(\overline{P}_L')$ will be higher than the old one. The different equilibrium combinations of price and quantity supplied by the industry determine the increasing-cost industry's long-run supply curve.

- The **long-run supply curve** (LRS) in *increasing-cost industries* is *positively sloped*.

Figure 10 Long-Run Supply Curve: Increasing-Cost Industry

Decreasing-Cost Industries. In a few industries, costs for individual firms may even fall as the industry expands. Expansion of an industry that is a very large user of electric power, for example, could permit an expansion of electric power plants, and the resulting economics of scale could lower the price of electric power. The lower price of electric power would lower the AC and MC curves of the firms in the industry. Industries of this sort are called *decreasing-cost industries*.

- Expansion of a *decreasing-cost industry* causes a decrease in the costs of production for firms in the industry.

In Figure 11, an increase in demand disturbs an initial long-run

Figure 11 Long-Run Supply Curve: Decreasing-Cost Industry

equilibrium at $\overline{P}_L$ and $\overline{Q}_L$, as in the previous examples, and the same market period and short-run adjustments take place. In the long run, however, as firms enter and push the SRS to the right, the firms' AC and MC curves shift *downward* to AC' and MC'. The decline in the firms' costs pushes SRS further to the right, and a new long-run equilibrium will be reached at a lower price than the old one—$\overline{P}_L'$ in Figure 11.

- The **long-run supply curve** in *decreasing-cost industries* is *negatively sloped*.

Decreasing-cost industries are unusual, and many economists doubt that they can exist at all in the long run. The source of lower costs as the industry expands generally is exhausted at some point or offset by other changes that raise costs.

Changes in Long-Run Supply

Changes in input prices, technology, quality of resources, taxes on the firm or its output, or any of the determinants of production and cost relationships in a perfectly competitive industry will cause the industry's long-run and short-run supply curves to shift.

Higher fuel and energy prices, for example, have increased the costs of producing just about everything. In Figure 12, suppose that higher input prices move the firm's AC and MC curves to AC' and MC'. Firms respond to higher costs by reducing output and leaving the industry, shifting the short-run supply curve to the left until a new long-run equilibrium is reached at $\overline{P}_L'$ and $\overline{Q}_L'$. In other words, the increased input prices shifted the industry's LRS curve upward to LRS'.

Figure 12 Changes in Long-Run Supply

Applying the Tools

Competition and Policy in U.S. Agriculture

The agricultural sector is the closest to perfect competition of any industry in our economy. There are more than 2.5 million farms in the United States, over 80 percent of which are owner-operated (or *family*) farms. Even the largest single farm is too small to have any impact on the market in which it operates. In a good year, for example, the yield of corn per acre could be about 100 bushels. A farm with 300 acres in corn would thus have a crop of 30,000 bushels, but this would be only a tiny fraction (0.000005 percent) of the 6 billion bushels produced by all farms in the United States in a good year. This farm could expand its size and output tenfold or shut down completely and the market wouldn't even notice the difference.

The average size of farms and the average value of farm assets have been rising steadily over time, but there aren't any significant barriers to entry or exit. It's very easy for one farm to shift from production of one commodity to another, so entry is virtually free. Market information is readily available, and price quotations from agricultural commodity markets are broadcast over rural radio stations several times daily.

The market structure of the agricultural sector, however, coupled with some unique characteristics of agricultural production have created a number of economic problems for farmers. The analytical tools studied in this chapter can be useful in understanding these problems and evaluating potential remedies.

Unstable Prices and Incomes

For most agricultural goods, such as wheat, the demand and supply curves are inelastic, as in Figure A. In addition, exogenous and largely unpredictable changes in weather and exogenous changes in foreign demand for exports contribute to in-

Figure A

stability of demand and especially supply. Since it is a highly competitive sector of the economy, prices are flexible in both directions. Putting all of this together, relatively small changes in supply or demand will produce relatively large changes in price, as in Figure A.

Suppose that year 1 is an average year (although most farmers claim that they never have *average* years): the supply of wheat is shown by S_1 and the price of wheat is $\overline{P}_1$. Now, suppose that the weather in year 2 is exceptionally good, and that the crop is much larger than the farmers expected when they planted. The supply curve shifts to S_2, driving the price in year 2 to $\overline{P}_2$. The low price in year 2 encourages farmers to produce less wheat in year 3, and the supply shifts to S_3, driving the price to $\overline{P}_3$.

Since demand is inelastic, price and total revenue move in the same direction, and large fluctuations in price will cause large fluctuations in farm incomes as well.

- In the absence of government stabilization policies, agricultural prices and incomes will be unstable over time.

This instability in the agricultural sector will contribute to unstable food prices (although the fluctuations in food prices at the retail level are smaller than at the farm level), and instability in the industries and markets related to agriculture (such as the farm equipment industry).

"Crime Doesn't Pay (Neither Does Farming)"

Farming is perhaps the least profitable industry in the economy, and economic losses are chronic (paticularly for small farms). Yet, farmers continue to produce —even when they expect at best to minimize their losses. The reason for this behavior—apart from noneconomic attachments to farming—is the high fixed cost of operating a farm. Depreciation of buildings and equipment, loan and mortgage payments, and other fixed costs go on in the short run even if the farm ceases to produce.

To stay in operation in the long run, the farm in Figure B has to cover its average cost (AC), but in the short run, it will continue to produce as long as price

Figure B

at least covers average variable cost (AVC). Unless the equilibrium price (P) fell below P_0 = minimum AVC, this farm would produce in the short run because its losses would be less than its fixed costs.

Government Price Supports

Agricultural price support programs have been one of the most controversial aspects of government agricultural policy since their introduction in the 1930s. There are three basic types of agricultural price supports—supply restriction, purchase of surplus output, and direct price subsidies. The choice of the means of supporting agricultural prices, and the choice to support them at all, have implications for farmers, for consumers, and for economic efficiency and community welfare.

Supply Restriction

In Figure C, the equilibrium price and output of wheat are $\overline{P}$ and $\overline{Q}$. To maintain a guaranteed price of P^*, the government restricts supply to RS so that the market will be cleared at the support price. How will this affect farmers, consumers, and efficiency?

First of all, farmers' incomes will rise. Since demand is inelastic, price and total revenue move in the same direction: consumers will pay more and farmers will receive more total revenue at P^* than at the unregulated price and quantity. The change thus represents a redistribution of income from consumers to farmers.

Restricting supply has another effect. At the unrestricted equilibrium ($\overline{Q}$ and $\overline{P}$), the price represents the value of the last additional unit of wheat to consumers and the marginal cost of producing it (remember that $P = MC$ along the supply curve). **Marginal-cost pricing,** which is discussed in detail in Chapter 12, has important implications for economic welfare. If the value of an additional unit of wheat is greater than the marginal cost of producing it, society will gain if more wheat is produced. If the marginal cost of the last unit produced is greater than its value to consumers, society will gain by reducing output. A price equal to the marginal cost of the last unit produced ($P = MC$), then, is the best price for society.

Figure C

Figure D

With output restricted to Q^*, however, the price of an additional bushel of wheat (P^*) exceeds the marginal cost of producing it ($MC_Q{}^*$). Society would thus gain if more wheat were produced until the market were cleared with price equal to marginal cost. The solid shaded area represents an efficiency loss to the community as a result of producing with price greater than MC.

Guaranteed Purchase

Farmers often criticize crop and acreage restrictions for interfering with "free enterprise" and private markets. What they generally mean, however, is that they would rather be free to produce as much as they wish at the support price.

In Figure D, the SRS and D determine equilibrium price ($\overline{P}$) and quantity ($\overline{Q}$) as in the previous example. This time, however, the government agrees to purchase surplus output at the support price.[1] With no price support, total revenue received by farmers from consumers would be $TR_c = \overline{P} \times \overline{Q}$, as in the previous example. Because of inelastic demand, consumers pay more for wheat at the support price—$TR_c' = P^* \times Q_D$—as they did with restricted supply. However, the farmers' revenue increases to the entire area $P^* \times Q_S$—divided between payments by consumers (TR_c') and payments by government (TR_g). Farmers receive more revenue with the guaranteed purchase program than with supply restriction, and the cost to the community of the payments to farmers is greater. Furthermore, the government has to bear the cost of storing the surplus products in addition to the subsidy payments.

Compared with the no price support alternative, there is a net efficiency and welfare loss by *overproducing*. Beyond $\overline{Q}$, the marginal cost of additional wheat exceeds the value of additional wheat to the community. The solidly shaded area in Figure D, then, represents the loss of benefits to the community from overproducing wheat.

Direct Subsidies: The *Brannon Plan*

The third alternative for supporting agricultural prices is to allow the market price

---

1. Actually, the government agrees to extend loans through the Commodity Credit Corporation, but it amounts to the same thing.

and output to reach equilibrium, and pay farmers a subsidy equal to the difference between the support price and the market price per bushel of wheat sold. In Figure E, the price and quantity would adjust to $\bar{P}$ and $\bar{Q}$, and consumers would pay $TR_c = \bar{P} \times \bar{Q}$. Farmers would receive a subsidy of $(P^* - \bar{P})$ per bushel of wheat, or total subsidy payments represented by the shaded area TR_g.

This plan has some advantages over both supply restriction and guaranteed purchase. There isn't a storage problem because the market clears at $\bar{P}$. Furthermore, the value of the last additional bushel produced ($\bar{P}$) equals the marginal cost of producing it (MC), so there isn't an efficiency loss from overproduction or underproduction. Consumers are better off than with the other plans because they consume more wheat at a lower price and pay a lower total revenue than with either of the other plans.

Farmers tend to be less than enthusiastic about this plan, however. At $\bar{Q}$, the farmers' total revenue—consumers' expenditures (TR_c) plus subsidy payments (TR_g)—is less than with the guaranteed purchase plan. They could respond to the support price and produce Q_S anyway and let the price fall to $\bar{P}'$, but the subsidy payments would be larger than with the guaranteed purchase plan, and support for the program could well weaken as the costs of price supports increased.

Figure E

Who Gains Most from Price Supports?

One of the arguments for price support programs in the Great Depression was that they would help preserve small farms. Today, this argument is of questionable validity. Small farmers do benefit from price support programs, but the biggest winners are the largest and most efficient farms.

Figure F shows the effect of a support price (P^*) on a small farm and a large farm. Unless the support price is high enough to cover the small farm's average cost (AC), it won't preserve it beyond the short run. If it is high enough to preserve the small farm, the larger farm earns economic profit at the support price. If the support price is below the small farm's AC, the large farm is the only beneficiary in the long run.

Figure F

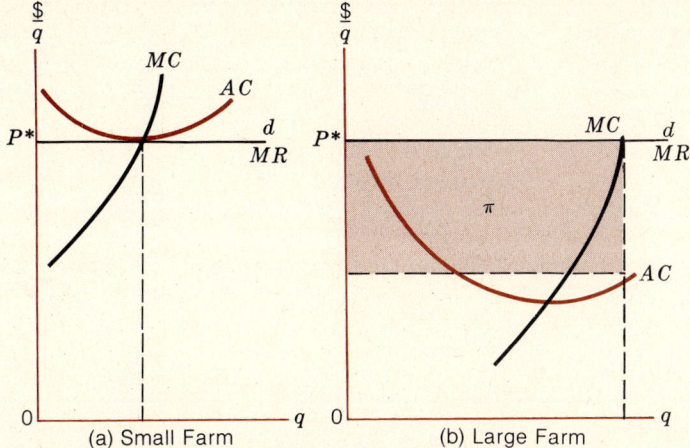

(a) Small Farm   (b) Large Farm

Of course, this doesn't mean that price supports should be abandoned just because they don't help the small farmer. The arguments for price supports as a way of aiding the small, generally low-income farmer should, however, be looked at very critically.

Summary

1. In the model of perfect competition, it is assumed that individual buyers and sellers are **price takers,** that all sellers within an industry sell **identical products**, that there is **no collusion** among individual buyers or sellers, that buyers and sellers have **market information**, and that there is **freedom of entry and exit** of sellers.
2. The demand for the output of a single firm in a perfectly competitive market is completely elastic at the equilibrium price determined for the market.
3. Price and marginal revenue are identical for perfectly competitive firms.
4. The firms will produce the output that maximizes profit—where $MR = MC$ and MC is rising.
5. A firm will remain in operation in the short run at a loss as long as it covers its variable cost.
6. The **firm's short-run supply curve** is the portion of its MC curve that lies above its average variable cost (AVC) curve. The **industry's short-run supply curve** is the sum of the quantities supplied by firms at each price.
7. A perfectly competitive industry can reach short-run equilibrium with firms in the industry earning economic profit, economic losses, or zero economic profit.
8. In the long run freedom of entry and exit will drive economic profit to zero in perfectly competitive industries. The **industry's long-run supply curve** shows the prices and quantities in which the industry is in long-run equilibrium.

Concepts for Review

price taker
atomistic competitor
market information
total revenue
average revenue
marginal revenue
total profit
shut-down point
short-run supply curve (firm)

market period
short-run supply curve (industry)
long-run equilibrium
long-run supply curve
constant-cost industry
increasing-cost industry
decreasing-cost industry
marginal-cost pricing
Brannon plan

Questions

1. "Perfectly competitive firms face completely elastic demand curves because the market demand curves in perfectly competitive industries are completely elastic."
   Is this statement generally correct or incorrect as an explanation of the elasticity of demand for a perfectly competitive firm? Explain your answer.
2. Explain why price and marginal revenue are identical for a perfectly competitive firm.
3. Many farms remain in production, even though the prices they receive don't cover the average cost of producing their crops.
   a. Why would a firm knowingly stay in production if it couldn't cover its costs?
   b. Is the situation described a short-run situation, a long-run situation, both long-run and short-run, or can't you tell?
4. Identify and explain the conditions in which:
   a. a firm will shut down in the long run;
   b. a firm will shut down in the short run;
   c. new firms will enter a perfectly competitive industry;
   d. firms will leave a perfectly competitive industry;
   e. the number of firms in a perfectly competitive industry will remain constant.
5. What are the conditions for short-run equilibrium and long-run equilibrium in a perfectly competitive industry? How does the industry adjust from a short-run to a long-run equilibrium?
6. Every long-run equilibrium for the firm or the industry is also a short-run equilibrium. Is every short-run equilibrium also a long-run equilibrium? Explain.
7. How (if at all) would each of the following affect long-run equilibrium and the long-run supply curve in wheat production?
   a. Innovations in tractor design make tractors 50 percent more efficient in using gasoline and diesel fuel.
   b. The OPEC oil cartel and domestic oil companies raise the price of petroleum products.
   c. Bad weather results in a smaller wheat crop than predicted.

Problems

1. The following table shows the relationship between output (q), total revenue (TR), and short-run total cost (TC) for a typical wheat farm.

q (tons/yr)	TR	TC
0	$ 0	$1000
10	500	1700
20	1000	2200
30	1500	2600
40	2000	2800
50	2500	3100
60	3000	3500
70	3500	4000
80	4000	4600
90	4500	5300
100	5000	6100

   a. Is this firm a price taker? How do you know?
   b. Calculate the firm's marginal revenue (MR) and average revenue or price (P) at the given outputs. Plot the firm's TR, MR, and demand (d) curves graphically.
   c. Find the firm's equilibrium output and its economic profit or loss (if any). Will this firm stay in operation in the short run? Will it stay in operation in the long run? How do you know?
   d. If this farm is typical of others in the wheat market, is the industry in a short-run equilibrium, a long-run equilibrium, both, neither, or can't you tell? Explain.
   e. What adjustments (if any) will take place in the industry to reach long-run equilibrium? Explain.

11

The Perfectly Competitive Resource Market

Preview: We turn now to the resource markets, to see how firms and households would behave as buyers and sellers of resources in a perfectly competitive economy, and how that behavior translates into resource prices and allocation. Since the distribution of income in a society depends ultimately on the prices of resource, we'll also want to look closely at how income would be distributed in a perfectly competitive economy.

In market economies, resource prices play a critical economic role. The cost of producing a good, you will recall from Chapter 8, is determined by a firm's production function and by the prices of resources used. Cost, in turn, is a determinant of the price at which the firm sells the good—in perfect competition, the sole determinant in the long run. Thus, the prices of resources have a strong effect on the prices of goods.

In competitive resource markets, prices reflect the scarcity of resources. Resource prices ration and allocate scarce resources among potential users, and encourage firms to minimize costs by economizing on the scarcest resources in producing goods.

Resource prices also determine the incomes of owners of resources. With the distribution of the ownership of resources—or the *distribution of wealth*—resource prices determine the pattern of *income distribution* in the economy. Coming full circle, income distribution will determine the pattern of demand for goods, which in turn determines the outputs of goods by firms.

Prices of scarce resources in market economies, like prices of scarce goods, are determined by demand and supply. In resource markets, however, the roles of households and firms are reversed from their roles in product markets. *Households are sellers* of the use of the resources they own, and the *supply* of resources reflects the utility-maximizing decisions of households. Firms are buyers of the use of resources, and the demand for resources reflects the profit-maximizing actions of firms.

Characteristics of Perfectly Competitive Resource Markets

Like the perfectly competitive model of the product market, the perfectly competitive resource market shows how resource markets would work in the absence of the imperfections that exist in the real world. Like the product market model, the resource market model is based upon a series of assumptions.

Price Takers

In perfectly competitive resource markets, individual buyers (firms) and sellers (households) are *price-takers*. A small "Mom & Pop" store in a large city couldn't possibly hire enough clerks to affect the market wage for retail clerks, and if the store fired all of its clerks, the market wage would not change. Similarly, an individual household couldn't possibly do anything that would affect the market prices of resources it owns. Firms and households thus make decisions in resource markets on the basis of given prices determined by the market.

Atomistic Competition

Perfect competition in resource markets assumes *atomistic competition* among buyers and sellers. Individual firms compete with each other in purchasing the use of resources. Individual households compete with each other in the sale of the use of the resources they own.

Market Information and Resource Mobility

Perfect competition in resource markets involves two additional assumptions. It is assumed that buyers and sellers have *market information*. Market information means that buyers and sellers won't pay more nor sell for less than the market dictates, and that sellers are aware of the advantages and disadvantages of alternative employments. The assumption of *resource mobility* means that resources can move freely from one employment to another, and that they are geographically mobile.

Homogeneous Resources

For purposes of analysis, we further simplify reality by assuming that all individual units of a given resource are identical, or *homogeneous*. Each unit of capital or labor is assumed to be identical to every other unit of capital or labor.

Equilibrium Resource Prices

The *equilibrium price* of a resource is reached when there is no tendency for the price to change, or where the quantity of the resource supplied by all households in the market is just equal to the quantity demanded by all firms. The equilibrium price clears the market of buyers and unsold resource services.

In Figure 1, the equilibrium wage or price of labor is $\overline{W} = \$30$. At $\overline{W}$, there is neither excess supply of labor nor excess demand. If the wage were above $\overline{W}$—$W_2 = \$50$, for example—the quantity of labor supplied is greater than the quantity demanded. The excess supply of labor at W_2 represents unemployment. In a perfectly competitive labor market, the sellers of labor would compete with each other, bidding the wage downward from W_2. If the wage is below equilibrium—$W_1 = \$20$ in Figure 1—there is excess demand for labor, and competition among firms will bid the wage upward from W_1.

Figure 1 Equilibrium Wage Determination

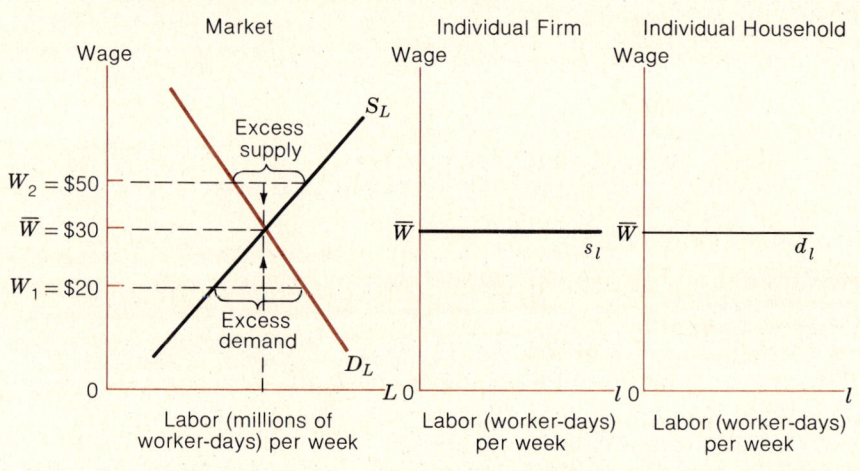

As price-takers, individual firms and households can't affect resource prices. In Figure 1, the perfectly competitive buyer of labor (the firm) faces a completely elastic supply of labor (s_ℓ) at the equilibrium wage for the market, $\overline{W} = \$30$. The perfectly competitive seller (the household) faces a completely elastic demand (d_ℓ) for its resources at the market price.

Resource Demand: A Closer Look

Generally, firms purchase the use of resources in order to produce and sell goods and services from which they earn profits. The basic goal of the firm is to maximize profit, and this goal overrides any other motives that may affect the firm's decision on the amount of a resource to employ.

- The quantity of a resource that a firm will employ at a given price, other things equal, is the quantity that maximizes the firm's profit.

The other things that are held constant in deriving the firm's demand for a resource (such as labor) are the production function, the prices of other resources, and the demand for the firm's product.

Changing the input of a resource has two effects on the firm's profits. Resources are scarce and command prices, so changing a resource input changes the firm's costs. In addition, the amounts and kinds of resources the firm uses in production determines its level of output, so changing those inputs will change both the level of output and the firm's revenue.

Firms arrive at the quantities of resources that maximize by *marginal decisions*—changing the quantity of resource input until profits are maximized.

- Profits are maximized when the last unit of a resource employed adds the same amount to the firm's cost that it adds to the firm's revenue.

To understand the firm's behavior in the resource market, we have to understand two important variables—*marginal factor cost* and *marginal revenue product*.

Marginal Factor Cost (MFC)

If more of a variable resource is employed, the firm's costs will rise because it must pay for the additional units of the resource it uses. If less is employed, costs will fall for the same reason.

- **Marginal factor cost** (MFC) is the change in the firm's total cost that results from a change in its variable resource input. If the firm uses one more unit of the variable resource, MFC shows how much TC will increase as a result. In other words, MFC is the *rate* at which cost changes as the input of a resource changes.

Algebraically, MFC is

$$MFC = \frac{\text{change in total cost}}{\text{change in variable resource input}}. \qquad (1)$$

In Table 1, the firm can purchase any meaningful number of worker-days of labor at $50 per worker-day. Changing the labor input by one unit (from 2 to 3 worker-days), MFC_ℓ is

$$MFC_\ell = \frac{(\$50 \times 3) - (\$50 \times 2)}{3 - 2} = \frac{\$150 - \$100}{1} = \$50.$$

Table 1 Revenue and Costs in a Perfectly Competitive Resource Market

Labor input (ℓ)	Output (q)	Product price = MR (p)	$P_\ell = MFC_\ell$	TR	MP_ℓ	MRP_ℓ
0	0	$10	50	$ 0		
					5	$ 50
1	5	10	50	50		
					8	80
2	13	10	50	130		
					10	100
3	23	10	50	230		
					9	90
4	32	10	50	320		
					8	80
5	40	10	50	400		
					7	70
6	47	10	50	470		
					6	60
7	53	10	50	530		
					5	50
8	58	10	50	580		
					4	40
9	62	10	50	620		
					3	30
10	65	10	50	650		
					2	20
11	67	10	50	670		
					1	10
12	68	10	50	680		
					0	0
13	68	10	50	680		

If the firm in Table 1 increased its labor input by more than one unit, say from 2 to 10 worker-days, we can compute the MFC_ℓ as

$$MFC_\ell = \frac{(\$50 \times 10) - (\$50 \times 2)}{10 - 2} = \frac{\$500 - \$100}{10 - 2} = \frac{\$400}{8} = \$50.$$

These results illustrate an important and unique relationship between the price of a resource and its MFC:

- The price and MFC of a resource are *identical* for a firm that is a *price-taker in the resource market*.

This means that the supply of the resource faced by a price-taker in the resource market is the same as the firm's MFC curve, as shown in Figure 2.

Marginal Revenue Product (MRP)

Changing a resource input also changes the level of output and therefore affects the firm's total revenue.

- The **marginal revenue product** (MRP) is the change in total revenue

Figure 2 Marginal Factor Cost Curve Resource Supply Curve

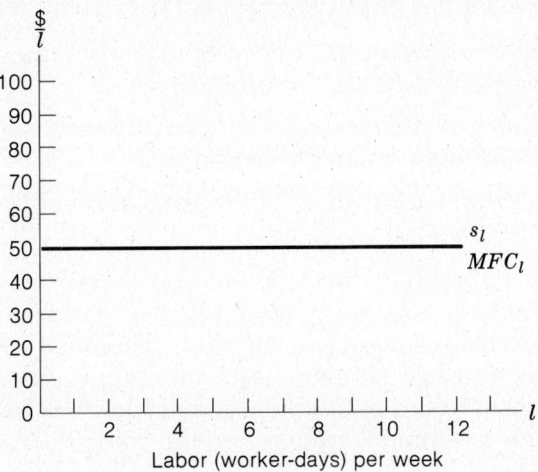

that results from a change in the variable resource input. If the firm adds one additional unit of the variable resource, MRP shows how much TR will increase as a result. In other words, MRP is the *rate* at which TR changes as the resource input changes.

Algebraically, marginal revenue product is the ratio

$$MRP = \frac{\text{change in total revenue}}{\text{change in resource input}}. \quad (2)$$

If labor is varied by some $\Delta \ell$, for example, the marginal revenue product of labor (MRP_ℓ) is

$$MRP_\ell = \frac{\Delta TR}{\Delta \ell}$$

The same definition applies to MRP of any variable resource.

The MRP of a resource depends on the amount of additional output produced by additional units of the resource (*marginal product*, MP) and the additional revenue earned from the sale of the additional output (*marginal revenue*, MR). Specifically,

$$MRP = MP \text{ of the resource} \times MR \text{ from the sale of the product.} \quad (3)$$

You can easily verify this definition by multiplying the MP figures in Table 1 by the MR figures.[1]

---

1. You can also prove it algebraically:

$$MP_\ell \times MR = \frac{\Delta q}{\Delta \ell} \times \frac{\Delta TR}{\Delta q} = \frac{\Delta TR}{\Delta \ell} = MRP_\ell.$$

Increasing and Diminishing Returns Again

If a firm is a price-taker in the product market, the behavior of the marginal revenue product (*MRP*) of a variable resource is determined by the marginal physical product (*MP*) of the resource.

- With *increasing returns*, *MP* of the variable resource rises as more of the resource is used, so *MRP* also rises.
- At the *point of diminishing returns*, *MP* reaches its maximum value, and *MRP* also reaches a maximum.
- With *diminishing returns*, *MP* falls as more of the resource is used, so *MRP* also falls.

Figure 3 plots various labor inputs and the corresponding *MRP*s from Table 1, and thus illustrates the relationship between the input of a variable resource and its *MRP*. Note that *MRP* reaches zero at an input of 13 units of labor. With this input, the firm's total revenue is at the maximum possible with fixed inputs of other resources. This is thus the maximum amount of the variable resource that the firm would use.

The Firm's Demand

A profit-maximizing firm will hire a resource until its profits reach a maximum. This occurs when the last additional unit of the resource

Figure 3 Marginal Revenue Product Curve

input costs the firm exactly as much as it returns to the firm in revenue. This observation leads us to a single rule for employment of a resource which is valid for *all* profit-maximizing firms, regardless of whether they are price-takers in the resource market or the product market.

- A profit-maximizing firm will hire additional units of a resource up to the point where the *MFC* of the last unit hired equals its *MRP*, and *MRP* is falling.

If the firm is a price-taker in the product market, its $MFC = P$, so the firm will hire a resource until $P_\ell = MFC_\ell = MRP_\ell$.

In Table 1 and Figure 3, the price of labor (P_ℓ) is $50 per worker-day. Notice that $MFC = MRP$ at two different inputs of labor—1 unit and 8 units. At 1 unit, however, *MRP* is rising, and every additional unit of labor between 2 and 8 units causes profits to rise because *MRP* is greater than *MFC*. The firm would thus stop hiring additional labor at an input of 8 units, where *MFC* is again equal to *MRP*, but *MRP* is now falling.

- The **firm's demand for a resource** is the negatively sloped portion of its *MRP* curve of the resource.

The firm's demand curve for labor is shown in Figure 4.

Figure 4 Firm's Demand for a Resource

Market Demand

The market demand for a resource is the sum of the quantities demanded by firms at various prices. Market demand for a resource may shift as a result of technological changes that alter the firms' production functions, changes in the demand for the firms' products, changes in other resource prices, and changes in the number of firms bidding for the use of the resource.

Elasticity of Resource Demand

Elasticity of resource demand measures the responsiveness of quantity of a resource demanded to changes in its price. Specifically, elasticity of demand for a resource (e_{dr}) is

$$e_{dr} = -\frac{\%\text{ change in quantity of resource demanded}}{\%\text{ change in resource price}}. \quad (4)$$

Most of the mechanics and analysis of elasticity of demand for a product apply to elasticity of demand for a resource. To find e_{dr} for a given change in price and quantity demanded, use the *arc approximation* approach introduced in Chapter 4. The relationship between elasticity of resource demand and total payments for a resource is similar to that between elasticity of product demand and total revenue.

- If *resource demand is elastic* (e_{dr} greater than 1), changes in the price of the resource will cause total payments for the resource to move in the opposite direction.
- If *resource demand is inelastic* (e_{dr} less than 1), changes in the price of the resource will cause total payments for the resource to move in the same direction.
- If *resource demand is unitarily elastic* ($e_{dr} = 1$), total payments for the resource are constant or at a maximum.

Elasticity of resource demand, like elasticity of product demand, depends on the ease of substitution.

- Demand for a resource is *more elastic*, the *easier it is to substitute other resources* for it.

For example, the demand for unskilled harvest labor, such as fruit pickers, is elastic because of the ease of substituting mechanized pickers for human labor or even converting orchards to "pick-your-own" operations. On the other hand, the demand for highly skilled labor in occupations where it is difficult to substitute other resources for labor—for example, airline pilots—tends to be inelastic.

Other things equal, the elasticity of demand also varies with the price of the resource.

- Generally, the demand for a resource is *more elastic at high prices* than at low prices.

In Figure 5, raising the wage rate from $1.50 to $2.50 causes total wages to rise from $270 to $400 because demand is inelastic over this range of wages. However, raising the wage rate from $8.50 to $9.50 reduces total wage payments from $340 to $190 because demand for labor is elastic over this range of wages.

If a resource accounts for a large part of a firm's total costs, changes in the price of the resource will have a more obvious effect on the firm's costs than would be the case if the resource accounted for only a small part of the firm's costs. Changes in costs reflected in changes in prices of goods. The effect of changes in the price of a resource on the quantity of the resource demanded, then, depends on the impact of the change in resource price on total cost and on the elasticity of demand for the goods produced by the resource.

- Resource demand is *more elastic the more important the resource is in the firm's total cost*.
- Resource demand is *more elastic the more elastic the demand for the firm's product*.

Figure 5 Elasticity of Demand for a Resource

Resource demand would be most elastic in industries in which the resource accounted for a large portion of total cost and in which the demand for the output of the industry is highly elastic. Resource demand would be the least elastic where the resource accounted for a small part of total cost and demand for the product is inelastic.

Applying the Tools

The Economics of Minimum Wages

Imposing or raising a legal minimum wage is often seen as a way to raise the incomes of the lowest-paid workers. However, unless the demand for low-wage labor is completely inelastic, imposing or raising a minimum wage has another negative effect: it creates excess supply of labor, or unemployment, at the minimum wage. In Figure A, for example, imposing a minimum wage of W^* above

Figure A

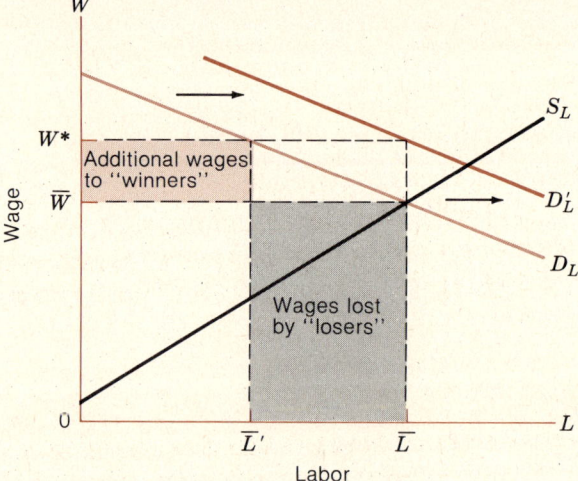

the equilibrium wage $\overline{W}$ reduces number of labor-hours employed from $\overline{L}$ to $\overline{L}'$. The workers who remain employed (*winners*) gain income due to the higher wage. The workers who become unemployed at the higher wage (*losers*) lose wages. A value judgment is required to say whether the gains to the *winners* are more important than the losses to the *losers*.

An intelligent value judgment should consider the sizes of the gains and losses, and this involves the elasticity of demand for low-wage labor. Some low-wage workers are employed by firms that are on the verge of shutting down, and higher minimum wages may precipitate shut-downs by pushing VC above TR. Many low-wage jobs are in firms where the demand for the product is relatively elastic (textile plants, retail establishments, farms, etc.). Many low-wage jobs can be mechanized or eliminated completely. Some fruit farms, for example, have mechanized many operations that previously required labor, and have even eliminated some jobs completely—for example, converting to "pick-your-own" operations instead of hiring pickers.

Low wages and unemployment are most serious among young workers, and particularly among young nonwhite workers. In 1977, for example, U.S. Department of Labor data showed an overall unemployment rate of 7 percent of the labor force, but the unemployment rate for workers ages 16-19 was 15.4 percent and for black workers ages 16-19 the unemployment rate was an astounding 38.3 percent. Workers in this age group typically don't have the training, experience, or job skills that are in demand and are limited to unskilled jobs with no specific skills.

Nearly every empirical study of the impact of minimum wages has shown that the demand for workers affected by minimum wages is quite elastic. This means that imposing or raising the minimum wage reduces total wages received by low-wage workers—or that the *losers* lose more than the *winners* gain.

Guaranteeing employment at a minimum wage requires improvement in the quality and productivity of the workers affected through improved educational and training programs, as well as policies to keep the overall unemployment rate low and the demand for labor high. Such programs would shift the demand for low-wage labor to the right (to D_L') in Figure A and offset the effects of the minimum wage.

Resource Supply: A Closer Look

The goal of the household in selling the use of its resources is to maximize utility. Selling the use of its resources allows the household to earn income. The income is used to buy goods and services that give the household utility. In selling the use of its resources, however, the household bears an *opportunity cost* because it has to give up the benefits from alternative uses of its resources.

Wages, Leisure, and the Household's Supply of Labor

In selling the use of its labor to earn income, the household must give up some leisure, and leisure, like income, yields satisfaction or utility. An *indifference map* can be constructed to show the utility of various combinations of income and leisure. In Figure 6, combinations of income and leisure along the same indifference curve yield the same utility, and indifference curves indicate higher levels of utility the further they lie from the origin. Thus all combinations along U_1 give this particular household the same amount of satisfaction, and any combination on U_2 gives it more satisfaction than any combination on U_1.

Earning income and consuming leisure require time, and a person's time is limited by the number of hours in a day and the minimum amount of time needed for sleep. If a person needs 8 hours sleep per day, the maximum leisure per day is 24 hours − 8 hours = 16 hours. The person can work a maximum of 16 hours per day, and if the wage is $2.50 per hour the maximum income per day is $2.50 per hour × 16 hour = $40. The line between the maximum leisure and maximum income shows all the possible combinations of income and leisure that are available to the person. The rate at which income can be substituted for leisure is the slope of that line.

- At a given wage, the household will supply the quantity of labor that maximizes its utility.

Figure 6 The Household's Supply of Labor

In Figure 6, the household maximizes its utility by supplying 6 hours of labor and consuming 10 hours of leisure per day—where an indifference curve is tangent to the income-leisure constraint. No other combination of leisure and income on the constraint gives more utility. This means that the wage of $2.50 and labor of 6 hours per day defines a point on the individual's supply curve of labor in Figure 6.

If the wage rises to $3.50 per hour, the opportunity cost of leisure rises to $3.50 per hour. At the higher wage, the opportunity cost of an additional dollar of income falls because it requires less time to earn it. The maximum leisure remains at 16 hours per day, but the higher wage increases the maximum income per day to $3.50 per hour × 16 hours = $56. The income-leisure line now connects the maximum leisure per day (16 hours) and the maximum income per day ($56). The household adjusts its income and leisure to maximize utility where an indifference curve is tangent to the new income-leisure line—at 8 hours of leisure and income of $28 which it earns by supplying 8 hours of labor at $3.50 per hour. Since the wage rate is the only thing that has changed, we have another point on the household's supply of labor curve at a wage of $3.50 per hour and 8 hours of labor per day.

As the household works more and earns more income, and has less and less leisure, the marginal utility of income will tend to fall and the marginal utility of leisure will tend to rise. At some point, the household's supply curve of labor may actually become negatively sloped, or "bend backward," as in Figure 6. This will occur if the household feels that its income is high enough, and it can earn the same income by working fewer hours at a higher wage, or if it can't purchase additional goods with its extra income.

The **market supply of labor** is simply the sum of the quantities of labor supplied by all workers at each wage, other things constant. To find the quantity supplied by all workers at a wage of $3.50, we'd add the 8 hours supplied by the household in Figure 6 to the quantities supplied by all other households at that wage.

Interest and the Supply of Capital

A unit of capital isn't as easy to define or visualize as a worker-hour of labor or an acre of land.

- **Capital** is a class of resources that are produced by the economic system and used in the production of other goods and services.

Many things fall under the heading of capital. A factory's plant and equipment, inventories of materials and goods, a carpenter's tools, the classrooms in which you are enlightened daily, and even the skills you acquire in your education are forms of capital.

Where does capital come from, and how is the supply of capital affected by utility-maximizing decisions of households?

- *Capital* represents decisions to *wait*—i.e., to withhold some income from current consumption to provide capital for future production.

To illustrate with a simple example, suppose a wheat farmer spends all of his income from this year's crop on current consumption. With no funds to purchase seed, fertilizer, machinery, fuel or other capital inputs, the farmer couldn't produce a crop next year. The capital to produce next year's crop must come out of this year's revenue, and this requires the farmer to withhold some of his revenue from current consumption. Of course, the farmer could borrow to finance his capital purchases to produce next year's crop, but the ability to borrow depends on a supply of **loanable funds** available to borrowers. Where do the loanable funds come from?

Households supply *loanable funds* in the form of savings deposits and the purchase of bonds and other financial securities. This, of course, requires the households to forego some current consumption in order to save. Giving up current consumption is a real cost or sacrifice for the household, and the **interest rate** is the price that compensates households for giving up the use of their loanable funds. For example, if a household decides to purchase a $1,000 corporate bond at a 10 percent interest rate, it receives $100 per year in future income for the use of its $1,000.

As the interest rate rises, there is a greater incentive to supply more loanable funds. Spending $1,000 on a vacation trip, for example, involves an opportunity cost to the household of $50 per year of future interest income if the interest rate is 5 percent, but the opportunity cost of the $1,000 vacation trip rises to $100 per year in foregone interest if the interest rate rises to 10 percent. The household would be more likely to withhold the $1,000 from current consumption at an interest rate of 10 percent than 5 percent, so we can expect a direct relationship between the interest rate and the quantity of loanable funds supplied by the household, as in Figure 7a. The **market supply of loanable funds** in Figure 7b is the sum of the loanable funds supplied by all households at each interest rate.

Loanable funds are an important source of funds for capital expenditures, and we can expect a direct relationship between the interest rate and the supply of capital, but the relationship between the interest rate and the supply of capital isn't very stable or predictable. Some capital expenditures are financed directly by firms out of their profits rather than through loans. Also, the relationship between interest rates and the supply of capital is affected by a number of exogenous variables—such as changes in corporate and personal tax laws and economic expectations.

Figure 7 Supply of Loanable Funds

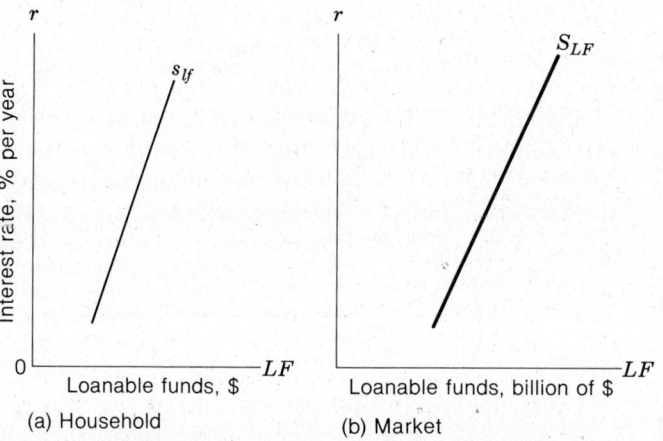

(a) Household (b) Market

Rent and the Supply of Land

Land is unique as a resource because its total supply is permanently fixed. Land can be shifted from one use to another—for example, turning a farm into a residential subdivision—but the amount of land of a given quality or in a given geographic region is fixed. The amount of land in the grain belt of the American Midwest won't change regardless of the price that's offered for its use.

Land and other resources that are fixed in supply earn *rent* or *economic rent*.

- **Rent,** or **economic rent,** is the price paid for the use of land and other resources permanently fixed in supply.

If the prices of agricultural products didn't allow landowners a normal return on labor and capital, the land would lie idle. If agricultural prices allowed farmers a normal return on their labor and capital—i.e., to cover their opportunity costs—the land wouldn't earn any rent, but would nonetheless be brought into production. If agricultural prices allowed farmers more than normal wages on their labor and more than normal returns on their capital, the land would earn an *economic rent*, but this wouldn't change the quantity of land supplied. Unlike economic profit, economic rent *can* exist in the long run in a perfectly competitive economy because the supply of land of a given quality is permanently fixed.

All land isn't alike. Some is very fertile, some is barren. Some is located near large market areas, some is located in remote areas. The price of an agricultural crop (such as wheat) will just cover opportunity costs (average cost) on the *marginal land*—the worst land in production. Owners of better land will be able to produce at lower costs, because of the superior quality of the land, and will earn a *differential rent* on their land.

In Figure 8, the equilibrium price of wheat is $20 per ton, which compensates the owners of marginal land for their opportunity costs. The *marginal land earns no rent*. However, a farm on superior land will produce where $MR = MC = \$20$, and will be more than compensated for the costs of its labor and capital because of the quality of its *land*.

The difference between the labor and capital costs per ton on the marginal and superior land represents a *differential rent* for the superior land. Of course, the market places a rental value on the superior land, so the owner of the better land has an opportunity cost that the owner of the marginal land doesn't have.

Figure 8 Land Quality and Economic Rent

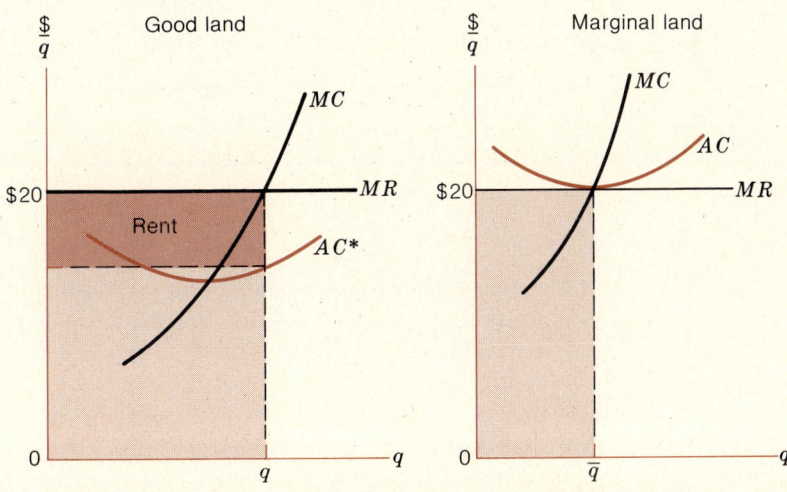

Output per acre can be raised on marginal land by irrigation, drainage, fertilizers, etc., but this requires more labor and capital per unit of output and raises the labor and capital cost per unit of output. Because its *land* is less productive, the farm on marginal land can't achieve the same returns on its labor and capital as the farm on better land.

Nonagricultural land may earn rent because of its location or **site value**—distance from population centers, shipping routes, etc. The rental value of an acre of land in the fashion district of New York City is astronomical, while the rental value of an acre of land in the business district of Homer, Michigan (population 1,690) is *much* lower. The 5th Avenue shops are in the center of a huge population, and attract many customers willing and able to pay high prices for the shops' wares. In Homer, even Main Street is not in the center of a large population of affluent buyers, and the site value of the land is much lower than in New York City.

Figure 9 Economic Rent and the Reservation Price

The **reservation price** on land just compensates owners for the benefits they'll receive from letting the land lie idle or using it for their own recreational purposes. Rents above the reservation price (above R_0 in Figure 9), however, do not increase the quantity of land. Taxing rents down to the reservation price (R_0) won't reduce the quantity of land supplied.

Close-up

The Single Tax Movement in the United States

The idea of a single tax on the pure rent from land is an old one in economics, going back to the eighteenth century. In the United States, a political movement grew around the idea and the works of Henry George. In 1879, George published a book entitled *Progress and Poverty* in which he advocated the replacement of all taxes on income from labor and capital with a single tax on the rental value (or site value) of land.

George's argument was simple, and rested on the concept of land rent as a price-determined, unearned return to the owners of land. Pure rent doesn't reflect any sacrifice or opportunity cost, in this context, but is the natural result of increasing demand for a fixed amount of land of given quality in a given location. If rent were taxed away, George asserted, the land would still be there anyway, and the single tax wouldn't upset production incentives. Expending labor and capital, however, do involve opportunity costs, and people have to have incentives to employ labor and capital in production. Taxing the income from labor and capital, according to George, would affect the supply of these resources and the output of goods and services.

Rent on Special Abilities and Talents

Some individuals earn *rents* due to their unusual talents, physical characteristics, natural abilities, and other special circumstances. These special characteristics of individuals are similar to the natural quality of a given piece of land—they are "gifts of nature" and their supply is fixed.

Vladimir Horowitz, for example, earns a high annual income because he may well be the greatest living pianist in the world. Certainly, Horowitz has spent many long hours of hard work to develop his talent, but without his great natural talent no amount of hard work would have brought him to his current level of perfection. Thus, a substantial portion of Horowitz's income represents an economic rent.

Horowitz's income is far above his **transfer income**—i.e., the income that would just compensate him for not accepting alternative employment. In Figure 10, W_0 represents Horowitz's *reservation price*, or **transfer wage**. The demand for the use of his talent is represented by the demand curve, D. The supply of his talent doesn't depend on the price offered for the use of it, so the supply of Horowitz's talent (S) is completely inelastic. The equilibrium price for the use of Horowitz's talent ($\overline{W}$) is above the reservation price, allowing him to earn a substantial economic rent. Like rent on land, rent on unusual natural gifts is earned on a resource that is fixed in supply. Also like the rent on land, rent on natural gifts of individuals is determined by the demand for the use of these gifts.

Figure 10 Rent and Special Talent

Close-up

Two "Big *E*'s": Elvin and Evert

In 1978 Elvin Hayes, the star forward of the Washington Bullets professional basketball team, signed a contract in which his annual salary was reported to be $450,000. In the year before, Chris Evert-Lloyd's earnings as a professional tennis player were $503,134. In addition, each of these stars was able to earn even more income by endorsing products, doing commercials, etc.

Were these lofty sums required to keep Hayes and Evert-Lloyd employed in their respective occupations? Could they have earned similar incomes in their next best occupations? The answer to both of these questions probably is the same—no. These and other "superstars" earned very high incomes because of truly unique gifts of natural athletic ability—and in Elvin's case, size. Very few of us could hope to attain their levels of performance in their sports, regardless of how hard we tried.

Changes in Resource Supply

The supply of a resource may change as a result of changes in one or more of the determinants of supply other than the price of the resource. If households develop a stronger preference for leisure over income, this will shift the households' supply curves of labor and the market supply of labor will shift as well. Changes in the number of sellers of a resource will cause the market supply to change at any price.

Households may change the supply of one resource as a result of changes in other resource prices. A farmer with a part-time or full-time nonfarm job may give it up and supply less nonfarm labor at any wage if agricultural prices and the rent from his land rise enough to allow him to earn a high income from the farm.

Markets for resources aren't independent of each other, nor are they independent of markets for goods. A change in the supply of labor, for example, will affect not only the equilibrium price of labor but the demand for other resources as well. Changes in the supply of labor and its price also will show up as changes in costs of production and prices of goods.

Perfect Competition and Income Distribution

How does a perfectly competitive economy answer the *for whom* question? Will incomes tend toward equality in a perfectly competitive economy? Does every person in a perfectly competitive economy receive the income that he or she *deserves*? These questions involve the *distribution of income*. We'll examine the distribution of income in a perfectly competitive economy from two angles—the *functional distribution of income* and the *size distribution of income*.

Functional Distribution of Income

The **functional distribution of income** is the distribution of income among the owners of different resources. In a competitive economy, the functional distribution of income depends on the prices of resources and the marginal products of resources. Firms hire resources until the *MRP* of each resource equals its *MFC*. In the product markets, long run equilibrium is reached with zero economic profit ($TR = TC$). The perfectly competitive firm's total costs and its total revenue, then are divided among wages, interest, and rent.

In Figure 11, at the given prices of resources, the firm hires $\bar{\ell}$ units of labor, $\bar{k}$ units of capital, and $\bar{t}$ units of land. The firm's total cost (TC) is

$$TC = (\overline{W} \times \bar{\ell}) + (\bar{i} \times \bar{k}) + (\overline{R} \times \bar{t}). \tag{5}$$

The firm will hire each resource until its price is equal to its *MRP*, and in the long run the firm's profits are zero, so

$$TC = TR = (MRP_\ell \times \bar{\ell}) + (MRP_k \times \bar{k}) + (MRP_t \times \bar{t}). \tag{6}$$

If the entire economy were perfectly competitive, there would be no economic profits in the long run, and the national income (Y)—the value of the products produced by all firms—would be divided among wages, interest, and rent. Specifically,

$$Y = (W \times \overline{L}) + (i \times \overline{K}) + (R \times \overline{T}) \qquad (7)$$
$$= (MRP_\ell \times \overline{L}) + (MRP_k \times \overline{K}) + (MRP_t \times \overline{T}), \qquad (8)$$

where $\overline{L}$, $\overline{K}$, and $\overline{T}$ are the quantities of labor, capital, and land employed in the whole economy.

Each household's income depends in turn on the prices (or MRP's) of resources and the quantity of each resource that the household sells at these prices. If a household sells $\bar{\ell}$ units of its labor, $\bar{k}$ units of its capital, and $\bar{t}$ units of its land, its income (y) will be

$$y = (W \times \bar{\ell}) + (i \times \bar{k}) + (R \times \bar{t}). \qquad (9)$$
$$= (MRP_\ell \times \bar{\ell}) + (MRP_k \times \bar{k}) + (MRP_t \times \bar{t}) \qquad (10)$$

This result is called the **marginal productivity theory of income distribution**. It has some interesting implications, and has been a source of controversy among economists and others. Some have asserted, either in attacking or defending the theory, that the marginal productivity theory assigns a clear, monetary value to the *worth* of a person in terms of his marginal productivity, and that it justifies any pattern of income distribution because everybody gets what he or she "deserves" (as indicated by his or her marginal productivity). However, marginal productivity theory can't answer the philosophical and theological question of the worth of human beings, nor does it answer the basically normative questions concerning the incomes that persons deserve. It simply shows how income would be distributed in a perfectly competitive economy.

Figure 11 Functional Distribution of Income

Size Distribution of Income

The degree of equality or inequality of income among households is the **size distribution of income**. Size distribution is important because it determines the distribution of *dollar votes* among households, and *dollar votes* ultimately determine what goods will be produced in a perfectly competitive economy. There is nothing inherent in perfect competition to guarantee any particular degree of equality or inequality of income among households. Resource markets determine resource prices, and each household's income is determined by the prices of resources and the quantities of resources it supplies at these prices.

One source of inequality in a competitive economy is inequality in the distribution of ownership of resources, or the **distribution of wealth.** Suppose that Smith and Jones work in the same occupation, that they both work 200 days per year, and that they both earn $40 per day from their labor. Smith owns only his own labor, so his entire income is from wages, and his income (y_s) is

$$y_s = \$40/\text{day} \times 200 \text{ days/yr.} = \$8,000 \text{ per yr.}$$

Jones, on the other hand, has $30,000 of capital on which he earns 10 percent per year interest and 100 acres of land which he rents at $50 per year. Jones's income (y_j) is

$$\begin{aligned} y_j &= (\$40/\text{day} \times 200 \text{ days/yr.}) + (.10/\text{yr.} \times \$30,000) \\ &\quad + (\$50/\text{acre/yr.} \times 100 \text{ acres}) \\ &= \$8,000 \text{ per yr.} + \$3,000 \text{ per yr.} + \$5,000 \text{ per yr.} \\ &= \$16,000 \text{ per yr.} \end{aligned}$$

There is nothing inherent in perfect competition that would alter the *distribution of wealth*, or differences in incomes that result from the distribution of wealth. Inequality of income due to unequal distribution of wealth won't go away in the long run—even in perfect competition.

Wage Differences

A second source of inequality of income in a perfectly competitive economy is differences in wages for different occupations. Competition in labor markets won't result in equal money wages for all occupations because all occupations aren't equally attractive. If all occupations offered the same wage, nobody would enter the occupations that are physically exhausting, dirty, require extensive training, carry low status, or are otherwise unpleasant. The economy might be without ironworkers, steeplejacks, physicians, plumbers, morticians, garbage collectors, etc.

With competition, market information, and mobility of labor among occupations, wage differences in competitive labor markets will just compensate for differences in the attractiveness or costs of learning for different occupations. In the long run, the **net advantages** (monetary and nonmonetary) will be equal in all occupations in a perfectly competitive economy.

If labor were free to move between biology teaching and the practice of medicine, for example, physicians would earn higher incomes than biology teachers to compensate for the higher costs of training and the mental and emotional pressures inherent in the practice of medicine. In the long run, however, the difference in income would just compensate physicians for their costs—there would be no reason for biology teachers to enter medical school or for physicians to look for jobs teaching biology.

Suppose that $10,000 would just compensate physicians for the costs and difficulties involved in medical practice. In Figure 12, this is shown with an equilibrium wage of $10,000 per year for biology teachers and $20,000 per year for physicians. If an increased demand for physicians' services drove the salary of physicians to $30,000 per year, physicians would be more than compensated and biology teachers would seek medical training, in much the same way that new firms will enter an industry where firms are currently earning an economic profit. In the long run, the supply of biology teachers would decline and the supply of physicians would increase until the difference in income just compensated physicians for the cost and difficulty of practicing medicine. In Figure 12, a new equilibrium would be reached at $15,000 per year for biology teachers and $25,000 per year for physicians.

This chapter has examined resource pricing and income distribution in an idealized, perfectly competitive economy. Two important questions emerge from this.

1. Does a perfectly competitive economy guarantee a distribution of income that is fair to all members of society?
2. Do the predictions of the competitive model (for example, equality of net advantages among occupations) hold up in an imperfect real world?

Figure 12 Equality of Net Advantages

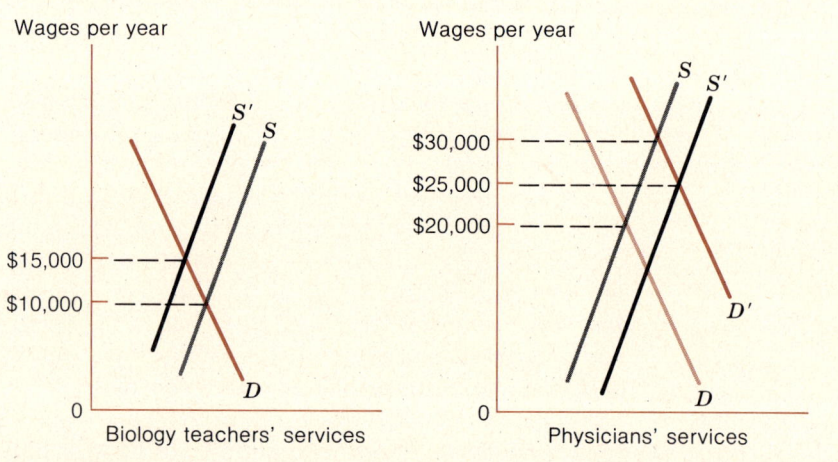

The next chapter tackles the first question. The second is taken up in Chapters 16 and 17 which focus on the effects of market imperfections in the real world.

Summary

1. In perfectly competitive resource markets, individual buyers (firms) and sellers (households) are price-takers, have market information, and compete atomistically in the purchase and sale of resource services.
2. The demand for resources is derived from the firm's goal of maximizing profit, its production function, and the demand for its product.
3. The supply of resources is derived from the household's goal of maximizing utility and its utility function.
4. **Wages** represent the price of labor, and compensate households for sacrificing their leisure. **Interest** is the price of using capital, and compensates the owners of capital for sacrificing current consumption and liquidity. **Rent** is the price of using land or other resources that are fixed in supply.
5. **Rent** is also income earned from unusual physical or intellectual traits or conditions of birth that are free gifts to the individual.
6. Perfectly competitive markets reach equilibrium on the basis of given resources, technology, preferences, and distribution of income. The perfectly competitive economy is amoral with regard to normative standards of equity and social justice.

Concepts for Review

resource mobility
marginal factor cost
marginal revenue product
market supply of labor
loanable funds
market supply of loanable funds
economic rent
differential rent
marginal land

site value
reservation price
transfer income
transfer wage
functional distribution of income
marginal productivity theory
size distribution of income
distribution of wealth
net advantage

Questions

1. Most official definitions define unemployment as workers willing and able to work at the going wage, but unable to find employment.
   a. In what sense does the equilibrium wage in a competitive labor market generate full employment?
   b. What characteristics of perfectly competitive labor markets cause it to reach equilibrium without unemployed labor?
2. Explain the relationship between the price of a resource and its marginal factor cost (MFC) to a perfectly competitive buyer in the resource market.
3. Many economic thinkers, from Adam Smith in the eighteenth and David Ricardo in the nineteenth century to a substantial number of

232 PART FOUR   PERFECT COMPETITION

contemporary economists, have been critical of minimum wage laws. Their views have led to a widespread public opinion that economists are hopelessly insensitive to the problems of the poor and the pawns of the business establishment. What is the basic criticism of minimum wages by economists? Explain carefully.

4. Explain how household preferences and utility-maximizing behavior determine the supply of labor.
5. What are the problems in defining capital as an economic resource? What do different types of capital have in common as a class of resource? What does the price of capital, or the interest rate, pay for?
6. Retailers in exclusive suburban shopping malls or the fashion districts of large metropolitan areas pay high rents, and often use their high rents to justify their high prices. Is this a correct statement of the relationship between rent and product prices? Explain carefully.
7. In what sense are rents "unearned income"?
8. How, and in what sense (if at all), does perfect competition cause individuals to receive incomes proportional to their effort and sacrifice (or cost)? Explain carefully.

Problems

1. The Adam & Eve Fig Leaf Co. uses labor and capital to produce fig leaves. The firm can sell any output (q) at a price of $10 per unit, and can hire any amount of labor at $20 per unit. With a fixed capital input, varying the labor input causes output to vary as follows:

Labor Input per day (ℓ)	Output per day (q)
0	0
1	5
2	14
3	27
4	34
5	40
6	45
7	49
8	52
9	54
10	55

a. Calculate marginal revenue product (MRP) for each labor input.
b. Find the firm's demand schedule for labor. Explain.
c. What is the relationship between MRP and the marginal physical product (MP)? Explain, and verify with the data in the table.
d. How much labor will this firm hire, and how much output will it produce? Explain carefully.
e. If the wage increased from $20 to $30, find the new equilibrium labor input and the new equilibrium output. Is the firm's demand for labor elastic, unitarily elastic, or inelastic over this range of wages? Explain.
f. If the wage increased to $100 per day, would the firm stay in operation in the short run? Why?

12

Perfect Competition: The Best of all Worlds?

Preview: We have seen in the last two chapters how prices, output, resource allocation, and income distribution would be determined in a perfectly competitive economy. This chapter tackles the issue of whether these results are "best" for society in terms of **efficiency** and **equity**. We'll also take a look at the question of whether there would be any useful economic role for government in a perfectly competitive economy.

In 1776, a Scottish "moral philosopher" named Adam Smith published a remarkable book, *An Inquiry Into the Nature and Causes of the Wealth of Nations*, which marked the beginning of modern economics. Economics has become less "philosophical" since 1776—and, some assert, less "moral" as well. Smith's basic argument about economic policy, however, is as controversial now as it was in 1776.

Smith argued that by leaving individuals free to pursue their self-interest in freely competitive markets, society would be led ". . . as though by an Invisible Hand" to its maximum economic welfare. This ran counter to the orthodox economics of Smith's time, which promoted an active role for the government in the economy. Many economic issues today still involve this basic question of the proper roles of markets and government policy in guiding economic activity.

The perfectly competitive model shows how a market economy would operate in the absence of many real-world imperfections—such as market power in the hands of firms and trade unions, immobility of resources, and various legal and economic restraints on the free operation of markets. These imperfections alter the results of the perfectly competitive model, and will be discussed in the following chapters.

Before moving to that discussion, however, there is an important question that must be addressed. Is perfect competition "best" for society economically? If perfect competition really existed, would the "Invisible Hand" lead us as a society to our highest level of economic welfare? The answer to these questions involves two types of considerations: efficiency and equity.

The Meaning of Efficiency

Without making value judgments, we can make only limited statements on the effects of economic changes on the community's economic welfare.

- A change that makes everybody better off, or at least makes somebody better off without hurting anybody else, raises the community's economic welfare.

It requires no value judgments or peculiar assumptions of additive utilities to say that the community is better off if everybody is better off or some people are better off and the other members of society are no worse off. However, if something happens that makes some people better off and others worse off, we can't say anything about society's economic welfare unless we can add up gains and losses of subjective utilities of different persons (which is impossible), or make value judgements concerning the winners and losers (which can't be proven or disproven by fact and logic).

To understand the efficiency implications of perfect competition, we have to understand the meaning of the term and the relationship between efficiency and economic welfare. Efficiency simply means producing the best combination of outputs possible within the limits imposed by given resources and technology. A complete definition of the *best* combination ultimately requires a value judgement, so we'll define efficiency in a narrower sense. If an economy is producing efficiently:

1. The combined output of each good by all firms producing it must be produced at the lowest possible combined cost.
2. Firms must be operating at their optimum size, and producing their optimum output—i.e., short-run and long-run average costs must be at their minimum.
3. Each good must be produced and sold at a price that reflects the marginal benefit of the last unit to society and the marginal cost of producing it.
4. It is impossible to reallocate resources among producers without causing the output of some good to fall—i.e., the economy can't produce more of one thing without reducing output of another.

Before we examine the ability of perfect competition to achieve these

Minimizing the Cost of a Given Output

conditions, we should take a closer look at each one outside the context of the perfectly competitive economy.

The combined output of a good by a number of firms is produced at the lowest combined cost when the marginal cost (MC) of the last unit produced is equal for all firms. Suppose that one farm (call it Farm A) produces an output of 6 tons of corn, and that the marginal cost of the last unit produced is $MC_A = \$40$. Farm B produces an output of 14 tons, and the marginal cost of the last unit produced is $MC_B = \$100$. Now, let Farm A produce one more ton of corn and Farm B produce one ton less. The combined output of A and B is unchanged.

$$\Delta q_{A+B} = \Delta q_A + \Delta q_B = 1 + (-1) = 0.$$

However, the cost of their combined output *has* changed. The additional cost of the additional ton produced by A is

$$\Delta TC_A = MC_A \, \Delta q_A = \$40(1) = \$40.$$

For B, reducing output by one ton causes cost to fall by

$$\Delta TC_B = MC_B \, \Delta q_B = \$100(-1) = -\$100.$$

The change the combined cost for the same combined output is

$$\Delta TC_{A+B} = \Delta TC_A + \Delta TC_B = \$40 + (-\$100) = -\$60.$$

The combined cost of a combined output of 20 tons of wheat will be minimized when

$$MC_A = MC_B. \tag{1}$$

Optimum Firm Size and Output

If firms are producing with *economies of scale*, they will become more efficient as they get larger, and their products will be produced at a lower cost. Similarly, if firms are experiencing *diseconomies of scale*, their products would be produced if the firms adjusted to a smaller, more efficient size. The *optimum size of firm*, as was explained in Chapter 9, is the size that produces a good most efficiently—large enough to have exhausted economies of scale, but not so large that diseconomies of scale have set in.

The *optimum output* is simply the output that minimizes short-run and long-run average costs, or the output that uses the optimum size of firm most efficiently. The optimum output is produced when the AC and LRAC curves are at their minimum points, as at q_2 in Figure 1. At the optimum output,

$$MC = AC = LRAC. \tag{2}$$

At outputs greater than the optimum (q_3) or less than the optimum (q_1), the firm is producing less efficiently and at a higher average cost than at the optimum.

Figure 1 Optimum Firm Size and Output

Marginal Cost Pricing

A **marginal-cost price** is a price equal to the marginal cost of the last unit of a good produced. The price that households would be willing and able to pay for a given quantity of a good reflects the value of the last unit to the households, or the value of the benefits that the community received from the last unit produced. The cost to the community of the last unit produced is the *marginal cost* of producing it.

- For society, the best price and output of a good is where the price equals the marginal cost ($P = MC$).

Suppose that Farm A in our example produced 26 tons of corn, but this price, $P = \$60$, is greater than $MC = \$40$ for the last unit produced. In this case the value of the additional benefits of an additional ton of wheat from Farm A is greater than the additional cost of producing it, and the community would gain welfare as A increased output. If A increased output beyond 12 tons—where $MC_A = \bar{P}$—the community would be worse off because the additional cost of A's corn beyond this point is greater than the value of the benefits from the additional corn. If all farms produced corn where $\bar{P} = MC$, then, the value of the last unit produced to the community would equal the additional cost of producing it, and the total corn output would be produced at the lowest possible cost.

Efficiency of Resource Allocation

If resources aren't allocated among producers as efficiently as possible, it is possible to produce more of one good without reducing the output of the others by reallocating resources.

- Resources are allocated as efficiently as possible among firms if the *marginal rate of technical substitution* (MRTS) *is equal* for all users of the resources.

The MRTS, as explained in Chapter 9, is the rate at which firms can substitute resources for each other in the long run without changing output.

We can verify this rule by looking at a situation in which it isn't met. Suppose that food producers and clothing producers both use labor and capital in production, and that they're combining labor and capital so that the MRTS is different in food production and clothing production. Let's say that the MRTS in food production is

$$MRTS_F = -\frac{4\ell}{1k}$$

and that the MRTS for the typical clothing producer is

$$MRTS_C = -\frac{1\ell}{1k}.$$

This allocation of labor and capital between the two producers isn't efficient.

If we take 1 k away from a clothing producer and give it to a food producer, the level of food production could be maintained by substituting the unit of capital for 4 units of labor. The clothing producers need only *one* additional unit of labor to maintain clothing production at the previous level. So, by reallocating resources, we have the same output of food, the same output of clothing, and 3 units of labor left over, which could be used to produce more food or more clothing. This analysis applies to allocations of resources among all users of the resources, whether in the same industry or different industries.

The Efficiency of Perfect Competition

With a grasp of the meaning of efficiency and the basic conditions that have to be met to achieve efficiency, we can now turn our attention to the implications of perfect competition for efficiency. In a market economy, any industry or market will move toward an equilibrium price and output where the price clears the market, and there is no tendency for firms to adjust output. If the goal of the firms is maximum profit, then equilibrium will be reached when the firms are producing and selling where $MR = MC$. In a long-run equilibrium, there will be no tendency for firms to make any long-run adjustments—size of firm, entry, or exit. Two basic assumptions about perfect competition—that individual firms are price-takers, and that freedom of entry and exit of firms drives economic profit to zero in the long run—have important efficiency implications.

Efficiency in Pricing and Output

A perfectly competitive firm, like any other profit-maximizing firm, is interested in producing where $MR = MC$ to maximize profit. However, because the perfectly competitive firm is a price taker, it must sell at a constant price $(\overline{P})$ dictated by the market, and $\overline{P} \equiv MR$ for the firm. Since $\overline{P} \equiv MR$ for the firm, when the firm produces where $MR = MC$, it also produces where

$$\overline{P} = MC. \tag{3}$$

All firms in a competitive industry must sell their products at the same price, so the marginal cost of the last unit produced will be equal for all firms in the industry. For the two farmers Adams (A) and Brown (B) in Figure 2, each sells at a price dictated by the market, and produces an output where $\overline{P} \equiv MR = MC$, so as these firms seek to maximize profit, they end up producing where

$$\overline{P} = MC_A = MC_B.$$

This minimizes the combined cost of their combined output.

In competitive markets, the market supply curve shows the sum of the quantities supplied by all firms at various prices. Since each firm adjusts output until $P = MC$, it follows that $P = MC$ at every point on the industry's short-run supply curve (SRS) in Figure 2. The equilibrium price is reached when the quantity demanded equals the quantity supplied—at $\overline{P}$ and $\overline{Q}$ in Figure 2. Thus, in a perfectly competitive market, equilibrium will be reached with

$$\overline{P} = MC_{\overline{Q}},$$

or where the value of the last unit produced $(\overline{P})$ equals the marginal cost of producing it $(MC_{\overline{Q}})$.

As explained above, a price equal to the marginal cost of the last unit produced is the best price for society. The perfectly competitive firm is interested in its own profit, not society's economic welfare.

Figure 2 Marginal Cost Pricing

It is the assumed nature of the perfectly competitive market that results in $P = MC$.

Zero Profit, Optimum Firm Size, and Optimum Output

Because of the absence of barriers against entry and exit of firms, a perfectly competitive industry will reach a long-run equilibrium in which all firms are earning zero economic profit and are producing where price is equal to the average cost per unit of output. If the price is above the average cost, firms in the industry will be earning an economic profit, and new firms will enter the industry, driving the price down. If price is below average cost, firms will be suffering economic losses and will leave the industry, driving prices up. In long-run equilibrium, then, $\overline{P} = LRAC$: at this point, there will be no entry or exit of firms in the industry because economic profit is zero—firms are just compensated for opportunity costs.

If the firm in Figure 3 is typical of others in the industry, the industry is in a long-run equilibrium. Firms won't adjust output because $MC = MR$. There won't be entry of new firms or exit of firms in the industry because $\overline{P}_L = AC = LRAC$, and economic profit is zero—firms are just compensated for opportunity costs.

Of course, earning zero economic profit isn't the firm's objective. The reason that economic profit is driven to zero in perfect competition in the long run is the absence of barriers against entry and exit of firms.

If we combine zero profit in long-run equilibrium with marginal cost prices, we have

$$\overline{P}_L = MC = AC = LRAC \qquad (4)$$

when the perfectly competitive industry reaches long-run equilibrium.

Figure 3 Zero Economic Profit

This only occurs at the minimum points on the firms' AC and LRAC curves, as shown in Figure 3. At this point each firm has reached its most efficient size and is producing at the lowest possible cost per unit.

Efficiency in Resource Allocation

Resource markets also contribute to economic efficiency in the perfectly competitive economy. Resource prices in competitive resource markets indicate the relative scarcities of resources and encourage profit-maximizing firms to economize in their use of the scarcest resources. Changes in resource scarcity will be reflected in changes in relative resource prices, and firms will alter their combinations of resources to minimize the cost of producing any given level of output.

It was shown in Chapter 9 that firms will minimize costs in the long run by combining resources so that the marginal rate of technical substitution (MRTS) is equal to the ratio of resource prices, or

$$\frac{P_\ell}{P_k} = \frac{MP_\ell}{MP_k} = MRTS. \qquad (5)$$

Since all users of resources pay the same prices for resources in competitive markets, MRTS will be equal for all users of resources as they minimize costs in the long run. Returning to Farm A and Farm B, if they pay uniform prices for resources, in the long run they will combine resources so that

$$MRTS_A = \frac{P_\ell}{P_k} = MRTS_B.$$

Thus, perfect competition ensures that productive resources will be allocated among users as efficiently as possible in the long run.

Efficiency of Information

Perfect competition contributes to economic efficiency by its ability to gather, synthesize, and transmit a fantastic amount of information through markets and prices. Each household's actions in product and resource markets reflect its preferences and income. Each firm's actions in product and resource markets reflect its production function and its goal of maximizing profit.

The unrelated actions of individual households and individual firms determine equilibrium prices in product and resource markets, allocation of resources among firms, outputs of goods and services, and distribution of this output among the members of the community. Any changes—in tastes, quality of resources, production functions, income, etc.—will be transmitted through the market system and produce a new equilibrium.

To get an idea of the amount of information involved in this process, imagine trying to reproduce the results of perfect competition by a computer solution. First, we'd have to have enough information to construct equations for each household's utility function and each firm's production function. From these equations, we could derive equations representing the household's demand function for each good and its supply function for each resource it owns. From the firm's production function, we could derive its supply function in the product market and its demand function for each resource it uses. Aggregating all of this information, we could derive an equation for the demand for each good, an equation for the supply of each good, an equation for the demand for each resource, and an equation for the supply of each resource.

To find the equilibrium prices and outputs, we'd have to solve simultaneously the demand and supply equations for goods and resources. Consider the number of equations that would have to be solved for unknown prices and quantities. In a small economy producing only 200 goods with only 5 resources, there would be 410 equations to solve—200 demand equations for goods, 200 supply equations for goods, 5 demand functions for resources, and 5 supply equations for resources.

Computers can solve large numbers of equations quickly and accurately, but the trick is getting information. The best computer techniques are no better than the information that is fed into the computer, and it would take a considerable period of time to gather all of the necessary information and put it into usable form. In an economy that is continually changing, much information would be obsolete by the time it's fed into the computer.

The lack of conflict between the interests of the firms and economic efficiency and welfare in a perfectly competitive economy does *not* mean that *laissez faire*, or leaving firms alone to pursue their own self-interest, would yield similar results in the U.S. economy of the 1980's. When we move to more realistic market structures in the following chapters, the link between the interests of the firm and the welfare of the community weaken.

Market Failures

There are a number of situations in which even perfectly competitive markets may fail to give accurate scarcity prices or may lead to inefficiency by producing too much or too little of certain goods. Such situations are called *market failures*. Their two most common sources are *public goods* and *externalities*.

Public Goods

Private markets do a poor job of providing the proper signals for the production of a class of goods called *public goods*.

- A **public good** is a good that is indivisible among members of the community. Individual members of the community cannot be excluded from the benefits of a public good.

National defense is an example of a public good. Modern defense technology and weapons systems make it impossible for every household to provide its own guns, missiles, tanks, and planes to defend itself. Individuals cannot be excluded from the benefits of national defense. If national defense protects your neighbors, it protects you as well.

Private markets give signals to producers based on household income and what households feel various goods and services are worth. But how much should an individual household pay for a good or service that can't be divided among individual households and whose benefits the household enjoys whether or not it pays for these benefits? To put it more clearly, how much would you be willing to pay to get into a movie or ballgame if you knew you could get in free? Clearly, assuming that they wish to get maximum utility at minimum cost, *individual households will pay nothing voluntarily for public goods*.

This does not mean that public goods have no value to the households. Defense, highways, police and fire protection, and other public goods add greatly to our welfare. Because of the unique characteristics of public goods, however, there is no meaningful market demand for them that represents their value to the community. If public goods are to be provided at all, then, they must be provided through the public sector and paid for by all members of the community. In other words, the government must tax all of us to provide the funds for public goods rather than depending on voluntary decisions and private markets.

Close-up

"Please Help Us Stay on the Air"

The broadcasting operations of commercial radio and T.V. stations are supported by revenue from advertisers. Noncommercial, public radio and T.V. broadcasting is financed by grants from private foundations and corporations and by donations from listeners and viewers. Public radio and T.V. have small but loyal groups of followers, but the broadcasters have to make numerous public appeals for funds and some are in chronic financial trouble. If the stations were forced off the air, their viewers and listeners would lose something they value, but only a small percentage of them typically contribute to the fund-raising campaigns.

The problem in trying to get donations for noncommercial broadcasting is that the stations are asking people to pay for something they can enjoy whether they pay anything or not—i.e., for a public good. If individual viewers could be excluded, by some form of "pay" T.V., or "pay" radio, the fund-raising drives wouldn't be necessary—but, of course the benefits would go to a smaller segment of the community.

Externalities

The benefits that households receive as a result of consuming goods (utility) and that firms receive as a result of producing and selling goods (profit) are called **private benefits.** The costs of goods to the households that consume them and to the firms that produce them are **private costs**. Equilibrium in competitive private markets comes about as households and firms seek to *maximize their private benefits* and *minimize their private costs*.

This result is economically efficient *only if* all scarce resources are privately owned and controlled and if production and consumption of goods has no *external effects* or **externalities** on other members of the community. When externalities do exist and are not taken into account, private markets will produce inefficient results.

External Social Costs

Problems associated with environmental pollution are **external social costs.** People who live near factories, airports, or congested highways bear social costs in the forms of noise, air pollution, TV interference from aircraft, etc. Since nobody "owns" the environment in a private economy, private markets don't assign prices for using the environment. The environment has been treated as a free resource when it is in fact scarce. This has encouraged producers and consumers to use the environment as a dump for industrial and household waste.

The effect of ignoring social costs on economic efficiency and community economic welfare is illustrated in Figure 4. The MC curve represents marginal private costs only, with no external costs included. The industry's supply curve, S, also excludes external costs. If the firm responds only to private costs, it will produce $\bar{q} = 24$, where $\bar{P} = MC$, and the industry will be in equilibrium at $\bar{P} = 12$ and $\bar{Q} = 40{,}000$.

If we evaluated the external costs of producing and consuming this good to the community, and added them to the private costs incurred by firms, the firm's MC curve would shift upward to MC'. If the firm still produces $q = 24$ at $\bar{P} = \$12$, the **marginal social cost** (MC') is greater than the value of an additional unit of output to the community. More concisely, by ignoring external social costs, the firm ends up producing where $MC' > \bar{P}$.

Including external social costs moves the industry's supply curve upward to S', and the industry would reach equilibrium with a smaller output ($\bar{Q}' = 30{,}000$) and a higher price ($\bar{P}' = \$16$). Ignoring external costs, then, causes this industry and the firms in it to produce more than the output that equates the value of an additional unit to the community and the marginal social cost to produce it.

- Private markets tend to overproduce goods that generate external social costs.

Figure 4 External Social Costs and Efficiency

Close-up

Smoking Grass or: "How Green Was My Valley"

The Willamette Valley in Oregon is one of the largest producers of grass seed (the legal variety that people grow in lawns) in the country. About 250,000 acres of the valley are used to produce seed. In 1972, the grass seed industry generated about $35 million in sales, and the community received external benefits from the industry in the form of employment and wages, demand for retail goods and services, and government tax revenue.

However, seed producers burned their fields periodically to remove grass debris and to eliminate some diseases and pests from the fields and the grass seed. This practice generated significant external social costs in the form of air pollution, respiratory problems, declines in property values, and even safety hazards due to the poor visibility with heavy concentrations of smoke in the air.

The Oregon legislature passed a law against open-field burning, and levied an excise tax on the grass seed producers to finance the enforcement of the law.

To the extent that this raised the cost of producing grass seed and the price of grass seed to consumers, it represents payment for external social costs that aren't included in private evaluations of products.[1]

---

1. The facts on the grass seed producers are from Dick Wedin, "Externalities and Open Field Burning: A Case Study," *American Journal of Agricultural Economics*, vol. 55, no. 5 (December 1973), pp. 1026–1027.

External Social Benefits and Efficiency

Some of the external effects of production and consumption are beneficial to the community. These are called **external social benefits.** If one of your neighbors, I. Sore, paints his house and landscapes his lot, he will probably gain some utility from improving the appearance of his property, and you and your neighbors will benefit as well. Your neighborhood will be more attractive, and (if Mr. Sore's property was a mess originally) his improvements could make your property more valuable.

On a larger scale, building a new industrial park in a deserted city slum or on the site of a former garbage dump would generate external benefits to the community—more attractive neighborhoods, better jobs and income, more retail sales, appreciation of property values, perhaps reduced crime and social discord. The construction of several new mass transit systems—the BART system in San Francisco and the Metro Subway in Washington, D.C., for example—have generated external benefits such as reduced auto traffic and increased sales for retailers convenient to mass transit.

External social benefits generally aren't considered by firms and households, so private markets provide no signals on the value of these external benefits to the community. Excluding external social benefits will lead to inefficient results.

In Figure 5, D is the demand for a certain product by utility-maximizing households, with no consideration of the external social benefits. Now, suppose that the value of the external benefits can be calculated, and that the value of the external benefits per unit of output is added to the price, shifting the demand curve upward to D'. At a price of $\overline{P}' = 70$ and a quantity of $\overline{Q}' = 1100$, the price reflects the total social benefits of an additional unit of output—including a value for external benefits. Since the firms consider only the price called out by the market $(\overline{P})$, their equilibrium output $(\overline{q})$ is reached when the MC of the last unit produced is less than the value of the benefits to society as a result of producing it—or MC is less than $\overline{P}'$. The community would gain welfare by increasing production of the good until $MC = \overline{P}'$.

- Private markets tend to underproduce goods that generate external social benefits.

Figure 5 External Social Benefits and Efficiency

Externalities and Government Policy	External effects generally don't enter into the decisions of individual producers and consumers. The private firm is interested in maximizing profit, the individual household in maximizing utility—not in maximizing the community's economic welfare. Since externalities aren't considered by firms and households, they don't show up in the demand side or the supply side of the market, and hence the market signals exclude the values of external effects.

In some cases, therefore, there may be a need for a determination of the value of externalities outside the market system, and an active role of the government in estimating these values and in enacting policies that add these values to the market signals. Such policies aim at reducing the output of goods with high external costs and at increasing the production of goods with high external benefits.

- Production or consumption of goods with high external costs can be reduced through taxation.
- Production or consumption of goods with high external benefits can be increased through subsidization.

Levying a tax on the output of the firms in the industry in Figure 4, for example, would raise the firms' MC curves to MC', and the industry supply curve from S to S'. This adds the external costs to the calculations of firms and households in the market, and the result is a higher price and lower output.

Contrary to popular arguments against taxes on pollution-creating industries and activities, such taxes do not create an *additional* cost to producers and consumers. They merely force producers and consumers to include the value of external costs that had been there all the time.

In cases where markets fail to take into account external social benefits (as in Figure 5), the government can subsidize the producers or consumers to encourage greater output until the marginal cost of the last unit produced equals its marginal benefit to society. Most mass transit systems operate with subsidies, and this fact is frequently used as evidence that "nobody really is willing to pay the service costs," and thus that the subsidy or the service should be discontinued. Again, what the subsidy does in this case is to equate social costs and social benefits. One way to get a good grasp of the benefits of public transit to the community is to note what happens to traffic congestion and pollution during a transit strike.

This does not mean that the government can correct for external benefits and costs simply by picking subsidies and taxes arbitrarily. If a tax on polluting industries exceeds the external costs, output will fall too much. Excessive subsidies can lead to inefficiently large production of goods that create external benefits—if the subsidy exceeds the value of these external benefits.

Applying the Tools

Making Polluters Pay

Cleaning up the environment is an expensive proposition, as we are becoming painfully aware. We tend to associate pollution with large, smoky industrial plants, but perfect competitors—even farmers—can create pollution in producing their goods. The runoff from fields into rivers and other bodies of water from farms contains chemicals from fertilizers and pesticides that contribute to water pollution.

Suppose that a community is experiencing water pollution as a result of farmers' chemical fertilizers in their water supply. Having estimated the annual cost of cleaning up the water supply, two proposals are made to finance the clean-up by taxing farms—an annual tax that doesn't depend on output and a variable tax per unit of output or per unit of fertilizer used.

In the short run the annual tax won't affect the farms' output. The annual tax is a fixed cost, and an increase in fixed cost doesn't affect MC. In Figure A(i), the annual tax moves AC to AC', but doesn't affect MC. At the equilibrium price, $\overline{P}$, the best the firm can do is to continue to produce the same output after the tax—$MC = MR$ doesn't change.

A tax on the farm's output or on a variable input—such as chemical fertilizers and pesticides—has a different impact. This tax raises variable costs and thus the MC of each unit produced. In Figure A(ii), the tax on output raises MC to MC' and AC to AC'. At any given price, the firm will reduce its output until $MR = MC'$. Some farms may even cease production if the tax has raised AVC above price.

Which type of tax is better? The answer depends on the goal of the community. If the object is to get the farms to pay for cleaning up the water supply

Figure A

(i) Graph showing MC, AC, AC′ curves with $\bar{P} = d = MR$ and output $\bar{q}$.

(ii) Graph showing MC, MC′, AC, AC′ curves with $\bar{P} = d = MR$ and outputs $\bar{q}'$ and $\bar{q}$.

without reducing output or employment (at least in the short run), the fixed annual tax is better. If the object is to reduce the volume of pollutants entering the water supply in the first place, the variable tax is better.

Perfect Competition and Welfare: Equity

Economic efficiency isn't the only dimension of economic welfare. Equity and social justice are important also. In fact, equity may be the more important dimension for social and economic stability. Equity is basically a normative concept, but there are some questions related to equity that we can deal with analytically. Does perfect competition ensure that persons are rewarded on the basis of their effort and sacrifice? Whose needs will be served best by perfect competition? These are questions that positive analysis can't answer completely because they involve value judgments.

The perfectly competitive economy is amoral: it literally "grinds out" a combination of goods and allocation of resources that reflects the pattern of dollar votes cast by consumers in the market place.

Competitive markets respond to demands and needs that are backed up by dollar votes, which means that the needs of those with low incomes and few dollar votes to cast will have little weight in determining how resources are allocated and what goods will be produced. If a small economic and social elite controlled a large percentage of a society's wealth, income, and dollar votes, competitive markets would respond to the needs of the elite. If the majority of the population had a small percentage of the income and dollar votes, their needs wouldn't have much impact on competitive markets.

If differences in income reflected differences in effort and sacrifice, then we could say that competitive markets would respond to the needs of those who have exerted the greatest efforts. In competitive labor markets, wages adjust so that the net advantages (monetary and nonmonetary) of all occupations are equal in the long run. Pleasant, high-status, nondemanding jobs requiring little training or responsibility would receive relatively low wages. Difficult, physically exhausting jobs, low-status jobs, and jobs requiring extensive training and responsibility would receive high wages to compensate for the greater effort and sacrifice required. If labor markets were competitive, then in the long run *low-wage* workers would be no better or worse off than *high-wage* workers. However, this doesn't mean that *low-income* households would be no worse off than *high-income* households in a perfectly competitive economy, because wages aren't the only source of inequality of incomes.

The distribution of wealth—i.e., the distribution of ownership of resources—also affects the distribution of income in a perfectly competitive economy. Heirs to large fortunes can earn high rental and interest incomes without sacrificing much leisure or expending much effort. Unusual physical and mental abilities that are in great demand earn economic rents for their owners that don't represent compensation for effort or sacrifice.

We thus can say very little about the equity of perfect competition without making value judgments. What seems perfectly equitable by one person's normative standards may seem grossly inequitable by another person's. It is clear, however, that extolling the virtues of perfect competition because it "gives all individuals what they deserve" is hopelessly simplistic.

Does Competition Destroy Itself?

Karl Marx, the great critic of nineteenth-century capitalism, argued that one of the great contradictions of the competitive capitalist economy is that competition destroys itself. According to Marx, competition leads to monopoly as stronger firms drive weaker firms from the market. Was he right?

Perfect competition leads to long-run equilibrium with firms producing at the lowest point on their long-run average cost curves. If the optimum size of a firm is small relative to the size of the market, there will be room for many firms, and competition won't be self-destructive. As long as economies of scale exist, however, larger firms are more efficient than smaller ones, and firms will tend to get larger as the industry moves toward long-run equilibrium. If there is no limit on economies of scale—if larger firms are always more efficient than smaller ones—the end result of competition will be one large surviving firm. With only one firm in the market, of course, we don't have perfect competition any more, but a monopoly.

Competition—more accurately, *atomistic competition*—may be eliminated before there's only one firm left in the market. If the optimum firm size is large relative to the market, and there are only a few firms in the market, the firms cease to be price-takers, and the decisions of one firm will affect the other firms in the industry. In this case, the firms may find it desirable to reach agreements that limit competition among them.

In most markets in our economy, firms have some *market power*, that is, they have some power to set their prices as well as their outputs. These markets will produce results that are quite different from the perfectly competitive equilibrium, and the differences are significant, as we'll see in our analysis of other market structures.

Summary

1. In perfect competition, the profit-maximizing actions of firms can lead to economically efficient results for the economy.
2. Perfectly competitive firms will produce where the price of the last unit produced is equal to its marginal cost.
3. In long-run equilibrium, firms will adjust to their most efficient size and produce their most efficient output.
4. Competitive resource markets assign scarcity prices to resources, and this leads to economic efficiency in production, and in the allocation of resources, and this leads to economic efficiency in production and in the allocation of resources among firms and industries.
5. Perfectly competitive markets are very efficient in gathering and transmitting market information.
6. Market failures are sources of inefficiency in private markets—even perfectly competitive markets.
7. Private markets don't assign accurate scarcity prices to public goods, and public goods have to be provided through government policies.
8. Private markets tend to overproduce goods with external social costs, and to underproduce goods with external social benefits.
9. It is difficult to make statements concerning equity in perfect competition without bringing in value judgments.

Concepts for Review

efficiency
equity
market failure

public good
externality
external social costs

external social benefits
marginal social cost

Questions

1. In perfect competition, the actions of firms in seeking their own profit, and the adjustments of perfectly competitive markets to long-run equilibrium, produce some other results that are important for economic efficiency and community economic welfare. For each of the following, explain how perfect competition leads to these results, and why each is important for efficiency and community economic welfare.
   a. $MR = MC$ for all firms
   b. $P = MC$
   c. $P = AC = LRAC$
2. Some economists—most notably, the *market socialists*—have argued that an economic planning agency could simulate competitive market

relationships with equations and solve the equations with computers to arrive at equilibrium prices, outputs, and allocation of resources. Furthermore, they argue that this would be faster and more efficient than arriving at equilibrium through the adjustments of markets. Do you agree or disagree with this? Explain.
3. Many hospitals are at least partially dependent on voluntary private contributions for financial support. Can you see any potential difficulties with this approach to financing? Explain.
4. How many of the things you consume generate externalities? Which are external social benefits and which are external social costs? Do you take these external effects into account in making your consumption decisions?
5. Critics of the Metro subway system in Washington, D.C., argue that the subway won't generate enough revenue from passengers to cover its costs, and therefore that the benefits from the subway don't justify the cost of constructing and maintaining it.

   Is this argument valid if the subway generates no externalities? Is the argument necessarily valid or invalid if the external effects generated by the subway are considered?
6. Many steel producers have blamed inflation in part on the government pollution standards and the necessity of installing scrubbers and other equipment to clean up their emissions. They claim that these regulations have placed additional costs on the community because steel is more expensive to produce.

   Do the costs of pollution abatement represent additional costs on steel producers? If we consider externalities, do these represent additional costs on the community? Explain.
7. Overfishing of ocean fishbeds by commercial fishermen is a growing problem in many areas. How effective do you think each of the following alternatives would be in alleviating this problem? Explain carefully with analytical tools. (Hint: Individual fishermen can be considered price-takers.)
   a. an annual license fee
   b. restriction of fishing hours
   c. a tax per 100 lb. of fish taken

Problems

1. Ajax (A) and Bonanza (B) are two perfectly competitive chicken farms. The relationship between output (q) and total cost (TC) for each is given below.

Ajax		Bonanza	
q	TC_A	q	TC_B
0	$ 100	0	$ 50
50	300	50	200
100	450	100	300
150	650	150	500
200	900	200	800
250	1200	250	1200
300	1550	300	1700
350	1950	350	1800
400	2400	400	2500

a. If an equilibrium price is determined by the market at $P = \$6$, how much will each farm produce? What is their combined output? What is their combined cost? Could this combined output be produced at a lower combined cost? Why?
b. In what sense is the price and output you found in (a) *best* for the community?
c. Suppose that every additional chicken produced and consumed creates external social costs which are evaluated at $2. What does this do to the efficiency of the result you found in (a)? What is the implication of this for the community's economic welfare? Explain carefully.
d. Suppose that an excise tax of $2 per chicken is imposed to take account of these social costs. What will happen to the outputs of A and B at $P = \$6$? What will happen to the industry's short-run supply curve and the equilibrium price of chickens? Explain.

Appendix

Benefit-Cost Analysis

Many projects undertaken by private organizations and public agencies generate substantial external social benefits and social costs for the community, in addition to the internal (or direct) benefits and costs to those directly involved in the projects.

- **Benefit-cost analysis** is a technique that tries to quantify the benefits and costs of alternative courses of action, and to provide a criterion for the best course of action.

As individuals, we do dozens of unconscious or conscious benefit-cost calculations every day. A student with a chemistry exam directly after an economics class may calculate the benefits of cutting the economics class (an extra hour's study or rest to prepare for the chemistry exam, probably a higher score on the chemistry exam, etc.) and the costs of this course of action (missing important material from the economics class, the probability of a lower score on the next economics exam, loss of intellectual stimulation and entertainment from the wise and witty economics professor, etc.). The choice of the appropriate course of action depends on the estimated costs and benefits of the alternatives—in this case, of course, the appropriate action is to attend the economics class.

Identifying and quantifying the costs and benefits of large projects—such as building a superhighway, constructing a professional sports complex, expanding a hospital, instituting a large-scale remedial education program—isn't as easy as identifying the costs and benefits of cutting an economics class to study for a chemistry exam. Benefit-cost studies tackle the problem through a number of steps to provide information to those who have to decide whether to undertake a project or not, or which of a number of alternative projects to undertake.

Defining Objectives

The first step is to define the objective or objectives of the project or alternative projects. This seems obvious, but stating objectives is important. If the objective of a dam is to control flooding, for example, its accessibility as a recreational site isn't crucial. If the objective of a medical research project is to reduce economic losses from illness, emphasis will be on diseases (such as colds) that cause the greatest loss of worker days and output.

Identifying Benefits and Costs

Unless all of the benefits and costs of projects are considered, including external social benefits and costs, benefit-cost analysis will yield misleading results. If the external social costs of highway projects were ignored, for example, benefit cost analysis would nearly always indicate that highway projects should be undertaken. If the external benefits of projects were excluded, on the other hand, many projects with large external benefits wouldn't be undertaken.

Some benefits and costs are relatively easy to identify. A new superhighway will benefit commuters who use it frequently, commercial shippers who can reduce costs of shipments and delivery time, and the contractors and construction workers employed in the construction of the highway. Likewise, some of the costs are easy to identify—the cost of purchasing the land, the funds required to build the highway, and the interest that must be paid on borrowed funds.

Some benefits, however, extend beyond those directly involved in the construction and use of the project. Some land will appreciate in value as a result of the highway. Lower shipping costs may result in lower costs and prices of some goods. Retail sales in areas served by the highway may increase. Communities affected by the highway may gain other external benefits—increased employment and income, greater local tax revenue, etc.

Costs also extend beyond the direct costs of building the project. Communities in the path of the highway will experience more noise and air pollution as a result of greater auto and truck traffic. Some property will depreciate in value as a result of the highway—commercial properties bypassed by the highway and farms cut in two by the highway, for example. The construction itself will impose some external costs in the form of congestion, detours, loss of retail sales in the construction area, and increased pollution associated with construction. In addition, there may be a loss of aesthetic quality of some of the areas through which the road is built.

Quantifying Benefits and Costs

Identifying the benefits and costs is only part of the task. To make intelligent choices, we need to know the magnitudes of the benefits and costs. Quantifying direct costs of a project—the cost of the land, construction, and financing—is fairly straightforward, although estimates are subject to error. Assigning accurate values to the external costs is more difficult, and there is a considerable amount of discretionary but presumably informed "guessing" involved. Some of the external costs, such as the loss of aesthetic surroundings or historical landmarks, may not be quantifiable at all in meaningful monetary terms.

Assigning values to the benefits has some unique problems. The benefits from a project to be undertaken now will be realized in the future—even the direct benefits. The first question, then, is the reliability of present estimates of future benefits. Critics of projects tend to make rather pessimistic estimates of the benefits to expect in the future, and those who want a project to be undertaken will tend to be optimistic in estimating future benefits.

The second problem associated with future benefits is that $1 of promised benefits in the future is not worth $1 today (even in the absence of inflation). To compare the dollars required to build a project now with the value of the future benefits from the project, we have to *discount* the future benefits to find their present value. The **discount rate** indicates the strength of preference for income now over income in the future, and is expressed as a percentage rate per year. The rate will be higher the greater the preference for current income. To find the present value (PV) of benefits (B) to be received any number (n) of years in the future, simply substitute the values in the formula

$$PV = \frac{B}{(1+r)^n}. \qquad (1)$$

Suppose that a project would yield expected benefits of $1000 a year from now. If this benefit is discounted at a discount rate of 10 percent, the present value of this benefit today is

$$PV = \frac{B}{(1+r)^n} = \frac{\$1000}{(1+.10)^1} = \$909.09.$$

The choice of discount rate affects the present value of the future benefits. If the $1000 benefit a year from now were discounted at 20 percent per year, present value would be

$$PV = \frac{B}{(1+r)^n} = \frac{\$1000}{(1+.20)^1} = \$833.33.$$

If the discount rate were 5 percent per year, the present value of the same future benefit would be

$$PV = \frac{B}{(1+r)^n} = \frac{\$1000}{(1+.05)^1} = \$952.38.$$

As in the case of external costs, some of the external benefits are difficult to quantify accurately, and some discretion is involved in estimating such things as the increased retail sales in a city as a result of the construction of a new sports complex. Some of the external benefits, such as community pride as a result of an elaborate project, are very hard to quantify accurately as monetary values. For example, a benefit-cost study of a program aimed at preventing school dropouts in St. Louis in the early 1960s could not assign measured values to such things as the self-esteem of the students in the program, increased social and political consciousness and participation, decreased social costs associated with crime and delinquency, decreased social costs of public assistance for participants, or benefits that the current generation of participants would pass on to their children.[1]

---

1. Burton A. Weisbrod, "Preventing High School Dropouts," in Robert Dorfman, ed. *Measuring Benefits of Government Investments* (Washington, D.C.: Brookings Institute, 1965), p. 148.

Benefit-Cost Ratios

The ratio of the value of benefits from a project over its cost is called, to no great surprise, the **benefit-cost ratio.** The benefit-cost ratio is a criterion, but not the only criterion, to determine whether or not a project should be undertaken or which of a number of alternative projects should be undertaken.

- Benefit-cost ratios greater than one (1) indicate that the value of the benefits of a project is greater than the cost of the project.

- Benefit-cost ratios less than one (1) indicate that the value of the benefits from a project is less than the cost of the project.

Suppose that a benefit-cost study of a proposed flood control project shows the following:

Present value of benefits	$8 million
Cost of project	$6 million
Benefit-cost ratio	1.33.

This doesn't necessarily mean that the project should be undertaken without asking a number of questions. Are the benefit and cost estimates reasonable? What rate of discount was used to discount the future benefits? Were all of the costs and benefits identified?

There is considerable room for discretion in estimating costs and benefits, and it should be recognized that many benefit-cost studies are conducted or paid for by those with a vested interest in undertaking or not undertaking a project. A different benefit-cost analysis of the same flood control project based on different (but still reasonable) estimates of benefits and costs could very well show something like the following:

Present value of benefits	$ 7 million
Cost of project	$10 million
Benefit-cost ratio	0.7.

Differences of this magnitude among different benefit-cost studies of the same project aren't unusual. A benefit-cost study of a cross-Florida barge canal by the Army Corps of Engineers, for example, showed a benefit-cost ratio of 1.20, while another study by consultants retained by the affected railroads showed a benefit-cost ratio for the same project of 0.13![2]

The benefit-cost ratio isn't of great importance if the cost of a project or an alternative project exceeds the community's ability to incur the cost. Suppose that a city has two alternative projects for improving the cultural life of the city—build a new concert hall, or renovate an existing hall. The costs and benefits of the two alternatives are

	New Hall	Renovation
Present value of benefits	$25 million	$11 million
Cost of project	$20 million	$10 million
Benefit-cost ratio	1.25	1.10

Advocates of the new hall will insist that the higher benefit-cost ratio demonstrates that the hall is "cost-effective" and should be built. The commu-

---

2. A. R. Prest and Ralph Turvey, "Applications of Cost-Benefit Analysis," *Economic Journal*, vol. 75, no. 300 (December, 1965), p. 718.

nity, however, has alternative uses for its funds in other programs—education, police and fire protection, public assistance, housing, and others—and may very well decide that a maximum of $12 million should be spent on the concert hall. With this constraint, the city would choose renovation over construction of a new hall.

In some cases, particularly in choice among alternative medical research projects, there are enormous normative issues that aren't resolved by benefit-cost analysis. Suppose that a foundation has $5 billion to allocate for medical research, and that the two most promising projects are a five-year project aimed at reducing the incidence of colds and flu, and a five-year project aimed at reducing the incidence of breast cancer.

Fortunately, breast cancer affects fewer people than do colds, and colds are seldom more than a nuisance. However, many more working days are lost due to colds than to breast cancer, and therefore there is a greater loss of measured output due to colds. Besides the loss of working days in the female work force, the losses of housewives' services to the household as a result of breast cancer is substantial, but the value of these services is difficult to evaluate accurately. The pain, uncertainty, and suffering that accompany breast cancer are nearly impossible to evaluate and measure in monetary terms. Suppose that benefit-cost studies of the alternative projects yield the following results.

	Cancer Project	Colds Project
Present value of benefits	$5.5 billion	$7.5 billion
Cost of project	$5. billion	$5 billion
Benefit-cost ratio	1.10	1.50

The higher benefit-cost ratio does not resolve the normative issues involved in choosing one project over the other!

Finally, benefit-cost studies generally don't tell us how the benefits and costs of a project will be distributed among members of the community. Generally, some of the people who share the greatest share of the cost of a project enjoy the smallest share of its benefits—such as the farmer who has to put up with the noise and pollution of a limited access highway, but doesn't have convenient access to it. Similarly, some of those who enjoy a disproportionate share of the benefits don't share proportionately in the cost. A high benefit-cost ratio only shows the possibility of compensating those who bear the costs of a project, not that they will be compensated for these costs.

The Usefulness of Benefit-Cost Analysis

The limitations of benefit-cost analysis should not be interpreted as showing that it is useless. In fact, benefit-cost analysis is far superior to casual perusal of projects or making decisions on the basis of emotion, incomplete evidence, or political influence alone. Communities that undertake large projects solely because of civic pride or because traditional thinking has always held that some projects are inherently good, may find themselves saddled with costly and wasteful white elephants—the overconstruction of hospital facilities and duplication of expensive hospital services is a case in point. Failure to consider and at least try to quantify all costs and benefits of alternative courses of action can lead to the construction of some projects that impose huge external costs that were overlooked or understated, or rejection of some others in which external benefits were ignored or understated.

If nothing else, benefit-cost analysis attacks allocation problems and external effects systematically. However, there is nothing "magic" in a benefit-cost study or in a benefit-cost ratio. There are sources of error and discretionary estimates, as discussed above. Furthermore, benefit-cost studies do not resolve the normative and equity questions that must be handled through the political process.

PART FIVE

Monopoly and Imperfect Competition

Few serious economists would argue that the perfectly competitive model presented in the last section represents an accurate picture of the world as it really is. A number of economic and noneconomic "imperfections" make the real world considerably messier than the model. In many industries, firms have some degree of market power which allows them to set the prices at which they sell. In others, barriers against the entry of new firms allow firms already in the industry to earn economic profits in the long run. In organized industries and firms, collective bargaining by unions has replaced wage and employment competition among individual workers.

In this section, we'll examine a variety of such imperfections. The first two chapters look at imperfections in products markets, beginning with the most extreme kind of imperfection—**pure monopoly**—and then moving to the more frequently encountered sorts of imperfect markets. Since market imperfections create potential conflicts between the interest of firms and the economic welfare of society, we'll want to look closely in Chapter 15 at the methods the government uses to control these conflicts. Finally, in Chapter 16, we turn our attention to resource markets, looking in particular at imperfections in the labor market and how those imperfections affect wages, employment, and income distribution.

13

Monopoly

Preview: Like perfect competition, **pure monopoly**—a market with only one firm—is an "ideal" economic model for which there are few if any real-world counterparts. The model is useful, however, in showing the implications of less extreme market imperfections on pricing, output, resource employment, efficiency, and the economic welfare of society. It thus serves, like perfect competition, as a sort of touchstone by which to judge a wide variety of real-world market structures.

In popular usage, *monopoly* is often applied rather liberally to General Motors, U.S. Steel, Alcoa, and other very large firms. The strict definition of monopoly, or *pure monopoly*, however, is narrower than this.

- **Monopoly** exists when there is only one seller in the market or industry.

A very small firm can be a monopolist if it's the only firm in the market. The only hardware store and the only barber in a small town, for example, are monopolists.

Some pure monopolies do exist in the real world. Your community probably is served by one telephone company, one electric company, and one railroad (if any). Except for such public utilities, however, pure monopoly is uncommon. Some elements of the monopoly model, however, can be used to analyze the behavior of firms that aren't pure monopolies.

Monopoly exists because of barriers against the entry of new firms into the market. The barriers to entry may be legal or economic barriers. Patents and copyrights give a seller a monopoly over a product because no other seller can legally sell the protected product or use the copyrighted brand name. Licensing requirements restrict entry into some professions and occupations (such as medicine, law, and plumbing), and restrict entry into certain types of businesses (such as liquor stores or taxis). Public utility regulations generally establish local monopolies for telephone service, mass transit, and electric power generation.

Economic barriers can restrict entry, even in the absence of legal barriers. If the most efficient size of firm is large enough to serve an entire market, no new firms can enter. Smaller, less efficient entrants won't survive against the larger and more efficient firm already in the market. If another optimum-sized firm entered such a market, only one firm would survive, and there would be a monopoly again.

Close-up

28 Varieties of Ice Cream, One Variety of Restaurant

From the opening of the Pennsylvania Turnpike in 1940 until January 1979, the Howard Johnson Company operated all of the restaurants on the Pennsylvania Turnpike. Howard Johnson's even had a monopoly on restrooms on the Turnpike. This arrangement isn't unique to the Pennsylvania Turnpike or to Howard Johnson's. Howard Johnson's also has monopolies on toll-road restaurants in Maine. Gladieux Food Services has monopolies on toll-road restaurants in Florida, Indiana, Kentucky, and on the New York State Thruway.[1]

Exclusive franchises to operate restaurants on toll roads create pure monopolies —literally, one seller. There is no possibility of entry by new firms because they are excluded during the term of the contract. For the consumer who is less than enthralled with the price, quality, and service at toll-road restaurants, the only alternatives are to leave the road or to carry along food for the trip.

1. These facts are from Deborah A. Randolph, "Howard Johnson's 38-Year Monopoly on the Pennsylvania Turnpike Could End," *Wall Street Journal*, October 18, 1978.

The Monopolist's Demand and Revenue

Unlike the perfectly competitive firm, a monopolist isn't a price taker. As the only seller in the market, the monopolist faces the market demand curve for its product, and the monopolist's output decision affects the price of the product.

- A monopolist faces a downward-sloping demand curve for its product.

To sell a larger output, the monopolist has to lower its price. If the monopolist decides to reduce output, the price rises. Table 1 is a demand schedule for a hypothetical monopolist. The monopolist's demand curve is shown graphically in Figure 1.

Table 1 Cost, Revenue, and Profit Figures for a Monopoly

P	Q_d	TR	MR	TC	MC	π
$40	0	$ 0		$ 50		$–50
			$38		$ 6	
38	1	38		56		–18
			34		10	
36	2	72		66		6
			30		14	
34	3	102		80		22
			26		18	
32	4	128		98		30
			22		22	
30	5	150		120		30
			18		26	
28	6	168		146		22
			14		30	
26	7	182		176		6
			10		34	
24	8	192		210		–18
			6		38	
22	9	198		248		–50
			4		42	
20	10	200		290		–90

Close-up

"We're the Only Phone Company in Town"

Virtually every community in the United States has a single telephone company; thus, your telephone company is a monopoly and faces the market demand curve. The following item appeared in the *Wall Street Journal* on December 12, 1978:

A . . . 7% rate increase would add about $201.5 million to the (telephone) company's annual revenue, New York Telephone said. The . . . figure takes into account the attrition in telephone use that is expected to follow the rate increase.

This excerpt shows clearly that the New York Telephone Company is not a price taker. If it had been, raising its price would have caused its sales to fall to zero.

Figure 1 Monopolist's Demand and Marginal Revenue Curves

The Monopolist's Marginal Revenue

The definition of marginal revenue—change in total revenue over change in quantity—is the same for a monopolist as it is for a perfect competitor. Because the monopolist isn't a price taker, however, the relationship between price and marginal revenue isn't the same for a monopolist as it is for a perfect competitor.

- For a monopolist, marginal revenue (MR) is less than price at all levels of output.

Suppose, for example, that the firm in Table 1 lowers its price from $38 to $36, and sells one more unit of output: The firm gains revenue from the additional unit sold, but it also loses revenue by reducing the price on the units it was already able to sell at the higher price. In this example, the marginal revenue (MR) from the additional unit of output is

$$MR = \frac{\Delta TR}{\Delta Q} = \frac{72 - 38}{2 - 1} = \$34.$$

This is less than the price at the new output of 2 units. In fact, MR is less than price for all quantities in Table 1.

Figure 1 shows graphically the relationship between price and marginal revenue for a monopolist. With any downward-sloping demand curve, MR falls faster than P as output increases, and the MR curve lies below the demand curve (D).

Marginal Revenue and Elasticity of Demand

Unless market demand is completely inelastic, increasing the price of its product won't always increase the monopolist's revenue. To sell additional output, the monopolist in Table 1 and Figure 1 must lower price, and lowering price increases TR only when demand is elastic. When demand is elastic, MR is thus positive. When demand is inelastic, increasing output and lowering price lowers TR, and MR is thus negative. This suggests the following relationship between MR and elasticity of demand, and TR.

- If *demand is elastic*, price and TR change in opposite directions, and MR *is positive*.
- If *demand is inelastic*, price and TR change in the same direction, and MR *is negative*.
- If *demand is unitarily elastic*, TR is at its maximum or constant and MR = 0.

You can verify these statements for yourself by comparing the elasticity of demand for a pair of prices and outputs where MR is positive and where MR is negative.

The Monopolist's Equilibrium

The goal of the monopolist is the same as the goal of the perfectly competitive firm—*to maximize its profit*. Like the perfect competitor the monopolist will maximize its profit by changing output until profit stops rising. Unlike the perfectly competitive firm, however, the monopolist's choice of output affects the market price. The monopolist, then, reaches both an *equilibrium output* and an *equilibrium price*.

In reaching an equilibrium output, the monopolist follows the same rule as the perfect competitor.

- Increasing output causes profit to rise if the marginal revenue from the last unit produced (MR) is greater than the marginal cost of producing it (MC).
- Reducing output causes profit to rise if the marginal revenue from the last unit produced (MR) is less than the marginal cost of producing it (MC).

In Table 1, the monopolist's profit rises until it increases output from 4 to 5 units. If it goes beyond 5 units, profit falls. The firm's equilibrium output, then, is $\overline{Q} = 5$. It will sell this output at its demand price, so the equilibrium price is $\overline{P} = \$30$.

This equilibrium is shown graphically in Figure 2. The firm's economic profit of $\pi = \$30$ is shown by the shaded area. You should verify for yourself that selling an output other than $\overline{Q}$ and charging a price other than $\overline{P}$ would result in a lower profit for the firm.

In this example, we have varied output in one-unit intervals, and we found that MR = MC somewhere between outputs of 4 and 5 units. The firm produces the fifth unit because the rise in profit as a result of producing the fourth unit indicated that this was the proper course

Figure 2 Monopolist's Equilibrium

of action. If the firm could change its output by smaller amounts, it would produce the exact output where $MR = MC$ and charge the market demand price for it, as shown by the broken brown lines in Figure 2. In all subsequent examples, we'll assume that the firm can change output and prices by such small amounts, so that equilibrium output and price will be where $MR = MC$.

- A profit-maximizing monopolist will produce an equilibrium output where $MR = MC$, and will charge an equilibrium price that clears the market.

In perfect competition, freedom of entry and exit and atomistic competition drive economic profit to zero in the long run. Because of the barriers to entry in a monopoly, however, a monopolist may earn economic profit in the long run as well as in the short run. If a firm earns a positive economic profit, it is more than compensated for its opportunity cost, so the monopolist's economic profit in the long run can't be explained in terms of costs or normal returns on resources. Monopoly profits, then, are similar to a rent because they represent a return on the firm's unique position as the only firm in the industry rather than compensation for cost. If pure economic profit were taxed away, the firm would not be forced to shut down, since it would still be compensated for its opportunity costs.

The *possibility* of a positive economic profit for a monopolist doesn't *guarantee* it, however. In Figure 3a, the monopolist is in equilibrium with $MR = MC$ and $\overline{P} = AC$, and is earning zero economic profit. In Figure 3b, the firm produces where $MR = MC$ and charges $\overline{P}$ to minimize its economic loss.

A monopolist may even have to shut down in the short run if it can't cover its variable cost. The firm in Figure 3c is a monopolist that is at its short-run shut-down point because its equilibrium price ($\overline{P}$) just covers its AVC.

Figure 3 Monopoly Equilibrium Without Profit

(a) Zero Economic Profit (b) Economic Loss (c) Monopolist's Shut-Down Point

Monopoly, Competition, and the Community

As we saw in the last chapter, when a perfectly competitive industry reaches long-equilibrium, there are a number of favorable implications for efficiency and the economic welfare of the community. The price of the good will equal the marginal cost of the last unit produced, so total combined output is produced at the lowest possible cost. Firms will be just compensated for opportunity costs with $\overline{P} = AC = LRAC$, and firms will adjust to their most efficient size and their most efficient output ($AC = LRAC$ = minimum). However, the implications of a monopolist reaching equilibrium where its profit is maximized are quite different.

Price and Marginal Cost

A monopolist maximizes profit where $MR = MC$, but P is always greater than MR for a monopolist. If the firm reaches equilibrium with $MR = MC$, and $\overline{P}$ is greater than MR at this output, P *must be greater than MC at the monopolist's equilibrium*.

- A monopolist can't maximize its profit and sell at a price that reflects the marginal cost of the last unit produced.

In terms of the community's economic welfare, the profit-maximizing decisions of a monopolist will thus lead to underproduction of its product. In Figure 4, the value to the community of an additional unit of output ($\overline{P}$) exceeds the marginal cost of producing it ($MC_{\overline{q}}$). The

Figure 4 Monopolist's Price Greater Than Marginal Cost

monopolist wouldn't produce Q' and sell at a price of $P' = MC$, because this wouldn't maximize profit (MR is less than MC at this point).

Efficiency and Economic Profit

A monopolist may adjust to the optimum firm size and produce where the long-run and short-run average cost curves are at their minimum points, but there's nothing in the structure or operation of the market to guarantee that this will occur. Likewise, a monopolist may end up just compensated for its opportunity cost ($\overline{P} = AC = LRAC$) in the long run, but again there isn't anything in the monopoly market to ensure that profits go to zero.

In Figure 5a, the monopolist's marginal revenue curve (MR) happens to pass through the minimum point on its $LRAC$ curve where $AC = LRAC = MC$. The firm will produce $\overline{Q}$, where $MR = MC$, and this is the firm's most efficient output. There *is* a catch, however. The monopolist won't sell at a price equal to average cost, but rather at the price that the market will bear for its equilibrium output—$\overline{P}$ in Figure 5a. The equilibrium price is greater than the average cost, and the firm earns an economic profit which more than compensates it for its opportunity costs.

Figure 5b shows a monopolist in a long-run equilibrium with zero economic profit—$\overline{P} = AC = LRAC$. This firm is just compensated for its opportunity costs, but it isn't at the minimum point on its AC or its $LRAC$ curve. The firm could realize economies of scale if it expanded, and in the short run the firm is underutilizing its capacity by producing above the minimum point on its AC curve.

Figure 5 Efficiency, Economic Profit, and Monopoly

(a) Optimum Size with Profit   (b) Suboptimum Size with Zero Economic Profit

As in all of the monopoly examples, the firms in Figures 5a and b maximize their profits by selling at a price greater than the marginal cost of the last unit produced.

Consumer Surplus and "Deadweight Loss"

There is an additional cost of monopoly that is not always obvious. To see it, we'll have to tackle an important but rather slippery concept called *consumer surplus*.

- **Consumer surplus** is the difference between the absolute maximum amount consumers would be willing and able to pay for a given quantity of a good and the amount they actually spend by purchasing at a uniform price.

The demand curve in Figure 6 shows the quantities of a good demanded at various prices. It also shows the amount that households would be willing and able to pay for each unit—$10 for the first unit, $9 for the second, and so on.

Suppose that the price of the commodity in Figure 6 is $6, and that the household buys 5 units at this price. The household pays, and the seller receives *total revenue* of

$$TR = P \times q = \$6 \times 5 = \$30.$$

However, the first unit is worth $10 to the consumer, the second is worth $9, the third is worth $8, and so on. If the household had paid a price for each unit equal to the value of that unit, it would have paid the *maximum revenue* for 5 units, and this maximum revenue would be

Figure 6 Consumer Surplus

$$TR^* = \$10 + \$9 + \$8 + \$7 + \$6 = \$40.$$

Consumer surplus is the difference between the maximum revenue (TR^*) and the actual total revenue paid (TR), or

$$CS = TR^* - TR = \$40 - \$30 = \$10.$$

In Figure 6, the consumer surplus from purchasing 5 units at a price of $6 per unit is the shaded area above the price of $6.

With this basic notion in mind, compare a competitive long-run equilibrium with a monopolist's equilibrium under the same cost conditions. To keep things simple, assume that the industry operates with *constant returns to scale*—all firms are equally efficient regardless of size. With constant returns to scale, $LRAC$ and $LRMC$ are constant and equal to each other at all outputs.

If the industry were perfectly competitive, long-run equilibrium would be reached at $\overline{P}_c = LRAC = LRMC$ and an output of $\overline{Q}_c$ in Figure 7. The consumer surplus with perfect competition is the triangular area $A\overline{P}_cC$.

Now, suppose that the industry is monopolized by a single large firm. The large firm is neither more nor less efficient than the small competitive firms. The monopolist faces the entire market, so the market demand curve is the monopolist's demand curve, D_m. Since the monopolist isn't a price taker, its marginal revenue (MR_m) lies below the demand curve. The monopolist's equilibrium output is $\overline{Q}_m$ where $MR_m = MC$, and the monopolist will charge a price of $\overline{P}_m$. Monopoly results in a smaller quantity and a higher price than perfect competition in this industry, and the monopolist earns a profit of π_m.

Monopolization reduces consumer surplus from the area $A\overline{P}_cC$ to the smaller area $A\overline{P}_mB$. Some of the lost consumer surplus is redistributed to the monopolist as profit, but not all of it. The gray shaded area EBC in Figure 7 is a **deadweight loss**, or lost consumer surplus that doesn't add to anybody else's benefits.

The deadweight loss can also be explained in terms of price and marginal cost. In the competitive equilibrium in Figure 6, $\overline{P}_c = MC$ of the last unit of additional output, or the value to the community of the last unit produced equals the additional cost of producing it. In the monopoly equilibrium of Figure 7, the value of the last unit produced by the monopolist $(\overline{P}_m)$ is greater than the marginal cost of producing it. For all outputs between $\overline{Q}_m$ and $\overline{Q}_c$, the value of additional units to the community exceeds their marginal cost, and the gray shaded area EBC represents a net loss of benefits to the community. The monopoly profit (π_m) represents a redistribution of benefits from consumers to the monopolist, as before.

To say that redistribution of benefits from consumers to the firm is good or bad requires a value judgment. The deadweight loss represents a net loss of benefits, however, and no value judgement is required to say that this represents a loss of economic welfare to the community. The economist's concern with monopoly thus has little to do with notions of "robber barons" or with any inherent ideological hostility toward the free enterprise system. The concern is with the effects of monopoly on economic efficiency and economic welfare and the costs borne by the community as a result of monopoly.

Figure 7 Deadweight Loss

Price Discrimination

A simple monopolist charges the same price for each unit of its output that it sells. All of the examples so far have been of simple monopolists. Some monopolies and other firms that aren't price takers can charge different prices for different quantities of their products or charge different buyers different prices for the same product. This practice is called **price discrimination.**

Price discrimination isn't unique to monopoly, but it requires that the firm have some control over its price. A price taker has to sell at a price determined by the market and thus can't be a price discriminator because it can't affect the price at which it sells.

Examples of price discrimination are abundant, and most price discrimination is considered to be a perfectly legitimate practice. In fact, price discrimination makes some consumers better off than they would be without it. Making some consumers better off, however, isn't the purpose of price discrimination: the firm's objective is to maximize profit.

Market Splitting and Peak Load Pricing

Anybody who has been to a movie, sent a telegram, or made a long-distance telephone call has observed price discrimination. Many movie theaters charge different prices for matinees and weekday performances than they charge for evenings on the weekend. A telegram on "night rates" is less expensive than using the service during business hours. These are examples of **market splitting:** the firm identifies different segments of its market, and sets prices in each segment to maximize profit.

One common example of market splitting is called **peak-load pricing:** the firm charges more for its services during periods of high demand, and less during periods of low demand. The rate for long-distance telephone calls, for example, is higher during periods of heavy demand (business hours weekdays and after 5:00 P.M. Sunday) than during periods in which demand is lower (after 5:00 P.M. weekdays, all day Saturday, and until 5:00 P.M. Sundays).

Why would the telephone company adopt such a pricing strategy? The telephone system must have enough capacity to provide adequate service during the period of high demand. If it adjusted its rates so that it maximized its profits during the period of peak demand, and charged the same price (P_1) at all times, however, the number of calls per hour would be very low during periods of slack demand, and the telephone company would incur losses during the slack period. The total profits from long-distance service with uniform rates would be the profit earned during the peak demand less the losses incurred during the slack period. Obviously, the firm's total profits would increase if it could increase its profits during the slack period without lowering peak-demand profits.[1]

---

1. For the sake of simplicity, assume that cost relationships are the same during the periods of high demand ("weekdays") and the periods of lower demand ("nights and weekends").

Figure 8 Peak-Load Pricing

In Figure 8, the telephone company would maximize profit during the slack period by charging $\overline{P}_2$ where $MR = MC$ during this period. By charging $\overline{P}_1$ during the peak demand period and $\overline{P}_2$ during the slack period, total profit would increase. The motivation of the telephone company isn't to provide a "bargain" for callers during the slack period, but to increase profit.

Some customers will substitute cheaper night and weekend calls for weekday calls due to the lower rates. This would cause the demand curve to shift to the left during the peak demand period. This wouldn't be an unfavorable result for the telephone company, since it would even out the utilization of its capacity and reduce losses during the slack period. If the telephone facilities were utilized more evenly, the telephone company could handle the same total flow of calls with a smaller capacity.

Close-up

Peak-Load Pricing: Water Rates

Many metropolitan areas face chronic shortages of water and overloaded sewage treatment capacities, particularly during period of peak demand—mornings, evenings, and weekends, when all family members are home. Overloading sewage treatment plants can cause serious environmental damage, but building sufficient capacity to handle peak demand would be wasteful because the capacity would be underutilized except during peak demand periods.

One solution being examined in several cities is peak-load pricing in water and sewage charges—charging higher rates during peak demand periods to discourage unnecessary use of water and lower rates during the off periods. The object in this case is *not* to maximize profit, but to even out the utilization of water and sewer capacities. To the extent that peak-load pricing works, it would make it possible to handle a given population's needs with a smaller capacity than if a single rate were charged.

Block Pricing

A second type of price discrimination common in monopoly markets is called **block pricing:** the buyer is charged a high price per unit for some initial quantity or block of units purchased, a lower price per unit for the next block of units, and so on. This type of price discrimination is very common, and is practiced by just about every gas and electric company in the country. Consider the following highly simplified rate schedule for electric power consumption.

kilowatt hrs. (kwh) per month	price per kwh
0–50	$ .25
50–75	.20
75–100	.15
100–125	.10

This isn't a simple quantity discount, in which the price per unit falls as the consumer buys more. The household pays $.25 per kwh for the *first* 50 kwh consumed, $.20 per kwh for the *next* 25, and so on. In a simple quantity discount, the buyer would pay $.25 per kwh if it consumed 50 kwh or less, $.20 if it consumed 75 or less, etc.

Suppose that a household would be willing and able to purchase 125 kwh per month at a price of $.10 per kwh, as in Figure 9. If it paid a uniform price of $.10 per kwh, the household's monthly electric bill would be $12.50 ($.10 per kwh × 125 kwh). However, the same amount of electricity with the sliding scale would come to $23.75—($.25 per kwh × 50 kwh) + ($.20 per kwh × 25 kwh) + ($.15 per kwh × 25 kwh).

In Figure 9, the household's total expenditure with a uniform price of $.10 per kwh is the area labeled *TR*. With the sliding scale, the household's total expenditure is the area *TR* plus the darker shaded area above it. In other words, the sliding rates allow the electric company to capture some of the consumer surplus as additional revenue. The darker area, then, represents a redistribution of benefits from consumers to the firm as a result of the price discrimination.

The sliding rate scales for gas and electric companies seem to be on the way out—but not because they're discriminatory or because they allow gas and electric companies to earn more revenue than single rates. Critics argue that the sliding rate scales encourage households to use more electric power and natural gas than they would with a single rate, and that a higher single rate would put less pressure on energy resources and the environment. In fact, there have been proposals to reverse the sliding scale and have gas and electric companies charge the lowest rate for the first units, higher rates for the next, etc.

Figure 9 Block Pricing

Applying the Tools

Natural Monopoly and Public Utilities

Sometimes, monopoly is more efficient than competition among many small firms in an industry. Suppose that two or more telephone companies, electric companies, or railroads competed with each other in the same area. Each company would have to build its own facilities to serve customers—each electric company would string its own lines, each railroad would run its own track, and so on. Except in *very* large population centers, there wouldn't be enough customers to justify more than one set of electric and telephone lines or railroad tracks. Even if there were enough customers, duplication of these facilities would be wasteful. Likewise, in some industries there may be *economies of scale* up to the point where one large, efficient firm could serve an entire market. If the large firm were broken up into many smaller firms, production would be less efficient.

These are examples of *natural monopolies*. In such cases, monopoly is the most efficient market structure. The traditional approach to natural monopolies in the U.S. has been to regulate them as public utilities. A public utility is a legal monopoly that is subject to regulations on the price and quantity (and, in some cases, quality) of its product.

Finding the Right Price

The firm in Figure A is a monopolist in the sale of electricity. If the firm were free to choose its own output and price, it would produce $\overline{Q}_m$, where $MR = MC$, and sell at a price of $\overline{P}_m$. The monopolist's profit (the shaded area) is a return to the firm in excess of its opportunity costs. Also, $\overline{P}_m$ exceeds the MC of the last unit produced, indicating that the community would gain if the firm increased output beyond $\overline{Q}_m$.

In a case such as this, the community may allow the firm to continue operating as a monopolist in order to realize the benefits of its efficiency over smaller sizes of firm. However, the community will regulate the firm's price to make the community better off than it would be at the monopolist's equilibrium output and price. The public utility regulators will try to set a price for the utility that will accomplish three goals: to clear the market, to allow a normal return on resources used by the utility, and to maximize the community's economic benefits from the utility. In this particular case, however, the regulators can't achieve all of these objectives.

If the price were set at P_1 to clear the market where $P = MC$, the firm will incur a loss because P_1 is below AC where $P = MC$. To keep the firm running at this price in the long run would require either a subsidy from the community to the utility (which takes funds from alternative public and private uses) or some type of *price discrimination* to increase the firm's revenue to cover its costs where $P = MC$ for the last unit produced.

Figure A

In this case, perhaps the best the community can hope for is a regulated price of P_2 that clears the market where $P = AC$. This isn't the ideal price for the community because P_2 exceeds MC at Q_2. The community does, however, benefit from a larger output and lower price than it would get with an unregulated utility or a large number of small, inefficient competing firms, and the owners of the company are compensated for their opportunity costs.

Figure A is only one possible combination of cost and revenue curves, and doesn't mean that a public utility never could get a regulated price equal to marginal and average cost. Another possibility, shown in Figure B(i), is that the demand curve (D) happens to pass through the minimum point on the AC curve, where $MC = AC$. Setting a regulated price of $P_R = MC = AC$ in this case allows a normal return on the firm's resources, and is the best price for the community.

Figure B

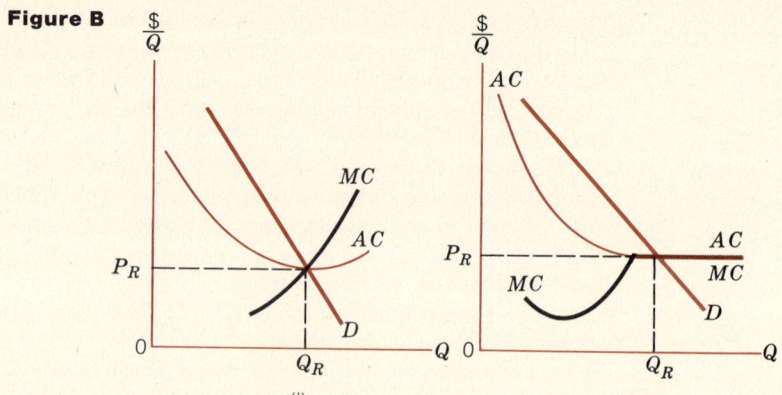

A more realistic possibility is the L-shaped AC curve in Figure B(ii). There is, in fact, some empirical evidence that electric power generation has this sort of AC curve, in which average cost falls until output reaches a certain level and beyond this level is constant. Where the AC curve is horizontal in Figure B(ii), AC is constant, and $MC = AC$. Setting a regulated price of P_R in this case gives us $P_R = MC = AC$.

In the real world, of course, regulating public utilities isn't as precise or straightforward as in these examples. In seeking a price which covers costs and offers owners a fair rate of return, regulators are forced to define answers to two basic questions:

1. *Which* costs of the utility should be covered by the price?
2. *What* rate of return is *fair* to both owners and consumers?

Defining Costs

In setting a price that covers the firm's costs, the most obvious question is what costs to allow. Wages are cost, but what is the appropriate wage to allow? Should unusually high wages and salaries be allowed as costs? How about bonuses and incentive payments? How should travel allowances and expense accounts be treated in figuring costs?

If the firm buys its materials exclusively from another firm that it owns or controls, how are material costs to be figured? American Telephone & Telegraph (AT&T) operates the Bell Telephone System as well as Western Electric Company, which supplies telephones and other equipment to the Bell System. If Western Electric charges inflated prices on the equipment it "sells" to Bell, are these prices a valid basis for figuring materials costs? If not, how is the *normal* cost of telephone equipment to be determined? The only other large telephone system in the country is the General Telephone System which is owned by General Telephone & Electronics (GTE), which in turn owns the Automatic Electric Division which supplies equipment to the General Telephone System.

"Fair" Rate of Return and the Rate Base

Opportunity costs include a "normal return" on the firm's resources. What is the *normal* rate of return for a public utility? Public utilities are unique, and it's difficult to find similar alternative employments for the firm's resources—except *other* public utilities. The term *fair* or *normal* return is vague in public utilities, and it is in the firm's interest to get the highest rate of return possible and then justify it as *fair*.

Suppose that the regulators have decided that 10 percent is a fair rate of return. There still remains the additional problem of determining the *rate base* on which this rate of return is to be calculated. Suppose, for example, that a regulated monopoly has plant and equipment which had an original cost of $10 million. The replacement cost of the same plant and equipment in 1981 is $15 million.

A 10 percent rate of return on the *replacement cost* of the firm's plant and equipment would allow the firm a return of $1,500,000 ($15,000,000 × .10). However, this is a 15 percent rate of return on the *original cost* of the plant and equipment. If the rate were calculated on the *original cost*, the firm would be allowed earnings of $1,000,000 ($10,000,000 × .10), but this is only a 6.7 percent rate of return on the replacement cost of the firm's plant and equipment.

There's no clear and simple answer to the question of the appropriate rate base. The basic problem is that the best rate base for consumers (original cost) is not the best one for the firm (replacement cost).

Unprofitable Public Utilities

Unprofitable public utilities pose some special problems for the community. If some of a public utility's operations are unprofitable—passenger service on an otherwise profitable railroad, for example—like passenger rail service, should the firm be allowed to abandon them or should the regulators look only at the profitability of all of the firm's operations taken together?

Figure C

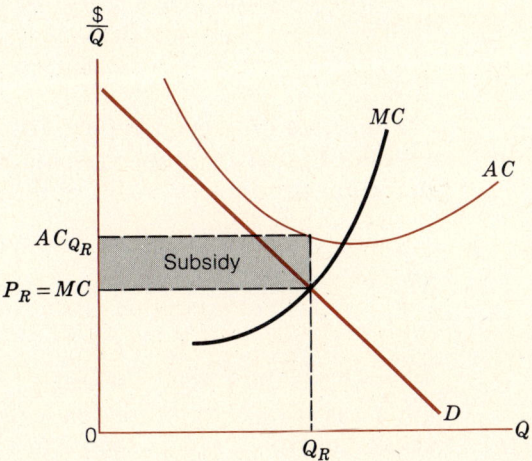

In Figure C, there is no single price that would allow the firm to cover its opportunity costs. If the firm provides important social benefits to the community, but can't cover its costs, it may be necessary to subsidize its losses. This might be desirable in cases where the losses are due to the existence of *external* social benefits that aren't calculated by consumers or reflected in the market demand. In these cases, the subsidy simply adds in the value of the external benefits.

The decision to subsidize unprofitable public utilities depends on the benefits and the costs to the community of keeping the firm in operation and providing its product or service. The community also has to evaluate the benefits from alternative uses of public funds to provide the subsidy. Finally, if the firm can be assured that its losses will be subsidized, there is a real possibility that it will have little incentive to operate as efficiently as possible to minimize costs.

Impact of Monopoly on the Labor Market

Any profit-maximizing firm will hire a resource until the additional revenue from the last unit hired (*marginal revenue product*, or *MRP*) equals the additional cost of the last unit of the resource (*marginal factor cost*, or *MFC*). However, the existence of monopoly or other markets in which firms aren't price takers in the product market has significant implications for resource markets.

VMP and MRP for a Monopolist

You will recall from Chapter 11 that the additional revenue from an additional unit of a resource is the *marginal revenue product* of the resource, and the *MRP* of a resource such as labor is the *marginal product* (MP_ℓ) multiplied by the firm's marginal revenue from the sale of its product (MR_q), or

$$MRP_\ell = MP_\ell \times MR_q. \tag{1}$$

The price of a good reflects its value. The value of the additional inputs of labor or other variable resources is called the **value of the marginal product,** or *VMP*, of the resource. Algebraically,

$$VMP = MP \text{ of resource} \times \text{price of product}. \tag{2}$$

The *VMP* of labor in the production of wheat would be

$$VMP = MP \times P_w,$$

where P_w is the price of wheat.

For a price taker in the product market, VMP and MRP are identical because the firm's *MR* is identical to its price. For a price taker in the product market, then,

$$MRP_\ell \equiv MP_\ell \times MR_q \equiv MP_\ell \times P \equiv VMP_\ell. \tag{3}$$

For a monopolist, however, with a downward-sloping demand curve for its product, *MR* is always less than price, so MRP_ℓ is less than VMP_ℓ at any input of the resource.

- For a monopolist in the product market, the *MRP* of a resource is less than the *VMP* of the resource.

Table 2 Monopolist's Use of Labor

Labor	Output	MP_ℓ	Price of product	TR	VMP_ℓ	MRP_ℓ
0	0		$20	$ 0		
		20			$360.00	$360.00
1	20		18	$360.00		
		18			291.60	255.60
2	38		16.20	615.60		
		16			272.80	233.60
3	54		14.60	788.40		
		14			184.80	109.20
4	68		13.20	897.60		
		12			144.00	62.40
5	80		12.00	960.00		
		10			110.00	30.00
6	90		11.00	990.00		
		8			81.60	9.60
7	98		10.20	999.60		
		4			39.20	0
8	102		9.80	999.60		

The *MRP* and *VMP* of labor for a monopolist in the product market are shown in Table 2 and in Figure 10. Note in both cases that *MRP* falls more rapidly than *VMP* as the input of labor increases.

Employment and Exploitation of Labor

If the firm in Figure 10 is a monopolist in the product market, but a price taker in the purchase of labor, it will hire ℓ units of labor where $P_\ell \equiv MFC_\ell = MRP_\ell$. If the firm had been a price taker in the product market as well as in the labor market, its *MRP* and *VMP* would be identical, and it would hire ℓ_c units of labor. Thus, the first consequence of monopoly in the product market is to reduce the employment of labor at any given price.

- A monopolist in the product market employs less labor at a given price than does a price taker in the product market.

Notice also that at $\bar{\ell}$ in Figure 10, the firm pays a wage equal to the *MRP* of the last unit of labor hired, and total wages of $P_\ell \times \ell$ shown by the solid shaded area in Figure 10. At this input of labor, however, the *VMP* of the last unit of labor hired (VMP_ℓ) is greater than $MRP_{\bar{\ell}}$.

- A monopolist in the product market will pay suppliers of labor a price less than the *VMP* of their labor.

The value of the output added by the last worker is the *VMP*. Since all individual units of labor are assumed identical, labor's contribution to the firm's revenue is $VMP_{\bar{\ell}} \times \bar{\ell}$, or the entire shaded area in Figure 10. However, the monopolist's total wage payments are less than this because $MRP_{\bar{\ell}}$ is less than $VMP_{\bar{\ell}}$. In this sense, the monopoly in the product market *exploits* labor.

Figure 10 Monopoly and Exploitation

Note that these impacts of monopoly are not limited to the labor market. Since profit-maximizing firms employ *any* resource until $MFC = MRP$ for the last unit employed, the implications of monopoly in the product market are similar for owners of other resources.

The Monopoly Model: A Final Note

So far, we have analyzed the least common market structures in our economy—perfect competition and pure monopoly. The monopoly model's usefulness extends beyond markets that are pure monopolies, however. In any market in which firms don't have to take the price dictated by the market for their product, the firm will face a downward sloping demand curve, and many of the concepts and results developed for monopolies will apply to these cases as well.

Summary

1. A **monopoly market** is one in which there is only a single seller. The monopolist faces the market demand for its product, and is not a price taker.
2. A monopolist will maximize its profit by producing where its marginal revenue is equal to its marginal cost. Unlike perfect competitors, the monopolist sets its equilibrium price as well as its equilibrium quantity.
3. The monopolist cannot both maximize its profit *and* sell at a price equal to marginal cost. It may or may not earn economic profits in the long run, and may or may not produce its most efficient output in equilibrium.

4. Some monopolists (and other firms with monopoly power) can split their markets and engage in **price discrimination** by charging different prices to different buyers. This generally allows the seller to earn more revenue and a greater profit than it could by charging a single price for all units sold to all buyers.
5. A **natural monopoly** may earn an economic profit, but also produces and sells its product at a lower price than would be possible by breaking the firm up into a number of smaller competing firms. Most public utilities are natural monopolies and are regulated by public agencies.
6. For a monopolist in the product market, the **marginal revenue product** (MRP) of a resource is always *less than* the **value of the marginal product** (VMP). At any given price of a resource, a monopolist will hire where $MRP = MFC$, but will pay a wage below the VMP of the last unit employed.

Concepts for Review

monopoly
consumer surplus
deadweight loss
price discrimination

market splitting
peak-load pricing
block pricing
natural monopoly

rate base
value of the
 marginal product
exploitation

Questions

1. Many people associate monopoly with huge firms. Can you think of any very large firms that aren't monopolies? Can you think of any small firms that are?
2. Since a monopolist doesn't have any competition in its market, it can charge whatever price it wishes, and can always raise its profits simply by raising its price. Is this an accurate statement? Why?
3. Which (if any) of the following are possible with a monopoly?
    a. Equilibrium with the monopolist earning zero economic profit;
    b. Equilibrium with the monopolist earning zero economic profit and charging a price equal to marginal cost;
    c. Equilibrium with the monopolist producing at the minimum points on its long-run and short-run average cost curves;
    d. Answer (c), plus zero economic profit;
    e. Equilibrium price and quantity that force the monopolist to shut down in the short run.
4. Could a monopolist maximize its profit by producing and selling at a price and quantity where demand for its product is inelastic? Explain.
5. Luke Hippocrates Christian, M.D., charges fees which vary directly with his patients' incomes. He tells his friends and colleagues that he's helping his low-income patients by charging lower fees to them than he charges his higher-income patients. What else is he doing?
6. The Bell Telephone System is a regulated monopoly in the areas it serves, but it engages in extensive advertising to encourage consumers to use their telephones more.
    a. Does it make any sense for a regulated monopolist to advertise? Why?
    b. Much of the Bell System's advertising tries to get people to use their telephones for long-distance calls during the times when rates are lowest. Does this make any sense?

7. In 1976, the Federal Communications Commission (FCC) recommended a large reduction in the rate base for the American Telephone & Telegraph Co. (AT&T).
   a. What is the rate base?
   b. How would a reduction of the rate base affect AT&T?
8. In 1978, the New York Telephone Co. estimated that a 7% increase in its rates would add $201.5 million to its annual revenue.
   a. What does this indicate about the elasticity of demand faced by N.Y. Telephone?
   b. How can you reconcile this result with your answer to question 4?
9. How does the existence of monopoly in the product market affect employment and wages paid by the firm? In what sense are resource owners "exploited" by monopolies? Does exploitation of resources by a monopolist necessarily mean that the monopolist earns high profits by exploitation?

Problems

1. Given the following information for the Y. C. Spotts Optical Company

Output	Total Revenue	Total Cost
0	$ 0	$ 2
1	11	4
2	20	7
3	27	11
4	32	16
5	35	22
6	36	29
7	35	37
8	32	46
9	27	56
10	20	67

   a. Calculate the firm's marginal revenue (MR), marginal cost (MC), and profit (π) at every level of output.
   b. Is this firm a perfect competitor in the product market? How do you know?
   c. Find the firm's equilibrium output and equilibrium price.
   d. What is the firm's economic profit at its equilibrium output? Could this be a long-run equilibrium? Explain.
   e. Will this firm produce where price equals marginal cost? Why? Why is this significant?
   f. Could this firm ever maximize profit at an output of 10? Explain.
2. The Baltimore Baseball Club, Inc. owns the Baltimore Orioles professional baseball team. Like other professional teams, the Orioles pay annual salaries to players and staff, and pay an annual rent for the use of Memorial Stadium for their home games. Also like other professional teams, they have a local monopoly.

a. Because the stadium is seldom filled to capacity during the regular season, it has been suggested that ticket prices should be lowered to fill the stadium to increase revenue and profit. Is this necessarily the proper course of action? Why?
b. The Orioles charge different prices for different types of seats. They also charge lower prices for children, high school students, college students, and senior citizens for certain types of seats. They also have a number of bargain nights (usually Mondays) with low ticket prices. Why don't they make their lives more simple by charging a single price for all tickets?
c. Draw a graph representing the Orioles demand and cost situation, and find equilibrium output. Explain your answer.
d. (Extra tough) Suppose that the demand for Orioles tickets is unitarily elastic for all prices. What special problems does this create in finding maximum profit?

14

Imperfect Competition in the Product Market

Preview: The perfect competition and pure monopoly models show how the profit-maximizing decisions of firms affect economic efficiency and the community's economic welfare when individual firms have no impact on the market (perfect competition) and when the firm is the only one in the market (monopoly). In reality, anything resembling perfect competition is nonexistent in the U.S. economy (except to some extent in agriculture), and monopoly is common only in regulated public utilities. Most real-world industries and markets fall into a very broad category called *imperfect competition*, which combines elements of perfect competition and monopoly. In this chapter, we'll look closely at the behavior of imperfectly competitive firms and industries and see how it differs from that of the pure monopolist or the perfect competitor.

What Is "Imperfect" Competition?

Perfect competition and monopoly are specific types of markets, but the term **imperfect competition** does not denote a single well-defined type of market. Just about every nonagricultural firm that isn't a public utility—from the corner grocery to General Motors—is an imperfect competitor.

Some imperfectly competitive markets have many of the characteristics of perfect competition—large numbers of firms, ease of entry, and atomistic competition. Others are characterized by significant barriers of entry and domination of the market by a few firms.

The basic distinction between perfect and imperfect competition is that the firms in an imperfectly competitive market aren't price takers. An imperfect competitor can raise its price without losing all of its customers, and can increase sales by lowering price. Unlike the monopolist, however, the firm in imperfect competition faces some competition from other firms in the industry.

Traditionally, imperfect competition has been treated as two distinct types of market structure—**monopolistic competition** and **oligopoly**. Actually, this distinction isn't necessary since all imperfectly competitive markets have some common traits, and there isn't any clear dividing line between the two types. *Oligopoly*—a market dominated by a few firms—is a special and important case within the general category of imperfect competition.

The degree of concentration of market power in the largest firms in an industry is an important dimension of the market structure of the industry. In industries made up of a few firms, or in which production is concentrated in a few firms, the largest firms are likely to have considerable market power. If production is more evenly distributed among a large number of firms, individual firms are likely to have relatively little market power.

One important indicator of the concentration of market power within an industry is the industry's *concentration ratio*.

- The **concentration ratio** is the percentage of the value of all shipments of an industry made by the largest firms in the industry.

The most commonly used concentration ratio is the "four-firm" ratio—the percentage of the value of shipments made by the four largest firms in the industry.

The Department of Commerce publishes concentration ratios for over 400 manufacturing industries. Table 1 is a list of selected industries and concentration ratios for 1972. If you're interested in a more complete list—and a lot of other information as well—consult the latest *Census of Manufactures*, published by the Department of Commerce and the Bureau of the Census.

Economists disagree about the relationship between the concentration ratio and monopoly power of firms in an industry. Concentration ratios and changes in concentration ratios do, however, serve as important criteria for investigating possible violations of antitrust laws.

The Firm and the Industry

Imperfectly competitive firms, even the small Mom & Pop retail stores, aren't price takers, but rather face downward-sloping demand curves for their products. The output decision of a firm that supplies a large proportion of the industry's output—such as General Motors or Alcoa—will affect the market price.

Small firms in imperfectly competitive markets aren't price takers because they don't sell identical products. One Ford dealer may make his product different from the Fords sold by other dealers by offering better service, a better location, a nice showroom, or more pleasant salespersons. A "Mom and Pop" store may enjoy customer loyalty, may be more conveniently located than other stores selling the same brands of products, or may simply be operated by pleasant people. In any event, by differentiating their products, imperfect competitors are able to raise price without losing all of their customers and can sell more by lowering their prices.

Table 1 Concentration Ratios, Selected Industries, 1972

Industrial Classification	Percent of value of shipments by 4 largest companies
Cellulose manmade fibers	96
Telephone & telegraph equipment (1970)	94
Primary lead	93
Flat glass	92
Motor vehicles & car bodies	93
Hard surface floor coverings	91
Cereal breakfast foods	90
Electric lamps	90
Cigarettes	84
Tire cord & fabric	84
Household refrigerators & freezers	80
Primary aluminum	79
Chocolate & cocoa products	74
Photographic equipment & supplies	74
Aircraft	66
Roasted coffee	65
Soap & detergents	62
Synthetic rubber	62
Glass containers	55
Malt beverages	52
Radio & T.V. receiving sets	49
Farm machinery & equipment	47
Construction machinery	43
Weaving mills, manmade fibers	39
Softwood veneers & plywood	37
Petroleum refining	31
Periodicals	26
Pharmaceuticals	26
Meat packing plants	22
Canned fruits & vegetables	20
Book publishing	19
Sawmills & planing mills	18
Newspapers	17
Bottled & canned soft drinks	14
Women's & misses' dresses	9
Concrete blocks & bricks	5
Commercial printing, lithographic	4

Source: U.S. Department of Commerce, Bureau of the Census, *1972 Census of Manufacturers.*

Most imperfect competitors, then, face demand curves similar to demand curve *d* in Figure 1. Since they aren't price takers, the imperfect competitor's marginal revenue (*MR*) is less than price. Unlike a monopolist, however, an imperfect competitor does face competition from other firms in the market. The products offered by one firm in an imperfectly competitive market are close substitutes for products of other firms, so the demand for the product of a given firm will be more elastic than the market demand.

Figure 1 Demand and Marginal Revenue Curves for an Imperfect Competitor

Interdependence of Firms' Demand

One of the most important features of imperfect competition is that a firm's demand curve is affected by the actions of other firms in the market, and that the firm's actions may produce reactions by other firms that ultimately affect its demand. Suppose that two used-car dealers—Honest John and Crazy Carl—operate in the same market and face the demand curves in Figure 2. Now, suppose that Honest John lowers his price from P_j to P_j', increasing the quantity of his cars

Figure 2 Interdependence of Imperfect Competitors' Demand

demanded. Honest John's cars are a substitute for Crazy Carl's, so the lower price of Honest John's cars reduces the *demand* for Crazy Carl's cars from d to d' in Figure 2.

Entry and exit of firms may also affect the demand curves of the firms in the market. If a third dealer—Philanthropic Phyllis—entered the used-car market, the demand for both Honest John's *and* Crazy Carl's used cars will fall. If one of the dealers left the market, the demand curves for the remaining dealers would shift to the right.

If the number of firms in the market is small, the effect of one firm's actions on the others' demand is obvious. With many firms in the market, however, the actions of one firm would have a less obvious impact on demand for the products of other firms. If one small used-car dealer in Los Angeles lowered its prices, the other dealers in the area probably wouldn't notice any change in the demand for their cars.

The Firm's Equilibrium

We assume that an imperfect competitor has the same goal as other firms—to maximize profit. Like other firms, it will maximize profit by producing the output where $MR = MC$.

In Figure 3, the firm produces $\bar{q}$, where $MR = MC$, and sells at an equilibrium price of $\bar{P}$. Like the monopolist, the imperfect competitor cannot both maximize profit *and* sell at a price equal to the marginal cost of the last unit produced, and this has the same unfavorable implications for efficiency and the community's economic welfare as was the case with monopoly.

Figure 3 Equilibrium for an Imperfectly Competitive Firm

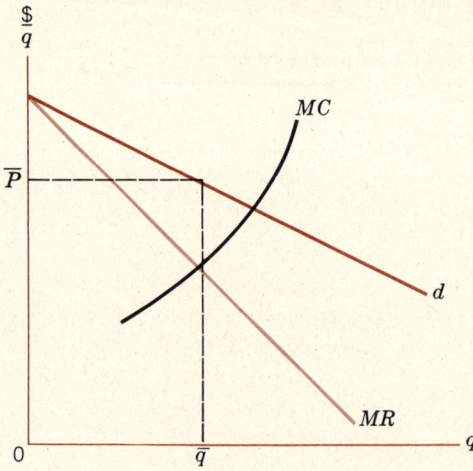

Short-Run Industry Equilibrium

Since there's more than one firm in an imperfectly competitive industry, we have to look at the industry's equilibrium as well as the firm's. The adjustment of an imperfectly competitive industry to equilibrium is a little more involved than it is for perfect competitors or monopolists because the firms' demand curves are interrelated.

Suppose that the firm in Figure 4 acts independently, and doesn't try to guess what other firms are going to do. Initially, the firm sells 40 toasters per day at a price of $20 each. This, of course, isn't an equilibrium because marginal revenue (MR) exceeds marginal cost (MC) at this quantity. This firm's course of action is obvious—increase quantity and lower price until $MR = MC$ and profits are maximized. If this firm were the only one in the industry that lowered its price, it would move to a price of $17 and a quantity of 100, where $MR = MC$.

Figure 4 Short-Run Industry Equilibrium Under Imperfect Competition

If other firms in the industry were in a similar initial position, and they all lowered prices to maximize profit, this firm's demand curve (d) and its marginal revenue curve (MR) would shift to the left, as in Figure 4. Short-run equilibrium will be reached in the industry when all firms stop making adjustments and their demand and marginal revenue curves stop shifting, with the firm in Figure 4 selling 80 toasters per day at a price of $15. As in other market structures, short-run equilibrium can be reached with firms in the industry earning economic profit, incurring economic losses (as long as they cover variable cost), or zero economic profit.

Close-up

NOW Accounts and Price Wars in Banking

One of the things that can cause an outbreak of price competition in imperfectly competitive markets is the introduction of a new product or service. In 1972, commercial banks in New England were authorized to offer *Negotiated Order of Withdrawal* (or *NOW*) accounts to the customers. *NOW* accounts are essentially interest-bearing checking accounts.

Many banks offered *NOW* accounts to attract more customers and deposits. To attract customers away from other banks that also offered the accounts, the banks engaged in a price war that resulted in lower minimum balances for the accounts and lower (eventually elimination of) service charges on the accounts. As one bank lowered its charges others followed to keep their customers and their deposits.

Eventually, the banks' losses on *NOW* accounts forced them to reinstate minimum balances and service charges on the accounts. When the authorization to provide versions of *NOW* accounts was extended to other parts of the country, many banks feared the kind of price war that accompanied the introduction of the accounts in New England.

Long-Run Industry Equilibrium

If there are effective barriers against the entry of new firms, it's possible to have firms in an imperfectly competitive industry earning economic profit in the long run, as in Figure 5a. As in monopoly, however, the *possibility* of economic profit in the long run doesn't necessarily mean that the firms *will* earn an economic profit in the long run.

With freedom of entry, economic profit will be driven to zero in the long run in imperfect competition. Suppose that the firm in Figure 5a is in an industry with no barriers to entry of new firms. In the short run, the firm is in equilibrium and earning an economic profit. Economic profits attract new firms to the industry, reducing the demand for this firm's product from d in Figure 5a to d' in Figure 5b. If firms in the industry had been making economic losses, some would leave in the long run and demand would increase for those that remained. Long-run equilibrium with freedom of entry will be reached with the firms maximizing profit ($MR = MC$) and zero economic profit ($\overline{P}' = AC = LRAC$) as in Figure 5b.

There are some important differences between the long-run equilibrium with zero profit in imperfect competition and long-run equilibrium with zero profit in perfect competition. Because perfect competitors are price takers, long-run equilibrium is reached with $\overline{P} = MR = MC = AC = LRAC$. Community welfare is maximized because $\bar{P} = MC$, and the firms produce at the minimum points on their AC and $LRAC$ curves because $MC = AC = LRAC$.

Figure 5 Short-Run vs. Long-Run Equilibrium

(a) Short-Run (b) Long-Run

In Figure 5b, however, things are quite different. First of all, there is a welfare loss compared with perfect competition because price exceeds the marginal cost of the last unit produced. Secondly, since the firm is producing along the downward-sloping portion of the AC curve, it is underutilizing its capacity. Finally, since the firm (and others in the industry, if this is a typical firm) is producing along the downward-sloping portion of its $LRAC$ curve, it is smaller than the most efficient size. A monopolist or a firm in imperfect competition with barriers against entry *might* produce where AC and $LRAC$ are at their minimum points. However, where there is imperfect competition and freedom of entry—as in Figure 5b—the firm *can't* do this.

In most imperfectly competitive industries, legal or economic barriers against entry protect the firms and enhance their chances of earning economic profits in the long run. The prohibitive financial barriers against the entry of a new automobile company, for example, protect the firms in the industry from entrants. "Fast-food" franchises, on the other hand, are relatively inexpensive (especially when compared to the cost of a new automobile company), and when "fast-food" restaurants in an area earn economic profits, others are attracted into the market—as a drive down a highway in any reasonably heavily populated area will show.

Oligopoly: Competition Among the Few

Oligopoly is a special and important case of imperfect competition.

- **Oligopoly** refers to control of an industry by a few firms.

Oligopoly is the market structure of many of our basic industries. In Table 1, the industries with the highest concentration ratios tend to be the most clearly oligopolistic.

Interdependence and Strategic Decision Making

In an oligopoly, each firm is large enough relative to the market that its actions have a clear impact on other firms in the market. Each firm, then, must consider the effects of its actions on other firms in the industry, as well as the possible reactions of other firms. Thus, firms in an oligopolistic industry have a common interest in reducing the uncertainty surrounding price and output decisions and the reactions of other firms.

For example, let's return to Crazy Carl and Honest John, and assume that they are the only used-car dealers in the market. (This is a special type of oligopoly called **duopoly**—two sellers.) In Figure 6, the two dealers initially sell at the same price—$P_c = P_j$.

At P_j, however, Honest John isn't maximizing his profit because his marginal cost (MC_j) is smaller than his marginal revenue (MR_j). To maximize profit, Honest John lowers his price to $\overline{P}_j$ and increases his sales to $\overline{q}_j$ where $MR_j = MC_j$.

Honest John's used cars are a close substitute for Crazy Carl's, so Crazy Carl's demand will fall from d_c to d_c', and his marginal revenue shifts to MR_c' in Figure 6. Now Crazy Carl has to adjust his price and

Figure 6 Price War

sales to maximize his profit. He lowers his price to $\bar{P}_c'$ and adjusts sales to $\bar{q}_c'$ where $MR_c' = MC_c$. So, Honest John's actions have had an impact on Crazy Carl, forcing him to alter his price and sales. This is only the beginning!

When Crazy Carl lowers his price to $\bar{P}_c'$, Honest John's demand and marginal revenue curves shift to the left to d_j' and MR_j', since Crazy Carl's used cars are a close substitute for Honest John's. Honest John will now have to adjust his price and sales *again* to maximize his profit where $MC_j = MR_j'$—at $\bar{P}_j'$ and $\bar{q}_j'$. Crazy Carl's demand and marginal curves shift to the left again, requiring him to adjust his price and sales again, which in turn shifts Honest John's demand and marginal revenue curves to the left again, etc., etc.

When Honest John first lowered his price to maximize his own profit, he set off a series of reactions which could be unfavorable for both firms. Prices might fall until one or both of the firms were forced to leave the market. At least, the *price war* initiated by Honest John's cut in price could cause substantial economic losses—or reductions in profit—until the price stabilized again. With these possible results in mind, *each firm has to consider the possible impact of its price and output decisions on the other and the possible reaction of the other firm.*

The *Kinked* Demand Curve

Existing theories of oligopoly don't give a "neat" picture of oligopolists' behavior, and each theory has some shortcomings. This doesn't mean that economics can't tell us anything about oligopoly. The answers just aren't very neat. The standard textbook explanation of oligopoly pricing is the **kinked demand curve**, introduced by Paul Sweezy in 1939. The theory of the kinked demand curve has been remarkably durable, in spite of some significant shortcomings as an explanation of oligopoly behavior.

This model sees the oligopolist as facing *two demand curves* at the existing price of its product. In Figure 7, the oligopolist sees itself on demand curves d_1 and d_2 at its initial price of $\bar{P}_0 = \$85$. The two demand curves represent different expectations concerning the reactions of other firms in the industry to a change in this firm's price. If the firm doesn't expect any other firms in the industry to follow a change in its price, it sees itself as being on d_1. The other demand curve, d_2, reflects this firm's expectation that all other firms in the industry would follow an increase or decrease in its price.

The "kinked demand curve" arises because the oligopolist is basically pessimistic. The firm assumes that *no other firms will follow if it raises its price*, and it will be on the more elastic d_1 if it raises its price. On the other hand, the firm assumes that *all other firms will follow it in a price reduction*, so it faces the less elastic d_2 for price reductions. In short, the firm's demand curve is d_1 for prices above \$85 and d_2 for prices below \$85.

Figure 7 *Kinked* **Demand Curve**

Since the firm is on two demand curves at $\bar{P}_0$, marginal revenue has two values at this price and output $\bar{q}_0$. MR_1 is the marginal revenue curve corresponding to d_1, and MR_2 is the marginal revenue curve corresponding to d_2. The firm sees its marginal revenue as MR_1 above $85 and MR_2 below $85. The firm will seek to maximize its profit, and to do this it must produce where $MR = MC$. However, at the price $\bar{P}_0 = \$85$ and quantity $\bar{q}_0 = 150$, MR is indeterminate between $30 on MR_2 and $70 on MR_1. If the MC curve lies between MR_1 and MR_2, the firm won't alter its price or its output in response to changes in costs. If the curve shifted from MC to MC' or to MC'', the firm wouldn't alter price or output.

The kinked demand curve helps to explain two important characteristics of oligopoly—the interdependence of firms' price and output decisions and the relative stability of prices in oligopolistic industries compared with prices in industries characterized by atomistic competition. The kink exists because the firm recognizes and considers the interdependence between its decisions and the decisions of other firms in the industry. The prediction that oligopolistic prices tend to be more rigid than in competitive markets is generally borne out by the evidence, although there is some disagreement among economists concerning the degree of price rigidity in oligopoly compared with other market structures.

The kinked demand curve suffers from some serious shortcomings as "the" theory of oligopoly, however. First of all, it doesn't explain how the original price was determined. It would help if a theory of oligopoly pricing could explain how the price got there in the first place, but the kinked demand curve doesn't.

Secondly, the kinked demand curve theory is based on simplistic assumptions concerning the expected responses of other firms. The firm in Figure 7 expects an all-or-nothing response from other firms in the industry—*all* firms will follow a price reduction, and *no* firms will follow a price increase. In fact, there are many possible responses between these extremes. Some firms may follow a price increase as well as a price decrease, some firms may follow neither a price increase nor a price decrease, and still others will follow the pattern assumed in the "kinked demand curve."

If the firm sees many possible reactions by other firms, many demand curves would have to be drawn through P_0, and MR would have many possible values at P_0. The "kinked demand curve" is cumbersome enough *with* the assumption of an "all-or-nothing" response by other firms! Because of such problems with the kinked demand curve, some economists have suggested other, simpler explanations of the behavior of prices in oligopolistic industries.

The Cost of Changing Prices

Many oligopolistic firms are very large enterprises which produce many different products and have extensive price lists. For small changes in costs, it may be cheaper for the firm to absorb the change without altering its entire price list, which could be a very expensive process. This is certainly a simple enough explanation of oligopoly price behavior, but it only explains price rigidities for small cost changes in firms with very extensive price lists.

Some firms with very large price lists cut the cost of changing prices by publishing index numbers that change all prices by the same percentage. A firm that produces hundreds of machines and parts, for example, can change the prices of all machines and parts in its catalog simply by revising the index. An announced index of 150 means that all of the firm's previously published prices have been raised by 50 percent, or that all revised prices are 150 percent of the published prices. A machine with a listed price of $1,000 would have a new price of $1,000 × 1.50 = $1,500. The index thus obviously reduces the cost of revising hundreds of prices and publishing new catalogs, and also announces the firm's new prices to its competitors in the industry.[1]

---

1. I am indebted to Professor Bruce T. Allen of Michigan State University for this example.

Formal Collusion and Cartels

The term **collusion** refers to agreements among firms in an industry on price or output. In its extreme form, collusion takes the form of a **cartel** in which firms agree formally to behave as a single monopoly to maximize joint profit and then decide how output and profit will be divided among members of the cartel.

Return again to Honest John and Crazy Carl. Tired of competition, threats of competition, and continual efforts to guess what the other is going to do, they decide to form a cartel. They agree to charge a common price that maximizes their joint profit, and to sell the quantities dictated by the cartel. In Figure 8, the cartel faces a single market demand curve (D) and marginal revenue curve (MR) rather than individual demand curves. The firms will produce a joint output, Q^*_{j+c}, where their joint marginal cost (MC_{j+c}) equals the marginal revenue from the last unit produced (MR) and will sell at a common price of P^*. The joint marginal cost curve (MC_{j+c}) is the sum of the quantities produced by both firms at any given MC—not the sum of the marginal costs of the firms in producing any given output.

The firms have to decide how the total output for the market will be split between them. One way to do this would be for each firm to produce where its MC equals the MR from the last unit sold on the market. If they did this, Honest John would produce and sell q_j^* where $MC_j = MR$.

Cartels eliminate the uncertainty of the price and output decisions of the firms in the industry, but cartels are rare. For one thing, in

Figure 8 Cartel

Used cars per week

the United States, cartels are illegal and a formal cartel isn't easy to disguise. More importantly, there is an incentive for some (or all) individual members of the cartel to cheat or *chisel*. In Figure 9, for example, Honest John isn't maximizing profit by abiding by the cartel agreement on price P^* and output q_j^*. If he lowered his price to $\overline{P}$ and increased quantity to $\overline{q}_j$, his profit would increase from π^* to π. One way he could do this secretly would be to offer his customers under-the-table discounts or "kickbacks." Generally, cartels are stable arrangements only if supported by some outside authority or if the costs of not belonging (such as uncertainty) are worth more than the loss of profit by belonging to the cartel and abiding by the agreement.

Figure 9 "Chiseling"

Used cars per week

Close-up

Cartels: The Shakiest of Marriages

Until the Arab oil producers imposed a boycott on oil shipments to the U.S. in 1973, most Americans gave little thought to cartels and probably weren't even aware of the existence of the Organization of Petroleum Exporting Countries (OPEC). Since the oil boycott, however, we have moved nearly to the opposite extreme in our attitude toward cartels and see them as the driving force in the world economy. Of course, OPEC is too significant to ignore as a world economic force because of the critical importance of oil. On the other hand, it's wrong to attribute too much power to cartels (even OPEC).

In fact, cartels are unstable arrangements because they require at least some members to cut back on output and sacrifice profit in order to maximize the cartel's joint profit. In the 1950s, there was a *de facto* (and illegal) cartel arrangement in the electrical generating equipment industry. Even before the conspirators were caught and convicted, the cartel had been through frequent periods of conflict, breakdown, and price wars as a result of individual members trying to cheat the cartel by increasing output and sales.

Even OPEC's power depends heavily on the willingness of the largest producers—Saudi Arabia, Kuwait, Iran (except in 1978-79 because of political strife), and the Arab Emirates—to hold down production. The reason that the large countries tend to be the moderates in OPEC price discussions is their interest in being able to sell larger outputs of oil. During periods of abundant supply, the cracks within OPEC start to show and to widen. In periods of tight supply, or when the outside forces that hold the cartel together are strong, OPEC's solidarity is much greater. In 1979, for example, OPEC was relatively stable because the oil glut of 1977 was gone, Iranian production fell off sharply following a revolution, and the Arab members of OPEC shared a common hostility to Israel and the treaty between Egypt and Israel.

CIPEC is an international alliance of copper exporting countries. The small producers in the Third World have been trying for some time to get CIPEC to set a common price and output restrictions and operate as an international cartel similar to OPEC. However, Chile and the other large producers have refused to reach such an agreement because it would limit their ability to determine their own prices and levels of production. If such a cartel were to be formed in copper, the conflicts of interest between the large and small producers would be a constant source of instability.[1]

---

1. The facts on CIPEC are from Alan Spence, "Free Markets, Not Producer Agreements," *Wall Street Journal*, December 7, 1978.

Informal Collusion: Gentlemen's Agreements and Price Leadership

In the late nineteenth century, Elbert Gary, the president of U.S. Steel, held frequent meetings in his home with the heads of other steel companies. At these meetings, or "Gary Dinners," the steel companies agreed on the prices of steel. For each of the companies, the "gentlemen's agreements" eliminated much of the uncertainty concerning the pricing decisions of other firms in the industry.

Price fixing, formal or informal, is illegal under our antitrust laws, and the definition of illegal activity even extends to communication among the top managers of firms in an industry. In one of the most famous antitrust cases in recent years, some executives in the electrical equipment industry actually served prison terms for illegal price-fixing activities.

One type of informal collusion is fairly common in oligopolistic industries—**price leadership**. With price leadership, one firm in the industry—usually the most powerful—is regarded as the price leader. The price leader can initiate a price change which other firms follow, or it can veto attempts by other firms to change prices. Price leadership has the dual advantages of reducing uncertainty and being almost impossible to detect.

For many years, U.S. Steel was the price leader in the steel industry. If U.S. Steel changed its prices, the other steel companies generally followed suit. If another company announced a price change and U.S. Steel didn't go along, none of the other firms did either, and the original price change was canceled.

What keeps the firms from ignoring the price leader and acting on their own? In the first place, price leadership reduces each firm's uncertainty about the pricing behavior of others in the industry, and breaking away from the pattern set by the price leader may initiate a general price war in the industry. Also, the price leader and other firms may retaliate against potential price competitors.

A firm's decision to follow the leader or ignore the price leadership pattern requires the firm to calculate the probable costs and benefits of each course of action. Staying with the pattern reduces uncertainty, but may result in a loss of potential profit. Breaking away from the pattern may increase a firm's potential profit, but it also increases uncertainty and risk.

As a general explanation of oligopoly pricing, price leadership has some significant advantages over the "kinked demand curve." For one thing, there is no cumbersome analytical device based on simplistic assumptions concerning expectations. In addition, empirical evidence strongly suggests that oligopolistic firms do in fact follow each other in price increases as well as price cuts. This is consistent with some type of informal collusion, such as price leadership, rather than with the kinked demand curve, which suggests that firms only follow each other in price cuts.

Close-up

How "Kinky" Is Oligopoly Demand?

The kinked demand curve as an explanation of oligopoly behavior appeared first in the economic literature in 1939. In 1947, Professor George J. Stigler of the University of Chicago published a critical article that questioned the validity of the kinked demand curve as an explanation of oligopoly behavior. Stigler used examples from the 1920s and 1930s that questioned the very existence of the kink. Who is right today? Have oligopoly markets become more "kinky" over the past 30 years? The following examples are from news items which appeared in the *Wall Street Journal* during September and October of 1978.

In September 1978, Alcan Aluminum announced a price increase on aluminum ingot. The Aluminum Company of America (Alcoa) refused to go along with the price increase, and this refusal put pressure on Alcan to return to the original price. This case is consistent with the kinked demand curve model, but it also is consistent with some form of collusion or price leadership pattern.

On September 6, 1978, Alcoa increased its price on beverage-can sheet by 5.5 percent. On September 13, 1978, Alcan raised its price on beverage-can sheet by 5 percent.

On September 12, 1978, Asarco, Inc., and NL Industries, Inc., raised the price of lead to 35¢ per pound. On September 14, 1978, Amax, Inc., Bunker Hill Co., Homestead Mining Co., and St. Joe Minerals Corp. increased lead prices to 35¢ per pound.

In October 1978, General Motors raised the price of its 1979 models by an average of 4.1 percent. Ford Motor Co. increased its price by an average of 4.2 percent. Chrysler Corp. followed with an average price rise of 4.2 percent.

In short, as in Stigler's and other more exhaustive studies, the behavior of oligopolists in making price changes can't be explained in the majority of cases by the kinked demand curve model. Apparent kinks in oligopoly demand curves can, however, be explained in terms of collusion or price leadership.

The efficiency of production in perfect competition rests heavily on the assumption that firms maximize profit. Even in the monopoly case, profit-maximization implies production of the monopolist's equilibrium output at the lowest possible cost to maximize profit. In markets where each firm tries to guess what the others are going to do, however, firms seek the best combination of uncertainty and profit, rather than simply maximum profit. This goal in turn may weaken the incentive for efficiency inherent in profit-maximizing behavior.

How Imperfect Competitors "Compete"

Fear of adverse reactions of other firms in the industry or a general price war, or simply the desire to minimize uncertainty, tends to discourage vigorous price competition in oligopolistic industries. As a result, imperfectly competitive firms often try to attract buyers to their products through devices other than lower prices: superior quality and service, advertising, innovation, or even outright deception.

Quality and Service Competition

"Build a better mousetrap," goes the old bromide, "and the world will beat a path to your door." Differences in the quality of products and customers' awareness of these differences may cause buyers to beat a path to the sellers of better automobiles, apparel, appliances, cereal, industrial machinery, and even mousetraps.

From the seller's point of view, quality competition increases the demand for its product without initiating a potentially destructive price war in the industry. From the buyers' point of view, quality competition can improve the quality of products, and can thus be beneficial even if the price of the product doesn't fall.

Customer service is another constructive form of nonprice competition. Drugstores offer free delivery service, free tax records, and other services to customers. At least a few gasoline stations wash windshields, check tire pressure, and perform other services along with the sale of gasoline. A large automobile dealer in the Washington, D.C., area offers a laundromat, a barbershop, transportation, and a T.V. lounge to its repair service customers.

By differentiating quality and customer service, imperfect competitors differentiate their products and try to increase demand. The same appliance or automobile from different dealers may be seen as quite different products by consumers if the quality of customer service differs. Consumers can thus choose among products or dealers to get their best combination of price, product quality, and service. This choice doesn't exist in perfect competition—where the products of individual firms are assumed to be identical in all respects—nor in a monopoly where there is only one seller.

Advertising and Product Differentiation

Some differences among the products of different firms in an imperfectly competitive industry are real: organizations like Consumers' Union work to point out these differences to potential buyers. But imperfect competitors may also use advertising and marketing techniques to exaggerate small differences or even to create nonexistent differences in the eyes of the consumer. The actual differences among different brands of the same product—deodorants, detergents, shampoos, corn flakes, furniture polishes, political candidates—are often not nearly as great as the advertisements suggest.

In some cases, advertising even tries to create differences among brands of products that really are identical. In the bleach case discussed in Chapter 6, advertising was able to shift the demands for Clorox and Purex, despite the fact that both are 5 percent solutions of sodium hypochlorite. The situation is similar for many pharmaceuticals. Prescription drugs are more expensive when prescribed by brand names or trade names than when prescribed by their chemical or *generic* names. The pharmaceutical firms claim that brand name compounds are of higher clinical quality than generic drugs, but this assertion has been challenged by government agencies and consumer groups in recent years.

Close-up

An Aspirin Is an Aspirin Is an Aspirin

Several years ago, Bayer aspirin ran a series of T.V. ads in which a procession of obviously unenlightened characters proclaimed that "the earth is flat" (as Columbus pulled out of port), that "man will never fly," that "women shouldn't vote," and, finally, that "all aspirin is alike." A scholarly gentleman holding an impressive-looking folder replied "bunk" to all of these obviously neanderthal notions.

In fact, except for the wrapping, all aspirin *is* chemically identical—crystals of salicylic acid ($C_9H_8O_4$). Furthermore, the U.S. Food and Drug Administration (FDA) has established quality standards for aspirin. The only differences are those asserted by the "national brand" producers (Bayer and St. Joseph) concerning the "clinical" quality of the aspirin.

Some patented analgesics are basically aspirin under an assumed name. Anacin, for example, correctly claims that it contains more of the leading pain reliever than other products. What is the "leading pain reliever"? Aspirin. An Anacin tablet contains 400 mg. of aspirin (and a little caffeine), compared with 325 mg. of aspirin in the standard aspirin tablet.

There is one important difference among different brands of aspirin—price. The heavily advertised "national brands" have higher prices than store brands of aspirin. Successful advertising and promotion have created differences in the minds of consumers that are absent in the products themselves.

Some advertising provides important benefits for consumers, informing us of the availability of a product and providing useful information on its characteristics. Some advertising has intrinsic entertainment value (such as the performances of the late Morris the Cat), or even artistic value (such as some of the advertising work done by great photographers). Our lives would be duller if all we had were want ads, or if we bought everything under the same conditions under which grain is bought and sold at grain elevators. It is important to realize, however, that the goal of the advertiser is to create demand for his product, and that advertising adds to the cost and hence the price of the product.

An effective advertising campaign increases the demand for an imperfect competitor's product, as in Figure 10. The advertising campaign shifts the firm's demand and marginal revenue curves from d to MR in Figure 10a to d' and MR' in Figure 10b.

Large-scale advertising is expensive, however, increasing the firm's costs as well as the demand for its product. Suppose that the

Figure 10 Effects of Advertising

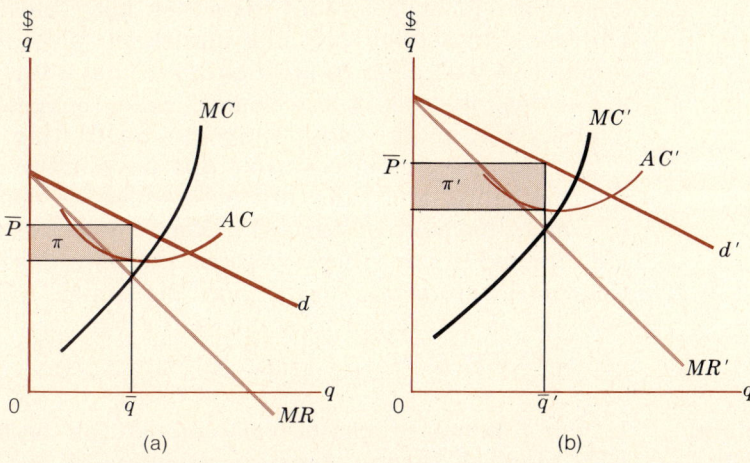

firm in Figure 10 purchases a fixed quantity of T.V. time and newspaper advertising space. This is an additional fixed cost, and it shifts the AC curve from AC in Figure 10a to AC′ in Figure 10b without affecting the MC curve.

Now look at the net effect of the advertising campaign in Figure 10. Output increases from $\bar{q}$ to $\bar{q}'$ because of the increased demand. The firm's profit is greater as a result of the advertising campaign—note the shaded areas in Figure 10a and 10b. From the consumer's side, however, the price is higher as a result of advertising—from $\bar{P}$ to $\bar{P}'$.

If the other firms in the industry engage in similar advertising campaigns, the effect of any one firm's advertising will decline. As a result, firms may increase their spending on advertising, adding even more to the cost of the products. Keep this fact in mind the next time you hear someone extol the virtues of "free" commercial television.

Deception and Consumerism

Much of the consumerism that has grown up since the 1960s is the result of some of the less savory forms of nonprice competition in imperfectly competitive markets.

In their zeal to attract customers and increase sales and profits through aggressive advertising and marketing, some firms resort to fraud and deception. Deceptive packaging—large packages holding small quantities of everything from children's toys to cereal—leads consumers to expect more than they get. Television advertising of children's toys often presents unrealistic pictures of the advertised product. It isn't clear to most children that a toy car may travel only a few feet instead of the several miles suggested by low camera angles, wide-angle lenses, slow-motion filming, and spliced films.

Competitive pressures in retailing have led to a number of deceptive marketing and sales practices—such as the "bait and switch," in which items are advertised at very low prices and then customers are directed to other items because the advertised item is "sold out." Consumer protection laws and consumer interest groups have emerged as a reaction to some of the excesses that competition for sales has produced.

Innovation and Competition

In the folklore of capitalism, competition breeds innovation and technological change. Owner-entrepreneurs are constantly looking for ways to improve their products and produce at lower costs. Innovations in products or production technique are imitated by others in the industry, and eventually consumers benefit from more goods at lower cost.

There are, however, plausible arguments that innovation and technological change aren't associated with competitive industries at all, but with large firms that have monopoly power. This is the basic view of such writers as Professor John Kenneth Galbraith and the late Joseph A. Schumpeter. According to this line of argument, the costs of research and development (R & D) and of the innovations themselves, as well as the time and cost required to implement technological innovations, are far too great for small firms to undertake. Only large firms in concentrated industries, it is asserted, have the resources to finance, implement, and bear the risks associated with technological change.

In fact, there isn't a neat general relationship between market structure and innovation—except that small firms in competitive industries and very large firms protected by high entry barriers into their industry do not tend to be very active innovators.

Some innovation and R & D are too expensive for all but the largest firms—such as developing new types of commercial aircraft—but not all of it. In the 1960s, for example, the small Control Data Corporation made significant innovations in computers that allowed it to compete successfully in an industry dominated by the giant IBM Corporation.[2]

---

2. For an excellent discussion of the relationship between market structure and innovation, see F. M. Scherer, *Industrial Market Structure and Economic Performance* (Chicago: Rand McNally, 1973), Chapter 15.

Galbraith and others have argued that oligopoly is most conducive to innovation in products or in production technique. With price competition minimized, innovation is an important and attractive form of nonprice competition. In addition, large oligopolistic firms have the resources to finance extensive innovative activity. This view is plausible, but there isn't overwhelming evidence to support it.

In some cases, such as automobiles, the costs of changing the product—such as major changes in cars or power plants—are so high that they discourage innovations. The important innovations in U.S. automobiles since the mid-1970s have come in reaction to external forces—the oil boycott, continuing energy problems, the popularity of energy-efficient imports, and government regulations on fuel efficiency and pollution. From the late 1950s through the mid-1970s, the innovations in American autos were size, accessories, and larger engines to power the large accessory-laden vehicles.

The technologically moribund American steel industry is another piece of sobering evidence for those who associate oligopoly with innovation and technological progress. Of the major innovations in steelmaking since World War II, none has been made by a U.S. firm. Instead, American firms have sought government protection from the imported steel produced by "unfair" foreign competitors.

The determinants of technological change and innovation are too complex to associate them with a particular type of market structure. To do so would ignore too many things—creativity and luck, for example—that aren't unique to any one market structure. Except for identifying certain types of firms and certain market characteristics in which innovation isn't very likely, the evidence doesn't point to a general relationship between market structure and technological progress.

Summary

1. **Imperfect competition** refers to the market structures that lie between the extremes of perfect competition and pure monopoly.
2. Imperfectly competitive firms aren't price takers, but the actions of other firms in the market affect each firm's demand.
3. Short-run equilibrium in imperfect competition is reached when the firms in the industry are producing where $MR = MC$. There may be economic profit, economic losses, or zero economic profit in imperfect competition in the short run. If there is freedom of entry, economic profit will be driven to zero, but if there are barriers to entry economic profit will be zero or greater in the long run.
4. **Oligopoly** is a special case of imperfect competition in which the market is controlled by a few large firms. Each firm has to consider the effects of its decisions on other firms and the possible reactions of other firms.
5. To reduce uncertainty, oligopolistic firms may form **cartels**, enter into collusive arrangements (both illegal in the U.S.), or follow a **price leadership** pattern.

6. Nonprice competition—quality, service, and product differentiation are common in imperfectly competitive markets.
7. There is no neat, general relationship between market structure and innovations in products or production methods.

Concepts for Review

imperfect competition
monopolistic competition
oligopoly
concentration ratio
kinked demand curve
collusion
cartel
"gentlemen's agreement"
price leadership
price war
quality competition
service competition

Questions

1. Why do we consider a small retail store an imperfect competitor, while a single farm with much larger assets and sales is considered a perfect competitor?
2. In perfect competition, freedom of entry leads to long-run equilibrium in the industry with firms earning zero economic profit, producing where price equals marginal cost, and producing their most efficient output. Compare these results with long-run equilibrium in an imperfectly competitive industry with freedom of entry. Why are the differences significant economically?
3. At various times in the 1970s, the automobile companies offered cash *rebates* or refunds to buyers of cars. Why didn't the firms simply lower automobile prices to increase sales?
4. The kinked demand curve is one of the possible explanations of oligopoly price and output behavior.
   a. Explain what the kinked demand curve is, and what is assumed about the oligopolist that gives the demand curve its kink. How does the kink affect the firm's marginal revenue curve?
   b. What general predictions follow from the kinked demand curve concerning price and output in oligopoly? Explain.
   c. Evaluate the kinked demand curve as a general explanation of oligopoly behavior.
5. What are cartels? How do they operate, and what do they try to do? What factors contribute to the stability or instability of cartel arrangements?
6. Suppose that you tried to get the students in your classes to get together and agree to keep examination scores low so that "curving" the scores would give everybody a better grade with less effort.
   a. What kind of arrangement is this? (Hint: "Clever" isn't a sufficient answer.)
   b. Would this arrangement be more likely to work in a class of 20 students or a lecture class of 200 students?
   c. Which students will be most likely to comply with the agreement? Which will be the least likely to comply?
   d. What is the relationship between this arrangement and the instability of cartels?

7. For many years, U.S. Steel was clearly the price leader in the steel industry. In the farm machinery industry, Deere & Co. is generally recognized as the price leader by the other firms in the industry.
   a. What is price leadership?
   b. Why would firms in the industry "follow the leader" even if it didn't maximize the followers' profit?
   c. How does price leadership differ from formal collusion or cartel arrangements? What are the advantages of price leadership?
8. Evaluate the ability of the kinked demand curve, collusion, and price leadership to explain each of the following.
   a. In the 1950s, American electrical generating equipment firms agreed on common prices for their products.
   b. In the fall of 1978, Copper Range Co., Louisiana Land & Exploration Co., and Texas Gulf raised copper prices to 73¢ a pound.
   c. In September 1978, Deere & Co., Allis-Chalmers, and International Harvester Co. raised prices on tractors.
   d. In 1977, the members of OPEC agreed to raise the price of exported oil by 10 percent.
   e. After deregulation of air fares in 1976 and 1977, all major carriers reduced air fares dramatically.
9. How many examples of nonprice competition have you observed? How do the types of nonprice competition you've observed affect consumers?
10. Why are advertising and marketing promotions likely to be more prevalent in imperfect competition than in monopoly or perfectly competitive markets?
11. Prescription drugs can be prescribed by their "brand names" or by their chemical (or "generic") names. Almost without exception, the brand name prescriptions are more expensive than generic prescriptions for the same drug. The large pharmaceutical firms that produce the brand name drugs also manufacture the same drugs under generic names.
    a. How do you explain economically the difference in price between generic and brand name prescription drugs?
    b. In response to legislation encouraging substitution of generic drugs for brand name drugs, the major drug companies began advertising their brand name drugs more aggressively and began marketing "branded generics" (generic drugs branded with the company name). How do you explain these actions? What effect could they have?

15

Market Power and the Role of Government

Preview: In monopolistic and imperfectly competitive markets, concentrations of market power create potential conflicts between the economic interests of firms and the economic welfare of society. Reducing such conflicts is one of the primary roles the government plays in the economy. In this chapter, we'll explore three alternative tools the government can use to deal with undesirable concentrations of market power: **antitrust**, **public regulation**, and **nationalization**.

Market power is the ability of individual firms to affect the market in which they operate. Concentration of market power is a fact of modern economic life with some important consequences.

At first glance, one might conclude that concentration of market power is not a growing trend. The average concentration ratio for all manufacturing industries hasn't changed much over the past 30 years. Some industries—such as malt beverages, an industry dear to the author's heart—have become more concentrated. Others, such as chemicals and related products, have become less concentrated.

But simple concentration ratios actually tend to hide the trend toward greater concentration of production in the largest firms. Table 1 shows the percentage of all value added (a measure of production) in manufacturing by the largest companies. The main reason this increasing concentration of market power in the largest companies is hidden by industry concentration ratios is the growth

Table 1 Percent of Value Added by Largest Manufacturing Firms, U.S., 1947–1972

	Percent of Value Added in Manufacturing by			
Year	Largest 50 Firms	Largest 100 Firms	Largest 150 Firms	Largest 200 Firms
1947	17	23	27	30
1954	23	30	34	37
1963	25	33	37	41
1972	25	33	39	43

Source: U.S. Department of Commerce, Bureau of the Census, *1972 Census of Manufacturers*.

of the **conglomerate merger**, which merges firms in different industries together as subsidiaries of a single conglomerate firm. The Transamerica Corporation, for example, owns such diverse firms as the Transamerica Insurance Company, Transnational Airlines, and United Artists Pictures. Montgomery Ward & Co. is now a subsidiary of the Mobil Corporation. Esmark Industries owns a number of subsidiaries ranging from the Greyhound Bus Co. and Swift & Co. meat packers to Playtex Co.

When firms have market power, there are potential conflicts between the economic interests of the firms, economic efficiency, and community economic welfare. These potential problems have been discussed in the analysis of monopoly and imperfect competition—prices above marginal costs, the possibility of economic profit in the long run, and the possibility that firms will produce above the minimum points on their short-run and long-run average cost curves.

Concentration of market power in the hands of large and powerful firms has some important political consequences as well. Large firms generally have the resources to protect their interests by influencing political leaders. The influence of multinational corporations has even extended to foreign governments. An American aircraft company recently admitted to carrying the Vice-President of France on its payroll. Deals between the Japanese government and American corporations and between Prince Bernard of the Netherlands and American corporations created governmental crises in these countries.

Because of the obvious economic, social, and political impact of concentrations of market power, measures are necessary to control the market power of firms or the degree to which firms may exercise their market power. This chapter takes a brief look at three alternative ways of dealing with market power—antitrust, regulation, and nationalization. Each approach has some unique advantages and some unique problems, and choosing the best approach involves value judgments.

Antitrust Policy

Perhaps the dominant means of limiting market power in the United States today is through *antitrust*.

Antitrust policies are policies aimed at preventing or breaking up concentrations of market power.

Antitrust Laws

The late nineteenth century was a period of dramatic change in the American economy. One of the most significant developments in this period was the rapid growth of large corporations—United States Steel, Standard Oil, the du Pont chemical empire, and the railroads. These firms had substantial financial resources, political influence, and, in some industries, the power to destroy all competition. By the end of the century, there was widespread public sentiment for breaking up some of the large corporations and combinations of corporations ("trusts").

Between 1890 and 1914, the three acts that form the cornerstone of our antitrust law were passed by Congress and signed into law—the **Sherman Antitrust Act** (1890), the **Clayton Antitrust Act** (1914), and the **Federal Trade Commission Act** (1914). The antitrust legislation that has followed these acts basically elaborates, clarifies, and makes the provisions of these acts more specific.

The Sherman Act is simple and straightforward. Based upon the British Common Law tradition against "restraint of trade" and "conspiracy to restrain trade," the Sherman Act outlaws "every contract combination in the form of a trust or otherwise, or conspiracy, in restraint of trade or commerce . . ." (Sec. 1), and makes it illegal to ". . . monopolize, or combine or conspire with any other person or persons, to monopolize any part of the trade or commerce among the several states, or with foreign nations . . ." (Sec. 2).

Early antitrust policies weren't very effective in stemming the growth of the large corporations or concentration of market power. The problem wasn't the legislation as much as the failure of the government to enforce the laws vigorously.

The Clayton Act of 1914 was built on the Sherman Act. The Clayton Act specified the kinds of business behavior that would be interpreted as monopolizing an industry, or "restraining trade." Furthermore, the Clayton Act outlawed practices that might *lead to monopolization* as well as dealing with monopoly after the fact. More specifically, the Clayton Act outlawed certain kinds of price discrimination (mostly by wholesalers) that would give large firms a competitive advantage, prohibited one corporation from purchasing the stock of a competing corporation, and made it illegal for several firms in an industry to share the same board of directors (interlocking directorates). The act also contains one very broad prohibition against ". . . unfair methods of competition in commerce." The Clayton Act was tightened by the Celler-Kefauver Amendment to it in 1950.

The third piece of basic antitrust legislation, the Federal Trade Commission Act, was also enacted in 1914. This act defined a number of unfair business practices and prohibited "unfair methods of competition." In addition, the act set up the Federal Trade Commission (FTC) as a quasi-judicial body to enforce the Federal Trade Commission and Clayton Acts. The Sherman Act remained under the jurisdiction of the Antitrust Division of the Department of Justice.

The language of the antitrust laws emphasizes monopoly and monopolization, and in the early years, antitrust policy was aimed at monopolies and formal cartels ("trust-busting"). Over the years, however, further antitrust legislation has supplemented the Sherman, Clayton, and Federal Trade Commission Acts to give us a fairly specific and well-defined body of antitrust law, and has broadened the scope of antitrust activity to include the prevention of excessive concentration of market power in a few firms in an industry. The concentration ratios introduced in Chapter 14 are important criteria for the authorities in identifying possible areas in which antitrust laws are being violated and in which concentration is excessive.

"Workable Competition"

Modern antitrust policies seek to achieve something called *workable competition* in our imperfectly competitive economy. Workable competition sounds like a reasonable and desirable goal, but defining it in meaningful terms is difficult.

How much competition is *best* for society? We tend to be conditioned to think that more competition is better than less, unless it's more competition for the products and services that we happen to be selling. In some cases, however, competition leads to wasteful proliferation of firms, facilities, and products. Ironically, the pressures for fraud and deception are greatest in some of the most intensely competitive markets—such as retailing.

What kind of behavior is consistent with workable competition? *Predatory pricing* by a large firm to drive smaller competitors out of the market by temporarily cutting prices below cost isn't consistent with maintaining workable competition. However, it isn't always easy to distinguish predatory pricing from legitimate, vigorous price competition.

In short, there's no simple and straightforward answer to the basic questions of what kind and how much competition is consistent with workable competition. Establishing workable competition as a goal for antitrust policy requires answers to these very basic questions.

Problems of Antitrust

Although antitrust remains the predominant means of limiting market power, there are a number of practical and analytical problems associated with its use.

Antitrust enforcement costs can be high. The Justice Department and the FTC maintain large research and legal staffs, and even with such large staffs, the agencies sometimes can't allocate the same resources and funds to prosecution of antitrust cases that the large firms can allocate to the defense.

Antitrust cases often take a long time to resolve—to compile evidence, to bring cases to court, and, if there is a conviction, to go through the long appeals procedures. For example, the government brought suit against International Business Machines (IBM) for monopolizing the market in computers in 1969, but experts predict that the case won't be settled until the 1980s.

Close-up

The Wheels of Antitrust Justice Grind Exceedingly Slow

The 20 to 25 years it will take to dispose of the IBM case is perhaps unusually long, but long periods of time in antitrust litigation are the rule. In 1972, for example, the Federal Trade Commission brought an antitrust suit against the four major breakfast cereal firms for restricting competition. The case was delayed by legal maneuvers and the defendants' resistance to producing evidence. In 1978, the FTC dropped its charges against one of the firms (Quaker Oats Company). When the case was filed, it was expected that it wouldn't be resolved until 1982 or 1983. By the fall of 1978, complications surrounding the retirement of the FTC administrative judge in charge of the case raised the possibility that the case wouldn't be resolved until the late 1980s.

The ability of antitrust to control concentration of market power via conglomerate merger isn't clear. The legislation is vague on this point, and there have been some problems in blocking conglomerate mergers that threaten competition in the industries involved.

The economic effects of concentration and restraints on competition are crucial, but the disposition of antitrust cases rests on economic and legal interpretation by the courts. The judicial system is burdened enough without expecting judges to be economic experts, but strictly legal interpretations may lead to economically undesirable results—such as punishing efficient firms and raising costs to consumers in the interests of preserving competition.

Close-up

A Case of Mistaken Identity?

U.S. v. The New York Great Atlantic & Pacific Tea Co. (the "A & P case") is one of the classics in antitrust law. It illustrates the difficulty of attempting to distinguish between legitimate price competition and predatory pricing, the vagueness of the notion of workable competition, and the economic consequences of strictly legalistic interpretations of firms' behavior.

After reducing prices and cutting profit margins in the 1930's, A & P sought quantity discounts from its suppliers, and threatened to cease dealing with buyers that didn't give the discounts. These actions led to a conviction of A & P in 1949 for "monopolizing" the market in retail food sales. Most economists have been highly critical of this decision.

Retail food sales was (and remains) a highly price competitive market. Seeking quantity discounts from suppliers and cutting prices are perfectly consistent with legitimate price competition—unless a firm lowers its prices far below cost temporarily to drive a weaker competitor out of the market to gain a monopoly position. A & P's prices were above cost, however, and the firm sought to increase its profit by increasing the volume of sales. Also, A & P accounted for only about 10 percent of retail food sales at the time. Its share of the retail sales market was 21 percent or below in every urban area, and reached 40 percent only in a few small towns. There were virtually no barriers to entry into retail food sales in the 1930s and 1940s.[1]

---

1. There are many good sources on the A & P case. Good, brief summaries can be found in F. M. Scherer, *Industrial Market Structure and Economic Performance* (Chicago: Rand McNally, 1973), p. 461; and Leonard Weiss, *Case Studies in American Industry*, 2nd edition (New York: Norton, 1971), pp. 247-249.

Breaking up *natural monopolies* in the interests of competition wouldn't be a desirable course, because it would eliminate the benefits of the natural monopolist's economies of scale. In Figure 1, for example, the monopolist would produce an equilibrium output of $\bar{Q}$, sell at a price of $\bar{P}$, and earn an economic profit shown by the shaded area. Now, suppose that the monopoly is broken up into a number of small firms, each of which would operate on the short-run average cost curve AC'. If the smaller firms operated as efficiently as they could and earned no economic profit, each would sell at a price of $\bar{P}_c$. In other words, the small firms would sell at a higher price than the monopolist because of economies of scale. Furthermore, there would have to be some restrictions in the long run to keep the firms from getting larger and more efficient!

Some critics of antitrust policies apply the natural monopoly argument to virtually all antitrust cases. In this context, antitrust is portrayed as punishing the most innovative and efficient firms,

Figure 1 Natural Monopoly vs. Competition

stifling the incentive for efficiency, and denying consumers the benefits of lower costs and lower prices. This argument is valid *if* there are economies of scale in production, and *if* these economies are passed on to consumers as lower prices. Obviously, these are big *if*'s.

Critics of the natural monopoly argument contend that as concentration increases and firms get larger, pricing and output decisions become more interdependent, and the common interest of firms in avoiding price wars may not (and probably will not) result in lower prices to buyers.

The apparent economies of scale of large firms in concentrated industries must be closely examined. It's one thing for a merged company to be more efficient in producing its goods. It's quite another if the cost savings are in advertising and marketing advantages over smaller firms. In 1967, the U.S. Supreme Court ruled against the merger of Clorox and Procter & Gamble largely on the grounds that the only savings were in advertising and marketing, and that the ability of the merged company to realize economies of scale in advertising would stifle competition in the already concentrated bleach industry.

With excessive concentration firms may avoid vigorous quality and service competition as well as vigorous price competition. If there are no close substitute goods produced by other industries, the incentive for production and profit innovation may be weakened with concentration.

Public Regulation

The scope of public regulation by local, state, and federal governments goes well beyond the pricing in natural monopolies discussed in Chapter 13. Pharmaceuticals, interstate trucking, interstate buses, airlines, and banking are all subject to some form of public regulation. Some regulations are aimed at minimizing such external social costs as pollution. Other are directed at the health and safety of workers and consumers. Still others are directed at market performance by regulating prices, entry, and standards of services or products.

Health and Safety Regulations

If new and untested products with potential health hazards are introduced and promoted, the results can be tragic. Shortly after the discovery of radium, for example, some patent drug companies added it to patent medicines as a miracle cure. Many of the so-called "female remedies" of the past century were generously laced with addictive narcotics. In the 1930s and 1940s, many shoe stores used unsafe X-ray machines to aid in fitting shoes. An anti-miscarriage drug, DES, has caused uterine cancers in the daughters of the women who took it.

Similarly tragic consequences can result if firms skimp on employee safety in order to gain a competitive edge. Unregulated and inadequately regulated working conditions have caused serious health problems for workers (lead poisoning, lung cancer, silicosis, and others). Numerous industrial disasters, such as the Triangle Shirtwaist Factory fire in 1911, in which over one hundred young female garment workers perished, could have been avoided with better regulation.

Health and safety regulations aren't free, however. There are enforcement costs, and compliance with regulations generally adds to the cost of production and thus to the prices paid by consumers. In addition, the resources allocated to enforcement and compliance have alternative uses, and society must bear an opportunity cost.

Regulations and Externalities

As was shown in Chapter 12, private markets do a rather poor job of assigning values to external social benefits and external social costs. Awareness of external social costs, in the form of environmental pollution in particular, has brought a number of regulations that seek to minimize these costs. Government agencies have established standards for noise pollution by cars, airplanes, and factories, have placed restrictions on dumping refuse into the air and water, and have required environmental impact studies for major public and private construction projects.

As with the health and safety regulations, regulations on acceptable levels of air and water pollution by factories, households, and communities, emissions controls on automobiles, and other environmental regulations involve substantial costs. We pay for the reduced emissions from our cars with lower performance and the cost of emission control systems. We pay for the pollution controls of industry and agriculture with higher prices on products. We pay for cleaner water with taxes for improved sewage and waste disposal systems. The old dictum that "there ain't such a thing as a free lunch" applies to environmental quality as well as to other scarce goods.

Regulation of Markets, Industries, and Firms

The economic regulations that have been the most controversial and under the closest scrutiny in recent years are those that regulate prices, quality of service, and entry of firms in specific industries. The first major regulatory agency charged with this type of regulation in the United States was the Interstate Commerce Commission (ICC), established in 1887 to regulate pricing and other practices of the railroads.

The ICC is still alive and well, regulating railroads, interstate buses, trucks, and other common carriers. It has been joined by an alphabet soup of regulatory agencies—the FCC (which regulates communications and the electronic media), the CAB (which regulates commercial air travel), the Federal Maritime Commission (which regulates maritime shipping), and others. In addition to the federal agencies, there are numerous state and local regulatory bodies that regulate building codes, public utilities, mass transit, etc.

Regulatory agencies were ostensibly established to protect the public from abuses of market power by the sellers in highly concentrated markets, to ensure minimum standards of performance, and to act as "watchdogs" over firms in regulated industries. If this is their purpose, their record has been far from acceptable.

Agencies have spent significant time and resources haggling over authority in areas of overlapping jurisdiction, or over new technological innovations where the regulatory authority isn't clear. For example, one of the more interesting innovations in transportation is the hover craft—a vehicle that travels on a cushion of air over land or water. Since it travels above ground, it might be classified as an aircraft and be subject to regulation by the Federal Aviation Agency (FAA) and the Civil Aeronautics Board (CAB). If it operated commercially over land in interstate commerce, it would be regulated by the Interstate Commerce Commission (ICC). If it crossed bodies of water, it could be classed as a maritime vessel and be subject to regulation by the Federal Maritime Commission. A colleague has suggested that a hover craft that operated commercially and crossed bridges over bodies of water that define state or international boundaries could be a regulatory nightmare (or dream, depending on how you choose to look at it). This frivolous, but not trivial, hypothetical example illustrates the potential for red tape and proliferation of regulations of dubious value in protecting the public interest.

Close-up

"Who's in Charge Here?" (Regulating the Safety of Kitty Litter Miners)

When Merle Travis wrote about the pain and dangers of mining in "Dark as a Dungeon Way Down in the Mine," it's clear what kind of mine he meant. When Congress passed legislation and established agencies to enforce mine safety standards, it's clear what it meant. However, when Southern Clay, Inc., learned that the federal Mine Safety and Health Administration (MSHA) had divined that it was subject to regulation as a mining operation, it was shocked. Southern Clay produces cat-box filler—"Kitty Litter." The image of miners risking life and limb to support the comfort of a few fat cats took on a new meaning.

Southern Clay was classified as a mine because it digs its own clay, which is the base of the cat litter, at its own quarry some distance from the factory. As a "mine," Southern Clay was required to provide mine safety training for all of its employees, even though their actual jobs bore no resemblance to mining.

In addition to producing a lot of tasteless jokes, the mine safety training involved costs—the costs of enforcing the rules by the MSHA and the cost to Southern Clay of freeing workers on company time to attend the training sessions. Southern Clay may be one of the few firms asking to be taken into the jurisdiction of another federal safety regulatory agency, OSHA.[1]

1. The facts on this "mine" are from Urban C. Lehner, "Just Who Regulates the Kitty Litter Factory?" *Wall Street Journal*, November 14, 1978.

The most serious economic problem with regulation is that it frequently prohibits competition in industries that need it. This has the effect of protecting the firms in the industry from competition at a cost to the community in the form of inefficiency, high prices, and monopoly power of the protected firms.

Interstate trucking, for example, is regulated by the ICC. ICC licensing of truckers who operate in interstate commerce serves as a barrier to entry. Interstate trucking rates are regulated and truckers can't compete with each other on the basis of price. Some regulations require a number of inefficient practices by truckers that add to shipping costs and the prices of goods.

Restricting entry isn't limited to the ICC, or even to federal regulatory agencies. Some cities, such as New York, have fixed the number of taxi licenses (or *medallions*), effectively establishing a barrier against entry of competing taxi operators. State and local laws in some areas limit the number of liquor stores, alcoholic beverage permits, and beer carry-outs.

Restricting entry into industries that aren't clearly natural monopolies, or where there would be no wasteful duplication of facilities and service simply enhances the monopolistic position of the firms in the industry. There may be good reasons for having a single gas and electric company in an area, but the reasons for having a fixed number of taxi companies are dubious at best (unless, of course, you happen to operate one of the taxis).

In some cases, regulatory agencies have been more concerned with the problems of the firms in their industries than with those of the consumers whom they are supposed to protect. Until recently, the regulatory agencies did little to protect consumers, and their current actions have been largely in response to pressure from consumer groups. Until 1975, for example, the ICC had no quality standards for railroad passenger service.

How Much and What Kinds of Regulation?

There is some danger that recent criticism of regulatory agencies and the well-known difficulties with public regulation may lead us to throw the baby out with the bath water, and try to get rid of all forms of regulation. Society does gain some significant benefits from some regulations. It would be of dubious value, for example, to eliminate all safety regulations on commercial aircraft and let poor performance and air crashes eliminate the worst planes and airline companies. Do we really want to allow any and all drugs and food additives on the market without testing for health hazards, or to eliminate all safety standards on consumer goods? Would gains in efficiency (if any) and lower costs justify doing away with all regulations on occupational health and safety and environmental protection?

Some types of regulations could be scrapped with little sense of loss, because they serve only to restrict competition and generate inefficiency. The deregulation of interstate air fares by the CAB after 1976—under the direction of the *enfant terrible* of the regulators, Alfred E. Kahn—is a big step in the direction of getting rid of this type of regulation. Similar moves are being made in interstate trucking and some other regulated industries.

Close-up

The Dismantling of the C.A.B., 1976-85

One of the things that keeps anticompetitive regulations and regulatory agencies intact after their usefulness has been exhausted is the vested economic interest of those who gain most from the regulations—the employees and owners in regulated industries and the employees of the regulatory agencies. When the Civil Aeronautics Board (CAB) was established in 1938, commercial aviation was still in its infancy, and regulations were necessary to protect consumers and set standards for carriers. By the 1970s, however, the CAB's primary function was one of restricting competition in commercial aviation.

Until 1976, airlines seeking new routes had to file applications with the CAB. Applications could be held up almost indefinitely by hearings, protests from competing airlines in the proposed routes, and bureaucratic red tape. Airlines' fares were regulated by the CAB, and any changes in fares or new types of fares had to be approved by the CAB after lengthy hearings and administrative procedures. By restricting entry and eliminating price competition in commercial aviation, the CAB made the industry an oligopolist's dream.

Attempts to deregulate the industry, or even to liberalize regulations in the direction of more competition were resisted by the carriers, their allies in Congress, and many within the agency. The most frequent argument for maintaining controls was that deregulation would lead to price wars, chaos, deterioration of service, a halt in service to smaller markets, and massive bankruptcies of airlines.

As liberalization and deregulation gained some momentum after 1976, some airlines did much better financially than they had under regulation—in spite of much lower fares and new types of fares and service. In the fall of 1978, the CAB made all unused routes available to airlines on a first-come–first-served basis, and airline representatives lined up at the CAB headquarters like teenagers at the box office of a rock concert.

By October 1978, the ranks of opponents of deregulation had dwindled, and Congress passed the Airline Deregulation Act of 1978. The act will reduce the authority and functions of the CAB until 1985, when the agency will be eliminated.

While deregulation was underway in airlines, moves were initiated to reduce the scope of regulation of interstate land transportation—trucks, buses, and railroads. The issues in interstate trucking—assigning routes, regulating rates, restricting entry, etc.—were about the same as in commercial aviation, as were the arguments for and against deregulation. Again, support for deregulation came from shippers and consumers, opposition from truckers and their allies in government. At this writing, the issue of interstate trucking deregulation hasn't been resolved, but the "deregulators" are already looking at railroads and some other regulated industries.

Support for deregulation came from consumers (whom the regulations were supposed to protect), while most of the opposition came from the airline companies (from whom the regulations were supposed to protect consumers). As it turned out, however, the deregulation not only benefited consumers (by lowering fares) but also increased airline profits (due to the increased volume of air travel).

Clearly, some agencies and regulations can be abolished to the benefit of both society as a whole and the regulated industry. But what about the "good" regulations on health, safety, and the environment? Very few people besides those with unbounded faith in private markets advocate complete abolition of these regulations. However disturbing it might be, though, we do have to recognize some basic realities:

1. A completely safe, orderly, and clean world is impossible with or without regulation.
2. Regulations—even "good" regulations—are expensive and require resources that could be used for other things.
3. Eventually, additional resources devoted to regulation yield diminishing returns in terms of benefits—every $1 worth of additional benefits from regulation costs more to obtain.

This brings us back to marginal analysis. If we increase regulation, will the marginal benefits from the regulations be worth the marginal cost? If we reduce regulation, will the marginal savings in cost be worth the marginal loss of benefits?

To illustrate, suppose that the monetary value of social costs and social benefits from regulation could be quantified. The optimal degree of regulation would be reached where the net benefits of regulation (social benefits minus social costs) are maximized. In Figure 2, the optimal degree of regulation is $\bar{R}$, where the *marginal benefit of regulation* equals the *marginal cost of regulation*—or where the slopes of the value of benefits curve equals the slope of the cost of regulation curve.

It's hard to say where the optimum degree of regulation for the U.S. is today, but recent evidence and the trend toward deregulation strongly indicate that we have moved considerably beyond it.

Figure 2 Costs and Benefits of Regulation

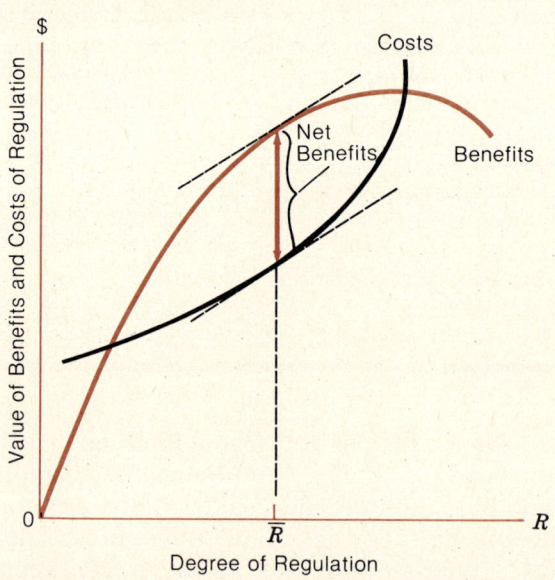

Nationalization and Public Ownership

A third alternative for controlling concentration of market power is **nationalization** or public ownership of firms in industries where competitive forces are weak. Unfortunately, a detailed appraisal of nationalization is difficult because our experience with public ownership is so limited—the Tennessee Valley Authority and the Postal Service are about the only familiar examples of publicly owned firms in the U.S.

In addition, the issue of nationalization invariably gets bogged down in purely ideological assertions of questionable relevance. Some political conservatives paint nationalization as an unqualified boondoggle or as a step on the "road to serfdom" (Professor F. A. Hayek's term), Stalinist dictatorship, or some other end too terrible to contemplate. Some of the supporters of nationalization see it as part of a revolutionary political and social change and tend to be euphoric about its social and economic benefits, without giving adequate attention to problems or costs associated with nationalized firms.

Limited nationalization—of some industries, or of some firms within industries as a means of improving market performance—doesn't imply massive changes in the economic system as a whole. This type of nationalization is relatively common in the mixed capitalist countries of Western Europe.

Some proponents of nationalization argue that the conflict between private profit-maximization, economic efficiency, and community economic welfare would be absent in a nationalized firm. Figure 3 shows a firm with some monopoly power producing an output of $\overline{Q}$ and selling at a price of $\overline{P}$ to maximize profit. Firms like this one that aren't price takers won't produce where $\overline{P} = MC$ voluntarily. If the firm in Figure 3 were nationalized, however, it would be possible to get it to produce where $P = MC$—at P' and Q'. Compared with the private equilibrium, society benefits from a greater output at a lower price and realizes a gain in efficiency in moving to the price and output that clears the market where $P' = MC$. The net gain in efficiency is indicated by the shaded area in the diagram.

If a nationalized firm earned economic profits where $P = MC$, these profits could be distributed to consumers as rebates or simply used as a source of revenue for other public projects and services. If a nationalized firm earned an economic loss where $P = MC$, the choices are about the same as they are for a privately owned public utility that operates at a loss—subsidize it, institute some form of price discrimination to raise revenue, or shut it down.

The necessity of subsidizing an industry or firm to produce where $P = MC$ doesn't necessarily result in economic inefficiency or loss of economic welfare. The demand curve doesn't include the value of external social benefits to the society. Some advocates of limited

Figure 3 Effects of Nationalizing a Monopoly

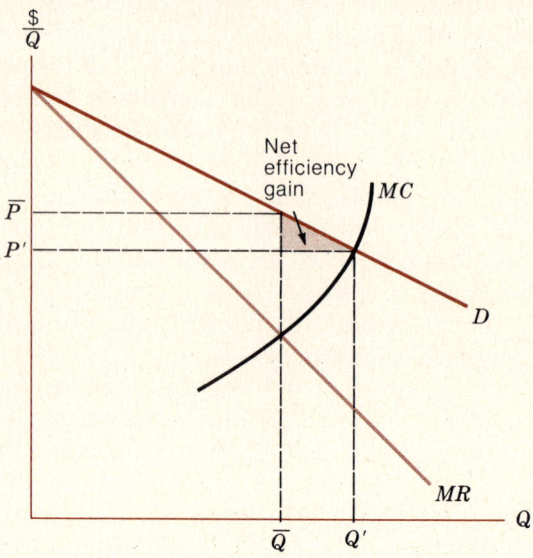

nationalization argue that a public firm would be in a better position to calculate social benefits and costs than a private firm. In Figure 4, for example, the demand curve D excludes the value of external benefits and the demand curve D' includes the value of the external social benefits per unit consumed—or D' shows the *marginal social benefit* to society of an additional unit of this good. The nationalized firm produces Q^* where the value of an additional unit to society (including external benefits) equals marginal cost. To clear the market, the firm sets a price of P^*.

Since the market-clearing price is less than average cost, this firm has to be subsidized. The subsidy is shown by the shaded area. However, the subsidy is also the value of the external social benefits that weren't included in the market-clearing price. In short, the total social benefits to society of producing Q^* equals the total revenue paid by consumers (TR) plus the subsidy.

Critics of nationalization are quick to point out, however, that inefficiency would be chronic in public enterprises because the managers of such enterprises would have little need to be efficient. Their own jobs as civil servants are so secure that there may be no incentive to provide high quality products at the lowest possible cost. In addition, ready access to public funds may reduce the incentive for efficiency even further. It should also be noted, however, that some private firms (such as Lockheed) have been bailed out by public funds in the form of government loans.

The viability of public enterprise also depends on some political considerations. If public enterprises become part of the political patronage system or pork barrel, there may be serious economic consequences. Some areas may receive or lose services as a form of political reward or punishment. Staffing public enterprises on the basis of political patronage may worsen the problems of efficiency.

Realistically, control of concentration and market power—at least for the immediate future—will involve improvements in antitrust legislation and enforcement and in a more efficient regulatory system. Public ownership in some cases could serve as an effective means of controlling market power, but public ownership is no panacea. The problem of scarcity and the necessity of choices are as present for nationalized firms as they are for private firms. Final decisions on the best balance of antitrust, public regulation, and public ownership must be reached on the basis of costs, benefits, and informed value judgements—not on the basis of emotion, ideology, and prejudice.

Figure 4 Subsidized Nationalization

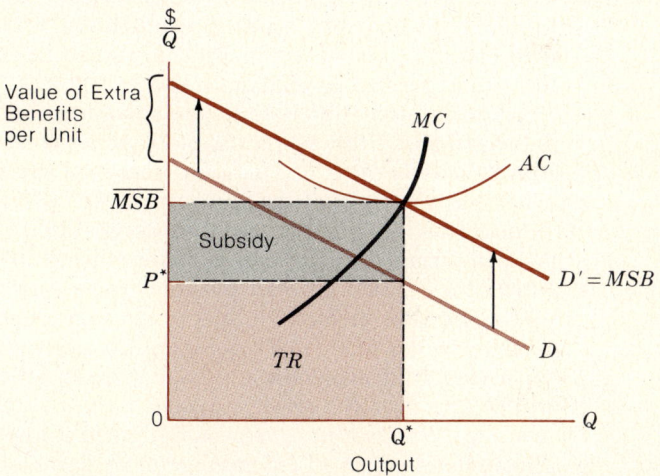

Summary

1. Concentration of production in the largest firms has been increasing, but the average concentration of industries has been about the same for the last 30 years. This odd combination can be explained in part by conglomerate mergers that include subsidiaries in more than one industry.
2. **Antitrust policies** try to promote and preserve competition by preventing or breaking up concentrations of market power. The basic antitrust laws are the **Sherman Antitrust Act**, the **Clayton Antitrust Act**, and the **Federal Trade Commission Act**.

3. Public regulations on economic activity deal with health and safety, externalities, and market performance. Many public regulations dealing with pricing and entry have served to restrain competition in regulated industries.
4. Regulations that do nothing more than restrain competition can be scrapped easily. For the rest, the proper degree of regulation has to be decided on the basis of the costs and the benefits of regulation.
5. **Nationalization** or public ownership is a highly controversial and untried (in the U.S.) way of dealing with market power.

Concepts for Review

market power
antitrust
Sherman Antitrust Act
Clayton Antitrust Act
Federal Trade Commission Act
workable competition
nationalization

Questions

1. What are the most important economic and social consequences (positive and negative) of increased concentration of market power in the largest firms?
2. Critics argue that vigorous antitrust prosecution stifles firms' incentive to succeed, penalizes success in competition, and leads to economic inefficiency by protecting inefficiently small firms rather than allowing firms to expand to an efficient size.
   How much merit is there to this argument as a general criticism of antitrust policy? Can you think of examples where the argument is valid? Can you think of examples where it's invalid?
3. What is meant by the term "predatory pricing"? How can it be distinguished from legitimate price competition? What problems does it pose for formulating policies to achieve "workable competition"?
4. After a long period of retail gasoline "price wars" in the Detroit area in the early 1960s, gasoline dealers in the area proposed that gasoline retailing be designated as a public utility and regulated by the state. What would the economic results of such an action have been? Who would have been the greatest gainers from the regulation of gasoline retailing? Who would have been the greatest losers?
5. The annual budgets of federal regulatory agencies total about $5 billion. In addition, there are state and local expenditures for various kinds of regulation.
   a. What would be the benefits and costs to society of complete (100%) deregulation of economic activity?
   b. Some public opinion polls in 1978 suggested that Americans would prefer more economic regulation. Identify the costs and benefits to society of more economic regulation.
   c. Suppose that the President has appointed you as his new "regulation czar," and made you responsible for designing programs that would lead to the optimum level of regulation. What kinds of analytical information would you look for? What kinds of regulation would you keep or expand? What kinds of regulation would you contract or eliminate? What value judgements would be necessary?

6. Amtrak has operated at a loss every year of its existence, and in 1978 the chairman of the board of Amtrak said that neither Amtrak nor any other intercity rail passenger service could operate at a profit. In 1978, Amtrak received about $500 million in subsidies.
   a. Does this mean that the benefits society realizes from the existence of Amtrak aren't worth the cost of maintaining it?
   b. Amtrak officials argue that if the financing situation doesn't improve, Amtrak will have to be nationalized. What would you predict as the economic effects (positive and negative) of nationalizing intercity rail travel?
7. The U.S. Postal Service is everybody's favorite horrible example of the inefficiency inherent in publicly owned and operated enterprises. What would you expect to be the major economic consequences of breaking up the Postal Service and relying on competition among private firms to perform the Postal Service's functions?

16

Imperfections in Labor Markets

Preview: With perfect competition in resource markets, individual buyers and sellers are price takers and have market information, resources are mobile among employers and occupations, and no collusion occurs among buyers or sellers of resources. In the real world, of course, there are a number of imperfections in the markets for labor and other resources, imperfections which affect resource prices and employment, efficiency, and income distribution. In this chapter, we'll examine three types of imperfection in resource markets—market power in the purchase of resources, market power in the sale of resources, and "institutional" imperfections. Although the analysis of the chapter focuses upon labor markets, many of the concepts and issues we will explore apply to other resource markets as well.

Monopoly in the Sale of Labor: The Economics of Labor Unions

Perhaps the most important labor market imperfection in the U.S. economy is the existence of labor unions.

Labor unions are important social, political, and economic institutions. Economically, a trade union is a form of monopoly. When union members formally agree to sell their labor at a common wage, they are, in fact, forming a *cartel*.

Legal Status of Trade Unions

For many years, the courts applied the Common Law *conspiracy doctrine* against trade unions as illegal conspiracies to restrain competition in the sale of labor. In fact, many of the early prosecutions under the Sherman Antitrust Act were against trade unions. It wasn't until the passage of the Norris-La Guardia Act in 1932 and the National Labor Relations (or Wagner) Act in 1935 that the legality of unions was firmly established.

The legality of unions as monopolies in the sale of labor and the illegality of monopolies in the sale of goods and services raises the question of an apparent double standard in the law. The double standard may be justifiable, however, because individual workers are at an inherent disadvantage in bargaining with large firms for wages, working conditions, and other benefits. In a large firm, the actions of one worker have no obvious effect on the firm's operations (unless the action is something as drastic as blowing up the plant). Many production jobs in factories require little specialized skill or training, and it's easy to replace an unhappy or troublesome worker with somebody else. If an individual worker tried to press demands by staying away from work or by some other form of job action, the most likely result would be the replacement of the worker with another.

Concerted actions by all employees through a union can offset the inherent advantages of the firm over the individual worker. If all workers in a plant stay off the job or stage some other job action, the effect on the firm is more dramatic. It would be much more difficult for a firm to replace all of its workers and hire a new labor force. The workers as a group are likely to have the resources and influence to publicize their grievances and can pool their resources to support those on strike.

What Do Unions Maximize?

It's far less reasonable to pick a single variable that unions maximize than it is to assume that firms try to maximize profit. Individual union members have different economic goals and interests. Some may prefer higher wages to job security. Others may prefer more job security, and be willing to sacrifice somewhat on wage increases. Still others may find improved fringe benefits more important than wage increases or job security.

Unions are complex political organizations, and union leaders try to satisfy the largest number of workers possible. This generally means getting a package of wages, fringe benefits, job security, and work rules that is acceptable to a majority of members.

Other things equal, however, it is safe to predict that union members will prefer higher wages to lower wages, and greater wage increases to smaller wage increases. One of the main selling points of American unions has been their ability to command high wages in periods of increasing demand for labor and to protect against wage reductions in periods of sagging demand for labor. The ability of unions to affect the wages paid to their members depends on the type of union and the characteristics of the workers they represent.

Unions and Wages: Craft Unions

Craft unions organize workers in a single craft—carpenters, barbers, bricklayers, plumbers, etc. All unionized workers in a given craft in a given area generally belong to the same union local, regardless of employer.

Craft unions generally have some form of control over the supply of labor in the craft. Becoming a journeyman plumber, for example, requires completion of an apprenticeship prescribed by the plumbers' union. Craft unions often influence the supply of labor in the craft through their influence on licencing requirements.

In Figure 1, S_L is the supply of plumbers' labor in the absence of any restrictions on the number of plumbers in the market. By restricting entry into the craft, the plumbers' union restricts the supply of labor, and shifts the market supply curve to the left to RS_L. The restriction on the supply of plumbers' labor drives the wage of plumbers upward from $\overline{W}$ (the equilibrium wage without restricted supply) to $\overline{UW}$ (the wage which results from the union's restriction of the supply of labor).

Because they control the supply of labor in the craft, craft unions can maintain wages above the competitive level and full employment of their members. In Figure 1, the quantity of labor demanded with the restricted supply of labor and higher wage ($\overline{N}_u$) is less than the quantity that would be demanded in the absence of the restriction of labor supply and the lower "competitive" wage ($\overline{N}$). However, because the supply of labor *is* restricted by the union, there is no excess supply (or unemployment) of union plumbers' labor at $\overline{UW}$.

The demand for labor in some crafts has declined severely in recent years due to technological change. Wet plaster has been replaced in construction by "drywall" (a prefabricated substitute for wet plaster). This has driven the demand for plasterers' labor downward, as shown by the shift of the demand curve to the left to D_L' in Figure 2. Faced with declining demand for their labor, many craft unions have accepted somewhat lower wages to minimize the unemployment of their members. Over the longer haul, however, the unions generally impose further restric-

Figure 1 Union Restriction of Labor Supply

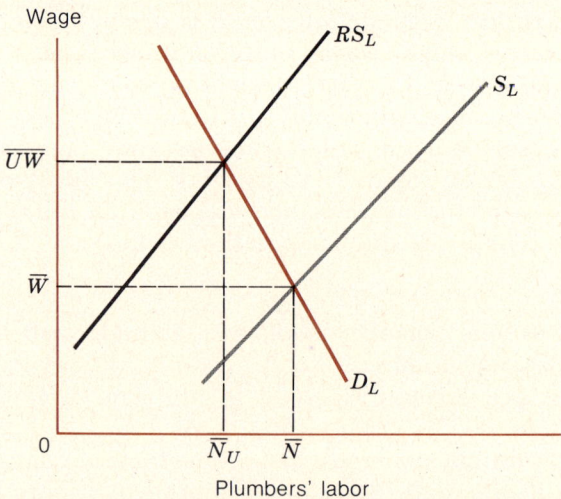

Figure 2 Declining Demand for Labor

tions on the supply of labor in the craft to maintain wages and minimize unemployment.

To maintain wages and full employment for their members, craft unions may insist on strictly defined "work rules"—strict definitions of "plumbers' work," "carpenters' work," etc. This often leads to "work-rules disputes" among the various crafts. They may also insist on specific provisions in public regulations (such as building codes and minimum-crew requirements) to bolster the demand for the labor of their members.

Unions and Wages: Industrial Unions

Industrial unions, such as the United Steelworkers (USW), the United Autoworkers (UAW), or the Teamsters, represent all workers within a unionized company or industry regardless of the workers' specific skills or training. Unlike craft unions, industrial unions generally have no control over the supply of labor to the industry or firm. Employers are free to hire whomever they want, but the union may require union membership or payment of a *maintenance fee* as a condition of continued employment.

Members of industrial unions agree collectively to offer their labor only at a wage specified in a contract between the union and the firm. The bargaining is **collective bargaining** between the employer and the workers as a group rather than individual bargaining between the employer and each worker. Unions typically bargain for a wage which is higher than the "competitive" wage which would be paid in the absence of the union. In Figure 3, the competitive wage for steelworkers' labor is $\overline{W}$. The union bargains for a wage (UW) which is above $\overline{W}$ and is

Figure 3 Unemployment at Union Wage

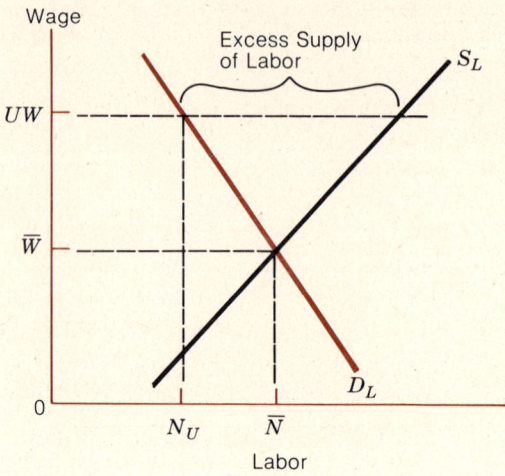

generally acceptable to union members. Since all workers agree to sell their labor at UW, the industry faces a completely elastic supply of labor at UW. The workers will not accept wages below UW, and it makes no sense for the firms to offer more than UW.

Industrial unions cannot obtain a wage above the competitive level and maintain full employment of all workers in the industry because they have no control over the supply of labor. In Figure 3, for example, there is an excess supply of labor available at UW, and this represents unemployment.

In periods of increasing demand for labor, industrial unions typically bargain for higher wages rather than allowing more employment at the original wage. Figure 4 illustrates the typical industrial union's wage and employment preferences. With an increase in the demand for labor from D_L to D_L' the union seeks higher wages for its members (UW'). On the other hand, when the demand for labor is falling, as in the shift from D_L to D_L'' in Figure 4, industrial unions generally try to maintain the wage rather than accepting a lower wage to maintain the same level of employment. This results in a *ratchet effect* in industrial union wages—they tend to be flexible upward in periods of high demand for labor, but inflexible downward in periods of slack demand for labor.

Bargaining Power

Why are some unions consistently able to achieve high wages and generous wage increases, while others aren't? Part of the answer lies in a complex concept called *bargaining power*—the ability of the unions to achieve their goals in bargaining. Bargaining power depends on a num-

Figure 4 *Ratchet Effect* in Industrial Union Wages

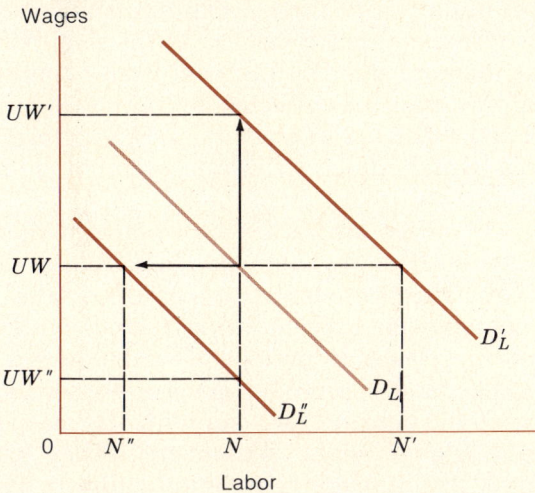

ber of variables—the organization of the industry (number of firms, degree of competition among firms, etc.), the elasticity of demand for the labor of union members, the ability of the union and the firm to impose and withstand economic hardship in holding out for a settlement, and the influence of community and political pressure on the firm and the union.

Other things equal, the ability of a union to achieve high wages is *greater* the *less elastic* the demand for the labor of its members. If the demand for labor is relatively inelastic, the cost of higher wages in terms of reduced employment is relatively small, and total wages paid to the union members will be greater than at lower wages. If the demand for labor is relatively elastic, the cost of higher wages is greater in terms of the reduction in employment, and total wage payments will be smaller.

On the basis of elasticity of demand of labor alone, then, it would be safe to predict that such unions as the plumbers' union and the Airline Pilot's Association will consistently be successful in their wage demands. The workers are skilled and difficult to replace, the demand for the products they provide (air travel, residential and commercial buildings) is not highly price elastic, and labor costs represent relatively small percentages of total costs in the construction and airline industries.

Bargaining power also depends on the ability of unions and firms to absorb economic hardship while imposing economic hardship on the other party during labor disputes. The union's ultimate weapon is the strike, which imposes economic hardship on the firm (lost sales and profit) and on the union members (lost wages). Firms may "lock out" union members simply by shutting down during the dispute. Like strikes, lockouts impose economic hardships on both parties. Large and powerful unions with large strike funds and large corporations with extensive financial resources are better able to withstand strikes and lockouts than are smaller, less well-heeled unions and firms.

Bargaining power is affected by the *outside pressure* exerted on the union and the firm to settle a dispute. Outside pressure is greatest in key industries which affect the whole economy and in industries where work stoppages inflict widespread discomfort, inconvenience, and hardship. Likewise, strikes are more potent weapons in periods of brisk demand for the firm's product than in periods of slack demand and high inventories. The firm stands to lose more sales and profits during a period of high demand than during a slump, and the costs of continuing the strike are greater in periods of brisk demand.

Unions generally promote government economic policies which would keep the demand for labor high and make it possible for unions to obtain higher wage settlements. They consistently advocate monetary, fiscal, and foreign trade policies which bolster the demand for goods and services and the labor to produce them. In fact, some economists argue that it is only through such policies that industrial unions can keep wages high for very long.

Monopsony in the Purchase of Labor

A second major form of labor market imperfection is the existence of *monopsony* in some markets.

The term *monopsony* means a *single buyer*.

- **Monopsony** exists in labor markets in which there is a single buyer of labor.

Just as a monopolistic seller faces the market demand curve for its product, a *monopsonistic buyer of labor faces the market supply curve of labor*. In Figure 5, S_F is the market supply of labor, and the supply curve faced by the monopsonistic buyer of labor.

Unlike a price taker in the labor market, when a monopsonist hires more labor, it must increase the wage to call out the additional labor and must pay all previously hired labor the higher wage. In Table 1, for example, if the monopsonist hires a fifth unit of labor, it raises the market wage from $30 to $35. The monopsonist, then, must pay the fifth worker—and all previously hired workers—a wage of $35. The MFC of the fifth unit of labor hired is the $35 paid to the fifth worker (i.e., the price of the extra unit), plus the additional $20 paid to the previously hired workers.

- For a *monopsonist in the resource market*, the MFC of a resource is greater than its price at all inputs of the resource.

Table 1 Costs for a Labor Market Monopsonist

Labor	Wage/Worker-Day	Wage Bill	MFC
0	$10	$ 0	
			$ 15
1	15	15	
			25
2	20	40	
			35
3	25	75	
			45
4	30	120	
			55
5	35	175	
			65
6	40	240	
			75
7	45	315	
			85
8	50	400	
			95
9	55	495	
			105
10	60	600	

The relationship between the supply of a resource and its MFC for a monopsonist is shown graphically in Figure 5. The MFC curve lies above the supply curve for all quantities of the resource.

Figure 5 Monopsony in the Labor Market

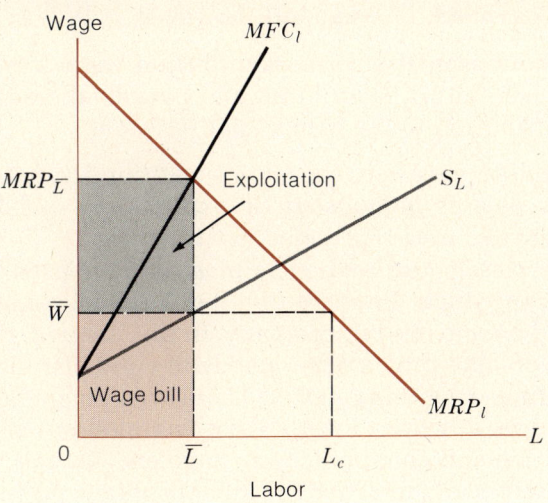

Monopsony and Employment

A monopsonist in the labor market, like any other firm, will maximize profit by employing labor to the point where the amount of additional revenue generated by the last unit hired (the marginal revenue product, or *MRP*) equals the additional cost of hiring the last unit (the marginal factor cost, or *MFC*).

- The profit-maximizing employment of labor is where *MRP* = *MFC*.

In Figure 5, the monopsonist would hire $\bar{L}$ units of labor, where MRP_ℓ = MFC_ℓ. However, the wage that the monopsonist must pay is determined by the supply of labor (S_L)—not the *MFC*. The monopsonist decides on the amount of labor to hire, and then pays the wage that will call out the desired quantity of labor. The monopsonist thus reaches both an equilibrium level of employment ($\bar{L}$) and an equilibrium wage ($\bar{W}$).

One implication is obvious.

- A monopsonist will pay a lower wage for a given quantity of labor or hire less labor at a given wage, than would a price taker in the labor market.

If the firm in Figure 5 were a price-taker at $\bar{W}$, for example, it would hire L_c units of labor where $\bar{W} = MFC_\ell = MRP_\ell$.

Monopsony and "Exploitation"

In maximizing profit by hiring labor to the point where *MRP* = *MFC* for the last unit hired, *a monopsonist pays a wage below the MRP of the last unit hired*. If all units of labor are identical, the *MRP* of the last worker hired shows the contribution of every unit of labor to the firm's revenue, and labor's contribution to the firm's revenue is *MRP* × *L*. At $\bar{L}$ in Figure 5, $MRP_{\bar{L}} \times \bar{L}$ is labor's contribution to the firm's revenue. The firm's total wage payment, or **wage bill**, however, is $\bar{W} \times \bar{L}$.

- A monopsonist pays an equilibrium wage less than the *MRP* of the last unit of labor hired and pays total wages less than labor's contribution to the firm's total revenue.

The difference between labor's contribution to total revenue and total wages paid is monopsonistic exploitation of labor. In Figure 5, the gray shaded area represents "exploitation."

The classic textbook examples of monopsony are remote mining towns in which there are no alternative jobs and all workers are employed by one mining company. In this context, monopsonistic exploitation of labor can be illustrated with vivid historical examples of living conditions in mining towns. There aren't many labor markets like this any more, however. People have migrated out of them, and improved education and communication have encouraged workers to seek other alternatives and lessened the monopsonistic power of the mine owners.

Monopsony still exists, and it still exploits resources. As the following example shows, however, this "exploitation" doesn't necessarily mean that the affected workers are driven to abject poverty.

Close-up

Monopsony and Professional Sports

Before 1975, many professional athletes weren't free to sell their services to the highest bidder. *Reserve clauses* bound players to a single team for a specified period of time (in pro football) or forever (in professional baseball). Teams could release players or trade them to other teams, but the players weren't free to seek employment with the highest bidder for their talents. For the players, the choice was to play for the team that held their contracts or not to play at all. Player drafts even eliminated the athletes' freedom of negotiating with different teams on entering the market.

When Curt Flood, the star outfielder for the St. Louis Cardinals, led his unsuccessful court fight against the reserve clause, his reported salary was about $90,000. It was difficult for anybody to believe that a person could be exploited and earn such a high salary. However, the salaries received by players since the demise of the reserve clause after 1975 indicate how exploited Flood and the other superstars were under the reserve clause.

In 1975, Jim "Catfish" Hunter—the ace pitcher of the Oakland A's—became a free agent after a court invalidated his contract with the A's. After a fierce bidding war, Hunter signed a five-year, $3.5 million contract with the New York Yankees. Other free agents have followed Hunter in obtaining very lucrative contracts—Vida Blue, Reggie Jackson, Andy Messersmith, and Tommy John, to name a few. The all-time record was reached in 1978, when Pete Rose left the Cincinnati Reds and signed at a salary of $800,000 per year with the Philadelphia Phillies. In 1979, Bill Walton did even better by signing with the San Diego Clippers of the National Basketball Association for a reported $850,000 a year.

Many critics of the high salaries for free agents argue that the players aren't worth the high salaries they receive and point to the lower salaries received by superior players when the reserve clauses were intact. In reality, what has happened is that the elimination of the reserve clause has reduced the monopsonistic power of the teams dramatically and has brought salaries of big-name players closer to their worth to the team.

Could anybody—even Pete Rose—have a marginal revenue product of $800,000? Consider the following facts. At an average ticket price of $4, the Phillies will have to draw an additional 200,000 fans at home per year to pay Rose's salary. This represents only about a 10% increase in home attendance for the Phillies, and Rose has been a big draw for over a decade. In addition, since Rose will be playing more games in the National League East, his presence can be expected to increase crowds at Phillies' games on the road as well, and the Phillies get 40¢ of every dollar of ticket revenue from their road games. In short, the *MRP* of Pete Rose is probably at least as high as his salary.

Institutional Imperfections

In the long run, in perfectly competitive labor markets, wage differentials among occupations should just compensate for differences in costs of training and differences in the nature of the work. In the real world, however, some of the lowest paid occupations are the least attractive, and some highly paid occupations are relatively attractive.

Migrant farm labor, for example, involves long hours of physically exhausting, dirty work. Migrant workers have no social status in their communities because of the transient nature of their work. It would be hard to think of a more difficult and unattractive occupation, yet it's one of the lowest paid occupations in our society.

Medicine, on the other hand is a relatively lucrative occupation. This would be the case even in the absence of market imperfections because of the long and expensive training required and the unusual emotional and mental strain involved in medical practice. There are, however, many attractive aspects of medical practice: the work is challenging and rewarding, and doctors enjoy high status in their communities.

If the relatively high wages of doctors merely equalized the net advantages of doctors and persons employed in other occupations, the competition among qualified candidates for admission to medical school would not be so fierce. The excess supply of qualified persons seeking to enter the profession suggests that the incomes of physicians more than compensate them for the unusual training, emotional pressures, responsibility, and other costs of medical practice.

Among some closely related occupations, there does appear to be a tendency toward equalizing of net advantages. Wages of craftsmen and some types of highly skilled labor, for example, have been increasing relative to the wages in some managerial and white-collar occupations. There isn't conclusive evidence, however, that this is happening across the board for all occupations. Many of our least attractive and most physically exhausting occupations remain the lowest paid.

Some of these wage differences may reflect rent earned by persons with natural abilities. Some of it can be explained by monopsony power of some employers (such as large "contractors" who hire migrant farm workers) and the monopoly power of some unions (such as the restrictions on entry into certain crafts). In addition, however, there are a number of institutional imperfections in labor markets that contribute to wage differentials which are more than compensating.

Lack of Market Information

If workers in an occupation aren't aware of their alternatives, there's no reason to expect wage differentials to compensate for differences in the attractiveness of work in different occupations. The typical worker's job search isn't very systematic or exhaustive. Many workers search for and choose jobs on the basis of informal and incomplete information. Advice from friends or relatives often is the only information the worker has to go on. Persons who are reasonably satisfied in their current job generally don't survey the job market regularly.

Geographic Immobility

Geographic immobility of labor is a complex problem with many economic and noneconomic facets. Moving from one area to another involves costs: the cost of the move itself, and the possible loss on the sale of a residence.

Some other costs of geographic mobility are real, but difficult to express in meaningful monetary terms. Giving up attachments to a community and long friendships to move to a new community are real costs. There may be additional costs in the uncertainty that typically surrounds moving to a new community. If the move involves a new type of community as well as a new job—from a rural community to an urban area, for example—these subjective costs include major changes in lifestyle.

Occupational Immobility

Long periods of training often limit occupational mobility. If physicians earn wages that more than compensate for the greater training and responsibility of medical practice, this differential can't be reduced until substantial numbers of students complete medical school. The training required to move between occupations is also costly in many cases, including the cost of the training itself, plus the additional opportunity cost of lost wages during the training period. These costs tend to limit the mobility of labor among occupations with different educational and training requirements.

Restrictions on entry into some occupations also limit mobility. Craft unions limit access to the craft by restricting entry into apprenticeship programs. Where practicing a craft requires a license, people in the craft generally can control entry by controlling licensing requirements. For many years, the American Medical Association opposed the expansion of medical schools and thus restricted the supply of physicians. Furthermore, the A.M.A. was influential in setting standards for internships, residencies, and licensing, which further restricted entry.

Immobility, Transfer Price, and Rent

Occupational immobility in the labor market has some of the same effects as barriers to entry in the goods market. Workers in the higher-wage occupations receive wages that are higher than necessary to keep them from moving to another occupation. Workers excluded from higher wage occupations because of immobility are less than compensated for their opportunity costs.

Suppose, for example, that an annual wage of $50,000 would just compensate physicians for the costs of training and the difficulty of their craft. This wage is called the *transfer price*.

- The **transfer price** is the minimum wage that would keep persons in an occupation from moving to their next best alternative.

If, because of immobility and restrictions on entry into medical practice, the average physician earns an annual wage of $75,000, physicians are earning a form of *rent*—income in excess of their opportunity costs or transfer price. This rent isn't unlike the rent earned by a monopolist by virtue of its unique position as the only firm in the market or the rent that accrues to the person who holds an unusually good piece of land.

Discrimination

Discrimination is a special kind of market imperfection that warrants special attention. It is one of the most emotionally charged areas covered by economics, and separating the positive analytical questions from the normative issues isn't easy. In addition, discrimination in the labor market is only part of a complex pattern of interrelated types of discrimination.

Discrimination may occur on the basis of nationality ("No Irish Need Apply"), religion (Catholics and Jews), race, sex, or just about anything else. There is even evidence that obese persons are discriminated against for promotion to top managerial positions in business and government. The most serious forms of discrimination in America today are against women, nonwhites, and some nationalities (such as Hispanics).

Independently of the normative issues, there are two important economic effects of discrimination in labor markets. First, it limits the choice of occupations open to certain groups in society. Those who are discriminated against aren't likely to be compensated for their opportunity costs in the occupations that are open to them. Secondly, excluding qualified persons from some occupations and relegating them to occupations that underutilize their abilities underutilizes the human resources and productive capacity of the economy as a whole.

Suppose that a qualified woman is excluded from medical school and enters a related occupation—medical technology or nursing. She won't be fully compensated for the lost income and satisfaction from practicing medicine, and the community loses the benefits of her talents as a physician. Society places a higher price and therefore a higher value on physicians' services than on those of medical technicians or nurses. By forcing some qualified persons to remain in occupations on which society has placed a lower monetary value, discrimination deprives society of some services on which it places a high value.

Discrimination: What Is It?

Surprisingly, although discrimination is a controversial and volatile issue, there isn't a single, clear-cut meaning for the term. For our purposes, however, we can turn our attention to two forms of discrimination in the labor market—exclusion of persons from certain occupations or access to those occupations on the basis of race, sex, or age; and paying different workers different wages for the same work on the basis of race, sex, or age.

Figure 6 represents the demand and supply of labor of two groups of workers—"whites" and "blacks"—in the same occupation. Actually,

Figure 6 Effects of Discrimination

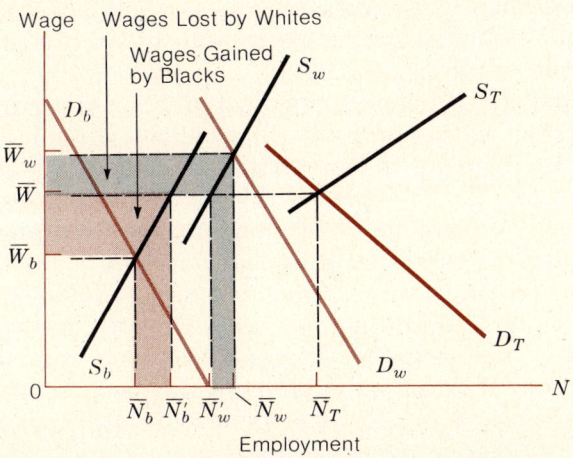

the analysis can apply to any pair of groups—male and female, Anglos and Hispanics, etc. Employers in this example are free to hire whomever they wish and to pay whatever wage the employer and worker agree on.

For whatever reason, employers demand more white labor than black labor at any given wage, or would be willing to pay a higher wage to whites than to blacks for any given quantity of labor. In addition to racist attitudes, there are other possible explanations for the greater demand for white workers. Blacks may have a lower marginal revenue product than whites because of inadequate educational backgrounds or lack of access to training in occupational skills. There may be a history of different labor force participation patterns of blacks and whites. If the employers perceive a greater risk of loss due to turnover or absenteeism of black workers, for example, black workers will seem less attractive to employers at any given wage. Of course, these other possibilities don't exclude the possibility of racial prejudice or stereotyping (defining blacks and whites as being "naturally suited" to different occupations).

Traditional attitudes also affect the supply side of the labor market. Racial prejudice among white workers may preclude them from working with blacks at the same wage. If an occupation is stereotyped as a *black* occupation, this may deter whites from entering the occupation. In low-wage occupations, the supply of blacks may be greater because of the lack of alternatives due to exclusion from other occupations.

With no restrictions on employment and wages in this occupation, $\overline{N}_w$ white workers will be hired at a wage of $\overline{W}_w$ and $\overline{N}_b$ black workers will be hired at a wage of $\overline{W}_b$. In other words, there is unequal pay for equal work.

Equal Pay for Equal Work

One possible remedy for discrimination of the type portrayed in Figure 6 is simply to require employers in this occupation to pay the same wage to all workers—or *equal pay for equal work*. As in all economic policy issues, some complications can arise from a seemingly simple solution.

First of all, there is a practical problem of accurately defining "equal work" in an economy with thousands of different occupations. If a firm employs persons in more than one occupation—say tool and die maker and millwright—is the work *equal* in the two occupations? Also, enforcing an equal pay requirement can be complex and costly.

Another issue is whether the equal pay is to be the higher wage previously paid to whites, the lower wage previously paid to blacks, or a common equilibrium wage reached by the interaction of demand and supply of all workers. If nothing is done to eliminate discriminatory attitudes or other factors affecting the demand for blacks, requiring that employers pay $\overline{W}_w$ for all workers will simply result in reduced employment of blacks in this occupation.

Another possible result of equal pay for equal work is that a common equilibrium wage will be reached where the quantity of black and white workers demanded (D_T) equals the quantity of black and white workers supplied (S_T). This result would yield a total employment of $\overline{N}_T$ at a wage of $\overline{W}$. The equilibrium wage would call out $\overline{N}_b'$ black workers (from the supply curve S_b) and $\overline{N}_w'$ white workers (from the supply curve S_w).

In purely economic terms, the gainers from the equal pay for equal work are the blacks whose employment and wages increase, the losers are the whites whose employment and wages fall. In Figure 6, the brown shaded area represents wages gained by blacks—higher wages for those originally employed and the wages of the additional blacks employed. The gray shaded area represents the wages lost by whites—lower wages for those who remain employed plus wages lost by the reduced employment of whites.

Education, Productivity, and Mobility

Any lasting solution to the economic burdens of discrimination must improve the productivity and occupational mobility of those discriminated against. If the economic status of women and racial minorities is to improve, their access to more highly paid occupations is essential.

Nonwhite workers made up 10.8 percent of the employed persons in the United States in 1977. However, the percentage of nonwhites in the total employment in low-wage, unattractive, and menial jobs was higher than this—for example, 55.4 percent of household cleaners and servants, 42.4 percent of the commercial lodging cleaners, 41.7 percent of clothing ironers and pressers, and 37 percent of the garbage collectors in the United States in 1977 were nonwhite. In contrast, nonwhites accounted for only 1.6 percent of the airline pilots, 2 percent of the real estate agents, 2.1 percent of the millwrights, 2.1 percent of the tool and die makers, and 3.2 percent of the lawyers in 1977.[1]

At least part of this concentration of nonwhites in low-paid and unattractive occupations is due to discrimination in higher-wage occupations or lack of access to education, training, and skills that would make nonwhites more employable in higher-wage occupations. Improved access to education and training and greater occupational mobility would improve the economic status of racial minorities in two ways—it would increase the demand for them in higher-wage occupations and it would reduce the supply of nonwhites in the low-wage occupations in which they have been heavily concentrated.

Of course, no programs or legislation aimed at discrimination can force people to abandon racial or sexual prejudice, but this isn't the issue. The issue is the degree to which persons are compensated for their opportunity costs in their occupation and the efficiency in using our human resources. Eliminating discrimination in employment and pay will require short-term measures (equal pay for equal work and possibly even employment quotas) and longer-range programs aimed at increasing the productivity of labor and providing equal access to training and education.

Applying the Tools

Discrimination and Women's Wages

World War II revolutionized the American labor force by simultaneously increasing the demand for labor and removing large numbers of males from the civilian labor force. "Rosie the Riveter" and her sisters entered the labor force in large numbers, many in traditionally male occupations. Since 1947, female employment has risen absolutely and as a percentage of the labor force, as have female labor force participation rates (the percentage of the female population over age 16 in the labor force). In 1977, females made up 41.1 percent of the civilian labor force.

Despite rising female participation in traditionally male jobs and the efforts of the feminist movement, however, the average earnings of employed women in 1977 ($6,345) were only 60.4 percent of the average earnings of employed men ($10,509). Some but not all of this difference can be explained in terms of discrimi-

---

1. These are government statistics from U.S. Department of Labor, Bureau of Labor Statistics, *Employment and Unemployment Trends in 1977* (Special Labor Force Report No. 212). Washington: Government Printing Office, 1978, pp. A22–A23.

nation against women in employment and pay. To get an idea of how much is due to discrimination, we have to look first at some other factors that contributed to higher wages for men than women.

Hours Worked

If two persons work at the same job for the same hourly wage, but work different numbers of hours, their incomes will be different. In 1977, 28.6 percent of the women and only 10.6 percent of the men employed in nonagricultural industries worked part time for voluntary or economic reasons. Women worked an average of 34.2 hours per week, while men worked an average of 41.6 hours per week—a difference of 21.6 percent. For full-time workers, the difference in hours is smaller. Full-time women worked an average of 40.2 hours per week while their male counterparts worked an average of 44.2 hours per week, or about 10 percent more hours. Table A shows average hours per week for males and females on full-time schedules by rather broad occupational groupings. Males worked more hours per week than females, but the difference isn't sufficient to explain a 40 percent difference in earnings.

Table A   Average Hours per Week in Nonfarm Occupations, Full-Time Male and Female Employees, 1977

Occupation	Males	Females
White-collar workers	45.7	40.2
Professional & technical	44.8	40.6
Mgr. & administrators	48.2	43.6
Sales workers	45.5	40.6
Clerical workers	41.9	39.2
Blue-collar workers	43.0	39.8
Craft & kindred workers	42.9	41.0
Operatives, ex. transp.	42.9	39.5
Transp. operatives	45.5	41.6
Nonfarm laborers	41.1	40.1
Service workers	43.8	40.6
Private household	48.1	43.2
Other services	43.7	40.4

Source: U.S. Department of Labor, Bureau of Labor Statistics, *Employment and Unemployment Trends in 1977*, Special Labor Force Report No. 212, Washington: Govt. Printing Office, 1978.

Industry and Occupation

Women are more heavily concentrated in low-wage industries and occupations than are men, and this too lowers their average earnings compared with men's earnings. Table B ranks broad industrial classes by the percentage of females employed in the industry and by average weekly earnings. The pattern is so clear that little elaboration is necessary, although it should be pointed out that some types of discrimination may account for the concentration of women in the low-wage industries.

Experience and Labor Force Participation Patterns

Within industries and occupations, earnings are related positively to experience.

New workers start at the bottom of the seniority ladder in the lowest paid jobs, and access to better jobs and training depends on seniority. This works against women in two ways.

Table B Females as Percentage of Employment and Average Weekly Earnings, 1977

Industry	% Female	(Rank)	Average Weekly Earnings	(Rank)
Services	58.8	1	$157.31	7
Finance, Insurance, & Real Estate	54.1	2	168.36	6
Whlsle. & Retail Trade	44.3	3	142.52	8
Mfg., Nondurable Gds.	39.3	4	199.76	5
Mfg., Durable Gds.	23.4	5	245.81	4
Transp. & Publ. Util.	22.3	6	277.60	3
Mining	8.5	7	302.97	1
Construction	6.4	8	295.87	2

Source: U.S. Department of Labor, Bureau of Labor Statistics, *Employment and Unemployment Trends in 1977,* Special Labor Force Report No. 212. Washington: Government Printing Office, 1978, pp. A27–A29, A46.

In jobs where female employment is new—such as police work—most women are going to be at the bottom of the pay and seniority ladder. As they acquire more experience and seniority, differences in average wages of men and women will narrow.

In addition, labor force participation patterns of women over their working lives are different from the labor force participation pattern of men. Male participation rates rise and level off in the 25–35 and 35–44 age groups, while female participation rates drop and level off over the same span of ages. The biggest factor here has been the demands of child-rearing and family responsibilities. No discovery has been made to date to get men to share equally in the task of child-bearing, and in spite of changing sex-roles, attitudes, and family arrangements, the responsibilities associated with children fall more heavily on women than on men.

If employers see a greater risk of women leaving employment than men—even temporarily—they will tend to invest less in specific job-related training for women. Also, if women have more in-and-out patterns of labor force participation than men, female employees will (on the average) have less experience than male employees of the same age. This difference could be reduced significantly by expanding child-care facilities.

Education and Training

Education and training affect employment and wages in a number of ways. In occupations requiring specialized education or training—such as surgeons and plumbers—persons without the training and education can't do the work. A well-educated worker may be more easily trained and more dependable than a worker with a poor educational background. Staying in high school or college to complete a program of study may be an indicator of stability on the job. In short, it's reasonable to expect workers with more education to earn more than workers with less (with a few notable exceptions, such as college teachers).

Table C Average Earnings of Year-Round Full-Time Employees by Sex, Race, and Years of Education, 1976

Educational Level	Both Sexes All Races	Males			Females		
		Total	White	Black	Total	White	Black
Total: All Educational Levels	12,959	15,022	15,414	10,680	8,603	8,669	8,071
Elementary: Total	9,280	10,284	10,632	8,670	5,946	6,101	5,425
Less than 8 yrs.	8,435	9,228	9,608	8,192	5,471	5,628	5,098
8 yrs.	10,065	11,316	11,474	9,787	6,319	6,429	5,770
High School: Total	11,236	13,133	13,424	10,130	7,823	7,889	7,380
1–3 yrs.	10,425	11,900	12,292	9,466	6,882	7,011	6,360
4 yrs.	11,475	13,545	13,776	10,556	8,040	8,072	7,810
College: Total	16,363	18,793	19,081	13,917	10,500	10,484	10,460
1–3 yrs.	13,287	15,280	15,512	11,898	9,041	9,029	9,060
4 yrs.	16,677	19,193	19,459	14,356	10,672	10,673	1,082
5 yrs. or more	21,702	24,192	24,484	20,012	13,842	13,808	13,338

Source: U.S. Department of Commerce, Bureau of the Census. *Money Income in 1976 of Families and Persons in the United States*, Current Population Reports, Series P-60, No. 114. Washington: Government Printing Office, 1978.

The evidence doesn't suggest that earnings differences between men and women can be explained in terms of educational differences. In Table C, women earn less than men at every level of educational attainment. Table D shows that educational differences are much smaller than earnings differences in various occupations.

Broadly Defined Occupations

Broad categories of occupations include a number of different occupations within them. For example, within the classification "Professional and Kindred Workers," there are over sixty fairly broad occupational subgroups ranging from recreation worker to physician. Generally, as the definition of occupations is narrowed, more and more of the difference in wages of men and women can be explained by factors other than discrimination.

Last, But Not Least, Discrimination

The existence of other factors that contribute to higher wages for men than women doesn't exclude discrimination as a cause. What is the nature of this discrimination?

Some employers have prejudicial, "sexist" attitudes in employment, pay, and promotion. This is the case with employers who don't hire female applicants for such reasons as "women aren't as strong as men," "women aren't as coordinated as men," "women can't think systematically or deal with figures," "women are emotionally unstable," etc. There may be some jobs that aren't well suited for many women—for example, jobs that require hours of heavy physical work—but the number of such jobs is quite small. This basic kind of discrimination is covered by civil rights and equal employment legislation.

But discrimination may be much subtler than the above expressions of sexual bigotry. Stereotyping and traditional sex-occupational roles have become ingrained

Table D   Median Earnings and Years of Education, Year-Round Full-Time Employees, 1977

	Median Earnings		Median Years Education		Female, % of Male	
	Male	Female	Male	Female	Earnings	Education
Total Employed	13,945	8,376	12.5	12.5	60	100.0
White-Collar (Total)	16,366	9,144	NA	NA	55.9	NA
Prof., Technical & Kindred	17,431	11,365	16.6	16.3	65.2	98.2
Managers & Administrators	17,351	10,069	13.3	12.7	58.0	95.5
Sales Workers	15,198	6,701	13.0	12.4	44.1	94.4
Clerical & Kindred	13,323	8,369	12.7	12.6	62.8	99.2
Blue-Collar (Total)	12,716	7,043	12.1	11.8	55.3	91.5
Craft & Kindred	13,962	8,026	12.3	12.3	57.5	100.0
Operatives	12,036	6,864	12.1	11.6	57.0	95.9
Except Transport	11,807	6,865	12.1	11.5	58.1	95.0
Transport	12,361	NA	12.1	12.4	NA	102.5
Nonfarm Laborers	10,310	7,728	11.4	12.1	75	106.0
Service Workers	10,547	5,945	12.1	12.0	56.4	99.2

Source: U.S. Department of Commerce, Bureau of the Census, *Money Income in 1976 of Families and Persons in the United States,* Current Population Reports, Series P-60, No. 114. Washington: Government Printing Office, 1978.

in our society, and in every society for that matter. A generation ago, "doctor's kits" with sugar pills, toy thermometer, toy stethoscope, and a picture of a male doctor on the box were popular toys—as were "nurse's kits" with the same sugar pills and paraphernalia and a picture of a female nurse on the box. In a "Dick and Jane" reader of the 1950s, Dick tells Jane that she can't play ball with him and his friend, but must play with "Baby Sally." In the old family "sit-coms," the wife stayed at home while the husband worked.

Such stereotyping has a number of negative effects on women's wages. A small group of occupations becomes "women's work," and women become concentrated in these occupations. In addition, some employers (and even some women themselves) come to believe that "a woman's place is in the home." Some employers may offer women lower wages because they think that women work for fulfillment and satisfaction, while men work for money to support their families. These stereotypes and traditional attitudes change very slowly, even in the face of contradictory evidence.

Improving the Economic Status of Women

Since discrimination is a complex pattern of behavior, it can't be dealt with simplistically. Where discrimination in hiring and pay can be identified, it can be prosecuted under the relevant civil rights and equal employment opportunity legislation. Where there is a history of discrimination, affirmative action programs that require active searches for qualified female candidates is a proper course, but such programs may not (especially in the short run) be able to equate the percentage of employment in every occupation with the percentage of females in the population or even in the labor force. Of course, this approach also applies to discrimination against women in access to education or training programs.

The root of the problem, however, goes much deeper than statistical discrepancies in employment or sexist attitudes of employers. Broad stereotypes of

Problems

1. The Aband & Hope Mining Company is the only employer of labor within a 30-mile radius of its location in Desolation, W. Va. As it hires more labor, its total revenue (TR) and the wage per worker behave as follows

Workers per day	Wage per worker	TR per day
10	$10	$ 180
11	15	305
12	20	425
13	25	540
14	30	650
15	35	755
16	40	855
17	45	950
18	50	1040
19	55	1125
20	60	1205

   a. Is this firm a perfectly competitive buyer of labor services? How do you know?
   b. Calculate the firm's marginal factor cost (MFC) and marginal revenue product (MRP) of labor.
   c. Find the firm's equilibrium level of employment.
   d. Find the firm's equilibrium wage.
   e. In what sense does this firm exploit its labor? Identify the exploitation.

Table D Median Earnings and Years of Education, Year-Round Full-Time Employees, 1977

	Median Earnings		Median Years Education		Female, % of Male	
	Male	Female	Male	Female	Earnings	Education
Total Employed	13,945	8,376	12.5	12.5	60	100.0
White-Collar (Total)	16,366	9,144	NA	NA	55.9	NA
Prof., Technical & Kindred	17,431	11,365	16.6	16.3	65.2	98.2
Managers & Administrators	17,351	10,069	13.3	12.7	58.0	95.5
Sales Workers	15,198	6,701	13.0	12.4	44.1	94.4
Clerical & Kindred	13,323	8,369	12.7	12.6	62.8	99.2
Blue-Collar (Total)	12,716	7,043	12.1	11.8	55.3	91.5
Craft & Kindred	13,962	8,026	12.3	12.3	57.5	100.0
Operatives	12,036	6,864	12.1	11.6	57.0	95.9
Except Transport	11,807	6,865	12.1	11.5	58.1	95.0
Transport	12,361	NA	12.1	12.4	NA	102.5
Nonfarm Laborers	10,310	7,728	11.4	12.1	75	106.0
Service Workers	10,547	5,945	12.1	12.0	56.4	99.2

Source: U.S. Department of Commerce, Bureau of the Census, *Money Income in 1976 of Families and Persons in the United States*, Current Population Reports, Series P-60, No. 114. Washington: Government Printing Office, 1978.

in our society, and in every society for that matter. A generation ago, "doctor's kits" with sugar pills, toy thermometer, toy stethoscope, and a picture of a male doctor on the box were popular toys—as were "nurse's kits" with the same sugar pills and paraphernalia and a picture of a female nurse on the box. In a "Dick and Jane" reader of the 1950s, Dick tells Jane that she can't play ball with him and his friend, but must play with "Baby Sally." In the old family "sit-coms," the wife stayed at home while the husband worked.

Such stereotyping has a number of negative effects on women's wages. A small group of occupations becomes "women's work," and women become concentrated in these occupations. In addition, some employers (and even some women themselves) come to believe that "a woman's place is in the home." Some employers may offer women lower wages because they think that women work for fulfillment and satisfaction, while men work for money to support their families. These stereotypes and traditional attitudes change very slowly, even in the face of contradictory evidence.

Improving the Economic Status of Women

Since discrimination is a complex pattern of behavior, it can't be dealt with simplistically. Where discrimination in hiring and pay can be identified, it can be prosecuted under the relevant civil rights and equal employment opportunity legislation. Where there is a history of discrimination, affirmative action programs that require active searches for qualified female candidates is a proper course, but such programs may not (especially in the short run) be able to equate the percentage of employment in every occupation with the percentage of females in the population or even in the labor force. Of course, this approach also applies to discrimination against women in access to education or training programs.

The root of the problem, however, goes much deeper than statistical discrepancies in employment or sexist attitudes of employers. Broad stereotypes of women—or any other group—contribute to at least unconscious biases in employment and pay. Different labor force participation patterns and experience have contributed to lower pay for women. The solution to any form of discrimination involves expanded educational and training opportunities (particularly in skilled crafts where women haven't been employed traditionally), elimination of sexual-occupational stereotyping and widening access to occupations, and improvements in child-care services. These will reduce the supply of women in traditional, low-paid "women's" jobs and raise the productivity and demand for women in higher paid jobs.

In the end, ironically, the profit motive could be the force that will eliminate or reduce the effects of discrimination. As women and racial minorities become more trained and productive, it becomes more profitable for firms to hire them and less profitable to discriminate against them. As the occupational opportunities expand and occupational mobility increases, women and racial minorities will become less concentrated in a few occupations and industries, and it will become harder to discriminate against them in any given occupation.

Summary

1. Imperfections in labor markets affect resource prices, employment, income distribution, and economic efficiency.
2. A **labor union** is a cartel of sellers of labor. This type of monopoly in the sale of labor is legal because of the unique characteristics of labor as a commodity and the inherent disadvantages of individual workers in bargaining with large employers.
3. **Craft unions** organize workers within a craft, and try to keep wages high by restricting entry into the craft and the supply of labor in the craft.
4. **Industrial unions** organize workers within a given industry or within a given firm. Industrial unions have no control over entry of labor into the industry or the firm.
5. **Monopsony** in the purchase of labor refers to labor markets in which there is a single buyer of labor. A monopsonist is not a price taker in the purchase of labor services.
6. A monopsonist in the labor market will hire where the MRP of the last unit of labor equals the MFC of hiring it. This will be at a smaller quantity of labor than for a price taker in the labor market, and a monopsonist will pay a lower wage for a given quantity of labor than will a perfect competitor. Monopsony leads to exploitation as workers receive wages less than the MRP of the last unit of labor hired.
7. **Institutional imperfections** in labor markets—lack of information, geographic immobility, occupational immobility, and discrimination—weaken the relationship between wages and the relative attractiveness of employment and allow some workers in high wage occupations to earn a form of economic rent.
8. **Discrimination** affects wages and employment opportunities of women and racial minorities. It's not always easy to isolate the economic effects of discrimination from other factors that lead to differences in wages and employment opportunities for different groups within society.

Concepts for Review	craft union industrial union ratchet effect	bargaining power monopsony wage bill	immobility transfer price discrimination institutional imperfection

Questions

1. What is a monopsonist? What are the differences and similarities between a monopsonist and a monopolist? Compared with perfect competition, how does monopsony affect the wage paid to labor and the employment of labor? Explain your answers.
2. Many people consider Babe Ruth to be the greatest baseball player of all time. He hit 714 home runs in his career, had a .342 lifetime batting average, and even had a career earned-run average of 2.28 as a pitcher (0.87 in World Series competition). He was so popular that Yankee Stadium is still called "the house that Ruth built." Taking inflation and higher taxes into account, it has been estimated that the Babe's $80,000 salary in 1930 is equivalent to about $250,000 to $300,000 in the 1970s. Few people compare Pete Rose to the Babe as a baseball player, and almost nobody puts Reggie Jackson in the same category with the Babe, but they both make salaries in excess of $300,000 (Rose's 1979 salary with the Phillies was $800,000). Are Pete Rose and Reggie Jackson overpaid? How do you account for the fact that their salaries are so much higher than the modern equivalent of Babe Ruth's highest salary?
3. What is the difference between a craft union and an industrial union? How does each gain a wage above the competitive equilibrium wage? Which is more likely to be successful in getting higher wages and maintaining full employment for its members? Explain.
4. The monopolist in the product market was assumed to maximize profit. In what sense is a trade union a monopolist in the labor market? What are the difficulties in assuming that unions seek to maximize a single variable? Consider the following possibilities.
   a. Unions seek the maximum wage rate.
   b. Unions seek the maximum level of employment in their craft or industry.
   c. Unions seek the maximum total wage bill in their craft or industry.
5. Unions consistently support increases in the minimum wage—although relatively few union members actually work for the minimum wage—and general economic policies to stimulate the demand for goods and services. Is it in the unions' self-interest to support these types of policies? Explain.
6. How do imperfections in labor markets affect the relationship between wages and the relative attractiveness of work in various occupations? Why is this significant?
7. How does discrimination in labor markets affect wages, employment, economic efficiency, and community economic welfare? How could you identify discrimination and its effects?
8. What tools does the government have available to it in fighting discrimination? How effective are they?

Problems

1. The Aband & Hope Mining Company is the only employer of labor within a 30-mile radius of its location in Desolation, W. Va. As it hires more labor, its total revenue (TR) and the wage per worker behave as follows

Workers per day	Wage per worker	TR per day
10	$10	$ 180
11	15	305
12	20	425
13	25	540
14	30	650
15	35	755
16	40	855
17	45	950
18	50	1040
19	55	1125
20	60	1205

   a. Is this firm a perfectly competitive buyer of labor services? How do you know?
   b. Calculate the firm's marginal factor cost (MFC) and marginal revenue product (MRP) of labor.
   c. Find the firm's equilibrium level of employment.
   d. Find the firm's equilibrium wage.
   e. In what sense does this firm exploit its labor? Identify the exploitation.

PART SIX
Economic Challenges for the Eighties

Perhaps the most important reason for studying economics is to acquire a set of basic tools that can help us analyze the sorts of problems that confront us every day. In this section, we'll try to put all the tools together in order to focus on two problems that are central to the long-run survival of mankind: energy and poverty.

With the OPEC embargo of 1973, the energy problem suddenly and dramatically emerged on the scene as one of the most important issues of our time. Your study of economics should help you to understand that the problem is considerably more serious and complicated that a mere conspiracy of greedy oil companies and Arabs. Whether and how the problem can be solved represents one of the greatest economic challenges of the 1980s.

The problem of poverty is hardly a new one. In the final chapter of this section, we'll take a hard look at the facts of poverty. Economic analysis can identify some possible approaches to solving it and can identify the strengths and weaknesses of the alternatives, but it can't itself resolve the issue of poverty because of the many normative questions involved.

17

Energy and the Economy

Preview: Many Americans believe that the energy crisis began with the OPEC oil boycott in 1973 and that the problem is simply a conspiracy of "oil companies and Arabs" to keep prices high. In fact, the current energy crisis is a complex problem with a variety of roots: a traditional belief that resources are unlimited, a lifestyle centered on cheap energy, and a number of selfish and unselfish actions by producers and government regulators. In this chapter, we'll take a close look at the energy problem and at a variety of strategies for dealing with it.

In November of 1973, an embargo on oil shipments to the United States by the Arab members of the Organization of Petroleum Exporting Countries (OPEC) caused an "energy crisis" to emerge seemingly out of nowhere. Long lines formed at gasoline pumps, gas stations stopped giving away free glasses and checking oil, and many stations simply closed down. As the crisis spread to other fuels, many businesses reduced hours or closed due to fuel and energy shortages, and households were exhorted to cut down on home heating by keeping thermostats at a lower setting.

Various short-lived attempts were made to conserve energy. Demand for small cars became so strong that it became difficult to trade in large luxury cars for subcompacts. Commuters formed car pools and even started riding buses and trains again. Highway speed limits were lowered, and (at least initially) the lower speed limits were vigorously enforced.

By the end of the decade, however, many of the pre-embargo patterns had returned, due, at least in part, to some softening of oil prices in 1975 and 1976 and to a widely held belief that the "crisis" was simply contrived by oil companies and Arabs in the first place. In Table 1, note that

Table 1 Trends in U.S. Energy Consumption, 1958–1977

	Average annual percent change		
	1958–1973	1973–1976	1976–1977
Total Energy Consumption	4.0	−0.1	4.3
Petroleum and natural gas liquid	4.1	0.2	6.1
Natural gas	4.9	−3.4	1.1
Coal	2.0	3.2	6.1
Net electric power generated	7.3	3.2	6.1

Source: *Economic Report of the President.* Washington: Government Printing Office, 1978, p. 181.

the percentage increases in energy consumption, except for natural gas and electricity, are higher during the late 1970s than during the "cheap energy" years between 1958 and 1973.

Per capita energy consumption in the United States and some other industrialized countries are compared in Table 2. The energy consumption figures are kilogram of coal equivalent—i.e., per capita energy consumption in the United States in 1976 was equivalent to the energy in 11,554 kg. of coal. One possible explanation of the difference between energy consumption in the United States and other countries is the historic abundance of energy resources in the United States and the resulting low energy prices that have locked us into a relatively "energy intensive" lifestyle. As our domestic reserves have become depleted, however, we have been forced to increase oil imports to take the place of domestic production. By the end of 1978, imports accounted for about 45 percent of the crude oil consumed in the United States.

Table 2 Per Capita Energy Consumption, United States and Selected Industrialized Countries, 1976

Country	Per capita energy consumption (kg. of coal equivalent)	Percent change, 1973–1976
United States	11,554	−1.6
Sweden	6,046	1.4
West Germany	5,922	0.6
United Kingdom	5,268	−5.9
France	4,380	−2.2
Japan	3,679	−6.1
Switzerland	3,340	−13.8

Source: *U.N. Statistical Yearbook, 1977.* New York: United Nations, 1978, pp. 385-387.

Cheap Energy and the Depletion of Reserves

Cheap energy has been an important source of economic growth, and has played a major part in our high living standards. For many years, government policies and tax laws promoted oil exploration and extraction. Tax laws allowed write-offs of exploration costs and the deduction of a 27 percent "depletion allowance" from the incomes of oil companies. The incentives for exploration and extraction were so strong that gasoline, fuel oil, and natural gas could be sold at very low retail prices —with the loss of profit at the retail level more than made up for by the profits and tax savings from exploration and extraction.

Households responded to cheap energy with an energy-using lifestyle. The availability and low price of gasoline encouraged daily migrations from "bedroom communities" to jobs in the cities—mostly via the private automobile, a notoriously inefficient energy user. Until the late 1970s, our cars themselves reflected the cheapness of gasoline— large, accessory-laden, over-powered vehicles.

Suburban communities were likewise designed with little regard for energy efficiency. Heating the standard suburban single-family house, for example, requires more energy than heating a townhouse of the same size because the single-family house has four outside walls while townhouses have only two or three.

The public utilities did their part to encourage energy use among households. With cheap fuel and economies of scale, many gas and electric companies used block pricing which charged lower rates as more gas or electricity was used. With lower rates for additional energy consumption, electric dishwashers, water heaters, air conditioners, lawnmowers, etc., became more attractive.

Firms also responded to cheap energy. The availability of fuel and its cheapness made it profitable for industry and agriculture to substitute machinery for labor. In agriculture, petrochemicals have replaced manure as the basic fertilizer. The products firms manufacture— plastics, synthetic fabrics, and numerous other household products derived from oil—reflected the cheapness of oil.

These forces led to dramatic increases in the demand for oil and other fossil fuels. Unfortunately, these are "wasting resources" which are consumed far more rapidly than nature replenishes them. Many of the best sources of oil are already becoming worked out, and in the future more and more oil will have to be extracted from less productive sources at increasing cost. As oil and energy become more expensive—which they certainly will—the effects will show up as higher costs and prices of most of the things we buy.

Dealing with the Problem

There are no neat, painless solutions to the energy problem and certainly none that don't involve normative considerations. Any policies to deal with energy problems have to recognize two basic (and usually unpleasant) facts. First, energy resources are becoming more scarce; as a result, energy will become more expensive in the future. Secondly, the demand for energy and energy resources will continue to increase with the spread of energy-using techniques in agricultural production, with rising incomes which increase the demand for goods and services.

Price Deregulation

Until the late 1970s, regulations established ceiling prices on *old* domestic oil—i.e., oil from existing wells and fields—and on interstate sales of natural gas. These prices were below equilibrium world oil and gas prices. For natural gas, the regulated interstate price was also below the price on gas sold within gas-producing states.

Regulated prices contributed to high energy consumption by providing insufficient incentives for firms and households to economize in their use of energy. Firms have little incentive to undertake the cost of innovations that make production more energy efficient if the price of energy is low. Similarly, households are less likely to economize on energy if it is relatively inexpensive as a result of regulation of prices. The household in Figure 1, for example, allocates its income (I) between energy (gasoline, home heating fuel, and electricity) and other goods (y). At the regulated price P_e^*, the household maximizes utility by consuming $\bar{e}$ units of energy and spending $\bar{y}$ on other goods. At the higher equilibrium price, the household's real income is lower and it will substitute other goods for energy. The household's energy consumption falls to $\bar{e}'$ as a result.

Regulated prices also lead to periodic shortages by keeping the price of fuel stable in the face of increasing demand and rising production costs. The impact of price regulations on consumption and shortages can be shown with a simple supply-and-demand model. In Figure 2a, the market supply (S) and demand (D) curves determine an equilibrium price of $\bar{P}$ and equilibrium output of Q_S. Suppose that the price is frozen at $\bar{P}^* = P$. As income and population rise, causing greater demand for the things that make up the "good life" (air conditioning, big cars,

Figure 1 Household's Response to Regulated Fuel Prices

Figure 2 Impact of Regulation of Fuel Prices

(a) Increase in Demand

(b) Decrease in Supply

houses in the suburbs, etc.), the demand for oil and natural gas increases, as shown by the shift of the demand curve from D to D' in Figure 2a. At the regulated price, P^*, the increase in demand creates a "shortage," because the price isn't allowed to rise to its new equilibrium level ($\bar{P}'$).

Regulated prices also contribute to shortages by keeping prices stable in the face of rising costs. As the best oil and gas fields are worked out, increasing amounts of labor and capital are required to produce each additional unit of oil and gas. This raises the marginal cost of oil and natural gas, and therefore the supply price. The effect of rising costs is shown in Figure 2b by the shift of supply from S to S', which raises the equilibrium price still further to $\bar{P}''$. Rising costs have thus increased excess demand at a regulated price.

Some form of energy price deregulation was a key part of the energy program of the Ford administration after 1974 and the Carter energy proposals after 1977. However, widespread doubts about the cause or even the existence of genuine energy shortages have made price deregulation less attractive to Congress than to the Executive branch. President Ford and the Congress reached deadlocks on the issue between 1974 and 1976, and the provisions of the Natural Gas Act of 1978 are so complex that its effectiveness in deregulating prices and encouraging greater output isn't certain. In 1979, President Carter couldn't convince many Democrats in Congress of the merits of deregulating oil prices.

Advocates of price deregulation argue that it will reduce enforcement machinery required with regulated prices and will eliminate the resulting excess demand and energy shortages. On the demand side, rising prices would reduce excess demand by reducing quantity demanded. On the supply side, it is argued that deregulation and higher prices would attack excess demand by encouraging greater output.

Arguments for deregulation or other means of bringing prices up to their scarcity levels have considerable merit. By setting a maximum price below equilibrium, effective price ceilings tend to cause overconsumption and underproduction. Price regulations also involve efficiency losses by keeping the price below the value of additional units to the community. In Figure 3, the supply price of any quantity of natural gas reflects the marginal cost (MC) of the last unit produced—the supply curve (S) is the total production by all producers at the same MC. At the regulated price, P^*, there is excess demand for natural gas and the value of the last unit produced (P') exceeds its MC. If the price regulation were lifted, the price and output would adjust to $\overline{P}$ and $\overline{Q}$, clearing the market where $\overline{P} = MC$, and a net gain in efficiency would be realized.

However, the immediate effects of deregulation aren't always those predicted for the long run, after markets have had time to adjust. When legislation was passed in 1978 that raised natural gas prices, a natural gas "glut" appeared almost overnight. Gas producers and experts preferred to call it a "bubble" or (in fluent bureaucratese) "an overdeliverability situation."

What seems to have happened is the following. Gas producers, expecting prices to rise with deregulation, increased production but held some of their gas off the market. In Figure 4, expectations of a price of P' after deregulation encouraged production to Q', but producers supplied only Q^*, holding the remaining gas in anticipation of higher prices. Meanwhile, high oil prices and policies to encourage greater domestic production resulted in more oil exploration and the drilling of new wells. One of the byproducts of these efforts was the discovery of new natural gas wells.

When gas prices were allowed to rise, the gas that had been held back, as well as the newly discovered gas, hit the market. The result was

Figure 3 Efficiency Gain from Deregulation

excess supply at the "incremental cost" or marginal cost price. This doesn't necessarily mean that there is a long-term abundance of natural gas or that the shortage never existed. High gas prices and uncertain supplies had caused many large users to shift to other fuels, coal in particular. As producers adjust output levels and as the stored gas reserves are consumed, the equilibrium price of natural gas will most likely remain considerably above the old regulated price.

Even after markets have adjusted to deregulation, we may get dramatic increases in prices without similar increases in production. As production is pushed to less productive oil and gas fields and as more oil has to be "stripped" from old wells, the supply becomes less and less elastic, as indicated in Figure 4. Removing the regulated price P^* and allowing price to adjust to equilibrium in this case would cause a large price increase but only a small increase in production.

One of the criticisms of deregulation is that it will lead to high prices and windfall profits for producers. If barriers to entry of new producers are relatively low, excess profits will attract new producers, increasing supply and reducing economic profit. However, substantial barriers to entry can protect the economic profits of producers already in the market even in the long run. Although the concentration ratios in the various stages of petroleum production aren't unusually high, there are substantial barriers against the entry of new independent firms—especially in refining. This isn't sufficient reason for maintaining artificially low regulated prices, however, since it would be possible simply to tax excessive windfall profits that result from higher prices. However, many in the oil industry and in Congress who supported

Figure 4 Market Adjustment to Deregulation

Natural Gas, billions of cubic feet/year

President Carter's deregulation of oil prices opposed the imposition of his proposed excess profits tax.

In Figure 5, the supply curve (S) is the sum of the quantities produced by individual producers at every level of MC. At the regulated price P^*, there is excess demand and the value of the last unit produced is greater than the MC of the last unit produced. The unregulated price, $\overline{P}$, clears the market with $\overline{P} = MC$, but the equilibrium price is greater than the average cost per unit of oil produced.[1] At the unregulated price, then, oil producers receive an aggregate economic profit shown by the shaded area π. With freedom of entry, the supply curve would move to the right and economic profits would fall. However, if there are significant barriers against the entry of new firms, as in oil refining and pipelines, there is no reason to expect entry and competition to drive economic profits to zero for the industry.

Figure 5 Windfall Profits and Excess Profits Tax

Oil, billions of barrels per year

The economic profit in Figure 5 could be taxed away, giving a new wholesale price of P_W'. Consumers, of course, would still have to pay a higher price than they did before deregulation.

Deregulation alone probably won't be sufficient to "solve" the energy problem. Many of us are locked into energy consumption patterns by the lifestyle that developed during the days of cheap energy. Empirical evidence indicates low elasticity of demand for energy, so it would take

---

1. The total cost (TC) of Q barrels of oil is the sum of the marginal costs of additional units between zero and Q. The average cost per barrel of all oil produced is $AC = TC/\overline{Q}$.

enormous increases in price to reduce energy consumption dramatically. While the experience of most European countries where energy prices are much higher than in the United States indicates that such a solution is possible, such increases probably would be politically unacceptable in the United States in the immediate future.

Reducing Demand

Little can be done about depletion and rising prices of crude oil and natural gas, but it may be possible to supplement the effects of higher prices with an attack on the demand side of the problem. Tougher standards on insulation and building design, for example, could make homes and factories more energy efficient and reduce the demand for energy for home heating and cooling.

A technological revolution would be required to make private autos very energy efficient per passenger mile—a point made by Secretary of Transportation Brock Adams in 1978 when he told American automobile producers that they would have to "reinvent the automobile." In the meantime, lower speed limits (or strict enforcement of existing 55 mile per hour limits), tighter fuel economy standards, and perhaps mandatory weight and horsepower limits for autos could reduce the demand for gasoline. Expansion and improvements in the quality of public transit could aid in this effort.

Recognizing ways of reducing the demand for energy is easy enough, but actually reducing demand isn't easy. With a basic lifestyle tied to energy consumption, it's difficult to convince people to do without things they are used to in the interests of energy conservation. Mandatory weight and horsepower limits on cars are unpopular with auto producers and with those who wish to have the freedom to choose large automobiles. Building adequate public transit networks is very expensive, and massive spending to construct such facilities isn't likely to be very popular.

Relaxing Environmental Standards

Many experts estimate that the United States has enough coal to last up to 500 years. As oil becomes more scarce and expensive, there will be increasing pressures to return to coal to fire electric generators, to serve as an industrial fuel where possible, and even to serve as a source of natural gas through a process called "gasification." Innovations have made it possible to extract more oil from largely depleted wells, and the search for new oil has been extended into the sea. Mining and refining oil from shale and oil-bearing sands are possible ways of increasing oil output.

These programs would make more energy available, but the social and environmental costs would be substantial. Strip mining of coal has a devastating effect on the landscape—even when the mined areas are "recontoured." Coal mining also discharges acid mine wastes into lakes and streams. Mining enough oil-bearing shale to make it a significant source of oil would have many of the same environmental effects as strip mining.

When being "pro-environment" ceased to be fashionable, and when it became clear that cleaning and preserving the environment would be costly and would force us to alter our lifestyles, environmental programs and restrictions were portrayed as an important cause of the energy crisis, unemployment, and inflation. Many firms lobbied hard for a moratorium on new environmental restrictions and elimination of some of the existing restrictions. Relaxing and reversing environmental standards and restrictions may reduce the demand for energy and reduce cost pressures slightly, but experts estimate that the effects of environmental standards on inflation in the mid-1970s are very small. Since many of the firms affected by environmental standards are oligopolists, it isn't clear that any cost reductions from looser environmental standards would be passed on as lower prices of products. Allowing firms and households to dump more pollutants into the environment increases the risk of pollution-related illness and even death, and this additional cost would be borne by the community.

Alternative Energy Sources

Another means of escaping our great dependency on oil is to develop new means of generating energy. Most of the public attention in this area has focused on nuclear power. Nuclear-powered electric generators use very little fossil fuel, and don't create smoke or smog, but they do generate a lot of heat. Water from surrounding rivers and bodies of water is used to cool the generators, and the warmed water is returned to the rivers and lakes. This upsets a delicate ecological balance by promoting the growth of vegetation in the water, and it speeds the aging (eutrophication) of lakes and rivers.

Nuclear power plants use enriched uranium and create plutonium as a waste product. Disposing of the plutonium, which remains radioactive for many years, could become a major problem and could lead to radioactive contamination of rivers, lakes, and even land. In the hands of terrorists, plutonium can be fabricated into crude nuclear weapons. The thermal pollution and risk of disaster from plutonium are thus important social costs of nuclear power.

Other alternative energy sources—solar power, wind power, geothermal energy, etc.—have been suggested as cures for the energy problem. Unfortunately, at present all such sources are either unreliable, not universally acceptable, or still in the experimental stage. Expenditures for research in these fields could pay high dividends in the future, but not in the next few years.

Close-up

The Three-Mile Island "Incident" and the Costs of Nuclear Power

The merits and dangers of nuclear power have been debated almost continuously since the end of World War II. In the early postwar period, optimism on the "peaceful uses of atomic energy" was at its peak—some people even arguing that nuclear power would be so cheap to generate that it wouldn't be worth metering. In the late 1960s and 1970s, the debate turned to the merits of using nuclear power to reduce oil consumption vs. the environmental and health hazards associated with nuclear power plants.

On March 28, 1979, what the government called an "incident" at the Three-Mile Island nuclear generating facility near Harrisburg, Pennsylvania, may have changed our views on the costs and benefits of nuclear power for the next generation. Through a combination of human error and mechanical failure, there was a partial "meltdown" of the plant's nuclear fuel which filled the reactor room with radioactive water and steam and caused some radiation to leak into the surrounding area. Apparently, the "incident" didn't turn into the full-fledged disaster that many fear in nuclear accidents, but the people who live in the vicinity of the facility have been exposed to increased radiation, and the effects of this exposure won't be known for years. Experts project a "slightly higher" incidence of cancer in the future among those exposed to the radiation—hardly comforting, since the health effects of radiation exposure during nuclear weapons tests in the 1950s are now becoming obvious.

Experts argue that we have the technology to make nuclear generating plants safer than they are. However, according to some of these experts, the additional devices and controls necessary to make the plants safe would make them too complex to operate.

If all nuclear generating plants were shut down, the external social costs that became so obvious in the Three-Mile Island incident would be gone, but so would the benefits of nuclear power. Reduced generating capacity would increase the probability of power blackouts or brownouts as the capacity became overloaded. Turning to fossil-fueled generators would bring us up against the high prices of oil and gas, or would require the conversion of more generators to coal (which also imposes social costs in the form of health hazards due to air pollution). The third possibility is to reduce energy consumption, but this would take time given our entrenched energy-intensive life-style. Even the advocates of nuclear fusion, solar power, wind power, and other alternative sources of energy concede that these wouldn't supply a very substantial portion of our energy needs until the turn of the century.

Nationalization of Energy

As the energy crunch gets tighter and affects larger numbers of people, nationalization will probably receive more attention as an approach to the energy problem. Advocates of nationalization argue that publicly owned producers would be more likely than their private counterparts to set prices that reflect the marginal social costs of energy.

The traditional nationalization proposals would establish a public monopoly in oil and gas production (with compensation to the private companies for their nationalized property). Figure 6 shows a public monopoly in oil production. The firm would try to set the price of oil equal to the marginal social cost (MSC), including the external social costs associated with the production and consumption of oil. Since we almost certainly are producing oil in the rising portion of the average cost curve, the price set by the public monopoly would exceed average social cost (ASC). This surplus could be simply refunded to taxpayers or used in a number of other ways to support energy related research or to offset the impact of high energy prices on low-income users.

The potential problems of nationalization were discussed in Chapter 15. One important problem is that the public managers might be under heavy political pressure to provide cheap energy and rely on government subsidies to make up any losses. Such policies would be disastrous in the long run, although probably quite popular in the short run. Suppose that the public oil monopoly sets its price at P^* and produces an annual output of Q^* in Figure 7. There is an efficiency loss due to overproduction (P^* is less than MC at Q^*), and if P^* is less than AC, there is a loss that would have to be made up with subsidies—at the

Figure 6 Public Monopoly in Oil Production

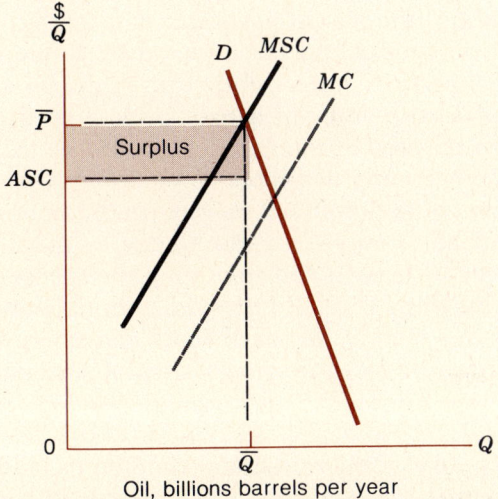

Oil, billions barrels per year

Figure 7 Efficiency Loss Due to Overproduction by Public Monopoly

expense of other government programs or higher taxes. Furthermore, the artificially low price would encourage overconsumption and accelerate the depletion of reserves.

A somewhat less dramatic proposal has been made to establish one publicly owned oil firm to compete with the private producers and provide public officials with accurate data on the costs of producing oil. Entry into oil production is restricted by a number of economic and institutional barriers, but a public firm might be able to bring about the same result as the entry of a new private producer. In addition, the information on production and cost would be valuable, since the only information currently available comes from private producers.

Some form of nationalized energy production, if properly managed, could be a viable course of action to deal with the energy problem, but we have very little basis for predicting the success of such a venture in advance. One thing is clear, however: nationalization would not change the increasing scarcity of fossil fuels and energy, and a nationalized energy firm would face the same basic problems and choices as a private firm.

Won't Anything Work?

Economists are at their worst, and economics is its most discouraging, when looking at seemingly straightforward solutions to complex economic problems. There is no way of dealing with the energy problem that doesn't impose some costs on the community, and the people who bear the brunt of the costs aren't necessarily those who enjoy the greatest benefits from any given approach. The energy crisis isn't a temporary problem that will go away quickly with peace in the Middle East, the enactment of (or failure to enact) new legislation, wishful thinking, or simply ignoring it.

Any successful approach to the energy problem will have to do a number of things:

1. *Reduce demand for energy and energy resources* by improved residential construction techniques, more energy-efficient housing design, more efficient automobiles, expanded mass transit, etc.
2. *Encourage energy conservation* by high prices or high taxes on energy-inefficient activities.
3. *Develop new sources of energy* which don't accelerate the depletion of fossil-fuel reserves.

Additional specific measures will be needed to deal with special problems and cases. Where the production and sale of fuels or other types of energy is highly concentrated and barriers to entry are prohibitive, antitrust measures may be necessary to maintain competitive pressure. Windfall profits taxes may be required to prevent any segment of the community from bearing an unfair share of the burden of higher energy prices or reaping windfall gains by virtue of market power. As energy prices rise, the lowest income households will find it increasingly difficult to provide even the barest energy needs—such as heating and cooking—and some form of assistance may be necessary in these cases.

A Very Short Conclusion

Political rhetoric and public relations campaigns notwithstanding, it's impossible to find energy or environmental policies that make everybody better off. The problem cannot be left completely to private markets, because even competitive private markets do a poor job of dealing with externalities and social costs. Policies will have to be based on extensive empirical research that identifies "winners" and "losers" from alternative policies and programs. The policymakers will still have to wrestle with difficult normative questions. The course taken will affect the environmental and energy problems, the basic macroeconomic problems of unemployment and inflation, and even our long-term economic welfare and survival.

Summary

1. Historically, energy prices have been relatively low in the United States, due to our extensive deposits of oil, gas, and coal, and because of government policies that encouraged extraction and underpricing.

2. Low energy prices led to an energy-intensive lifestyle and the adoption of energy-intensive production methods that have made energy consumption less responsive to increasing scarcity and rising prices than in the other industrialized countries.
3. Regulated maximum prices on crude oil and natural gas have encouraged overconsumption, underproduction, and led to chronic shortages.
4. Complete deregulation would reduce excess demand for energy and improve efficiency by bringing prices closer to marginal costs, but probably wouldn't lead to dramatic increases in production.
5. Reducing the demand for energy will require major changes in the American lifestyle or major energy-saving technological changes and innovations.
6. Partial or complete nationalization of energy production may be able to bring prices closer to marginal social costs, but there are potential practical problems of management and administration. Nationalized firms will have to make choices similar to those facing private firms.

Questions

1. One part of the Carter administration's National Energy Plan in 1978 was to raise all domestic crude oil prices to world levels.
   a. What would be the most likely consequences of this action on prices to users of crude oil in the U.S.? How would it affect the domestic production of oil?
   b. How would the policy affect the prices of other goods?
2. In the 1960s, the coal-mining regions of the U.S. were economically depressed areas. In the late 1970s, many coal-mining areas experienced almost unprecedented prosperity. How can you explain this economically?
3. The 1978 *Economic Report of the President* states one of the central goals of the National Energy Plan is to "... bring prices and social costs of energy together."
   a. What are some of the social costs of production and consumption of energy? How would you go about quantifying them?
   b. Why have U.S. energy prices diverged from social cost?
   c. How would you assess the costs and the benefits of achieving this objective?
4. In 1978, legislation established "incremental cost" as the basis for natural gas pricing.
   a. What is "incremental cost"?
   b. How would "incremental cost" pricing of gas affect economic efficiency and welfare, compared with pre-1979 regulated prices?
   c. Who stands to gain and who stands to lose economically as a result of this program?
   d. How would you go about compensating the losers for their losses?
5. One of the criticisms of deregulation of oil and gas prices is that the only results will be higher prices for consumers and windfall profits for producers. Evaluate the economic merits of this argument. Under what conditions would it be valid, and under what conditions would it be

invalid? Is this a correct prediction for the U.S. in the 1980s? To the extent that this result occurs with deregulation, how could it be corrected?
6. What are some of the economic costs and benefits of reconversion to coal and the expansion of nuclear power capacity as solutions to the energy problem?
7. Evaluate the economic merits of nationalization of oil and natural gas production as a means of dealing with the energy problem. Would this action mean lower energy prices?
8. In what sense are energy conservation and environmental preservation compatible goals? In what sense are they competing goals?

18

Poverty

Preview: Individuals and societies have been concerned with the problem of poverty for centuries, and numerous programs have been proposed, debated, and attempted to reduce the problem. Yet poverty persists. In this chapter, we'll take a close look at the economic roots of poverty and at the characteristics of those we classify as "poor." We'll also examine the strengths and weaknesses of a number of alternative strategies for dealing with the problem of poverty.

The problem of poverty is, unfortunately, never out of date. When John Stuart Mill wrote his *Principles of Political Economy* in 1848, one of his prime concerns was applying economic analysis to the problem of poverty. The great nineteenth-century British economist Alfred Marshall asserted that all of the great economists are "social reformers at heart"; for Marshall in 1890, the most important social problem was poverty. Professor R. M. Hartwell of Oxford, a widely respected contemporary economic historian, has written that "economics is, in essence, the study of poverty; economic history, similarly, is largely the history of poverty."[1]

Poverty is not the exclusive domain of economics, however. Virtually all of the social sciences—psychology, sociology, history, political science, and (of course) economics—can tell us something about the problem. Such questions as the effect of nutrition and health on economic performance and the recent inflammatory issue of the role of heredity as determinants of success even give the problem a biological dimension.

---

1. R. M. Hartwell, "The Consequences of the Industrial Revolution in England for the Poor," in R. M. Hartwell et. al., *The Long Debate on Poverty* (London: The Institute of Economic Affairs, 1972), p. 3.

This chapter is directed at the economic aspects of the problem of poverty in America and an economic analysis of some of the alternative ways of dealing with it. It isn't easy to divorce the economic analysis of poverty from the normative side of the problem because poverty hits some of our most fundamental values and attitudes—such as social justice, equity, the work ethic, etc.

How Poor Is Poor?

Calvin Coolidge is alleged to have proclaimed that when people are out of work, unemployment results. In this vein, we could say that when people have low incomes, poverty results. This statement isn't as ridiculous as it sounds—or as Coolidge's trenchant analysis of unemployment. Unless all households or persons receive equal incomes, some are going to be "poorer" than others in the sense that they have a smaller share of the community's income.

There are a number of ways to show the degree of inequality in the distribution of income. One way is to compare the cumulative percentage of families with the cumulative percentage of income received. Table 1 shows the percentage of national income received by the poorest 20 percent of the populace, the poorest 40 percent, and so on. With *complete equality*, 20 percent of the families would receive 20 percent of the aggregate income, 40 percent of the families would receive 40 percent of the income, etc. With *complete inequality*, one family would receive all of the income. Table 1 shows complete equality, complete inequality, and the distribution of income among families in the U.S. in 1976.

The information in Table 1 is presented graphically in the *Lorenz curve* in Figure 1.

- The **Lorenz curve** shows the cumulative percentage of national income received by cumulative percentages of families.

With complete equality, the Lorenz curve would be a straight 45° line

Table 1 Percentage Distribution of Income

	Percent of Aggregate Income Received		
Percent of Families	Complete Equality	Complete Inequality	United States, 1976
20	20	0	5.4
40	40	0	17.2
60	60	0	34.8
80	80	0	58.9
100	100	100	100.0

Source: U.S. Department of Labor, *Handbook of Labor Statistics, 1977*. Washington: Government Printing Office, 1977, p. 33.

Figure 1 Lorenz Curve

from the origin to the point defined by 100 percent of national income and 100 percent of families. With complete inequality, the Lorenz curve runs along the horizontal axis and then jumps up to the point defined by 100 percent of the national income and 100 percent of the families.

- The closer the Lorenz curve lies to the 45° complete equality line, the greater the equality of income distribution.

In Figure 1, the broken Lorenz curve for Sweden in 1972 shows a more equal distribution of income than the Lorenz curve for the U.S.

The degree of inequality of income distribution is also reflected in the value of the *Gini index*.

- The **Gini index** is the ratio of the area between the Lorenz curve and the complete equality line over the entire area between the complete equality line and the complete inequality line.

The value of the Gini index will lie between zero (complete equality, with the Lorenz curve on the complete equality line) and one (complete inequality, with the Lorenz curve on the complete inequality line). Figure 2 shows values of the Gini index between 1947 and 1976, and indicates somewhat less inequality in 1976 (Gini index = .359) than in 1947 (Gini index = .375). However, the path of the Gini index over time hasn't been smooth, and inequality of income distribution increased between the mid 1960s and the mid 1970s.

"Relative Poverty"

One way to define the dividing line between the poor and the nonpoor is with a **relative poverty standard.** One type of relative poverty standard picks some cutoff in the size distribution of income—say, the lowest 20 percent of families ranked by income—and defines all families below this cutoff as "poor." Another relative poverty standard defines the poverty line as incomes below a certain percentage of the average or median income of all families.

One advantage of a relative poverty standard is that the poverty line is adjusted over time not only for changes in average or median income, but also for changes in the real standard of living of the family earning the average or median income. Families who could consume only half of the goods and services of the typical family would probably consider themselves poor, even if their living standards were above some rigidly defined "subsistence" level.

There are, however, some problems with relative poverty standards. For one thing, the poverty line varies with economic conditions. During serious recessions or depressions when the average income is low, some families may be above the poverty line who are in real need. In periods of high average incomes, some families who aren't in real need may be below the poverty line.

Relative poverty standards also lead to a number of irrelevant "red herring" arguments. If poverty is only judged by relative standards, for example, it could be argued that we can reduce or eliminate it by confiscating wealth and income from the rich and destroying it. Or, if

Figure 2 Concentration of Income (Gini Index) United States, 1947–1976

Source: U. S. Department of Commerce, Bureau of the Census. *Money Income in 1976 of Persons and Families in the United States*, Current Population Reports, Series P-60, No. 114. Washington: Government Printing Office, 1978.

the typical family can afford a four-bedroom house and two cars, households who could purchase only a three-bedroom house and one car may be judged poor. These arguments are correct semantically, but they aren't relevant to realistic relative poverty standards. The median income of a four-member family in the U.S. in 1976, for example, was about $17,300. If we define the poverty standard as 50 percent of the median income, the poverty line for a four-member family in 1976 would have been about $8650, or about 86 percent of the Bureau of Labor Statistics' estimate of $10,040 as the low-income budget for a four-member family in 1976.

"Absolute Poverty"

Traditionally, most economists have defined *subsistence* as an **absolute poverty standard**. In 1817, David Ricardo, one of the major figures in the development of economics, defined subsistence as the "power of the labourer to support himself and the family which may be necessary to keep up the number of labourers."[2] In this context, *subsistence* consists of the goods and services, or *real wage*, to maintain a minimally acceptable standard of living.

- **Absolute poverty standards** define poverty in terms of the income necessary to maintain a subsistence or minimally acceptable standard of living.

The official poverty standard used by various federal agencies is an absolute standard derived by the U.S. Bureau of the Census. The official **poverty-level income** is based on the cost of the food necessary to maintain an "emergency" level of nutrition, and an assumption that this food budget represents one-third of the total poverty-level income. In 1978, for example, it was estimated that the cost of the "emergency" food for a family of four was about $2100 per year, so the official poverty line income was

Cost of "emergency" nutritional level, or food budget	$2100
+ Food budget × 2	4200
Poverty-line income	$6300.

The only adjustments in the poverty line income are those due to changes in prices. There is no alteration of the real poverty-line standard of living. This is significant because the poverty-line is based on a nutritional standard that families couldn't be expected to survive on for an extended period of time. In other words, the poverty line is an income that would barely maintain minimum standards of health and decency.

---

2. David Ricardo, *Principles of Political Economy and Taxation* (London: J. M. Dent & Sons, 1911), p. 52.

The Poor: Who and How Many?

If we look at the number of families below the poverty line, both in absolute numbers and as a percentage of the total number of families, it appears that the "war on poverty" is being won. Between 1959 and 1975, the number of families with incomes below the poverty line fell from about 8.3 million (or 18.5 percent of all families) to 5.05 million (or 9 percent of all families). These figures are misleading, however. Table 2 is a more detailed picture of poverty in the United States in 1975.

It's important to remember the extremely low standard of living on which the poverty line is based. Being slightly above the line doesn't imply much in the way of comfort or quality of life. Over half of the persons and families below the poverty line had incomes below 75 percent of the poverty line. In the same year, 16.5 percent of persons and 13.2 percent of all families had incomes below 125 percent of the poverty line.

Furthermore, notice that the incidence of poverty is very uneven among various subgroups in the population. Blacks and Hispanics are much more likely to be below the poverty line than whites, as are persons in families headed by females and some segments of the popula-

Table 2 Poverty Rates for Various Groups, United States, 1975

Population Group	Poverty Rate (% of Group below Poverty Level)	Percent of Group with Incomes below Specified % of Poverty Level		
		75%	125%	150%
All Persons	11.4	6.7	16.5	21.7
White	8.8	5.0	13.4	18.1
Black	29.6	18.5	38.8	47.3
Hispanic	23.1	12.7	32.0	41.0
Persons over 65	14.0	5.6	23.6	32.1
White	12.1	4.7	21.4	29.7
Black	34.8	15.2	47.7	59.0
Hispanic	23.1	10.5	36.8	45.5
Persons in Families	10.0	5.9	14.7	19.6
White	7.4	4.2	11.4	15.9
Black	28.7	18.0	38.0	46.5
Hispanic	22.7	12.3	31.6	40.6
Persons in Families with Female Head	32.6	20.3	42.4	50.4
White	26.2	15.8	35.8	43.3
Black	50.6	33.0	61.1	70.8
Hispanic	52.1	34.6	71.5	80.9
All Families	9.0	5.2	13.2	17.7
Head White	7.0	3.9	10.7	14.8
Head Black	25.8	15.9	34.0	42.3
Head Hispanic	22.1	12.0	30.9	38.5

Source: U.S. Department of Commerce, Bureau of the Census, *Money Income and Poverty Status in 1975 of Families and Persons and Families in the United States* (Current Population Reports, Series P-60, nos. 112 and 113). Washington: Government Printing Office, 1978.

tion over age 65—even after including transfer income from various public assistance programs.

Poverty, Race, and National Origin

Although some people are quick to point out that there are more poor whites than blacks or Hispanics, the important statistic is the *poverty rate*, or the percentage of the persons or families with incomes below the poverty line. In every subgroup in Table 2, blacks and Hispanics show much higher poverty rates than whites.

Poverty and Sex

The sex of the head of a family is strongly related to the poverty rate. The general poverty rate among persons in families in 1975 was 10 percent. For persons in families headed by females, the rate was 32.6 percent, and for the persons in families headed by black or Hispanic females, over 50 percent.

Education and Poverty

Beyond a point, as every disappointed Ph.D. knows, more education doesn't guarantee more income. Lack of a high-school education (12 years), however, does enhance the chance of ending up below the poverty line, particularly for blacks and Hispanics. In Table 3, note the higher poverty rates in every group for heads of households with less than 4 years of high-school education.

There are several reasons for the strong relationship between poverty and lack of education. Access to education has been tied to race or national origin in some cases. Persons without basic educational skills in reading and mathematics may not be able to complete occupational training programs. In addition, employers may use education as an indicator of a potential employee's reliability and diligence.

Unemployment and Poverty

Groups that suffer high unemployment rates also show a high incidence of poverty, a fact that should hardly be surprising. Table 4 shows the

Table 3 Poverty Rate and Education

Educational Level of Head of Family	Poverty Rate, % of Families Below Poverty Line			
	All Races	White	Black	Hispanic
Elementary: Less than 8 yr.	21.3	18.1	32.6	33.6
8 years	10.5	9.0	24.3	23.9
High School: 1–3 yrs.	11.9	8.4	30.6	19.0
4 yrs.	6.2	5.0	19.5	12.5
College: 1 or more yrs.	2.8	2.4	7.8	5.9

Source: Same as Table 2.

Table 4 Poverty Rate and Work Experience

	Poverty Rate, % of Families Below Poverty Line			
Work Experience of Head	All Races	White	Black	Hispanic
Worked	5.5	4.5	15.3	13.2
50–52 weeks	2.8	2.4	8.0	7.3
Full time	2.5	2.2	6.5	7.0
49 weeks or less	13.9	11.3	30.4	27.6
Did not work	24.5	18.9	55.5	54.2
Main reason did not work				
ill or disabled	29.4	24.3	50.3	46.8
keeping house	54.9	46.2	78.6	73.3
unable to find work	51.7	42.6	69.9	61.5
all other reasons	39.5	32.6	60.6	NA

Source: Same as Table 2.

poverty rates for families headed by persons 25 years of age or older with various levels of work experience. Excluding retirees, the largest groups in the *did not work* category are those who couldn't work because of disability or family responsibilities and those unable to find work. *Did not work*, in other words, isn't synonymous with *leisure*.

The Economic Roots of Poverty

In a perfectly competitive economy, inequality of labor income is in the long run *purely* the result of households' voluntary choices and so cannot be viewed as a problem. If a biology teacher earns less than a physician, it is because the teacher has *voluntarily* sacrificed some potential income in return for a less pressured lifestyle. If a woman who works six hours a day earns less than a man who works twelve, it is because she has *voluntarily* sacrificed some potential income in return for extra leisure hours. In such an economy, any poverty resulting from differences in labor income is purely voluntary; the society need not concern itself with the poverty of a person who chooses to work only one hour a day.

Inequality of income is thus a problem only insofar as it is *not* voluntary. One source of such inequality is the unequal ownership of nonlabor resources and of the resulting nonlabor income. As we saw in Chapter 12, there is nothing inherent in the perfectly competitive model that will equalize the ownership of nonlabor wealth. Households that own no nonlabor resources won't earn any nonlabor income (dividends, interest, or rent).

Some nonlabor wealth, of course, is accumulated by sacrifice and frugality, and the ownership or lack of ownership of such wealth *does* represent a household's voluntary decision. But a great deal of nonlabor wealth is inherited, and in paying an income to the owners of resources, resource markets make no distinction between inherited and noninherited wealth. Unless *all* nonlabor wealth is accumulated by effort and sacrifice, inequality of total income ceases to be voluntary.

A second source of income inequality in the real world is the kind of resource market imperfections discussed in Chapter 16. Many low-wage workers are trapped below the poverty level by a combination of labor market imperfections—geographic immobility, occupational immobility, market power in the hands of unions and professional organizations, and discrimination. It is no coincidence that the subgroups of the population that suffer the highest incidence of poverty—blacks, women, and Hispanics—are the same groups that were singled out in the discussion of discrimination in Chapter 16.

Historically, monopsony power of employers has also contributed to low wages and poverty for some workers. In cases where there was a single employer in a labor market, the workers were in debt to the employer, communication was difficult, and geographic mobility was low, employers exercised considerable monopsony power in employment and wages. This was true in many of the company towns run by mining companies in the nineteenth and early twentieth centuries.

With a few exceptions, however, monopsony probably isn't a very important cause of poverty today. One possible exception may be some contractors of migrant agricultural labor. Many migrant workers have little education, little or no fluency in English, and very little occupational mobility (especially illegal aliens).

Searching for Solutions

Since there isn't a single cause of poverty or a uniform group of persons classified as poor, there isn't a single solution to the problem. What is needed is a coordinated set of policies to deal with the diverse causes of poverty.

Full Employment and Economic Growth

Poverty is worse in periods of high unemployment. The incidence of poverty is highest among the unemployed, and many workers whose incomes are above the poverty line fall below it if they become unemployed. Others who remain employed during high unemployment periods may fall below the poverty line due to shorter hours.

One approach to the problem of poverty is to keep the demand for goods and services and the labor to produce them high in order to reduce the poverty associated with unemployment. This is implicit in the "Humphrey-Hawkins" bill enacted in a watered-down version in 1978. Humphrey-Hawkins sets goals for unemployment rates for the economy as a whole and for heads of households and commits the government in principle to pursuing policies to achieve these goals.

Unless the capacity to produce goods and services increases, however, simply stimulating demand will lead to inflation. Furthermore, experience indicates that inflationary pressures will set in before the desired rate of unemployment is reached. For these reasons, there are some important limitations in relying too heavily on stimulating demand and increasing capacity as a solution to the problems of poverty.

First of all, inflation imposes costs on some members of society—all of those whose money incomes don't keep up with price increases. If a policy of stimulating demand raises the incomes of the unemployed and underemployed and leads to more rapid price increases, we have to make a value judgment to evaluate the importance of the gains and losses.

Expanding the capacity to produce, or *economic growth*, is the only way that the incomes of the poor can be raised without lowering the incomes of the nonpoor, but there are some limitations of economic growth as the painless solution to the poverty problem. First, some economists see absolute limits on economic growth imposed by the supplies of such basic resources as fossil fuels. Furthermore, economic growth imposes *external costs* on the community—most notably environmental damage—in addition to its benefits. Again, value judgements are required at some point to say whether the gains are more important than the costs.

Even after all of the value-laden cost-benefit questions have been answered, there is a more fundamental issue concerning the ability of full employment and economic growth policies to deal with the specific problem of poverty. Many of the low-wage workers have little education and no productive skills in demand in the labor market. Many of the low-income female heads of families are unable to work because of the lack of day-care facilities. Simply raising the demand for all labor may not increase the demand for these specific groups of workers who suffer a high poverty rate. By increasing the demand for more skilled workers, and not the demand for unskilled workers, these policies could actually increase the gap between low-wage workers and high-wage workers.

Figure 3 shows a hypothetical demand for unskilled labor and for skilled labor. The most likely result of raising the overall demand for labor would be a large increase in the demand for skilled labor and a smaller (if any) increase in the demand for unskilled labor, as shown in Figure 3. The wage of unskilled labor rises from $3 to $3.50 per hour, while the wage for skilled rises from $5 to $7 per hour. The ratio of skilled to unskilled wages rises from $5/$3 to $7/$3.50, or from 1⅔ to 2.

Many of the technological changes that increase productivity and capacity and are the main source of economic growth tend to reduce the demand for unskilled labor. Such changes would thus reduce the employment opportunities for low-wage workers, further aggravating their problems of unemployment and poverty.

No antipoverty program can succeed without a high demand for labor. Retraining unemployed agricultural workers to be unemployed maintenance persons makes little sense. However, policies aimed at the

Figure 3 Demand for Skilled vs. Unskilled Labor

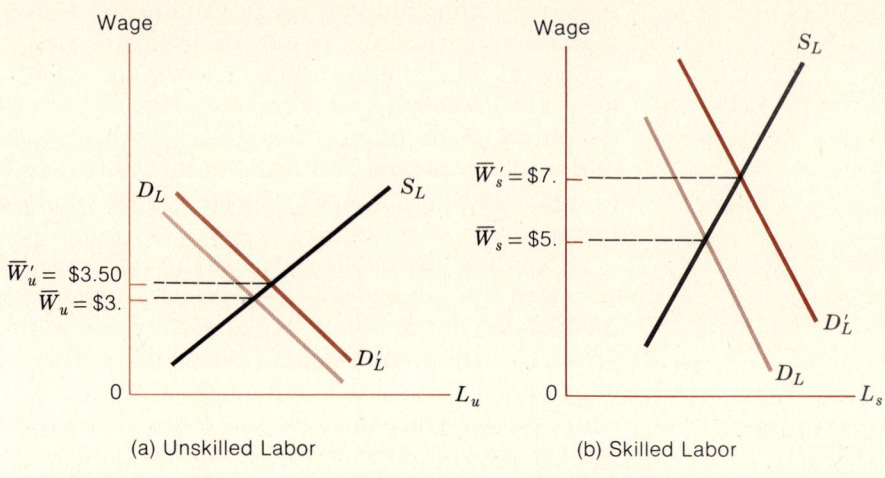

(a) Unskilled Labor (b) Skilled Labor

overall demand for labor and economic growth alone aren't sufficient to deal with the problem of poverty.

Investing in Human Capital

Acquiring employable skills through education and training represents an investment in human capital. That the lack of human capital investments by the poor represents a major cause of poverty has been recognized by economists for a long time—from John Stuart Mill in the mid-nineteenth century to Professor Gary Becker and other modern human capital theorists.

Programs to increase the human capital of low-income persons and families would include such things as greater access to education, expanded vocational education and training, and expanded manpower retraining programs. Where discrimination has been a factor limiting access to such programs, affirmative action will be required.

By increasing employable skills and raising productivity, education and training can give many low-wage workers a way out of the unskilled labor market and the poverty associated with it. Even the workers who remained in the unskilled market could benefit. By enhancing the occupational mobility of low-wage workers, these programs could reduce the "rent" component of higher wages, and promote wage differentials that more accurately reflect differences in costs of working in different occupations.

In Figure 3, as more workers are able to obtain the education and training required for skilled jobs, the supply of unskilled labor falls and the supply of skilled labor increases. This raises the wages not only of the unskilled workers who become skilled workers, but also the wages of those who remain in the unskilled labor market. Also, this reduces the difference between skilled and unskilled wages.

There are, however, some limitations on human capital programs. First of all, their success depends on the overall demand for labor. Secondly, since the returns from the human capital programs will be realized in the future, there are some potential problems in trying to estimate future patterns of demand for various types of labor and future returns on current expenditures in the education and training programs. Finally, the cost of these programs is high, including the cost of the educational and training programs themselves, plus the opportunity cost borne by the low-wage workers who participate. These opportunity costs to the low-wage worker may not be very great in terms of forgone wages, but the family income and living standard may be so low that many workers couldn't afford to participate without financial assistance.

Geographic Mobility

Migration in response to high wages and employment opportunities played a crucial role in populating the United States in the nineteenth and early twentieth centuries. Massive international migration, of course, isn't a realistic solution to the poverty problem in the United States today, but the inability to escape depressed areas is a cause of poverty for some people. There are two basic ways to attack poverty that accompanies geographic immobility—stimulating economic development and employment in depressed areas, and/or increasing mobility of families out of these areas.

There is, in fact, some evidence that labor will respond to geographic differences in wages and employment opportunities. From the beginning of the century until the 1960s, for example, many black and low-income white workers migrated from the South to the Northeast, and in the mid-1970s many of them are migrating from the Northeast to the "Sun Belt" states where wages are now higher and employment opportunities greater. Many people even migrated to Alaska in search of employment and high wages during the construction of the Alaskan pipeline.

The effect of geographic mobility is similar to the effect of occupational mobility. In Figure 4, the movement of labor out of a low-wage area to a high-wage area raises the wages of those who find employment at higher wages as well as those whose wages raise with the reduction in the supply of labor in the low-wage area.

As always, however, there is a catch. The sociological factors that affect geographic mobility are very strong. Many families in the 1950s and 1960s were subsidized for the economic costs of moving out of depressed areas and assisted in their employment search in more prosperous areas, but moved back to the depressed areas after a few years. In addition, geographic mobility from low-wage areas to high-wage areas reduces wages (or slows wage increases) in the high-wage areas. Workers already in high-wage areas have seldom welcomed newcomers. Finally, geographic mobility isn't a very effective solution for

Figure 4 Geographic Mobility

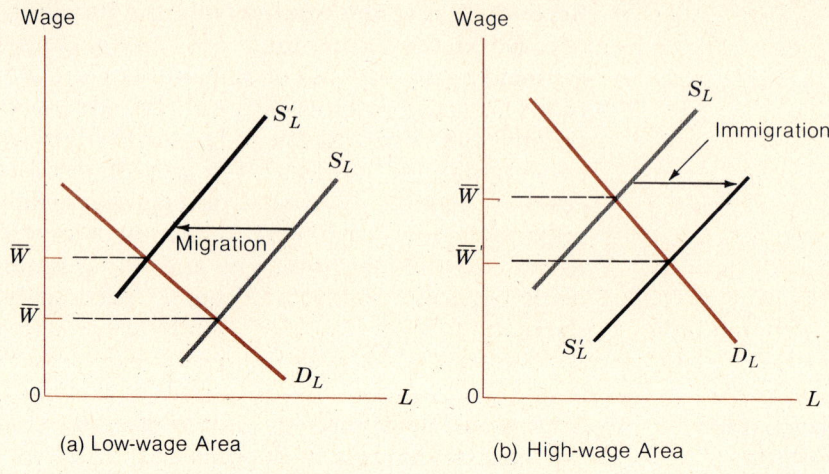

(a) Low-wage Area

(b) High-wage Area

many of the poorest families who can't afford to move at all or for poorly educated workers without employable skills.

Equal Employment Opportunity

The link between poverty and discrimination is too strong to be explained away as a statistical "fluke." To reduce the poverty that is related to racial, ethnic, and sexual discrimination, those who are discriminated against must have equal access to training, education, and employment. The specific remedies for discrimination discussed in Chapter 16 are also relevant to the problem of poverty.

Public Assistance and Transfers

So far, the possible solutions discussed are related to raising the incomes of the poor by improving their wages and opportunities for employment. However, dealing with poverty will also require continuation of various types of *public assistance*, or *transfers* of income to the poor. Employment-oriented programs may not raise the incomes of all of the working poor to a level that would allow a minimally acceptable standard of living. For the poor who can't work—the elderly, the ill and disabled, and single-parent heads of families with small children—transfer programs are the only means of raising incomes and living standards.

The major issues in public assistance in the 1980s are basically three —the type of transfers, the level of benefits, and the effect of transfers on the incentive to work.

Transfers in Kind vs. Cash Transfers

Transfers in kind provide benefits in the form of specific goods and services. Free medical care (Medicare and Medicaid), housing subsidies, and food stamps are examples of *transfers in kind*. *Cash transfers*, on the other hand, are simply assistance in the form of direct cash payments. The traditional approach to public assistance has been to provide transfers in kind, and these transfers have improved the incomes and living standards of the poor.

A major problem with transfers in kind, however, is that they restrict the low-income household's economic choices, compared with cash transfers of equal value. In Chapter 5, it was shown that a household's utility would be higher with a cash payment than with food stamps that raised its real income by the same amount. This also applies to other transfers in kind. Changing from transfers in kind to cash transfers could raise the low-income households' level of satisfaction at the same level of public expenditure or could reduce the level of public spending to maintain the same level of satisfaction.

Many transfer-in-kind programs are inequitable because they exclude some of the poor from benefits. Public housing, for example, is allocated on the basis of family size, thus excluding many poor individuals or childless couples. With cash transfers, benefits per person don't depend on the size of the family or the age of the head of the family, so the benefits would be more equitably distributed among the low-income population.

Most existing transfer-in-kind programs also have complicated definitions of need, eligibility, and benefits, making them very inefficient and expensive to administer and enforce. Costs of administering cash transfer programs should be considerably lower than for transfers in kind because of the simplicity of the definitions of needs and benefits.

The Negative Income Tax (NIT)

One of the most publicized proposals for cash transfers is the so-called **negative income tax** (*NIT*). There are a number of versions of the *NIT*, but they are very similar on the main points. A negative income tax simply establishes a minimum guaranteed income, and pays families whose income is below this level a refund (or "negative tax") equal to the full guaranteed income minus a certain percentage of earned income. For example, if the guaranteed annual income for a family of four were $6000 (approximately the "poverty line") and a family of four had *no* earned income, it would receive a "negative income tax" of $NIT = \$6000 - \times \%(0) = \$6000$.

Most existing welfare programs reduce benefits by $1 for every $1 for earned income, in effect levying a 100% tax on the earnings of the poor. *NIT* proposals specify reductions of the *NIT* payment by 30 percent to 50 percent of earned income, thus providing a positive incentive to work and earn income. For example, suppose that a family of four earned income of $4000 and the guaranteed income were $6000. If the NIT payment were reduced by 50 percent of the family's earned income, its NIT income would be $6000 − (.50 × $4000) = $6000 − $2000 = $4000. Adding the NIT payment to its earned income of $4000, the household ends up with a total income of $8000.

Most NIT proposals advocate replacing existing transfers in kind with the NIT, not adding on to the existing programs. This could save a great deal of administrative and enforcement expense. Professor Milton Friedman has argued that the program could be administered by the Internal Revenue Service. A simple definition of needs and benefits in terms of money per person would replace the complex and sometimes bizarre eligibility standards of existing programs.

Some critics of the NIT proposals argue that the cost of administration and enforcement would be considerably greater than proponents predict. Another more serious and normatively "loaded" issue is whether the low-income households will allocate their NIT payments "correctly," or whether they will spend the payments on items not directly related to the family's needs—in short, whether the poor know what's best for them.

In 1978, the results of a 10-year experiment with negative income tax programs in Denver and Seattle also raised the possibility that the work incentive isn't very great with NIT. The Denver and Seattle experiments guaranteed a minimum income equal to the poverty-line income, and reduced benefits by 50 percent of earned income. Instead of working more, heads of families in the experiment worked less. Instead of becoming more stable, families in the experiment were less stable and a larger percentage broke up compared with a control group of families that didn't participate.

The results of the Denver-Seattle experiments have been interpreted and misinterpreted in a number of ways—from proof of the failure of NIT programs to generate incentive to proof of the inherent laziness of the poor. In fact, the experiments didn't provide conclusive proof of the merits of NIT compared with traditional welfare programs, since the levels of benefits as well as the types of transfers differed between the two programs.

For the same level of guaranteed benefits, the incentive to work and earn income is greater with some form of NIT than with a traditional welfare program with its implicit 100 percent tax on earned income. The annual reductions of hours worked in the experiment—from 96 for white husbands to 230 for black husbands, in a full-time work year of 2000 hours—don't support the claim that the participants in the experiment stopped working and accepted the guaranteed poverty-line income. The experiment does suggest that low-income households with an NIT will probably take some of their expanded income-leisure possibilities as additional leisure.

Close-up

Welfare, Negative Income Taxes, and Incentive

In 1976, an Illinois family of four that received Aid to Families with Dependent Children (AFDC) benefits, free medical care under the Medicaid program, and food stamps received benefits valued at $6412. If the same family had earned the minimum wage for full-time work for the year and received food stamps, its total income (including the value of the food stamps) would have been $5958. In other words, the family would have "paid" $454 for working full time.

Suppose that this family could have been guaranteed an annual income of $6000 through a negative income tax program, and the NIT payment would be reduced by 50 percent of earned income. Taking away the value of the food stamps, the annual earnings from full-time work at the minimum wage would have been $4966. With the hypothetical NIT program, the family would receive an NIT payment of $6,000 - (.50 \times 4066) = \$3517$ by working full time at the minimum wage, and its total income would be NIT + earned income = $3517 + $4966 = $8483.

The cost of subsidizing the household's income with the NIT would be $3517, compared with $6412 with the AFDC and other transfers in kind. The household's income would be $8483, compared with $6412 with the AFDC program—and its income would be in cash, which has higher utility than transfers in kind of equal monetary value.[1]

---

1. The facts on the actual benefit program are from the *Economic Report of the President* (Washington: Government Printing Office, 1978), p. 226.

The Level of Transfer Benefits

The issue of the proper level of transfer benefits is at least partially separable from the issue of the type of transfers made. Raising the level of transfer benefits is the only way to raise the incomes and living standards of the elderly, ill, disabled, and other poor who are unable to work or benefit from employment-oriented programs.

In 1978, the Carter administration proposed a *two-tier* system of cash assistance to replace existing programs. The upper tier would include those not expected to work (aged, blind, disabled, and single-parent families with children under age 7). The lower tier would include persons who could be expected to work. The basic federal benefit would be $4200 per year for the upper tier, and $2500 per year for the lower tier. For the lower tier, benefits would be reduced by no more than 50 percent of earned income over $3800 per year. The federal benefits could be supplemented by states, with federal subsidies on state supplements that raised total income to the poverty line.

This approach has some positive incentives to work, and would focus benefit payments on those in most need and least likely and able to earn income. However, for those in the upper tier, there is an implicit statement that federal benefits and state supplements will add up to the poverty line. This may be an improvement in the level of benefits for many of the recipients, but it should not be forgotten that this is a survival level of income.

The proper level of benefits requires both analysis and value judgments. The funds that are used for transfer benefits to the poor have alternative uses—either for other public uses or for private uses. Just as all other economic choices, the question is whether the benefits to the winners are more important than the losses to the losers.

Welfare Fraud

Welfare cheating—people receiving benefits who aren't entitled to them or people receiving greater benefits than they are entitled to—is an issue that's generally been blown out of proportion. Welfare fraud is a fact, but the popular image of most welfare families as able to work but living comfortably on welfare instead is a myth.

First of all, the typical level of benefits hardly suggests a "comfortable" way of life for the typical welfare family. In addition, most estimates of the percentage of persons on welfare rolls who receive more benefits than they are entitled to or who receive benefits to which they aren't entitled at all are in the range of 5 percent to 10 percent. If the overpayments were eliminated, more funds would be available to those really in need or as tax relief, but *completely* eliminating all overpayments would save the average taxpayer no more than $10 to $15 per year or 20¢ to 30¢ per week.

One of the most effective ways to eliminate the fraud that does exist is to simplify the system. This could be done by consolidating the complicated and administratively separate programs into a single cash transfer program with simple definitions of need and benefits.

The Road Ahead

Getting people "off the welfare rolls and on the payrolls" has broad appeal. It appeals to the work ethic ingrained in most of us from childhood—the basic lesson that those who don't work or contribute shouldn't eat. It appeals to those of us in the middle class who feel overworked, underpaid, and overtaxed to pay for welfare cheaters and the tax loopholes of the rich. In some circles, attacking the welfare system is a socially acceptable outlet for racial, ethnic, or sexual bigotry.

Actually getting people off the welfare rolls and on the payrolls is a difficult, expensive, and complex task. It requires vigorous enforcement of equal opportunity legislation in employment, wages, and access to education and training. It requires additional day-care facilities to expand employment opportunities for single parents with small children. Genuine equality of opportunity may require some redistribution of income among families. For that element of the low-income population that is unable to work, the level of transfer benefits should allow something better than an income that most of us couldn't survive on for an extended period of time.

Because alternative approaches to the poverty problem hit so many of our basic attitudes and normative values, there probably never will be a consensus on exactly what ought to be done, and perfectly reasonable people can come up with quite different solutions. However, effective attacks on poverty require more than simplistic thinking, scapegoats, and slogans. They require careful analysis of the problem, calculation of costs and benefits of alternative solutions, and intelligent and informed value judgments on the proper course of action.

Summary

1. Unless every person receives an equal income, some persons and families will be "poor" relative to others.
2. The **Lorenz curve** and the **Gini index** are two means of showing the degree of inequality in income distribution.
3. **Relative poverty standards** define poverty as the lowest part of the income distribution or as a percentage of the median or average income.
4. **Absolute poverty standards** define poverty as the money value of goods and services to maintain some minimum standard of living.
5. Although the number of families below the poverty line and the overall poverty rate have been falling, the incidence of poverty remains high among blacks, Hispanics, families headed by females, the ill and disabled, and some of the elderly. Most poverty is due to imperfections in resource markets and inadequate levels of public assistance.
6. For the employable poor, anti-poverty programs should maintain a low overall unemployment rate; should expand education, training, and retraining programs; should reduce immobility out of low-income areas; and should ensure equal employment opportunity.
7. For the poor who are unable to work or highly unlikely to be able to earn enough to maintain a minimum standard of living, public assistance or transfer programs are necessary. The questions in public assistance are the level of benefits and the form of the transfers (transfers in kind or cash).

Concepts for Review

Lorenz curve
Gini index
relative poverty standard
absolute poverty standard

poverty-level income
human capital
transfer in kind
negative income tax (*NIT*)

Questions

1. How is the official federal poverty line derived? Is this an absolute or relative poverty standard? Explain.
2. Since 1963, the poverty-line income has more than doubled. Does this reflect a higher minimum standard of living to divide the poor from the nonpoor? Explain.

3. Explain the differences between relative and absolute poverty standards. What are some of the advantages and disadvantages of each?
4. Some people point to the declining poverty rate for the general population as evidence that the "war on poverty" is being won. To what extent is this assessment justified? What qualifications (if any) should be made? What other evidence (if any) should be examined to evaluate our success in eliminating poverty?
5. To what extent, if at all, are income inequality and poverty consistent with perfect competition? Explain.
6. Explain how the severity of the poverty problem and the poverty rate are affected by the unemployment rate, and the potential of reducing or eliminating poverty by policies that maintain a high overall level of demand for labor.

Problems

1. Consider the following income transfer programs
   Plan A: Basic benefits in cash and in kind valued at $5000 per year for a family of four. Benefits are reduced by $1 for every $1 of earned income.
   Plan B: Basic cash benefit of $4000. Cash benefits are reduced by 30¢ for every $1 of earned income.
   Plan C: Similar to Plan B, except that the basic cash benefit is $5000, and is reduced by 50¢ for every $1 of earned income.
   In no case will cash benefits be less than zero. A full-time worker working 2000 hours per year at a minimum wage of $3.50 per hr. would earn an annual income of $7000. The poverty standard is $6500 per year.
   a. Calculate the total income of a head of a family of four who is employed full time at the minimum wage under each of these plans.
   b. The net earnings from working are the difference between the earnings from working and income without working. What are the net earnings and net earnings per hour of a worker who works full time at the minimum wage under each of these plans?
   c. Which plan provides the greatest incentive to work? Which plan provides the least incentive to work?
   d. For households that don't earn any income, the money value of the benefits of Plans A and C are equal. Does this mean that households with no earned income would be indifferent between these two plans?

PART SEVEN
Understanding the Aggregate Economy

The study of economics has traditionally been broken down into two main parts. **Microeconomics** explores the interactions between buyers and sellers in the market for a *particular* good or resource, and analyzes how those interactions determine price, output, and employment in that market. **Macroeconomics** explores the interactions between *all* buyers and sellers in *all* markets and analyzes how those interactions determine a price level and a level of output and employment *for an entire economy*. In other words, macroeconomics deals with the same basic variables as microeconomics, but it does so on an **aggregate** level—for the economy as a whole.

The central problems we will explore in macroeconomics are ones we read or hear about nearly every day: inflation, unemployment, recession. This section presents a general overview of these problems and of the macroeconomist's approach to them. Since most of our attention in subsequent sections of the text will focus on how aggregate output, prices, and employment are determined, we'll also look closely in this section at how the levels of these key macroeconomic variables can be measured empirically.

19

Introduction to Macroeconomics

Preview: We now turn our attention from *microeconomics* to *macroeconomics*—the study of the economy as a whole. Instead of the market demand for a particular good, we'll look at the *aggregate demand* for *all* goods and services by *all* consumers; instead of the market supply of a particular good, we'll look at the *aggregate supply* of *all* goods and services by *all* producers and suppliers. In this first chapter, we'll focus upon some of the key theories, problems, and issues of modern macroeconomics.

Since the 1940s, economic analysis has developed two main branches—*microeconomics* and *macroeconomics*.

- **Microeconomics** deals with the parts of the economy—households, firms, and markets.
- **Macroeconomics** deals with the economy as a whole, or with economic aggregates.

It's very important that the distinction and degree of separation between microeconomics and macroeconomics not be either overstated or understated. Nearly every economic problem and issue has both a macroeconomic and a microeconomic side. For example, inflation, the hottest issue of the late 1970s, has traditionally been classified as a macroeconomic problem. If it were strictly macroeconomic, however, the problem would be very easy to solve—simply freeze all prices at current levels. The aggregate price level would stop rising and the problem of inflation would be solved. As we saw in Chapter 3, however, prices perform the critical economic functions of rationing and allocating scarce goods and resources, so freezing prices would require some nonprice means of performing this function. Excess demand and excess supply would develop in various markets, and *black markets* for goods in excess demand would become a problem.

At the other extreme, if we understate the distinction between microeconomics and macroeconomics, we are in danger of falling into either the *fallacy of composition* (what's true for the part is true for the whole) or the *fallacy of division* (what's true for the whole is true for the parts), discussed in Chapter 1. The steel industry, for example, has been faced with chronic unemployment in recent years because of competition from more efficient foreign producers. Protection of the steel industry from foreign competition—by imposing tariffs or import quotas—would increase output, employment, and profits in the American steel industry. What's good for the steel industry, however, won't necessarily be good for everybody. Consumers will have to pay higher prices for all goods that require steel in their production. If we were to restrict *all* imports, we would probably find that we had fewer goods and services available at higher prices.

Similarly, we can't turn a macroeconomic result around and conclude that what's true for the economy as a whole will necessarily be true for every part of the economy. For example, increasing the money supply and government spending can increase the demand for goods and services and lower the overall unemployment rate in the economy. However, some elements of the unemployed population won't be affected by the increase in demand: workers without necessary skills, education, and experience to perform the jobs most needed won't suddenly become employable as a result of greater demand.

In short, microeconomics and macroeconomics are related parts of the same basic subject—branches of the same tree—but they aren't identical. We can't generalize results in specific industries and markets to the economy as a whole, and we can't attribute macroeconomic results for the economy as a whole to all individual markets, firms, and households.

The Villains: Unemployment and Inflation

The main concern of macroeconomics is two fundamental economic problems that have plagued nearly all of the world's economies in recent years: unemployment and inflation. Each is bad enough alone, but the challenge in the past two decades has been to understand and deal with unemployment and inflation at the same time.

Politicians, commentators, newspapers, and economists tell us again and again that unemployment and inflation are bad for the economy and the community. Promises to deal with unemployment and inflation have become as established in campaign lexicon as defense of the flag and "Mom's apple pie." What is it about unemployment and inflation that makes them so bad economically? Why is there so much controversy over the appropriate policies to deal with them?

An old bromide asserts that "it's an ill wind that doesn't blow somebody some good." Unemployment or inflation may not be bad for everybody economically. Unemployment generally is the most serious problem for the segment of the economy that's unemployed and suffers a loss of income. Inflation is most harmful to those whose money incomes are fixed or don't rise as fast as the prices of the goods and services they buy, and for creditors (people and institutions to whom debts are owed).

The aggregate problem of unemployment generally doesn't have a very heavy impact on those who remain employed and those whose incomes aren't interrupted or reduced. Inflation doesn't harm those whose money incomes at least keep pace with the prices of the goods and services they buy, nor does it harm those firms whose profits rise more rapidly than prices. In fact, inflationary periods are actually beneficial to people and institutions that owe large debts because the debts are repaid in cheaper dollars as prices rise.

Of course, unemployment and/or inflation can reach such extreme levels that they threaten the entire social, political, and economic fabric of society. Masses of unemployed workers may form a potent revolutionary force. **Hyperinflation**—very rapid increases in prices—can lead to economic, social, and political chaos, as it did in Germany in the 1920s and more recently in Argentina. Short of these extremes, unemployment and inflation cause some potential difficulties for the community economic welfare.

Unemployment represents unused productive capacity, and the community loses the goods and services that could have been produced by this unemployed capacity. If society is to do the best it can with what it has, resources and technology must be employed fully.

Inflation doesn't always hurt everybody economically, but it "taxes" the community in the form of higher prices of goods and services, and it tends to redistribute income from those who are hurt by the inflation to those who benefit from it. The problem with inflation as a tax or a means of redistributing income is that its effects aren't always precise or predictable.

The Aggregate Demand–Aggregate Supply Model: A Sneak Preview

In order to get a very basic understanding of the sources of inflation and unemployment, we're going to take a brief look at a model of the economy that will be developed in detail in the course of this text: the **aggregate demand–aggregate supply (*YD-YS*) model.** Don't expect to understand it fully yet: it is only meant to provide you with a general picture of the direction we will be taking in the remainder of the text.

The *YD-YS* model describes the interaction between two variables that lie at the heart of modern macroeconomics:

- **Aggregate demand** (YD) is the total demand or intended expenditure for all goods and services by all buyers—private households, firms, the government, and foreign buyers.
- **Aggregate supply** (YS) is the total supply of all goods and services by all producers.

In Figure 1, the horizontal axis represents the **aggregate output** of the economy as a whole, while the vertical axis shows the average price of goods and services produced, or the **aggregate price level**, as defined by a price index. The **aggregate demand curve (YD)** shows the total output of goods and services the public would wish to purchase at any given price level, *ceteris paribus*. The **aggregate supply curve (YS)** shows the price level consistent with any given level of total output, *ceteris paribus*. The economy reaches **equilibrium aggregate output** when the aggregate demand for goods and services equals the aggregate supply—where YD intersects YS in Figure 1. Here the aggregate output of the economy depicted will be $\bar{Y}$ and the price level will be $\bar{P}$.

Inflation and Unemployment in the YD-YS Model

Inflation is defined as a sustained rise in the price level. In the aggregate demand–aggregate supply model, there are two basic causes or types of inflation.

- *Increasing aggregate demand* causes the price level and aggregate output to rise.
- *Decreasing aggregate supply* causes the price level to rise and aggregate output to fall.

Figure 1 The Aggregate Demand–Aggregate Supply Model

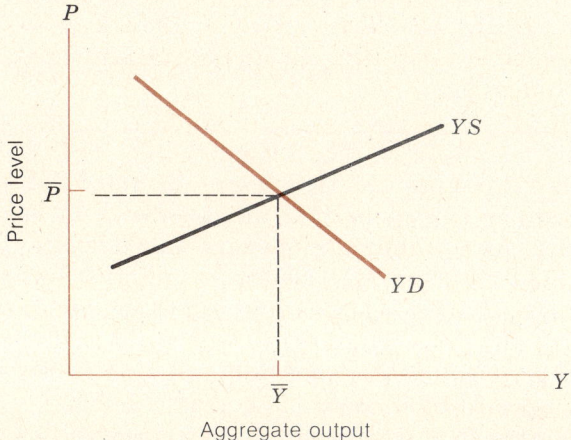

Figure 2 Inflation and Unemployment

(a) Demand-Pull Inflation

(b) Cost-Push Inflation + Unemployment

(c) Demand-Deficiency Unemployment

These two types of inflation are illustrated in Figure 2. In Figure 2a, increases in aggregate demand are shown by shifts of the aggregate demand curve to the right. As aggregate demand increases from YD_0 to YD_1, YD_2, YD_3, and YD_4, aggregate output increases from Y_0 to Y_1, Y_2, Y_3, and Y_4. As aggregate output increases due to increasing aggregate demand, the price level rises as well, as shown in Figure 2a. This type of inflation is called **demand-pull inflation** because the price level is *pulled* upward by increasing aggregate demand.

In Figure 2b, the aggregate supply curve shifts upward, or to the left, indicating a higher aggregate price level at each level of aggregate output or a smaller aggregate output at every price level. As the aggregate supply curve shifts from YS_0 to YS_1, YS_2, YS_3, and YS_4, aggregate output falls and the price level rises. This type of inflation, which originates from the supply side, is called **cost-push inflation** because the price level is *pushed* upward by shifts of the aggregate supply curve to the left.

The level of employment and therefore the severity of the unemployment problem depends on the level of aggregate output. As aggregate output increases, employment increases and unemployment generally declines. As aggregate output falls, so does the level of employment, and unemployment increases.

Changes in aggregate supply and aggregate demand, then, will also affect the level of unemployment.

- A *decrease in aggregate demand* lowers aggregate output, employment, and the price level.
- A *decrease in aggregate supply* lowers aggregate output and employment, but causes the price level to rise.

The effect of a decrease in aggregate supply on the price level and aggregate output is shown in Figure 2b. As aggregate output falls, so does the level of employment, and the level of unemployment rises. In Figure 2c, aggregate demand falls from YD_4 to YD_3, YD_2, YD_1, and YD_0, causing aggregate output and the price level to fall. As aggregate output falls, the level of employment declines and unemployment increases.

But what causes these changes in aggregate demand and aggregate supply? Why are the curves in the *YD-YS* model shaped the way they are, and how will our predictions of inflation and unemployment be different if the shapes of the curves are different? What does it mean to say that aggregate demand *depends* on the price level? Why does the level of output vary with the price level? What can we *do* about inflation and unemployment, and how will our policies differ according to the sources of the problems?

By now, you've probably asked yourself some or all of these questions—and maybe a few more besides. Our goal in the remainder of this text will be to try to come up with some satisfactory (if not always satisfying) answers to them. In the next chapter, we'll look at how we measure the quantities on the two axes of the *YD-YS* model: aggregate output and the price level. After that, we'll spend a number of chapters looking closely at aggregate demand: what determines its level, what changes it, and how the government can manipulate it (through fiscal and monetary policies) in order to fight inflation and unemployment.

For many years, most orthodox economists felt that the demand side of the economy was all that really "mattered," and that *demand management* policies were the key to combating inflation and unemployment.

Unfortunately, many of the economic problems our economy has faced in recent years—oil embargoes, productivity slowdowns, stagflation—have been *supply* problems. Thus, after thoroughly reviewing the successes and failures, problems and issues surrounding the use of demand management policies, we'll return to the question of aggregate supply, rebuilding the YD-YS model from scratch and seeing what the model can tell us about the policy directions that must be taken in the continuing fight against inflation and unemployment.

Varieties of Macroeconomics Thinking

Modern economics, macroeconomics in particular, is hardly characterized by universal agreement on the basic questions and analytical approaches. It probably never has been, but there have been periods in which orthodox economic ideas—what Professor John Kenneth Galbraith has called the *traditional wisdom*—have been more widely accepted by economists than is the case in modern macroeconomics.

Classical Macroeconomics: The Old Orthodoxy

The term *classical economics* has several meanings. In the history of economics, it refers to a school of economic thought that dominated economics from the late eighteenth century until the last quarter of the nineteenth. As an approach to macroeconomics, however, the term **classical macroeconomics** refers to the orthodox economic analysis that was generally accepted between the late eighteenth century and the analytical revolution started by John Maynard Keynes in the late 1930s.

A cornerstone of classical macroeconomics is a proposition known as *Say's Law*:

- **Say's Law** argues that in a competitive market economy, supply creates its own demand.

This rather puzzling little proposition has an important implication. Since producers can be assured of demand for all additional output, they will increase output until their capacities to produce are fully utilized. Aggregate output will thus reach equilibrium only when the economy is at full employment. Turning Say's Law around, the existence of unemployed resources and capacity indicates *disequilibrium*, and if market forces aren't interfered with, full employment would be reached as aggregate output and prices adjusted to equilibrium.

The full-employment equilibrium in classical macroeconomics depends on flexible wages and prices. Classical economists viewed the use of labor as any other commodity that is bought and sold in the marketplace. If the price of labor is too high, there will be *excess supply* or unemployment. In the long run, however, adjustments of markets to equilibrium with flexible wages and prices would cause the wage to fall. As the wage falls, the quantity of labor demanded increases and the

Figure 3 Varieties of Macroeconomic Thinking

(a) Extreme Classical View (b) Extreme Keynesian View

quantity supplied falls until the labor market is cleared at the equilibrium wage.

Similar arguments apply to other markets as well. If there is overproduction of a particular good, its price will fall relative to other prices until the excess supply is eliminated at equilibrium. Excess demand for goods or resources will drive their prices up relative to other prices, eliminating the excess demand. When all competitive markets are in equilibrium, there will be no excess demand or supply for goods or resources and no unemployed productive capacity.

In the long run, according to classical macroeconomics, equilibrium aggregate output will be reached only at full employment, so in the long run aggregate output is determined by productive capacity, not by aggregate demand. In terms of the YD-YS model, this suggests an aggregate supply curve that is vertical at the level of output consistent with full employment of productive capacity—Y^* in Figure 3a. Notice that such a curve implies that changes in aggregate demand will affect only the price level in the long run, and will have no long-run effect on the levels of aggregate output and employment. If this analysis is accurate, there is no role for the government in determining the level of output and employment, and government intervention will tend only to interfere with the adjustment of the system to full-employment equilibrium.

Keynesian Macroeconomics: The "New Orthodoxy"

Much of the macroeconomic orthodoxy of the 1970s has evolved from ideas introduced by the late British economist John Maynard Keynes in his *General Theory of Employment, Interest, and Money*, published in 1936. In fact, the contemporary mainstream in macroeconomics is called **Keynesian economics**.

One of the central assertions of *The General Theory*, and a continuing source of disagreement and controversy, is that macroeconomic equilibrium *can* be reached with unemployed productive capacity or with chronic inflationary pressures, as well as at the classical full-employment level. This notion ran head-on into the classical position that in the long run private market forces would lead to equilibrium at full employment—an argument to which Keynes offered his famous reply that "in the long run, we all are dead."

In Keynesian macroeconomics, the critical variable determining equilibrium aggregate output and employment is aggregate demand. In fact, the most extreme Keynesian view implied that the aggregate supply curve was virtually horizontal, as in Figure 3b, until full employment is reached.

The classical full-employment equilibrium would be reached only if aggregate demand were YD_2 in Figure 3b. This is a possibility in the Keynesian analysis, but clearly not the only possibility. If aggregate demand falls at YD_1, the economy is underutilizing its capacity and workers are unemployed. On the other hand, if aggregate demand were at YD_3, the economy would experience rising prices or inflation because the output of goods and services can't increase beyond the full employment level (Y^*).

Keynes' major point of departure with the classical analysis was his contention that there are no automatic forces operating within the economy to drive aggregate demand to YD_2 or equilibrium aggregate output to Y^* without inflationary pressures. According to Keynes, prices are not sufficiently flexible to achieve the classical result automatically. If equilibrium is reached with unemployment, the only way to eliminate the unemployment is to increase aggregate demand. Similarly, chronic inflation as a result of excess aggregate demand can be dealt with only by policies that lower aggregate demand.

Thus the Keynesian approach provides for active government intervention in the economy to stimulate or dampen aggregate demand in order to deal with unemployment or inflation. Keynes tended to advocate the use of government spending and taxation (*fiscal policies*) over manipulation of the money supply (*monetary policies*), particularly to stimulate aggregate demand in periods of severe economic depression.

Monetarism: The Classical Resurgence

For many years Professor Milton Friedman, now retired from the University of Chicago, has been the leading spokesman for an approach to macroeconomics called **monetarism**. In fact, Friedman and the University of Chicago have been so closely identified with modern monetarism that it has been called **Chicago-school monetarism.**

Not surprisingly from its name, monetarism identifies the money supply as the critical variable in macroeconomics. There is more to monetarism than a heavy emphasis on the money supply, however. Like classical macroeconomists, monetarists usually argue that the private sector is inherently quite stable and that competitive market forces and flexible prices will generate equilibrium aggregate output at full employment of resources and capacity.

According to the monetarists, active government intervention in the economy, particularly to stimulate aggregate demand and reduce unemployment, generally does more harm than good—if it has any effect at all. In the long run, they argue, real aggregate output is determined by productive capacity, and government attempts to stimulate aggregate demand in the short run won't affect long-run equilibrium anyway. Attempts to stimulate aggregate demand in the short run by fiscal policies won't be very effective unless they are supported by appropriate changes in the money supply; this is because, in the long run, fiscal policies affect only the distribution of output between the public and private sectors of the economy, not the total aggregate output.

Monetarists have argued further that, because of incomplete information on the size or the timing of the effects of changes in the money supply, monetary authorities should do as little as possible. With incomplete information, there's a very good chance that attempting to reduce unemployment by expanding the money supply or reduce inflation by reducing the money supply will end up doing too much, too little, or the wrong thing entirely. Thus, like the classicists but in sharp contrast with the Keynesians, monetarists tend to advocate *laissez faire* as the appropriate strategy for government in the economy.

Macroeconomics in the 1980s: Sound and Fury Signifying Much

The above sketches of various schools of macroeconomic thought are hardly exhaustive descriptions or analyses, but only broad characterizations. Furthermore, most economists' ideas on macroeconomic problems fall somewhere between the extreme Keynesian and monetarist positions. However, the debates between basically monetarist and basically Keynesian economics will be one of the central themes of macroeconomics in the 1980s. Within this theme, the central issues are the following:

1. Can the economy sustain acceptably high levels of output and employment with stable prices?
2. What are the proper roles of private market forces vs. public policy in achieving price stability, full employment, and a stable trend of aggregate economic activity over time?
3. How important is money as a determinant of aggregate output, income, employment, and prices?
4. What is the proper relationship between policies dealing with government spending and taxes vs. policies dealing with the money supply in achieving economic objectives?

5. How important is aggregate supply vs. aggregate demand in causing unemployment and inflation, and what is the role of supply management vs. demand management policies in dealing with those problems?

The chapters that follow, unfortunately, won't provide answers to all of the unresolved questions in macroeconomics. They do, however, provide a basic grasp of the tools and concepts that are essential for evaluating the arguments and recognizing the relevant questions.

Summary

1. **Microeconomics** analyzes the parts of the economy—markets, firms, and households. **Macroeconomics** analyzes economic *aggregates*, or the *economy as a whole*. **Inflation** and **unemployment** are the key problems explored in the study of macroeconomics.
2. **Aggregate demand** is the total expenditure for all goods and services at any given level of **aggregate output**, or **real national income**. **Aggregate supply** is the total supply of goods and services by all producers. The interaction between aggregate supply and aggregate demand can result in unemployment and inflation.
3. In **classical macroeconomics**, flexible prices and **Say's Law** lead to equilibrium aggregate output only at full employment in the long run.
4. In **Keynesian macroeconomics**, the level of aggregate demand determines equilibrium aggregate output, which may or may not be at full employment. Keynes' analysis allows government a much larger role in the economy than does the classical analysis.
5. Modern **monetarism** is built on the classical foundation and represents a reaction to Keynesian macroeconomics. Monetarists tend to argue that freely operating markets and flexible prices will cause aggregate output to move toward a full-employment equilibrium in the long run. Attempts by government to regulate demand or change equilibrium will upset this adjustment.

Concepts for Review

microeconomics
macroeconomics
inflation
unemployment
aggregate demand

aggregate supply
aggregate output
price level
demand-pull inflation
cost-push inflation

classical macroeconomics
Say's Law
Keynesian macroeconomics
monetarism

Questions

1. What is the relationship between microeconomics and macroeconomics? Are they separate subjects? Is it sufficient to understand either microeconomics or macroeconomics, but not both, to deal with current economic problems?

2. What (if anything) is wrong with the following statements?
   a. "We should limit bids for public construction projects to local contractors, since the economic health of the community is determined by the economic health of local businesses."
   b. "Since automation makes it possible to produce more goods at a lower cost, it is good for the economy and therefore good for every worker."
3. Looking at Figure 1, explain how each of the following occurrences (*ceteris paribus*) will affect the price level, aggregate output, and the level of employment:
   a. An increase in aggregate demand.
   b. An increase in aggregate supply.
   c. A decrease in aggregate demand.
   d. A decrease in aggregate supply.
4. David Ricardo (a leading classical economist of the early 19th century), John Maynard Keynes, and Milton Friedman each made one of the following statements. Match each statement with its author, and explain your choices.
   a. "(The) only effective way to stop inflation is to restrain the rate of growth of the money supply."
   b. "(There) is no limit to demand—no limit to the employment of capital while it yields any profit."
   c. "(There) will be only one level of employment consistent with equilibrium. . . . This level cannot be greater than full employment, . . . But there is no reason in general for expecting it to be equal to full employment."
5. Compare the points of similarity and disagreement among classical, Keynesian, and monetarist macroeconomics.

20

Measuring Aggregate Output, Income, and Prices

Preview: Basic to the understanding of macroeconomic problems and issues are three variables: *aggregate output, income,* and *price level*. In this chapter we'll see how aggregate output and income are defined and measured, we'll look at the meaning of price levels, and we'll examine the usefulness of measures of aggregate output as guides to a country's economic welfare.

Anybody who follows the economic news, even casually, will be bombarded with macroeconomic data. The federal government gathers, estimates, and publishes a vast array of information on output, income, prices, economic growth, and other indicators of economic performance. Economic performance and problems occupy a prominent place in political debates and issues, and most economic policy arguments are bolstered by economic data.

It's important to have a basic understanding of the meaning of the economic data to which we're exposed continually. What does it mean if somebody argues that the economy is doing poorly because Gross National Product didn't increase significantly in the last quarter? When an increase in the nation's personal income is announced, what does this mean in terms of the economic welfare of the typical family? If the Consumer Price Index increases by 10 percent in a year, how accurately does this measure any specific family's increase in cost of living?

The Flow of National Income and Output: An Overview

The first step in measuring national income and output is to recognize the distinction between *stocks* and *flows*.

- **Flows** are quantities per unit of time.
- **Stocks** are simply quantities that are not expressed with any reference to time.

For example, the *flow* of water through a pipe is measured in gallons per hour, per day, etc., while the *stock* of water in a reservoir is simply expressed in gallons.

Output and income are *flows*. As individuals, our incomes are weekly, monthly, or annual *flows*—$250 per week, $1,000 per month, or $12,000 per year—not a single lifetime figure (stock) of $500,000. One of the more depressing things to do is to look back over the past several years and add all of your annual incomes together, and wonder where all of that money went.

The answer is quite simple, if not reassuring. The weekly, monthly, and annual flows of income were accompanied by weekly, monthly, and annual *expenditure flows*—for food, housing, clothing, etc.

In its simplest representation, an economy is a circular flow of goods and services and of *productive resources* or *factors of production* between households and firms, such as the one shown in Figure 1. In the absence of coercion, we can expect households and firms to exchange goods and resources of equal value. For households, the benefits or satisfaction from the goods they receive will just equal the real costs of the resources they give up. For firms, the resource services they purchase will equal the value of the goods they offer in exchange.

- In the circular flow, the value of the goods flow equals the value of the resource flow.

Instead of exchanging resources directly for goods, households exchange their resources for money and the money for goods. Firms will

Figure 1 Simple Circular Flow in a Barter Economy

Figure 2 Simple Circular Flow in a Money Economy

purchase resource services for money and sell goods to households for money. In Figure 2, the quantities of food and clothing in the flow and the prices of food and clothing determine the size of the expenditure (consumption) flow from households to firms. The **consumption expenditure flow** in this system represents the money value of the goods and services produced for consumption by all firms.

- **Aggregate output**, or **national product**, is the aggregate value of goods and services produced for final use in the economy per year.

In the lower loop of the circular flow, the quantities of resources in the flow and the prices of resources determine the **factor payments** or **income flow** from firms to households. This is the money value of the resource flow from households to firms.

- **National income** is the sum of the values of the factors of production or resources employed in production of goods and services.

Since households and firms exchange equal values, it follows that

$$\text{Aggregate output} = \text{National income}$$

and

$$\frac{\text{Aggregate expenditure}}{\text{for goods and services}} = \frac{\text{Aggregate}}{\text{factor payments}}$$

Measuring National Income and Output

In a single industry or market, finding the aggregate quantity supplied by all sellers and the aggregate quantity demanded by all buyers is conceptually quite simple. The quantities supplied by individual sellers or demanded by individual buyers can simply be added up.

However, adding the outputs of all firms in all industries or the quantities of all goods demanded by all buyers together to get aggregate figures for the economy as a whole isn't quite so simple. Physical units of different products can't be added together—5 billion bolts + 5 billion nuts = 5 billion bolts + 5 billion nuts. Adding outputs of different goods and services together to get a meaningful sum requires a common denominator. The only useful common denominator for this purpose is the *money value*, or the *price*.

Measuring aggregate output and income is thus basically a very large accounting problem. In a vast and complex economy, however, since it's impossible to gather all of the detailed information on economic activity from all producers, most of the measurements in the national income accounts are estimates. In addition, unavoidable errors, clerical and otherwise, inevitably affect the accuracy of the figures.

Gross National Product (GNP)

Gross National Product (GNP) is the most comprehensive measure of economic activity in the national income accounts.

- **Gross National Product** (GNP) is the value of all goods and services produced for final use in a given year, expressed in current market prices.

In 1978, the U.S. GNP was $2,106.6 billion, or $2.1 trillion. This was the value of goods and services produced for final use in 1978, expressed in 1978 prices.

The values of *intermediate goods* are not included as separate items in calculating GNP.

- **Intermediate goods** are goods that are used in the production of other goods that are ultimately sold for final use by households.

The value of intermediate goods *is* included in the values of goods produced for final use. To include the values of all intermediate goods, and the value of final goods and services, would include the values of intermediate goods more than once. This is called *double counting*.

Each stage of the production process adds value to the materials and intermediate goods produced at previous stages of the production process. Table 1 is a simplified hypothetical example of the values added at various stages of production of an automobile with a retail price of $5000.

- The **value added** at each stage of production is the value of the product at the end of that stage less the value of the materials at the beginning of that stage.

In Table 1, mining adds $100 to the value of the unmined ore used to produce one automobile, smelting adds $100 to the value of the mined ore, etc. The final value of the automobile is the sum of the values added at each stage of production. The sum of the values of all final

Table 1 Price vs. Value Added

	Sales Price	Value Added
Miner sells ore to pig-iron factory	$ 100	$ 100
Pig-iron factory sells refined iron to steel manufacturer	$ 200	$ 100
Steel manufacturer sells steel to General Motors	$ 500	$ 300
General Motors sells Chevette to dealer	$3800	$3300
Dealer sells Chevette to customer	$5000	$1200
TOTAL	$9600	$5000

goods and services, then, is the sum of the values added by all producers of raw materials, intermediate goods, and final goods.

- *GNP is the sum of the values added* by all producers at all stages of production.

If all of the items in the left-hand column of Table 1 were included as separate items in calculating GNP, the value of the iron ore would be counted five times, the value of the pig iron four times, the value of the steel three times, etc. Double counting would show the contribution of one $5000 automobile to GNP as $9500.

Close-up

The *Value Added* Tax

The tax revolt in the United States in the late 1970s made politicians very wary of raising taxes, and led to renewed interest in a **value added tax** (VAT) as a means of raising government revenue or as a substitute for some direct taxes on individuals. One politically appealing aspect of the VAT is that not many people would understand what is being taxed. Everybody understands and feels the impact of a direct tax on income, but a small percentage levy on something as obscure as value added isn't likely to generate much rebellion among taxpayers.

A value added tax is an excise tax on the value added to materials and intermediate goods by a producer, so a 10 percent VAT would levy a 10 percent excise tax on the values added by all producers at all stages of production. In other words, a 10 percent VAT would be a 10 percent excise tax on the entire GNP! A seemingly innocuous 10 percent VAT on a GNP of $2 trillion would yield $200 billion in revenue.

The VAT raises the producers' costs at each stage of production, and the producers pass the cost of the tax on to the next stage of production, until the consumers end up paying the VAT as part of the retail prices of the goods and services they buy.

There are two basic measures of GNP—the **expenditure approach** and the **factor-payments approach.** Since they are alternative measures of the same thing, both methods give the same final figure for GNP. However, the two approaches provide somewhat different information.

Measuring GNP: The Expenditure Approach

The expenditure approach to measuring GNP measures the expenditure flows for goods and services purchased by households, firms, the public sector (federal, state, and local governments), and net expenditure flow from the international sector. In other words, this approach treats GNP as a measure of aggregate output.

Personal consumption is the largest component of GNP on the expenditure side. In 1978, personal consumption amounted to $1,339.7 billion, or 63.6 percent of the 1978 GNP of $2,106.6 billion. Total consumption expenditures by households are broken down into three broad categories of expenditures, based on the types of items consumed. Expenditures on *consumer durables* are expenditures on such items as appliances, automobiles, and other durable consumer goods. In 1978, expenditures on consumer durables amounted to $197.6 billion, or 14.8 percent of total consumption expenditures by households. *Nondurable consumer goods*—such as food, utilities, etc.—are consumed in short periods of time and generally don't last from one year to the next. In 1978, *nondurables* accounted for $525.8 billion in consumption expenditure, or 39.2 percent of total consumption. The third component of consumption expenditure is for *services* (such as haircuts, repair and maintenance services, medical care, etc.), and in 1978, expenditure for services was $616.3 billion, or 46 percent of total consumption.

The other expenditure flow from the private sector is *gross private domestic investment* or *gross investment*, which includes investment expenditures by households and firms. Investment expenditures differ from consumption expenditures in that they are expenditures for goods that give firms and households future benefits, which generally extend over a period of time. For households, the major investment item is new residential construction. Investment expenditures by firms include plant, equipment, and inventory adjustments. In 1978, gross private domestic investment expenditure amounted to $344.5 billion, or 16.4 percent of GNP measured from the expenditure side.

As defined in national income accounts, investment does *not* include the purchases of financial securities (stocks and bonds) or deposits in savings accounts. These transactions simply transfer cash into other financial assets. They add nothing to the stock of housing, plant, equipment, inventories, or other forms of capital used in production.

For households, the dividing line between consumer durables and investment is somewhat arbitrary. Residential housing is a component of the investment expenditure flow because housing provides benefits for a long period of time, while the purchase of an automobile is a

Table 2 U.S. Gross National Product, 1978, Expenditure Approach (billions of $)

Personal Consumption			1,339.7
Durable goods		197.6	
Nondurable goods		525.8	
Services		616.3	
Gross Private Domestic Investment			344.5
Nonresidential structures		77.5	
Producers' durable equipment		146.2	
Residential structures		105.0	
Changes in business inventories		15.7	
Government Purchases of Goods & Services			434.2
Federal		154.0	
Defense	99.5		
Nondefense	54.5		
State and local		280.2	
Net Exports of Goods and Services			−11.8
Exports		205.2	
Imports		−217.0	
GROSS NATIONAL PRODUCT			2,106.6

Source: *Economic Report of the President, 1979.*

consumer durable expenditure. But how long is *long*? The author's new 1965 Dodge served him well until 1977, and some of the old "monitor top" refrigerators of the 1930s lasted for a generation.

The GNP also includes expenditures from the public sector for purchases of goods and services by federal, state, and local governments—payrolls, public buildings, roads, military hardware, etc. In 1978, *government purchases* amounted to $434.2 billion, or 20.6 percent of GNP from the expenditure side. This does *not* include such things as government-financed pensions or welfare payments—these are *transfer payments* for which the public sector receives no goods and services in return. Transfer payments will be treated later.

The final component of GNP from the expenditure side is *net exports*, or the *balance of trade*, from the international sector. When foreign buyers purchase U.S. exports, their payments to American sellers enter our expenditure stream, and add to our GNP. When a U.S. buyer pays a foreign seller for imported goods, these expenditures leave our income stream and diminish GNP. *Net exports*, or the *balance of trade*, is simply the difference between export expenditures and import expenditures—or exports minus imports. This shows the net effect of the international sector on the domestic GNP.

The attention given to specific issues involving imports and exports—the effect of import competition on specific industries, oil imports, "defending the dollar," etc.—tends to create the impression that the balance of trade is a much larger component of GNP than it actually is. In 1978, net exports were −$11.8 billion (we imported more than we exported), and this amounted to less than 1 percent of U.S. GNP from the expenditure side.

Adding consumption, gross investment, government purchases, and net exports together gives us GNP by the expenditure approach. This is summarized for the U.S. in 1978 in Table 2. Note that these expenditures are for goods produced in 1978. The purchase of a house built in 1958 wouldn't be included in the investment flow for 1978, because the house isn't part of the 1978 output of goods and services.

Measuring GNP: The Factor Payments Approach

In the circular flow, total expenditure for goods and services is equal to the total payment by firms for the use of resources or factors of production employed to produce those goods and services. GNP measured from the *factor payments* side represents the value of the resources used to produce goods and services, and compensation to resource owners for the use of their resources. In other words, this approach views GNP as a measure of national income.

The largest item in the factor-payments flow is *compensation of employees*—wages, salaries, and supplements paid to employees in the private and public sectors to compensate for the use of their labor. In 1978, compensation of employees amounted to $1,301.2 billion, or about 61.8 percent of GNP.

Compensation for the use of the labor and resources of self-employed persons—farmers, self-employed professionals, and self-employed proprietors—is included in the category of *proprietors' income*.

Corporate profits compensate owners of corporations. Some of this profit goes to pay *corporate profit taxes*, some is distributed to stockholders as *dividends*, and some is saved by the corporations as *undistributed corporate profits*.

Rental income compensates the owners of land and rental business and residential properties. The national income accounts also include imputed rents on owner-occupied housing—imputed rents are simply estimates of the "rent" the homeowner pays himself or herself as his or her own "landlord."

Net interest represents payments by firms for borrowed funds, and is included in the national income accounts as part of the factor payments flow. However, it should be noted that this does not include all interest payments. Interest payments on consumer loans and interest payments by the government are excluded from the definition of net interest.

The value of the capital that wears out, or is consumed, in the course of production during the year is included in the factor payments flow as *capital consumption* or *depreciation*. The size of the capital consumption component of GNP depends heavily on tax laws governing depreciation allowances, and isn't necessarily an accurate picture of the actual loss of capital equipment.

Part of the retail price or value of final goods represents *indirect taxes*

Table 3 Gross National Product, 1978, Factor Payments Approach (billions of $)

Compensation of Employees		1,301.2
Wages and salaries	1,100.7	
Wage and salary adjustments	200.5	
Proprietors' Income		112.9
Farm	25.1	
Nonfarm	87.8	
Rental Income		23.4
Corporate Profits, Adjusted		160.0
Before-tax profits	202.4	
Corporate profit taxes	84.1	
Dividends	49.3	
Undistributed corp. profit	69.1	
Capital consumption adjustment	−18.1	
Inventory valuation adjustment	−24.3	
Net Interest Payments		106.1
Indirect Business Taxes		178.2
Depreciation		216.9
Statistical Discrepancies & Misc.		7.9
GROSS NATIONAL PRODUCT		2,106.6

Source: *Economic Report of the President, 1979*

which are levied on sellers and passed on to consumers. These indirect taxes include such items as general sales taxes, special excise taxes on some goods, gasoline taxes, etc.

There are more details in the national income accounts on the factor payments side, but the additional detail isn't essential for a basic understanding of the accounts. In addition, there are clerical and estimation errors in the data. All of these items will be lumped together in a catch-all category, *statististical discrepancies and misc*. The GNP for the U.S. in 1978 measured by factor payments (or income) is summarized in Table 3.

Close-up

Are the National Income Accounts *Sexist*?

Few occupations make more demands than that of the housewife. Housewives perform many of the duties of chefs, maids, teachers, managers, purchasing agents, counselors, and paramedics. It has been estimated that a full-time housewife works 2,500 hours per year at her profession, which works out to 52 48-hour weeks. Estimates of the value of housewives' services to the household range from about $4,800 per year to over $16,000 per year.[1] It has also been estimated that the value of housewives' services is about 20 percent of the Gross National

---

[1] Some of the facts in this example are based on information in Juanita M. Kreps, *Sex in the Marketplace* (Baltimore: Johns Hopkins University Press, 1971), pp. 69–73.

Product. What, then, is the value assigned to housewives' services in the GNP accounts? Zero!

Some feminists have argued that the exclusion of housewives' services from the national income accounts is "sexist," and that it reflects the low status of traditional women's roles in our society. Sexual stereotyping and sexual discrimination in education, employment, and pay are serious economic problems, but the treatment of housewives' services in the national income accounts isn't related to this.

The national income accounts exclude the value of *all* unpaid family services to the household. The value of the bachelor's housekeeping services and the household services provided by the growing number of husbands who share in household duties are excluded as well.

There are two rather simple, and non-"sexist," reasons for excluding the value of unpaid family services to the household. First of all, it would be difficult if not impossible to gather reasonably accurate data on the value of everything from the tomatoes in the backyard garden to the major do-it-yourself home improvements provided by family members. Secondly, there isn't any meaningful "market test" of the value of these services because the relationship among family members is more emotional than economic.

Although GNP is the most convenient and comprehensive summary measure of aggregate output and income of the economy, it can be misleading as the sole indicator of economic performance. Other national income aggregates that are derived from GNP are useful for a more complete picture.

Net National Product (NNP)

GNP, whether measured from the expenditure or factor payments side, includes the value of the capital that is used up in the course of production during the year as part of aggregate income. In fact, this *depreciation* or *capital consumption* represents a loss of productive resources during the year.

- **Net National Product** shows the net value of final goods and services produced during the year, after deducting the value of capital consumed.

Algebraically, if D is depreciation,

$$NNP \equiv GNP - D.$$

In 1978, for example, deducting depreciation of $216.9 billion from the GNP of $2106.6 billion gives us

NNP = $2106.6 billion − $216.9 billion = $1889.7 billion.

National Income (NI)

National income is often used as a general expression synonymous with GNP or NNP. However, in the national income accounts, the term *national income* (NI) has a rather precise meaning.

- **National Income** (NI) is the aggregate income earned by factors of production.

To calculate national income from the national income accounting data, simply deduct indirect business taxes (IBT) from net national product. Algebraically,

$$NI \equiv NNP - IBT.$$

To avoid confusion, all future references to "national income" in the text will be to national income in the general sense (i.e., *GNP*) and not to this specific accounting definition, unless otherwise noted.

Personal Income (PI)

We still don't know the aggregate income received by households because not all of the national income produced by factors of production actually goes to the households. In addition, households receive income that hasn't been included in the definitions of GNP, NNP, or NI.

- **Personal Income** (PI) is the aggregate income actually received by households.

The first step in calculating PI is to deduct the items included in NI that aren't received by the households. First there are *corporate profits*, which represent income to corporations. *Social insurance contributions* are paid out of the income produced, but aren't received as income by persons, so they are excluded from Personal Income. *Net interest* isn't paid to households or individuals, so it isn't included in Personal Income.

Now, we have to add income that is received by households and persons, but wasn't included in the definitions of GNP, NNP, or NI. The big item here is *transfer payments*, of which the largest portion are government transfer payments for pensions, welfare programs, and survivors' benefits. Transfer payments aren't included in the definition of factor payments because they simply transfer income, and aren't payments for the use of productive resources. However, they are included in the definition of Personal Income because they represent income received by persons.

Dividends are the portion of corporate profits that are distributed to stockholders, and therefore represent income to persons. *Personal interest income* is the interest income of persons from all sources. These items have to be added to the definition of Personal Income. Summing all of this up, then, Personal Income (PI) is

$$PI \equiv NI - (\text{corporate profit} + \text{social insurance contributions} + \text{net interest})$$
$$+ (\text{transfer payments} + \text{dividends} + \text{personal interest income}).$$

Disposable Personal Income (DI)

Disposable Personal Income, or *Disposable Income* (*DI*), is the aggregate "take-home pay" of households to allocate and spend as they wish.

- **Disposable income** (DI) is personal income (PI), minus *direct taxes*.

Direct taxes are levied directly on households. Personal income taxes, property taxes, and other taxes paid directly by households are direct taxes.

There are only two possible uses for disposable income—it must be spent for personal consumption or saved. In other words,

$$DI \equiv C + S,$$

where C is personal consumption and S is personal saving.

Table 4 summarizes the relationship between GNP and the other national income accounting aggregates for the U.S. in 1978.

Table 4   U.S. National Income Aggregates, 1978 (billions of $)

Gross National Product			2,106.6
Less: Depreciation	216.9		
Equals: *Net National Product*			1,889.7
Less: Indirect business taxes	178.2		
Misc.	7.9		
Equals: *National Income*			1,703.6
Less: Adjusted corporate profits	160.0		
Net interest	106.1		
Social insurance contribution	164.3		
Plus: Transfer payments		226.0	
Personal interest income		158.9	
Dividends		49.3	
Equals: *Personal Income*			1,707.4
Less: Direct personal taxes	256.2		
Equals: *Disposable Personal Income*			1,451.2
Less: Personal outlays	1,374.4		
Consumption 1,339.7			
Other 34.8			
Equals: *Personal Saving*			76.8

Source: *Economic Report of the President, 1979*

Measuring Changes in Prices and Output

Index numbers express GNP, prices, industrial production, and other variables in a given year as a percentage or proportion of their value in a base year. The index for the base year is 100 or 1.0. For example, the index of industrial production for the U.S. expresses industrial production as a proportion of industrial production in 1967 (1967 = 100). In 1978, the industrial production index stood at 145 (1967 = 100). This simply means that industrial production in 1978 was 145 percent of industrial production in 1967, or 1.45 times as large as it was in 1967.

Real and Nominal Income

The economy's *real GNP* is the circular flow of goods and resources. The flow of money expenditures for goods and services and factor payments is *money income*, or *nominal GNP*. Real GNP can't be calculated by adding up different physical quantities of different goods and resources, and money prices have to be used as a common denominator. However, changes in prices can cause the money income flow to change with no change, or even an opposite change in the real income flow.

For example, suppose that the output of food and clothing remain constant in two years (call them year 1 and year 2), while the prices of food and clothing increase by 50%. In *current prices*, or *current dollars*,

GNP in yr. 1 = (5 billion C × $20/C) + (10 billion F × $10/F)
= $200 billion.
GNP in yr. 2 = (5 billion C × $30/C) + (10 billion F × $15/F)
= $300 billion.

The 50% increase in nominal income in this case means very little in terms of living standards or economic welfare because the outputs of goods, or *real GNP* didn't change.

To measure the real output of goods and services, or real GNP over a period of years, each year's income is expressed in *constant prices*, or *constant dollars*.

- Real GNP is the value of goods and services produced per year in *constant prices*.

In the above example, if GNP is expressed in constant prices (use prices from year 1),

GNP in yr. 1 = (5 billion C × $20/C) + (10 billion F × $10/F)
= $200 billion.
GNP in yr. 2 = (5 billion C × $20/C) + (10 billion F × $10/F)
= $200 billion.

Using constant prices, there was no change in real GNP.

In practice, it's impossible to assign constant prices to the millions of goods and services produced to find real GNP in constant prices. Instead, **price indexes** are estimated which show the average price level in a given year as a percentage, or proportion of the price level in some base year.[1] For example, if we used year 1 from the previous example as the base year, the price index in year 1 would be 100 (or 1.0), indicating that prices in year 1 are 100 percent of prices in year 1. In year 2, with prices 50 percent higher than in year 1, the price index for year 2 would be 150 (or 1.5), indicating that prices in year 2 are 150 percent of prices in year 1, or 1.5 times as high as prices in year 1.

- To find real GNP in a given year in constant prices, divide the money GNP by the price index for the given year.

---

1. For more details on price indexes, see the appendix to this chapter.

In the previous example, real GNP in year 2, in constant prices from year 1 is

$$\text{Real GNP (in constant prices)} = \frac{\text{Money Income}}{\text{Price Index}} = \frac{\$300 \text{ b.}}{1.5} = \$200 \text{ b.}$$

Two of the more important price indexes published by the government are the **consumer price index** (CPI) and the **implicit price deflator** (IPD).

Consumer Price Index (CPI)

The *consumer price index* (CPI) is perhaps the most commonly used price index. It is estimated by the U.S. Bureau of Labor Statistics from data gathered in a scientifically designed statistical sample of 85 urban areas. The most commonly used version of the CPI is the index for all items in all urban areas.

- The **consumer price index** (CPI) estimates the cost of a constant *basket* of goods as a percentage of the cost of the same basket of goods in the base year.

Traditionally, the basket of goods chosen by the BLS was supposed to approximate the consumption pattern of typical urban households headed by wage earners and clerical workers. Since January 1978, an additional CPI has been estimated to show changes in cost of living for all urban households. The basket is modified at ten-year intervals to reflect changes in typical consumption patterns. The 1968 revision, for example, deleted men's pajamas and added motel rooms to the basket.

The CPI is a good indicator of inflation and changes in cost of living, but it doesn't measure the change in every household's cost of living. If you happen to live in an area where prices are rising more rapidly than the average of all urban areas, the change in the CPI will understate the change in your cost of living. If your consumption pattern differs from that of the average urban household, the CPI will give an inaccurate picture of the change in your cost of living. Table 5 shows the CPI for various classes of expenditure. If you happen to spend a larger share of your income than the average household for goods whose prices have increased most rapidly, such as medical care, the CPI for all items will understate the increase in your cost of living. The BLS also publishes CPI data for individual cities. To estimate the change in your cost of living, look at the CPI for the items that make up the largest proportion of your budget and the CPI for the nearest city for which the BLS publishes CPI data.

The CPI isn't a very accurate measure of changes in prices over very long periods of time, such as 1929–1978. The basket of goods in the CPI for 1978 is quite different than the 1929 basket, so the CPI doesn't measure the change in the cost of a constant basket of goods. Many

Table 5 Consumer Price Index for Selected Items, 1978 (1967 = 100)

ALL ITEMS	195.4
Commodities	187.1
Food	211.4
Housing	202.8
Fuel & Utilities	216.0
Household Furnishings	177.7
Apparel	159.6
Services	210.9
Medical care	219.4
Rent	164.0

Source: U.S. Department of Commerce, *Survey of Current Business*, April, 1979. Actual price indexes are compiled and published by the U.S. Department of Labor, Bureau of Labor Statistics.

products are available today that didn't even exist in the 1920s or 1930s, and there may not even be a close equivalent—for example, the 1929 equivalent to a color T.V. set. In some cases, changes in quality over long periods change the commodity dramatically. A 1980 Ford is quite different from a 1929 Model A Ford.

Implicit Price Deflator (IPD) and Real GNP

As was explained earlier, the relevant GNP comparisons over time are comparisons of *real* GNP. To find GNP in constant prices, or real GNP, current nominal GNP is deflated by a price index called the *implicit price deflator for GNP (IPD)*.

- The **Implicit Price Deflator** *(IPD)* for GNP estimates the average change in prices of all items in GNP between a base year and a given year.

The Department of Commerce publishes GNP in current dollars (or *nominal* GNP) and in "1972 dollars." To find real GNP in 1972 dollars, the nominal GNP is divided by the implicit price deflator which shows the proportional change in prices since 1972. For example, the implicit price deflator for 1978 was 152.09, or 1.5209, and GNP in current-year (1978) prices was $2106.6 billion. In 1972 prices, the real GNP in 1978 was

$$\text{GNP in 1972 prices} = \frac{\text{GNP in current prices}}{\text{implicit price deflator}} \qquad (1)$$

$$= \frac{\$2106.6 \text{ billion}}{1.5209} = \$1385.1 \text{ billion}.$$

Figure 3 shows the behavior of nominal and real GNP between 1960 and 1978. Some additional topics on index numbers are included in the appendix to this chapter.

Figure 3 Real vs. Nominal GNP

Source: *Economic Report of the President*, 1979.

GNP as a Measure of Economic Welfare

GNP is often used as an indicator of economic performance and welfare. Real GNP is a convenient and comprehensive measure of aggregate output of goods and services, and the size of the flow of goods and services produced has strong implications for economic welfare. Other things equal, the community will generally be better off economically with a large output of goods and services than with a small one. However, there isn't a one-to-one relationship between GNP and economic welfare, or between changes in GNP and changes in economic welfare. We have to look beyond the GNP figures to get a clearer picture of economic welfare.

Per Capita Income

A doubling of GNP doesn't necessarily mean a doubling of economic welfare or dramatic increases in living standards of the population. If population doubles at the same time, there is no increase in the average output of goods and services per person, or *per capita real GNP*.

- **Per capita real GNP** is the average output of final goods and services per person, or the ratio of GNP over population.

Pattern of Income Distribution

If income is very unevenly distributed among persons in a country, real GNP and even per capita real GNP doesn't tell us much about the living standards of the average person in a country. The small sheikdom of Kuwait, for example, has the highest per capita national income in the world—owing to its small population and its extensive oil reserves—but the living standard of the typical Kuwaiti citizen is more modest than the average living standards in countries with lower per capita national income but a less uneven pattern of income distribution.

Associating economic welfare with a particular pattern of income distribution requires a normative value judgement at some point. To say that greater equality or inequality of income distribution is more equitable or better requires some normative standards of equity.

Composition of GNP

The types of goods and services produced obviously affect the community's economic welfare and living standards. Suppose that two countries—A and B—have the same real GNP per capita and the same pattern of income distribution. However 70 percent of A's GNP is made up of heavy industrial machinery and military goods, while 70 percent of country B's GNP is made up of consumer goods. Obviously, households in country B will have higher living standards than those in country A.

Similarly, the relationship between growth of GNP over time and increases in community economic welfare and living standards depends heavily on the types of goods whose output is growing the fastest. For example, the Soviet Union experienced dramatic increases in GNP between 1928 and 1953, but living standards didn't grow proportionately because the growth of GNP was accomplished by squeezing the production of consumer goods to produce more heavy industrial equipment.

GNP and Gross National Cost

The value of goods and services produced, and therefore GNP, depends on costs of producing goods and services. The value added at any stage of production also reflects the cost incurred at that stage of production. In other words, we can think of GNP as a measure of the costs borne by society in producing goods and services. However, GNP is not a very accurate measure of aggregate cost because some important costs borne by society never enter the GNP calculations.

Production and consumption of goods imposes *external social costs* on the community.

- **External social costs** are costs of production and consumption of goods borne by persons not directly involved in their production or consumption.

Environmental pollution is one of the most serious forms of external social cost.

Building a nuclear power plant increases the output of electric power for consumers and provides more electrical power to be used in production of other goods, but it also contributes to thermal pollution of surrounding bodies of water as the heated water from the power plant is discharged into lakes and rivers. This accelerates the aging of bodies of water, and generally reduces the recreational value of lakes and rivers. These are external social costs borne by society, but they don't enter into the cost calculations of firms or into the final value of goods and services.

In other words, by excluding social costs, GNP and the measures of income related to it tend to understate the costs borne by society in producing its annual output of final goods and services.

Summary

1. **Real national income** or **output** is the annual circular flow of goods and services and resource services, or the annual flow of expenditures for goods and services and payments to factors of production.
2. Measuring national income and output is a large accounting problem, and the national income data are based on data gathered from producers and by statistical estimation.
3. **Gross National Product** (GNP) is the value of all *final* goods and services produced in a given year. It is the most comprehensive measure of economic activity. Other national income aggregates derived from GNP are Net National Product (NNP), National Income (NI), Personal Income (PI), and Disposable Personal Income (DI).
4. **Index numbers** express prices, output, or other variables in any given year as a percentage or proportion of their value in a base year.
5. The **Consumer Price Index** (CPI) and the **Implicit Price Deflator** (IPD) are price indexes. They express prices in a given year as a percentage of prices in a base year.
6. National income aggregates alone aren't indicators of economic welfare. Population, the composition of real GNP, the pattern of income distribution, and unmeasured social costs all must be considered in assessing the economic welfare of a country.

Concepts for Review

stock
flow
circular flow
aggregate output
national product
national income
factor payments flow
income flow
expenditure flow

Gross National Product (GNP)
intermediate goods
value added
Net National Product (NNP)
National Income (NI)
Personal Income (PI)
Disposable Income (DI)

real GNP
nominal GNP
price index
consumer price index (CPI)
implicit price deflator (IPD)
per capita real GNP
external social costs

Questions

1. The Minnow family is being visited by I. M. Sharkey, a life insurance salesman. Part of Mr. Sharkey's pitch is that the Minnows will earn $1 million in their lifetimes. Is this a very meaningful way to express a family's income? Why?
2. If Gross National Product is defined as the value of the annual output of goods and services for final use, what happens to the values of the raw materials and intermediate goods produced during the year?
3. The Soviet government defines the aggregate output of industry as the "sum of the values of the outputs of all industrial enterprises." Is this the same as defining the aggregate output of industry as the sum of the values added by all industrial enterprises? Is the distinction between the two (if any) significant?
4. Senator I. M. Phogbound has told his constituents in Temperance, Mich., that he will oppose any increases in taxes on individuals. Instead, he argues heatedly, additional revenue could be raised by a 15 percent tax on the values added by producers.
   a. What is the senator talking about?
   b. If he voted for such a tax, would he be keeping his promise to oppose additional tax burdens on individuals?
   c. About how much revenue would such a tax raise in the U.S.?
5. The Nerd and Schnook families are next-door neighbors in Drab, Pa. The Nerds have hired the Schnooks to do all of their domestic work at an annual salary of $10,000. The Schnooks have hired the Nerds to do the same thing for them at an annual salary of $10,000.
   What effect would this arrangement have on GNP? Explain.
6. As a full-time housewife, Ms. Jane Good worked a 40-hour week in the home, and served as a volunteer aide in a nursing home for 10 hours per week. In 1980, she took a full-time job at an annual salary of $15,000. Because of the demands of her job, she has less time to work in the home, and has to give up her volunteer activities.
   As GNP is defined and measured, what effect would Ms. Good's employment have on GNP? Would the change in GNP accurately reflect a change in the economy's aggregate output of goods and services? Explain.

Problems

1. The following national income data are for Lower Slobovia in 1980 (all figures are billions of dollars)

   Gross Investment 250
   Net Interest 150
   Indirect Business Taxes 150
   Corporate Profits 175
   Dividends 75
   Transfer Payments 275
   Personal Consumption 1200
   Imports 100
   Proprietors' Income 75
   Personal Taxes 175
   Government Purchases 250
   Exports 200
   Wages and Salaries 1050
   Undistributed Corporate Profits 100
   Social Security Taxes 100
   Depreciation 200

a. Calculate the following:
   GNP by the expenditure flow
   GNP by the factor-payment flow
   NNP
   National Income
   Personal Income
   Disposable Personal Income
   Personal Saving
b. The GNP of Upper Slobovia in 1980 is twice as great as Lower Slobovia's. Does this mean that the citizens of Upper Slobovia are twice as well off economically as the citizens of Lower Slobovia? Explain carefully.

APPENDIX

How Not to Be Fooled by Growth Indexes

Index numbers are convenient and useful ways to show growth in GNP or other aggregate measures of output over time. However, the apparent clarity and convenience of index numbers hide some important subtleties that make it very easy to be misled by them. The first lesson is to be skeptical of any single index of growth of income that doesn't provide some information on the type of index it is or how it was calculated.

Real and Nominal Growth

Be sure that the index shows real growth, and not simply the growth in nominal or money GNP. It was explained in the chapter that the real GNP—i.e., the output of goods and services in constant prices—is more important for changes in economic welfare than the money value of this flow in current prices.

For example, the U.S. GNP in 1978 in current (1978) prices was $2106.6 billion, and the U.S. GNP in 1968 in current (1968) prices was $868.5 billion. The change in GNP over this period, expressed as an index number is

$$\frac{GNP_{78}}{GNP_{68}} \times 100 = \frac{\$2106.6 \text{ billion}}{\$868.5 \text{ billion}} \times 100 = 242.6$$

This does not mean that the ouput of goods and services in 1978 was 242.6 percent of the level of output in 1968, because prices changed over this period as well as output.

Constructing an index of GNP in constant prices—i.e., an index of *real* GNP— would be a more meaningful comparison because prices would be the same in both years. Comparing U.S. GNP in 1968 and 1978 in constant 1972 prices, for example, yields the following index of growth

$$\frac{GNP_{78} \text{ (in \$1972)}}{GNP_{68} \text{ (in \$1972)}} \times 100 = \frac{\$1385.1 \text{ billion}}{\$1051.8 \text{ billion}} \times 100 = 131.7$$

However, even indexes of growth in real terms can be misleading.

Look at the Base Year

Growth between a base year and a given year can be overstated or understated by the choice of the base year. Choosing an unusually bad year with an unusually low GNP as the base year will overstate growth, and an unusually good base year with an unusually high GNP will tend to understate growth.

Price Weights and the "Index Number Problem"

Index numbers can be manipulated through the choice of price weights. This is a little technical, but the following example will show how the choice of price weights affects the result.

Assume a very simple economy, producing only two goods—widgets and gadgets. We want to compare GNP in two years—a *base year* (year 0), and an *end year* (year 1). The actual number of years between 0 and 1 need not be one year, year 1 is simply to identify the end year.

Gadgets were a new item in the base year, and their output between year 0 and year 1 grew much faster than the output of widgets. By simple supply and demand reasoning, if the output of gadgets grows more rapidly than the output of widgets, gadgets become less scarce relative to widgets, and their relative price falls—as shown in Table A-1a.

Table A-1 Base-Year vs. End-Year Price Indexes

(a) Basic Data	Year 0		Year 1	
	P_0	Q_0	P_1	Q_1
Widgets	$1	5,000	$2	5,000
Gadgets	$100	100	$20	1,000

(b) Base-year Index	Year 0		Year 1	
	P_0	Q_0	P_0	Q_1
Widgets	$1 × 5,000 = $5,000		$1 × 5,000 = $5,000	
Gadgets	$100 × 100 = $10,000		$100 × 1,000 = $100,000	
GNP in Year 0 Prices	$15,000		$105,000	

(c) End-year Index	Year 0		Year 1	
	P_1	Q_0	P_1	Q_1
Widgets	$2 × 5,000 = $10,000		$2 × 5,000 = $10,000	
Gadgets	$20 × 100 = $2,000		$20 × 1,000 = $20,000	
GNP in Year 1 Prices	$12,000		$30,000	

To construct an index of growth of real GNP for this period, we have to express GNP in both years in the same prices. We have two choices—express GNP in both years in base-year prices, or express GNP in both years in end-year prices. Table A-1b shows GNP in both years in base-year prices (P_0), and Table A-1c shows GNP in both years in end-year prices (P_1).

The index of growth in *base-year prices* is called a *base-year index*, or **Laspeyere index** (I_L). It compares GNP in year 1 in base-year prices as a percentage of GNP in year 0 in base-year prices. In this case,

$$I_L = \frac{\$105,000}{\$15,000} \times 100 = 700.$$

An index of growth in *end-year prices* is an *end-year index*, or **Paasche Index** (I_P).

Assigning end-year prices to the same physical outputs in the two years in the example gives

$$I_P = \frac{\$30,000}{\$12,000} \times 100 = 250.$$

Both indexes are equally correct and equally truthful, but they show much different rates of growth. This illustrates the **index number problem**. Base-year indexes tend to overstate growth and end-year indexes tend to understate it. It's a "problem" because there isn't any way to eliminate it. The distortion becomes greater the greater the difference in relative prices in the two years. It would become very great if the base year were a year in the distant past.

The existence of an index number problem doesn't mean that growth indexes are useless or that they are only tools of the devious. However, the moral is clear. There are many ways to be fooled by indexes, so be wary of index numbers that don't give you any information on such things as the base year, price weights, etc.

PART EIGHT

Aggregate Demand: The Goods Market

We have now seen how the interaction of aggregate supply and aggregate demand determines equilibrium levels of prices and output. In the past, most activist Keynesian economists have considered aggregate demand the more important factor and have urged the use of **demand-management policies** to stabilize economic conditions. The next two sections of the text explore this notion of **aggregate demand**.

Traditionally, economists have analyzed aggregate demand by dividing the entire economy into two basic markets or sectors: the market for goods and services (the **goods market**) and the market for money and financial assets (the **money market**). In this section, we'll focus on aggregate demand in the goods market. To do this, though, we have to assume that no changes occur in the money market, that everything there remains constant. We also have to assume that prices remain constant up to full employment—in other words, that the aggregate supply curve is horizontal up to that level. Given these major assumptions, of course, aggregate demand in the goods market becomes the sole determinant of equilibrium aggregate output.

We begin our analysis by building a simple model of the economy to show how the level of aggregate demand is determined and how that level in turn determines the economy's output. We'll then look at various factors that affect the stability of aggregate demand and output over time. Finally, we'll explore the government's use of fiscal policy in its effort to stabilize aggregate demand and achieve full employment without inflation.

21

Aggregate Demand and Income Determination: The Private Sector

Preview: In order to understand the role of aggregate demand in determining the levels of aggregate output and national income, we have to construct a model of the economy. The model is usually referred to as the **simple Keynesian model**, and is used to predict changes in output and income due to changes in aggregate demand in the goods market. In this chapter, we will build a simplified version of the model, representing an economy with no public sector (and therefore no government spending or taxes) and no international sector (and therefore no import or export expenditures).

In this chapter, we examine the role of aggregate demand for goods and services in determining the level of aggregate output (or real GNP). This has implications for the level of employment, since the level of aggregate output affects the level of employment of labor to produce the goods and services. Aggregate demand also has implications for inflation. If the demand for goods and services exceeds the economy's capacity to produce, the result is *demand-pull inflation*. If aggregate demand and output aren't sufficient to generate full employment, the result is *demand-deficiency unemployment*.

This chapter focuses on the relationship between aggregate demand (AD) and aggregate output or real GNP (Y). More specifically, we're interested in aggregate demand as a determinant of *equilibrium* aggregate output or GNP. To isolate the relationship between aggregate demand and output, we have to make some simplifying assumptions. First, we'll assume that the price level is constant, so that changes in GNP represent changes in real GNP or aggregate output.

This chapter and several that follow it deal with aggregate demand and equilibrium aggregate output, or equilibrium in the goods sector of the economy. For the time being, we'll leave money and financial markets (the monetary sector) out of the analysis. The effects of money and monetary phenomena will be introduced and integrated into the analysis of income and employment in the next section of the text.

The income determination model uses the expenditure concepts introduced in national income accounting, but with an important difference. In the income determination model, consumption, saving, and investment are *desired* or *intended* expenditures—i.e., they are *ex ante* quantities. In national income accounting, expenditures are *measured*, or *ex post*, quantities. The task of the income determination model is to predict equilibrium income and changes in income, not simply to measure income after the fact. In the analysis of income determination that follows, investment and saving will refer to intended investment and intended saving unless noted otherwise.

Aggregate Demand and Output in the Circular Flow

Figure 1 illustrates the circular flow of real GNP in a simple economy composed of *private households*, *private firms*, and a *financial sector* (banks, capital markets, etc.). National income or aggregate output (Y), you will recall from the last chapter, is equal to the sum of factor payments or the sum of expenditure on final goods and services:

$$Y = \text{sum of factor payments} = \text{sum of expenditures} \qquad (1)$$

Since there is no public sector, there are no taxes on firms or households, and all factor payments accrue to households as income. The

Figure 1 The Circular Flow of Real GNP

households allocate this income between *consumption* (C) and *saving* (S) which flows out of the expenditure stream to the financial sector. Investment (I) flows from the financial sector into the expenditure flow as firms and households purchase investment goods (capital equipment, new residential housing, etc.). The firms receive all expenditures for consumption and investment as receipts, so measured GNP (Y) in a closed, private economy can be expressed as

$$Y = \text{Consumption} + \text{measured Investment}. \quad (2)$$

Now, we must look at the aggregate demand (AD) for goods and services in the closed private economy. There are only two expenditure flows, consumption (C) and investment (I), so aggregate demand (AD) at any level of aggregate output or real GNP is

$$AD = C + I. \quad (3)$$

Now, from equations (2) and (3), it appears that aggregate demand is identical with GNP at any level of GNP. However, the two equations say two quite different things. The key is that *investment* in equation (2) is actual or measured investment. In equation (3), however, investment is intended investment—the amount of investment that households and firms are willing and able (or intend) to undertake at any level of aggregate output or real GNP. Thus, equation (2) says: "GNP is the sum of consumption expenditures and the measured level of investment." Equation (3), on the other hand, says: "At any level of aggregate output or real GNP, the aggregate demand for goods and services is the sum of intended consumption and intended investment expenditures."

Now, we're faced with an apparent puzzle concerning GNP and aggregate demand. Suppose that the economy had an actual GNP of $500 billion—consumption of $300 billion and measured investment expenditures of $200 billion. In other words

Measured GNP = C + measured I = $300 billion + $200 billion
= $500 billion.

However, at a GNP (or aggregate output) of $500 billion, suppose that aggregate demand is

AD = C + intended I = $300 billion + $150 billion = $450 billion.

How could aggregate demand be less than the level of real GNP? The answer is quite simple. Measured investment includes *all* investment, *unintended* as well as intended.

- **Unintended investment** is the difference between the actual or measured level of investment and intended investment.

How could investment be unintended? Is this type of investment made by accident? Most unintended investment is unintended or unexpected accumulation of inventories by firms. If AD isn't sufficient to purchase the entire aggregate output or real GNP, some of it remains unsold and is added to inventories of producers and sellers. To reduce their inventories to normal or desired levels, the firms will cut back on current output, and this will cause aggregate output to fall.

- If aggregate demand is less than the level of aggregate output, unintended inventory accumulation will cause aggregate output or real GNP to fall.

What would happen if aggregate demand exceeded aggregate output? Let's reverse the previous example, and suppose that at a real GNP of $450 billion, aggregate demand is $500 billion. In other words, households are willing and able to spend more than the current aggregate output. This will cause some **unintended disinvestment** as firms find their inventories falling in order to meet their customers' demands. As firms find their inventories below normal or desirable levels, they will increase inventories. To do this, they have to increase output, so aggregate output (real GNP) will rise.

- If aggregate demand exceeds aggregate output, unintended inventory depletion will encourage firms to increase output and cause aggregate output to increase.

Equilibrium Output

Aggregate output or real GNP reaches equilibrium when there is no tendency for it to change. As long as there is unintended accumulation or depletion of inventories (intended investment or unintended disinvestment), aggregate output will not be in equilibrium. Unintended inventory investment as a result of aggregate demand less than aggregate output or real GNP will encourage firms to reduce output to reduce their excessive inventories. If there is unintended inventory depletion because aggregate demand exceeds aggregate output, firms have an incentive to increase their output to satisfy customers and to replenish inventories.

Thus aggregate output or real GNP will be in equilibrium only if there is no unintended investment. This occurs only when intended expenditures (aggregate demand) equal aggregate output.

- **Equilibrium real GNP** is reached when the sum of intended expenditures equals real GNP, or GNP $(Y) = AD$.

Equilibrium can also be analyzed and understood in the context of the circular flow in Figure 1. Outflows from the income stream make the stream smaller, and inflows make it larger. Therefore, the size of the income stream will remain constant only if expenditure outflows and inflows are equal.

Figure 2 Equilibrium Real GNP: $Y = AD$

- Equilibrium GNP is reached when the sum of expenditure outflows from the income stream equals the sum of expenditure inflows into it.

In a closed, private economy, saving is the only expenditure outflow and investment is the only inflow. It follows, then, that

- Equilibrium GNP is reached in a closed private economy when the intended savings flow equals the intended investment flow, or $S = I$.

The distinction between *ex ante* (or intended) and *ex post* (or measured) saving and investment is important here. Equilibrium is reached when intended saving equals intended investment. However, if we look at measured GNP, measured saving is always equal to measured investment. With measured GNP,

$$\text{measured } Y = C + \text{measured } I.$$

The portion of GNP that isn't consumed is saved—i.e.,

$$\text{measured } S \equiv \text{measured } Y - C \equiv C + \text{measured } I - C \equiv \text{measured } I,$$

or

$$\text{measured } S \equiv \text{measured } I. \qquad (4)$$

Equilibrium GNP is approached graphically in Figure 2. In Figure 2, the horizontal axis is real GNP or aggregate output and the vertical axis is intended aggregate spending, or AD—both axes would be expressed in constant dollars. We have established that equilibrium GNP requires $Y = AD$. This condition is met at all points[1] on the 45° line in Figure 2. To verify this, note that any positively sloped straight line in Figure 2 would conform to the equation

$$AD = a + bY.$$

Since the 45° starts at the origin, $a = 0$. The slope of a positively sloped 45° line is 1, so the equation for the 45° line in Figure 2 is

$$AD = 0 + (1)Y, \text{ or } AD = Y.$$

In other words, all points on the 45° line fulfill the equilibrium condition $Y = AD$.

Aggregate demand, or intended spending, is represented in Figure 3 by the aggregate demand (AD) function. This shows the level of intended spending at each level of aggregate output or real GNP. In our closed private model,

$$AD = C + I.$$

Consumption and intended saving (S) vary directly with real GNP or aggregate output. As aggregate output increases, the size of the factor payments flow—and therefore incomes received by households—increases. Some of the additional income will be consumed and some will be saved.

For the time being, to keep our analysis simple, we'll assume that intended investment is an *autonomous expenditure flow*.

Figure 3 Aggregate Demand Function

---

1. Remember, however, that it is impossible for the economy to produce more than full-employment real GNP or Y^*, regardless of the level of aggregate demand. For this reason, the equlibrium line becomes vertical at Y^*. For simplicity, this change to a vertical equilibrium line will be shown only when necessary in this text.

- **Autonomous expenditures** are determined by variables other than real GNP, and don't vary with the level of real GNP.

Some investment *is* autonomous—such as annual investment expenditures in the course of completing long-term investment projects—but some varies with income. The assumption that all investment is autonomous is made only to make the analysis simpler at this point, and more realistic cases will be analyzed later.

The sum of consumption and intended investment expenditures at each level of aggregate output or real GNP is aggregate demand (AD) at that level of GNP. The AD function in Figure 3 shows the relationship between real GNP and aggregate demand, other things constant. With all investment autonomous and consumption varying directly with real GNP, AD will vary directly with real GNP.

Figure 4 analyzes equilibrium real GNP by combining $Y = AD$ from Figure 2 and $AD = C + I$ from Figure 3. At equilibrium real GNP ($\overline{Y}$), intended spending must equal aggregate output, or

$$\overline{Y} = AD = C + I.$$

This is attained where the $AD = C + I$ function intersects the $Y = AD$ (or 45°) line. At this intersection, we have

$$\overline{Y} = C + I.$$

In Figure 4, then, equilibrium GNP is $\overline{Y} = AD = 600$.

Figure 4 The Simple Keynesian Model

Figure 5 Saving and Investment at Equilibrium Real GNP

If aggregate output exceeds aggregate demand, as it does at $Y_2 = 800$ in Figure 4, aggregate demand isn't sufficient to purchase aggregate output and there is unintended investment in inventories of unsold goods. As was explained earlier, this will encourage firms to reduce their output to bring inventories back down to normal or desired levels and aggregate output will fall.

At an aggregate output of 400, where AD exceeds aggregate output, we have the opposite situation. In this case there is unintended saving because output isn't sufficient to accommodate all intended expenditure and unintended disinvestment in the form of inventory depletion. This will encourage firms to increase output to meet demand and to restore normal inventories, and aggregate output will rise.

Figure 5 looks at equilibrium GNP in terms of intended saving (S) and investment (I). It has already been explained that GNP will be in equilibrium when expenditure outflows from the income stream equal expenditure inflows into it. This occurs at $\overline{Y} = 600$ in Figure 5, where intended saving equals intended investment. At $Y = 800$, intended saving exceeds intended investment, and the income stream (GNP) will contract. At $Y = 400$, intended investment exceeds intended saving and the income stream will get larger.

The key, then, to maintaining a stable economy is the ability to predict accurately the level of aggregate demand, and then produce a level of output that will just satisfy that demand. The key to predicting the level of aggregate demand in our closed, private economy, in turn, is the ability to predict the levels of the two kinds of expenditures that make up aggregate demand, *consumption* and *intended investment*. To understand aggregate demand in more depth, then, we have to take a closer look at consumption and investment.

Consumption

Consumption is the largest component of aggregate demand, so the more we know about consumption, the better we will be able to predict aggregate demand. It should come as no surprise that, in general, the more income a household has, the more it will spend. In other words, the level of consumption (C) varies directly with the level of disposable income (Y_d). This relationship is expressed by the *consumption function*.

- The **consumption function** shows the relationship between income and consumption expenditures.

The consumption function can be written algebraically as

$$C = a + bY_d. \qquad (5)$$

Note that in a private economy with no taxes, GNP and Y_d are identical, so the consumption function can be written more simply as $C = a + bY$. When taxes are introduced into the model in the next chapter, however, the relationship between consumption and disposable income will no longer be exactly the same as the relationship between consumption and GNP.

The a in the function represents autonomous consumption—consumption expenditure determined by variables other than aggregate output or GNP. Autonomous consumption could go on even if aggregate output and income dropped to zero through borrowing or consuming out of accumulated savings. The b in the consumption function is the slope, and it shows the rate at which consumption varies with income, or the fraction of additional income that is consumed; it is called the *marginal propensity to consume*.

The consumption function is shown graphically in Figure 6. When income (Y) is zero, the only consumption expenditure is autonomous

Figure 6 The Consumption Function

consumption (a). This autonomous consumption is determined by variables other than current income and doesn't vary with the level of income.

A world in which all consumption is autonomous would be a very peculiar world. If the level of income dropped to zero or rose astronomically, the level of consumption wouldn't change. In reality, the largest component of the consumption expenditure flow is *induced consumption*, or consumption that varies with national income and GNP.

- **Induced expenditures** are expenditures that vary directly with aggregate output or GNP.

If we add induced consumption to autonomous consumption in Figure 6, we have the consumption function, $C = a + bY$, which shows the level of total consumption expenditure at every level of GNP.

Clearly, the values of a (autonomous consumption) and b (the slope of the consumption function, or marginal propensity to consume) are critical in determining the relationship between aggregate output, or GNP, and consumption. This warrants a closer examination of these elements of the consumption function.

Marginal Propensity to Consume

The term *propensity* literally means tendency or leaning. Keynes used the term in *The General Theory* to refer to the proportion of income consumed and the rate at which consumption changes with income. Its continuing use in macroeconomics is one of Keynes' more durable, if not enlightening, contributions to the field.

- The **marginal propensity to consume** (*mpc* or b) is the change in the level of consumption that results from a given change in income. If income increases by $1, *mpc* tells how much consumption changes as a result of that $1 increase. In other words, *mpc* is the *rate* at which consumption changes as income changes.

Graphically, *mpc* represents the slope of the consumption function. It can be written algebraically as

$$mpc = \frac{\text{change in consumption}}{\text{change in income}} = \frac{\Delta C}{\Delta Y}. \tag{6}$$

For a given consumption function, holding all of the exogenous variables that affect consumption constant, *mpc* can't be negative or greater than 1. A negative *mpc*, or an inverse relationship between consumption and the level of income, makes no sense at all if you think about it. If *mpc* = 0, this means that all consumption is autonomous and doesn't depend on income at all—this also is quite strange.

Only a society of spendthrifts would have $mpc = 1$—all changes in income matched by equal changes in consumption and no change in saving.

- For all practical possibilities, the value of the mpc lies between 0 and 1.

The mpc determines the shape of the consumption function. Both of the consumption functions in Figure 7 obey all of the rules we normally expect consumption functions to obey, but they indicate quite different relationships between consumption and the level of income. Along C_1, a *linear* consumption function, the slope or mpc is constant and consumption is equally responsive to changes in income at all levels of income. Along C_2, on the other hand, the slope or mpc diminishes as income increases. Not only is consumption lower at any level of income along C_2 than along C_1, but aggregate consumption becomes less and less responsive to changes in income as the income rises.

Many economic and noneconomic variables affect the marginal propensity to consume. Keynes' explanation of the marginal propensity to consume relied on several propositions that he presented *a priori* (as valid without proof).

> The fundamental psychological law, upon which we are entitled to depend with great confidence both *a priori* from our knowledge of human nature and from the detailed facts of experience, is that men are disposed as a rule, and on the average to increase their consumption as their income increases, but not by as much as the increase in their income.[2]

A great deal of research has been done on the consumption function since Keynes wrote, and we can identify several somewhat more precise determinants of the marginal propensity to consume. The marginal propensity to consume is affected by economic expectations. If people have optimistic expectations about future economic conditions, they will tend to consume a larger portion of additional income than they would if their economic expectations were pessimistic. The distribution of income among groups with high marginal propensities to consume and those with low marginal propensities to consume affects the aggregate mpc. The observed or estimated marginal propensity to consume tends to be higher for long periods of time than it is for short periods of time.

Autonomous Consumption

Autonomous consumption is determined by variables other than disposable income or GNP. For a given consumption function, these other variables are assumed constant; and changes in these other vari-

---

2. John Maynard Keynes, *The General Theory of Employment, Interest, and Money*. New York: Harcourt, 1936, p. 96.

Figure 7 Consumption Functions: Constant vs. Diminishing *mpc*

ables will change the level of autonomous consumption and cause the level of consumption expenditure to change at any level of income.

Autonomous consumption is only a small part of total consumption in the U.S. In fact, when the relationship between consumption and disposable income is estimated over a long period of years, there appears to be virtually no autonomous consumption. There may, however, be year-to-year changes in autonomous consumption, and because of the size of the consumption flow even small percentage variations in consumption involve large absolute changes in aggregate spending.

Economic expectations of consumers are important determinants of autonomous consumption and short-term shifts of the consumption function. Economic pessimism and uncertainty tend to discourage current consumption and encourage saving to meet possible future needs due to unemployment or reduced income. Economic optimism has just the opposite effect: if households are confident of future employment and income, they tend to save less and consume more at every level of income.

Expectations of future prices also affect consumption behavior, particularly expenditures for consumer durables. Expectations of rapid price increases encourage current consumption and discourage current saving. Expectations of falling prices tend to encourage current saving and to discourage current consumption in the hope of being able to make purchases at lower prices in the future.

The *availability and terms of consumer credit* affect the level of consumption. For many people, readily available credit encourages greater consumption expenditures because it allows more consumption at every level of income. Many "large ticket" consumer durables (such as automobiles) are purchased on credit, and expenditures for these items may be sensitive to the interest rates or cost of borrowing.

Expected living standards affect the level of autonomous consumption. If current disposable income falls below the level necessary to maintain a *normal* or *expected* standard of living, consumers may make up the difference between desired consumption expenditures and current income by *dissaving*—i.e., consuming out of accumulated savings and/or borrowing.

Consumption is affected by the *distribution of income* among households or groups of households with different consumption patterns. Suppose for example, that $800 billion of a total aggregate disposable income of $1000 billion is received by the upper half of households ranked by income, and that these households consume 50% of their aggregate disposable income. The remaining $200 billion is received by the lowest half of the households ranked by income, and they consume 90% of their aggregate disposable income. With this distribution of disposable income, total consumption would be

$$\text{consumption by upper half} = \$800 \text{ billion} \times .50 = \$400 \text{ billion}$$
$$+$$
$$\underline{\text{consumption by lower half} = \$200 \text{ billion} \times .90 = \$180 \text{ billion}}$$
$$\text{total consumption} \qquad\qquad\qquad\qquad\qquad\qquad \$580 \text{ billion}$$

Now, suppose that the same aggregate disposable income of $1000 billion is redistributed so that all households get an equal share, and that with their new levels of disposable income all households consume 70 percent of their aggregate disposable income. As a result of the change in income distribution, total consumption changes to

$$\text{total consumption} = \$1000 \text{ billion} \times .70 = \$700 \text{ billion}$$

This list of determinants of autonomous consumption is illustrative, and not exhaustive. Other variables that determine autonomous consumption include population, changes in the price level, sudden or *windfall* gains or losses of income, etc. Detailed statistical estimates of consumption functions typically contain dozens of variables in addition to the current level of disposable income or GNP. Some of the determinants of consumption other than current income are more rooted in the psychology and perception of consumers than in strictly economic motives—in fact, Keynes devoted an entire chapter of *The General Theory* to psychological or subjective determinants of consumption.

Estimates of the Consumption Function, 1929–1978

It is possible to estimate the consumption function over the last half century using statistical techniques and historical data.[3] Each of the points in Figure 8 represents disposable income (Y_d) and consumption (C) for one of the years between 1929 and 1978 in 1972 dollars.

---

3. Statistical estimation is explained briefly in the appendix to Chapter 1.

Figure 8 Consumption Function, 1929–1978

Source: *Economic Report of the President.*

The estimated consumption function, C_{29-78}, is the line that *fits* these points best. The equation for the estimated consumption function for this period is

$$C_{29-78} = -3.1 + 0.93\, Y_d.$$

For the entire period 1929–78, the estimated consumption function in 1972 dollars shows virtually no autonomous consumption ($a = -3.1$ can be interpreted as $a = 0$) and a very high mpc ($b = .93$). However, estimated consumption functions for shorter periods of time show a somewhat different picture.

The estimated consumption function for 1930–39 in 1972 dollars is

$$C_{30-39} = 36.1 + 0.78\, Y_d.$$

The 1940s can be excluded here because of the dramatic effects of World War II on income and the restrictions on consumption during the war. For 1950–59, the estimated consumption function is

$$C_{50-59} = 12.4 + 0.89\, Y_d.$$

For the 1960s,

$$C_{60-69} = 28.2 + 0.87\, Y_d.$$

Finally, for the period 1970–75,

$$C_{70-75} = 12.6 + 0.89\, Y_d.$$

These short-run consumption functions suggest that the determinants of consumption other than disposable income are more important in the short run than in the long run. The most dramatic period, of course, is the decade between 1930 and 1939. This was a period of rapidly changing economic conditions, and most of the changes were for the worse. In constant (1972) dollars, per capita disposable income fell by about 28 percent between 1929 and 1933. In nominal terms, the decline was even greater (46 percent). For many people, the most important determinant of consumption spending during this period was the level of consumption to maintain an acceptable standard of living, hence the high level of autonomous consumption (36.1 billion 1972 dollars).

Consumption and Saving

A **saving function** shows the relationship between disposable income and intended saving. It can be derived easily from the consumption function. Since all income in a private economy must be saved or consumed,

$$S = Y - C. \tag{7}$$

Substituting the consumption function $C = a + bY$ for C,

$$\begin{aligned} S &= Y - (a + bY) = Y - a - bY \\ &= -a + (1 - b)Y. \end{aligned} \tag{8}$$

For example, if $C = 100 + 0.6\, Y$,

$$S = -100 + (1 - 0.6)Y = -100 + 0.4\, Y.$$

These consumption and saving functions are shown in Figure 9. Any shift in the consumption function will cause the saving function to shift in the opposite direction.

The slope of the saving function is the **marginal propensity to save** (mps). It shows the response of intended saving to changes in income. Like the mpc, the mps will lie between 0 and 1. Also, since every \$1 in additional income must be consumed or saved, the portion that isn't consumed will be saved,[4] or

$$mpc + mps = 1;\ \text{and}\ mps = 1 - mpc. \tag{9}$$

---

4. A simple proof for the wary skeptics:

$$C + S = Y$$

$$\frac{\Delta(C + S)}{\Delta Y} = \frac{\Delta Y}{\Delta Y};\ \frac{\Delta C}{\Delta Y} + \frac{\Delta S}{\Delta Y} = \frac{\Delta Y}{\Delta Y};\ \text{or}\ mpc + mps = 1.$$

Figure 9 Consumption and Saving Functions

Intended saving may be positive, negative, or zero, depending on the consumption function and the level of income. At any point on the 45° line in Figure 9, $C = Y$. At $Y = \$250$ billion, where the consumption function intersects the 45° line, $C = Y$, and $S = 0$. At all levels of Y greater than \$250 billion, Y is greater than C, and the difference is positive saving. If Y is less than \$250 billion, saving is negative, and this **dissaving** represents consumption out of accumulated savings or borrowing.

Investment

The second major component of aggregate demand is *investment*. Some investment—called *induced investment*—is determined by the level of GNP; we'll look closely at induced investment in a later chapter. For now, we'll simply assume that all investment is *autonomous*—determined by variables other than GNP. In order to predict the level of autonomous investment, we will have to discover what those variables are and how they affect investment.

As defined in the national income accounts, **investment** includes three broad categories of expenditures—new capital equipment or producer durables purchased by firms, new residential and nonresidential construction, and inventory adjustments. These seemingly different types of expenditures have several things in common.

1. Investment expenditures increase the economy's capital stock—i.e., the stock of productive equipment, buildings, and finished goods.
2. Investments have current costs, and require current expenditures.
3. Investments yield their returns (if any) in the future.

In a complex economy, there are hundreds of thousands of alternative investment projects with different expected future returns, different initial costs, and different productive lifetimes. Investments will be undertaken until the productivity, or return, from the last investment made just equals the cost of undertaking it.

- The **marginal efficiency of investment** (*MEI*) is the productivity of the last investment made, expressed as an annual expected rate of return.

If alternative investment projects are ranked by expected annual rates of return, the most productive investment projects would be undertaken first. As investment increases, the rates of return on successive investment projects made will be lower, or the expected rate of return on additional investment will fall as the level of investment increases. Put another way,

- The marginal efficiency of investment varies inversely with the level of investment, other things held constant.

Potential investors consider the benefits from alternative uses of their funds—either making an investment or depositing the funds in a savings account to earn *interest*. A rational investor will only invest if the return he expects on his investment is greater than the interest rate—his opportunity cost. A firm will only invest in a project if the return from the project is greater than the interest rate on funds borrowed to finance the project. Clearly, then, the interest rate is of major importance in determining the level of investment.

Suppose that an investor is considering an investment project with a current cost (V) of \$10,000, an expected return (R) of ten percent after one year. The interest rate (r) reflects preference for current income over future income. If the interest rate is 5% per year, should the investment be undertaken?

If the investment were made, the investor would realize

$$V(1 + R) = \$10,000 \,(1.10) = \$11,000.$$

Depositing the money in a savings account at the going rate of interest would yield

$$V(1 + r) = \$10,000 \,(1.05) = \$10,500.$$

Since R is greater than r, the investment should be undertaken because the return from the investment is greater than the return by depositing the money in a savings account.

If the interest rate were 15%, the investment project should not be undertaken because R is less than the interest rate. With an interest rate of 15%, depositing the funds in a savings account would realize a return of

$$V(1 + r) = \$10{,}000\,(1.15) = \$11{,}500.$$

The marginal efficiency of investment shows the return from the last (and least profitable) investment in the economy. Thus, the relationship between *MEI* and the interest rate will determine the level of investment in the economy.

- If *MEI* is greater than r, investment will tend to increase.
- If *MEI* is less than r, investment will tend to fall.
- The equilibrium level of investment will be reached when *MEI* = r.

The relationship between the interest rate and the level of investment is shown graphically in Figure 10. Since the interest rate and *MEI* are expressed as % per year, they can be shown on the same axis. Given the interest rate $r = 10\%$, investment will stabilize at I where *MEI* = r = 10%. At I_1, *MEI* is greater than r, and investment will tend to rise. At I_2, *MEI* is less than r, and investment will tend to fall.

Changes in the interest rate will alter the level of investment. In Figure 10, for example, if the interest rate rose from r to r', the level

Figure 10 The Marginal Efficiency of Investment

of investment would fall to I_1 where $MEI = r'$. If the interest rate fell from r to r'', the level of investment would increase to I_2 where $MEI = r''$.

Other things equal, the level of autonomous investment and aggregate demand will vary inversely with the interest rate. We can plot investment demand graphically against GNP much as we plotted the consumption function. In Figure 11, the horizontal function I_r represents investment demand at interest rate r. The line is horizontal because we are looking only at autonomous investment, which doesn't change with GNP. A decline in the interest rate will cause investment demand to rise to I_r''. A rise in the interest rate will cause investment demand to fall to I_r'.

The Simple Keynesian Model

With a basic grasp of the relationship between aggregate output or real GNP and the components of aggregate demand (consumption and intended investment), the pieces can be put together into an income determination model. First of all, we can write the *aggregate demand equation* to express the relationship between aggregate output or real GNP (Y) and intended spending ($C + I$). At any level of Y, AD is

$$AD = C + I,$$

as was shown at the beginning of the chapter.

Now, we'll simply fill in some more specific information on consumption and investment. The relationship between consumption and GNP is shown by the consumption function, $C = a + bY$. So far, we have assumed that investment is autonomous, and we will express

Figure 11 Interest Rate and the Level of Autonomous Investment

autonomous investment as I_a. Substituting this information for C and I, we now have

$$AD = C + I_a = a + bY + I_a$$
$$= a + I_a + bY. \qquad (10)$$

To estimate AD at any level of Y, we need to know the values of a, I_a, and b in the AD equation. If the known or estimated values of a and b are $a = \$100$ billion and $b = 0.6$, then the consumption function becomes

$$C = a + bY = 100 + 0.6\ Y.$$

To predict the level of consumption expenditure at any level of GNP (Y), simply plug the value of Y into the equation. For example, at $Y = \$600$ billion, consumption expenditure will be

$$C = 100 + 0.6\ (600) = 100 + 360 = \$460 \text{ billion.}$$

If the level of autonomous investment is known or estimated to be $I_a = 100$ billion, this is substituted for I_a in the AD equation. With the given consumption function and the given level of autonomous investment, aggregate demand or intended aggregate spending at any level of GNP is

$$AD = a + I_a + bY = 100 + 100 + 0.6\ Y = 200 + 0.6\ Y.$$

This aggregate demand function (AD) and its components are shown graphically in Figure 12.

Figure 12 Aggregate Demand = Consumption + Investment

To predict aggregate demand at any given level of income (Y = $600 billion, for example), simply find the expenditure coordinate of Y = $600 billion in Figure 12, or plug the given value of Y into the aggregate demand equation and solve for aggregate demand as follows:

$$AD = 200 + 0.6\,Y = 200 + 0.6(600) = \$560 \text{ billion.}$$

Equilibrium in the Simple Keynesian Model

Whenever the economy is *not* at equilibrium, that is, when aggregate demand is greater or smaller than aggregate output (GNP), real GNP will tend to change to move the economy toward equilibrium. At a GNP of Y_1 = $700 billion in Figure 12, we can see from the aggregate demand function that *ex ante* aggregate demand is only $625 billion. This means that $75 billion worth of goods won't be sold. As inventories rise above normal or desired levels, firms will reduce their output to reduce inventories to normal, and real GNP will fall, moving the economy toward equilibrium.

At a GNP of Y_2 = $200 billion in Figure 12, the aggregate demand (AD) exceeds aggregate output by $120 billion. Put another way, buyers will purchase more goods and services than are being produced. This causes inventories of goods to fall—the only way one can sell more than he or she produces is to reduce inventories. As inventories fall below normal or desired levels, output must increase to restore inventories to their normal levels.

At $\overline{Y}$ = $500 billion, the aggregate demand for goods and services produced (AD) is equal to the aggregate output of goods and services or real GNP. At this point, there will be no tendency for inventories, output, or real GNP to change, and therefore $\overline{Y}$ is the equilibrium GNP.

- *Equilibrium real GNP* is reached when the aggregate demand for goods and services is equal to real GNP.

This is not a different equilibrium condition than we saw in the circular flow. Common sense suggests that if GNP is at its equilibrium level, the expenditure inflows into the income stream must equal the expenditure flows out of the income stream.[5]

Calculating Equilibrium GNP in the Simple Model

In reality, economists don't estimate or predict equilibrium GNP by drawing graphs. Instead, they derive empirical estimates of the various expenditure flows that make up aggregate demand, and express

---

5. A more formal verification is easy for those skeptics for whom common sense isn't enough. Since there are no taxes in the closed private economy, all factor payments (GNP) represent disposable income (Y_d), or $Y = Y_d$. All disposable income, and GNP in this case, must be consumed or saved by households—$C + S = Y$. At $\overline{Y}$, then $S = \overline{Y} - C$. At $\overline{Y}$, $\overline{Y} = AD = C + I$. Thus, at $\overline{Y}$, we have

$$S = Y - C = I, \text{ or } S = I.$$

Remember that S and I are *ex ante* saving and investment. If $Y \neq AD$, intended $S \neq$ intended I.

these flows as equations. The equations are then solved to estimate equilibrium GNP. To get an idea of how this works, we can solve our known AD equation to find equilibrium GNP.

We know that at any level of aggregate output or GNP, intended spending (AD) is

$$AD = 200 + 0.6\,Y.$$

We also know that equilibrium GNP (Y) requires that intended spending equal aggregate output, or

$$\overline{Y} = AD.$$

Substituting the AD equation in the equilibrium condition, and substituting Y for $\overline{Y}$ in the AD equation, equilibrium GNP will be reached when

$$\overline{Y} = 200 + 0.6\,Y.$$

Equilibrium GNP is found by solving this equation for Y, and this involves only simple algebra and arithmetic. First, subtract $0.6\,\overline{Y}$ from both sides, giving us

$$Y - 0.6\,Y = 200$$

or

$$0.4\,\overline{Y} = 200.$$

Dividing both sides of this expression by 0.4,

$$\overline{Y} = 200/0.4 = 500.$$

Figure 13 Equilibrium Real GNP in the Simple Keynesian Model

Not surprisingly, this is the same result that is shown graphically in Figure 13 which combines the equilibrium condition $Y = AD$ (the 45° line) and the AD function $AD = 200 + 0.6\,Y$.

Aggregate Demand, Unemployment, and Inflation

We now have the tools to identify possible sources of unemployment and inflationary pressure that are related to the level of aggregate demand. In Figure 14a, equilibrium GNP ($\overline{Y}$) is less than the real GNP that would generate full employment (Y^*). In this case, the economy would experience *demand-deficiency unemployment*.

- **Demand-deficiency unemployment** of resources and capacity results from inadequate aggregate demand to generate equilibrium GNP at full employment.

In Figure 14a, the aggregate demand (AD) and the expenditure inflows and outflows determine equilibrium GNP at Y, which is less than the full employment GNP, Y^*. At the full-employment GNP, Y^*, there is a *demand deficiency* or *deflationary gap*.

- The **deflationary gap** is the amount that aggregate demand would have to increase to achieve equilibrium at full employment GNP.

In Figure 14a, equilibrium GNP will remain at Y unless the aggregate demand curve shifts. To achieve equilibrium at full employment, the aggregate demand curve would have to shift upward to AD' to close the deflationary gap.

If equilibrium GNP is greater than the full-employment GNP, this will generate inflationary pressures. In Figure 14b, the high level of aggregate demand would (if it could) generate an equilibrium GNP, Y, greater than full-employment GNP (Y^*). In this case, there is excess demand or an *inflationary gap* at the full employment GNP.

Figure 14 Unemployment and Inflation in the Simple Keynesian Model

(a) Demand-Deficiency Unemployment (b) Demand-Pull Inflation

- The **inflationary gap** is the amount that aggregate demand would have to be reduced to eliminate demand-related inflationary pressure.

To eliminate the demand-related inflation in Figure 14b, aggregate demand would have to be shifted downward to AD'.

This has been a rather long journey through an unrealistically simple economy, but this trip *was* necessary. We now have the basic tools we need to understand, analyze, and predict equilibrium aggregate output. This offers some insight into the aspects of unemployment and inflation that are related to the level of aggregate demand. The chapters that follow simply add the public sector to this simple model to analyze the impact of government on aggregate demand and equilibrium aggregate output.

It is worthwhile, however, to recall what we're doing in the analysis of income determination so far. First of all, we're looking only at the aggregate demand side, so we don't have all of the tools we need to analyze unemployment and inflation that are caused on the aggregate supply side. Also, we haven't included the impact of the monetary sector. Be patient—we can't do everything at once, and the rest follows.

Summary

1. The theory of income determination and income determination models are concerned with the variables that determine equilibrium national income or GNP, and with predicting equilibrium GNP and changes in equilibrium GNP. The variables in income determination models are *ex ante*, or intended, quantities.
2. In a closed private economy, there is no public sector and no international sector. The only expenditure flows in this simple economy are consumption, investment, and saving.
3. The **consumption function** shows the relationship between GNP or disposable income and the level of consumption. In the short run, some consumption may be autonomous, but in the long run, virtually all consumption is explained by the level of income.
4. The **marginal propensity to consume** (mpc) is the rate at which consumption changes as disposable income or GNP change. It is the slope of the consumption function.
5. Since disposable income equals saving plus consumption, the consumption function also determines the relationship between disposable income and saving, or the **saving function**. The **marginal propensity to save** (mps) is the rate at which intended saving varies with GNP.
6. The **marginal efficiency of investment** is the expected annual percentage rate of return on the last investment made. Since the most productive investments are made first, the MEI falls as the level of investment increases. Investments will be made for which the MEI is greater than the interest rate.

7. **Equilibrium GNP** is reached when the expenditure outflows from the income stream equal the expenditure inflows into it, and when the aggregate demand for goods and services equals the aggregate output of goods and services.
8. According to the Keynesian income determination model, equilibrium GNP may be reached with unemployment or with inflationary pressure.

Concepts for Review

unintended investment
unintended disinvestment
equilibrium real GNP
autonomous expenditure
induced expenditure
consumption function
marginal propensity to consume
autonomous consumption
dissaving

saving function
marginal propensity to save
investment
marginal efficiency of investment
simple Keynesian model
demand-deficiency unemployment
deflationary gap
inflationary gap

Questions

1. Explain the distinction between intended saving and investment, and measured saving and investment. Why is this distinction significant?
2. Economic forecasters and policymakers pay a lot of attention to business inventories as an indicator of future aggregate output and employment. What predictions of future real GNP and employment follow from rising inventories? What predictions follow from falling business inventories? Explain in the context of the income determination model.
3. During an economic recession in 1958, the automobile companies launched a large advertising campaign telling consumers that they "auto buy now." Apart from the obvious effect of increased demand for automobiles on the automobile industry, how would increases in automobile sales affect aggregate demand, equilibrium GNP, and the level of employment?
4. What are autonomous expenditures? Can you think of any examples of autonomous consumption and autonomous investment?
5. In 1933, disposable personal income in the United States was $45.5 billion, while personal consumption expenditures amounted to $45.8 billion. How could you explain this?
6. In constant (1972) dollars, U.S. disposable personal income increased from $859.7 billion to $890.1 billion between 1975 and 1976. In the same period, personal consumption in constant (1972) dollars increased from $774.6 billion to $819.4 billion.
   a. How could consumption expenditures rise by a greater amount than disposable income?
   b. In the context of the theory of the consumption function what could explain the behavior of consumption between 1975 and 1976?
7. It has been argued that expectations of future economic recessions (falling real GNP) or future inflationary pressure are *self-fulfilling prophecies*—i.e., things that happen by virtue of the fact that we expected them to happen. Evaluate and explain this argument in the context of the income determination model.

AGGREGATE DEMAND AND INCOME DETERMINATION: THE PRIVATE SECTOR

Problems

1. You are given the following information on consumption (C) and disposable income (Y_d) for the small peanut republic of Cartermania.

Y_d	C	mpc	S	mps
0	50			
100	140			
200	230			
300	320			
400	410			
500	500			
600	590			
700	680			
800	770			
900	860			
1,000	950			

   a. Fill in the figures for intended saving (S). How did you get the figures?
   b. Explain the marginal propensity to consume (mpc). Calculate mpc for all levels of disposable income in the table.
   c. Explain the marginal propensity to save (mps). Calculate mps for all levels of income in the table.
   d. Write the equations for the consumption and saving functions. On graph paper, draw the consumption and saving functions from the data in the table.
   e. Suppose that all intended investment is autonomous, and that I_a = 50. Write the equation for the aggregate demand function, and draw the aggregate demand function in the graph you drew for part d.
   f. Find equilibrium GNP algebraically and graphically from the above information.

2. The Adam & Eve Loose-Leaf Binder Co. is considering the purchase of a machine that would produce an expected $100,000 worth of binders over its productive lifetime of 2 years.

   a. The machine has a purchase price of $85,000. Should Adam & Eve purchase the machine if the interest rate is 10% per year? Should they purchase the machine if the interest rate fell to 5% per year?
   b. What variables other than the interest rate could affect Adam & Eve's decision to purchase the machine?

22

Aggregate Demand and Income Determination: Completing the Model

PREVIEW: The simple model introduced in the last chapter has taken us a long way in understanding the basic effects of aggregate demand in the goods markets on real GNP. In this chapter, we will complete the model by adding in the government and international sectors to it. We'll then look closely at how changes in the variables that comprise aggregate demand cause changes in the level of real GNP.

The Public Sector

The public sector includes all levels of government—local, state, and federal. All levels of government affect aggregate demand and income by spending and taxing, but macroeconomic policy is the nearly exclusive domain of the federal government. Adding the public sector adds three basic types of expenditures to the circular flow—government spending for goods and services, government transfer payments (pensions, income maintenance payments, etc.), and taxes. In the Keynesian model, these are reduced to two—*government spending* and *net taxes*.

Government Spending

When the government purchases a piece of equipment or hires an employee, this has the same effect on the spending flow as if a private employer had purchased the same equipment or hired the same employee. However, not all outlays by the government are included in the government spending flow in the expanded model. **Transfer payments** don't represent government purchases of productive services or of goods and aren't included as government spending in the model.

- **Government spending** includes all purchases of goods and services by local, state, and federal governments from the private sector.

Government spending is an inflow into the income stream. When the government increases its purchases from the private sector this increases the size of the aggregate spending flow.

- Other things equal, aggregate demand and equilibrium income will change in the same direction as changes in government spending.

Net Taxes

Income taxes, property taxes, sales taxes, excise taxes, and other taxes all represent expenditure outflows from the income stream to the government. Taxes reduce disposable income and thus reduce the level of consumption. Taxes on firms' profits reduce the funds that firms can distribute as dividends or reinvest in production.

The transfer payments that were excluded from the definition of GNP and from the definition of government spending in the Keynesian model do affect aggregate demand. Transfer payments are income to the households that receive them, so transfer payments tend to increase total disposable income. In the analysis of income determination that follows, the tax flow will be the **net tax flow,** which shows the net effect of taxes and transfer payments on the income stream. Specifically,

$$\text{Net taxes } (T) = \text{total taxes} - \text{transfer payments}.$$

Since transfer payments are smaller than total tax payments, the net tax flow in the model is an expenditure outflow.

- Other things equal, aggregate demand and equilibrium income will change in the opposite direction of changes in net taxes.

The International Sector

When a domestic buyer purchases an imported good, the expenditure to pay for the import represents an outflow from the domestic economy's income stream. On the other hand, when a domestic seller exports goods to foreign buyers, the expenditures to pay for the exports represent an expenditure inflow into the domestic economy's income stream. The *net effect* of the international sector is the difference between exports and imports, or **net exports.**

$$\text{net exports} = \text{export expenditures } (X) - \text{import expenditures } (M).$$

The net export flow may be positive (inflow) or negative (outflow), depending on the size of the export and import expenditures.

Equilibrium in the Complete Model

The circular flow of income in an economy with a public sector and an international sector is shown in Figure 1. The basic condition for equilibrium income in the complete model is the same as it was for the closed, private economy.

Figure 1 The Complete Circular Flow

- **Equilibrium GNP** will be reached when *total expenditure inflows* into the income stream equal *total expenditure outflows* out of the income stream, and when the *aggregate demand* for goods and services is equal to the *aggregate output* of goods and services.

The only difference between this and equilibrium in the closed private economy is the additional inflows and outflows and the additional components of aggregate demand as a result of adding the public and international sectors.

The expenditure inflows and outflows in the complete model are summarized below.

	Inflow	Outflow
Private Sector	Investment (I)	Saving (S)
Public Sector	Government Spending (G)	Net Taxes (T)
International Sector	Net Exports ($X - M$)	
Entire System	$I + G + (X - M)$	$S + T$

The condition for equilibrium income in this model, then, is
$$I + G + (X - M) = S + T. \tag{1}$$
This can also be expressed as
$$\overline{Y} = C + I + G + (X - M). \tag{2}$$

Aggregate Demand in the Complete Model

At any level of GNP (Y), aggregate demand will be the sum of expenditures from the private sector (consumption and investment), the public sector (government spending), and the international sector (net exports).
$$AD = C + I + G + (X - M). \tag{3}$$
To keep the following analysis simple, two assumptions will be made in analyzing aggregate demand.

- All expenditure flows except consumption and saving will be considered *autonomous* expenditures.
- Until the international sector is analyzed in detail later in the text, we will assume that $(X - M) = 0$, and thus disregard the international sector.

Given these assumptions, the equation for aggregate demand can be rewritten as
$$AD = C + I + G. \tag{4}$$
Since we already know the relationship between the components of aggregate demand and the level of real GNP, it is possible to determine the level of aggregate demand at *any* level of real GNP.

The first step is to substitute the consumption function for C in the aggregate demand equation, giving us
$$AD = a + bY_d + I + G.$$
In the model, we'll use a simplified definition of disposable income—GNP (Y) less net taxes (T), or
$$Y_d = Y - T. \tag{5}$$
Assuming investment, government spending, and net taxes to be autonomous, the aggregate demand equation becomes
$$AD = a + b(Y - T_a) + I_a + G_a = a + bY - bT_a + I_a + G_a.$$
Grouping all of the autonomous expenditures together,
$$AD = (a + I_a + G_a - bT_a) + bY. \tag{6}$$

In Figure 2, the consumption function (C) shows the level of consumption expenditure at any level of GNP (Y). Since intended investment and government spending are assumed autonomous ($I = I_a$ and $G = G_a$), we simply add the sum of these expenditures to consumption at every

Figure 2 Aggregate Demand in the Complete Model

level of GNP to get the aggregate demand function (AD) in Figure 2.

Not surprisingly, if all of the components of AD are autonomous except consumption, the slope of the AD curve is the *mpc* (b in the consumption function and AD equation).

The aggregate demand function tells us what information to look for to predict aggregate spending. If the expenditure flows in aggregate demand are known or estimated, we can predict the level of aggregate expenditure at all levels of GNP. Suppose, for example, that the following information is known—or at least that it's the best estimate we have.

$$\text{Consumption: } C = 100 + 0.6\,Y_d$$
$$\text{Intended Investment: } I = I_a = 110$$
$$\text{Govt. Spending: } G = G_a = 100$$
$$\text{Net Taxes: } T = T_a = 50.$$

All of the numbers represent billions of dollars per year. From this information, the economy's aggregate demand function is

$$\begin{aligned}AD &= a + bY - bT_a + I_a + G_a \\ &= 100 + 0.6\,Y - 0.6(50) + 110 + 100 \\ &= 280 + 0.6\,Y.\end{aligned}$$

This aggregate demand function is shown graphically in Figure 3.

To predict aggregate demand at any given level of GNP, substitute the value of GNP for Y in the aggregate demand equation and solve for AD. For example, at a GNP of $Y_1 = \$400$ billion per year,

$$AD_1 = 280 + 0.6\,Y_1 = 280 + 0.6(400) = \$520 \text{ billion per year.}$$

This same solution can be arrived at graphically. Simply find the aggregate demand coordinate of $Y_1 = 400$ in Figure 3. Notice that we get the same answer by this method: $AD_1 = \$520$ billion per year.

If GNP increased from $Y_1 = \$400$ billion to $Y_2 = \$600$ billion per year, aggregate spending would increase to

$$AD_2 = 280 + 0.6Y_2 = 280 + 0.6(600) = \$640 \text{ billion per year.}$$

The change in aggregate demand per dollar change in GNP is the slope of the aggregate demand function. When GNP increased from $Y_1 = 500$ to $Y_2 = 600$, aggregate demand increased from $AD = 520$ to $AD' = 640$, and the slope of AD is

$$\frac{\Delta AD}{\Delta Y} = \frac{AD_2 - AD_1}{Y_2 - Y_1} = \frac{640 - 520}{600 - 400} = \frac{120}{200} = 0.6.$$

Aggregate Demand and Equilibrium GNP

The condition for equilibrium in the economy with a public sector is the same as the condition for equilibrium in the closed, private economy.

$$\overline{Y} = AD.$$

The addition of autonomous government spending (G_a) and autonomous net taxes (T_a) to the aggregate demand function simply adds two more terms to the equilibrium condition.

Figure 3 Aggregate Demand and Equilibrium GNP

$$\overline{Y} = (a + I_a + G_a - bT_a) + b\overline{Y}.$$

To find equilibrium GNP, we simply have to solve the above equation for $\overline{Y}$, as we did in the last chapter. Subtracting $\overline{Y}$ from both sides,

$$\overline{Y} - b\overline{Y} = (a + I_a + G_a - bT_a)$$
$$(1 - b)\overline{Y} = (a + I_a + G_a - bT_a).$$

Finally, equilibrium GNP ($\overline{Y}$) becomes

$$\overline{Y} = \frac{1}{(1 - b)}(a + I_a + G_a - bT_a). \tag{7}$$

This equation has a lot of terms to remember, but this will be easier if you simply note that the parentheses contain all autonomous expenditures. So equilibrium in this model is found simply by dividing the sum of the autonomous expenditures by $(1 - b)$ or the *mps*.

To predict a specific equilibrium GNP from a known or estimated aggregate demand function—$AD = 280 + 0.6Y$, for example—simply plug the known or estimated values for autonomous spending and the *mpc* into the expression for $\overline{Y}$ that was derived above, and solve for $\overline{Y}$.

$$\overline{Y} = \frac{1}{(1 - 0.6)}(280) = \frac{280}{0.4} = 700.$$

This equilibrium is shown graphically in Figure 3, where the aggregate demand function ($AD = 280 + 0.6Y$) intersects the equilibrium (45°) line labeled $Y = AD$.

Changes in Equilibrium Income

National income or GNP will remain in equilibrium unless something happens that alters the expenditure flows and aggregate demand.

- Equilibrium GNP will change in the same direction as shifts of the aggregate demand function.

If aggregate spending increases at every level of GNP, the aggregate demand function shifts upward, increasing equilibrium GNP, as shown by the shift of AD to AD' and GNP from $\overline{Y}$ to $\overline{Y}'$ in Figure 4. If the level of aggregate spending falls at every level of GNP, the aggregate demand function shifts downward and reduces equilibrium GNP, as shown by the shift of aggregate demand from AD to AD'' and equilibrium GNP from $\overline{Y}$ to $\overline{Y}''$ in Figure 4.

The list of exogenous changes that disturb aggregate demand and equilibrium GNP is nearly endless. The outbreak of a war generates large increases in government spending that raise aggregate demand and equilibrium income, and sudden reductions of government spending at the end of a war can lower aggregate demand and equilibrium income. Increases in taxes reduce disposable income, consumption,

Figure 4 Changes in Aggregate Demand and Equilibrium GNP

and aggregate demand at any level of GNP and tend to reduce equilibrium GNP. Optimism or pessimism about future economic conditions affect the behavior of consumption, saving, and investment and shift aggregate demand.

We can make two broad generalizations about the effects of changes in expenditure flows on equilibrium GNP.

- Aggregate demand and equilibrium GNP will change in the same direction as the expenditure flows with positive signs in the aggregate demand equation—i.e., consumption, investment, government spending, and net exports—and in the opposite direction of changes in expenditure flows with negative signs (saving and net taxes).

Applying the Tools

Aggregate Demand and World War II

Although there had been several halting recoveries and improvements in economic conditions in the 1930s, the recovery from the Great Depression was in fact brought about by the dramatic increases in government spending during World War II. In constant (1972) dollars, federal purchases of goods and services from the private sector increased about 8.4 times between 1940 and 1945, from 26.3 billion

Figure A

1972 dollars to 264.3 billion 1972 dollars. The effect of this increase in aggregate demand from the public sector is shown in Figure A.

Increased government spending to prosecute a war is an increase in autonomous government spending—the war wasn't related to our GNP. Increasing government spending from G to G' per year increases the expenditure inflow from $I + G$ per year to $I + G'$ per year, and the aggregate demand from $AD = C + I + G$ at every level of income to $AD' = C + I + G'$. This dramatic increase in aggregate demand increases equilibrium income from $\overline{Y}$ to $\overline{Y}'$. In fact, the general prediction that the increased aggregate demand would raise equilibrium GNP was borne out by the behavior of U.S. GNP during this period. In constant prices, U.S. GNP increased from $344 billion 1972 dollars in 1940 to $559 billion 1972 dollars in 1945.

Toward the end of the War, there was considerable disagreement among economists over how the economy would respond to peace. Many economists felt that the end of the War would bring back Depression levels of unemployment. They argued that the dramatic increases in government spending during the War had reduced unemployment, but if government spending fell dramatically after the War, aggregate demand, GNP, and unemployment would return to prewar levels.

Other economists predicted that the most serious problem after the end of the War would be inflation, and not depression. Although government spending would fall after the War, they predicted that a dramatic upward shift of the consumption function would offset the effect of reduced government spending on aggregate demand. Because of the unusually high rates of unemployment during the Depression, many households had to postpone purchases of automobiles and appliances. During the War, these goods were in very short supply because of the allocation of resources to producing military goods, and this forced households to save during the War. As the forced savings from the War years were unloaded to buy the goods that many couldn't find during the War, the consumption function would shift upward.

Both predictions were theoretically correct, but the facts clearly support the inflationary prediction. The unemployment rate did rise after the war (to 3.9 percent in 1948), but didn't even come close to the unemployment rates of the 1930s. Consumption expenditures increased in constant dollars between 1945 and 1948, despite the fact that disposable income declined during this period in constant prices. Finally, the inflationary prediction was confirmed by an increase in the Consumer Price Index by about 38% between 1945 and 1948.

Changes in Savings and the *Paradox of Thrift*

The **paradox of thrift** refers to a conflict between individual motives for saving and the macroeconomic consequences of changes in saving. If an individual has pessimistic or uncertain economic expectations, this tends to encourage him or her to save more and consume less at any given level of disposable income. It should be noted here that "saving more" could take the form of "dissaving less" by reducing consumer borrowing. What the individual is trying to do by saving more is to "hedge" against future unemployment or reduction of income.

If the uncertainty or pessimism that encourages individuals to save more at every level of income is widespread, aggregate saving (S) will increase at every level of income, as shown in 5a. If more is saved at every level of income, consumption and aggregate demand will fall at every level of income, so the increase in aggregate saving to S' and the increase in expenditure outflows to $S' + T$ causes consumption to fall to C' and aggregate demand to fall to $AD' = C' + I + G$. The paradox, of course, is that at this new level of aggregate demand there will actually be *less* saving than there was before the upward shift in

Figure 5 The Paradox of Thrift

the saving function. Also, the likelihood of unemployment and loss of income that prompted the increased saving by individuals is greater as a result of the lower level of aggregate output and real GNP.

In periods of inflation, the paradox of thrift tends to contribute to the inflationary pressure. Inflationary expectations tend to discourage current saving and encourage greater consumption. The future purchasing power of current saving is eroded by rising prices, and consumers may even find it worthwhile to borrow in order to purchase some consumer durables (such as autos) to avoid future price increases. If the economy is already in an inflationary equilibrium, as in Figure 5b, the inflationary pressures are made worse as a result of the reduction of saving and increase in consumption and aggregate demand.

The Multiplier Effect

If GNP reaches equilibrium $100 billion short of the full-employment GNP, will aggregate demand have to be increased by $100 billion to get GNP to the full employment level? If the government spends an additional $100 million per year, how much will this increase equilibrium GNP? If households decide to reduce consumption by $10 billion at every level of aggregate income, what effect will this have on equilibrium GNP? All of these questions involve an important but rather tricky concept called the *multiplier*, or to be more specific, the *autonomous expenditure multiplier*.

- The **autonomous expenditure multiplier** shows the change in equilibrium GNP as a result of a given change in autonomous spending.

Changes in autonomous spending shift the aggregate demand function, and this will cause equilibrium GNP to change by some multiple of the change in autonomous spending. The *multiplier* (k) is the ratio

$$k = \frac{\text{change in equilibrium GNP}}{\text{change in autonomous spending}} = \frac{\Delta \overline{Y}}{\Delta AD}. \qquad (8)$$

How It Works

The basic concept and mechanics of the multiplier effect aren't hard to master. Suppose that government spending increases by $20 billion per year, and that the higher level of government spending is maintained over an extended period of time.

Raising government spending by $\Delta G = \$20$ billion per year obviously adds $20 billion to the spending stream and increases aggregate spending by $20 billion per year. However, the increase in spending doesn't stop here. The additional government spending and GNP increases disposable income, and part of the additional disposable income will re-enter the income stream as additional consumption—in addition to the initial increase of government spending.

For example, if the marginal propensity to consume is $mpc = 0.6$, and all expenditures except consumption and saving are autonomous, increasing government spending by $\Delta G = \$20$ billion per year increases disposable income by $\Delta Y_d = \Delta G = \$20$ billion. This increase in disposable income will cause consumption to increase by

$$\Delta C = mpc\,\Delta Y_d = mpc\,\Delta G = 0.6 \times \$20 \text{ billion} = \$12 \text{ billion}.$$

Adding the additional consumption to the additional government spending, the income stream has increased by

$$\begin{array}{ll} \Delta G & \$20 \text{ billion per year} \\ +\,\Delta C = mpc\,\Delta G = & \underline{12 \text{ billion per year}} \\ & \$32 \text{ billion per year} \end{array}$$

The increased consumption in the first "round" of spending represents an increase in disposable income in the second "round." Thus, for the second round there is additional disposable income of $\Delta Y_d = mpc\,\Delta G$, or \$12 billion per year. Part of this additional disposable income will re-enter the spending stream as additional consumption. The additional consumption in the second "round" of spending is

$$\Delta C = mpc\,\Delta Y_d = mpc\,(mpc\,\Delta G) = mpc^2\,\Delta G =$$
$$0.6 \times 0.6 \times \$20 \text{ billion} = \$7.2 \text{ billion per year.}$$

The increase in aggregate spending after two "rounds" of spending is thus

$$\begin{array}{ll} \Delta G & \$20 \text{ billion per year} \\ +\,mpc\,\Delta G & 12 \text{ billion per year} \\ +\,mpc\,(mpc\,\Delta G) = mpc^2\,\Delta G & \underline{7.2 \text{ billion per year}} \\ & \$39.2 \text{ billion per year} \end{array}$$

The increase in spending through four "rounds" is shown in Figure 6.

At each "round" of spending, some of the additional disposable income re-enters the income stream as additional consumption, and some leaks out of the income stream as saving. The income stream will continue to increase until all of the additional spending has leaked out. From an initial change in government spending of ΔG per year for a period of years, the increase in equilibrium GNP will be

$$\Delta \overline{Y} = \Delta G + mpc\,\Delta G + mpc^2\,\Delta G + mpc^3\,\Delta G + \ldots$$
$$= \Delta G\,(1 + mpc + mpc^2 + mpc^3 + \ldots).$$

If the rounds of spending approach infinity, and additions to disposable income and consumption approach zero, the sum in the parentheses becomes an *infinite series*, which can be written as $1/(1 - mpc)$. Thus, as the number of rounds approaches infinity, the increase in GNP as a result of an increase in government spending (or other autonomous expenditure) over an extended period approaches

Figure 6 The Multiplier Effect

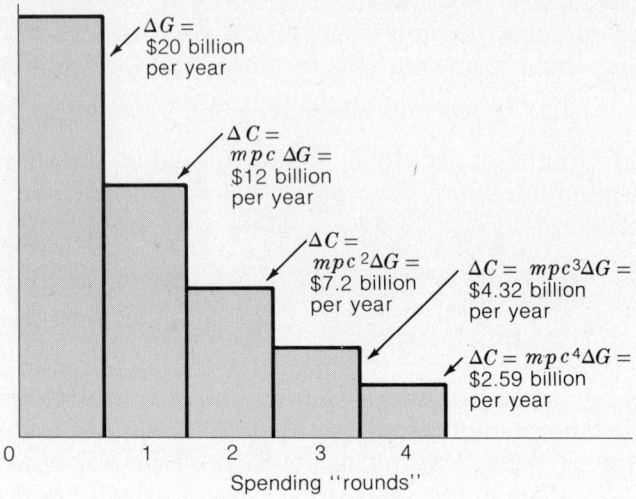

$$\Delta \overline{Y} = \frac{1}{(1 - mpc)} \times \Delta G.$$

The multiplier, then, is

$$k = \frac{\Delta \overline{Y}}{\Delta G} = \frac{1}{(1 - mpc)}. \tag{9}$$

In our example, if $mpc = 0.6$ and all expenditures are autonomous except consumption and saving, the maximum increase in equilibrium GNP as a result of additional government spending of $\Delta G = \$20$ billion per year over an extended period is

$$\Delta \overline{Y} = k \Delta G = \frac{1}{(1 - 0.6)} \times 20 = \frac{1}{0.4} \times 20 = \$50 \text{ billion/year}.$$

The Multiplier in the Keynesian Model

The multiplier is easily shown in the context of the aggregate demand function and equilibrium GNP. With all components of aggregate demand autonomous except consumption, the aggregate demand function is

$$AD = (a + I_a + G_a - bT_a) + bY,$$

and equilibrium GNP is reached when

$$\overline{Y} = \frac{1}{(1 - b)} (a + I_a + G_a - bT_a).$$

Changing any of the autonomous expenditure flows in the parentheses will cause equilibrium to change by

$$\Delta \overline{Y} = \frac{1}{(1-b)} \text{ (change in autonomous spending)}.$$

The multiplier in the model is

$$k = \frac{1}{(1-b)}.$$

In Figure 7, with an aggregate demand function of

$$AD = 280 + 0.6Y,$$

equilibrium GNP was

$$\overline{Y} = \frac{1}{(1-0.6)} \times 280 = \frac{1}{0.4} \times 280 = \$700 \text{ billion per year}.$$

Increasing government spending by $\Delta G = \$20$ billion per year shifts the aggregate demand function to

$$AD' = 300 + 0.6Y$$

in Figure 7. The new equilibrium income is

$$\overline{Y}' = \frac{1}{(1-0.6)} \times 300 = \frac{1}{0.4} \times 300 = \$750 \text{ billion per year}.$$

The change in GNP (ΔY) is the change in autonomous spending ($\Delta G = \$20$ billion per year), multiplied by the multiplier $1/(1-b)$.

$$\Delta \overline{Y} = \frac{1}{(1-0.6)}(300-280) = \frac{1}{0.4}(20) = \$50 \text{ billion per year}.$$

The multiplier works in both directions. If autonomous spending falls, the multiplier determines the decline in equilibrium GNP.

The Size of the Multiplier

The value of the multiplier and the strength of the multiplier effect are determined by the proportion of additional income that is consumed and the proportion of additional income saved at each "round" of spending. The higher the *mpc*, the greater the value of the multiplier coefficient. Since we normally expect the *mpc* to lie between 0 and 1, the multiplier will be finite and greater than 1 for all practical possibilities.

For example, with $mpc = 0.6$ in the previous examples, the multiplier was

$$k = \frac{1}{(1-mpc)} = \frac{1}{(1-0.6)} = \frac{1}{0.4} = 2.5.$$

Figure 7 The Multiplier in the Keynesian Model

If the *mpc* were 0.8 instead of 0.6, the multiplier would be

$$k' = \frac{1}{(1 - 0.8)} = \frac{1}{0.2} = 5.$$

Obviously, the accuracy of our estimate of the aggregate demand function and the value of the *mpc* are crucial for the accuracy of predicted changes in income.

The Keynesian Model: Some Precautions

Predicting equilibrium GNP and the effects of changes in autonomous spending on equilibrium GNP in the real world isn't as simple, mechanical, or precise as in the model. Very few expenditure flows are in fact completely autonomous. We don't have completely accurate information, and in any given year short-term changes in expenditures make longer-term statistical estimates less reliable. The multiplier effect takes considerable time to work itself out completely—most empirical estimates of the multiplier effect estimate it for a period of 2 to 3 years—and while the multiplier effects are operating on one disturbance in the expenditure flows, other disturbances may come along. Again, keep in mind that we're still looking only at the aggregate demand side of income determination, and that our analysis still doesn't include the impact of the monetary sector. This makes the model a highly imperfect tool for predicting exact levels of GNP or exact changes in GNP. However, it doesn't mean that the model is practically useless. It shows important economic relationships and gives us an analytical approach to macroeconomic problems.

Summary

1. The complete Keynesian model includes expenditure flows from the private, public, and international sectors. Adding the public sector to the closed private model adds expenditure inflow (government spending) and an expenditure outflow (taxes). The impact of the international sector on aggregate demand is through net exports (exports − imports), which may be positive, zero, or negative.
2. Expanding the model doesn't change the conditions for equilibrium GNP—where inflows = outflows, and where $AD = Y$—but simply adds more components to inflows, outflows, and AD.
3. Aggregate demand and equilibrium GNP change in the same direction as changes in consumption, investment, and government spending; and in the opposite direction of changes in saving and taxes.
4. The multiplier effect shows the change in equilibrium GNP as a result of a given change in autonomous spending. The size of the multiplier effect depends on the proportion of the increased spending that re-enters the expenditure flow and the proportion that leaks out.

Concepts for Review

government spending
transfer payments
net taxes
net exports
paradox of thrift
autonomous expenditure multiplier

Questions

1. Explain how each of the following would affect aggregate demand and equilibrium income.
   a. Adding a 10 percent surcharge to all federal income tax liabilities.
   b. Increasing and extending public assistance programs to low-income families.
   c. Purchasing a new weapons system.
   d. Reducing federal employment.
2. What are autonomous government purchases and autonomous taxes? List some examples of each and explain.
3. What is the distinction between taxes and net taxes in the income determination model? Why is the distinction important in defining the tax flow in the model?
4. Some critics of the Keynesian income determination theory argue that World War II, and not policies based on Keynesian notions of aggregate demand, explain the end of the Great Depression. Is this a valid criticism? Explain.
5. What is the *paradox of thrift*, and why is is a paradox?

Problems

1. Adding a public sector to the closed private economy in Problem 1 from the previous chapter adds the following autonomous expenditures:

   Government purchases: $ 90 billion per year
   Taxes: $110 billion per year
   Government transfer payments: $ 30 billion per year

   a. Calculate the size of the net tax flow.
   b. Combining this information and the information on consumption and saving from Problem 1 from the last chapter, write the equation for the economy's aggregate demand, expenditure inflow, and expenditure outflow functions. Show these relationships graphically.
   c. Find the level of aggregate demand at a real GNP of $1000 billion per year. Could this be equilibrium GNP? Explain.
   d. Find equilibrium GNP. If the economy requires a real GNP of $1100 billion per year for full employment, would you predict that the economy will experience unemployment, demand-pull inflation, or neither? Explain.

2. As a result of the end of the Great War between Cartermania and Reagania, government purchases of goods and services are reduced by $20 billion per year.
   a. Find the maximum change in equilibrium GNP as a result of this change in government spending, using information from the previous question.
   b. What factors would determine the actual change in equilibrium GNP as a result of this change in government purchases?

23

Fluctuations of Aggregate Demand and GNP

Preview: Aggregate demand and output change constantly over time. Because such changes have such a major impact upon society's welfare, economists and others have been trying for many years to understand and predict fluctuations in economic activity. In this chapter, we'll look closely at how the components of aggregate demand in the goods market—consumption, investment, government spending, and taxes—contribute to the volatility of demand and output over time.

Although GNP may continually be seeking equilibrium, equilibrium GNP is probably the exception rather than the rule. Figure 1 shows the path of real GNP, consumption, investment, and government purchases in 1972 dollars for the period 1929 through 1978. For the two decades between 1958 and 1978, real GNP follows a relatively smooth path, but for the other years, the path of real GNP —like that of true love—is rough.

Fluctuations of economic activity over time have important implications for economic welfare. Drastic swings from prosperity to depression mean wide swings in living standards, and create an unstable and uncertain environment for economic decision making. Stabilization of real GNP around a long-term trend will tend to stabilize employment and inflationary pressures, and minimizing fluctuations is one of the central goals of macroeconomic policy.

There is considerable disagreement over the nature and cause of fluctuations of output and income, and this disagreement leads to disagreements over the proper policy approach to minimize instability. Controversies over stabilization policies center around several basic questions.

Figure 1 Gross National Product, Consumption, Investment, and Government Purchases 1929–1978

1. What causes fluctuations in economic activity and real GNP over time?
2. Can fluctuations be predicted and timed relatively accurately?
3. Is active intervention by the government to stabilize real GNP over time likely to increase, decrease, or not affect the degree of instability?

Business Cycles

Fluctuations of economic activity have been common for as long as economic data have been recorded. Over the years, economists have advanced a number of alternative explanations of fluctuations. In the classical analysis of the nineteenth century, fluctuations of economic activity were viewed as short-term adjustments to sudden economic shocks. Karl Marx saw cycles as the result of "fits and starts" in investment and the accumulation of capital, and a symptom of the internal contradictions of the capitalist system. Some economists, such as the great nineteenth century British economist William

Stanley Jevons, even explained fluctuations in terms of the cyclical pattern of sunspot activity and its effects on crops.

For many years students of business fluctuations treated them as cyclical fluctuations, or *business cycles*.

- **Business cycles** are self-reversing fluctuations in economic activity.

A very simple sketch of the phases of the business cycle is shown in Figure 2. Once an economic expansion begins, forces are set in motion that cause the expansion to continue. Rising personal income causes the demand and orders for consumer goods to increase. Sellers of consumer goods increase their orders, and producers increase output and employment. The increased output of consumer goods increases the demand for investment goods. Rising profits generate optimism that encourages further investment. Employment and income rise, keeping the expansion going.

Expansion can't go on indefinitely because the capacity to produce is limited, and some sectors of the economy reach full employment of capacity sooner than others. At high levels of output and employment, bottlenecks and shortages of basic industrial goods and resources increase the firms' costs. Higher costs lead to disappointed profit expectations and cause some firms to cut back. This reduction in demand spreads to other industries and to resource markets. Investment falls off, employment falls off, incomes fall, and the forces of contraction or **recession** spread. The point at which the expansion ends and the contraction begins is called the **upper turning point,** or **peak,** of the cycle.

Figure 2 Phases of the Business Cycle

Eventually, however, the contraction will stop and another expansion will begin. Inventories eventually become depleted, capital equipment and consumer durables (automobiles and appliances, for example) wear out and must be replaced. If prices fall during the contraction, the purchasing power of accumulated savings increases, and this may encourage higher levels of consumption. These forces cause the contraction or recession to reach a **lower turning point**, or **trough**, and a new expansion begins.

Cycles don't have to be symmetrical. There may be long or short periods of expansion or contraction. A deep trough may be followed by a weak recovery and a low peak. Long periods of expansion and a high or prolonged peak may be followed by a mild recession and a shallow trough.

Measuring and Defining Business Cycles

The National Bureau of Economic Research (NBER) is a private research organization, and much of its research activity is directed at fluctuations and cycles. It was founded by the late Wesley Clair Mitchell, a major figure in the study of business cycles.

One of the most important functions of the NBER is to measure and define cyclical fluctuations.

- A **reference cycle** is defined by the NBER as an expansion and a contraction, or a cycle from trough to peak to trough.

The NBER dates the peaks and troughs of each reference cycle. Table 1 is a summary of the NBER's postwar reference cycles. Although there is a repeating pattern of expansion followed by contraction, the reference cycles aren't symmetrical.

Table 1 Postwar Recessions

Peak	Trough	Length of recession (months)
Oct. 1948	Oct. 1949	12 months
July 1953	May 1954	10 months
Mar. 1957	April 1958	13 months
April 1960	Feb. 1961	10 months
Oct. 1969	Nov. 1970	13 months
Nov. 1973	Mar. 1975	16 months

Source: U.S. Department of Commerce, *Handbook of Cyclical Indicators* (Washington: May, 1977). Also, *Business Conditions Digest*, vol. 19, No. 3 (March, 1979).

Some research on business cycles seeks to predict fluctuations, or at least turning points. This is important information. For example, if the government is following a policy of stimulating demand to minimize unemployment during a recession, it's important to know when to stop. If the stimulation of demand stops too soon, the recovery could halt before unemployment reaches an acceptably low level. If it continues too long, it could intensify inflationary pressures during an expansion.

Leading indicators reach their turning points before real GNP and can predict future peaks or troughs. For example, new orders for capital goods generally peak before real GNP, and a downturn in orders for capital goods generally suggests a future contraction or recession.

Are There Business Cycles?

Although the pattern of fluctuations shows a steady pattern of expansion, peak, recession, trough, expansion, etc.—and although most economists use the term *business cycles* loosely to refer to fluctuations—there is not widespread agreement on the causes of these fluctuations. Most business cycle theories give the heaviest weight to cyclical variations as the main cause of fluctuations. There are, however, other events that can affect the size and duration of expansions or contractions.

The economy is constantly bombarded by exogenous shocks that could cause instability in aggregate demand. Looking back over the historical record, many of the fluctuations in economic activity could be explained as the response to dramatic shifts in aggregate demand due to some important exogenous shocks—World War I, postwar demobilization, the Stock Market crash followed by drastic tightening of the money supply that discouraged investment and brought on the Depression, World War II, demobilization and reconversion after the war, the Korean War and demobilization, a large increase in demand for capital goods (explained in part by the shortages during World War II and the Korean War), and finally, the Vietnam War and its aftermath in the 1970s.

The instability or stability of real GNP over time is ultimately determined by the instability or stability of the determinants of aggregate demand over time—consumption, investment, government spending, etc. Figure 3 shows year-to-year percentage changes in real GNP, consumption, gross private domestic investment, and government purchases for the period 1950 to 1978. Even a casual look at these figures shows that consumption is the most stable component of aggregate demand over time, and investment is the least stable. Government purchases are relatively unstable over time, but this reflects the effects of exogenous events (wars and demobilizations, for example).

Figure 3 Changes in GNP and Components of GNP, 1950–1978

Source: *Economic Report of the President*, 1979.

Consumption and Instability

Consumption is the largest component of aggregate demand and GNP. Dramatic changes in employment, incomes, and expectations can cause the consumption function to shift. General optimism, pessimism, or uncertainty about future economic conditions, employment, and income particularly affect *consumer durables* spending—purchases of "big ticket" items like cars, furniture, and appliances. If households are generally optimistic about their future economic condition, they will be more likely to make purchases of large consumer durables than if they are pessimistic or uncertain about the future economic prospects. Expenditures for consumer durables accounted for only about 16 percent of total consumption expenditures in 1978, however. The other basic types of consumer expenditure—purchases of *nondurables* (like food and clothing) and *services*—tend to be much less volatile. In fact, the most notable characteristic of consumption over time is its stability around its long-term trend, and the relatively small percentage changes in consumption from year to year—smaller even than the changes in GNP.

The Relative Income Hypothesis

One of the earliest explanations of the stability of household consumption behavior over time was the **relative income hypothesis**, formulated by Professor James Duesenberry of Harvard in 1952. Briefly, the hypothesis asserts that people gear their current consumption expenditures to their peak income achieved so far.

Figure 4 illustrates the relative income hypothesis by looking at a hypothetical household. In 1970, the household earned its highest disposable income to date ($15,000), and its 1970 consumption was 90 percent (.9) of its 1970 income, or $13,500. Now, suppose that the household's income falls from $15,000 in 1970 to $12,000 in 1974. If the household adjusted its consumption to 90 percent of its current income, its consumption spending would drop to $10,800 in 1974. However, according to the relative income hypothesis, the household wouldn't reduce consumption proportionally to a decline in disposable income below a previous peak. In Figure 4, then, the household reduces its consumption from $13,500 to $12,000 in 1974. This suggests that the household's consumption function for the period 1970-74 is C_{70-74}.

In 1975, the household's disposable income reaches a new historic high—$18,000. Consistent with the relative income hypothesis, the household adjusts its consumption in 1975 to 90 percent of its peak income, or $18,000 \times 0.9 = $16,200. If the household's income declined again from $18,000 in 1975 to $15,000 in 1980, the household would reduce its consumption spending less than proportionally because income in these years is below the historic peak.

Figure 4 Relative Income Hypothesis

In short, as income moves to higher and higher peaks over time, households adjust consumption to the peak income. However, if it falls below the peak, consumption is reduced less than proportionally. This suggests a **rachet effect** that moves the household's short-run consumption function upward over time, but not downward.

If households' consumption behavior were consistent with the relative income hypothesis, we should expect that consumption will be more stable than disposable income over time, that the relationship between consumption and income over long periods of time will likewise be quite stable, and that the *mpc* will be lower in the short run than in the long run. All of these predictions are generally consistent with the empirical evidence on consumption presented in an earlier chapter. However, there is a serious analytical flaw in the relative income hypothesis: the implicit assumption that households never expect their long-term income trend to be below a historic peak.

The Permanent Income Hypothesis

In 1957, Professor Milton Friedman introduced the **permanent income hypothesis** according to which households gear their current consumption expenditures to their **permanent income**, or their expected average income over a period of years. As a result, there will be a more stable relationship between consumption and permanent income than between consumption and current income.

To explain permanent income in simple terms, imagine a person who receives a monthly salary of $1000 on the first day of each month. On the first of the month, the person's *measured* (or actual) daily income is $1,000. If the person geared his or her daily consumption to measured daily income—say, daily consumption = 90 percent of measured daily income—consumption expenditures would be $900 on the first of the month and zero for the rest of the month. To avoid this feast on the first and famine on the other days of the month, the typical household spreads its consumption expenditures more evenly over the month. In Friedman's terminology, the paycheck on the first of the month would be the person's *permanent income* for the entire month.

Having established that households will tend to smooth out their consumption expenditures over time, Friedman argues that there is no reason to believe that households will necessarily gear their annual consumption in any given year to their measured income in that year. Rather, he argues, households will gear their annual consumption to their *permanent income*, which Friedman defines as the expected average income over a three-year period. To illustrate, suppose that a household expects to earn an average income of $20,000 per year for the period 1980–1982—its permanent income is $20,000 per year. If it consumed 90 percent of its permanent income in each year, then, its consumption expenditures would be $18,000 in each of the years in the period. The household's actual measured income isn't constant, but varies from $18,000 in 1980 to $22,000 in 1981 and $20,000 in 1982. Thus, even though measured income fluctuates, consumption expenditure (which is geared to permanent income) is stable.

	1980	1981	1982
Measured Income	$18,000	$22,000	$20,000
Permanent income	$20,000	$20,000	$20,000
$C = .9 \times$ Permanent Income	$18,000	$18,000	$18,000

The permanent income hypothesis predicts that the ratio of consumption to disposable income may vary from year to year, but that C/Y_d will be stable over long periods of time. It also predicts that C/Y_d will be higher if measured over long periods of time than if measured over shorter periods. This prediction is consistent with the empirical relationship between consumption and disposable income. The permanent income hypothesis places a heavy emphasis on the stability of expectations over time on stabilizing consumption. Unlike the relative income hypothesis, the permanent income hypothesis doesn't preclude households' expecting permanent income to fall.

The Life-Cycle Hypothesis

A third explanation of the greater stability of consumption than GNP over time is the **life-cycle hypothesis** of consumer behavior formulated by Professor Franco Modigliani of MIT. According to this hypothesis, the household gears its annual consumption behavior to its expected average income for its earning lifetime. Suppose a household expects an annual average income of $20,000 for its earning lifetime. Typically, a household's income is below average in the early years of its life cycle, at a peak in the middle years, and below average again after retirement. Our hypothetical household's earnings behavior is represented in Figure 5.

In the early years, the household can maintain relatively high levels of consumption by borrowing against future income. During its peak earning years, it can pay off debts incurred in the early years and save for the years of low income after retirement. After retirement, the household can maintain its normal consumption and standard of living by spending the savings accumulated during the peak earning period. If the household geared consumption to its average annual income for its lifetime, year-to year changes in income would have relatively little effect on its consumption. However, over a long period of time, there will be little consumption that can't be explained by disposable income, a high *mpc*, and a very tight relationship between consumption and disposable income.

Figure 5 Life-Cycle Hypothesis

Investment and Instability

Although investment is a smaller expenditure flow and a smaller component of aggregate demand and GNP than consumption, it contributes more instability. Figure 3b shows that gross investment (*I*) was the least stable component of GNP during the period 1950–1978.

There are three basic reasons for the instability of investment—the existence of *induced investment* that varies with GNP, the so-called *accelerator effect*, and the effects of uncertainty and shifts in investors' *expectations*.

Induced Investment

Up to this point, all investment has been assumed to be autonomous. In fact, some investment depends on the level of output and real GNP.

• **Induced investment** is investment that varies with GNP.

Some investment is financed out of firms' profits, and some is financed by loans. The source of loanable funds to finance investment loans is the saving by households. Since profits and savings vary with GNP, it's reasonable to expect at least some investment expenditures to vary directly with GNP.

The rate at which investment varies with GNP is the **marginal propensity to invest** (*mpi*). Algebraically, *mpi* is the ratio

$$mpi = \frac{\Delta I}{\Delta Y}. \tag{1}$$

Other things equal, the *mpi* will lie between its extreme values of 0 (all investment autonomous) and 1 (all additional GNP invested).

With the addition of induced investment, the relationship between investment (*I*) and GNP (*Y*) can be expressed by an investment function

Figure 6 Aggregate Demand and Induced Investment

$$I = I_a + mpi\,(Y). \tag{2}$$

This investment function is shown graphically in Figure 6. At any level of GNP, total investment is composed of autonomous investment (I_a) and induced investment.

The addition of induced investment also affects the aggregate demand function. If we assume government spending and net taxes to be autonomous ($G = G_a$ and $T = T_a$), and substitute the consumption and investment functions for C and I, aggregate demand is

$$\begin{aligned}
AD &= C + I + G \\
&= (a + bY_d) + (I_a + mpiY) + G_a \\
&= (a + bY - bT_a) + (I_a + mpiY) + G_a \\
&= (a + I_a + G_a - bT_a) + (b + mpi)Y.
\end{aligned} \tag{3}$$

Recall that with only autonomous investment, the slope of the aggregate demand function was b, the same as the slope of the consumption function. The addition of induced investment has increased this slope to $(b + mpi)$, as illustrated in Figure 6.

The addition of induced investment contributes to instability by strengthening the multiplier effect. With consumption the only non-autonomous expenditure, the multiplier is

$$k = \frac{1}{(1 - mpc)}.$$

If consumption and investment both vary with GNP, the multiplier becomes[1]

$$k = \frac{1}{1 - (b + mpi)}. \quad (4)$$

This difference may look small at first glance, but its effects are really quite large. If $mpc = 0.6$, $mpi = 0.2$, and all other expenditures are autonomous, the multiplier with no induced investment is

$$k = \frac{1}{(1 - mpc)} = \frac{1}{0.4} = 2.5.$$

With induced investment added, the multiplier becomes

$$k = \frac{1}{1 - (mpc + mpi)} = \frac{1}{1 - (0.6 + 0.2)} = \frac{1}{0.2} = 5.$$

The addition of induced investment in this particular case actually *doubles* the multiplier effect.

Figure 7 Induced Investment and the Multiplier

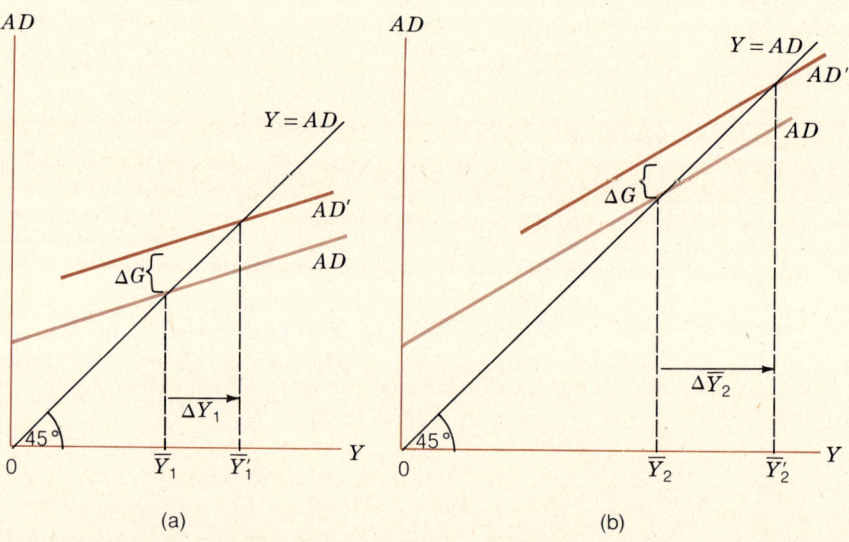

1. This multiplier can be derived algebraically by setting $AD = \overline{Y}$ and then solving equation 3 for $\overline{Y}$:

$$\overline{Y} = (a + I + G_a + bT_a) + (b + mpi)\overline{Y} \quad (3)$$
$$\overline{Y} - (b + mpi)\overline{Y} = (a + I_a + G_a - bT_a)$$
$$(1 - b - mpi)\overline{Y} = (a + I_a + G_a - bT_a)$$
$$\overline{Y} = \frac{1}{(1 - b - mpi)}(a + I_a + G_a - bT_a)$$

The multiplier with induced investment is thus

$$k = \frac{1}{(1 - b - mpi)} = \frac{1}{1 - (b + mpi)}.$$

The effect of this change can be seen graphically in Figure 7. In part a (no induced investment), an increase in autonomous government spending from G_a to G_a' shifts the aggregate demand function upward by that amount and causes equilibrium GNP to rise from $\overline{Y}_1$ to $\overline{Y}_1'$. In part b (induced investment added), the slope of the aggregate demand function is now greater ($b + mpi$ instead of just b). As a result, though the increase in government spending shifts the function upward by the same amount as before, equilibrium GNP this time rises from $\overline{Y}_2$ to $\overline{Y}_2'$—about twice as much as before.

This stronger multiplier effect of shifts in autonomous spending will strengthen the destabilizing effects of economic shocks (sudden changes in expectations, wars, embargoes, etc.). It will also amplify the effects of changes in government spending and mistakes in economic policies.

The Accelerator and the Stability of Investment

Another cause of the instability of investment over time is a phenomenon known as the *accelerator effect*.

- The **accelerator effect** is the tendency of the capital stock and investment to change by greater proportions than changes in real GNP or real output.

Imagine an economy that always invests just enough to keep its stock of capital fully employed. Assume that 5 percent of the capital stock wears out every year and has to be replaced. Assume also that every $1 worth of output requires $5 worth of capital stock—i.e., that the **capital-output ratio** or ratio of required capital stock to real GNP is 5:1.

Initially, in year 0, real GNP is $500 billion, and the capital stock (KS) is 5 × $500 billion = $2,500 billion. In year 1, GNP remains at $500 billion. The only investment in year 1 is the 5 percent of year 0's capital stock ($125 billion) that wore out and had to be replaced—i.e., all investment in year 1 is *replacement investment*. In Table 2, *gross investment* = replacement investment + net investment = $125 billion + 0 = $125 billion.

In year 2, real GNP increases by 10 percent to $550 billion. This will require 5 × $50 billion = $250 billion in *net investment* to produce

Table 2 The Accelerator Effect

Yr.	Real GNP	Capital Stock	Replacement Investment	Net Investment	Gross Investment
0	500	2500	—	—	—
1	500	2500	125	0	125
2	550	2750	125	250	375
3	550	2750	137.5	0	137.5

the additional output. This net investment is in addition to the replacement investment of $125 billion (5 percent of the capital stock in year 1). So the 10 percent increase in real GNP causes gross investment to increase from $125 billion to $375 billion—an increase of 300 percent!

In year 3, real GNP stabilizes at $550 billion. Will this stabilize investment? No! Net investment falls to zero, because no additions to the capital stock are required to produce the same level of output. The only investment is the replacement investment to replace the capital stock from year 2 that wore out—in this case replacement investment is 5% × $2,750 billion = $137.5 billion. So, when real GNP stabilized after an increase, gross investment fell from $375 billion to $137.5 billion—a decline of about 63 percent.

This is a very simple example of the accelerator effect. In reality, the size of the accelerator may be smaller if there is unemployed capital in the economy. The example does, however, make some important points about the stability of the investment flow over time.

1. A stable investment flow over time will require steady growth of real GNP.
2. If GNP stabilizes after a period of growth, the level of investment will fall.
3. Fluctuations in investment will be greater than fluctuations in real GNP over time.

Expectations, Uncertainty, and Investment

A third force behind the instability of investment is something everyone has heard a good deal about in recent years: investor uncertainty. Investments are made on the basis of *expected* future returns. Nobody knows for sure what's going to happen in the future—not even self-styled mystics, prophets, astrologers, and wizards. In periods of particular uncertainty, investors tend to wait and see before tying their resources up in investment projects. This makes sense. A 90 percent chance that an investment would yield a return of 10 percent per year is more attractive than a 40 percent chance that it would yield the same annual rate of return.

If such "chances" were *objective*, investor uncertainty would contribute little to investment instability. Expectations about the future are *subjective*, however, and the state of investors' economic expectations can thus have a strong influence on the level of stability of investment. Suppose that with normal economic expectations, an investment project would be expected to return $1000 on a $10,000 outlay after one year—a 10 percent return. However, with more *optimistic* expectations, suppose that the same project would be expected to return $2000 after a year, or 20 percent. Suppose that the *pessimistic* expected return from the same project is $500 or 5 percent after one year. If the interest rate (r) were 10% per year, this would

Figure 8 Expectations, Investment, and Aggregate Demand

be a marginal project with normal expectations. It would definitely be undertaken if investors were more optimistic and definitely would not be undertaken if investors were pessimistic.

Expectations of all investors affect the *MEI* and the level of investment for the entire economy. Optimistic expectations of future returns tend to raise the *MEI* at all levels of investment and increase the level of investment at any interest rate. In Figure 8a, the *MEI* curve reflects "normal" expectations, *MEI'* reflects more optimistic expectations, and *MEI"* reflects more pessimistic expectations. At a given interest rate (r), investment would be $\bar{I}$ with normal expectations where $MEI = r$. Optimism would drive the level of investment to $\bar{I}'$ at the same interest rate. Pessimism would drive the level of investment to $\bar{I}"$.

The role of expectations in the stability of investment and GNP is important. Unstable expectations lead to unstable investment, aggregate demand, and equilibrium GNP. If optimism raises investment to $\bar{I}'$ in Figure 8a, aggregate demand increases to AD' in Figure 8b and GNP rises by $\Delta Y = k \Delta \bar{I}$. Pessimism drives investment to $\bar{I}"$ and equilibrium GNP to $\bar{Y}"$. Unstable GNP, in turn, makes expectations and investment even more unstable.

Government Spending and Instability

One of the recurring controversies in the debate over the proper role and scope of government intervention in the economy is the ability of government policies to stabilize aggregate demand and GNP over time through government spending and tax policies that stimulate aggregate demand during recessions and dampen demand-related inflationary pressures during economic expansions. This question is taken up in the analysis of fiscal policy in the next chapter.

The question of the effect of government purchases on the stability of income isn't the same as the question of the possibility of stabilizing income through government spending policies. Government purchases fluctuate for a variety of reasons other than attempts to stabilize income—wars and their aftermaths being the most obvious examples. Even since 1950, the Korean War and the Vietnam War had dramatic effects on government purchases of goods and services. In nonwar years since 1950, government purchases haven't fluctuated wildly. Furthermore, as shown in Figure 3b, fluctuations in government spending tend to run against the direction in fluctuations in investment, and may have a stabilizing effect on income.

Built-in Stabilizers

Even when economic problems are the most puzzling and disturbing, very few economists seriously expect a repeat of the economic disaster of the 1930s. In fact, many economists feel that the economy is "depression-proof," because of a number of **built-in stabilizers** that dampen expansions and contractions even in the absence of changes in economic policies.

Figure 9 Aggregate Demand and Induced Taxes

Induced Taxes

Up to this point, taxes have been treated as an autonomous flow. In fact, while some taxes (such as real estate taxes) *are* autonomous, most of the taxes that we pay vary with GNP. When GNP rises, personal income and the revenue from personal income taxes also rise. Since not all of the additional GNP and personal income is taxed away, disposable income also rises, and some of the additional disposable income is spent for consumption, increasing the revenue from sales taxes. Thus, the total tax flow contains *induced taxes* as well as autonomous taxes.

- **Induced taxes** are taxes that vary with income and GNP.

In periods of expansion and rising GNP, the induced tax flow increases, dampening the increase in aggregate demand and GNP. In recessions, falling GNP causes the induced tax flow to fall, dampening the decline in disposable income and aggregate demand.

The rate at which induced taxes vary as GNP varies is called the **marginal tax rate** (*mtr*). Algebraically, the marginal tax rate is

$$mtr = \frac{\Delta T}{\Delta Y}. \tag{5}$$

If induced taxes are *proportional taxes*, all income is taxed at the same rate, and the *mtr* is constant. A **tax function** showing the relationship between GNP (Y) and the level of tax payments could be expressed by the equation

$$T = T_a + mtr\,(Y). \tag{6}$$

This tax function is shown graphically in Figure 9. The distance between the autonomous tax flow (T_a) and total taxes (T) at any level of income represents the induced tax flow.

Adding induced taxes changes the aggregate demand function. If we assume for simplicity that investment and government spending are again autonomous ($G = G_a$ and $I = I_a$), we can substitute the consumption and tax functions for C and T in the aggregate demand equation.

$$\begin{aligned}
AD &= C + I + G \\
&= (a + bY_d) + I_a + G_a \\
&= [a + bY - b\,(T_a + mtr\,Y)] + I_a + G_a \\
&= a + bY - bT_a - b \cdot mtr\,Y + I_a + G_a \\
&= (a - bT_a + I_a + G_a) + (b - b \cdot mtr)\,Y. \tag{7}
\end{aligned}$$

Just as the addition of induced investment *increased* the slope of the aggregate demand function from b to $(b + mpi)$, so the addition of induced taxes *reduces* the slope from b to $(b - b \cdot mtr)$ in Figure 9.

Induced taxes likewise change the multiplier effect, reducing its strength and thus making equilibrium GNP less responsive to changes in autonomous spending. With induced taxes and consumption the only non-autonomous expenditures, the multiplier becomes[2]

$$k = \frac{1}{1 - b + b \cdot mtr}. \tag{8}$$

Suppose that the *mpc* is $b = 0.8$, and that induced taxes are 25 percent of GNP ($mtr = .25$); the multiplier is

$$k = \frac{1}{1 - 0.8 + 0.8(.25)} = \frac{1}{0.4} = 2.5.$$

With the same *mpc*, but no induced taxes ($mtr = 0$), the multiplier would be

$$k = \frac{1}{1 - 0.8 + 0.8(0)} = \frac{1}{0.2} = 5.$$

Thus, the addition of induced taxes in this case has cut the multiplier in half.

Figure 10 Induced Taxes and the Multiplier

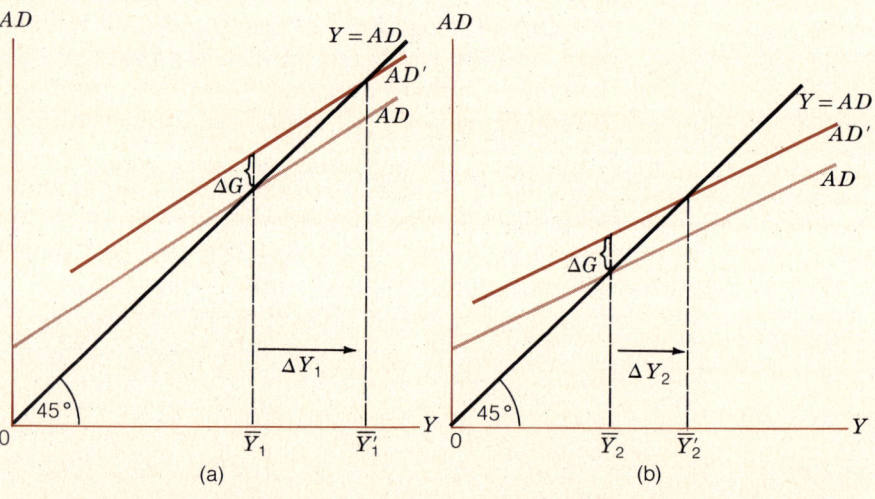

2. As with induced investment, the multiplier can be derived algebraically by setting $\bar{Y} = AD$ and then solving Equation 7 for $\bar{Y}$:

$$\bar{Y} = (a + I_a + G_a - bT_a) + (b - b \cdot mtr)\bar{Y}$$
$$\bar{Y} - (b - b \cdot mtr)\bar{Y} = (a + I_a + G_a - bT_a)$$
$$[1 - b + b(mtr)]\bar{Y} = (a + I_a + G_a + bT_a).$$
$$\bar{Y} = \frac{1}{1 - b + b(mtr)} (a + I_a + G_a - bT_a)$$

The multiplier with induced taxes is thus

$$k = \frac{1}{1 - b + b(mtr)}$$

This difference is illustrated graphically in Figure 10. In part a (no induced taxes), the increase in autonomous government spending raises equilibrium GNP to $\overline{Y}_1'$. In part b (induced taxes added), the same increase in government spending raises GNP only to $\overline{Y}_2'$—about half as far. Thus, adding induced taxes has the opposite effect of adding induced investment, as a quick comparison of Figures 7 and 10 will clearly show.

Progressive taxes, such as the Federal Income Tax and some state and local income taxes, tax higher incomes at higher rates than lower incomes. As a result, progressive taxes have a stronger dampening effect on changes in aggregate demand than do proportional taxes. During expansions, the rising marginal rate of progressive taxes causes disposable income to rise more slowly relative to GNP than would be the case with proportional taxes. During recessions, the drop in the marginal tax rate causes disposable income to fall more slowly than with proportional taxes.

Unemployment Insurance

Most workers are covered by some form of **unemployment insurance** which subsidizes their income if they become unemployed. Some unemployment programs are public programs financed by payroll taxes paid by employers. In some industries, there are private programs which supplement or expand the benefits from the public programs.

Unemployment insurance dampens fluctuations in personal and disposable income, consumption, and aggregate demand. This has a stabilizing effect on GNP over time. In periods of falling aggregate demand and rising unemployment, more and more people qualify for benefits from unemployment insurance. This dampens the decline in personal income, disposable income, and consumption expenditures during recessions. When aggregate demand and GNP are rising and unemployment is falling, fewer and fewer people receive unemployment insurance benefits. Employers' payrolls increase during periods of expansion, and so do payroll taxes. So, the benefits that bolster income and aggregate demand during recessions don't continue to stimulate aggregate demand in periods of economic expansion.

Economic Fluctuations: What Can the Government Do?

One of the central goals of government *demand management* policies is to stabilize aggregate demand, employment, and output over time. Although an active economic role for the government is widely accepted, the controversy over the necessity, effectiveness, and desirability of government policies to regulate aggregate demand continues to divide economists and politicians.

The government has basically two bags of tools to regulate aggregate demand—monetary policies and fiscal policies. Since we have been analyzing the role of aggregate demand in determining aggregate output and equilibrium in the goods sector, we'll examine the fiscal tools (government spending and taxes) in the next chapter. Monetary policies will be analyzed after the monetary sector has been introduced into the analysis.

Summary

1. As long as economic data have been gathered and recorded, economic activity has shown a pattern of fluctuations over time.
2. Fluctuations are commonly referred to as **business cycles**, but strictly defined, business cycles are self-reversing fluctuations. Most modern theories of economic fluctuations try to explain fluctuations in terms of the stability or instability of the components of aggregate demand.
3. **Consumption** is the largest component of aggregate demand, but (except for consumer durables) contributes little to instability because of the stability of consumption around its long-term trend.
4. The **relative income hypothesis**, the **permanent income hypothesis**, and the **life-cycle hypothesis** are all economic theories which attempt to explain the long-term stability of consumption.
5. **Investment** is the least stable component of aggregate demand, and contributes the most to instability. The instability of investment reflects the importance of expectations in investment decisions.
6. **Induced investment** varies with GNP and makes GNP less stable by strengthening the multiplier effect.
7. Except for war years, **government spending** doesn't appear to be a major source of instability in aggregate demand or GNP.
8. **Built-in stabilizers** tend to dampen expansions and recessions automatically. **Induced taxes** and **unemployment insurance** are two important built-in stabilizers in the economy.

Concepts for Review

business cycle
recession
peak
trough
reference cycle
leading indicator
relative income
 hypothesis
ratchet effect
permanent income
 hypothesis
life-cycle hypothesis
induced investment
marginal propensity
 to invest
accelerator effect
capital-output ratio
investor expectations
built-in
 stabilizers
induced taxes
marginal tax rate
unemployment
 insurance

Questions

1. What are the *phases* of the business cycle? What are the implications of the predictability of fluctuations and turning points?
2. To what extent has each of the components of aggregate demand—consumption, investment, and government spending—contributed to the stability or instability of GNP over time?
3. How do business and consumer attitudes and expectations affect the stability of aggregate demand and GNP?
4. Evaluate the following statement by the President's Council of Economic Advisers: "As inflation abates . . . , consumer confidence in the economy should improve and thus strengthen consumer markets. . . . The saving

rate is consequently expected to decline...." (*Economic Report of the President, 1979*).

5. If the level of consumer debt and the stock of consumer durables are unusually high, what does this imply about the future behavior of consumption?
6. How would each of the following affect equilibrium GNP and the stability of GNP? Explain your answers.
   a. A 10% value-added tax is levied.
   b. A 10% tax is levied on personal property.
   c. The marginal propensity to invest increases.
   d. A progressive tax is levied on personal income.

Problems

1. The following expenditure flows are given for the economy of Macroland:

   $$\text{Consumption: } C = 50 + 0.6Y_d$$
   $$\text{Investment: } I = 50 + 0.2Y$$
   $$\text{Govt. Purchases: } G_a = 75$$
   $$\text{Net Taxes: } T_a = 50$$

   a. Calculate the equilibrium GNP ($\overline{Y}$) from the above data.
   b. Find the levels of consumption, autonomous investment, induced investment, government purchases, and saving at equilibrium GNP.
   c. If full-employment is reached at a real GNP of $Y^* = 1175$, does Macroland face an inflationary gap, a deflationary gap, or neither? Explain.
   d. Is equilibrium GNP in this economy more or less responsive to disturbances of aggregate demand than it would be without induced investment? Explain.

2. You are given the following expenditure flows for the small totalitarian country of Akademiia:

   $$\text{Consumption: } C = 50 + 0.75Y_d \quad \text{Investment: } I_a = 55$$
   $$\text{Govt. Purchases: } G_a = 75 \quad \text{Net Taxes: } T = 20 + 0.4Y$$

   a. Calculate equilibrium GNP ($\overline{Y}$) from the above information.
   b. What is the level of induced taxes at the equilibrium GNP?
   c. If full-employment GNP is $Y^* = 500$, does the economy face an inflationary gap, a deflationary gap, or neither?
   d. How do induced taxes affect the degree to which equilibrium GNP responds to disturbances of aggregate demand?

3. In addition to the expenditure flows for Akademiia in Problem 2, suppose that induced investment is 20 percent of GNP—i.e., induced investment = $0.20Y$.
   a. Write the equation for Akademiia's aggregate demand function.
   b. What is the value of the multiplier in Akademiia with the addition of induced investment? Why is it different from the value of the multiplier in problem 2?
   c. Find equilibrium GNP ($\overline{Y}$) and the levels of induced investment and induced taxes at equilibrium GNP.
   d. If full-employment GNP is $Y^* = 500$ as before, does the economy face an inflationary gap, deflationary gap, or neither? Does it face the same problem it did in problem 2?

24

Fiscal Policy: Mechanics, Problems, and Issues

Preview: The government has at its command two basic tools for controlling or offsetting disturbances in aggregate demand. **Discretionary fiscal policies** involve manipulation of *government spending* and *taxes*. **Discretionary monetary policies** involve manipulation of the *money supply* and *interest rates*. In this chapter, we'll look closely at some of the problems and issues surrounding the use of fiscal policies, delaying our analysis of monetary policies until we have had a chance to set up a framework in the next section of the text. Keep in mind, though, that the effectiveness of any particular fiscal policy will depend heavily on the monetary policies that accompany it.

Fiscal policies are enacted to provide and pay for government programs and to regulate the level of aggregate demand. These two goals aren't mutually exclusive. Some people who advocate increased government spending to stimulate aggregate demand and reduce unemployment may object to particular spending programs. Others who think that government spending should be reduced may support maintaining or expanding spending on specific programs (often the ones from which they benefit).

In analyzing the role of the government in the determination of aggregate demand, unemployment, and inflation, we're primarily concerned with the issue of *discretionary fiscal policy*.

- **Discretionary fiscal policies** are government spending and tax policies whose *main aim* is regulation of aggregate demand in order to minimize demand-related unemployment, inflationary pressure, and instability.[1]

---

1. Since the primary interest here is the effect of fiscal policy on aggregate demand and equilibrium GNP, the analysis will be almost exclusively on federal fiscal policies. State and local governments also spend and tax, of course, but these fiscal policies are directed primarily at providing and paying for specific programs and services and not regulating aggregate demand.

In the Keynesian model, equilibrium GNP ($\overline{Y}$) may fall short of full-employment GNP (Y^*), as in Figure 1a. The resulting *deflationary gap* causes underutilization of resources and unemployment. To achieve full employment, aggregate demand would have to shift to AD' in order to raise equilibrium GNP to Y^*. If the private sector's intended consumption and investment spending is insufficient, *expansionary fiscal policies* by the government may be necessary to raise aggregate demand and close the deflationary gap.

- **Expansionary fiscal policies** are increases in government spending and cuts in taxes meant to stimulate aggregate demand and relieve unemployment.

It is also possible in the Keynesian model that equilibrium GNP ($\overline{Y}$) may fall *above* full-employment GNP (Y^*), as in Figure 1b. The resulting *inflationary gap* and excess demand mean that individuals in the private sector will bid against each other for scarce goods and resources, raising the price level. In such cases, the government may be forced to use *restrictive fiscal policies* to lower aggregate demand to AD' and close the inflationary gap.

- **Restrictive fiscal policies** are cuts in government spending and increases in taxes meant to dampen aggregate demand and relieve inflationary pressures.

Whether the real world will actually behave the way the Keynesian model suggests is, of course, another question entirely. The necessity or desirability of discretionary fiscal policy is a long-standing

Figure 1 Effects of Discretionary Fiscal Policy

(a) Expansionary Policy   (b) Restrictive Policy

source of dispute among economists, and the experiences of the past decade have convinced a small but significant contingent of the economics profession that fiscal (and, for that matter, monetary) policies are ineffective in controlling aggregate demand, inflation, and unemployment. The possibility of achieving equilibrium GNP with less than full employment or with chronic inflationary pressure is perhaps the most important question that divided Keynes from the economic orthodoxy of the 1930s, and it is at least one of the most important questions that divide modern Keynesians and monetarists.

Government Spending vs. Taxes

It takes more than a flip of a coin to choose between fiscal policies that regulate aggregate demand through government spending and those that regulate aggregate demand through taxes. A number of important considerations are involved in making the choice between government spending and taxes.

Taxes, Government Spending, and Ideology

Modern political liberals tend to accept or advocate a broader range of services provided through the public sector and a more active role for the government in the economy than do modern conservatives. The "tax revolt" that gained widespread attention in the late 1970s had the strongest support from political conservatives and the strongest opposition from political liberals. Different political ideologies dictate different fiscal policies for raising or lowering the level of aggregate demand.

During periods of high unemployment, liberals tend to favor increased government spending through the undertaking of new public programs and expansion of existing programs. To reduce inflationary pressures, liberals tend to advocate tax increases over spending reductions, so as to avoid reducing the size and role of the public sector.

Close-up

The Democrats' Free Lunch: The Humphrey-Hawkins Bill

The famous economic saying, "There's no such thing as a free lunch," means that every benefit carries an associated cost. At election time, however, many politicians seem to disbelieve this notion, supporting bills that promise a free lunch to the voters. One such bill of major importance was the Full Employment & Balanced Growth Act of 1976, sponsored by the late Senator Hubert Humphrey (D-Minn.) and Representative Augustus Hawkins (D-Calif.) and thus known as the *Humphrey-Hawkins Bill*. The bill would establish "the right of all adult Americans able, willing, and seeking work to opportunities for useful paid employment at fair rates of compensation." In its original form, the bill required the government to pursue policies which would bring unemployment down to 3 percent by 1980; if traditional monetary and fiscal policies were insufficient to achieve this goal through the private sector, the government would act as employer of last resort, using public service job programs.

Supporters of the bill claimed that the huge expenditures necessary to hire millions of workers would not require a tax increase. Why? Because the growth in GNP and the tax base resulting from the much larger work force would mean an increase in tax revenues sufficient to pay for the new jobs. Most economists, however, including such prestigious liberals as Arthur Okun, James Tobin, and Franco Modigliani, didn't buy that logic, contending that the bill would be hugely inflationary and could not possibly achieve its objectives. By the time Jimmy Carter came to support the bill in 1978, it had been thoroughly watered down: the 3 percent goal had risen to 4 percent, no specific measures of money figures were spelled out for achieving that goal, and the President was even permitted to suggest changes in the goal after two years if he felt the economic situation required such changes.[1]

1. See "What Humphrey-Hawkins Would Mean," *Business Week*, May 31, 1976, pp. 66–67.

Political conservatives that accept *any* role for fiscal policy in stimulating aggregate demand tend to favor tax cuts over increased government spending. Tax cuts stimulate aggregate demand and at the same time achieve the conservatives' objectives of reducing the impact of the public sector. In inflationary times, conservatives tend to favor cuts in government spending, which both dampen inflationary pressures and reduce the size and role of the public sector.

Close-up

The Republicans' Free Lunch: The Kemp-Roth Bill

If our examination of the Humphrey-Hawkins Bill made you want to rush out and vote Republican, wait a moment. The "Kemp-Roth" Bill, introduced in 1978 by Representative Jack Kemp (R.-N.Y.) and Senator William V. Roth, Jr. (R-Del.), is the Republican version of the "free lunch." The bill would cut all personal taxes by one-third over a three-year period, at a cost of roughly $125 billion in lost tax revenues. Unlike more typical conservative tax-cutters, however, supporters of Kemp-Roth claim that this huge cut would require *no* cut in government spending. The reason: the tax cut would provide incentive for firms and households to work harder and spend and invest more, thus increasing national income and the tax base and entirely offsetting the original deficit. In other words, the government would be getting a proportionately smaller piece of a much larger pie.

Like the Humphrey-Hawkins Bill, the Kemp-Roth Bill rests on a kind of "fly now-pay later" theory of economic policy-making. Also like Humphrey-Hawkins, Kemp-Roth was rejected as unfeasible and highly inflationary by most economists, including such major conservative economists as George Stigler, Martin Feldstein, and Herbert Stein, who estimated that it would take "about 30 years to regain the revenue level that would have been achieved without the tax cut." Many of those Republican candidates who embraced the bill in the 1978 elections found that even in the midst of "Proposition 13 Fever," most voters agreed with the economists and demanded that any tax cuts be tied to equivalent cuts in government spending.[1]

---

1. See Seymour Zucker, "The Fallacy of Slashing Taxes Without Cutting Spending," *Business Week*, August 7, 1978, pp. 62, 64.

These generalizations don't mean that liberals will approve every proposed increase in spending or that conservatives will approve every proposed decrease. Political liberals, for example, tend to be critical of increased military spending, and every elected official or candidate for office (liberal or conservative) has to be sensitive to the spending and tax programs that are most important to his or her constituents. Also, since Congress is made up of representatives with diverse ideologies, the process of debate and compromise generally results in policies that combine some of the liberal and conservative fiscal strategies.

The Multiplier Effect of Government Spending and Taxes

Political considerations aside, does the choice of manipulating government spending or taxes *really* make any difference in regulating aggregate demand? Figure 1a is the familiar picture of an economy with equilibrium GNP ($\overline{Y}$) below the full employment GNP (Y^*). Suppose that the government has an either-or choice between taxes and government spending to close the deflationary gap. How much additional government spending (ΔG) would get equilibrium GNP ($\overline{Y}$) up to Y^*? The change in government spending will generate a greater change in equilibrium GNP ($\Delta \overline{Y}$) because of the multiplier effect. If k is the multiplier, then

$$k \Delta G = \Delta \overline{Y}. \tag{1}$$

Given $\overline{Y}$ and Y^*, the desired change in GNP is $\Delta \overline{Y} = Y^* - \overline{Y}$. This value can be substituted for $\Delta \overline{Y}$ in equation 1:

$$k \Delta G = (Y^* - \overline{Y}). \tag{2}$$

The change in government spending that yields this change in GNP will thus be

$$\Delta G = \frac{(Y^* - \overline{Y})}{k}. \qquad (3)$$

The deflationary gap could also be closed by cutting taxes. For simplicity, assume a change in autonomous taxes—for example, a change in property taxes. The autonomous tax term in the consumption and aggregate demand functions, you will recall, is $(-bT_a)$, so changing autonomous taxes by ΔT_a will cause GNP to change by

$$-k\,b\,\Delta T_a = \Delta \overline{Y} \qquad (4)$$

Again, the desired change in GNP is $(Y^* - \overline{Y})$, so we can substitute that term for $\Delta \overline{Y}$ in equation 4:

$$-k\,b\,\Delta T_a = (Y^* - \overline{Y}). \qquad (5)$$

The change in taxes (ΔT) which would yield the desired change in GNP $(\Delta \overline{Y})$, then, is

$$\Delta T = -\frac{(Y^* - \overline{Y})}{kb}. \qquad (6)$$

The negative sign in this result shows that a desired change in GNP will require a change in taxes in the opposite direction. Notice that unless $b = 1$, kb will be less than k, and it will thus take a larger reduction in taxes to raise GNP by a given amount than the increase in government spending that gives the same result.

This result can be reinforced with a numerical example. Suppose that full-employment GNP $(Y^*) = \$500$ billion, equilibrium GNP $(\overline{Y}) = \$400$ billion, mpc $(b) = 0.8$, and $k = 5$. The desired change in GNP is $Y^* - \overline{Y} = \$500$ billion $- \$400$ billion $= \$100$ billion.

The change in government spending that would yield full-employment GNP is

$$\Delta G = \frac{\$500\text{b.} - \$400\text{b.}}{5} = \frac{\$100\text{b.}}{5} = \$20 \text{ billion.}$$

The change in taxes (ΔT) that would give the same result is

$$\Delta T = -\frac{\$500\text{b.} - \$400\text{b.}}{5 \times 0.8} = -\frac{\$100\text{b.}}{4} = -\$25 \text{ billion.}$$

Increasing equilibrium GNP by $100 billion, then, would require a *$20 billion* increase in government spending or a *$25 billion* cut in taxes.

- A given change in GNP will require a larger change in autonomous taxes than the change in government spending that would yield the same result.

If full-employment real GNP is $Y^* = \$500$ billion and equilibrium real GNP is $\overline{Y} = \$600$ billion, the economy faces an *inflationary gap* and demand-pull inflation, as shown in Figure 1b. In this case, the desired change in GNP ($\Delta \overline{Y}$) is negative—$Y^* - \overline{Y} = \$500$ billion $- \$600$ billion $= -\$100$ billion.

To reduce equilibrium GNP by reducing government spending only,

$$\Delta G = \frac{\$500 \text{b.} - \$600 \text{b.}}{5} = \frac{-\$100 \text{b.}}{5} = -\$20 \text{ billion.}$$

To achieve the same result by increasing taxes,

$$\Delta T = -\frac{\$500 \text{b.} - \$600 \text{b.}}{5 \times 0.8} = -\frac{-\$100 \text{b.}}{4} = \$25 \text{ billion.}$$

In this case the tax increase is greater than the reduction of government spending that would achieve the same result.

Discretionary Fiscal Policy and Balanced Budgets

The *balanced budget* (government tax revenues equal to government spending) is one of the most durable of economic issues. Some people revere the balanced budget with a fervor usually accorded only to religious relics. Balanced budgets are typically identified with fiscal responsibility and *surpluses* with unusual restraint and self-discipline by public officials.

The disdain for government budget *deficits* (government spending exceeding tax revenues) seems to be nonpartisan. Republicans associate budgets deficits with Democratic administrations, and Democrats seldom miss a chance to point to budget deficits under Republican administrations.

Close-up

Should an Unbalanced Budget Be Unconstitutional?

One of the ways in which the public sentiment against "Big Government" and taxation in the late 1970s made itself felt was in the drive for a constitutional amendment to ban deficit federal spending. By mid-1979, 26 of the required 34 state legislatures had passed resolutions calling for a constitutional convention to draft such an amendment. Amendment proposals ranged from those which would ban deficit spending altogether to those that would limit spending to a set percentage of the previous year's growth in real GNP. Supporters claimed that only through the external pressure of an amendment could the Federal government be forced to limit its spending. Opponents, on the other hand, argued that such a ban would straitjacket the government in times of economic "emergency" and would be impractical or impossible to enforce.

Although the drive for a convention began as a nonpartisan, grass-roots movement, the issue was taken up by candidates for the presidential nomination in both major political parties. Former Governor John B. Connally of Texas made the balanced budget amendment part of his platform in his drive for the 1980 Republican nomination. On the Democratic side, Governor Edmund G. ("Jerry") Brown—who had been unsuccessful in his fight against "Proposition 13" in California in 1978—jumped on the amendment bandwagon to gain support in his drive for the 1980 Democratic party nomination for the presidency. Brown declared that "the time has come for this nation to balance what it produces with what it spends."[1]

---

1. "A Constitutional Ban on Red Ink?" *U.S. News and World Report*, January 29, 1979, p. 27.

One way to balance the budget is to separate government spending and taxes from the issue of full employment. In fact, some monetarists argue that government spending should be determined only by the merits of specific spending programs, and tax revenue should be sufficient to balance the budget. Full-employment and price stability would be achieved in the long run through the adjustments of prices and outputs in freely operating markets.

Unless the economy generated full employment and price stability on its own, however, we shouldn't expect discretionary fiscal policy to give us *annually balanced budgets*—i.e., government spending equal to taxes every year. Of course, if the economy generated full employment and price stability on its own, there would be no need for discretionary fiscal policies to regulate aggregate demand in the first place.

A more flexible version of the balanced budget arguments calls for *cyclically balanced budgets*, or total government spending equal to total taxes over the course of a business cycle. The argument here is that deficits will shorten and reduce the seriousness of recessions, and surpluses will dampen inflationary pressures in periods of excess demand. A major problem with this approach is that instability is not caused by cyclical changes alone, and random economic shocks appear to explain much more instability than cyclical forces. Moreover, the cyclically balanced budget would be achieved only if fluctuations were symmetrical—which they aren't. We don't find recessions and troughs offset by expansions of equal duration and peaks of equal height to the depth of the trough.

The Full-Employment Budget

When the President presents his proposed budget in January of each year, reference is often made to the *full-employment* budget. It is most commonly invoked to minimize the significance of a projected deficit in the proposed budget.

- The **full-employment budget** estimates government spending and tax revenue for the economy operating at full employment or at an acceptably low rate of unemployment.

Budgets show a *full-employment balance* if tax revenues would equal government spending if the economy were operating at full employment. Figure 2a illustrates a full-employment balanced budget graphically. Real GNP (GNP in constant prices) is shown on the horizontal axis, and government spending and taxes ($) are on the vertical axis. In the diagram, government spending (G) is autonomous, and taxes (T) vary directly with GNP. The predicted GNP (Y_p) is less than full-employment GNP (Y^*), and predicted tax revenue (T_p) is less than tax revenue at full employment (T^*), and less than government spending. The budget shows a deficit in the projected budget, but a *full-employment balance* ($T^* = G$).

If tax revenues exceed government spending at full-employment (T^* greater than G), as in Figure 2b, the budget shows a *full-employment surplus*, even though the actual budget would show a deficit. In Figure 2c, the budget shows a *full-employment deficit* (T^* less than G) as well as an actual deficit.

Figure 2 The Full-Employment Budget

At first glance, the full-employment budget looks like nonsense. To say that we have a deficit, but would have a balanced budget at full employment seems to make about as much sense as the assertion that if my grandmother had had wheels she'd have been a car. On closer examination, however, the full-employment budget is a useful device in the design and evaluation of fiscal policy. The full-employment budget indicates whether or not a projected budget would be expansionary or restrictive at high levels of employment. Changes in the actual budget surplus or deficit may or may not indicate expansionary or restrictive changes in fiscal policy. For example, in Figure 2b, tax revenues vary with income along T as income changes. With no change in spending, tax rates, or types of taxes—i.e., no change in the direction of fiscal policy—the actual deficit will increase as GNP (Y) falls and will shrink as Y rises. However, the full-employment deficit or surplus will change only if the tax (T) or government spending (G) curves shift due to changes in fiscal policy.

A balanced full-employment budget suggests that an actual deficit is adequate to generate full-employment GNP without contributing to excess demand and inflationary pressure at high levels of employment—*if* the estimates are correct.

The full-employment budget, although a handy device for political deception (by calling nearly everything a *balanced budget*), *is* useful for fiscal policy. If the goal is to stimulate aggregate demand to reduce high unemployment, it indicates whether or not actual deficits are adequate to reduce unemployment to an acceptably low level without intensifying inflationary pressures as unemployment falls.

The Balanced-Budget Multiplier

Could discretionary fiscal policy be used to alter aggregate demand if the proposed balanced-budget amendment to the Constitution were ratified? The first impression is that it couldn't because the possibility of stimulating aggregate demand with deficits and dampening it with surpluses would be removed. However, it *is* possible to change aggregate demand and equilibrium GNP via equal changes in government spending and taxes.

Suppose that the government increases government spending and taxes by an equal amount ($\Delta G = \Delta T$) to maintain a balanced budget. For simplicity, assume that the entire ΔG enters the income stream and stimulates aggregate demand. However, increasing taxes lowers disposable income, and a reduction in disposable income (ΔY_d) reduces consumption only by a proportion of the change in disposable income ($\Delta C = mpc \, \Delta Y_d$). In other words, the change in government spending would have a greater effect on aggregate demand and equilibrium GNP than would the equal change in taxes.

The effect of an equal change in government spending and taxes on equilibrium GNP is called the *balanced-budget multiplier effect*.

- The **balanced-budget multiplier** is the change in equilibrium GNP resulting from equal changes in government spending and taxes.

The value of the balanced-budget multiplier can be derived formally using a little simple algebra. Given an autonomous expenditure multiplier k, and $mpc = b$, the effect of a change in government spending is

$$\Delta \overline{Y}_G = k \Delta G. \tag{7}$$

The effect of an equal change in taxes is

$$\Delta \overline{Y}_T = -k\, b\, \Delta T. \tag{8}$$

The net effect of these changes on equilibrium GNP is

$$\Delta \overline{Y} = \Delta \overline{Y}_G - \Delta \overline{Y}_T = k \Delta G - k\, b\, \Delta T. \tag{9}$$

Since $\Delta G = \Delta T$ in this example, they can be substituted for each other in equation 9, giving us

$$\Delta \overline{Y} = k \Delta G - k\, b\, \Delta G = (1 - b)\, k \Delta G. \tag{10}$$

Recall, however, that the autonomous expenditure multiplier k is equal to $1/(1 - b)$. Substituting this ratio into equation 10, we get

$$\Delta \overline{Y} = (1 - b) \cdot \frac{1}{(1 - b)} \Delta G = \frac{(1 - b)}{(1 - b)} \Delta G = \Delta G. \tag{11}$$

The balanced-budget multiplier, k_B, in this simple case then will be

$$k_B = \frac{(1 - b)}{(1 - b)} = 1. \tag{12}$$

The fact that the balanced-budget multiplier is 1 means that the change in GNP will be equal and in the same direction as the equal changes in government spending and taxes. If government spending increases by $10 billion, and taxes increase by $10 billion, equilibrium GNP will increase by $10 billion. Conversely, if taxes and government spending are both cut by $10 billion, equilibrium GNP will fall by $10 billion.

Whether the balanced-budget multiplier in any *particular* equal change in government spending and taxes will actually equal 1 depends on the proportion of the additional government spending that represents a *net* increase in aggregate spending. The increase in taxes to cover an increase in government spending reduces disposable income. This reduction in turn reduces consumption, so a portion of the increased government spending simply replaces private spending.

In reality, the balanced-budget multiplier is probably quite small, and there is even some disagreement concerning its very existence. This suggests that, while not quite impossible, the continued use of discretionary fiscal policies while maintaining a balanced budget would be difficult at best. The kinds of massive changes in government spending and taxes that would be needed to offset even relatively minor disturbances in aggregate demand would be politically unacceptable to most elected officials. As a result, an unbending requirement (through legislation or constitutional amendment) that Congress balance the budget would virtually eliminate the role of discretionary fiscal policy in regulating aggregate demand.

Close-up

The Vietnam Tax Surcharge

In 1968, President Johnson proposed, and Congress enacted, a 10 percent surcharge on individual and corporate income taxes. The object was to dampen the inflationary pressures generated by the increasing expenditures of the Vietnam War without cutting back spending on the *Great Society* programs.

The tax surcharge was supported and opposed by rather strange ideological alliances. The supporters of the surcharge included political liberals who were concerned with maintaining civilian programs, as well as political liberals and conservatives who were hawkish on the war. The opposition included, predictably, many political conservatives who advocated reduced nonmilitary spending to dampen inflationary pressure and support the war effort without extending the scope of the government in the economy, and a strange alliance of political conservatives, liberals, and radicals who were dovish on the war and saw the tax surcharge primarily as a means of supporting the war.

Inflationary pressures worsened after 1968, even with the tax surcharge. The Consumer Price Index rose by 4.2 percent in 1968, 5.4 percent in 1969, and 5.9 percent in 1970—leading many to argue that the economists were wrong again (or "wrong, as usual"). What the worsening inflation showed, however, wasn't that the prediction that rising taxes would dampen inflationary pressure was wrong, but that the tax increase wasn't sufficient to offset the inflationary impact of the war, the Great Society, and the economic expansion that had been going on since 1964.

Fiscal Policy and the National Debt

When government spending exceeds tax revenues, the government has to borrow, and this increases the *national debt*. The national debt, or the debt owed by the federal government, has been a source of controversy since the days of Hamilton and Jefferson. The great orator Daniel Webster is alleged, in the heat of debate and slightly in his cups, to have offered to pay off the national debt to eliminate it as an issue. However, Webster never made good on his offer, and the debt survives as the issue for which the shakiest economic arguments have attracted the largest popular following.

Government deficits and surpluses affect the size of the national debt. Budget surpluses can be used to repay or *retire* part of the debt. Deficits require government borrowing, and this increases the debt. Since deficits have been much more common than surpluses, as shown in Figure 3, the federal debt has been increasing, a cause of some concern but frequently for the wrong reasons.

"The National Debt Will Bankrupt the Country"

One of the most common concerns about the public debt is that it represents reckless government spending and that it will lead to national bankruptcy. The argument typically goes something like this: "As individuals we can't spend more than we make for very long without going bankrupt. Therefore, if the government continues to go in debt to finance deficits, the country will go bankrupt."

The argument seems to make sense, but there are a couple of things wrong with it. It obviously commits the fallacy of composition, as do many arguments that appeal to common sense alone. An increase

Figure 3 Surpluses (+) and Deficits (−) in Federal Budgets, 1920–1980

in the national debt may be undesirable economically, but the principles of household budgeting have little to do with the merits of running a deficit in the federal budget. For one thing, the government could simply print up money or raise taxes and pay off the debt—a course not open to households in financial trouble.

Bankruptcy of the federal government doesn't mean that creditors will descend on Washington to attach the Capitol and other government buildings and office equipment. Bankruptcy in this context would consist of the inability of the government to sell bonds and other government securities, or a general lack of acceptance of money issued by the government. This situation isn't impossible, but it *is* highly unlikely. If we ever reach this point, the national debt will be the least of our worries.

How "reckless" has federal spending been? How large is the debt? In absolute terms, the federal debt is an impressive figure. In fiscal 1979, the estimated federal debt was $839.2 billion, and the debt has been increasing over time. However, this isn't the entire picture. The federal debt jumped about 500 percent during World War II. Between 1946 and 1976, the net federal debt increased at an average annual rate of about 2.7 percent per year. In the same period, net private debt increased at an annual average rate of 9.78 percent per year. In this context the rise in the federal debt doesn't appear so alarming.

"The National Debt Is a Burden on the Community and on Future Generations."

This argument is more subtle than the bankruptcy arguments and is even valid under certain circumstances. It usually begins with an assertion that every baby born in the country is in debt at the moment of birth. The amount of this debt is the total outstanding federal debt divided by the total population—in 1978, about $3,840 per person. However, the validity of the argument depends on two things—to whom the debt is owed and the kinds of expenditures financed by the debt.

An *externally held* public debt is owed by the government to creditors in another country. Principal and interest payments on an externally held debt are leakages out of the domestic income stream. Since these payments are made out of the tax revenues of the debtor country, they are a real burden on the citizens of the country. The funds used to pay interest and principal on the external debt have uses in the domestic economy—they could have been used for consumption, for investments to increase productive capacity, or for other government programs that convey benefits to the citizens.

- An **externally held public debt** places a net burden on the citizens of the debtor country because the debt payments leave the country's income stream.

An *internally held public debt* is owed by the government to its own citizens. Every person or institution that owns bonds or other government securities holds a portion of the public debt. Interest and principal payments on an internally held debt stay within the country, and represent income to the holders of the debt.

- An **internally held public debt** doesn't impose a net burden on the country.

The federal debt of the U.S. government is an internally held debt. In fiscal year 1979, 78 percent of the outstanding federal debt was held by the public and 22 percent was held by government agencies.

An internally held debt does impose a *distributional burden* on some elements of society—those that don't hold any of the debt. It distributes income from the community as a whole to the holders of the debt, but because the gains and losses of benefits or satisfaction for different groups can't be added up or compared meaningfully, it's impossible to say that the internally held public debt imposes a net burden on the country.

Even an internally held debt *can* impose a net burden on future generations, however, if the debt finances *current expenditures*—i.e., goods and services that are used up in the current time period. Current expenditures don't confer benefits on future generations, who may be saddled with the debt.

Capital expenditures are on projects that last and provide benefits beyond the current time period. Future generations may bear the burden of a public debt that financed capital expenditures, but they also enjoy important benefits from the capital projects—highways, parks, schools, hospitals, and mass transit systems. The long-term U.S. debt represents almost exclusively debt incurred for capital projects. Most current expenditure projects are financed by current tax revenues or short-term borrowing, and therefore impose no burden on future generations.

Some Normative Aspects of Fiscal Policy

Fiscal policy requires choices—concerning private vs. public spending, the allocation of government spending among alternative programs, and the distribution of the tax burden. Most of these choices involve normative questions that can't be answered by analysis alone.

Spending Priorities

If you ask ten people on the street whether or not the level of government spending should be raised, the majority probably will answer no and may even suggest that it is already too high. However, the majority of your sample probably will feel that at least *some* public services are inadequate. This brings us to the messy question of priorities. With a fixed level of spending, spending more on some programs will require reductions in others.

In the late 1970s, fiscal austerity (at least in the abstract) became very popular politically. This was reflected in the federal budget for fiscal year 1980, which reduced real spending in some areas (mostly social services) and increased real spending for defense. The President was under pressure internationally and domestically to increase defense spending, but he was also under great political pressure to hold down the level of government spending.

Suppose that government spending is either for defense or "arms" (A) or for civilian programs or "butter" (B). The budget sets the level of spending. In Figure 4, the budget of $500 billion can be spent entirely on defense, entirely on civilian programs, or can be allocated between defense and civilian spending along the *budget line A*B**.

Figure 4 Spending Priorities

If the government initially spends $200 billion on arms and $300 billion on civilian programs, military spending can be increased to $240 billion only if civilian programs are cut to $260 billion, or the level of government spending increases to $540 billion. If there is additional pressure to hold down budget deficits, increasing government spending will require tax increases, reducing disposable income which households are free to spend as they wish. Dodging the tax increase and running up the deficit may be inflationary, and inflation taxes all members of the community whose money incomes don't keep up with price increases. There are no free lunches.

Eventually, deciding on priorities involves value judgments. Politicians advocating higher spending for specific programs at the expense of others generally make arguments that imply that the gains from expansion of the programs they advocate are greater than the losses from the programs that have to be cut or the evils of higher taxes. To say that the interests of the community are served best by spending more on defense and less on social programs, more on education and less on space research, or more on highways and less on mass transit involves value judgments on the importance of those who would benefit vs. those who would suffer.

Distributing the Tax Burden: Who Pays?

Having decided on the level of government spending and taxes, there is the question of the types of taxes that will be enacted, and how the tax burden will be distributed among members of the community. Obviously, to argue that some group should bear a larger or smaller share of the total tax burden requires value judgments.

A 10 percent tax on all income from all sources would take the same proportion of every person's income.

- **Proportional taxes** tax all levels of income at the same rate.

Most of the taxes we actually pay are nonproportional taxes that shift the tax burden among members of the community. Some taxes, called *regressive taxes*, shift the tax burden from high to low income groups.

- **Regressive taxes** tax lower incomes at a higher rate than higher incomes are taxed.

Retail sales taxes tend to be regressive. A person with an income of $5000 per year who consumed all of it would pay total sales taxes of 5 percent × $5000 = $250, which represents a full 5 percent of annual income. A person who earned $20,000 per year but consumed only $10,000 per year would pay a total sales tax of 5 percent × $10,000 = $500—only 2.5 percent of the higher total income.

Many local taxes are regressive. Per capita, *head* taxes are the most regressive because they tax every person the same *amount*, regardless of income. *Wage taxes*, or *earned income taxes* are regressive because they tax only wages and salaries and not nonwage income—and higher income households are more likely to earn rent, dividend, and interest income. *Real estate taxes* tend to be regressive, especially in areas where assessments and tax rates rise more rapidly than income.

The Federal Income Tax was a controversial issue when it was enacted in 1912, and has remained so in part because it is a *progressive tax*.

- **Progressive taxes** tax higher incomes at higher rates than lower incomes.

With a progressive tax, the marginal tax rate (the proportion of additional income taxed) increases as income increases. In the federal income tax schedules, single persons are taxed at 14 percent of the first $1000 of taxable income, 16 percent of the next $1000, 18 percent of the next $2000, and so on up to the highest marginal tax rate of 70 percent on all taxable income over $180,000 per year.

Arguments for and against progressive taxes are both positive and normative. One of the positive questions is the effect of rising marginal tax rates on the incentive to work harder to earn more income. Critics of progressive taxes argue that the higher marginal tax rate reduces the incentive to earn higher income because an increasing share or the additional income will be taxed.

The evidence on the effect of progressive taxes on incentives is mixed and inconclusive. Persons have turned down opportunities to earn income that involve more demanding work, but the effect of the marginal tax rate on such decisions is hard to identify and isolate. Many highly paid occupations and positions carry great prestige and satisfaction, and the marginal tax rate probably has little effect on decisions to enter these occupations or accept these positions.

The normative aspect of progressive taxes is the question of the fairness of taxing higher incomes at a higher marginal rate than lower incomes. Some people argue that progressive taxes are unfair because they tax the effort and sacrifice to earn higher incomes at an increasing rate. To the extent that income differentials do reflect differences in effort and sacrifice, progressive taxes tax effort at an increasing rate. However, income differences reflect more than differences in effort and sacrifice. Incomes reflect inherited wealth, talents, access to education, social status, and other factors (including simple luck) that don't involve effort or sacrifice.

Close-up

The 101 Percent Tax

Sweden is well known as a nation of high taxes, but early in 1976, the Swedish government carried the idea of high progressive taxes to new levels of absurdity. In a preelection move to attract working-class voters, Prime Minister Olof Palme shifted the burden of Sweden's cradle-to-grave social programs from individual wage-earners to companies and self-employed individuals. As a result, self-employed taxpayers were forced to pay 101.2 percent of all income above $35,000. In other words, disposable income would steadily *decrease* as pretax income rose above $35,000.

The results of the Swedish tax were hardly surprising. Film director Ingmar Bergman canceled all projects in Sweden. Numerous businesses were forced to shut their doors because the owners could not afford to earn a profit. Many singers, writers, and artists simply refused to produce (or to collect royalties on earlier work), because the royalties they might receive would be less than the tax they would have to pay on those royalties.¹

---

1. See "The 101.2% Solution," *Time*, April 5, 1976.

Is the burden of a progressive tax greater for high-income households than for low-income households? This one isn't as easy as it looks. In terms of percentage of income taxed, of course, a progressive tax obviously places a heavier burden on high-income households. However, there is also a question of the kinds of goods that have to be given up to pay the tax.

Consider two hypothetical households—a subsistence household whose income just allows it to buy basic necessities, and a higher income household whose income is substantially above the subsistence level. *Any* tax paid by the subsistence household will force it to reduce its consumption of necessities. However, the high-income household's disposable income after paying its tax will still be well above the subsistence level, and the higher marginal tax rate won't force the high-income household to reduce its consumption of basic necessities.

Loopholes and Tax Reform

A number of wealthy persons and large corporations pay very low percentages of their income as taxes or pay no income taxes at all, due to special tax treatments or *loopholes* in the income tax laws. Interest income from municipal bonds, for example, is not taxed, in order to allow state and local governments to borrow at lower interest rates. The major beneficiaries (in addition to the municipalities) are the very wealthy who have large sums of money to put into the bonds and are in the highest marginal tax rate brackets. Persons with modest incomes don't realize great tax savings from municipal bonds because they don't make large bond purchases, and because their marginal tax rates are lower. In the 20 percent marginal tax rate bracket, a 5 percent municipal bond pays the equivalent of a 6 percent return per year (interest plus tax saving). In the 50 percent tax bracket, the same 5 percent tax-free bond pays the equivalent of a 7.5 percent rate of return per year.

Not all loopholes benefit only the very rich. For example, federal income tax law allows the deduction of state and local taxes and interest payments from gross income in figuring taxable income. This subsidizes everybody who is paying for a home, because mortgage interest and real estate taxes are deductible. Renters can't make this deduction, even though they pay a share of their landlords' interest and property taxes in their monthly rents. However, even this loophole gives the greatest tax savings to persons in high tax brackets because they generally have more expensive property and the tax savings per dollar of interest and property tax paid are greater because of the higher marginal tax rate.

There is much to be said for reforms that simplify the tax system. On the side of equity, a simpler tax system with fewer (or no) loopholes would result in different families with the same income and dependents paying the same tax. A simpler system would allow lower and more meaningful tax rates. At present the high marginal tax rates on high incomes don't indicate the true tax burden, because they apply to taxable income. There is no question that simplified tax rules would make the existing income tax more progressive.

Promises and proposals for tax reform and closing tax loopholes have become part of the standard American political rhetoric, but really significant simplification of the tax system or large-scale closing of loopholes has yet to materialize. Every special interest tries to protect its own "tax incentives" while calling for elimination of somebody else's "loophole." Also, there are costs involved in elimination of loopholes. Eliminating tax-free interest on state and local bonds, for example, would require states and localities to pay higher interest on their obligations. The final solution of the "tax mess" requires analysis of the costs and benefits of the reforms and intelligent value judgements on equity and fairness of the tax system.

Practical and Political Problems

Fiscal policies aren't decided by economists and models, but by a political process in a very imperfect real world. In addition to all of the analytical and normative questions, there are some significant political and practical considerations.

Political Appeal

To be effective, discretionary fiscal policies have to be flexible. However, the flexibility of fiscal policy is limited by the necessity of coming up with policies that have broad political support. Unfortunately, the political mood and economic expectations of the electorate aren't always in tune with economic reality. Elected officials (like the rest of us) don't wish to be unemployed, so many fiscal policies tend to reflect political realities more than economic realities.

Fiscal policy is like a lever with a ratchet that makes it easy to turn in one direction, but difficult or impossible to reverse. Programs that are initiated or expanded as part of an expansionary fiscal policy develop constituencies that make it difficult to cut them in periods of fiscal restraint. It's easy politically to cut taxes to stimulate demand, but much harder to raise them to fight inflation.

The passage of "Proposition 13" in California in 1978 made fiscal austerity (reduced government spending and reduced taxes) politically popular because many people don't associate severe cuts in government spending with reductions in public services, or at least cuts in the programs that benefit them. Middle and upper income families may support cuts in welfare payments, but not in police and fire protection. Defense contractors may support reduced spending for environmental programs, but not defense. Environmentalists may support cuts in defense, but not in environmental programs. Social Security recipients may support cuts in highways, but not in Social Security benefits.

Time Lags and Information

Time and information are two practical difficulties in using fiscal policy to regulate aggregate demand to minimize unemployment and inflationary pressure. With inadequate information on the effects of changes in fiscal policy, and economic forecasting a highly imperfect art, fiscal policies may do too much or too little to achieve their objectives. Overstimulation of the economy to promote full employment will lead to excessive inflationary pressures; inadequate stimulation won't achieve the objective of full employment. Excessive fiscal restraint to reduce inflationary pressures will probably result in an unacceptably high unemployment rate.

Time lags also limit the success of discretionary fiscal policies. Economic theorists have defined two basic types of lag:

- The **inside lag** is the time that passes before policymakers take action.
- The **outside lag** is the time it takes for a policy to have its effect on the economy.

The inside lag itself has also been divided into three lags:

- The **recognition lag** is the period of time between the actual beginning of a problem and policymakers' recognition that the problem exists. This lag may be lengthened if policymakers for political reasons refuse to admit that there is a problem.
- The **decision lag** includes both the time it takes for policymakers to decide what policy action is needed, and the time needed for legislators to approve that policy.
- The **action lag** is the time it takes for the approved policy action to be put into effect.

Irregular and unpredictable time lags between the enactment of policies and their effects is one dimension of the overall problem of inadequate information which limits the effectiveness of policies and enhances the chance of error. We simply don't have all of the necessary information to predict the exact effects of fiscal policies or the timing of these effects, which would enable policymakers to hit specific targets for unemployment and inflation. By the time the policies actually affect aggregate demand, economic conditions may have changed, and the policies may end up worsening problems of unemployment and inflation.

Applying the Tools

The 1964 Tax Cut

John F. Kennedy's campaign for the presidency in 1960 hit hard on the Republicans' apparent inability to reduce the unemployment rate and "get the economy moving." During his campaign and after he took office, Kennedy's official and unofficial economic advisers included such prominent Keynesian economists as Professor Paul A. Samuelson and Walter Heller. Keynesian economics became the *New Economics* of the 1960s, even though it had been a generation since the publication of the *General Theory*.

For a year after taking office, the President followed a relatively orthodox, non-Keynesian, course in economic policy. The 1960 election was the closest in recent history, and Kennedy was sensitive to criticisms of fiscal irresponsibility. Although his advisers had called for an active expansionary fiscal policy in 1960, the Kennedy administration didn't pursue active expansionary fiscal policies until the summer of 1962. This was due to a combination of political prudence and recognition and decision lags on the part of the administration concerning the proper course for fiscal policy. From January of 1961 until June of 1962, there was mild fiscal expansion as military spending increased without increased taxes.

In the summer of 1962, Kennedy turned to more clearly expansionary fiscal policies that centered on reducing taxes. Investment tax credits and accelerated depreciation encouraged greater levels of investment to stimulate aggregate demand. In January of 1963, the administration pushed for substantial permanent cuts in personal income tax rates to increase disposable income and consumption expenditures.

Congressional reaction to the proposed tax cuts ranged from lukewarm to hostile, and the familiar criticism of fiscal irresponsibility emerged in the debate over the tax cut. The President went beyond Congress to appeal directly to the public for support for the tax cut, but at the time of his death in the fall of 1963, the tax cut still hadn't been enacted. The tax cut finally was enacted with the passage of the Revenue Act of 1964 in February 1964—three years after Kennedy's inauguration and over a year after his first proposal for tax cuts. The *action lag* between proposal and enactment of the tax cut legislation in this case had exceeded one year.

There was still an additional lag—the *outside lag* between enactment of the tax cut legislation and the effects of the tax cuts on aggregate demand and employment. For about three months, the tax cut had no noticeable effect. The short-term effects appeared over a six-month period following their enactment. By the third quarter of 1964, the short-term effect of the tax cut was an increase of GNP of about $1.50 per $1 of tax reduction. By the middle of 1965, this exceeded $2.50 of additional GNP per $1 of tax reduction. The middle of 1965 was a year and a half after the enactment of the legislation and nearly three years after Kennedy had proposed the cuts.[1]

---

1. Facts on the tax cut are from Rudiger Dornbusch and Stanley Fischer, *Macroeconomics*. New York: McGraw-Hill, 1978, Chapter 10.

In the period between Kennedy's inauguration and the full effect of the tax cut, economic conditions had changed. An economic recovery which had been under way in 1960 continued. The escalation of the Vietnam War after 1965 stimulated aggregate demand further as government military spending increased. On top of this, the Johnson administration expanded the number and scope of federal social programs under the banner of the Great Society. The following table summarizes the chronology of the tax cut program and the unemployment rate at each critical point. By the end of 1965, the expansionary effects of the tax cut, the Vietnam War, and the Great Society programs had driven the unemployment rate low enough that there were significant demand-pull inflationary pressures. In other words, by the time the stimulating effects of the tax cut were fully felt, the economy no longer needed stimulation.

	Year/Quarter	Unemployment Rate
Kennedy inaugurated	1961/I	6.8%
Decision to cut taxes	1962/I	5.6%
Tax cut passed	1964/II	5.2%
Tax cut effects	1965/IV	4.1%

Source: Unemployment data from U.S. Department of Commerce.

Summary

1. Fiscal policies are those dealing with government spending and taxes. **Discretionary fiscal policies** are aimed at regulating aggregate demand and GNP to minimize unemployment and inflationary pressures in the economy.
2. Aggregate demand and GNP vary directly with government spending and inversely with taxes. Generally, changes in government spending will affect GNP more than equal changes in taxes.
3. The choice between government spending and taxes depends in part on political ideology. Modern conservatives tend to prefer tax cuts to increased government spending as a means of stimulating aggregate demand, and spending cuts to dampen aggregate demand. Modern political liberals tend to prefer increased spending and expanded programs to stimulate demand and tax increases to dampen it.
4. Stimulating or dampening aggregate demand may require deficits or surpluses in the government's budget. The **full-employment budget** estimates taxes and spending if the economy were operating at full employment.
5. Deficits and surpluses affect the public debt. An **internally held public debt** which finances capital projects imposes no net burden on the community, but may impose a distributional burden on some members of the community.
6. With a **balanced-budget multiplier effect,** equal changes in government spending and taxes may change equilibrium GNP without creating or changing the national debt.
7. Fiscal policies generally require choices and value judgments that can't be evaluated analytically. Among the more important choices that must be made are the choice of priorities in government spending and the distribution of the tax burden.

8. The effectiveness and flexibility of discretionary fiscal policies are limited by **time lags** in the formulation and impact of fiscal policies, inadequacies in information, and the necessity of formulating policies with broad political appeal.

Concepts for Review

discretionary fiscal policy
cyclically balanced budget
full-employment budget
balanced-budget multiplier
national debt

externally held public debt
internally held public debt
proportional tax
regressive tax
progressive tax

inside lag
outside lag
recognition lag
decision lag
action lag

Questions

1. Explain the meaning of the term *discretionary fiscal policy*. Are all fiscal policies *discretionary*? Explain.
2. What are some of the considerations that would enter into a choice between changes in taxes and changes in government spending as a means of regulating aggregate demand?
3. Many state constitutions require that the state budget be balanced—receipts equal to expenditures. Does this make sense for a state government? Would the merits of requiring balanced state budgets apply to arguments that a constitutional amendment should be ratified which requires an annually balanced federal budget?
4. Emma I. Rich has willed her entire estate to the federal government to be applied to the federal debt to lighten the burden of the debt on the citizens instead of leaving her fortune to her spendthrift heirs. Evaluate the wisdom of this act.
5. In the 1976 presidential campaign, candidate Jimmy Carter promised to try to fight unemployment, fight inflation, and balance the federal budget by 1981. In his January, 1979, Budget Message, President Carter stated that the budget for the 1980 fiscal year ". . . meets my commitment to a deficit of $30 billion or less."

    Is the targeted deficit in the budget for fiscal year 1980 inconsistent with his promise to balance the budget? What are some of the implications of drawing up a budget around a long-term commitment to a balanced budget and an immediate commitment to keeping the deficit below some targeted maximum?
6. Some economists use the enormous federal debt incurred during World War II as an example of a public debt that imposes a net burden on future generations. Evaluate the validity of this argument.
7. Explain how each of the following would affect the progressivity of federal taxes.
    a. the imposition of a value added tax, or a national sales tax;
    b. imposing a value added tax in order to reduce income tax rates;
    c. elimination of the tax-exempt status of municipal bonds;
    d. elimination of all itemized income tax deductions, and substituting a standard deduction of 20 percent of all income;
    e. allowing tuition tax credits for college, secondary, and elementary school tuition.

Problems

1. The following data represent aggregate expenditure flows for the economy of Farcelonia (all figures are billions of Farcical dollars).

   Consumption: $C = 100 + 0.8\ (Y\text{-}T)$
   Intended Investment: $I = 50$
   Government Purchases: $G = 50$
   Taxes: $T = 40$

   a. The best estimate of the Farcical Council of Economic Advisors is that full employment would be reached at a GNP of $1000 billion. Should the government pursue an expansionary fiscal course to stimulate aggregate demand or a restrictive course to dampen inflationary pressure? Explain.
   b. What change in government spending would be necessary to move equilibrium GNP to the full-employment level?
   c. What change in taxes would move equilibrium GNP to the full employment level? How do you explain the difference between this answer and the answer to part b?
   d. Could the government achieve full employment by equal changes in government spending and taxes? If so, what change in government spending and taxes would be required?

2. The relationship between taxes and GNP in Utopia is $T = 20 + 0.2Y$. Government spending is $\underline{G} = 100$.
   a. If equilibrium GNP is $\overline{Y} = 300$, will the actual budget be balanced, show a deficit, or show a surplus?
   b. At what level of GNP will the actual budget be balanced?
   c. If full employment is reached at $Y^* = 500$, does the full-employment Utopian budget show a full-employment deficit or surplus? What does this mean?

3. In problems 1 and 2 at the end of the previous chapter, calculate the size of the inflationary or deflationary gaps.

PART NINE

Aggregate Demand: The Money Market

The chapters in this section bring money into our analysis of aggregate demand. Money is important to us as individuals, of course, but its importance to the economy as a whole is much greater. Without money, economic specialization and indeed modern civilization itself would be impossible. Further, money plays a critical role in determining the level of aggregate demand and is thus the basis of an important set of demand-management tools—**monetary policy**.

Like the product markets described in Chapter 3, the money market is one in which demand and supply interact to achieve an equilibrium. In the first chapter of this section, we'll examine the demand side of the money market by asking why people want to hold money (as opposed to, say, real estate or gold) and how much money they want to hold. The answers to those questions will allow us to construct a **demand curve for money** and to show how equilibrium in the money market affects aggregate demand in the goods market. In the next chapter, we'll look at how the banking system determines the **supply of money** in the economy, and how the money supply influences aggregate output and prices. Finally, we'll examine a variety of issues surrounding the government's use of its power over the money supply as a policy tool for "managing" aggregate demand.

25

Money: What It Is and What It Does

Preview: Money is only one of a variety of possible forms in which people can hold their wealth. In this chapter, we'll explore why people want to hold money. We'll begin by looking briefly at the history of money to see how its role in most modern economies has evolved over time. We'll then focus on the **demand for money** and examine how the interaction between the demand and supply of money in the money market affects aggregate demand and output in the goods market.

Few people need formal training in economics to recognize that money is important. An individual's economic welfare depends largely on his or her purchasing power, which in turn depends on his or her money and real income. The importance of money to individuals is so obvious that it tends to obscure the role of money and monetary policies in the determination of aggregate demand, aggregate output, and the seriousness of the problems of unemployment and inflation. Money and monetary issues have attracted the attention of the greatest economists, as well as the attention of an unusually large number of quacks.

A Brief History of Money

The origins of the use of money go back to the beginnings of economic specialization, exchange, and organized markets. In many primitive and feudal societies, households or small communities were self-sufficient, and the exchange that did take place was *barter exchange*.

- In **barter exchanges**, goods and services exchange directly for other goods and services.

As market economies developed, competition and exchange led to greater economic specialization, and greater specialization required the use of some form of money. By facilitating exchange, the use of money widened producers' markets, and encouraged greater specialization and efficiency than would be possible in a barter system.

If people specialize in producing the things they produce best, this increases the efficiency in the use of the economy's resources. However, the degree of specialization is severely limited in barter economies because of the difficulties of making exchanges. Suppose, for example, that you are a very good pig farmer. In a barter economy, if you needed cloth, you would have to find another person who had cloth to offer in exchange *and* would be willing to accept pigs in exchange. To guard against the possibility of not finding such a person, you'd have to provide your minimal needs of cloth by producing it yourself—i.e., divert some of your time and resources from raising pigs (which you do well) to producing cloth (which you might not do so well).

In a money economy, however, to exchange your pigs for cloth and other goods you need, all you have to do is find somebody who will exchange money for your pigs (whether or not he or she has cloth to offer in exchange). The money from the sale of the pigs could then be used to purchase the cloth and other goods you need from persons who may or may not want to buy pigs. This reduces the possibility that you would be deprived of some of the things you need if you specialized in pig production, and you would be more likely to specialize. If everybody specialized in producing the things he or she produced best and exchanged for other goods, this would make more efficient use of the economy's resources.

Commodity Money

The earliest money was **commodity money**—physical goods with the basic characteristics of money. The most common money commodities were precious metals, particularly gold and silver. These metals have been widely acceptable in exchange since ancient times. They are relatively durable, easily divisible into small units, and (despite the efforts of alchemists and mad scientists) impossible to reproduce.

With commodity money, the *value of money* is determined by the supply of and demand for the money commodity, just like the value of any other scarce commodity. The money prices of other goods and services reflect the relative prices of the goods and the money commodity. The *money price* of a pound of meat, for example, is the amount of money that has to be given up to get it. Changes in the scarcity of the money commodity relative to other goods and services appear as changes in the money prices of the other goods and services.

Close-up

The Price Revolution in Europe

After a long period of economic stability in the late medieval period, there was a rapid inflow of gold into Europe at the end of the fifteenth century as a result of Spanish discoveries in the New World. Some of the gold was brought by the Spanish, and some was brought by pirates who stole it from the Spanish.

Gold was commodity money in Europe, and the rapid influx of gold drove the price of gold downward relative to the prices of other goods. Since gold was less scarce relative to other goods, more gold had to be offered in exchange for goods, and the gold (money) prices of goods rose dramatically.

In a commodity money system, gold or silver currency or coin simply specified and guaranteed the quantity and quality of the gold or silver contained in the coin. In fact, in the British system, the denominations *pound* and *shilling* were originally measures of weight. Exchanging coins was more convenient than assaying and weighing gold and silver each time a purchase was made, but some problems emerged. Devious and enterprising persons would "clip" or shave the edges of coins and sell the gold or silver shavings. Most people can't tell the exact weight of a coin by feel, so the clipped coins could be exchanged at their full face value. Finely serrated edges on coins made it easier to tell whether or not a coin had been clipped. On a larger scale, governments often *debased* or adulterated their currency by reducing the weight of the gold in the coins or mixing other metals (such as lead) with the gold in the coins.

The practices of clipping coins, counterfeiting, and debasement encouraged people to hoard their gold coins (*good* money) or to use it for international purchases, and to use only the debased or adulterated coins (*bad* money) domestically. Several hundred years after this had become a familiar phenomenon, it was given a name—*Gresham's Law*.

- **Gresham's Law** states that *bad* money drives out *good*.

The Gold Standard

Initially, paper currency was fully backed by the money commodity (gold or silver). A piece of **fully backed currency** was a coupon which entitled the holder to a specified quantity of gold or silver. Before 1933, for example, U.S. Gold Certificates would be exchanged by the government for gold coin. Until the late 1960s, Silver Certificates were convertible to silver dollars or metallic silver by the government.

Paper money that was fully backed by gold or silver was, in fact, commodity money. This arrangement is commonly called the *gold standard*—or more generally the *commodity standard*.

- With a **gold standard**, the quantity of currency in circulation is tied to the quantity of gold held by the government.

Paper money is more convenient than gold coins, and the use of paper money kept much of the gold coin out of circulation. This reduced the loss of gold through wear and abrasion of coins in circulation.

Not all backed currency was fully backed by gold or another money commodity. The quantity of **partially backed currency** is limited to a multiple of the value of the gold held by the government. Until the late 1960s, for example, the maximum amount of U.S. currency that could be issued was limited to a rather large multiple of the value of U.S. government gold reserves. This wasn't a true commodity money system, since the currency wasn't converted by the government to gold, but it was designed to limit the discretionary power of the government over the quantity of currency issued.

By the late 1960s, however, the U.S. gold reserve had become so small that it threatened to constrain the money supply, so the last tie between the gold reserves and the quantity of currency issued was severed. Today, U.S. currency isn't backed by any commodity.

Fiat Money

U.S. currency is *fiat money*.

- **Fiat money** is money simply because the law (fiat) says it's money.

Just about every dollar bill in circulation today is a Federal Reserve Note. The government will not redeem a dollar bill for anything except other denominations of currency.

The value of fiat money, like the value of commodity money, is determined by its purchasing power over goods and services. The value of a dollar is the quantity of goods and services that can be purchased with a dollar. However, unlike commodity money, the value of fiat money doesn't depend on the value of any commodity.

Some people attribute every historical catastrophe since the fall of Rome to the abandonment of commodity money or the gold standard. Others are upset because a fiat money system removes a restraint on the power of the government to issue currency. Those who distrust the competence or intentions of government monetary authorities tend to be the most leary of fiat money.

Generally, however, people aren't terribly concerned about fiat money as long as their money is acceptable in exchange for goods and services or there isn't a complete economic and social collapse. If any readers of this book feel that their fiat money is worthless because it isn't backed by gold or silver, the author would be happy to take it off their hands.

The Basic Functions of Money

Money has two basic economic functions. It serves as a *unit of account and exchange*, and as a *store of value*. In fact, money can be defined in terms of these basic functions.

- **Money** is anything that serves as a **unit of account and exchange** and as a **store of value.**

Unit of Account and Exchange

As a *unit of account* or unit of value, money makes it possible to quantify costs, revenue, profits, and national income. Monetary values are common denominators that allow the addition of different goods, services, and resources. Oranges, apples, bobby pins, locomotives, hours of labor, etc., can't be added together without first expressing them as monetary values.

To perform its accounting and exchange function, money must have several basic characteristics. It must be *generally acceptable in exchange*, and it must be *divisible into small units*. If few people accepted money, it couldn't serve its exchange function. If it weren't divisible into small units, it couldn't be an accurate measure of value, nor could it ensure exchange of equal values.

In addition, money must be *scarce* and *difficult or impossible to reproduce*. If money weren't scarce or could be produced easily by individuals, it would not be a meaningful unit of value in exchange.

Store of Value

Generally, one's needs for goods and services don't coincide with the receipt of his or her money income. Money allows households and firms to "store" the values of the goods, services, and productive resources they sell. Obviously, to serve as a *store of value*, money must be relatively durable.

Storing the value of one's goods and services is cumbersome or impossible without money. It's much easier to store the value of a wheat crop by holding the money received from its sale than to store the wheat. The values of highly perishable goods can't be stored for more than a few days without money. The value of services (haircuts, for example) can't be stored at all without the use of money.

Defining Money Aggregates

Money, we have seen, can be just about anything that performs the basic functions of money. When examining the role of money in the aggregate economy, however, it is necessary to use somewhat narrower definitions of *money*.

- **Money aggregates** are formal definitions of money used for studying the influence of money in the economy.

Money aggregates are used in particular when studying the *supply of money* or the *demand for money* in an economy.

Most of us identify money as *currency*, and an increase in the supply of money is seen in our minds' eye as a change in the amount of currency in circulation—an image that is reinforced by the common phrase *printing money* to refer to an increase in the money supply. All money aggregates include currency in their definitions of money, but other things are also included. The dividing line between things that are considered money and those that aren't is drawn on the basis of the ability to be substituted for each other as money.

The Strict Definition

Demand deposits, or checking accounts, are nearly perfect substitutes for currency as money. Checks are generally acceptable in exchange, and can be written for just about any amount. Because demand deposits and currency are close substitutes as money, they are included in even the narrowest definition of money.

- The **strict definition of money** is currency plus demand deposits.

For years, monetary authorities and most economists adopted the strict definition as the relevant definition of the money supply. This definition excludes **time deposits**, or savings accounts, from the definition of money. The basic argument for excluding time deposits has been that time deposits aren't very close substitutes for currency and demand deposits as money. Until recently, persons couldn't write checks authorizing someone else to withdraw funds from a savings account. Some time deposits reserve the bank's right to require advance notice for withdrawals, and some time deposits require that funds remain on deposit for a minimum period of time from 90 days to several years. In short, time deposits generally are less *liquid* than currency or demand deposits—which is one of the reasons that they earn interest.

Recent dramatic changes in banking regulations and practices have caused monetary authorities to reexamine the traditional exclusion of time deposits from the definition of money. New types of savings accounts—Negotiated Order of Withdrawal (or *NOW*) accounts and Automatic Funds Transfer (AFT) accounts—transfer funds automatically from savings to checking accounts. Many banks will transfer funds from savings to checking accounts via depositors' telephone orders. Some savings and loan associations even have checkable savings accounts.

Broader Definitions of Money

The strict definition is, in fact, only one of five official definitions of the money supply. We need to concern ourselves with only three of these definitions.

M_1 (the strict definition) = currency plus demand deposits
$M_2 = M_1$ plus savings and time deposits in commercial banks
$M_3 = M_2$ plus savings and time deposits in nonbank thrift institutions

Because of the changes in banking practices and regulations that make some time deposits close substitutes for currency and demand deposits as money, the definition of M_1 is being altered, and the Federal Reserve has started publishing yet another money aggregate, M_1+

$M_1+ = M_1$ plus savings deposits at commercial banks and checkable deposits at nonbank thrift institutions.

Although all of the money aggregates show a similar pattern of growth over time in Figure 1, the strict supply of money has grown more slowly than the money supply more broadly defined.

Monetary authorities still generally consider M_1 (or M_1+) as the relevant definition of the money supply, but for some monetary policy questions, M_2 or M_3 may be the relevant definition. For example, the funds available for residential mortgages depend heavily on time deposits in commercial banks and savings and loan associations.

The specific monetary aggregate that we define as money isn't crucial for a basic understanding of the relationships between money and the price level and between money and real GNP. To keep the analysis simple, the term *money* in the following chapters will refer to M_1 unless noted otherwise.

Near Monies

Near monies are things with stable monetary values that are easily convertible into money at their full value. Government securities are an example of a near money. There is little risk of loss in holding government securities, and they can be sold for cash easily. Some government securities are *negotiable* and can be assigned from one person to another. However, government securities aren't close enough as substitutes or demand deposits to include them in the definition of money.

Economic uncertainty and inflation in the middle and late 1970s caused many people to turn their attention to gold as a store of value and a hedge against inflation. "Good as gold" is a common phrase, but one never describes something as "good as a Federal Reserve Note" or "good as a personal check." Yet, gold isn't included in any official definition of money. Gold is simply a commodity. In periods of inflation and uncertainty, its value tends to rise as people seek to hold gold rather than money or financial securities. Despite the gold mystique, most heavily promoted by sellers of gold, the value of gold has fluctuated significantly since 1974.

Figure 1 Changes in the Money Supply

Close-up

Are Credit Cards Money?

The credit card has become a familiar fixture in household finances. The use of credit cards has grown dramatically in the past twenty years, and some people even refer to them as "plastic money." One of the large bank credit card companies even tells its card holders to treat the card "like money."

However, credit cards are not money. When a person makes a purchase with a credit card, he or she simply agrees to pay for the purchase in the future, and to pay a substantial rate of interest (typically 18% per year). Like other forms of credit, credit card purchases are a loan to the consumer, and these loans are paid for with money (currency or check).

Credit and credit cards are substitutes for money, rather than a component of the money supply.

Basic Motives for Holding Money

The amount of money demanded for the economy as a whole is the sum of the quantities demanded by individual households, firms, and financial institutions. Households, firms, and financial institutions demand money for three basic reasons—to make transactions, to prepare for unexpected contingencies, and to protect against losses.

Households and firms have to hold some money to make transactions that require money payments—either in currency or by check. The amount of money that must be held for these transactions represents the **transactions demand** for money. The transactions demand for money is determined largely by institutional features of the economy—means of making payments, the availability of credit, etc.

The **precautionary demand for money** stems from uncertainty about the future. Except for a few self-styled clairvoyants, nobody knows when future needs for money will arise. Households and firms hold some money to take care of the unforeseen contingencies that may arise in the future. During periods of economic uncertainty and pessimism, the precautionary demand for money tends to increase.

The **speculative demand for money** also stems from economic uncertainty: the probability of incurring an economic loss by holding money compared with the probability of loss by holding stocks, bonds, and other assets. In periods when the risk of incurring such losses is high, the speculative demand for money tends to be high.

Although we are examining the demand for money, it should be clear that holders of money are interested in their *real balances*—the amount of transactions, precautionary, and speculative benefits that can be purchased with the money. The ability of money balances to purchase these benefits depends, in turn, on the level of prices.

- **Real balances** are money balances divided by the price index.

For example, $1000 in cash and demand deposits would represent a real balance of $1000 if the price index is 1.0.

$$\text{Real balance} = \frac{\text{Money balance}}{\text{Price index}} = \frac{M}{P} \quad (1)$$

$$= \frac{\$1000}{1.0} = \$1000.$$

If the price index rose to 1.25, the same $1000 represents a real balance of

$$\frac{M}{P} = \frac{\$1000}{1.25} = \$800.$$

For now, we'll assume that the price level doesn't change, so that changes in money balances represent equal changes in real balances.

Money thus offers households, firms, and financial institutions important benefits—the ability to make transactions, to meet future needs, and to minimize economic losses. Why, then, don't individuals simply hold their entire wealth as money? Why not simply fill the mattress with cash and enjoy the benefits? To understand the demand for money, particularly the precautionary and speculative demands, we have to take a closer look at money as an asset and the factors that contribute to choices to hold money and other assets.

Choice of Assets and the Demand for Money

Households, firms, and financial institutions hold their wealth in the form of assets. Money is one of these assets, but not the only one. Individual owners of wealth may decide to hold their wealth in real estate, in corporate bonds, in government securities, in savings accounts, in common stocks, and in many other types of assets in addition to money. Owners of wealth will try to hold the assortment of assets, or **portfolio of assets**, that strikes the best balance among liquidity, rate of return, and risk. Differences in individual circumstances among owners of assets—age, income, willingness to take risks, size of family, etc.—affect individual decisions on the best portfolio of assets. The demand for money depends heavily on the choices of individuals concerning the amount of money to hold in their portfolios.

Liquidity, Risk, and Rate of Return

Liquid assets are assets that can be converted easily into other assets. Money and negotiable securities are very liquid assets that can be converted easily into other assets at virtually no cost. Most owners of wealth will try to achieve some level of **liquidity**, or flexibility, in their asset portfolios. If a household held all of its wealth in real estate (the least liquid of assets), for example, it would be difficult to adjust to changing economic conditions by converting the real estate into other assets—i.e., selling the real estate and using the proceeds to purchase other assets.

Assets that involve a loss of liquidity, other things equal, aren't as desirable as more liquid assets. For example, few people would purchase a one-year certificate of deposit if the interest rate were the same as on passbook savings that can be withdrawn at any time without any interest penalty. To induce people to give up liquidity, then, banks have to pay a higher rate of return on funds that reduce the depositors' liquidity, and this rate of return is higher the longer the term that the money must remain on deposit.

- Other things equal, there is an inverse relationship between the liquidity of assets and the rate of return. The less liquid the asset, the higher the rate of return necessary to induce people to hold it.

Many assets also involve some risk of losing the value of the asset. Common stocks, for example, may depreciate in value after they are purchased, in which case the stockholder suffers a loss of the money value of his or her stock. Few people would accept the same rate of return for owning an asset that involved a low level of risk and another that involved a high risk of loss. Anybody who has gambled knows that high odds are necessary to induce people to bet long shots. Those who bet long shots and win do very well—for example, those who bet on Mohammed Ali (then Cassius Clay) in his first fight against Sonny Liston or who bet on Leon Spinks in his first fight against Ali. However, few successful gamblers bet only long shots because the risk of losing is so great.

- Other things equal, the rate of return on assets varies directly with the risk of loss from holding the asset.

There is a way to avoid risk—simply hold nothing but safe assets with a very small risk of loss. The catch is that these assets offer low rates of return. In inflationary periods, the rate of return on very safe assets may not even keep pace with prices.

Very few owners of assets hold portfolios that achieve the highest possible safety and liquidity, but earn the lowest possible rate of return. Similarly, very few maximize the rate of return on their assets by holding only assets that involve the maximum degree of risk and the minimum liquidity.

- Generally, owners of assets will choose portfolios of assets to achieve some combination of liquidity, safety, and rate of return.

Money as an Asset

Money would be a part of just about any portfolio of assets. The only exceptions would be for asset owners for whom liquidity and safety are unimportant. Money is the most liquid of assets. It can be converted into other assets instantly and at no cost. Holding money offers asset owners liquidity or flexibility to adjust to future needs and to future changes in economic conditions.

Money is also a safe asset, in the sense that the risk of losing the face value of money is nonexistent. Holding $1000 in currency and demand deposits involves no risk that this would be worth less money in the future. The same can't be said for a $1000 corporate bond or $1000 worth of common stock. With these assets, there is a risk of losing the face value of the assets. The corporation could go bankrupt, in which case it would pay off only a percentage of its bonds and other debts, and the stock of a bankrupt corporation is virtually worthless. The price of the bond or the common stock could fall in financial markets, in which case the assets couldn't be redeemed for their full face value.

Since money is the most liquid asset, and the asset with the minimum risk of loss of its face value, holding money involves no loss of liquidity and no risk of loss. Therefore, no return is required to induce people and institutions to hold money (currency and demand deposits). As a reasonable approximation of reality, then, money can be treated as an asset that is completely liquid, completely safe, and earns no interest. Remember that we're still looking at a world in which the price level is constant—rising prices would cause a loss of *real balances* from holding money.

With stable prices, the way to maximize liquidity and safety would be to hold all assets as money. However, money earns no interest. The benefits of liquidity and safety from holding money have a cost—namely, the interest that could be earned in alternative uses that involve no risk. At low interest rates, the opportunity cost of holding money is low, and households and businesses tend to hold relatively large amounts of money in their portfolios. For example, holding $10,000 as money for one year costs $500 if the interest rate is 5%. If the individual decides that it is worth $500 to hold $10,000 for one year, he will do so. However, if the interest rate increases to 8%, the cost of holding $10,000 for one year increases to $800, and the individual will reduce his holdings of money due to the higher cost, as shown in Figure 2a.

- The quantity of money demanded varies inversely with changes in the interest rate, other things constant.

Figure 2 The Demand Curve for Money

For the economy, the quantity of money demanded at a given interest rate, other things equal, is the economy's **liquidity preference**, or **demand for money**. In Figure 2b, the inverse relationship between the interest rate and the quantity of money demanded is shown by the negatively sloped **liquidity preference function** (L), which is the economy's **demand curve for money**.

Among the variables assumed constant for a given demand curve for money are the price level, aggregate output (or real GNP), nominal GNP (or money GNP), and expectations. Changes in any of these exogenous variables will cause the demand for money to change at any interest rate, and will shift the demand curve for money.

Changes in the Demand for Money

The demand for money will change, and the demand curve for money will shift, if *nominal* GNP changes. Nominal GNP (Y_n) is simply aggregate output (Y) evaluated in current prices (P), or

$$Y_n = P Y. \quad (2)$$

At any level of nominal GNP, firms and households will demand sufficient money to make transactions. The money demanded at any given level of nominal GNP will be a fraction or proportion (m) of the nominal GNP. The demand for money won't equal nominal GNP because money is spent more than once. Algebraically, the demand for money at any level of nominal GNP is

$$L = mPY. \quad (3)$$

From this equation, the demand for money at any interest rate would vary directly with the price level (P), the aggregate output (Y), and nominal GNP (PY). For example, if $m = 0.5$ and nominal GNP = \$2 trillion, the demand for money would be

$$L = mPY = 0.5 \times \$2 \text{ trillion} = \$1 \text{ trillion}.$$

If the price level doubled to $P' = 2P$, the demand for money with the same aggregate output (Y) would be

$$L' = mP'Y = 0.5 \times 2P \times Y = 0.5 \times \$4 \text{ trillion}$$
$$= \$2 \text{ trillion}.$$

Similarly, if aggregate output doubled to $Y' = 2Y$ at a constant price level (P), the demand for money would be

$$L' = mPY' = 0.5 \times 2 \times \$2 \text{ trillion} = 0.5 \times \$4 \text{ trillion}$$
$$= \$2 \text{ trillion}.$$

The effect of an increase in nominal GNP (through changes in the price level and in aggregate output) is shown graphically in Figure 3 by a shift of the demand curve for money to the right from L to L'. It should be obvious that declines in nominal GNP would cause the

Figure 3 Change in the Demand for Money

demand for money at any interest rate to fall and the demand curve for money to shift to the left.

Changes in the value of m can change the demand for money at any interest rate. The value of m, in turn, reflects a number of variables.

First of all, the institutional features of the economy that determine the efficiency of money in exchange affect the value of m. For example, if the established practice was for people to be paid their yearly salary once each year (on January 1), people would have to hold large average balances of money (probably in checking accounts) to make transactions over the course of the year. When people are paid monthly, the average amount of money they have to hold to make transactions over the course of the year is much less.

The efficiency of money and the value of m are affected by the ways that payment is made for purchases. In a cash-only society, in which all purchases had to be paid for in cash or check, everybody would have to hold relatively large amounts of currency and maintain large checking account balances to make their purchases. However, the availability of credit for making purchases reduces the amount of money that persons have to hold in order to make their purchases.

The value of m and the demand for money are also affected by economic expectations. If there is widespread economic uncertainty and pessimism, households and institutions may want to hold greater precautionary and speculative balances to provide for future contingencies and to reduce the risk of loss by holding more money. In periods of optimism when the risk from holding assets other than money is low, the owners of wealth will shift some of their assets out of money into other assets, and the demand for money will drop.

The institutional variables that affect the demand for money—such as the frequency of wage and salary payments and the system of making purchases and payments—are relatively stable, and change rather gradually over time. However, unstable expectations can create instability in the demand for money that has serious implications for the stability of aggregate output and employment in the goods sector of the economy and for the success of attempts to regulate aggregate demand through the monetary sector.

Equilibrium in the Money Market

Equilibrium in money markets has important implications for equilibrium aggregate output and employment in the goods sector. In fact, all of the analysis of equilibrium output and employment in the previous section of the text assumed equilibrium in the monetary sector. If money markets aren't in equilibrium, the goods sector won't be in equilibrium either, and disturbances in the monetary sector will affect the equilibrium in the goods sector.

Equilibrium in the money market is determined by the interaction of the demand for money and the supply of money. The basic mechanics are similar to the determination of equilibrium price in any market, except that the price in the money market is the interest rate.

The Supply of Money

We've had a good look at the demand side in the money market, but what about the supply of money? For simplicity, we'll assume that the supply of money (M) is a *policy variable*. This simply means that the supply of money is determined by government policy and not by the interest rate. This assumption is not quite accurate as a picture of the determinants of the money supply in the real world, but monetary policy by the government is the most important determinant of the money supply, and the assumption makes our analysis much simpler than a more comprehensive list of the determinants of the money supply.

If the money supply (M) is determined by government policy, and not by the interest rate, the supply of money doesn't vary with the interest rate. With no changes in monetary policy to alter the supply of money, then, the supply of money can be represented by the vertical supply function, M, in Figure 4.

The Equilibrium Interest Rate

Given the demand for money (L) and the supply of money (M) in Figure 4, the interest rate tends to move toward equilibrium at $\bar{r}$ where the quantity of money demanded along L equals the supply of money. If the interest rate were r_1, which is below the equilibrium rate, there would be excess demand for money balances, and this excess demand would drive the interest rate upward. If the interest rate were above equilibrium, say at r_2, excess supply of money would drive the interest rate downward.

The link between the demand for and supply of money and the interest rate is crucial, because the interest rate affects investment expenditures and some types of consumption expenditures. This gives us an important link between the money market and aggregate demand in the goods sector.

Money, Interest, Investment, and GNP: The "Keynesian Connection"

It was shown that the level of investment will increase or decrease until the marginal efficiency of investment (*MEI*)—the annual rate of return on the last investment made—equals the interest rate. The link between the money markets and aggregate demand is easy to establish. All we have to do is combine the demand curve for money, the marginal efficiency of investment, and the simple Keynesian model.

The demand curve for money (*L*) and the supply of money (*M*) determine the equilibrium interest rate ($\bar{r}$) in Figure 5a. In Figure 5b, the equilibrium interest rate ($\bar{r}$) and the marginal efficiency of investment (*MEI*) determine the equilibrium level of investment at $\bar{I}$, where $\bar{r} = MEI$. Combining the equilibrium level of investment with other expenditure flows gives us the aggregate demand function, $AD = C + \bar{I} + G$ in Figure 5c. Equlibrium GNP ($\bar{Y}$) is reached in Figure 5c where $AD = \bar{Y}$.

If the money market isn't in equilibrium, the interest rate won't be stable, but will be moving toward equilibrium. Without a stable interest rate, we can't have equilibrium in the goods market because the changing interest rate would lead to changes in the level of invest-

Figure 4 Money Market Equilibrium

Figure 5 Money Market Equilibrium and the Level of GNP

ment, aggregate demand, aggregate output, and employment in the goods sector until the interest rate stabilized at equilibrium and investment stabilized where $\bar{r} = MEI$.

Now, the importance of the stability and predictability of the demand for money should be clear. Suppose that we have equilibrium in the money market at $\bar{r}$ and in the goods market at $\bar{Y}$ in Figure 5. Shifts in the demand for money—due to a change in expectations, for example—will disturb the equilibrium in the money market and this will disturb the equilibrium in the goods market. An increase in the demand for money to L' will drive the interest rate to $\bar{r}'$, which will cause investment to fall to $\bar{I}'$ where $MEI = \bar{r}'$, and this will cause aggregate output to fall to $\bar{Y}' = C + \bar{I}' + G$. Instability in the demand for money over time will be translated into unstable aggregate demand, aggregate output, and employment in the goods sector.

Understanding equilibrium in the money market and the link between equilibrium in the money and goods markets sets the stage for analyzing the effects of changes in the money supply on aggregate demand, aggregate output, and the price level. This is important because government monetary policies seek to regulate or *manage* aggregate demand to minimize instability, unemployment, and inflationary pressure. The link between changes in the money supply and changes in output and prices is taken up in the next chapter.

Summary

1. The origins of money go back to the beginnings of economic specialization and exchange, and the development of the market economy. Money encourages greater specialization by facilitating exchange.

2. The earliest forms of money were **commodity money**—a commodity which possessed the basic characteristics of money. The value or purchasing power of commodity money is determined by the relative scarcity and relative price of the money commodity.
3. **Fiat money** is money because laws define it as money. It isn't backed by any money commodity. The value of fiat money is its purchasing power, but this purchasing power doesn't depend on the value of a money commodity.
4. As a **unit of exchange**, or **unit of account**, money makes it possible to quantify costs, profits, and aggregate output. To serve as a unit of account and exchange, money must be generally acceptable in exchange, divisible into small units, and scarce and difficult to reproduce.
5. As a **store of value**, money allows households to store the values of the goods and resources they sell.
6. The strict definition of the money supply includes currency and demand deposits. Broader definitions include some types of savings and time deposits.
7. **Near monies** have stable money values, and are easily converted to money at their full value. They aren't included in the definition of the money supply.
8. Money or **real balances** is only one of the assets individuals will hold in their portfolios of assets. Individuals hold money for transactions, precautionary, and speculative reasons. The quantity of money demanded tends to vary inversely with the interest rate, which is the opportunity cost of holding money balances.
9. Money affects aggregate demand and real GNP through its effect on interest rates and the level of investment. Changes in the demand for money cause changes in interest rates and thus result in changes in the levels of investment and equilibrium GNP.

Concepts for Review

barter exchange
commodity money
Gresham's Law
gold standard
fiat money
unit of account
unit of exchange
store of value

money aggregate
demand deposit
time deposit
near monies
transactions demand
  for money
precautionary demand
  for money

speculative demand
  for money
real balance
liquidity
portfolio of assets
liquidity preference
demand curve
  for money

Questions

1. Of all the villains in Ian Fleming's "007" novels, none was nastier or more cunning than the infamous Goldfinger, who attempted to make the U.S. gold stock radioactive and useless by detonating a nuclear device in the vault at Fort Knox. (Fortunately, he was foiled at the last moment by "007!")
   a. If a modern Goldfinger were to destroy the U.S. gold stock in Fort Knox today, how would this affect our money supply?
   b. Would the same heinous deed have had the same effect on the money supply if it had been pulled off 100 years ago?

2. Some people are upset because our money isn't backed by any *real* money (such as gold or silver). Is there any historical cause for this concern? Do you think that the fact that our fiat money isn't backed by gold or silver is a serious economic problem today?
3. The line between things that should be included in the definition of money and those that shouldn't is drawn on the basis of their substitutability as money.
   a. What functions does money perform, and what characteristics does money have to have to perform these functions?
   b. Which of the following would you include in the definition of money, and why?

currency	government securities
demand deposits	checkable savings accounts
savings accounts	gold
time deposits	credit cards

4. Deposits in insured passbook savings accounts earn an annual rate of 5¼ percent. Longer term certificates of deposit earn 6 percent if the funds are left on deposit for one year. High-grade, long-term corporate bonds earn about 10 percent per year. Bonds issued by the Last Gasp Uranium Mining Co. pay an annual interest rate of 20 percent.
   a. How do you explain the different annual rates of return for holding these assets?
   b. Which of the interest rates above are reasonable approximations of the opportunity cost of holding money as an asset?
   c. Suppose that the interest rate on insured passbook savings deposits increases to 6 percent. How would this affect individual portfolios of assets? What would you expect to happen to the interest rates on the other assets? How would this change affect the demand for money as an asset?
5. It is possible to have equilibrium aggregate output of goods and services if the money market isn't in equilibrium? How do disturbances of equilibrium in money markets affect equilibrium output of goods and services?
6. "Other things being the same, it is highly plausible that the fraction of assets individuals and business enterprises wish to hold in the form of money, and also in the form of close substitutes for money, will be smaller when they look forward to a period of stable economic conditions than when they anticipate disturbed and uncertain conditions." [Milton Friedman, A *Monetary History of the United States*. New York: National Bureau of Economic Research, 1963 (Published by Princeton University Press), p. 673.]
   a. Explain carefully how the stability of economic expectations affects the demand for money as an asset. How does this affect the stability of aggregate demand and aggregate output in the goods sector?
   b. Based on your knowledge of facts and monetary economics, how would economic expectations have affected the demand for money as an asset during the "new era" prosperity of the mid 1920s, the Great Depression of the 1930s, the World War II and early postwar period (1940–45 and 1945–48)? You can check your answer by consulting the relevant section of the *Monetary History*.

Problems

1. The relationships between the interest rate (r), the level of intended investment (I), and the demand for money balances (L) for the small country of Mammonland are as follows:

Interest Rate (r) (% per year)	Intended Investment (I) (billions $ per year)	Demand for Money (L) ($ billions per year)
20	0	0
18	10	5
16	20	10
14	30	15
12	40	20
10	50	25
8	60	30
6	70	35
4	80	40
2	90	45

a. Write an equation that expresses the relationship between the interest rate and the demand for money. The equation will be of the general form $r = a + bL$. Explain the relationship between the interest rate and the demand for money.

b. Write an equation that expresses the relationship between the interest rate and the level of intended investment. The equation will be of the general form $r = a + bI$. Explain this relationship.

c. If the supply of money is $M = \$20$ billion, find the equilibrium interest rate ($\bar{r}$). What will be the level of investment at this interest rate?

d. The consumption function in Mammonland is $C = 50 + 0.8\,Y$. Government spending is autonomous at $G_a = \$30$ billion. Intended investment is determined by the interest rate and the MEI. Write the economy's aggregate demand function as an equation. What is equilibrium aggregate output?

e. Worsening economic expectations double the amount of money that households and firms wish to hold at every interest rate. How does this affect the equilibrium in the money market and the level of GNP that you found in part (c)?

f. Show the effect of the increased demand for money as an asset in part (d) on the aggregate demand function and on equilibrium aggregate output.

26

The Supply of Money

Preview: The relationship between the money supply and the levels of aggregate output and prices is a controversial subject that has fascinated economists for centuries. In this chapter, we'll analyze that relationship as it is explained by the quantity theory of money. We'll also look closely at exactly how the supply of money is determined by the commercial banking system and the Federal Reserve.

The Supply of Money and Aggregate Output

The previous chapter established a link between equilibrium in the money market and equilibrium aggregate output in the goods market. The link is the interest rate. The demand for money and the supply of money determine the equilibrium interest rate, which determines the level of investment demand (and also affects some types of consumption spending). The level of investment, as a component of aggregate demand, is a determinant of equilibrium real GNP or aggregate output. Changes in the demand for money will upset the monetary equilibrium, upsetting equilibrium in the goods sector as well.

What about the supply side of the money market? How do changes in the supply of money affect equilibrium in the money market, aggregate demand, and equilibrium aggregate output in the goods sector? How do changes in the money supply affect the price level? The relationship between changes in the money supply and changes in output and prices has interested economists for centuries, and it continues to be a central issue that divides economists.

Recall from the previous chapter that the demand for money (L) and the supply of money (M) define the equilibrium interest rate ($\bar{r}$) in Figure 1a. At the equilibrium interest rate, investment will increase until the rate of return on the last investment made (MEI) equals the

Figure 1 Changes in the Money Supply and Changes in GNP

Money
(a)

Investment
(b)

Aggregate output
(c)

interest rate—$\bar{I}$ in Figure 1b. In Figure 1c, the equilibrium level of investment, along with the other intended expenditure flows, determines the level of aggregate demand (AD) and equilibrium aggregate output or real GNP (Y).

Now suppose that the money supply increases from M to M' in Figure 1a. The equilibrium interest rate falls to r'. As a result of the lower interest rate, investment increases to I' where $r' = MEI$. The increase in investment to $\bar{I}'$ causes the aggregate demand function in Figure 1c to rise to AD', and aggregate output to increase to $\bar{Y}' = AD'$. Verify for yourself that reducing the money supply from M' to M would cause aggregate demand and equilibrium real GNP to fall. We have thus identified an important link between changes in the supply of money and changes in aggregate output.

- At a constant price level, aggregate output will vary directly with changes in the money supply.

This relationship is obvious in Figure 2, which compares yearly changes in the money supply (M_1 and M_2) and changes in real GNP (Y) between 1929 and 1978.

The relationship between changes in the money supply and changes in aggregate output, with a constant price level, is easily verified by looking back at the demand for money and equilibrium in the money market. In the last chapter, we saw that the *demand for money at any level of nominal GNP* ($Y_n = PY$), other things constant, is a fraction (m) of nominal GNP, or

$$L = mY_n = mPY. \tag{1}$$

If the money market is in equilibrium, the supply of money equals the demand, or

$$M = mPY. \tag{2}$$

With given values of m and P, aggregate output will vary directly with changes in the money supply.

There is a qualification that has to be made concerning the effects of changes in the money supply on real GNP. If changes in the money supply cause the interest rate to change:

1. The interest rate will vary inversely with the money supply.
2. Investment will vary inversely with the interest rate, and directly with the money supply.
3. Equilibrium GNP will vary directly with investment, and directly with the money supply.

Money Supply, Output, and Prices: The Quantity Theory of Money

Most of us have an intuitive notion that the amount of money in circulation affects prices of goods and services. If the supply of money in circulation increased while the output of goods and services remained constant, or if the money supply increased more rapidly than the output of goods and services, goods and services would be more scarce relative to money. This means that goods and services will command more money in exchange, or more simply that the money prices of goods and services will rise.

If the quantity of money fell while real output remained constant or increased—or if it fell more rapidly than the output of goods and

Figure 2 Changes in the Money Supply and Changes in Real GNP, 1929–1978

Figure 3 Changes in the Money Supply and the Consumer Price Index, 1929–1977

services—money would become more scarce relative to goods and services. In this case, goods and services would command less money in exchange, or the money prices of goods and services would fall.

In the eighteenth century, the British philosopher and essayist David Hume wrote a fable in which everybody's money doubled overnight. As the people rushed out to spend their new wealth, however, the increased demand for goods and services doubled the prices of goods and services. *Hume's Fable* states the "crude" quantity theory of money.

- The *crude* **quantity theory of money** predicts that prices will change in the same direction and by the same proportion as changes in the money supply.

Modern monetary theory also predicts a direct relationship between changes in the money supply and changes in prices, but a less rigid relationship than the one stated in the crude quantity theory.

- The *modern* **quantity theory of money** predicts a direct, but not necessarily proportional, relationship between changes in the money supply and changes in prices.

If the money supply doubled overnight, the modern quantity theory would predict that prices would rise, but not necessarily double.

Figure 3 shows year-to-year changes in the money supply (M_1 and M_2) and the Consumer Price Index (CPI) for the period 1929–1977. Generally, but not always, prices tend to rise most rapidly during periods of rapid increase in the money supply, and tend to rise more slowly or fall in periods in which the money supply is increasing slowly or falling. This generally confirms the predictions that follow from the quantity theory, but it also indicates that the money supply isn't the only variable that affects prices.

The Velocity of Money

The quantity of money in circulation doesn't have to be as large as nominal GNP because money is spent more than once.

- The **velocity of money** is the rate at which money changes hands, or "turns over" in the economy.

If the velocity of money were 2, for example, this means that the supply of money would, on the average, change hands twice during the year. It would also mean that nominal GNP is twice as great as the money supply.

We can measure the velocity of money by dividing the nominal (or "money") GNP in current prices by the supply of money—i.e.,

$$V = \frac{\text{Nominal GNP}}{\text{Money Supply}}. \tag{3}$$

Nominal GNP is real GNP (Y), or aggregate output, multiplied by the current price level (P)—algebraically, *nominal GNP* $= PY$. Now, the expression for velocity becomes

$$V = \frac{PY}{M}. \tag{4}$$

As noted in the last chapter, there is some disagreement over the best measure of the supply of money—M_1 or M_2. We'll skirt the issue by examining two measures of velocity, V_1 and V_2, where

$$V_1 = \frac{PY}{M_1} \quad \text{and} \quad V_2 = \frac{PY}{M_2}.$$

For example, in 1977,

$$V_1 = \frac{\$1890.4 \text{ billion}}{\$324.5 \text{ billion}} = 5.83$$

$$V_2 = \frac{\$1890.4 \text{ billion}}{777.6 \text{ billion}} = 2.43.$$

Most early monetary theorists paid relatively little attention to velocity. They either ignored it or assumed that it was an institutionally determined constant. However, velocity may change for a number of reasons—institutional changes (such as new arrangements for making payments), changing economic conditions, changing expectations, and changes in households' and firms' preference for holding money over other assets. Figure 4 shows the behavior of V_1 and V_2 between 1929 and 1977.

The rise in V_1 in Figure 4, for example, reflects in part the growing use of checkable savings accounts (such as the NOW accounts). By making it easier to make payments out of savings accounts, the checkable savings account tend to reduce the households' and firms' need to hold currency and demand deposit balances. In other words, M_1 falls relative to nominal GNP, and $V_1 = PY/M_1$ rises.

Although V_2 has been considerably more stable over time than V_1, it hasn't been constant. Dramatic changes in economic conditions tend to increase households' and firms' demand for money balances, and this causes velocity to fall—as it did through much of the Great Depression, during and immediately following World War II, and less dramatically in several recessions since World War II (note 1974 in particular).

The stability and predictability of velocity is important economically. If velocity is unstable or unpredictable, it will be difficult to predict the effect of changes in the money supply on prices.

The Equation of Exchange

One way of expressing the quantity theory of money is with the *equation of exchange*.

- The **equation of exchange** states the relationship among the money supply, velocity, the price level, and real GNP.

Derivation of the equation of exchange is easy, and follows from

Figure 4 Velocity of Money, 1929–1977

the definitions of nominal GNP (PY) and velocity ($V = PY/M$). Multiplying the money supply (M) by velocity (V),

$$MV = M\left(\frac{PY}{M}\right) = PY.$$

The equation of exchange, then, is

$$MV = PY. \qquad (5)$$

Historically, the concern has been the effect of changes in the money supply on the price level, so we can write the equation of exchange as

$$PY = MV.$$

Dividing both sides by Y,

$$P = \frac{MV}{Y}. \qquad (6)$$

The general predictions from the equation of exchange are obvious.

1. Prices tend to vary directly with changes in the money supply.
2. Prices tend to vary directly with changes in the velocity of money.
3. Prices tend to vary inversely with changes in real GNP.

The crude quantity theory predicted proportional changes in the money supply and prices by assuming implicitly that output and velocity remain constant while the supply of money changed.

To illustrate the effect of changes in velocity, suppose that the initial supply of money is 200, velocity is 4, real GNP is 800, and the price level is 1—i.e.,

$$P = \frac{MV}{Y} = \frac{200 \times 4}{800} = \frac{800}{800} = 1.$$

Now, suppose that the money supply increases to 400 and that the velocity of money increases to 5. If Y remains at 800, the new price level will be

$$P = \frac{400 \times 5}{800} = \frac{2{,}000}{800} = 2.5.$$

Because of the change in V, doubling the money supply leads to a 2.5-fold increase in prices.

The equation of exchange predicts that the price level will vary inversely with changes in real GNP. For example, suppose that the money supply and velocity remain at their initial values, while real GNP increases from 800 to 1200. The new price level will be

$$P = \frac{MV}{Y} = \frac{200 \times 4}{1200} = \frac{800}{1200} = 0.75.$$

In reality, of course, these variables don't change one at a time as they did in the examples. If M, V, and Y are changing at the same time, the effect on prices depends on which variables are changing the fastest.

- If MV rises (falls) more rapidly than Y, prices will rise (fall). If Y rises (falls) more rapidly than MV, prices will fall (rise).

Close-up

The Free Silver Movement

Following the Civil War, the U.S. experienced rapid growth of real GNP. However, the supply of gold was fairly stable. Since the U.S. was on a "gold standard," the money supply increased more slowly than real output. In the context of the quantity theory and the equation of exchange, MV was increasing more slowly than Y, and the price level fell.

Inflation has been such a serious matter of concern in the 1970s that the problems of *falling* prices might not be obvious. As prices fall, the dollars that repay loans have greater purchasing power than the dollars originally borrowed. This increases the *real* burden of debts, and debtors (persons who owe debts) are worse off economically when prices are falling. Creditors (persons to whom debts are owed) benefit during periods of falling prices because they receive money in repayment of loans that has greater purchasing power than the money lent.

The *Free Silver* Movement in the U.S. was composed of advocates of greater coinage of silver. More silver money would increase the money supply, and this would stem the deflation. In the 1896 presidential election, the movement gained an eloquent spokesman in the person of William Jennings Bryan (the "silver-tongued orator of the Platte"), who ran on the Democratic ticket. Bryan declared that the gold standard was crucifying mankind on a "cross of gold."

Business and financial interests rallied around the Republicans' promise to preserve the gold standard and "sound money." Creditors who had benefitted from the deflation didn't want to end it by increasing the supply of silver money.

The Democrats' strongest support for "free silver" came from debtor classes—particularly farmers in the South and the West. They lost the election. However, by the end of the century, the deflation was stemmed—not by the free coinage of silver, but by increased production of gold.

The Equation of Exchange and Equilibrium in the Money Market

You may have noticed some similarities between the equation of exchange and the money market equilibrium discussed earlier. This isn't surprising since they are alternative ways of saying about the same thing concerning the effects of changes in the money supply. In fact, the equation of exchange can be derived easily from the equilibrium in the money market.

The money market reaches equilibrium when $M = L$, or

$$M = mPY. \tag{7}$$

The value of m is determined by the same variables that define velocity of money (V), except that the circumstances which define a low value for m define a high value for V. Specifically, m is the *reciprocal* of V. From the previous equation, m is found by dividing both sides of the equation by PY, or

$$m = \frac{M}{PY}. \tag{8}$$

From the equation of exchange, we established that velocity is

$$V = \frac{PY}{M}.$$

Therefore

$$m = \frac{1}{V}. \tag{9}$$

For example, if the velocity of money were $V = 2$, this is simply a way of saying that money changes hands twice during the year, or that the required supply of money would be ½ of nominal GNP, or $m = ½$.

The two expressions of the modern quantity theory are simply alternative ways of expressing essentially the same thing. If we start with the equation

$$M = mPY,$$

and substitute $(1/V)$ for m, we have

$$M = \frac{1}{V}PY.$$

Multiplying both sides of this equation by V,

$$MV = V\frac{1}{V}PY,$$

or

$$MV = PY.$$

Obviously, the importance of the stability and predictability of velocity applies with equal force to the stability and predictability of m. To the extent that m is unstable or unpredictable, it will be difficult to predict accurately the effects of changes in the money supply on the price level.

Having established the relationship between changes in the money supply and changes in aggregate output, we have to examine the way that the money supply is altered. The most important economic institutions, as far as the supply of money is concerned, are commercial banks and the Federal Reserve (the authority over monetary policy in the United States).

Commercial Banks and the Money Supply

The banking system plays a critical role in determining the supply of money. **Commercial banks** are particularly important. In addition to providing the familiar services of holding demand and time deposits and providing credit to households and businesses, commercial banks *create* money. To see how commercial banks can do this without printing currency and without any legal authority over the money supply, we have to examine the nature and functions of banks more closely.

Goldsmiths and the Origins of Commercial Banking

In addition to making and selling gold objects, goldsmiths were the first commercial bankers. They held gold for their customers for safekeeping against bandits, thieves, and tax collectors, and charged fees for this service similar to the fees charged by modern banks for safe-deposit boxes. The goldsmiths kept accounts showing each customer's deposits, withdrawals, and the balance of each customer's account.

The ancestors of modern checking accounts emerged as depositors wrote *drafts* authorizing third parties to make withdrawals from their accounts. Eventually, drafts played an important role as money. Buyers used them to authorize payments to sellers. Sellers deposited the drafts into their accounts, and the goldsmith simply deducted the amount of the draft from the buyer's account and added it to the seller's account. Very often, no gold physically changed hands. This had a very important result.

Goldsmiths soon discovered that they didn't have to hold all of the gold that had been deposited with them, but only enough to meet the normal demands of customers for withdrawals. As long as the goldsmiths could honor requests for withdrawals of gold, they could loan out the gold they didn't need and earn interest on the loans (in addition to the fees charged to depositors). This type of banking is called *fractional reserve banking*.

- **Fractional reserve banking** is a system in which banks hold only a fraction of their deposits as reserves.

By loaning out part of their reserves, the goldsmiths could *create* money. Say a goldsmith holds $100,000 worth of gold deposits for his customers. But suppose, the goldsmith decides that only 20 percent of this amount needs to be held as **required reserves** to cover normal demands for withdrawals of gold. This means that the goldsmith has $80,000 (80 percent of $100,000) in **excess reserves**—i.e., reserves in excess of those needed to meet customers' withdrawal requests.

Enterprising goldsmiths loaned out their excess reserves, and earned interest on the loans. This put more money into circulation, in addition to the original deposits. If our goldsmith-banker loaned out the $80,000 in excess reserves, the amount of money in circulation (the gold demand deposits, plus the money loaned out) would be

Initial Gold Demand Deposits	$100,000
Gold Loaned Out	80,000
Money in Circulation	$180,000

In other words, the goldsmith *created* an additional $80,000 in money by making loans from his deposits.

The Commercial Bank's Balance Sheet

Like the goldsmith bankers, modern commercial banks hold fractional reserves. Although commercial banks in the U.S. don't issue currency, fractional reserves allow the banks to alter the money supply by increasing or decreasing the quantity of demand-deposit money.

To see how banks can *create* money, we have to take a look at a highly simplified **balance sheet** for a hypothetical commercial bank. A balance sheet is simply an accounting statement that summarizes a firm's **assets**, **liabilities**, and **net worth** (or **equity**). One of the basic axioms of accounting is that *assets must equal liabilities plus owners' equity*. Every change in an asset is accompanied by an equal change in liabilities or equity or offsetting changes in other assets. For example, if you borrow $5000 to buy a new car, you'll acquire a $5000 asset (the car) and a $5000 liability (the loan). If you paid for the car out of your accumulated savings, you'd acquire a $5000 asset (the car), but you'd reduce another asset (savings) by $5000.

The simplified balance sheet for our hypothetical commercial bank —call it Bank A—is shown in Table 1. The bank's *reserves* are money held as vault cash and as a demand deposit with a central reserve bank. Suppose that Bank A must hold 20 percent of its demand deposits as *required reserves* to meet depositors' requests for withdrawals. This bank is *loaned up*—i.e., it holds no *excess reserves* above its required reserves.

Table 1 Simplified Balance Sheet for Bank A

ASSETS		LIABILITIES	
Reserves		Demand Deposits	$20 million
Required	$ 4 million	Time Deposits	5 million
Excess	0	Other Liabilities	5 million
Loans	16 million		
Government Securities	8 million	OWNERS' EQUITY	5 million
Other Securities	7 million		
	$35 million		$35 million

The bank's other assets include loans, government securities, and other securities. These represent obligations of others to make repayments to the bank. On the liabilities side of the sheet, demand deposits and time deposits are liabilities for the bank. They represent the bank's obligations to honor requests for withdrawals from these accounts. All other liabilities are lumped together in a catch-all category, *other liabilities*. The bank's *owners' equity* or *net worth* is the difference between assets and its liabilities, and represents the value of the owners' claims against the bank.

Initially, Bank A is loaned up and holds no excess reserves. This bank couldn't create any additional money unless something happened to increase its reserves.

Creation of Money by the Banks

Suppose that Bank A receives an additional $2 million in new reserves. This could happen if the bank acquired new demand deposits from new depositors or additional demand deposits from old depositors. This increases Bank A's reserves (an asset) by $2 million, and its demand deposits (a liability) by $2 million. If the bank holds 20 percent of its demand deposits as **required reserves**, the additional $2 million in demand deposits will increase required reserves by $0.4 million (20 percent of $2 million).

Additional reserves above required reserves are additional **excess reserves**. So the additional $2 million in demand deposits increase excess reserves by $1.6 million (80 percent of $2 million).

Bank A

ASSETS		LIABILITIES	
Reserves		Demand Deposits	+ $2 million
Required	+ $0.4 million		
Excess	+ $1.6 million		

The new excess reserves held by the bank can be loaned out to earn interest. Assume that the bank loans out the entire $1.6 million—after all, the excess reserves earn no income as reserves. After loaning out the new excess reserves, the bank is loaned up again. The bank has converted one asset (excess reserves) into another asset (loans).

Bank A

ASSETS		LIABILITIES
Excess Reserves	− $1.6 million	No Change
Loans	+ $1.6 million	

Firms and households generally take out loans to make purchases. It doesn't make a great deal of sense for a borrower to hold borrowed funds (on which interest must be paid) as currency (which earns nothing) or to deposit them in a savings account at a lower rate of interest than must be paid on the loan.

Whether borrowers deposit borrowed funds in their own accounts or make purchases with the borrowed funds and the sellers deposit them in their demand deposit accounts, the loaned funds eventually find their way back into the banking system as additional demand deposits.

Suppose that the entire $1.6 million in additional excess reserves in Bank A is loaned out, and that the funds are redeposited in Bank B as demand deposits. This increases Bank B's demand deposits and its *reserves* by $1.6 million. Bank B also holds 20 percent of its new demand deposits as required reserves, and the remaining 80 percent represents new excess reserves in Bank B.

Bank B

ASSETS		LIABILITIES	
Reserves		Demand Deposits	+ $1.6 million
Required	+ $0.32 million		
Excess	+ $1.28 million		

Like Bank A, Bank B loans out its new excess reserves, converting excess reserves into loans.

Bank B

ASSETS		LIABILITIES
Excess Reserves	− $1.28 million	No Change
Loans	+ $1.28 million	

If the $1.28 million loaned out by Bank B is deposited in another bank—Bank C—the process is repeated. Bank C's demand deposits and reserves increase by $1.28 million.

The additional reserves are broken down into $0.26 million in required reserves (20 percent of $1.28 million) and $1.02 million in new excess reserves (80 percent of $1.28 million).

Bank C

ASSETS		LIABILITIES	
Reserves		Demand Deposits	+ $1.28 million
Required	+ $0.26 million		
Excess	+ $1.02 million		

If Bank C loans out the entire $1.02 million in excess reserves, and these funds are deposited in yet another bank—Bank D—demand deposits and bank reserves will continue to increase. To verify your understanding of all of this, construct balance sheets to show the effect of Bank C's new loans on its assets and liabilities, and the effect of the additional demand deposits in Bank D.

In these examples, no bank loaned out more funds than it held as reserves—in fact each bank held some of its additional reserves as required reserves. However, *together* the banks created additional money as bank reserves and demand deposits increased. The total increase in reserves and demand deposit money from the initial increase of $2 million in Bank A's reserves is shown below.

New Reserves in Bank A	$2.0 million
New Reserves in Bank B	1.6 million
New Reserves in Bank C	1.28 million
TOTAL NEW RESERVES	$4.88 million

The banking *system* in this example has *created* nearly $3 million in additional demand deposit money over and above the original increase in bank reserves.

The Banking System Multiplier

How much money will eventually be generated by the initial increase in Bank A's reserves? This is determined by something called the *banking system multiplier*.

- The **banking system multiplier** determines the maximum supply of demand deposit money that can be generated from any level of bank reserves, and the maximum change in the supply of demand deposit money as a result of changes in bank reserves.

The size of the banking system multiplier effect depends on the *reserve ratio (rr)*.

- The **reserve ratio** is the proportion of demand deposits (*DD*) that banks must hold as required reserves (*R*).

The maximum supply of demand deposit money (DD_{max}) from any given level of bank reserves is

$$DD_{max} = \frac{1}{rr} R. \qquad (10)$$

If bank reserves change by some ΔR, the maximum change in the supply of demand deposit money (ΔDD_{max}) is

$$\Delta DD_{max} = \frac{1}{rr} \Delta R. \qquad (11)$$

The ratio ($1/rr$) is the banking system multiplier.[1]

---

1. The proportion of an initial change in bank reserves, ΔR, that can be loaned out is $(1 - rr)$. This represents additional reserves for the "second generation bank," and the second generation bank can loan out $(1 - rr)$ of these additional reserves, or $(1 - rr)(1 - rr)\Delta R = (1 - rr)^2 \Delta R$. This amount, in turn represents new reserves for the third generation bank, and the third generation bank can loan out $(1 - rr)(1 - rr)^2 \Delta R = (1 - rr)^3 \Delta R$. If no funds ever leak out of the demand-deposit credit flow, the maximum change in demand deposit money will be

$$\begin{aligned}\Delta DD_{max} &= \Delta R + (1 - rr)\Delta R + (1 - rr)^2 \Delta R + (1 - rr)^3 \Delta R + \cdots \\ &= \Delta R[1 + (1 - rr) + (1 - rr)^2 + (1 - rr)^3 + \cdots]\end{aligned}$$

As the number of rounds increases, the amount of new reserves entering the banking system gets

Bank reserves can fall as well as rise, of course, and the banking system multiplier works in both directions. If bank reserves declined, banks may have to reduce their loans to maintain their required reserves, and this would cause demand deposits in the banking system (and the level of total bank reserves in the system) to fall further.

If banks were required to hold *all* of their demand deposits as required reserves, we wouldn't have fractional reserve banking, but *100% banking*. With 100% banking, there would be no banking system multiplier effect, because the reserve ratio is $rr = 1$, and the banking system multiplier would be $1/rr = 1/1 = 1$.

The Banking System Multiplier: Some Qualifications

The banking system multiplier defines the maximum level of demand deposit money that can be generated by the banking system from a given level of bank reserves, or the maximum change in demand deposit money as a result of a given change in bank reserves, with a given reserve ratio. However, it's highly unlikely that this maximum would ever be reached in practice.

In the examples, no funds leaked out of the demand-deposit credit flow of the banking system. In fact, there are a number of possible leaks out of this flow which reduce the size of the banking multiplier. Leaks into currency are an important leak. To the extent that funds are held as currency instead of being redeposited as demand deposits in the banking system, this reduces the expansion of bank reserves and the banking system's ability to generate demand-deposit money.

In addition, the banks in the examples stayed loaned up, and never held excess reserves. This infers that banks are mechanical and passive in the creation or contraction of the money supply. In fact, banks aren't passive or mechanical in their decisions. Like households and firms, banks may desire to hold some excess reserves for precautionary or speculative reasons. If Bank A in the previous examples had diverted more than 20 percent of its additional demand deposits to reserves, less money would have been loaned out and redeposited in Bank B as demand deposits, and the expansion of demand deposits in Bank B and all subsequent banks would have been smaller.

These qualifications are significant, because the exact size of the banking system multiplier is not easy to predict precisely. The fol-

---

smaller and smaller. The expression in the brackets becomes an *infinite series*, which can be written

$$\frac{1}{1 - (1 - rr)} = \frac{1}{rr}.$$

The maximum change in demand deposits from an initial change in reserves is

$$\Delta DD_{max} = \frac{1}{rr} \Delta R.$$

lowing is a more realistic, but less precise statement of the banking system multiplier.

- With fractional reserve banking, banks can generate demand deposit money from their excess reserves, and changes in bank reserves will produce greater changes in demand deposit money.

But Is It Really Money?

The creation of money through a series of accounting operations looks like a sleight-of-hand trick that violates our common sense. Do the commercial banks really create money?

Demand deposits, as many people point out, are only "money on paper," but they *are* money. Demand deposits are very good substitutes for currency as a means of exchange and a store of value, and are widely acceptable in exchange. Except with *commodity money* (such as gold or fully backed gold certificates), all money is "money on paper." The folding money in your pocket is also "money on paper." In short, when banks alter the supply of demand-deposit money, they *do* alter the supply of money.

The Federal Reserve and the Money Supply

Unlike the hypothetical banks in the previous section of this chapter, commercial banks in the real world aren't completely free to set their own minimum required reserves or to determine the supply of money independently of any central control. In all industrialized countries, the actions of individual banks are restricted by the rules, regulations, and policies of a **central bank**. A central bank is the keystone of the commercial banking system. Central banks play three critically important roles—as the *government's bank*, as the *banks' bank*, and as the *authority over monetary policies*.

The United States hasn't had a true central bank since the demise of the Bank of the United States in 1836. Control over monetary policy and the actions of individual banks were decentralized in the United States through most of the nineteenth century. The United States was on a gold standard in this period, and this stabilized the money supply somewhat, but serious economic panics occurred in 1873, 1884, 1890, 1893, and 1907.

After the Panic of 1907, Congress appointed the National Monetary Commission to study the problem of monetary policy. Unlike most commissions, the National Monetary Commission had some impact. Largely as a result of the research and recommendations of the National Monetary Commission, the Federal Reserve Act was passed and enacted in 1913. This act established the **Federal Reserve System** to perform most of the functions of a central bank in the United States. The formal organization of the Federal Reserve System (the *Fed*) is about the same today as it was in 1913.

The Structure of the Federal Reserve

The country is divided into twelve Federal Reserve Districts, as shown in the map in Figure 5. Each district has a Federal Reserve Bank that serves as a central bank for the member commercial banks in the district. The Federal Reserve Banks hold demand deposits for the commercial banks, make short-term loans, and perform other banking services for member commercial banks.

Federal Reserve Banks act as clearinghouses for commercial banks. Suppose that Emma Turkey buys a new car from Saintly Sam and pays for it with a check drawn on her account at the Ebeneezer Bank & Trust Co. The dealer deposits the check in his account with the Legree Bank, which adds the amount of the check to the dealer's account. The Legree Bank then deposits the check in its reserve account with the Federal Reserve Bank in his district.

The Federal Reserve Bank *clears* the check by adding the amount of the check to the Legree Bank's reserve account and deducting it from Ebeneezer Bank & Trust Co.'s account. The check then proceeds to the Ebeneezer Bank & Trust Co., which deducts the amount of the check from Ms. Turkey's account and returns the paid (or cancelled) check as a receipt. The journey of the check is shown in Figure 6.

Figure 5 The Federal Reserve System

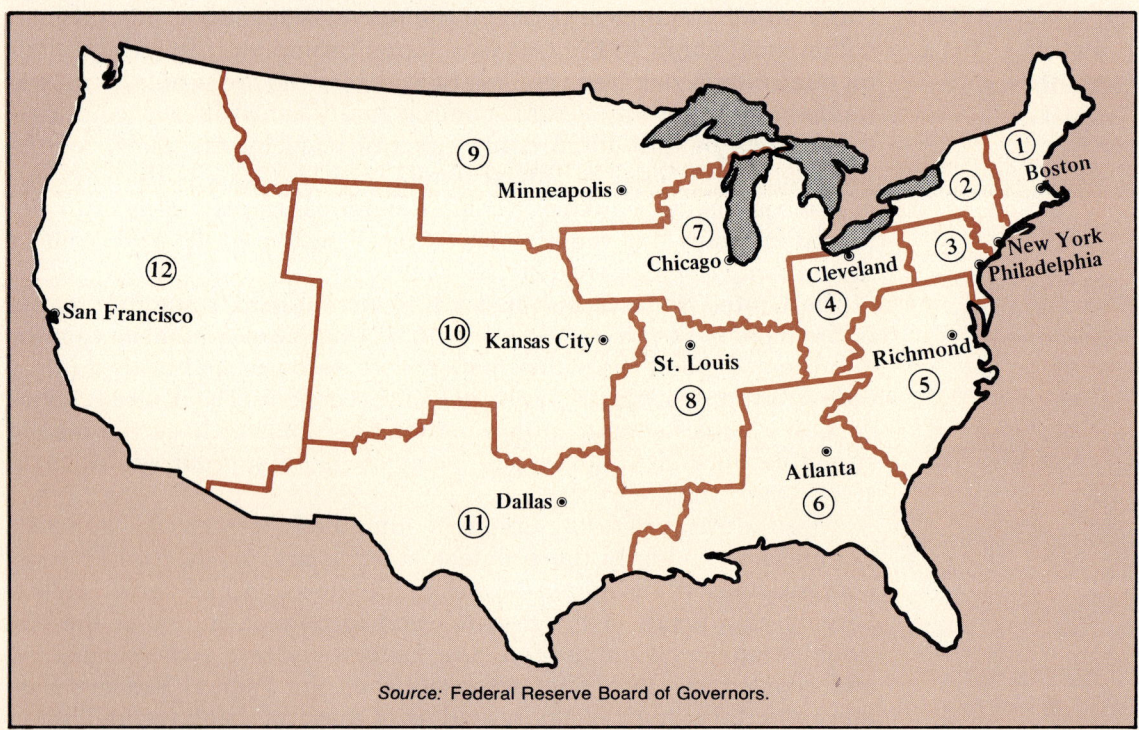

Source: Federal Reserve Board of Governors.

Alaska and Hawaii are in District 12, served by the Federal Reserve Bank of San Francisco.

Clearing operations are important economically. They make transactions by check much easier than they would be if each bank had to send all checks to other banks for payment. By facilitating exchanges by check, clearing operations enhance the monetary function of demand deposits.

Federal Reserve Banks are "owned" by the member commercial banks in their districts. The commercial banks are the "stockholders" in their Federal Reserve Banks, but they don't have all of the rights and powers of stockholders in private corporations. The commercial banks can't, for example, decide on the dividend that will be paid on their stock in the Federal Reserve Bank—this is limited by law to a 6 percent annual rate of return. Unlike private stockholders, commercial banks don't choose all of the directors of a Federal Reserve Bank. Each Federal Reserve Bank has a nine-member board of directors, three of whom are appointed by the Board of Governors of the Federal Reserve System.

Individual Federal Reserve Banks don't determine monetary policies for their districts independently. National monetary policy is determined by the Board of Governors and several committees.

The Board of Governors. The Federal Reserve System is directed by a seven-member Board of Governors, or the Federal Reserve Board. Members of the Board are appointed by the President, with confirmation by the Senate. The President appoints the Chairman of the Board when the post becomes vacant.

Figure 6 Movement of a Check Through the Banking System

Members of the Federal Reserve Board of Governors are appointed for 14-year terms. The terms of the Governors are staggered, with a vacancy on the Board in every even-numbered year. This seemingly trivial institutional detail is very significant. A President can't fire or demand the resignation of a member of the Board of Governors whose term has not expired, and a President's appointees to the Board of Governors will affect monetary policy after the President is out of office. Also, because the Board will be made up of appointees of at least two different Presidents, this makes monetary policy relatively independent of changing political moods that are reflected in changes in the occupants of 1600 Pennsylvania Avenue.

The Federal Open Market Committee (FOMC). The Federal Open Market Committee (FOMC) is a potent force in monetary policy. The majority of the twelve-member FOMC are the seven members of the Board of Governors. The other five members are the presidents of five of the twelve Federal Reserve Banks. This committee directs the Fed's purchases and sales of government securities in the open securities market. This is a very important monetary policy tool.

Centralization of Power in the Fed. On paper, the Fed looks relatively decentralized. However, the centralization of power and influence in monetary policy is considerably greater than the formal organization of the Fed suggests.

The chairman of the Board of Governors is more than the presiding member of the Board. Generally, chairmen dominate the Board, and strong Federal Reserve chairmen have been recognized as the most important spokesmen on monetary policy by the President, the Congress, the media, and the public.

Secondly, to borrow a phrase from George Orwell's *Animal Farm*, some of the Federal Reserve Banks are "more equal" than others in their ability to influence monetary policy. The Federal Reserve Bank of New York is the most influential of the 12 Federal Reserve Banks because New York is the financial capital of the country. The president of the Federal Reserve Bank of New York, is the only Federal Reserve Bank president that holds a voting seat on the FOMC every year.

How Does the Fed Control the Money Supply?

Article I of the U.S. Constitution gives Congress the power to "coin money and regulate the value thereof," but the authority to regulate the supply of money has been delegated by the Congress to the Federal Reserve. Changing the supply of money, however, involves more than coining or printing currency. The Fed has a number of tools that it can use to regulate the supply of money, but the tools aren't equally useful or effective.

The Quantity of Currency in Circulation. Common references in the media and political debates to "printing money" when the Fed expands the money supply are very misleading because they infer that the way the money supply is increased is simply by printing more currency. The Fed *can* order the Treasury and the Bureau of Printing and Engraving to print more currency, but the quantity of *currency* in circulation isn't very significant as a monetary policy tool.

The critical variable is the quantity of *money* in circulation, and currency isn't the largest component of the money supply. In December 1978, for example, currency was only about 27 percent of the narrowly defined money supply (M_1 = currency + demand deposits). Using the broader definition of money, M_2, currency accounted for only about 11 percent of the money supply in December 1978.

Furthermore, the mix of currency and demand deposits depends largely on the public's need or preference for currency and demand deposits. If the Fed tried to put more currency in circulation than firms, households, and financial institutions wanted to hold as money, the excess currency would end up in banks as demand deposits, and eventually back at the Fed.

The Required Reserve Ratio. Commercial banks that belong to the Federal Reserve System can't set their own *reserve ratios*—the proportion of demand deposits held as required reserves. The minimum reserve ratio for commercial banks in the United States is set by the Federal Reserve. Changing the reserve ratio is a powerful monetary tool which can have dramatic effects on the money supply.

The *banking system multiplier* is the ratio $1/rr$, where rr is the reserve ratio, and it defines the maximum amount of demand deposit money that banks can generate from a given level of bank reserves. Changing the reserve ratio changes the maximum amount of demand deposit money that can be generated from bank reserves.

The effect of a change in the reserve ratio on the banks' ability to generate money is shown below. At an initial reserve ratio of 10 percent of demand deposits, the bank below holds $2 million in excess reserves.

ASSETS		LIABILITIES
Reserves		Demand Deposits $20 million
Required	$ 2 million	
Excess	2 million	
Loans	$16 million	

If these reserves were loaned out and redeposited as demand deposits in the banking system, this would increase the supply of demand deposit money.

If the Fed raised the reserve ratio from 10 percent to 20 percent (this is an *enormous* change and is only illustrative), the bank's balance sheet would look like this:

ASSETS		LIABILITIES
Reserves		Demand Deposits $20 million
Required	$ 4 million	
Excess	0	
Loans	$16 million	

What happened to the excess reserves? They're gone, because the bank now has to hold the entire $4 million as required reserves (20 percent of $20 million). At the higher reserve ratio, the bank is loaned up, there are no excess reserves to loan out, and this bank can't contribute to an increase in the quantity of demand deposit money.

What if the bank had been loaned up at the lower reserve ratio?

ASSETS		LIABILITIES
Reserves		Demand Deposits $20 million
Required	$ 2 million	
Excess	0	
Loans	$18 million	

The bank holds no excess reserves, and if the reserve ratio rose to 20 percent it would have to increase its reserves to $4 million. The bank may have to take out a short-term loan from the Fed to meet its immediate need for reserves, but eventually it will have to convert some of its other assets (primarily loans) to reserves, and this takes money out of the demand-deposit credit flow.

With a reserve ratio of 20 percent of demand deposits, the bank is loaned up and can't create any demand-deposit money by extending loans from excess reserves. If the reserve ratio were lowered to 10 percent of demand deposits, however, the bank would have excess reserves. With the lower reserve ratio and reduced required reserves, the bank could create demand deposit money by loaning out its excess reserves.

All of this leads to two obvious conclusions.

- *Raising the reserve ratio* reduces the maximum amount of money that can be generated from bank reserves.

- *Lowering the reserve ratio* increases the maximum amount of money that can be generated from bank reserves.

The reserve ratio is a powerful tool with only limited usefulness as a monetary policy tool. Seemingly small changes in the reserve ratio can have dramatic, but not always accurately predictable, effects on the money supply. If banks desire to hold excess reserves or the public desires to hold some of the additional money as currency, the exact effect of changing the reserve ratio on the money supply is hard to predict.

The Fed is limited by law to reserve ratios between 7 percent and 22 percent of demand deposits, and the reserve ratio has been fairly stable around 15 percent in recent years, although the Fed can and does change it by a point or less from time to time. The reserve ratio is most useful for large changes in the money supply, and usually changes in the reserve ratio are accompanied by other monetary policies to soften its short-run impact.

Open Market Operations. The Fed is a large buyer and seller of government securities in the open market.

- **Open market operations** are the purchases and sales of government securities by the Federal Reserve.

The Fed differs from most private buyers and sellers of securities in two important respects. First, the Fed's purchases and sales are large enough to affect the market prices of securities. Secondly, unlike private traders, the Fed's main objective in open market operations isn't to earn the highest possible return on a portfolio of financial securities, but to change the money supply and the interest rate. Open market operations are the most important and widely used monetary policy tools.

- The Fed *buys securities* in the open market to *increase the money supply* and *lower interest rates*.

The sale of the securities to the Fed increases member banks' reserves, and reduces their holdings of government securities.

Member Banks

ASSETS		LIABILITIES
Government Securities	−$100 million	No Change
Reserves	+$100 million	

The purchase of government securities increases the Fed's holdings of government securities and increases member bank deposits.

Federal Reserve

ASSETS		LIABILITIES	
Government Securities	+$100 million	Member Bank Deposits	+$100 million

If the securities had been sold by households and firms, an extra step is involved. The Fed acquires $100 million in government securities, and pays the sellers by check. As the households and firms deposit their proceeds in commercial banks, bank reserves increase. If the households and firms purchase goods and services with the proceeds from the government securities and the sellers of these goods and services deposit the funds in their demand deposits, this also increases the banks' demand deposits and reserves.

- The Fed *sells securities* in the open market to *reduce the money supply* and *raise interest rates*.

When the Fed sells government securities, its holdings of government securities decline, and member bank deposits (bank reserves) decline as the banks purchase the securities. A sale of $100 million in government securities by the Fed to commercial banks increases the banks' holdings of government securities by $100 million, and reduces bank reserves (which are used to pay for the securities) by $100 million.

Member Banks

ASSETS		LIABILITIES	
Government Securities	+$100 million	No Change	
Reserves	−$100 million		

The sale of the securities reduces the Fed's holdings of government securities and member bank deposits (reserves) by $100 million.

Federal Reserve

ASSETS		LIABILITIES	
Government Securities	−$100 million	Member Bank Deposits	−$100 million

Again, the effect is similar if the government securities are purchased by households and firms. If the households and firms write checks to pay for the securities, demand deposits in commercial banks and the level of bank reserves fall.

Open Market Operations and Securities Prices. In addition to their effects on interest rates through changing the supply of money, the Fed's open-market operations affect interest rates and aggregate demand through their effects on the prices of securities.

The size of the Fed's open-market purchases and sales is great enough to affect the prices of securities, and the effective interest rate on a security is determined by its price. For example, a government bond that sells for $20,000 and pays $2000 per year in interest has an effective interest rate or yield of 10 percent per year ($2000 per year/$20,000). If the price of the bond fell to $16,000, the effective interest rate or yield would increase to 12.5 percent per year ($2000 per year/$16,000). If the price of the bond rose from $20,000 to $25,000, the effective interest rate would fall from 10 percent per year to 8 percent per year ($2000 per year/$25,000). Such changes may stimulate aggregate demand in two ways. First, higher securities prices mean lower interest rates, and lower interest rates stimulate investment spending and some forms of consumer spending. Also, the higher securities prices increase the wealth of the holders of the securities. Some of the additional wealth of securities owners may lead to increased spending, and this also stimu-

Figure 7 Effects of the Fed's Open Market Operations

lates aggregate demand. The effects of Fed purchases of government securities are illustrated in Figure 7a.

When the Fed sells government securities on the open market, this tends to dampen aggregate demand. In Figure 7b, the sale of government securities by the Fed lowers the price of securities from $\overline{P}_S$ to $\overline{P}_S'$. Lower securities prices dampen aggregate demand and economic activity by raising effective interest rates (which discourages investment and some consumer spending), and by reducing the wealth of securities owners.

The Discount Rate. Federal Reserve Banks extend loans to member commercial banks to meet short-term needs for funds, and charges interest on these loans. The **discount rate** is the interest rate which the Fed charges on loans to commercial banks.

Commercial banks are profit-seeking institutions. If they have to pay more for the short-term funds they borrow from the Fed, they will pass on this higher cost to their customers as higher interest rates on the loans they extend. Also, higher discount rates discourage the commercial banks from borrowing short-term funds from the Fed to cover reserves, and this reduces the availability of credit in the economy. In short, raising the discount rate tends to dampen aggregate demand and economic activity.

Reducing the discount rate tends to stimulate aggregate demand and economic activity. Lower discount rates may encourage commercial banks to lower interest rates on loans extended to their customers. Also, commercial banks may be encouraged to extend more loans and cover short-term reserve requirements with funds borrowed by the Fed if the discount rate and therefore the cost of short-term funds from the Fed is low. These effects of a lower discount rate tend to stimulate aggregate demand.

Direct Controls. The Fed sets maximum interest rates that commercial banks can pay on savings and time deposits—"the highest interest rates allowed by law." Interest rates on time deposits affect households' allocation of income between consumption and saving and firms' investment decisions. High interest rates on time deposits tend to encourage saving and discourage consumption and investment.

During World War II, the Fed had extensive direct controls over consumer credit, most of which were removed after the War. The Fed retained one important direct control over credit—*margin requirements* on purchases of stocks and other securities. The *margin requirement* is the percentage of a securities purchases that must be paid in cash to the broker. For example, a margin requirement of 50 percent means that a buyer of common stock would have to pay at least half of the amount of the purchase in cash at the time of the purchase.

Low margin requirements and large stock purchases on credit were among the causes of the financial panic and collapse of the stock market in 1929. Many people bought common stocks on very low margins, expecting the stocks to appreciate and to make large returns on their margins. When stock prices fell, the margins disappeared. Brokers sold stocks as losses wiped out the margins, and this drove stock prices even lower. To avoid a repeat performance of October 1929, the Fed has established fairly high margin requirements on most securities purchases.

The Fed's goal in manipulating the money supply is to regulate interest rates and aggregate demand to maintain low levels of unemployment, stabilize aggregate output, and dampen inflationary pressures. Whether or not monetary policies can accomplish these objectives is a central issue among economists, and this issue is examined in some detail in the next chapter.

Summary

1. If changes in the money supply cause changes in the interest rate, then they will also cause changes in the levels of investment and aggregate output.
2. The **quantity theory of money** states the relationships among the money supply, the velocity of money, the price level, and real GNP.
3. The **velocity of money** is the rate at which money "turns over" or changes hands during the year. It is determined by institutional arrangements, economic conditions, expectations, and the preference for money over other assets. Changes in velocity affect the relationship between changes in the money supply and changes in prices.
4. **Commercial banks** can create demand-deposit money because they operate with **fractional reserves,** holding only a fraction of their demand deposits as **required reserves.** The proportion of demand deposits that must be held as required reserves is the **reserve ratio.**
5. The banking system can *create* money as banks extend loans from their excess reserves and these loaned funds are redeposited as demand deposits in the system.

6. The **banking multiplier** is the maximum amount of demand-deposit money that can be generated from each dollar of bank reserves, or the maximum change in demand deposit money from each dollar's change in bank reserves. The banking multiplier varies inversely with the reserve ratio.
7. The exact size of the banking multiplier is hard to predict accurately because of numerous "leaks" out of the demand-deposit credit flow that creates money.
8. **Central banks** or their equivalent serve as the government's bank, the banks' bank, and as the monetary authority. The United States hasn't had a true central bank since 1836. The functions of a central bank are performed by the **Federal Reserve System,** which was established in 1913.
9. The Fed could alter the supply of money by changing the banks' reserve ratio, but this is a powerful and unpredictable tool. The Fed's most important means of regulating the money supply and interest rates is through **open-market operations.** The Fed also regulates interest rates by setting the discount rate on its short-term loans to member banks and to a lesser extent through its authority to set maximum interest rates on savings and time deposits.

Concepts for Review

crude quantity theory
modern quantity theory
Hume's Fable
velocity of money
equation of exchange
commercial bank
fractional reserve banking

required reserve
excess reserve
asset
liability
net worth
banking multiplier
reserve ratio

central bank
Federal Reserve System
Board of Governors
Federal Open Market
    Committee
open market operations
discount rate

Questions

1. What is the essential difference between the crude and modern versions of the quantity theory of money? Explain, and show that the crude quantity theory is a special case of the modern quantity theory.
2. What is the velocity of money? What determines velocity, and why is it important economically?
3. Following the November Revolution in 1917, the Soviet Union experienced serious economic problems. World War I had been an economic disaster, absenteeism among factory workers was very high, many people left the cities because of social and economic chaos, and productivity fell dramatically. In 1918, the government enacted legislation that authorized the printing of as many paper rubles as necessary. The currency in circulation increased from about 22 billion rubles in 1917 to about 61 billion by the end of 1918.
Using the quantity theory of money and the equation of exchange, what would you predict as the most likely effect of this increase in the money supply?
4. The "classical" economists' concern with the supply of money was almost exclusively a concern with the relationship between the money

supply and the price level. In fact, they generally argued that in the long run, changes in the money supply would affect only prices, and not real output.

How does classical macroeconomics, presented in earlier chapters, lead to this conclusion? Use the quantity theory and the equation of exchange in explaining your answer.

5. If you wrote a check for the full amount of your checking account balance, could your bank cash the check for you immediately? If all checking-account depositors wrote checks for the full amount of their checking account balances, could the banking system cash their checks for them immediately? Explain your answers.
6. When Franklin D. Roosevelt assumed the office of President in 1933, one of his first acts was to declare a "bank holiday" and close the banks.

    Based on your understanding of banking and your knowledge of economic conditions in 1933, explain the circumstances that made the holiday necessary.
7. Explain the basic functions of central banks. Why are central banks important economically?
8. When the Federal Reserve increases the money supply, does it simply order the Treasury to print more currency? Explain how the Fed can alter the money supply, and the effectiveness of its basic monetary tools.
9. What could you envision as possible economic consequences of dismantling the Federal Reserve System and decentralizing control over the money supply?
10. Suppose that the Federal Reserve sells $500 million worth of government securities on the open market.
    a. What would be the Fed's objective in making the sale?
    b. Explain how the sale would achieve the Fed's objective.
    c. Could the Fed achieve the same objective by any other means?

Problems

1. Suppose that an additional $10 million is deposited by millionaire-philanthropist Bruce Wayne in his checking account with the Gotham City Bank & Trust Co.
    a. Show and explain the effect on the bank's assets and its liabilities.
    b. The Gotham City Bank & Trust Co. is a member of a system of commercial banks, each of which holds 25 percent of its reserves as required reserves. What is the maximum change in demand deposit money that the banking system could generate from the additional $10 million deposited in the Gotham City Bank & Trust? Show the effect through 3 "generations" of banks in the system.
    c. What conditions are necessary for the change in demand deposit money to reach the maximum you identified in part b? Is it likely that the maximum would be reached? Explain carefully.

27

Monetary Policy: Mechanics, Problems, and Issues

Preview: Discretionary monetary policies are changes in the money supply and interest rates aimed at minimizing unemployment and inflation. Like fiscal policies, monetary policies are a form of **demand management**, whose usefulness as a tool in controlling the economy has been a subject of considerable controversy in recent years. In this chapter, we'll explore the basic mechanics of monetary policy and the controversies surrounding its use as a tool for controlling the economy.

For many years, a battle raged over the question of the effectiveness of discretionary monetary policies in achieving the objectives of full employment, stable prices, and stability. *Keynesians*, who emphasized the importance of fiscal policies, were portrayed as arguing that "money doesn't matter" (or "doesn't matter much"). *Monetarists*, who emphasized the importance of monetary policy, found themselves associated with arguments ranging from "money matters" to "money is all that matters."

Today, fortunately, there is little disagreement that money matters. However, the issue of the effectiveness and necessity of *discretionary* monetary and fiscal policies remains unsettled.

- **Discretionary monetary policies** alter the supply of money and the interest rate with the goal of altering aggregate demand, real GNP, employment, and inflation.

Discretionary Monetary Policy: The Mechanics

As you will recall from the last chapter, changes in the money supply affect aggregate demand, real GNP, and the strength of inflationary pressure primarily via their effects on interest rates.

$$\Delta M \longrightarrow \Delta r \longrightarrow \Delta I \longrightarrow \Delta \overline{Y} = k\Delta I$$

change in money supply — change in interest rate in the opposite direction — change in investment — change in equilibrium GNP (k is the multiplier)

The object of discretionary monetary policies is to change the money supply in a way that brings equilibrium real GNP to its full employment level (i.e., to achieve $\overline{Y} = Y^*$).

Unemployment and Expansionary Monetary Policy

If the economy experiences unemployment as a result of inadequate aggregate demand, monetary policies will seek to stimulate aggregate demand, and monetary authorities will pursue *expansionary monetary policies*.

- **Expansionary monetary policies** are deliberate increases in the money supply aimed at stimulating aggregate demand and relieving unemployment.

Increasing the money supply from M to M' in Figure 1a lowers the interest rate from $\overline{r}$ to $\overline{r}'$. In Figure 1b, the lower interest rate causes investment to increase to $\overline{I}'$, where the marginal efficiency of invest-

Figure 1 Effects of Expansionary Monetary Policy

ment (*MEI*) equals the lower interest rate. The increased investment, of course, raises aggregate demand (*AD*) in Figure 1c, narrowing or closing the *deflationary gap* and bringing GNP closer to the full-employment GNP.

$$+\Delta M \longrightarrow -\Delta r \longrightarrow +\Delta I \longrightarrow +\Delta \overline{Y} = k\Delta I$$

Inflation and Restrictive Monetary Policy

If the problem facing the monetary authorities is inflationary pressure as a result of excess aggregate demand, *restrictive monetary policies* may dampen aggregate demand and the inflationary pressure.

- **Restrictive monetary policies** are deliberate decreases in the money supply aimed at lowering aggregate demand and relieving inflationary pressures.

Reducing the money supply from M to M' in Figure 2a raises the interest rate from $\bar{r}$ to $\bar{r}'$. In Figure 2b, the higher interest rate reduces investment from $\bar{I}$ to $\bar{I}'$, where $MEI = \bar{r}'$. Finally, in Figure 2c, the lower level of investment lowers aggregate demand to AD', reducing equilibrium GNP and closing the *inflationary gap*.

$$-\Delta M \longrightarrow +\Delta r \longrightarrow -\Delta I \longrightarrow -\Delta \overline{Y} = k\Delta I$$

Of course, if the real world operated as neatly as the models, there wouldn't be any dispute over the effectiveness and necessity of discretionary monetary policies. Unfortunately, the real world is considerably "messier."

Figure 2 Effects of Restrictive Monetary Policy

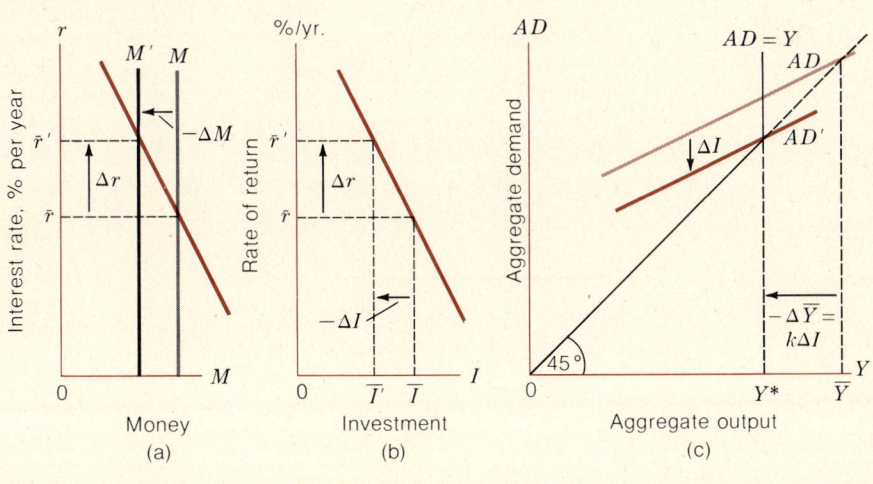

Close-up

Political Business Cycles?

Economic conditions play an important part in the political fortunes of incumbent presidents seeking re-election. Professor Ray Fair of Yale University has found that incumbents have traditionally had a much greater chance of re-election if aggregate output and employment are rising during the election year.[1] If this is in fact the case, an incumbent president seeking re-election would do well to pursue monetary and fiscal policies that would ensure the maximum rate of expansion during the election year. One way to do this would be to apply monetary and fiscal restraint to put the economy into a contraction in the year before the election year, and then pursue expansionary monetary and fiscal policies during the election year. This would generate what some observers have called *political business cycles*—fluctuations in economic activity that can be explained by the domination of political concerns of incumbents over other goals of discretionary monetary and fiscal policy (such as price stability).

There are a number of cases consistent with the political-business-cycle scenario. In 1972, for example, the money supply grew at a rapid rate—over 8 percent. In 1972, of course, Richard Nixon was also seeking re-election. The Chairman of the Board of Governors of the Federal Reserve, and the dominant voice in monetary policy at the time, was Arthur Burns. Burns and Nixon were very close ideologically and members of the same party. This combination of events, of course, doesn't necessarily mean that Burns' motives in monetary policy were to aid the re-election efforts of Nixon, but policy certainly was consistent with this aim.[2]

It is probably a bit of an exaggeration to predict that incumbents will invariably follow expansionary monetary and fiscal policies in election years, even at the expense of excessive inflation, or that such policies would be the most important factor affecting the outcome of the election. President Ford opposed many expansionary policies in 1975 and 1976, and the economic expansion in 1976 didn't result in his election. Many factors besides economic growth affect the outcomes of elections—ideology, candidates' personalities, foreign policy issues, and other political issues (such as President Ford's pardon of Richard Nixon). Also, after several inflationary expansions to gain voter support, excessive inflation may well become the dominant issue for voters—this clearly was the case by mid-1979 as the Carter administration geared up for the 1980 election.

---

1. Ray C. Fair, "Growth Rates Predict November Winners," *New York Times*, January 25, 1976.
2. On the 1972 election, see Carol J. Loomis, "The New Questions About the U.S. Economy," *Fortune*, Vol. 89, No. 1 (January 1974), pp. 69–73ff.

Choice of Objectives

The ultimate objective of discretionary monetary policy is to minimize unemployment and inflationary pressure. In pursuit of this goal, the

Federal Reserve has to shoot at two "targets" in its policy decisions—a **money supply growth target** and an **interest rate target**. Once it has determined the proper direction for monetary policy, the Fed establishes a targeted range for changes in the money supply and for the interest rate.

In some cases, the monetary and interest rate targets are competing goals. The Fed may have to sacrifice its targeted growth of the money supply to keep the interest rate in the desired range, or it may have to sacrifice its interest rate objective to keep changes in the money supply within the targeted range. When push comes to shove, the Fed appears more willing to sacrifice the money supply objective than the interest rate objective, and this willingness can have some serious consequences.

The basic economic logic behind reducing instability of interest rates is sound and easy to follow. Unstable interest rates lead to unstable investment, aggregate demand, and GNP, which in turn lead to unstable expectations and further instability of aggregate demand. However, if economic conditions dictate a change in the interest rate, trying to keep it from changing by adjusting the money supply can create problems. Suppose that the economy is experiencing rising aggregate demand and is approaching full employment. Since income is increasing, money demand will also be increasing, and interest rates will tend to rise (perhaps rather sharply). The Federal Reserve, concerned about the rising interest rates, may increase the money supply, thus intensifying inflationary pressures. If the interest rate had been allowed to rise, the increase in aggregate demand would have been dampened as the economy moved toward full employment.

Consider the opposite case. A sharp economic downturn reduces the level of investment and the demand for money. The decline in the demand for money reduces interest rates. If the Fed tries to stabilize interest rates, it will have to reduce the money supply. However, reducing the money supply in a recession will tend to amplify the deflationary forces—probably lengthening and deepening the recession. The proper course of action would be to let interest rates fall, which would dampen the decline in aggregate demand.

Close-up

The "Credit Crunch" of 1966

The period between 1960 and 1965 was one of steady and strong economic recovery and expansion. In 1964, demand was stimulated further by the enactment of a major cut in federal income taxes, and in mid-1965 the escalation of the Vietnam War caused still greater increases in aggregate demand. The economic expansion increased the public and private demand for funds in credit markets, and interest rates began to rise.

The Federal Reserve, concerned about the prospects of high interest rates, moved in mid-1965 to increase the money supply more rapidly to accommodate the increased demand for funds. Since the increase in the money supply added to the inflationary pressures building in the economy, the Fed moved in 1966 to reduce inflationary pressures by reversing their expansionary monetary policies. Between the second and third quarters of 1966, M_1 fell at an annual rate of 0.7 percent after four consecutive quarters in which M_1 had increased at annual rates in excess of 4.5 percent.

The sharp reversal of monetary policy created severe shortages of loanable funds in money markets—or, as it was called at the time, a severe **credit crunch**. The crunch undoubtedly would have been less severe had the Fed simply allowed interest rates to rise and restrained the growth of the money supply more gradually in 1965.

The Effectiveness of Monetary Policy

The effectiveness of monetary policy is a two-part question. First, there is the question of the strength of the effects of monetary policies on aggregate demand, output, employment, and prices. The second question is the practical usefulness of monetary policy as a means of regulating demand. Obviously, monetary policy wouldn't be very effective if it had very weak effects on aggregate demand. Nor would it be very useful if its effects on aggregate demand were erratic and unpredictable.

Money and Depression: The Liquidity Trap

In the depths of an economic disaster of the magnitude of the Great Depression of the 1930s, monetary policies alone may not be very effective in stimulating aggregate demand. In an extreme situation, called a *liquidity trap*, changing the money supply won't stimulate aggregate demand at all.

- A **liquidity trap** is a situation in which increasing the money supply *only* increases the amount of money held by households and firms and does not cause the interest rate to fall.

Bleak and uncertain economic expectations encourage firms, households, and financial institutions to be as liquid as possible—i.e., to hold money for precautionary and speculative reasons. In Figure 3, the money supply is increased from M to M' in an attempt to stimulate demand and output. However, worsening expectations increase the precautionary and speculative demands for money, shifting the money demand curve from L to L' in Figure 3. Instead of spending the money supplied, individuals simply hold the additional money as precautionary and speculative balances to provide for needs in a grim economic future and to minimize the risk of loss. As a result, the

Figure 3 Liquidity Trap

interest rate doesn't change and the increase in the money supply cannot stimulate aggregate demand via higher levels of investment.

The liquidity trap has been presented as a key concept in Keynesian economics and in the Keynesian explanation of the Great Depression. In fact, Keynes himself recognized only the theoretical possibility of liquidity traps and argued that liquidity traps probably never had been observed. The Great Depression is the only economic catastrophe in this century in which a liquidity trap might have been observed, but the money supply in fact *fell* during the worst years of the Depression.

Economists in the classical and monetarist tradition deny even the theoretical possibility of liquidity traps—except at interest rates approaching zero. The classical argument goes all the way back to Adam Smith's assertion that "A man must be perfectly crazy who, where there is tolerable security, does not employ all the stock which he commands."[1] This implies that people would put their money into interest-bearing assets as long as these assets earn any interest at all.

Weak Effects of Monetary Policy

Short of severe depressions and the highly unlikely liquidity trap situations, there are conditions in which monetary policy alone would have relatively weak effects on aggregate demand, real GNP, and employment. This situation is likely to occur when aggregate demand is low and GNP is considerably below the full employment level—as in Figure 4.

In Figure 4a, the low level of GNP generates a low transactions demand for money, and the interest rate ($\bar{r}$) is relatively low. Increasing

---

1. Adam Smith, *An Inquiry into the Nature and Causes of the Wealth of Nations*, Book II, Chapter 1.

Figure 4 Weak Effects of Monetary Policy

the money supply to M' lowers the interest rate to $\bar{r}'$, a small reduction from a substantial increase in the money supply. The small drop in the interest rate, coupled with the low response of investment to changes in the interest rate in Figure 4b, results in a small increase in investment from $\bar{I}$ to $\bar{I}'$. Thus, in Figure 4c, the large initial increase in the money supply has yielded a relatively small increase in equilibrium GNP from $\bar{Y}$ to $\bar{Y}'$.

In periods of low output and high unemployment, as portrayed in Figure 4, the Fed's other monetary policy tools may not be very effective either. The discount rate on loans from the Fed to commercial banks could be lowered, but the Fed can't force the banks to extend more loans at lower interest rates. In a severe recession, there may not be many opportunities to make loans at the banks' minimum acceptable interest rate, and banks won't lower the interest rate if the lower rates don't compensate them for the loss of liquidity.

The effectiveness of monetary policy in stimulating recovery from a recession has thus been described as trying to "push a string." Though the phrase is fairly descriptive of the problem, it shouldn't be interpreted as meaning that "money doesn't matter," but rather that monetary policy *alone* may not be very effective in these circumstances.

Strong Effects of Monetary Policy

Not surprisingly, the conditions in which monetary policies are likely to have strong effects on aggregate demand are basically the opposite of the conditions in which the effects are weak. High aggregate output, high transactions demand for money, a steep demand curve for money, a relatively flat *MEI* curve, and a strong expenditure multiplier will contribute to strong effects of monetary policy on aggregate demand.

In Figure 5a, the transactions demand for money is high relative to the supply of money, resulting in a high initial interest rate ($\bar{r}$) in the portion of the money demand curve (L) where the interest rate is most sensitive to changes in the money supply. A relatively small increase in the money supply from M to M' causes a substantial decline in the interest rate in Figure 5a, leading to a large increase in investment in Figure 5b. The increase in investment causes a large increase in equilibrium GNP from $\bar{Y}$ to $\bar{Y}'$ in Figure 5c as a result of the initial small increase in the money supply in Figure 5a.

Thus, the impact of monetary policies on aggregate demand, GNP, employment, and inflationary pressures varies with economic conditions. As a general rule, monetary policies have the weakest effects in periods in which aggregate demand, GNP, and initial interest rates are low; and the strongest effects when aggregate demand, GNP, and initial interest rates are high.

Another lesson is that discretionary monetary policies are more useful for some problems than others. Pushing the string to stimulate recovery from a deep recession by monetary expansion alone will be difficult. However, pulling on a string is more effective, and monetary restraint is a strong tool for dampening inflationary pressures caused by excess demand.

Figure 5   Strong Effects of Monetary Policy

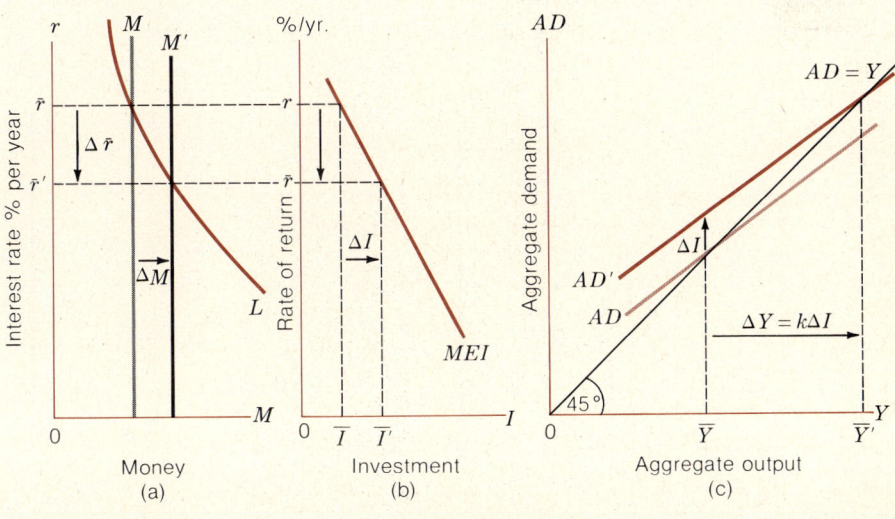

Information Problems

"The best laid schemes o' mice and men," wrote the Scottish poet Robert Burns, "gang aft agley" ("often go awry"). The same thing could be said of many of the best laid schemes of the Federal Reserve. One reason that many well-designed monetary policies "gang aft agley" is the inadequacy of information.

What pieces of information would be required to achieve minimum unemployment and inflationary pressures via monetary policies? First, a reasonably good estimate of the demand curve for money is needed to predict the effects of changes in the money supply on the interest rate. Policies should be based on the best empirical estimates possible, but even the best estimates may not be accurate.

In Figure 6a, suppose that the estimated money demand curve is L_e, but that actual money demand is represented by the darker curve L_a. The interest rate will be more sensitive to changes in the money supply than the estimate would predict. If the Fed increased the money supply from M to M' to stimulate aggregate demand, it would expect the interest rate to fall from $\bar{r}$ to $\bar{r}'$ in Figure 6a. However, such an increase in the money supply would actually cause the interest rate to fall from $\bar{r}$ to $\bar{r}''$, stimulating investment and aggregate demand more than the Fed's estimate. This overstimulus could lead to inflationary pressure, even if all of the other information required is 100% accurate (which it isn't).

What if the Fed tries to dampen aggregate demand and *underestimates* the sensitivity of the interest rate to changes in the money supply? In Figure 6b, the estimated money demand curve is L_e and actual

Figure 6 Information Problems: Estimating Money Demand

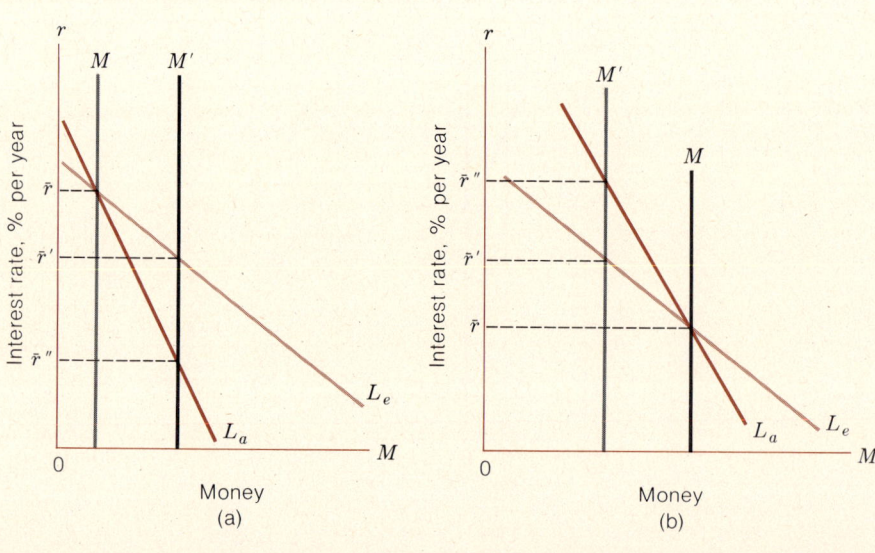

money demand is represented by L_a. If the Fed cuts the money supply from M to M', expecting the interest rate to rise from $\bar{r}$ to $\bar{r}'$, the interest rate would actually increase to $\bar{r}''$. In this case, the error in estimated money demand would depress investment and aggregate demand more than predicted, resulting in greater unemployment than expected.

Money demand is only one piece of the puzzle that monetary authorities must solve. The Fed also needs a good estimate of the responsiveness of investment changes in the interest rate, or the marginal efficiency of investment (MEI). In Figure 7, the estimated marginal efficiency of investment function is MEI_e, and the actual marginal efficiency of investment function is MEI_a. In this case the level of investment is more responsive to changes in the interest rate than the estimate suggests. If the Fed's actions lower the interest rate from $\bar{r}$ to $\bar{r}'$, in Figure 7, the expected increase in investment would be from $\bar{I}$ to $\bar{I}'$. However, because of the error in the estimated MEI curve, the level of investment actually increases to $\bar{I}''$—more than predicted and possibly enough more to create unacceptable inflationary pressure. Similarly, if the Fed tries to dampen inflationary pressure by increasing interest rates, the decline in investment would be greater than predicted, possibly resulting in an unacceptable rise in unemployment.

Even if the Fed knew the money demand and marginal efficiency of investment functions fairly accurately, there could be problems. To estimate the increase in aggregate demand that would yield an ac-

Figure 7 Information Problems: Estimating the Responsiveness of Investment

Expectations

ceptably low unemployment without excessive inflationary pressure or dampen inflationary pressure without creating an unacceptable unemployment rate, the Fed must have a good estimate of the multiplier effect of a change in investment on equilibrium GNP.

To make matters worse, the money demand and *MEI* curves have a nasty habit of shifting in response to changes in expectations, making even the best estimates from previous data inaccurate. Suppose that the estimated money demand curve (*L*) in Figure 8 is an accurate estimate based on data from past years. The Fed increases the money supply from M to M', expecting to lower the interest rate from $\bar{r}$ to $\bar{r}'$ and stimulate investment and aggregate demand. But if economic expectations have worsened, demand for precautionary and speculative balances will have increased, shifting the money demand curve to L'. Increasing the money supply to M' thus causes a smaller reduction of the interest rate (to $\bar{r}''$) than expected.

Expectations also affect the expected rate of return on investments and therefore the *MEI* curve. Suppose that monetary authorities increase the money supply and lower the interest rate from $\bar{r}$ to $\bar{r}'$, expecting that investment will rise to $\bar{I}'$ in Figure 9. If worsening expectations have shifted *MEI* leftward to *MEI'*, the increase in investment will be much smaller than expected.

Changes in expectations are hard to predict, and because they affect the responsiveness of interest rates and investment to changes in the

Figure 8 Effects of Expectations on Money Demand

Figure 9 Effects of Expectations on Investment Decisions

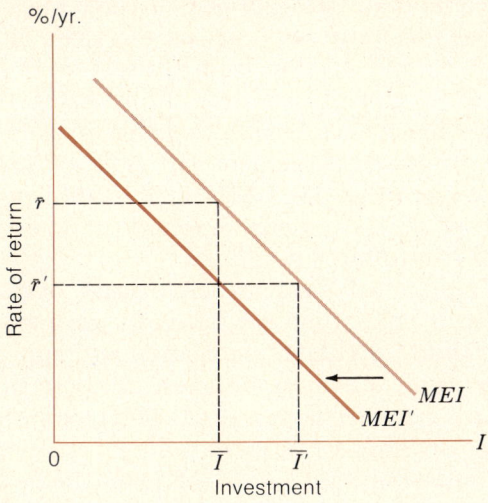

supply of money, unstable expectations increase the chance that monetary authorities will make mistakes. Frequent mistakes in monetary policy, in turn, make expectations still less stable.

Leads and Lags Imagine that you own an extremely powerful car that can reach speeds of over 200 miles per hour. The car has a strange quirk, however: when you step on the accelerator, the car will speed up, but you can't be sure when or how much. If you let up on the accelerator and apply the brake, the car will slow down, but you can't be sure when. Furthermore, the time lags between your actions and the car's reactions aren't always the same. How should you drive such a machine? If you drove it at all, you should do so *very* cautiously. In fact, many would urge you not to drive it at all.

What does all of this have to do with monetary policy? Like the car, money and monetary policy are powerful machines. Also like the car, there is generally some lag between a change in monetary policy and the full effect of this change. Finally, the lags between the policy and its full effect aren't always the same, and the same acceleration or braking of monetary policy won't always have the same ultimate effect. Monetary policy is thus a machine to be operated with some caution. Frequent rapid acceleration, deceleration, and braking can lead to serious accidents.

When aggregate demand and economic activity change, monetary authorities don't know about it immediately. The information doesn't reach the authorities until the relevant data has been compiled and published. This **data lag** is usually about two months—inflationary pressures that develop in January become apparent when January data becomes available in late February or early March.

Authorities generally don't act on the basis of a one-month change in economic conditions, but wait to see if there is a trend. If the data show very slow growth or a decline in aggregate output for January, for example, policymakers will probably wait for February and maybe March data to see if the economy is truly in a recession. In short, there is a **recognition lag** between the publication of data and the recognition of a need for discretionary policies. This lag may be on the order of two to three months.

For fiscal policies, there are significant **decision lags** and **action lags** because it takes time for Congress and the President to decide upon, enact, and implement legislation and appropriate spending and tax policies. With monetary policies, these particular elements of the **inside lag** are virtually nonexistent. The Open Market Committee and the Board of Governors can make policy decisions much more quickly than the Congress and the President. Once the Fed decides on a change in monetary policy, it can act almost immediately.

The inside lag thus tends to be much shorter for monetary policy than it was for fiscal policy. Unfortunately, the same cannot be said for the **outside** or **effectiveness lag**. The impact of fiscal policy on aggregate output is quite direct: an increase in government spending represents (in theory) a direct increase in aggregate demand which will lead directly to an increase in output. The effects of monetary policy, on the other hand, are indirect: a change in the money supply changes the interest rate, which changes the level of investment, which changes aggregate demand, which changes output. The outside lag between the implementation of a change in monetary policy and its full economic impact may be as long as six to ten months.

If all of these lags were regular, predictable, and short, they wouldn't pose a serious problem for discretionary monetary policy. However, if they are long, variable in length, and unpredictable, the problems of effective discretionary policy are much more serious. Adding the lags together, there may be a lag of a year or more between the time that economic conditions change and the full effects of corrective policies are felt. Many other changes can occur in the course of a year, and by the time that the full effects of a change in policy are felt, they may worsen a new problem that has arisen in the meantime.

Relationship Between Monetary and Fiscal Policies

Monetary and fiscal policies are under the jurisdiction of separate authorities—monetary policy under the Federal Reserve and fiscal policy under the President and Congress. However, the two are not independent economically. The economic effects of discretionary fiscal policies depend heavily—some argue exclusively—on supportive monetary policies. How are monetary and fiscal policy related? Can one work without the other?

Unsupported Fiscal Expansion

Suppose that the President and Congress embark on a course of expansionary fiscal policy—increasing government spending or cutting taxes—but the Fed doesn't go along. To stimulate aggregate demand, the government runs or increases a deficit in the Federal budget, and has to increase borrowing to finance the deficit.

To see how deficits and government borrowing affect interest rates and aggregate demand, we have to take a look at the market for **loanable funds**. Loanable funds are funds available for loans to borrowers. The price of loanable funds is the interest rate that has to be paid for the use of the funds.

As the interest rate rises, households and businesses reduce their holdings of money balances and convert more of their money balances into assets that earn interest. Thus, more loanable funds become available as the interest rate rises, so there is a direct relationship between the interest rate and the quantity of loanable funds supplied along S_{LF} in Figure 10a. But a rise in the interest rate also represents an increase in the price of loanable funds, so the quantity of loanable funds demanded will fall along D_{LF}. The loanable funds market is in equilibrium when the quantity of loanable funds demanded equals the quantity supplied—i.e., at the equilibrium interest rate ($\bar{r}$) in Figure 10a.

Figure 10 Unsupported Fiscal Expansion

If the government increases its borrowing to finance a larger deficit due to expansionary fiscal policies, the demand for loanable funds increases to D_{LF}' in Figure 10a and driving the interest rate upward to $\bar{r}'$. The rising interest rate chokes off investment, as shown in Figure 10b. As the interest rate rises to $\bar{r}'$, investment falls to $\bar{I}'$, dampening aggregate demand and working against the goal of expansionary fiscal policy. In other words, some private spending is *crowded out* by the higher interest rates that followed the fiscal expansion.

- **Crowding out** is the tendency of expansionary fiscal policies to reduce private investment demand by raising interest rates.

Expansionary monetary policies would increase the supply of loanable funds, shown in Figure 10b by the shift from S_{LF} to S_{LF}'. This would support the expansionary fiscal policy by reducing or offsetting the effect of government borrowing on the interest rate. By keeping the interest rate from rising, the supporting monetary policy reduces or eliminates the crowding out of private investment.

Unsupported Fiscal Restraint

Suppose that the President and Congress try to restrain inflationary pressure by reducing government spending or raising taxes. This would reduce the government deficit and government borrowing. Less government borrowing reduces the demand for loanable funds from D_{LF} to D_{LF}' in Figure 11a, causing the interest rate to fall to $\bar{r}'$. The lower interest rate encourages more investment in Figure 11b, and this at least partially offsets the dampening effect of fiscal restraint on aggregate demand.

Figure 11 Unsupported Fiscal Restraint

The Fed could support fiscal restraint by restrictive monetary policies. Restrictive monetary policies reduce the supply of money and the supply of loanable funds from S_{LF} to S_{LF}' in Figure 11a. By keeping the interest rate from falling, or at least reducing the decline in the interest rate, supporting monetary restriction reinforces the effect of the restrictive fiscal measures.

There is a fairly broad consensus that fiscal policy and monetary policy will be more effective if they aren't pulling in opposite directions. However, the question of the proper degree of coordination and consolidation of monetary and fiscal policy is not easy to answer.

Consolidation of Monetary and Fiscal Policy: Pro

Conflicting monetary and fiscal policies make both less effective. If the Fed were required to support fiscal policies with appropriate monetary policies, there would be no conflict between them and fiscal policy would be more effective. This would eliminate conflicts among the Fed, the Congress, and the President such as those in the 1930's, the mid-1960's, and the mid-1970's in which the Congress and the President followed expansionary fiscal policies to stimulate demand and reduce unemployment, while the Fed pursued anti-inflationary monetary policies.

Greater formal coordination of monetary and fiscal policy would make monetary policy more responsive to the electorate. The President and the Congress have the responsibility for fiscal policy and must run for re-election periodically. Therefore, fiscal policy is likely to follow as closely as possible the needs and wishes of a majority of voters. Monetary policy, on the other hand, is in control of the Board of Governors of the Fed, who are appointed (not elected) for long terms. This makes it much easier to pursue monetary policies that run counter to the views of the popular majority. If monetary policy were tied formally to fiscal policy, monetary policy would be more "democratic" in the sense of conforming more closely to majority sentiment.

Consolidation of Monetary and Fiscal Policy: Con

Consolidation of monetary and fiscal policy would indeed make fiscal policy more potent, but the negative side of this is that mistakes in monetary or fiscal policy would be magnified if the two were coordinated. If the President and Congress follow the wrong fiscal policies, the Fed would have to magnify the error by following a supportive monetary policy.

Making monetary policy more responsive to the popular will is consistent with the tradition of majority rule, but may not be a good thing economically. The long and staggered terms of the members of the Board of Governors of the Fed and the independence of the Fed give the Fed greater freedom to pursue monetary policies which may be necessary but unpopular. The long terms of members also contribute to greater consistency of monetary policy over time.

Political considerations make it difficult for Congress and the President to pursue necessary fiscal policies which may be unpopular—especially anti-inflationary policies which reduce government spending or raise taxes. To limit the flexibility of the Fed with similar political considerations would put similar pressures on monetary policy.

If frequent changes in the political climate led to frequent changes in monetary policy, monetary policy would be less consistent over time, thus contributing to instability and uncertainty. Uncertainty, especially if accompanied by pessimistic expectations, is not a favorable economic environment.

Formal consolidation of monetary and fiscal policy could have some disastrous economic effects. The President and the Congress could take a relatively casual view toward the enactment of new programs if they could be sure that the programs could be financed by expansionary monetary policy without following the politically dangerous course of raising taxes.

The question of the proper degree of consolidation of monetary and fiscal policy will not be settled overnight. The final solution ultimately depends on the strength of the positive and negative aspects of more or less coordination. If there is too little coordination and too much conflict between monetary and fiscal policy, both may be relatively ineffective. If there is too much coordination, mistakes in monetary or fiscal policy will be magnified.

Close-up

Carter and the Chairmen

Every President inherits Federal Reserve Board members who were appointed during previous administrations. When President Carter assumed office, he inherited not only Federal Reserve Board members who had been appointed by President Nixon, but one of the strongest willed Chairmen of the Federal Reserve Board, Arthur F. Burns. The politically and economically conservative Burns is a widely respected monetary economist, and a former director of the National Bureau of Economic Research. While the President followed an expansionary fiscal course in 1977 to stimulate aggregate demand and reduce unemployment, Burns not only didn't go along with supporting monetary policies, but followed his own independent course of monetary restraint to reduce inflationary pressure. When Burns' term as Chairman expired in 1978, President Carter's decision not to reappoint him surprised nobody (least of all Burns).

When President Carter appointed G. William Miller as Chairman, most observers saw this as a move that would reduce the Fed's independence from the Executive and Legislative branches of the government. Miller's scholarly credentials as a student of monetary theory and policy didn't approach those of Burns, and he was not a well-known public figure. However, Federal Reserve Board appointees have a way of surprising the President who appoints them.

Chairman Miller followed a monetary course which he described as "steady as you go," i.e., avoiding dramatic changes in the money supply. After having trouble getting Chairman Burns to go along with expansionary policies, the President had some trouble getting Chairman Miller to support fiscal restraint with discretionary restrictive monetary policies. The friction between the two was not enough, however, to prevent Miller's joining the Carter cabinet as Secretary of the Treasury in July, 1979.

The Monetarist Prescription

With a firm grounding in the economics of monetary and fiscal policy, we can take a closer look at **monetarism**, which was introduced briefly in an earlier chapter. Monetarism is a school of economic thought that emphasizes private market forces and changes in the money supply as the critical determinants of aggregate demand, output, employment, and prices. Monetarist economic arguments are based on several basic propositions.

1. In the long run, freely operating market forces will yield equilibrium real GNP at full employment.
2. In the short run, changes in the money supply can affect real GNP. The effects of fiscal policy on real GNP are weak and short-lived unless supported by monetary policy.
3. In the long run, real GNP is determined by the economy's capacity to produce, and changes in the money supply affect only prices and nominal GNP. Fiscal policy only determines the division of income and output between the public and private sectors.
4. Incomplete information and irregular lags between changes in monetary policy and the full effect of these changes make it hard to predict the size and timing of the effects of monetary policies.

These basic propositions have led the monetarists to a policy strategy that is dramatically different from the strategy followed by monetary authorities. This strategy is most fully and clearly developed and expressed in the works of the monetarists' most famous and eloquent spokesman, Milton Friedman.

No Discretionary Monetary Policy

One fundamental goal of the monetarist strategy is to strip the Fed of its discretionary power over the money supply. Friedman and many other monetarists would replace the discretionary power of the Fed with a legislative rule requiring a constant annual rate of growth of the money supply. The constant rate would be tied to the long-term trends in growth of real GNP and velocity of money.

If the money supply grew at a rate that just offset the effects of economic growth and changing velocity, it would have no long-range effect on prices. Temporary shifts of aggregate demand could cause short-term variation of prices, but inflationary or deflationary pressures wouldn't be worsened by monetary policy. Friedman has estimated that an annual rate of growth of three to five percent would accomplish this objective.

It might seem odd that Friedman and the other monetarists attach such great importance to changes in the money supply but advocate the elimination of discretionary monetary policy. Friedman's basic argument is that the history of discretionary monetary policy is one of mistakes by monetary policy authorities—"Too late and too much has been the general practice."[2]

Monetarists attribute the destabilizing effects of monetary policy to a number of causes—incompetence of monetary authorities, inadequate information, irregular and unpredictable lags between changes in policy and the effects of these changes, political pressure on monetary authorities, or some combination of these. In short, in the monetarist framework, the Fed is almost certain to make mistakes in monetary policy and the effects of these mistakes are destabilizing. Thus, the proposal to eliminate discretionary monetary policy isn't inconsistent with the view that money is the most potent economic variable.

Fiscal Policy

Most monetarists reject discretionary fiscal policies as a means of reducing unemployment and inflationary pressures. In the short run, fiscal policy has very little effect on aggregate demand, GNP, employment, or inflationary pressure unless it is supported by accommodating monetary policies—i.e., *crowding out* is virtually complete. In the long run, fiscal policy doesn't affect equilibrium real GNP because in the monetarist view of the world, real GNP tends toward the full employment level in the long run. Thus, the only effect of fiscal policy is to determine the division of aggregate output and income between the private and public sectors of the economy.

Monetarists generally advocate a minimal role for the government in the economy, so it isn't surprising that they would reject discretionary monetary and fiscal policies as a means of promoting full employment and stable prices. Friedman would limit fiscal policy to government spending projects that are determined by the community's need for them, and argues that all government spending should be financed by taxes—i.e., that the budget should be balanced. In fact, Friedman has advocated a form of "balanced-budget amendment" to the Constitution.

Employment

How would problems of unemployment be handled without discretionary monetary and fiscal policies to regulate the level of aggregate

---

2. Milton Friedman, "The Role of Monetary Policy," *American Economic Review*, vol. 58, no. 1 (March 1968), p. 16.

demand? Monetarists tend to accept the classical view that the economy will tend toward equilibrium at full employment in the long run if the government doesn't interfere in the free working of market forces. If the long-run level of employment is full employment without discretionary policies, the discretionary policies are unnecessary.

Of course, monetarists—like their classical predecessors—recognize the possibility of unemployment in the short run. However, if government tries to cure unemployment through discretionary fiscal and monetary policies, the long-run effect would be inflationary. Expansionary fiscal policies to reduce unemployment have to be supported by expansionary monetary policies to be effective, and expansionary monetary policies will contribute to inflation as the economy moves toward its long-run equilibrium at full employment.

Critique of the Monetarist Program

Monetarists constitute a minority of contemporary economists—an important minority, but still a minority. Most economists would accept some of the monetarists' arguments about the importance of money, but not their attachment to laissez faire and their desire to disarm monetary and fiscal policy authorities.

The monetarist program described briefly above rests on an implicit assumption that the private sector of the economy is inherently stable and that it would deal with unemployment and inflationary pressures on its own. However, as we have seen, some components of aggregate private spending—specifically, investment and consumer durables—tend to be unstable. To the extent that there is an *accelerator effect*, investment will tend to be less stable than GNP over time.

The monetarist-classical argument that the natural long-run equilibrium of the economy is only at full employment requires that prices of goods and resources be flexible—downward as well as upward. In a period of slack demand, for example, prices must move downward to clear goods markets of unsold goods and labor markets of unemployed workers. There are a number of forces in the economy, however, that contribute to price rigidity, or at least sluggish adjustments of prices, especially downward adjustments. In most basic industries, for example, there are only a few large firms, and these firms tend to avoid *price wars*. The aversion to vigorous price competition in these industries contributes to downward rigidity of prices.

Labor unions try to use their market power to get their members the maximum economic benefits possible in periods of brisk demand, and to guard against reductions in these benefits in periods of slack demand. This means that wages in organized industries where unions have bargaining power are likewise extremely slow to adjust downward.

Friedman argues that wages and prices can remain rigid downward only if they are supported by monetary policy. If wages are too high to clear the labor market, for example, monetary authorities are under pressure to pursue expansionary monetary policy to reduce full employment, thus supporting the high wages.

The monetarist view of the world is a long-run view. In the long run, market forces will deal effectively with unemployment and inflation without discretionary monetary and fiscal policies. However, as Keynes once observed, "In the long run, we all are dead." The monetarist program would eliminate some important policy tools to deal with short-run problems of unemployment and inflation.

The Monetarist Controversy: Who's Right?

The running debate between the monetarist minority and the nonmonetarist majority isn't between an entrenched intellectual establishment and a vocal but insignificant minority. The Presidency of the American Economic Association is perhaps the clearest evidence of esteem from the economics establishment. The following are excerpts from the 1968 Presidential Address of Professor Friedman and the 1976 Presidential Address of Professor Franco Modigliani of M.I.T.

> My own prescription is still that the monetary authority go all the way in avoiding swings in monetary policy by adopting publicly the policy of achieving a steady rate of growth in a specified monetary total. . . . It would be better to have a fixed rate that would on the average produce moderate inflation or moderate deflation, provided that it was steady, than to suffer the wide and erratic perturbations we have experienced.[3]

> All I am arguing is that (i) there is no basis for the monetarists' suggestion that our postwar instability can be traced to monetary instability—our most unstable periods have coincided with periods of relative monetary stability; and (ii) stability of the money supply is not enough to give us a stable economy, precisely because there are exogenous disturbances.[4]

In the currently unsettled state of the debate, is there any reason to accept the basic monetarist or basic nonmonetarist arguments? One possible reason to choose one over the other is a basic confidence that the private sector is inherently stable (which would lean one toward monetarism) or that the private sector is inherently unstable (which would lean one toward nonmonetarist activism in monetary and fiscal policy). Similarly, the choice between the monetarists' laissez-faire prescription and discretionary monetary and fiscal policies depends on one's confidence in the ability of monetary and fiscal authorities to gather and evaluate all of the necessary information and take the appropriate actions to deal effectively with unemployment and inflation.

A second basis for choosing monetarism or nonmonetarist activism is more political, ideological, and normative than analytical. If one feels that there are unmet social needs that can be dealt with effec-

---

3. Milton Friedman, "The Role of Monetary Policy," *American Economic Review*: vol. 48, no. 1 (March 1968), p. 16.
4. Franco Modigliani, "The Monetarist Controversy or, Should We Forsake Stabilization Policies?" *American Economic Review*: vol. 67, no. 2 (March 1977), p. 12.

tively only through the public sector—national health insurance, improved mass transit, etc.—this suggests an active role for fiscal policy in meeting social needs as well as promoting full employment. If, on the other hand, one feels that individuals should be free to spend their incomes as they see fit, and that the ultimate test of goods and services society should have is the market test, he or she will tend more toward the monetarist view of the world. These, obviously, are very important considerations. Unfortunately, there is no positive, analytical resolution of these types of issues.

Summary

1. **Discretionary monetary policies** try to regulate aggregate demand by changing the money supply and the interest rate.
2. Monetary policy affects aggregate demand, output, employment, and the price level through its effects on interest rates and investment expenditures.
3. The Federal Reserve gears its monetary policies to two targets—a targeted rate of growth of the money supply and an interest rate target.
4. A **liquidity trap** is a situation in which changes in the money supply have no effect on the interest rate, and therefore no effect on aggregate demand, output, or employment.
5. The effectiveness of monetary policy in regulating aggregate demand and achieving unemployment and inflation goals is limited by information problems and lags between changes in monetary policy and the economic effects of these changes in policy.
6. Without supporting monetary policies, fiscal policies may be relatively ineffective in regulating aggregate demand. Unsupported fiscal policies to stimulate aggregate demand tend to raise interest rates and crowd out some private spending. Unsupported fiscal restraint will cause interest rates to fall, at least partially offsetting the effects on aggregate demand.
7. Modern monetarism emphasizes the importance of private markets and changes in the money supply as the critical determinants of aggregate output, employment, and prices. Monetarists argue for a minimal role of government demand-management policies and a constant rate of growth of the money supply as an alternative to discretionary monetary policy.

Concepts for Review

discretionary monetary policy
expansionary monetary policy
restrictive monetary policy
money supply growth target
interest rate target
credit crunch
liquidity trap
crowding out
loanable funds
monetarist program

Questions

1. Suppose that the Federal Reserve sticks closely to a strategy of keeping interest rates stable by changing the money supply.
   a. In a period of rising aggregate demand and aggregate output, what should the Fed do to keep the interest rate stable? Explain how these policies would stabilize interest rates. Would the policies have any

effects beyond stabilizing the interest rate?
   b. Answer the questions in part (a) for a period of falling aggregate demand and aggregate output.
2. Stimulating recovery from severe recessions has been characterized as "pushing on a string," or, as Keynes advised President Roosevelt in 1936, "trying to get fat by buying a bigger belt."
   a. Explain why the effects of expansionary monetary policy tend to be weak in severe recessions. Under what circumstances might expansionary monetary policies alone be completely ineffective in stimulating aggregate demand and output?
   b. Do the weak effects of monetary policy alone in recessions apply to the effects of monetary policy in periods of high output and inflationary pressure?
3. Supporters of discretionary monetary policy have argued that monetary policy stabilizes aggregate demand and output by "leaning against the wind." Friedman and other monetarist critics of discretionary monetary policy have replied that monetary policy authorities have to decide now on policies to lean against whatever wind is blowing in the future.
   a. Explain the meaning of the term "leaning against the wind." How could monetary policy do this?
   b. Explain the basis of the monetarists' counterargument. What are the merits and weak points of the argument? What are the implications of the monetarist critique for discretionary monetary policy?
4. What is meant by the term *crowding out*? What does it imply about the effectiveness of unsupported fiscal policies in stimulating aggregate demand and output? What (if anything) could monetary policy do to reduce crowding out? Explain carefully.
5. "Restricted growth in Federal spending, combined with the revenues yielded by a moderately growing economy, will reduce the budget deficit to $29 billion in 1980, less than half its size in the year before I took office . . . These measures of fiscal policy are being complemented by firm and careful monetary restraint on the part of the Federal Reserve Board . . . ." (President Carter, January 1979).
   a. What kinds of monetary policy would support the efforts of restrictive fiscal policies in dampening aggregate demand?
   b. What would be the probable effects of the Fed's refusing to complement fiscal restraint?
6. If Friedman and the monetarists argue that the money supply and changes in the money supply are such potent economic variables, why do they advocate a constant rate of growth of the money supply to replace discretionary monetary policies?
7. Consider the following proposals:
   a. Make the Federal Reserve completely independent of the executive and legislative branches of the government—i.e., make it an institution similar to the Supreme Court.
   b. Make the terms of members of the Federal Reserve Board of Governors identical to the presidential term of office.
   c. Select members of the Federal Reserve Board of Governors by popular vote.
   What would you predict as the effects of these proposals on the nature and effectiveness of monetary policy? Explain.

APPENDIX

Money, Interest, and GNP: The *IS-LM* Approach

Equilibrium aggregate output of goods and services is reached when the aggregate demand for goods and services—or intended spending—is just equal to aggregate output or real GNP. Equilibrium also requires that the expenditure outflows (or leaks) from the spending stream equal the expenditure inflows into the spending stream. However, equilibrium in the goods sector and equilibrium aggregate output requires equilibrium in money markets as well. If money markets aren't in equilibrium, the interest rate will move toward its equilibrium, and this will affect investment, some consumption expenditures, and aggregate demand. In 1939, Sir John Hicks derived a model to show how equilibrium real GNP and equilibrium in money markets are interrelated, and to show how changes in one sector affect equilibrium in the other.

The Goods Sector and Real GNP

Recall that equilibrium GNP is reached in a closed private economy where *intended investment* (I) equals *intended saving* (S). Intended investment depends on the interest rate (r). Given an interest rate of 7% in Figure A–1a, intended investment comes to rest at $\bar{I} = 250$, where the interest rate (r) equals the *MEI*.

Equilibrium GNP ($\bar{Y}$) is reached when $I = S$. The saving function (S) in Figure A–1b shows the relationship between GNP (Y) and intended saving (S). Equilibrium GNP is reached at $\bar{Y} = 500$ in Figure A–1b where $\bar{I} = S = 250$. In other words, the interest rate, the *MEI* function, and the saving function have determined an equilibrium GNP that is consistent with an interest rate of 7%. In Figure A–1c, then, if the interest rate is $r = 7\%$, $I = S$ at $\bar{Y} = 500$.

If the interest rate fell to $r' = 6\%$ in Figure A–1a, intended investment would rise to $I' = 500$. Equilibrium GNP with $I = S$ would be reached at $\bar{Y} = 1000$ in Figure A–1b. In Figure A–1c, an interest of 6% is consistent with an equilibrium real GNP ($\bar{Y}$) of 1000. We now have two points on the *IS* curve in Figure A–1c.

- At all points on the *IS* curve, the goods sector is in equilibrium with $I = S$.

The Monetary Sector

Equilibrium in money markets is reached when the quantity of money (or liquidity) demanded equals the supply of money in circulation.

For a given level of GNP, the quantity of money demanded will vary inversely with the interest rate (r) along the demand curve for money (L) in Figure A–2a. At a higher level of GNP, the demand for money will be greater at every interest rate. Suppose that the supply of money is $M = 400$ in Figure A–2a. At a GNP of 1000, the money market would reach equilibrium where

Figure A–1 Deriving the IS Curve

$L = M$ at an interest rate of 5%. In Figure A–2b, then, we have a monetary equilibrium ($L = M$) at an interest rate of 5% and a GNP of 1000.

If GNP increased to 1500, the demand for money would shift from L to L' in Figure A–2a. With the same supply of money ($M = 400$), the money market would now reach equilibrium ($L' = M$) at an interest rate of 7%.

Combinations of GNP (Y) and interest rates (r) that generate equilibrium in money markets ($L = M$) with the given supply of money ($M = 400$) will define points on the LM curve in Figure A–2b.

Figure A–2 Deriving the LM Curve

- At all points on the **LM curve** the demand for money equals the supply of money ($L = M$), and the money market is in equilibrium.

A word of caution concerning the interpretation of IS and LM curves: they resemble supply and demand curves, but in fact they are entirely different. The IS curve represents combinations of GNP and interest rates that generate equilibrium in the goods market ($I = S$). Similarly, the LM curve shows combinations of GNP and interest rates that generate equilibrium in money markets ($L = M$).

Equilibrium in Goods and Money Markets

To have a macroeconomic equilibrium, we must have equilibrium in both the goods sector and the monetary sector. Equilibrium is reached at the interest rate ($\bar{r}$) and real GNP ($\bar{Y}$) where the IS and LM curves intersect in Figure A–3—i.e., at $\bar{Y} = 1000$ and $\bar{r} = 5\%$. Any other combination of interest rate and GNP will be unstable because of disequilibrium in goods or money markets.

For example, consider $Y = 500$ and $r = 7\%$ in Figure A–3. We have equilibrium in goods markets ($I = S$), but money markets aren't in equilibrium. Monetary equilibrium with a GNP of $Y = 500$ would be reached with an interest rate of only 3%. An interest rate of 7% at a GNP of 500 is above the interest rate that would clear money markets of excess demand or excess supply of money. In this case, with the interest rate above equilibrium, there will be an excess supply of money in money markets, and this excess supply will cause the interest rate to fall. As the interest rate falls, this tends to stimulate investment and aggregate demand, causing GNP to increase along IS.

If the initial interest rate were 7% and GNP were $Y = 1500$, we have equilibrium in money markets ($L = M$ on LM), but not in goods markets. At this GNP, goods market equilibrium would be reached at an interest rate of $r = 3\%$. In this case, at $Y = 1500$ and $r = 7\%$, the interest rate is too high to achieve equilibrium in the goods market at a GNP of 1500. Since the interest rate is above the interest rate necessary to get $I = S$ at $Y = 1500$, this means that the level of investment at an interest rate of 7% must be less than intended saving, and

Figure A–3 The IS-LM Model

unintended investment will cause GNP to fall. As GNP falls, the interest rate to maintain goods market equilibrium rises along *IS*, and the interest rate to maintain monetary equilibrium falls along *LM*.

All of this leads to an obvious condition for equilibrium in goods and money markets.

- Equilibrium in goods and money markets is reached at the interest rate and GNP where $I = S$ and $L = M$, or where $IS = LM$.

Effects of Fiscal and Monetary Policies

Adding the public sector to the income determination model, you will recall, adds expenditure flows for government spending (G) and net taxes (T) and changes the equilibrium conditions for real GNP from

$$I = S$$

to

$$I + G = S + T,$$

where I is intended investment, S is intended saving, G is government spending, and T is net taxes. The public sector is incorporated in the *IS–LM* model in Figure A–4.

In Figure A–4a, autonomous spending includes I, which varies with the interest rate (r), and government spending which is independent of the interest rate. At a given interest rate, $r = 6\%$, autonomous spending is the sum of equilibrium investment ($\bar{I} = 200$) plus government spending ($G = 100$), or $\bar{I} + G = 300$.

Equilibrium GNP ($\bar{Y}$) is reached in Figure A–4b where $\bar{I} + G = S + T = 300$

Figure A–4 Fiscal Policy and the IS Curve

at $\bar{Y} = 800$. Finally, in Figure A–4c, we have a point on the IS curve where GNP = 800 and $r = 6\%$.

Changes in Government Spending

Now, suppose that government spending increases from 100 to 200—i.e., $\Delta G = 100$ per year. This shifts the autonomous expenditure curve from $MEI + G$ to $MEI + G'$ in Figure A–4a, increasing autonomous spending to $\bar{I} + G' = 400$ in Figures A–4a and A–4b. In Figure A–4b, the new equilibrium GNP is at 1200 where $I + G' = 400 = S + T$. In Figure A–4c, equilibrium in the goods sector is now reached with an interest rate of $r = 6\%$ and an equilibrium GNP of 1200, so the IS curve has shifted to the right to IS'.

- Increases in government spending will shift the IS curve to the right. Reductions in government spending will shift the IS curve to the left.

You should be able to verify in Figure A–4 that reducing government spending from G' to G would bring IS' back to IS.

Changes in Taxes

Changes in taxes also affect the IS curve. Suppose that equilibrium is reached in Figure A–4b with $S + T = I + G'$ at 1200. Now suppose that taxes are increased, shifting $S + T$ upward to $S + T'$. Equilibrium GNP falls to 800. In other words, the tax increase reduces the equilibrium GNP to 800 at the interest rate $r = 6\%$, shifting the IS curve to the *left* from IS' to IS.

- Tax increases shift the IS curve to the left. Tax reductions shift the IS curve to the right.

You should be able to verify in Figure A–4 that cutting taxes sufficiently to bring $S + T'$ back to $S + T$ would shift the IS curve from IS to IS'.

The effects of shifts of the IS curve on equilibrium GNP and equilibrium interest rates are shown in Figure A–5.

Figure A–5 Shifts in the IS Curve

588 PART NINE   AGGREGATE DEMAND: THE MONEY MARKET

- If the *IS* curve shifts to the right, equilibrium GNP and the equilibrium interest rate will tend to rise.
- If the *IS* curve shifts to the left, equilibrium GNP and the equilibrium interest rate will tend to fall.

Changes in the Money Supply

At all points on the *LM* curve in Figure A–6, the monetary sector is in equilibrium. Changes in the money supply will disturb equilibrium in money markets and cause the *LM* curve to shift. Suppose that the supply of money is increased from M to M' in Figure A–6a. This causes the interest rate to fall to 5%, which is consistent with a GNP of 1500. In Figure A–6b, then, the effect of the greater money supply is a shift of *LM* to the right.

- The *LM* curve shifts in the same direction as changes in the money supply.

The effect of shifts of the *LM* curve on equilibrium GNP and the interest rate is shown clearly in Figure A–7.

- If the *LM* curve shifts to the right, equilibrium GNP tends to increase and the equilibrium interest rate tends to fall.
- If the *LM* curve shifts to the left, equilibrium GNP tends to fall, and the equilibrium interest rate tends to rise.

Unsupported Fiscal Policy

For GNP to be at its equilibrium level, both the goods sector and the monetary sector must be in equilibrium. Changes in fiscal policy will disturb equilibrium in the goods sector and cause shifts of the *IS* curve. However, shifts of the *IS* curve will cause disequilibrium in the monetary sector as well. The

Figure A–6   Monetary Policy and the LM Curve

Figure A–7 Shifts in the LM Curve

effectiveness of unsupported fiscal policies in altering equilibrium GNP and dealing with unemployment or inflation depends on the shape of the LM curve.

Unsupported Fiscal Expansion and "Crowding Out"

In Figure A–8, an expansionary fiscal policy (increased government spending or tax cuts) shift the IS curve to the right to IS'. However, the Fed decides not to change the money supply, so LM doesn't change.

If the interest rate remained at $r = 6\%$, the fiscal expansion would cause equilibrium GNP to increase to 1200. However at a GNP of 1200, an interest

Figure A–8 Unsupported Fiscal Policy

rate of 10% would be required for equilibrium in the monetary sector—i.e., there would be excess demand in money markets which would pull the interest rate upward toward 10% at a GNP of 1200. As the interest rate rises, the economy moves along IS' until equilibrium is reached at an interest rate of 8% and an equilibrium GNP of 1000. The rising interest rate has crowded out private spending of 200 (1200 − 200) as a result of the fiscal expansion.

The strength of the crowding-out effect and the effectiveness of expansionary fiscal policy in raising equilibrium GNP depends on the slope of the LM curve, and this slope isn't the same at all levels of real GNP and employment of capacity. In Figure A–9, the LM curve is relatively flat at low levels of output and employment. If there is a liquidity trap, it will be horizontal at the minimum interest rate. As real GNP and the employment of capacity increase, the LM curve generally gets steeper because it gets increasingly difficult to increase real output. At full employment, the LM curve becomes vertical because real GNP can't be increased at all.

In Figure A–9, if the initial position of the economy is with $IS_1 = LM$ at $Y = 400$, fiscal policy that shifts the IS curve from IS_1 to IS_2 will increase real GNP from 400 to 750, while increasing the interest rate from 4% to 5%. If the interest rate hadn't risen, the new equilibrium GNP on IS_2 would have been 800, so rising interest rates crowded out private spending of only 50.

However, if the initial position had been at $Y = 1600$ and $r = 12\%$—where $IS_3 = LM$—the same fiscal expansion would have a much smaller effect on real GNP and a much larger effect on the interest rate. Fiscal expansion that shifts IS from IS_3 to IS_4 (the same shift as from IS_1 to IS_2) causes the interest rate to rise to 18.5% while real GNP increases only from 1600 to 1700. If the

Figure A–9 The Strength of the *Crowding Out* Effect

interest rate hadn't risen, this fiscal expansion would have led to a real GNP of 2000, so rising interest rates due to the fiscal expansion crowded out private spending of 300.

- Unsupported fiscal policies have a smaller effect on real GNP, and crowding out is greater, the higher the level of real GNP and employment.

The strongest monetarist arguments that unsupported fiscal expansion can't affect real GNP at all implies that the economy will be operating in the vertical region of the LM curve. If unsupported expansionary fiscal policies shift the IS curve beyond IS_4 in Figure A–9, the only effect will be rising interest rates and crowding out will completely offset the expansionary effect of the fiscal policies. Of course, by crowding out private spending, the expansionary fiscal policy means that a larger share of aggregate output and income will be accounted for by public spending.

Unsupported Fiscal Restraint

The effectiveness of unsupported fiscal restraint in dampening demand-related inflationary pressure also depends on the responsiveness of GNP and interest rates to shifts of the IS curve. Since demand-related inflation occurs at high levels of output and employment, where the LM curve is steep, unsupported fiscal restraint is likely to have greater effects on interest rates than on reduced real GNP.

Suppose, for example, that the economy depicted in Figure A–9 is operating at $Y = 1700$ where $IS_4 = LM$, and that demand-related inflationary pressures are unacceptably great. Fiscal authorities estimate that these inflationary pressures would be minimized at a real GNP of 1200, and raise taxes and reduce government spending to shift IS from IS_4 to IS_3. However, shifting the IS curve to the left lowers interest rates from 18.5% to 12%, and GNP falls only from 1700 to 1600. Unless this fiscal restraint were supported by restrictive monetary policies, it would require a much larger shift of IS to get GNP to 1200—verify this in Figure A–9.

Even relatively mild fiscal restraint—cutting government spending or raising taxes—has serious political implications. The strong fiscal restraint necessary to curb demand-related inflationary pressures at high levels of output and employment may be politically impossible to achieve unless milder fiscal restraint is accompanied by supporting monetary restraint.

Supported Fiscal Policy

Expansionary or restrictive fiscal policies will have a larger impact on aggregate demand and real GNP if they are supported by monetary policies. In fact, monetarists argue that fiscal policy alone will be ineffective unless supported by monetary policy.

In Figure A–10, expansionary fiscal policy shifts IS to the right to IS'. To avoid rising interest rates and crowding out, the expansionary fiscal measures are supported by expansionary monetary policies that shift LM to the right to LM'. As a result of the fiscal expansion and supporting monetary expansion, GNP increases to 1200, while the interest rate remains at 8%. Because of the expansionary monetary policy, there has been no crowding out. If the monetary authorities hadn't gone along with the expansion, the interest rate

Figure A–10 Supported Fiscal Policy

would have risen to 10%, and crowding out would have resulted in a smaller increase in real GNP (to 1000 instead of 1200).

The same argument works in reverse. If fiscal restraint shifted IS to the left from IS' to IS, and the monetary authorities didn't cooperate, interest rates would fall to 6% and GNP would fall to 1000. However, with a restrictive monetary policy supporting fiscal restraint, LM also shifts to the left (from LM' to LM), and the fiscal restraint has a stronger effect on GNP.

The potential and the dangers of supporting monetary policy should be fairly obvious. Coordinating monetary policy with fiscal policy makes discretionary policies more potent. However, coordination will also amplify the effects of mistakes in policy. If there is a political bias toward the expansion of public programs and against increasing taxes, the ability to "finance" fiscal expansion with monetary expansion and inflation may be very tempting politically.

PART TEN
Inflation and Unemployment

The overriding economic theme of the 1970s was the problem of unacceptably high rates of inflation and unemployment occurring at the same time. The issue came to a head in the period 1974–75, when unemployment reached its highest level since the Depression, while the Consumer Price Index rose at its fastest annual rate since the lifting of price controls after World War II. The persistence of the problem raised serious doubts about the validity of a significant portion of traditional macroeconomic theory, and even led some critics to point to the 1970s as proof of the "death" of macroeconomics.

This view, like Mark Twain's premature obituary, appears to be somewhat exaggerated. Macroeconomics *is* in a state of flux, however, and many of the traditional analytical tools have had to be abandoned in favor of newer ones that more accurately describe the world as it really is. In this section, we'll explore the dual problem of inflation and unemployment, using the **aggregate demand–aggregate supply model** introduced earlier. We will examine the sources of the problem, some possible solutions to it, and the important question of whether policymakers can "trade off" higher rates of inflation for lower unemployment rates (and vice versa).

Several words of caution and encouragement are in order before you tackle this section. Some of the analysis approaches the frontiers of current economic thinking and can thus be quite tricky at times. Many of the waters are uncharted, and controversy in this area is the rule rather than the exception. However, your efforts in these chapters will reap substantial rewards in terms of understanding the contemporary problem of inflation and unemployment.

28

Inflation and Unemployment: Defining the Problem

Preview: The notion that inflation and unemployment *are* in fact problems is one that most people accept without very much question. But why exactly are they problems? Does an unemployment rate of five percent *really* mean that five million Americans can't find jobs? Is everybody *really* getting poorer during times of inflation? In order to gain a clearer picture of the costs these problems impose on society as a whole, we have to look at precisely how inflation and unemployment are defined and measured. This, in turn, will allow us to set reasonable policy goals for minimizing those costs.

The Meaning and Significance of Inflation

Inflation, as everybody knows, refers to rising prices. However, a rise in the price of baseball tickets or of any other single product isn't necessarily cause for concern about inflation.

- **Inflation** refers to a sustained rise in the general price level, as measured by some price index.

The two most common summary indicators of the price level are the Consumer Price Index (CPI) and the Implicit Price Deflator for GNP (IPD).

- The **Consumer Price Index** (*CPI*) estimates the cost of a given bundle of goods and services as a percentage of the cost of the same bundle in a base year.

- The **Implicit Price Deflator** (*IPD*) estimates the average change in prices of all final goods and services between a base year and a given year.

These price indexes were explained in some detail in a previous chapter. Since the CPI is used to estimate the change in the cost of living for a typical household, it is the most commonly cited price index.

In Figure 1, the black line shows the year-to-year percentage changes in the CPI. Obviously, *stable prices* (no change in the CPI from one year to the next) have been rare—1950 and 1955 are the only years in the past half-century in which prices remained virtually unchanged from the previous year. Most of us have lived our entire lifetimes in a period of rising prices. Figure 1 also explains our increasing concern with the problem of inflation over the past twenty years: since the mid-1950s, the trend in price changes has clearly been upward.

Inflation: Winners and Losers

In his 1979 *Economic Report*, President Carter suggested that "inflation injures every person in our country." This sort of statement makes good press when inflation is the most important problem of the day and solutions are likely to be unpopular, but it isn't accurate.

Figure 1 Unemployment and Inflation, 1930–1980

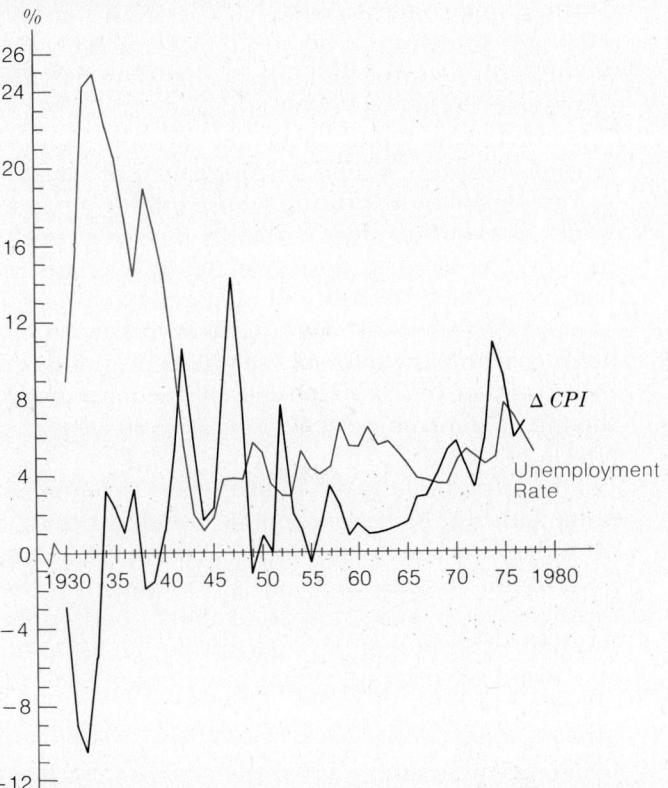

- Nobody whose money income at least keeps up with increases in prices is worse off economically during periods of inflation.

First of all, many persons are protected against inflation by *escalator clauses* that adjust their money incomes to changes in the CPI. Social security recipients, military and civilian federal pensioners, retired state government employees, and workers whose contracts contain cost-of-living-adjustment (COLA) clauses are not injured by inflation.

Furthermore, in some industries, the power of firms in the product market and of unions in the labor market can produce wage increases that exceed the rate of price increase; workers in these industries will be better off economically because their *real wages* are increasing. Such firms may also be able to protect the incomes of stockholders and suppliers of nonlabor resources by raising the prices of their products. The ability of firms and unions to push wages and prices upward depends heavily on outside support—from regulations that limit competition and allow firms to pass on higher costs as higher prices, or from government monetary and fiscal policies that accommodate their higher wages and prices.

Inflation also redistributes real income among various groups in the economy. Borrowers who owe long-term debts typically gain as a result of inflation because the dollars that they use to repay the loans have lower purchasing power (or are *cheaper*) than the dollars they borrowed. The borrowers' gains, of course, are the lenders' losses. The lender receives "*cheaper*" dollars in repayment of loans than were lent out.

Any person or institution whose money income rises *less* rapidly than prices does suffer a loss of real income as a result of inflation. Workers in weak bargaining positions, many welfare recipients and private pensioners, and probably the person teaching this course all lose real income during inflationary periods. Likewise, many banks and bondholders who earn interest income from bonds suffer real losses from inflation. Persons on fixed money incomes are hurt worst of all, since their money incomes don't increase to offset even partially the corrosive effects of inflation.

If inflation actually did injure "every person in our country," no value judgment would be needed to conclude that inflation is unambiguously bad for the country and that reducing it would be unambiguously good for the country. Since inflation *doesn't* injure all of us economically, however, such sweeping statements about inflation require at least implicit value judgments concerning the importance of those who lose as a result of inflation vs. those who don't.

Furthermore, some policies that reduce inflation will impose significant costs on some groups in the population—for example, those who become unemployed if the government decides to fight inflation through monetary and fiscal contraction. Thus, those who lose as a result of inflation may sometimes lose even *more* as a result of efforts to fight inflation.

Inflation and Savings

Inflation alters *real interest rates* and *real interest income*. It also erodes the purchasing power of savings and principal on loans. For example, suppose that a family of modest means has managed to accumulate savings of $10,000 which it has deposited in a savings account that pays an interest rate of 6% per year. At the end of a year, the money value or *nominal* value of the principal and interest is $10,000 × 1.06 = $10,600. This increase in the nominal value of principal and interest is an illusion, however, unless prices are stable. If prices rose by ten percent over the year, the purchasing power of $10,600 would be about $9600—$400 less than the purchasing power of $10,000 a year earlier. In other words, the saver has earned *real interest* of −$400, or a *real interest rate* of −4% per year. The effect would be the same on a lender who lent out $10,000 at 6% interest under the same conditions.

Obviously, the prospects of very low or negative real interest rates are a deterrent to saving and lending. Under the circumstances above, the household would have an incentive to consume its $10,000 rather than save it at a negative real interest rate. Inflationary expectations lead lenders to charge an *inflation premium* as part of the nominal interest rate on loans to protect against a loss of purchasing power. Even this premium, however, is no guarantee against loss if the rate of inflation turns out to be higher than anticipated by lenders.

Inflation and Taxation

Inflation imposes a tax on our incomes in two ways. In the first place, it reduces the purchasing power of the dollars we receive as money income. For example, if the price level rises by 10%, the purchasing power of a $300 per week wage is the same as the purchasing power of a $273 per week wage at the old price level.

But inflation imposes taxes in another, more subtle way. The Federal Income Tax is a *progressive tax*—i.e., high incomes are taxed at higher *rates* than low incomes. Income taxes are calculated on our money incomes, not our real incomes. The family of four in the table below, for example, has an income of $20,000 in year 1 and pays a federal tax of $2536, or about 12.7 percent of income. Suppose that in year 2 the household's money income rises 10 percent to $22,000, but that prices also rise 10 percent. The household's *real* income has remained constant, but the federal tax on $22,000 is $3036, or 13.8 percent. As a result, despite the apparent $2000 increase in the family's income, its *real* after-tax income has actually fallen $224, from $17,464 to $17,240.

	Money Income	Real Income	Tax Rate	Money Taxes Paid	Real Taxes Paid	After-Tax Money Income	After-Tax Real Income
Year 1	$20,000	20,000	12.7%	2536	2536	17,464	17,464
Year 2	$22,000	20,000	13.8%	3036	2760	18,964	17,240

Taxes that depend on money incomes create a windfall gain of tax revenue for the government during inflationary periods—a gain that requires no politically risky legislation. If and when public pressure to reduce the tax burden becomes irresistible, the government can enact popular "tax cuts" that don't cut taxes at all. If in the previous example the government cut taxes in year 2 by 5 percent, it would still receive about $2884, a *real* gain of $86 over the previous year's revenue.

Applying the Tools

The Granddaddy of Inflations

Hyperinflation, as its name implies, is extreme or super inflation. It is the bogey man of all persons who fear inflation. There isn't a clear-cut line to divide serious inflation from hyperinflation, although Professor Philip Cagan has drawn the line at annual price increases of 50 percent or more. However serious a 50 percent annual inflation might seem, though, some actual hyperinflationary episodes make Cagan's standard look modest. One of the most severe hyperinflations in history occurred in Germany between 1921 and 1923, in which prices rose by a factor of one trillion—or an average rate of 102 percent per *day*!

What Caused the Inflation?
Wars are generally inflationary, particularly for countries in which the war is fought. During World War I (1914-18), the Germans financed their wartime expenditures by government deficits and borrowing. Following the war, the German government continued to run budget deficits and to finance them by printing money.

The Germans ran balance of payments deficits in foreign exchange markets because the war had destroyed most international commercial relations and much of the ability to produce for export. In addition, the Germans had to make postwar reparations payments in *gold marks*—i.e., in currency that could be converted for gold in international markets. Since the Germans couldn't finance these payments by trade surpluses (excess of exports over imports), they sold paper marks (currency not backed up by gold) in international markets. This caused the value of the mark to fall in international markets, and this tends to be inflationary. After the mark had depreciated initially, foreign currency speculators bought the marks, expecting the value of the mark to rise (they were wrong). German currency speculators sold marks, betting that the value of the mark would continue to fall (they were correct). Eventually, all currency speculators dumped their paper marks in international markets, and the value of the mark fell to virtually nothing.

At home, the German government followed expansionary monetary and fiscal policies. The government budget continued to run deficits, the availability of credit to businesses was expanded dramatically, interest rates were too low to restrain aggregate demand, and printing money (literally running the printing presses to print paper marks) went on 24 hours a day. New currency, unbacked paper marks, removed all constraints on the government's ability to increase the money supply. All of this, you should keep in mind, was taking place in an economy whose productive capacity had *shrunk* as a result of the war effort.

Speculative business activity ran rampant in Germany. The availability of business credit, negative real interest rates on loans, and the government's seemingly unbounded commitment to increasing the money supply encouraged firms to finance speculative ventures on borrowed funds, since the marks they would use to repay the loans would have a tiny fraction of the purchasing power of the marks they had borrowed.

The rapid acceleration of the rate of inflation encouraged people to spend their marks as quickly as possible. Holding marks for a day or two would reduce their purchasing power by 50 to 75 percent. Workers were paid twice a day so that they could spend their morning's wages before their purchasing power evaporated. The velocity of money was basically the speed at which people could run to spend their marks. This, of course, added to the inflationary pressures.

Effects of the Hyperinflation

Surprisingly, not all of the effects of the inflation were bad—at least, not bad for everybody. During the 1920–1922 postwar depression in Europe, for example, employment and output rose in Germany in spite of the inflation. Businesses who read the signals correctly made enormous gains during the inflation through speculative ventures and acquisition of other firms. Landholdings that were financed by mortgages were paid for in worthless marks, and many landowners made out handsomely. Anybody who could earn foreign currency (for example, exporters) was in good shape, since small amounts of foreign currency could finance large purchases of property and assets in Germany.

Output wasn't growing fast enough to allow the great economic gains to some Germans without imposing losses on others. Persons whose incomes couldn't keep up with the rate of inflation suffered losses of real income, and persons who were on pensions or fixed salaries were quickly reduced to desperation. Most wage and salary workers and much of the German middle class suffered losses during the hyperinflation because their incomes couldn't keep up with prices, and they had to sell property and assets at a fraction of their value to survive. The group that suffered under the inflation was a large part of the German population, and this provided a political base for Hitler's National Socialists (Nazis).

Albert Speer, who later became Hitler's chief architect and city planner during the Third Reich, was a student during the inflation in 1923:

> I had to draw my allowance weekly; by the end of the week the fabulous sum had melted away to nothing. . . . shortly before the end of the inflation, a restaurant dinner cost ten to twenty billion marks, and even in the student dining hall over a billion. I had to pay between three and four hundred million marks for a theater ticket.[1]

The End of the Inflation

By the end of 1923, the German monetary system had simply collapsed. Money had become worthless, and many exchanges were barter exchanges. There was no

---

1. Albert Speer, *Inside the Third Reich.* New York: Macmillan, 1970, pp. 9–10.

way that monetary and fiscal policies could restore order to the economy with the worthless paper currency. In 1924 the German government issued new currency that could be converted for the old marks at a rate of 1 trillion old marks = 1 new mark. The new *reichsmark* was convertible to gold or dollars, and one *reichsmark* (which was equivalent to 1 trillion paper marks) could be converted for $0.24!

Most of the facts in this discussion are from Dudley Dillard, *Economic Development of the North Atlantic Community.* Englewood Cliffs, N.J.: Prentice-Hall, 1967, pp. 512–20.

The Meaning and Significance of Unemployment

Our concern with high unemployment rates goes back to the Great Depression of the 1930s when the unemployment rate reached astronomical levels (the highest was 25.2 percent of the labor force, in 1933). For many, unemployment meant real and severe economic hardships. Breadlines, displaced families, and economic desperation are indelible images of that era in the public mind.

Fortunately, the unemployment rate hasn't reached depression levels since the 1930s, although it did exceed 9 percent briefly in 1975. Does unemployment carry the same connotations of hardship in the 1980s that it did in the Depression?

How Unemployment Is Measured

Government labor force data are based on statistical estimates made by the Bureau of Labor Statistics. Each month, the BLS surveys a sample of households which reflects the characteristics of the total population. The sample is rotated so that any given household is in the sample for a few months.

Interviewers ask the sample households a series of questions, and the responses determine the labor force status of members of the households. The sample results are then "blown up" to estimate the size of the labor force, total employment, total unemployment, and the unemployment rate.

- Persons who were employed for pay are defined as **employed.**
- Persons who weren't employed for pay, but were able to work and actively seeking work or awaiting recall from layoffs are defined as **unemployed.**
- Persons who weren't employed for pay because of inability to work or weren't actively seeking work are defined as **not in the labor force.**

The **labor force** is the sum of total employment and total unemployment, and the unemployment rate is the percentage of the labor force that is unemployed. Persons who are disabled, have full-time home responsibilities, or are not able to work or seek work for any number of other reasons are not in the labor force, and therefore don't enter into the calculation of the unemployment rate.

Many people misinterpret unemployment data and the meaning of the unemployment rate—in particular, politicians and others who talk about achieving *zero* unemployment or equate all unemployment with suffering and misery. The fact that an average of six million persons was unemployed in 1978 doesn't mean that six million persons stood in breadlines or lived off their savings for the entire year. The overall unemployment rate hides two very important dimensions of the unemployment problem—the duration of unemployment and the reasons that persons were unemployed.

The Duration of Unemployment

If the unemployment rate is stable at, say, 6 percent of the labor force for a number of years, this does *not* mean that the same 6 percent of the labor force remains unemployed for the entire period. In 1978, the annual average number of unemployed workers was slightly more than six million persons (5.2 percent of the labor force), but the average duration of unemployment in 1978 was only 11.9 weeks. In other words, the same six million workers weren't unemployed for the entire year. In fact, 2.8 million persons (2.4 percent of the labor force) were unemployed for fewer than five weeks in 1978.

Over time, persons move among labor force categories, as summarized in Figure 2. There is a steady flow of *new entrants* into the civilian labor force—i.e., persons going to work for the first time. In addition, there

Figure 2 Changes in the Labor Force

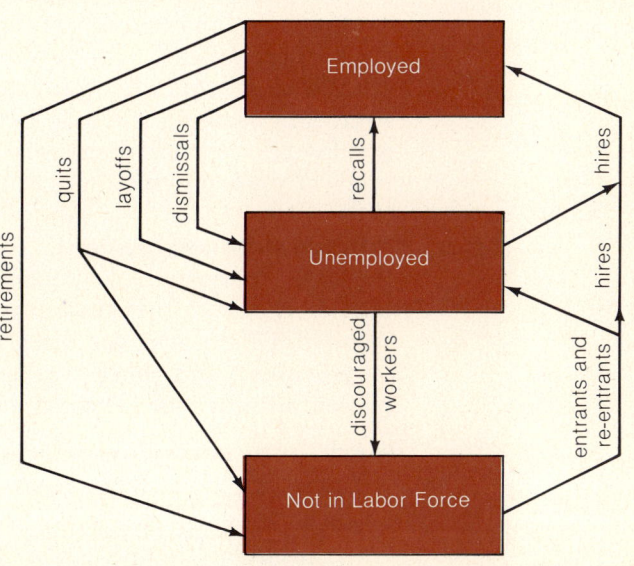

are *re-entrants*—persons who had been in the labor force but had dropped out temporarily. Some entrants and re-entrants will be hired immediately and others will be unemployed while they seek work.

If unemployed workers, new labor force entrants, or re-entrants are hired, the level of employment rises.

There are also flows of workers out of the labor force. Some persons quit their jobs to leave the labor force temporarily—for example, women who leave work during the periods of their lives when family demands are heaviest. Retirees represent another flow out of the labor force. Finally, discouraged workers who give up the search for employment represent a flow out of the labor force.

Quits, layoffs, and dismissals represent flows out of employment. Some of the persons who quit or are dismissed from employment leave the labor force completely, but most become unemployed as they seek other employment. Employment increases if laid-off workers are recalled by their employers.

The point here is that even in periods when the unemployment rate is stable, there are continual movements of persons among labor force categories. Seeking a goal of keeping the unemployment rate at 5 percent doesn't condemn a stable group of persons to perpetual unemployment. Also, because of the continual movements among labor force categories, the measured unemployment rate *cannot* be reduced to zero.

Kinds of Unemployment

Average unemployment figures can be misleading in another way. Although the same six million persons weren't unemployed for all of 1978, due to the relatively short duration of unemployment, more than six million persons experienced periods of unemployment during the year. If all of this unemployment could be explained by insufficient aggregate demand, it would be bad news, but at least such unemployment would respond to monetary and fiscal measures. However, several types of unemployment are not caused by low aggregate demand.

Frictional Unemployment. Some persons are unemployed because they are "between jobs," or temporarily unemployed. Workers on temporary layoff from their regular jobs are unemployed until they are recalled. Others who are dissatisfied with their jobs quit to seek other employment, and these workers are unemployed until they are employed on new jobs. These are examples of *frictional unemployment*.

- **Frictional unemployment** can be explained by imperfections, or "friction," in the labor market.

Specific causes of frictional unemployment include geographic or occupational immobility of labor, the time necessary to find new employment, the time required to acquire new skills, and inadequate market information. Because of these frictions, people don't move instantly from one job to another, and during the time between jobs they are frictionally unemployed.

Job Search Unemployment. Just because workers are unemployed doesn't mean they will necessarily take the first job they find. Most workers have a *reservation wage*, or a minimum acceptable wage. Jobs that offer wages below a worker's reservation wage will be rejected, and the worker will search for work until finding a job that offers a wage equal to or greater than the reservation wage. As long as the job search continues, a worker is considered unemployed.

- **Job search unemployment** is due to unemployed workers' choosing to continue their job searches until their reservation wage is met.

As long as the worker expects a wage offer equal to or greater than the reservation wage to turn up through continued searching, he or she will choose to continue to search rather than accept a wage offer below the reservation wage. However, as the number of weeks of unemployment and job search increases, the worker tends to lower the reservation wage.

The inverse relationship between the weeks of unemployment and the worker's reservation wage is shown graphically in Figure 3. At the end of week 1, the worker's reservation wage is $5 per hour. This is the wage that would be necessary to get the worker to cease searching

Figure 3 Time and the Reservation Wage

and accept employment. If a week of searching turns up a best wage offer of $3, the worker won't accept it because he or she expects to find a better wage offer by further searching. However, as further searching fails to turn up a $5 wage offer, the worker lowers his or her reservation wage. If after eight weeks of unemployment and searching, the best wage offer is still $3 per hour, the worker will accept the offer because the reservation wage has fallen to $3.

Structural Unemployment. Some unemployed workers don't have the skills and training necessary to fill the jobs that are in demand. For example, unemployed teenagers and persons with less than high-school educations won't be hired to fill vacancies for computer technicians, tool and die makers, accountants, or other jobs that require substantial education and training. Others with highly specialized skills are unemployed because technological change or shifting demand has eliminated the need for these skills. Revolutionary changes in typesetting and printing, for example, eliminated or sharply reduced the demand for many skilled printing crafts. These are examples of *structural unemployment*.

- **Structural unemployment** is the result of basic differences between the characteristics of unemployed workers and the characteristics of the jobs in demand.

The magnitude and significance of structural unemployment is a long-standing controversy among economists. In long periods of relatively high unemployment rates, the structural element tends to look quite large because of the large number of workers unemployed for long periods of time. In periods when the demand for labor is high, however, some of what appeared to be structural unemployment usually disappears. To the extent that structural unemployment does exist, stimulating aggregate demand will be ineffective in reducing unemployment because structural unemployment would exist regardless of the level of aggregate demand.

The key point of this discussion is that unemployment is due to a number of causes. The disturbing corollary of this is that no single approach will be effective against all types of unemployment. Stimulating aggregate demand will be effective against demand-deficiency unemployment, but not against structural unemployment. Retraining the structurally unemployed without adequate attention to aggregate demand won't do much to alleviate demand-deficiency unemployment. Too much attention to the overall unemployment rate probably won't do much to reduce the tragically high unemployment rates among specific groups in the labor force. In short, complex problems require complex solutions.

What the Unemployment Rate Hides

We have seen that, in one sense, the overall unemployment rate overstates the seriousness of unemployment because some unemployment is voluntary (for example, choosing to continue job search rather than accept employment at the best current wage offer), and because most persons are unemployed for short rather than long periods of time. However, the unemployment rate also *understates* some other serious dimensions of the problem of unemployment.

Minority and Female Unemployment. The unemployment rate for the total labor force is a convenient summary indicator of macroeconomic performance, but it doesn't tell us much about the employment status or the severity of unemployment for specific subgroups in the labor force. In 1978, for example, the unemployment rate for the total labor force was 6 percent. However, unemployment rates for individual subgroups in 1978 ranged from 3.7 percent for white males ages 20 and older to 38.4 percent for non-white females ages 16-19. For married men, the unemployment rate in 1978 was only 2.8 percent.

Unemployment rates have been consistently higher for blacks than for whites—a long-standing source of social tension. For many years, blacks were discriminated against in hiring and retention. Where workers were protected by seniority rules, blacks tend to be at the bottom of the seniority ladder and hence the first workers laid off in periods of slack demand. For young blacks, the unemployment rates in the 1970s were higher than the overall unemployment rates in the depths of the Great Depression.

Discouraged Workers. In some cases, when unemployment rates have remained unusually high for long periods of time, many unemployed workers become discouraged and stop looking for employment. These *discouraged workers* are officially defined as not in the labor force, even though they would be able to work and would be likely to seek employment if they were more optimistic about their prospects. The **discouraged worker effect** tends to understate the seriousness of unemployment in economically depressed geographic areas, during severe recessions and depressions when unemployment rates remain high for long periods, and among demographic groups where unemployment rates are chronically high.

Underemployment. Persons who are employed for pay are counted as employed whether or not they are fully employed. There are two basic types of **underemployment** of labor.

Some workers are underemployed because they are unable to find employment that utilizes their training, skills, and talents fully. Many Ph.D.s have been unable to find suitable academic or research employment because of the shrinking demand for college teachers and the overexpansion of graduate education in the 1950s and 1960s. A Ph.D.

in history who has to settle for a full-time job pumping gas or in routine clerical work is employed, but underemployed.

Part-time employment is another form of underemployment. Persons who are unable to find full-time employment may have to settle for part-time or casual employment. Since the BLS data don't measure underemployment—in fact, it may be difficult or impossible to measure accurately—the data don't reflect the loss of production of goods and services due to underemployment of labor.

The Costs of Unemployment

Unemployment imposes severe costs on the community. Some of the costs are borne by those who are unemployed. Persons who are unemployed as a result of layoffs, dismissals, and quits and are unable to find other employment suffer losses of income. Entrants and reentrants into the labor force who are unable to find employment are unable to earn income. Recent studies in other disciplines—sociology, psychology, and even medicine—have identified some other costs borne by the unemployed. Groups that suffer chronically high unemployment show higher incidences of mental disorders and physical illnesses than the general population. The suicide rate, for example, is considerably greater among the unemployed than it is for the general population. Social instability and tensions are common in urban ghettoes where high unemployment rates are the norm.

The community as a whole also loses economically when workers are unemployed—even when that unemployment doesn't mean economic desperation for the unemployed workers themselves. For example, relatively affluent housewives and teenagers who seek supplementary income probably won't be in a desperate situation if they don't find employment. However, their unemployment does impose a cost on the community. An unemployed worker, regardless of economic need, represents an unemployed resource, and the community loses the benefits of the goods and services he or she could have produced if employed.

The way the government estimates the value of these lost benefits to the community requires a bit of explanation. The President's Council of Economic Advisers (CEA) bases many of its predictions and policy recommendations on estimated *potential GNP*.

- **Potential GNP** is the estimated real GNP (in constant dollars) that would be produced with low unemployment rates and high rates of utilization of capacity.

The first step in defining potential GNP is to establish the measured unemployment rate that in fact constitutes full employment, or a **benchmark unemployment rate**. Since 1975, the benchmark unemployment rate for calculating potential GNP has been 5.1 percent.

Potential GNP isn't stable over time, but grows as a result of several economic forces. As population and the labor force grow, the capacity to produce expands due to the additional labor resources. Potential GNP also grows as a result of innovations, technological change, and other forces that increase the productivity of labor and other resources. The broken line in Figure 4 is the estimated trend of potential GNP between 1968 and 1978.

The solid line in Figure 4 is the path of actual real GNP (in 1972 prices) between 1968 and 1978. For brief periods, actual GNP exceeded potential GNP, which simply means that unemployment fell below the benchmark rate. For most of the period, however, actual GNP fell below potential GNP, creating a *GNP gap*.

- The **GNP gap** is the difference between potential GNP and actual GNP.

In 1978, for example, the GNP gap (in billions of 1972 dollars) was

$$\text{Potential GNP} - \text{Actual GNP} = \$1,422.9 \text{ billion} - \$1,385.1 \text{ billion} = \$37.8 \text{ billion}.$$

The GNP gap shows one of the costs of unemployment to the community—the loss of goods and services that would have been produced if the economy were at full employment. In other words, unemployment in 1978 cost the U.S. $37.8 billion (1972 dollars). The loss of goods and services due to excessive unemployment for the decade 1968–1978 is represented in Figure 4 by the shaded area *below* the broken line.

Figure 4 Actual and Potential GNP, 1968–1978

Setting an Employment Goal

Because unemployment is such a complex problem, setting a goal for policies to deal with the problem is no easy matter. Full employment is a desirable goal, but the definition and meaning of full employment isn't clear-cut. The only non-arbitrary definition is a measured unemployment rate of zero, but this is impossible to reach. The lowest measured unemployment rate recorded in the United States was 1.2 percent of the labor force in 1944, a year of peak wartime demand, a civilian labor force depleted by military manpower needs, complete mobilization, and extensive economic controls. Nobody reasonably expects to lower measured unemployment to the 1944 level, and we should be thankful that we don't face the situation that drove the unemployment rate so low.

Since a zero measured unemployment rate can't be reached, full employment has to be defined in terms of a measured unemployment rate that in fact constitutes full employment. This can be tricky. Depending on one's optimism and the weight one attaches to inflation as a problem, full employment may be defined very optimistically as a measured unemployment rate of 3 or 4 percent of the labor force, or less optimistically as 5, 6, or even 7 percent. Obviously, the measured unemployment rate that we accept as full employment isn't a precise standard.

One consideration in defining the measured unemployment rate that constitutes full employment is the rate of inflation we're willing to accept. Look back at Figure 1. Except in periods of stringent price controls during World War II, sudden drops in the unemployment rate generally have been accompanied by more rapid rates of price increase. In the late 1950s and 1960s, there was a clear pattern of falling unemployment rates and rising rates of increase in the Consumer Price Index.

- Most economists define **full employment** as the lowest measured unemployment rate that can be sustained without excessive inflation.

However, there is no unambiguous standard that defines the rate of inflation that is *excessive*. The historical record summarized in Figure 1 and common sense suggest that complete price stability is an unreasonable goal for an economy that is continually changing and buffeted by economic shocks. On the other hand, few would accept a sustained period of double-digit rates of price increase as a reasonable goal for price stability. Within this very broad range, what is an excessive rate of inflation—2, 4, 5, 8 percent per year? There is no absolute analytical standard.

A more fundamental question is whether there is, in fact, any long-run tradeoff between inflation and unemployment. That's a question we'll explore in some depth in the next chapter.

Summary

1. **Inflation** refers to sustained increases in the price level as measured by a price index.
2. Inflation imposes losses of income on those whose money incomes don't keep up with price increases. Those whose money incomes increase more rapidly than prices gain real income during inflationary periods. Inflation generally redistributes real income from those who lose real income to those who gain.
3. Since many taxes are tied to money income or the value of real estate, inflation generally increases government tax revenue without any alternation of tax rates. With progressive taxes, the effective tax rate on incomes rises with inflation.
4. **Unemployment** data are estimated from sample surveys of households which define persons into one of three categories—*employed*, *unemployed*, and *not in the labor force*. The overall unemployment rate doesn't show the seriousness of the unemployment problem for specific labor force groups, nor does it tell us much about the duration or type of unemployment.
5. Unemployment is caused by a combination of deficiency of aggregate demand, friction and immobility in labor markets, and structural mismatch between the characteristics of the unemployed and the jobs available.
6. Employment at jobs that don't utilize workers' skills or abilities fully and part-time employment are forms of underemployment. Unemployment data don't include the loss of employment or production from underemployment.
7. Unemployment imposes economic costs on those who are unemployed and on society in the form of lost production of goods and services that could have been produced by the unemployed workers. The loss of production due to unemployment is estimated as the difference between the estimated potential GNP and actual GNP.
8. As a practical goal, full employment with stable prices is unrealistic. Employment goals tend to be defined in terms of measured unemployment rates that we accept as full employment. There is no single, unambiguous analytical standard for defining a single rate of unemployment as "the" full-employment standard.

Concepts for Review

inflation	frictional unemployment	underemployment
real interest	job search unemployment	potential GNP
hyperinflation	structural unemployment	GNP gap
labor force	discouraged worker effect	full employment

Questions

1. Evaluate the following statement:
   "We know a lot about unemployment and how to deal with it, but we don't know much about inflation. Therefore, we should follow

a course of trying to achieve full employment and let the inflation take care of itself."
   a. What kinds of policies would follow from this way of looking at unemployment and inflation? What would be the effects of such policies?
   b. Are there any normative arguments implicit in the statement? Explain.
2. Job vacancy data estimate the number of unfilled jobs available. What would be the merits of defining full employment as a situation in which the number of unemployed equals the number of job vacancies?
3. What is *job search unemployment*? In what respect is it voluntary unemployment? How would each of the following affect the level and average duration of job search unemployment?
   a. Improved transmission of labor market information.
   b. Increased economic optimism concerning economic conditions in the near future.
   c. Increased economic pessimism concerning economic conditions in the near future.
   d. Higher unemployment compensation benefits and extended coverage under unemployment insurance.
4. Some critics of official unemployment data argue that the data overstate the seriousness of unemployment by including as unemployed many who don't suffer any financial hardship as a result of unemployment—teenagers living at home, middle-class housewives entering the labor force for the first time, etc.
   a. What would happen to the measured unemployment rate if definitions included financial need in the definition of unemployed—i.e., those not working who don't need the income would be classified not in the labor force?
   b. In terms of the economic welfare of society, and the costs of unemployment to society, is economic need a relevant criterion for defining unemployment?
5. The Council of Economic Advisers uses a *benchmark unemployment rate* of 5.1 percent in estimating potential GNP. Some critics argue that this benchmark is too high and others argue that it is too low.
   a. Why should any measured unemployment rate be accepted as *full employment*?
   b. What factors would affect the choice of a measured unemployment rate to serve as full employment?
   c. What are the implications of accepting a 7 percent unemployment rate as full employment? How about 4 percent as the full employment standard?
6. Although income tax rates were cut in 1979, many people found that they were paying more income tax in 1979 than they did in 1978, and that their after-tax incomes bought less in 1979 than in 1978. How could you explain this?

Problems

1. Suppose that prices rise by 8 percent this year. What effect will this have on each of the following people?
   a. A farmer who borrowed $10,000 at 10 percent interest for the year, and the banker who made the loan.
   b. A person with $10,000 deposited in a savings account that pays 6 percent annual interest.
   c. A person who pays an interest rate of 7 percent per year on the unpaid balance of a home mortgage.
   d. A person who received a raise from $20,000 annual salary last year to $21,000 this year.
   e. A pensioner who receives a fixed pension of $1,000 per month.
   f. Persons covered by escalator clauses that adjust their money incomes for changes in the price level.
2. The duchy of Idlehandia uses the same labor force definitions as the United States, since its earliest settlers were people who had retired from the U.S. Bureau of Labor Statistics. At the end of the year 1979, the labor force was 100,000 persons, of whom 95,000 were employed. During 1980, the following events occurred:
      i. 11,000 persons entered the labor force for the first time. Of these, 6,000 found employment immediately—although 1,000 of these were persons with Ph.D.s who took unskilled jobs. The remaining entrants continued to search for employment for the rest of the year.
      ii. A survey of households showed that 8,000 persons were willing to work, able to work, and desired to work, but didn't look for work because they were too pessimistic about their employment prospects.
      iii. Layoffs and dismissals totaled 5,000. Of these 3,000 found other work or were recalled during the year, 1,000 continued to search for employment for the rest of the year, and 1,000 gave up searching for employment.
   a. How many were unemployed and what was the unemployment rate at the end of 1979?
   b. Find employment, unemployment, labor force, and the unemployment rate at the end of 1980.

29

Aggregate Demand and Aggregate Supply

Preview: The Keynesian income determination model presented in earlier chapters showed how aggregate demand would determine equilibrium GNP or aggregate output at a *given* price level. But what if the price level isn't fixed? In this chapter, we'll "rebuild" the **aggregate demand–aggregate supply model** introduced earlier and show how and why aggregate output demanded and aggregate output supplied will vary with the price level, how the interaction of the two will determine equilibrium levels of GNP and prices, and how disturbances from either side of the economy will affect employment, output, and prices.

The great contribution of Keynesian economics was its explanation of aggregate demand and of the importance of aggregate demand as a determinant of aggregate output and employment. However, the basic Keynesian income determination model, with its assumption that the price level remains stable until full employment is reached, seriously understates the difficulty of our contemporary problems of unemployment and inflation. To understand the existence of unemployment and inflation *at the same time*, we have to drop the assumption of price stability and take a close look at the aggregate supply side of the economy, which is largely overlooked in the simple Keynesian model. This will allow us to see how aggregate demand and aggregate supply interact to determine the price level and the rate of inflation, as well as the level of aggregate output.

The first step is to restate aggregate demand and aggregate supply in terms of real GNP and the price level. The basic model was introduced briefly in Chapter 4, but without much explanation. This chapter takes a much closer look at aggregate demand and aggregate supply. Some of the analysis is difficult, but the rewards—in terms

Figure 1 Aggregate Output and the Price Level

of understanding contemporary problems of unemployment and inflation and evaluating policies to deal with them—are very great.

Another View of Aggregate Demand

In the analysis of aggregate demand up to this point, we have defined aggregate demand as the level of intended spending by households, firms, and the government at various levels of real GNP with a fixed price level. Equilibrium GNP was reached when intended spending equaled real GNP in the goods sector and when money demanded equaled money supplied in the money sector. A change in the price level disturbs this equilibrium and generally causes a change in the level of aggregate demand.

The initial money supply (M_1) and the price level (P_1) define the supply of real balances, M_1/P_1, in Figure 1a. Real balances, you will recall, represent the purchasing power of the money in circulation. Given GNP, the demand for real balances at any interest rate is shown by the demand curve for money (L). Equilibrium is reached in money markets when the quantity of real balances demanded equals the supply—at $\bar{r}_1$ in Figure 1a.

The interest rate, you will recall, is a major determinant of the level of investment. Investment will increase or decrease until the rate of return from the last investment (MEI) equals the interest rate—i.e., until investment reaches $\bar{I}_1$ in Figure 1b. Investment is a component of aggregate demand, along with consumption and government spending. In Figure 1c, consumption (C), investment (I_1), and government spending (G) define the aggregate demand function (AD_1) and determine aggregate output demanded[1] where $Y = AD$ at Y_1.

---

1. With a fixed price level, we could say that aggregate demand alone determined **equilibrium aggregate output**. If we allow the price level to change, then aggregate demand *alone* will only determine **aggregate output demanded**.

Aggregate Demand and the Price Level

Now, suppose that the price level falls from P_1 to P_0. The supply of real balances in Figure 1a will increase from M_1/P_1 to M_1/P_0—the purchasing power of the money in circulation is greater due to the drop in the price level. This increase in the supply of real balances causes the equilibrium interest rate to fall to $\bar{r}_0$, increasing the level of investment to $\bar{I}_2$ in Figure 1b. The higher level of investment in turn increases aggregate output demanded to Y_2 in Figure 1c.

If the price level rose from P_1 to P_2, the effects would be just the opposite. Real balances would fall to M_1/P_2, raising the interest rate to $\bar{r}_2$. The higher interest rate in turn would cause investment to fall, and aggregate output demanded would drop to Y_0.

In short, a decline in the price level increases the aggregate output demanded from Y_1 to Y_2, while an increase in the price level lowers aggregate output demanded from Y_1 to Y_0. This inverse relationship between the price level and aggregate output demanded defines the *aggregate demand curve* in Figure 2.

- The **aggregate demand curve** shows the level of aggregate output demanded at any price level.

To make it clear when *aggregate demand* refers to the relationship between aggregate output demanded and the price level, we will again label this curve YD instead of AD.

The aggregate demand curve in Figure 2 resembles the demand curve for a commodity, but there is an important difference. Points on YD represent equilibrium in the money market ($L = M/P$) and in the goods sector ($Y = AD$) at each price level. Thus, the points on YD and the shape of YD are determined for a given consumption function (C), a given aggregate demand function (AD), a given MEI function, and a given demand curve for money.

Figure 2 The Aggregate Demand (YD) Curve

The Slope of the Aggregate Demand Curve

The slope of the *YD* curve reveals the responsiveness of aggregate output demanded to changes in the price level. Along a steep aggregate demand curve like *YD* in Figure 3, large changes in the price level result in relatively small changes in the aggregate output demanded. On the other hand, if the aggregate demand curve is relatively flat like *YD'*, much smaller changes in the price level will result in relatively large changes in aggregate output demanded. What determines the responsiveness of aggregate output demanded to changes in the price level?

The demand curve for money. If the demand for real balances is highly responsive to changes in the interest rate—i.e., the demand curve for money is relatively flat—large changes in the price level and the supply of real balances with a given money supply will cause small changes in the interest rate. If the interest rate is highly responsive to changes in real balances—i.e., the demand curve for money is steep—small changes in the price level and real balances will cause relatively large changes in the interest rate. The size of the change in investment, aggregate demand, and equilibrium GNP as a result of a given change in the price level depends on the change in interest rates, so

- Aggregate output demanded is more responsive to changes in the price level the more responsive the interest rate is to changes in real balances.

The *MEI* curve. If the *MEI* curve is relatively flat, intended investment is more responsive to a given change in the interest rate than it is along a relatively steep *MEI* curve. The magnitude of the change in aggregate demand depends on the magnitude of the change in investment.

Figure 3 The Slope of the *YD* Curve

- Aggregate output demanded is more responsive to changes in the price level the more responsive investment is to changes in the interest rate.

The multiplier effect. If the multiplier effect is weak, aggregate output demanded is less responsive to a given change in investment than it is with a strong multiplier effect.

- Aggregate output demanded is more responsive to changes in the price level the greater is the multiplier effect of changes in investment.

Shifts of the Aggregate Demand Curve

Any exogenous change that affects aggregate demand will cause the aggregate demand curve to shift. Any number of exogenous changes can cause these shifts—shifts of the consumption function, altered expectations, different preferences for current consumption vs. future income, to name just a few. There is a simple, general rule for the effect of *any* exogenous change on the aggregate demand curve.

- Any exogenous change that increases aggregate demand shifts YD to the right, and any exogenous change that reduces aggregate demand shifts YD to the left.

From the policymaker's point of view, the most important changes are those in government monetary and fiscal policies. A close look at the mechanism by which such changes shift the aggregate demand curve will illustrate the effects of all exogenous changes. In Figure 4a, increasing government spending by ΔG raises AD to AD' and increases aggregate output demanded in Figure 4a to Y'. Thus, in Figure

Figure 4 Fiscal Policy and the YD Curve

4b, the increased government spending increases aggregate output demanded to Y' at price level P_1, shifting YD to the right to YD'.

- Expansionary fiscal policies—increasing government spending or cutting taxes—shift the aggregate demand curve (YD) to the right.

Restrictive fiscal policies—cutting government spending or raising taxes—will have just the opposite effect. You should verify and explain for yourself how a reduction of government spending of ΔG in Figure 4 causes the aggregate demand curve to shift from YD' to YD.

- Restrictive fiscal policies—cutting government spending or raising taxes—shift the aggregate demand curve (YD) to the left.

Changes in the money supply also cause the aggregate demand curve to shift. In Figure 5a, expansionary monetary policies increase the money supply from M to M' and the supply of real balances from (M/P_1) to (M'/P_1) at the given price level P_1. Increasing the supply of real balances lowers the equilibrium interest rate to $\bar{r}'$. The lower interest rate causes investment to increase to $\bar{I}'$, where $MEI = \bar{r}'$ in

Figure 5 Monetary Policy and the YD Curve

Figure 5b. The increased level of investment, in turn, causes aggregate output demanded to increase to Y' in Figure 5c. Thus, in Figure 5d, the aggregate demand curve shifts from YD to YD' as a result of the expansionary monetary policy.

- Expansionary monetary policies—increasing the money supply in order to reduce the interest rate—shift the aggregate demand curve (YD) to the right.

Again, you should verify and explain for yourself how reducing the money supply from M' to M would shift the aggregate demand curve in Figure 5d from YD' to YD.

- Restrictive monetary policies—reducing the money supply in order to raise the interest rate—shift the aggregate demand curve (YD) to the left.

Aggregate Supply: Output and the Price Level

With the wide acceptance of Keynesian economics in the 1940s, 1950s, and most of the 1960s, macroeconomics became preoccupied with aggregate demand. The high unemployment rates of the 1930s, wartime and post war inflationary pressures between 1940 and 1947, and the periodic episodes of recession and inflation in the 1950s and 1960s could be explained reasonably well in terms of aggregate demand. Furthermore, discretionary monetary and fiscal policies—**demand management policies**—did a fairly good job of regulating aggregate demand and keeping unemployment and inflation rates low.

In the past decade, however, aggregate demand has proved insufficient by itself as a means of explaining unemployment and inflation or of charting appropriate policies to deal with these problems. While changes in aggregate demand could explain rising prices with rising employment or falling employment with falling prices, they could not adequately account for falling employment with rising prices, a persistant problem in recent years. As a result, the *macroeconomics* of the 1970s has paid increasing attention to the *microeconomics* of aggregate supply in the search for an explanation of the problems of unemployment and inflation.

Employment and Output: The Aggregate Production Function

The first step in understanding aggregate supply is to understand the relationship between the employment of labor and the level of output. We can start with a simple example. Suppose a farmer uses labor (ℓ) and a fixed amount of capital (k^*) to produce wheat. The output of wheat (q) varies with the input of labor, and we can express this relationship with the function

$$q = f(\ell, k^*). \tag{1}$$

This is the wheat farm's **production function**.

Adding labor to a fixed input of capital won't yield equal increases in output for every additional unit of labor—if it did, an infinite amount of wheat could be produced by adding labor to a backyard garden. Eventually, the farm will produce under conditions of **diminishing returns**, with successive additional units of labor adding less and less output, as in Figure 6a. The **principle of diminishing returns**, one of the most universally valid propositions in economics, holds that eventually all goods must be produced under conditions of diminishing returns.

The relationship between the aggregate employment of labor (N) and the level of aggregate output (Y) is defined by the economy's *aggregate production function*.

- The **aggregate production function** shows the relationship between the level of employment and the level of aggregate output.

Since all goods must be produced under diminishing returns, it follows that the aggregate output of goods and services will show diminishing returns as employment increases with a given capital stock and a given state of technology, as in Figure 6b.

The aggregate production function defines a level of aggregate output (Y) for each level of employment (N), and conversely, a level of employment consistent with each level of aggregate output. In Figure 6b, for example, an aggregate output of Y_1 requires employment of N_1. At the level of employment that we accept as full employment (N^*), we have the full-employment real GNP (Y^*).

Figure 6 Aggregate Production Function

(a) Labor used

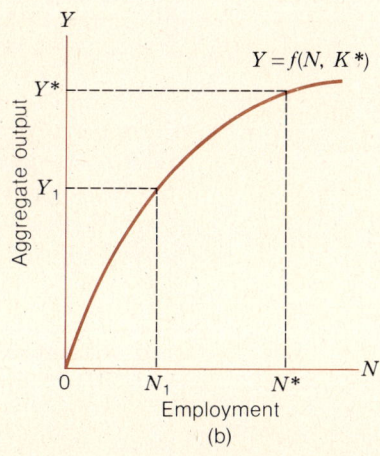

(b) Employment

Equilibrium in the Labor Market

In competitive labor markets, the supply of labor by households and the demand for labor by firms determine the equilibrium level of employment and the equilibrium wage. Profit-maximizing firms will increase or reduce the number of workers they employ until the last worker employed adds the same amount to the firm's revenue that he or she adds to the firm's cost. If adding a worker would increase the firm's revenue by $100 per day, and the firm would have to pay the worker a wage of $75 per day, hiring the worker would cause the firm's revenue to rise more than its costs, so profit would rise. Thus the firm should hire more labor until the last worker's addition to the firm's revenue is equal to the additional cost of hiring the additional worker.

The additional revenue from an additional unit of labor, or the revenue added by the last worker employed, is called the **marginal revenue product of labor** (MRP_N), and is $100 in the case above. The MRP of additional labor employed depends on the additional output produced by the additional labor, or the **marginal physical product** (MP_N), and the price at which that additional output is sold. For the economy as a whole, MP_N is the additional aggregate output produced by the additional labor employed. The value of this additional output is defined by the price level (P), so that

$$MRP_N \equiv MP_N \times P. \qquad (2)$$

With diminishing returns and a given price level, MP_N and MRP_N will both fall as employment increases, since each additional worker hired produces less additional output.

At any **money wage** (W), firms will maximize profit by hiring labor until

$$W = MRP_N. \qquad (3)$$

In other words, firms will hire workers until the value of the output the last worker produces is equal to the cost of hiring that worker. At any **real wage** (money wage divided by price level, or W/P), labor will be hired until[1],

$$\frac{W}{P} = MP_N. \qquad (4)$$

At a real wage of $(W/P)_1$ in Figure 7a, firms will want to employ N_1 units of labor, where the MP_N equals the real wage. If the real wage fell to $(W/P)_0$, firms would want to increase their employment to N_2. The falling MP_N curve thus represents the **demand curve for labor** (D_N).

---

1. These two conditions are really the same. Firms hire until $W = MRP_N = MP_N \times P$. Dividing both sides of the equation by P, we get

$$\frac{W}{P} = \frac{MRP_N}{P} = \frac{MP_N \times P}{P} = MP_N.$$

The decisions of households in allocating their time between leisure and working for pay determines the **supply of labor**. Workers try to allocate their time between work and leisure to achieve the combination of leisure and income that maximizes their utility. If the real wage rises, an hour's work for pay will buy more goods and services, and an hour's leisure will require a larger sacrifice of goods and services. The higher real wage will therefore encourage workers to consume less leisure and to work more.

At a real wage of $(W/P)_1$ in Figure 7b, workers will be willing to supply N_1 of labor. At a higher real wage of $(W/P)_2$, workers are willing to supply more labor, N_2 in Figure 7b. This direct relationship between the real wage and the aggregate quantity of labor supplied defines the **supply curve of labor** (S_N) in Figure 7b. It is important to note, though, that in the real world workers generally make labor-supply decisions on the basis of the money wage and an *expected* price level—i.e., on the basis of an **expected real wage**.

Figure 7c combines Figures 7a and 7b to show how demand and supply determine the equilibrium wage $(\overline{W/P})$ and the equilibrium level of employment $(\overline{N})$. At a higher real wage, such as $(W/P)_2$, workers are willing to supply more labor than firms want to hire. At a lower real wage, such as $(W/P)_0$, firms want to hire more labor than workers are willing to supply.

Prices, Employment, and Output

The key to aggregate supply is the relationship between the aggregate output supplied by all firms in the economy and the price level. This relationship is determined largely by the aggregate production function and the labor market equilibrium we've just looked at.

Figure 7 Labor Market Equilibrium

Given the price level P_1 in Figure 8a, labor market equilibrium will be reached at an equilibrium level of employment of $\overline{N}_1$ and an equilibrium real wage of $(\overline{W/P})_1$. Note, however, that this equilibrium real wage is in fact defined by an equilibrium money wage $(\overline{W})$ and the given price level (P_1). Thus,

$$(\overline{W/P})_1 = \overline{W}/P_1. \tag{5}$$

In Figure 8b, employment of $\overline{N}_1$ generates an aggregate output of Y_1 on the aggregate production function. Thus, the combination of aggregate output supplied (Y_1) and price level (P_1) define point A in Figure 8c.

Now suppose that the price level rises to P_2 and that workers' price level expectations do not adjust immediately. At the original equilibrium money wage $(\overline{W})$ and employment level $(\overline{N}_1)$, the real wage falls to $\overline{W}/P_2$. This change is represented graphically in Figure 8a as a downward shift in the labor supply curve to S_N'. In other words, workers are now supplying any quantity of labor at a lower real wage than before. Because of the lower real wage, firms will want to increase employment, but to do so they must raise the money wage, leading some workers to think they are getting a higher real wage and thus to supply more labor. A new equilibrium will be reached at employment level $\overline{N}_2$ and real wage $(\overline{W/P})_2 = \overline{W}'/P_2$ in Figure 8a. Notice that while the new equilibrium money wage is higher than it was before the increase in the price level (i.e. $\overline{W}' > \overline{W}$), the new real wage is lower than the original real wage (i.e., $(\overline{W/P})_2 < (\overline{W/P})_1$).

At the new level of employment $(\overline{N}_2)$, firms will produce a higher level of aggregate output (Y_2) in Figure 8b. Thus, this second combination of price level (P_2) and aggregate output supplied (Y_2) defines point B in Figure 8c.

Figure 8 Deriving the Aggregate Supply (YS) Curve

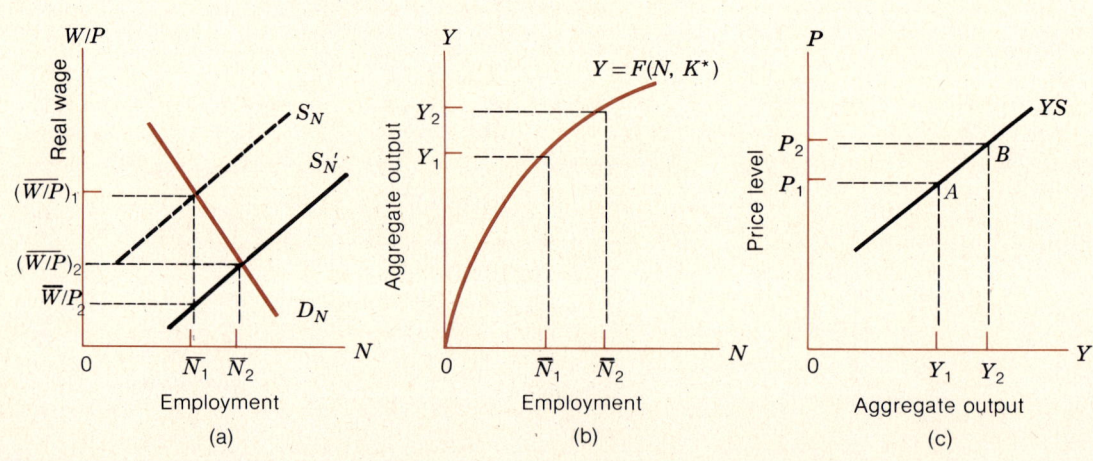

Any change in the price level should cause this same chain of events as long as workers' price level expectations do not adjust.

$$+ \Delta P \longrightarrow - \Delta(W/P) \longrightarrow + \Delta N \longrightarrow + \Delta Y$$

Increase in   Decrease in   Increase in   Increase in
Price Level   Real Wage   Employment   Aggregate
                                                                                  Output Supplied

Graphically, this chain of events defines the upward-sloping *aggregate supply curve* (YS) in Figure 8c.

- The **aggregate supply curve** (YS) shows the relationship between the price level and the aggregate output supplied, other things constant.

The aggregate supply curve in Figure 8c depicts a *short-run* relationship between the price level and aggregate output supplied. Initially, many workers may not recognize that rising prices have lowered the real wage. Unemployed workers holding out for a higher reservation wage, for example, generally respond to a higher money wage even if the real wage has fallen. For many employed workers, there may be a lag between a rise in the price level and a full recognition of the effect of higher prices on their real wage. Because of multi-year contracts, there may also be a lag between the workers' recognition of the drop in the real wage and their ability to demand a compensating change in the money wage. Once workers do catch on, however, raising their expected price level and demanding a higher money wage at every level of employment, the labor supply curve will shift upward from S_N'.

To keep our analysis simple, however, we'll assume for now that workers aren't aware of the effect of higher prices on the real wage, so that the labor supply curve remains at S_N' in Figure 8c. This assumption will be relaxed in the next chapter, which extends the analysis of prices, employment, and output to the long run.

The Shape of the Aggregate Supply Curve

There is little disagreement over the existence of an aggregate supply curve, but little agreement on its shape. The shape of the aggregate supply curve is not a trivial question, however. If the aggregate supply curve is vertical—as YS_1 in Figure 9—equilibrium aggregate output and employment will be the same regardless of the level of aggregate demand, and changes in aggregate demand will affect only the price level. At the other extreme, if the aggregate supply curve is horizontal—as YS_2 in Figure 9—changes in aggregate demand would cause aggregate output and employment to change without changing the price level. A relatively steep aggregate supply curve (YS_3) translates changes in aggregate demand into small changes in output and employment and large changes in the price level. A relatively flat aggregate supply curve (YS_4) would translate changes in aggregate demand into

Figure 9 The Shape of the YS Curve

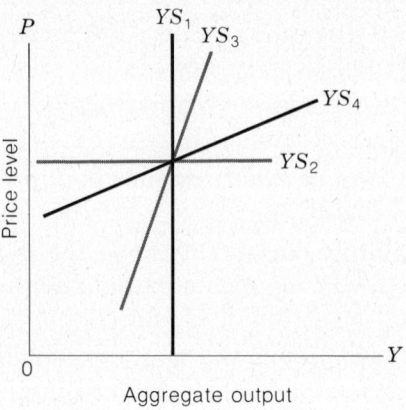

large changes in output and small changes in the price level.

Controversies among economists notwithstanding, empirical evidence strongly suggests (in the short run, at least) a direct relationship between the price level and the level of aggregate output. For this reason, we will make the not unreasonable assumption that the aggregate supply curve is upward-sloping, like YS_3 and YS_4 in Figure 9.

Shifts of the Aggregate Supply Curve

The relationship between aggregate output and the price level may change as a result of a number of exogenous changes. Higher input prices (for example, higher oil prices), changes in weather (such as prolonged drought), and changes in international relations that affect the supply of inputs are examples of **supply shocks** that would cause the aggregate supply curve to shift.

The dramatic rise in energy costs in the 1970s is one of the clearest examples of a supply shock. Just about every form of energy—oil, coal, gas, and nuclear—has become more expensive to produce in recent years. This has raised the price of energy and increased the cost of producing everything that requires energy in production—i.e., everything we produce. These higher costs of production are passed on to consumers as higher prices, so the price level rises at every level of aggregate output, shifting YS upward or to the left to YS' in Figure 10.

Changes in the labor market may also shift the aggregate supply curve. In Figure 11a, the labor supply curve shifts upward from S_N to S_N'. This shift could be due to any number of exogenous changes—stronger preference for leisure over income and other goods, greater optimism on the chance of finding higher wages through job searches, higher unemployment benefits, etc. To maintain employment at N_1

Figure 10 Shifts in the YS Curve

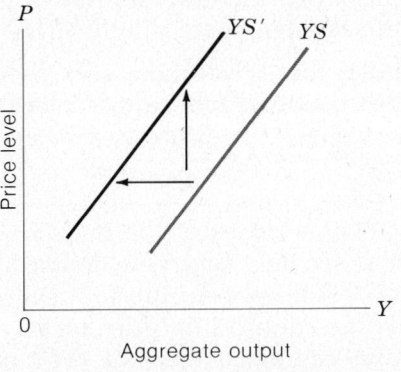

and real GNP at Y_1, the wage would have to rise from $(W/P)_1$ to $(W/P)_2$ on the new supply of labor $S_N{}'$. This would cause higher costs and higher prices at every level of aggregate output, shifting the aggregate supply curve to YS' in Figure 11b.

Technological change can also shift the aggregate supply curve. Suppose that a technological breakthrough results in a practical and inexpensive means of using solar energy to meet most of our energy needs for production and consumption. This would lower energy costs and thus the costs of producing goods and services, causing the price level to fall at every level of aggregate output. As a result, the aggregate supply curve would shift downward.

Figure 11 Labor Market Changes and the Aggregate Supply Curve

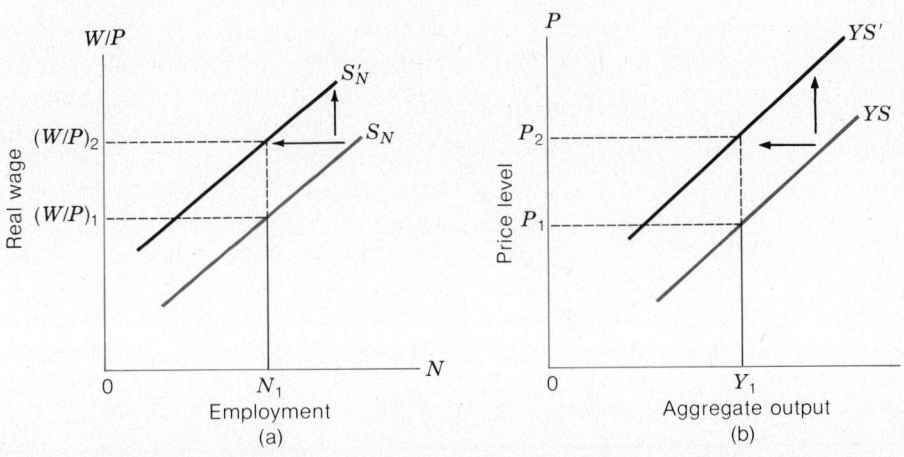

Summing all of this up,

- Exogenous changes that increase the cost of producing goods and services will shift the aggregate supply curve upward.
- Exogenous changes that lower the cost of producing goods and services will shift the aggregate supply curve downward.

Equilibrium Employment, Output, and Price Level

We now have all of the pieces of the puzzle. All that remains is to put them together to see how aggregate demand and aggregate supply interact to determine not only equilibrium aggregate output and employment, but also the equilibrium price level.

In Figure 12, the aggregate demand (YD) and aggregate supply (YS) curves determine equilibrium aggregate output at $\bar{Y}_1$ and an equilibrium price level at $\bar{P}_1$. If the price level were above or below $\bar{P}_1$, with the given YD and YS curves, the price level and aggregate output would not be in equilibrium. At P_2, for example, output supplied along YS exceeds output demanded along YD, and inventories of goods will increase. Firms will reduce their inventories by lowering prices to sell more and by reducing current output and employment. As prices fall real balances rise and more output will be demanded along YD.

At P_0 in Figure 12, current output falls short of aggregate demand, and inventories will fall. To maintain inventories and meet the demand for products, firms will increase current output and employment, causing wages and costs to rise with employment and raising the price level as output increases along YS. As the price level rises, real balances fall and the aggregate output demanded falls along YD.

Figure 12 The *YD-YS* Model

With flexible wages and prices, output will move toward $\bar{Y}_1$ and the price level toward $\bar{P}_1$. Once attained, there will be no tendency for output or the price level to change unless there is a shift in the aggregate demand or aggregate supply curves.

Demand Shifts

Suppose that an exogenous change—for example, expansionary monetary and fiscal policies—shifts aggregate demand from YD to YD' in Figure 13a. As a result of the increased demand for output, the economy faces demand-pull pressures on the level of output and on the price level. With YD' and YS, there is excess aggregate demand at Y_1 and P_1. As the producers increase employment and output and buyers compete for goods and services, the price level will rise until a new equilibrium is reached at $\bar{Y}_2$ and $\bar{P}_2$.

- Exogenous increases in aggregate demand generally cause aggregate output, employment, and the price level to rise.

If an exogenous change had caused aggregate demand to fall from YD' to YD in Figure 13a, the result would be just the opposite. Inventories would increase at Y_2 and P_2, the price level would fall and output would contract until equilibrium were restored at $\bar{Y}_1$ and $\bar{P}_1$.

- Exogenous decreases in aggregate demand generally cause aggregate output, employment, and the price level to fall.

Supply Shifts

In Figure 13b, an exogenous change causes the aggregate supply curve to shift upward from YS to YS'. Whatever the cause of this shift—more aggressive wage demands by workers, natural disasters that af-

Figure 13 Changes in Equilibrium Output and Price Level

(a) Demand Shift

(b) Supply Shift

fect production of critical goods, political and economic decisions by OPEC, etc.—the upward shift of YS means that every given level of aggregate output will be supplied only at a higher price level than before. At Y_1 and P_1, excess demand results from the shift of YS, causing the price level to rise until a new equilibrium is reached at a higher price level ($\overline{P}_2$) and a smaller aggregate output ($\overline{Y}_0$).

- Upward shifts of the aggregate supply curve, or reductions in aggregate supply, cause the aggregate price level to rise and the level of output and employment to fall.

If aggregate supply increases, or the aggregate supply curve shifts downward, the results would be just the opposite. If aggregate supply shifted from YS' to YS in Figure 13b, there would be excess aggregate supply and rising inventories at Y_0 and P_2. As the price level falls, aggregate output demanded will increase along YD until equilibrium is restored at $\overline{Y}_1$ and $\overline{P}_1$.

- Downward shifts in the aggregate supply curve, or increases in aggregate supply, cause the price level to fall and aggregate output and employment to increase.

We have come a long way on a rough road, but we now have a framework within which we can analyze the effects of aggregate demand and aggregate supply on output, employment, and the price level. We are no longer in the rarified world in which prices remain constant until full employment is reached. We can attack the real world problem of excessive unemployment and excessive rates of inflation.

One lesson is clear, and will preview the discussion in the next chapter. Since unemployment and inflation are determined by aggregate demand and aggregate supply forces, traditional demand-management policies—primarily discretionary monetary and fiscal policies—won't be adequate by themselves in attacking unemployment and inflation at the same time.

In the next chapter, we'll examine the relationship between the rate of inflation and the unemployment rate. For many years economists have argued that there is a trade-off between unemployment and inflation—i.e., to reduce unemployment we have to accept a greater rate of inflation, and vice versa. The next chapter tackles the nature of the unemployment-inflation trade-off and the question of whether such a trade-off exists at all.

Summary

1. The Keynesian income determination model and the analysis of equilibrium in money markets show how aggregate demand affects aggregate output or real GNP, assuming a fixed price level.

2. To understand contemporary unemployment and inflation, the first step is to drop the assumption of stable prices, and to examine the relationships between the price level and the aggregate demand for goods and services and between the level of output and the price level.
3. Other things equal, aggregate output demanded varies inversely with the price level. As the price level falls, money markets adjust to a new equilibrium interest rate, and investment, aggregate demand, and aggregate output demanded increase, defining an **aggregate demand curve**.
4. Exogenous changes that increase aggregate demand cause the aggregate demand curve to shift to the right. Exogenous changes that reduce aggregate demand shift the aggregate demand curve to the left.
5. Aggregate output supplied varies in the short run directly with the price level, defining an **aggregate supply curve**. When the price level rises, the **real wage** falls and firms will hire more labor to increase output and profit.
6. Exogenous changes that increase costs at any level of output or that reduce the output that will be produced at a given price level shift the aggregate supply curve upward or to the left. Exogenous changes that lower costs or increase the output that can be produced at a given level of prices shift the aggregate supply curve downward or to the right.
7. Aggregate output and the price level reach equilibrium when the aggregate output produced (aggregate supply) equals the aggregate output demanded.
8. Exogenous changes that shift aggregate demand or aggregate supply curves will disturb equilibrium aggregate output and the price level.

Concepts for Review

aggregate demand curve
aggregate supply curve
production function
diminishing returns

aggregate production function
marginal revenue product of labor

supply of labor
demand for labor
real wage
supply shock

Questions

1. Explain the relationship between the aggregate demand curve as it was presented in the discussion of income determination and as it is presented in this chapter.
2. How would each of the following affect the aggregate demand for goods and services? In each case, explain whether the changes are along the aggregate demand curve or are shifts of the aggregate demand curve.
   a. The Federal Reserve reduces the supply of money.
   b. Households increase consumption expenditures at every level of income.
   c. The Consumer Price Index rises from 200 (1967 = 100) to 210.
   d. Investors become more pessimistic about future economic conditions.
   e. The federal government increases its purchases of goods and services from the private sector.

3. Describe the conditions that would make aggregate demand highly responsive to changes in the price level, and the conditions that would make aggregate demand relatively unresponsive to changes in the price level. Why is the responsiveness of aggregate demand to changes in the price level significant?
4. What determines the economy's aggregate production function? What does it show? What are diminishing returns? How do diminishing returns affect the production function, and what do they imply about the relationship between aggregate output and the price level?
5. How would each of the following affect aggregate supply? Explain whether each would cause a change along an aggregate supply curve or would cause the aggregate supply curve to shift.
    a. OPEC raises the price of oil in world markets from $23.50 to $30.
    b. Output per worker and money wages both rise by 10 percent.
    c. Output per worker rises by 5 percent, and money wages by 10 percent.
    d. A technological breakthrough makes it possible to generate massive amount of electric power with solar powered generators at one-half the cost per kwh with existing methods.
6. If aggregate output is greater or less than its equilibrium level, explain how aggregate demand and aggregate supply will bring it to its equilibrium level. What is the significance of assuming that prices are flexible in this analysis?
7. What are the implications of each of the following for aggregate output and employment, the price level, and the ability of aggregate demand and aggregate supply to produce equilibrium aggregate output and prices?
    a. Firms in basic industries (steel, oil, aluminum, etc.) agree not to precipitate price wars and uncertainty by cutting prices.
    b. A comprehensive minimum wage law prohibits any employer from hiring any worker at less than $4 an hour.
    c. To avoid excessive inflation the government freezes all wages and prices at their current level.
    d. Maximum interest rates are imposed on time deposits and on business and commercial loans.

Problems

1. Econometricians in the small country of Aggregatania have found the following empirical relationships. The data are very accurate and the econometricians are very smart, so we can accept these as accurate relationships.
    Demand for money (real balances) (L): $r = 20 - 0.8\,(M/P)$
    Investment demand (MEI): $MEI = 20 - 0.5\,I$
    Government purchases: $G = 27$
    Consumption: $C = 50 + 0.8\,(Y - T)$
    Taxes: $T = 20$
    Price level: $P = 1.00$
    Money supply: $M = 20$.
    a. Find the equilibrium interest rate (r) and the level of investment (I) from the above information. This can be done algebraically or graphically by drawing an accurate demand curve for real balances (L) and an accurate MEI curve.

b. From the answer to part (a) and the other information given, find equilibrium aggregate output or real GNP ($\bar{Y}$). This can be done algebraically or graphically. What does this tell you about the aggregate output demanded at $P = 1.00$ with the other information given? Show *this* graphically.

c. Now, suppose that the price level rises to $P' = 2.00$, and that nothing else changes. Repeat parts (a) and (b) with the new price level.

d. Draw the aggregate demand (YD) curve, showing the relationship between aggregate output demanded and the price level over this range of price levels. How is this aggregate demand curve different from the demand curve for a single commodity that shows the quantity demanded at various prices?

e. The government increases the money supply to $M' = 30$. Repeat (a) and (b) with the new money supply and the price level $P' = 2.00$. What has happened to the aggregate demand curve you found in part (d)?

f. The government increases its spending to $G' = 40$. How does this affect the results you got from parts (a) and (b)? How has the change affected the aggregate demand curve? How would the existence of crowding out affect this result?

2. Given the following labor supply information for the economy of Ewessay.

Money wage per worker per year	Employment (N) (millions of workers)	Real output produced (millions)
$ 7,000	15	$200,000
8,000	20	300,000
9,000	25	390,000
10,000	30	470,000
11,000	35	540,000
12,000	40	600,000
13,000	45	650,000
14,000	50	690,000
15,000	55	720,000

a. Assuming that the economy's price level is equal to one, find the marginal product of labor (MP_N) at each level of employment. What is the demand for labor?

b. Find the equilibrium wage and level of employment in the economy. What level of aggregate output will be produced at this level of employment?

c. Suppose now that the price level doubles overnight, and that workers remain unaware of the change. At what real wage will the former equilibrium employment level be reached? How will firms react to this change? What will be the new equilibrium wage and employment level in the economy? How long would you expect this equilibrium to continue?

3. In the small country of Fernland, an aggregate output (or real GNP) of $600 billion (1972 dollars) is consistent with a price level of 2.80 on the YS function. However, the aggregate output demanded at this price level is $500 billion on the YD function. Every change in the price level by 0.2 points causes the aggregate output supplied to change in the same direction by $10 billion and the aggregate output demanded to change in the opposite direction by $10 billion.

a. Draw the economy's aggregate demand (YD) and aggregate supply (YS) curves for the range of aggregate output between $500 billion and $600 billion.
b. Is $600 billion the equilibrium aggregate output? Is $500 billion the equilibrium aggregate output? How do you know? What adjustments (if any) would bring aggregate output and the price level to equilibrium?
c. Find the equilibrium aggregate output and price level (if you haven't already).
d. An increase in energy prices adds 0.8 points to the price level at each level of aggregate output produced. What effect will this have on aggregate output and the price level? Find the new equilibrium aggregate output and price level.
e. Every increase or decrease of aggregate output by $1 billion causes employment to increase or decrease by 10,000 workers per year. What effect will the higher energy prices in part (d) have on employment in Fernland? If the government undertakes monetary and fiscal policies to bring employment back to the original level, what will happen to the price level? Why?

30

Inflation and Unemployment: Is There a Trade-off?

Preview: This chapter examines the relationship between the unemployment rate and the rate of inflation. The aggregate demand and aggregate supply model from the previous chapter is modified to show how aggregate demand and aggregate supply determine the level of aggregate output, employment, the unemployment rate, and the rate of inflation. The chapter also discusses the difference between the short-run and long-run relationships between unemployment and inflation.

Aggregate Demand, Aggregate Supply, Inflation, and Unemployment

The 1960s was a decade of steadily declining unemployment rates and increasing rates of inflation. In 1960, the unemployment rate was 5.5 percent, and the Consumer Price Index (CPI) was about 1.5 percent above it's level in 1959. In 1969, the unemployment rate had fallen to 3.5 percent, and the CPI had risen about 5.4 percent between 1968 and 1969.

The experience of the United States with unemployment and inflation in the 1960s—coupled with the pioneering studies in the 1950s by the late British economist, A. W. Phillips, of unemployment rates, wages, and prices in England—led many economists and others to see an inverse relationship or *trade-off* between the apparently conflicting goals of full employment and stable prices. The emphasis in economic policy discussions turned to finding the best, or most acceptable, compromise between low unemployment rates and low rates of inflation. Since the costs of unemployment and inflation aren't borne equally by all groups within society, finding the best trade-off between unemployment and inflation involves value judgments.

In the 1970s, the debate over the relationship between unemployment and inflation took a new twist. The data showed a very loose and unstable relationship between the unemployment rate and the rate of inflation, so that even identifying the trade-off is a sticky problem. Furthermore, new theoretical and empirical work in the 1970s suggests that there is no trade-off between unemployment and inflation in the long run—only the choice between higher and lower rates of inflation—and that the apparent trade-off in the 1960s had been a short-run phenomenon.

Obviously, the relationship (if any) between the unemployment rate and the rate of inflation is central to our ability to achieve an acceptably low rate of inflation and an acceptably low unemployment rate through discretionary policies. To understand how unemployment and inflation are affected by aggregate demand and aggregate supply, we have to restate aggregate supply and aggregate demand to show how aggregate output supplied (YS) and aggregate output demanded (YD) are related to the **rate of inflation**. These aren't different from the aggregate demand and aggregate supply relationships presented in the previous chapter, but merely a slightly different way of looking at them.

Aggregate Supply and the Inflation Rate

In the last chapter, we saw that when the price level rises and the real wage falls, firms will want to hire more labor and increase output, and by offering higher money wages, they will be able to do so until workers' expectations adjust to the higher price level. As the economy approaches full capacity, however, equal increases in the price level result in smaller and smaller increases in output. Conversely, equal increases in output require successively larger increases in the price level. In short, there is an apparent relationship between the level of aggregate output supplied and the percentage change in the price level, or the **inflation rate**.

This result occurs mainly for two reasons. In Figure 1a, the aggregate production function shows the relationship between employment

Figure 1 Aggregate Production Function and Employment Per Dollar of Real GNP

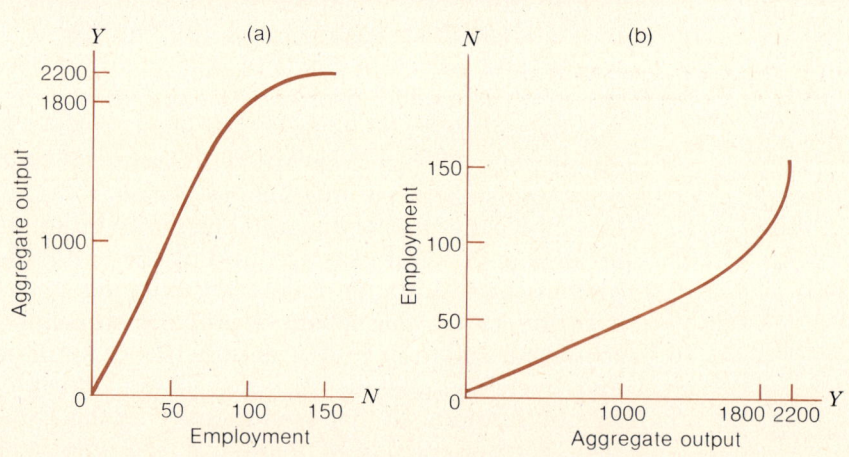

(N) and aggregate output or real GNP (Y). Because of diminishing returns, Y increases at a diminishing rate as N increases. Figure 1b is simply Figure 1a turned on its side. It shows that the number of workers required to produce an additional dollar of real GNP rises at an increasing rate as output increases. Such successively larger increases in employment can come about only through successively larger declines in the real wage. These, in turn, can result only from larger and larger increases in the price level.

The behavior of the money wage augments this effect. Figure 2 shows the quantity of labor supplied as a function of the money wage, with given price level expectations. To call out additional labor, firms must increase the money wage, partially offsetting the decline in the real wage. At low levels of output, with many unemployed workers holding out for reservation wages and employed workers anxious for overtime, relatively small increases in the money wage will be required to produce a given increase in employment. As the economy approaches full capacity, however, fewer workers remain unemployed and employed workers are less and less willing to sacrifice additional leisure time for additional income. As a result, equal increases in employment require successively larger increases in the money wage. Thus, the increase in the price level required to bring about a given decline in the real wage and corresponding rise in employment will be greater the closer the economy is to full capacity.

In short, with a large gap between actual output (Y) and full-capacity output (Y^*), aggregate output supplied will be relatively responsive to changes in the price level. As that gap shrinks, however, the combined effect of diminishing returns and rising money wages means that the price level must rise at an increasing rate with respect to aggregate output supplied. Therefore, given any gap between Y and Y^*, we can associate a percentage change in the price level, or *infla-*

Figure 2 Supply Curve of Labor

Figure 3 Aggregate Supply, Aggregate Demand, and the Rate of Inflation

tion rate (IR), with any change in the size of that gap. This, of course, allows us indirectly to relate a rate of inflation to the level of aggregate output supplied, as illustrated in Figure 3a. As aggregate output increases, the gap between actual and full-capacity output gets smaller and the rate of inflation rises.[1]

Aggregate Demand and the Inflation Rate

You will recall from the last chapter that aggregate output demanded (YD) varies inversely with the price level, other things constant. Suppose that the money supply this year is the same as it was last year, but that the price level has increased by 10 percent. This will produce the following familiar sequence of events:

1. A 10 percent increase in the price level with a constant money supply cause real balances (M/P) to fall by about 10 percent.
2. The 10 percent drop in real balances causes the interest rate to rise.
3. Higher interest rates reduce investment and aggregate spending and cause the aggregate demand for goods and services to fall.

Now, suppose that the price level had risen by 5 percent instead of 10 percent since last year, with a constant money supply. Compared with the effects listed above for a 10 percent increase in the price level,

1. There will be a smaller reduction in real balances—about 5 percent instead of 10 percent.
2. There will be a smaller rise in the interest rate.
3. There will be smaller reductions in investment, aggregate spending, and the aggregate demand for goods and services.

---

[1]. This relationship is meant only to simplify our analysis of unemployment and inflation, and should *not* be misinterpreted. The YS curve in Figure 3a shows the relationship between output and the inflation for *given values of Y and Y** and *given price level expectations*. Since Y, Y*, and price expectations are constantly changing, we can't interpret Figure 3a as saying that a particular level of aggregate output supplied (say, $2 trillion) will *always* be associated with a particular rate of inflation (say, 12 percent).

4. Aggregate output demanded this year will be greater than it would be with a 10 percent rate of inflation.

In short, given an initial level of aggregate output, we can define an inverse relationship between the rate of inflation (IR) and the level of aggregate output demanded.[2] This relationship is shown graphically by the negatively-sloped YD curve in Figure 3b.

Aggregate Output and the Inflation Rate

We now have the pieces to assemble part of the unemployment-inflation picture. Combining Figures 3a and 3b, aggregate demand (YD) and aggregate supply (YS) determine a level of aggregate output ($\overline{Y}_1$) and a rate of inflation ($\overline{IR}_1$) in Figure 4.

If aggregate output were greater than $\overline{Y}_1$—for example, Y_2 in Figure 4—the rate of inflation as a result of producing this level of output (IR_2 along YS) would be greater than the rate of inflation that would clear the market of this aggregate output. Looked at another way, the aggregate output demanded at a rate of inflation of IR_2 is less than Y_2—i.e., aggregate demand is insufficient to clear the market of the aggregate output produced. Unintended increases in inventories would cause the rate of inflation to fall as firms either lowered prices or reduced price increases to sell their unsold goods.

At an aggregate output below $\overline{Y}_1$ in Figure 4—for example, Y_0—the rate of inflation is IR_0 (from YS). At this rate of inflation, the aggregate output demanded (from YD) is greater than the output of goods and services, and the economy will experience excess aggregate demand. Producers will respond to unfilled orders and declining inventories by increasing output, causing the aggregate output to increase from Y_0 and the rate of inflation to rise above IR_0.

Figure 4 The YD-YS Model and the Rate of Inflation

---

2. In other words, aggregate output demanded *this year* depends on aggregate output *last year* and the rate of change in the price level *since last year*.

Figure 5 Unemployment and the Rate of Inflation

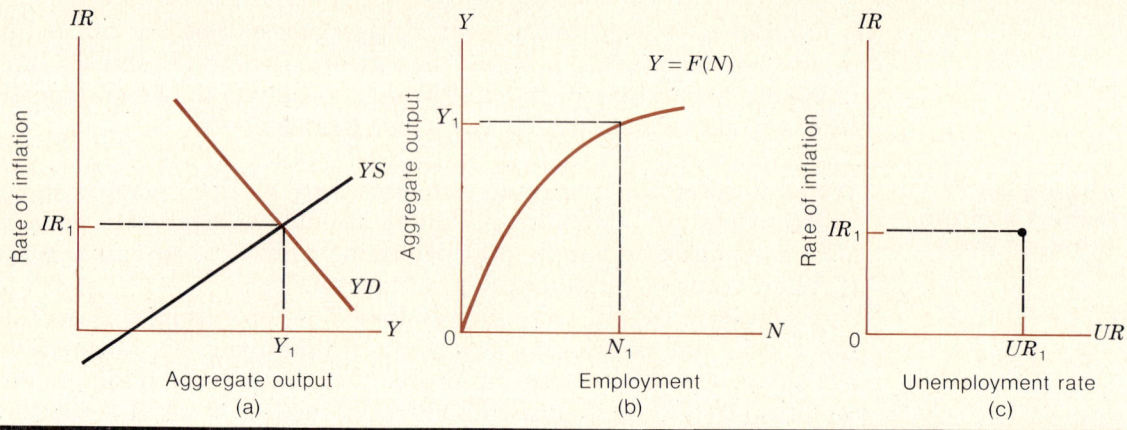

Inflation, Output, and Unemployment	The final piece that has to be put in place is the relationship between the rate of inflation and the unemployment rate. Actually, that is relatively simple. In Figure 5a, YS and YD determine the level of aggregate output (Y_1) and the rate of inflation (IR_1). The aggregate production function in Figure 5b shows the level of employment (N_1) consistent with an aggregate output of Y_1. We now know that a rate of inflation of IR_1 is consistent with aggregate employment of N_1.

What about inflation and *un*employment? If we let N^* be full employment, then unemployment at N_1 is

$$U_1 = N^* - N_1. \tag{1}$$

The **unemployment rate** is simply unemployment as a percentage of the labor force or full employment, so the unemployment rate at N_1 is

$$UR_1 = \frac{N^* - N_1}{N^*}. \tag{2}$$

Our basic model is now complete. Aggregate demand and aggregate supply determine aggregate output and the rate of inflation in Figure 5a and the level of employment in Figure 5b. The level of employment defines the level of unemployment and the unemployment rate in Figure 5c. Putting it all together, we have aggregate demand and aggregate supply determining the unemployment rate (UR_1) and the rate of inflation (IR_1) in Figure 5c. Now we are ready to turn to the trade-off between the unemployment rate and the rate of inflation.

The Phillips Curve	The **Phillips curve** shows the relationship between the unemployment rate (UR) and the rate of inflation (IR). The term recognizes the con-

tributions made by a British economist—the late A. W. Phillips—in the 1950s in his studies of the relationship between unemployment rates, wage increases, and inflation in Britain.

The Phillips curve can be derived directly from the **aggregate demand–aggregate supply model.** Aggregate demand (YD) and aggregate supply (YS) in Figure 6a determine a level of output $\overline{Y}_1$ (with an unemployment rate of 6 percent) and an annual rate of inflation of 5 percent. Now, suppose the government undertakes expansionary monetary and fiscal policies to lower the unemployment rate. Such policies shift the aggregate demand curve to YD' in Figure 6a, raising aggregate output to $\overline{Y}_2$ (with an unemployment rate of 5 percent) and the rate of inflation to 8 percent. These two combinations of inflation rate and unemployment rate (shown as points A and B) lie on the negatively-sloped Phillips curve PC in Figure 6b.

Figure 6 The YD-YS Model and the Phillips Curve

Unemployment and Inflation in the 1960s

The Phillips curve can be estimated empirically by constructing a scatter diagram with each point in the scatter representing the unemployment rate and the rate of inflation in a given year.[3] Figure 7 is a scatter diagram showing unemployment rates and the rate of inflation (percentage changes in the Consumer Price Index) for the United States in the years 1960–1969.

It's easy to see in Figure 7 why the notion of a trade-off between the unemployment rate was so prevalent in the 1960s. Simply connecting the points year-to-year traces out a Phillips curve for the 1960s, and shows a stable and predictable relationship between the unemployment rate and the rate of inflation.

---

3. For more detail on statistical estimation, see the appendix to Chapter 1.

The Breakdown of the Trade-off in the 1970s

The stable relationship between the unemployment rate and the rate of inflation that seemed so clear in the 1960s came apart in the 1970s. Figure 8 adds the unemployment rates and rates of inflation for the years 1970–1977 to the scatter diagram for the 1960s. It should come as no surprise after looking at Figure 8 that the notion of a stable and predictable trade-off between the unemployment rate and the rate of inflation lost ground rapidly in the 1970s. No single Phillips curve of the general shape of the Phillips curves in Figures 6 and 7 fits all of the points in Figure 8 very well—indicating a very loose relationship or an unstable trade-off.

If we continue the year-to-year path of unemployment and inflation from the 1960s to the 1970s, we get a very different picture for the 1970s than we saw for the 1960s. Between 1969 and 1970, the unemployment rate and the rate of inflation both increased. There was an apparent trade-off between 1970 and 1971, but both rates fell between 1971 and 1972. After an increase in the rate of inflation between 1972 and 1973, the pattern repeats in the period 1974–1978. If we put the 1960s and 1970s together, the path of unemployment and inflation traces out a *spiral*.

Amid all of the gnashing of teeth and breast-beating over how little we know about unemployment and inflation in the 1970s, several important points went largely unnoticed outside the ranks of professional economists. First, a stable and predictable Phillips-curve relationship between unemployment rates and the rate of inflation depends on a stable aggregate supply curve. In the 1970s, there were a number of supply shocks that made the relationship between aggre-

Figure 7 Phillips Curve, 1960–1969

gate output supplied and the price level unstable—for example, the imposition and removal of a price freeze in 1971–1972 and the dramatic increase in the prices of oil imports. Secondly, the inverse relationship between unemployment rates and the rate of inflation in the 1960s apparently was a short-run relationship. The long-run relationship between the unemployment rate and the rate of inflation is quite different from the short-run trade-off we saw in the 1960s—in fact, there may be no trade-off in the long run.

Figure 8 Phillips Curve, 1960–1977

Is There a Long-Run Trade-off?

Why would the relationship between unemployment and inflation be different in the long run than in the short run? What factors contribute to this difference? Is there a trade-off between unemployment and inflation in the long run? These questions are central to the success (or lack of success) of policies to combat unemployment and inflation.

Expectations, Aggregate Supply, and the Natural Unemployment Rate

What firms and households expect to happen in the economy has an impact on what actually does happen in the economy. For example, if firms expect a rapid increase in prices in the future, they may withhold products from market now in order to receive higher prices later. The resulting reduction in supply contributes to rising prices. Likewise, if unions expect rapid inflation, they will bargain for large money wage increases to offset the expected inflation. These reactions of firms and households to expected inflation will contribute to actual inflation.

Expecting something to happen, of course, doesn't mean that it will happen, and economic expectations may turn out to be wrong. People and businesses aren't dumb, and there is no reason to believe that they will cling indefinitely to unfulfilled expectations. Rather, individuals and firms will adapt their economic expectations to actual economic conditions. For example, if the expected rate of inflation is 5 percent per year, and the price level actually rises by 10 percent per year, businesses and households will adjust their inflationary expectations upward. These changes in expectations show up in our aggregate demand–aggregate supply model as shifts in the aggregate supply curve.

- Changes in the expected rate of inflation will shift the labor supply curve and the aggregate supply curve.

The labor supply and aggregate supply curves will stabilize only when the actual rate of inflation (IR_a) equals the expected rate of inflation (IR_e)—that is, when there are no unexpected changes in the price level. Suppose, for example, that the expected rate of inflation is $IR_e = 0$. In other words, households and firms expect stable prices.

Figure 9 The Natural Rate Hypothesis

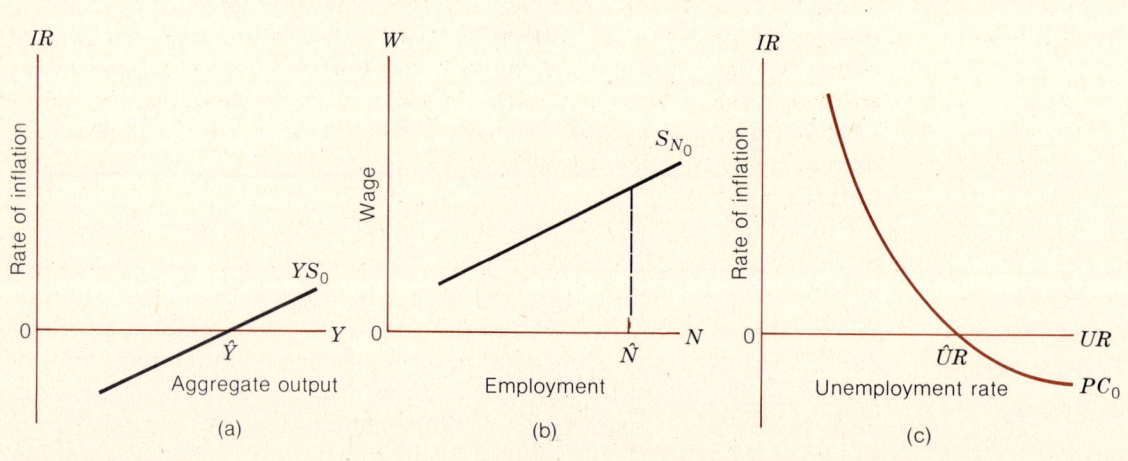

With $IR_e = 0$, the aggregate supply curve (YS_0) in Figure 9a shows the relationship between aggregate output (Y) and the actual rate of inflation (IR_a). At output $\hat{Y}$, the actual rate of inflation equals the expected rate ($IR_a = IR_e = 0$). $\hat{Y}$ is referred to as the *natural level of aggregate output*.

- When the actual rate of inflation equals the expected rate of inflation, the economy is producing its **natural level of aggregate output**.

The labor supply curve S_{N_0}, in Figure 9b shows the relationship between the level of employment and the wage level if workers expect stable prices ($IR_e = 0$). $\hat{N}$ in Figure 9b is the level of employment consistent with the natural aggregate output, or the level of employment at which the actual and expected rates of inflation are equal. $\hat{N}$ is referred to as the **natural level of employment**.

If the actual and expected rates of inflation are equal, the economy is producing the natural level of aggregate output, $\hat{Y}$ in Figure 9a, at the natural level of employment, $\hat{N}$ in Figure 9b. This means that the unemployment rate will also be at its natural rate in Figure 9c.

- The **natural unemployment rate** is the unemployment rate at which the actual rate of inflation equals the expected rate of inflation.

In Figure 9c, the natural unemployment rate is $\hat{UR}$, where $IR_e = IR_a = 0$. As long as the expected rate of inflation stays at $IR_e = 0$, there will be a trade-off between unemployment and inflation represented by the curve PC_0 in Figure 9c. Note that the rate of inflation equals the expected rate on PC_0 at the natural unemployment rate, $\hat{UR}$.

Before moving on, several points have to be cleared up concerning the natural unemployment rate. First of all, contrary to its name, it is not determined by natural forces. The natural unemployment rate is affected by such things as unemployment compensation laws, immobility and friction in labor markets, and institutional relationships in the economy. Secondly, the natural unemployment rate is not permanently fixed, but can be changed through changes in economic institutions, legislation, and improvements in the working of labor markets. Finally, the natural unemployment rate will never be zero, and may even exceed the unemployment rate that is politically acceptable as full employment.

In what sense are natural employment, output, and unemployment rate *natural*? These are simply the rates toward which the economy will *naturally* move as economic expectations adjust the expected rate of inflation to the actual rate. In Figure 10a, YD and YS_0 determine equilibrium aggregate output at $\overline{Y}$ which is greater than natural aggregate output ($\hat{Y}$). This means that the unemployment rate ($\overline{UR}$) is less than the natural rate ($\hat{UR}$) in Figure 10b, and that the actual rate of inflation ($IR_a = 3\%$) exceeds the expected rate ($IR_e = 0$). As workers find that prices are rising more rapidly than they expected, the money wage will rise at every level of employment, increasing costs and raising the aggregate supply curve in Figure 10a.

The aggregate supply curve will continue to shift upward until the actual and expected rates of inflation are equal—i.e., until aggregate output reaches its natural level. In Figure 10a, natural output is reached again when $IR_e' = IR_a = 6$ percent. In Figure 10b, the increase in the expected rate of inflation and the shift of the aggregate supply curve to YS_6 shifts the Phillips curve upward in Figure 10b until the actual and expected rates of inflation are equal, or until unemployment reaches the natural rate $(\hat{UR})$ with a $IR_e' = IR_a = 6$ percent.

Figure 10 Adjustment to the Natural Rate

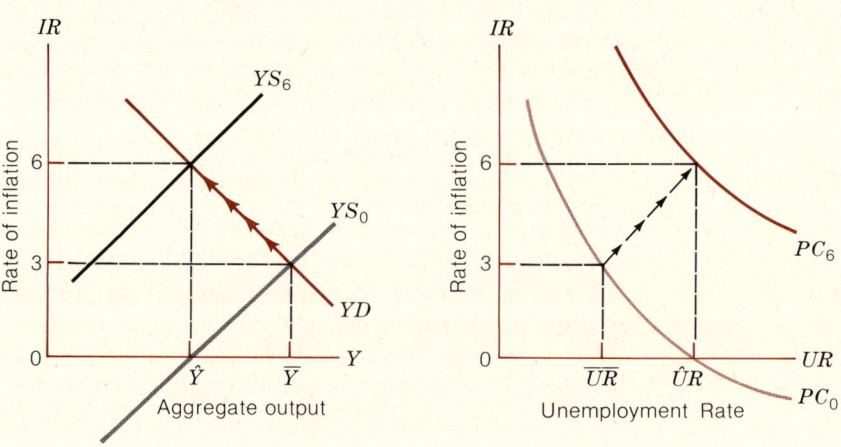

If aggregate demand and aggregate supply determine a level of aggregate output below the natural level, prices will rise more slowly than the expected rate of inflation, and the unemployment rate will exceed the natural rate. In Figure 11a, for example, the equilibrium aggregate output determined by YD and YS_6 ($IR_e = 6$ percent) is below the natural rate, and prices are rising at 4.5 percent rather than at the expected rate of inflation of 6 percent. In Figure 11b, the unemployment rate exceeds the natural rate with prices rising at 4.5 percent. As the expected rate of inflation adapts to the actual rate, the aggregate supply curve falls until the actual rate of inflation equals the expected rate at $IR_e' = IR_a = 3$ percent. The shift of the aggregate supply curve due to weaker inflationary expectations shifts the Phillips curve from PC_6 to PC_3. Again, it's important to note that $IR_e' = IR_a = 3$ percent on PC_3 at the natural unemployment rate $\hat{UR}$.

INFLATION AND UNEMPLOYMENT: IS THERE A TRADE-OFF? 645

Long-Run Aggregate Supply and the Long-Run Phillips Curve

In the long run, allowing enough time for expectations to adapt to actual rates of inflation, aggregate output will always readjust to its natural level. This suggests that the *long-run aggregate supply curve (LYS)* will be vertical at the natural level of aggregate output, as in Figure 11a. This implies that in the long run, aggregate output will be at $\hat{Y}$, regardless of the level of aggregate demand. The only thing that aggregate demand determines in the long run is the rate of inflation.

The long-run aggregate supply curve in Figure 11a also suggests a vertical *long-run Phillips Curve (LPC)* at the natural rate of unemployment, as in Figure 11b. The short-run Phillips curves, such as PC_4 and PC_3 in Figure 11b, indicate the inverse relationship between the unemployment rate and the rate of inflation that occurred in the United States in the 1960s. However, if expectations adjust fully to changing economic conditions, the vertical Phillips curve at the natural unemployment rate indicates that there is no long-run trade-off between the unemployment rate and the rate of inflation—only a choice between higher and lower rates of inflation at the natural unemployment rate.

The notion of a natural unemployment rate is a source of controversy among economists, and the lines in the controversy are fairly sharply drawn. The strongest supporters of the **natural rate hypothesis** are monetarists and others who are skeptical of the ability of discretionary monetary and fiscal policies to achieve full employment and price stability. Monetary and fiscal activists who assign a large role to discretionary monetary and fiscal policy are the most critical of the natural rate hypothesis.

The notion that the unemployment rate will move toward its natural rate in the long run has serious implications for the long-run effects

Figure 11 Long-Run Aggregate Supply and the Long-Run Phillips Curve

Figure 12 Inflation, Unemployment, and Government Policy

of discretionary monetary and fiscal policies—particularly if these policies are aimed at a target unemployment rate below the natural rate. Suppose that the desired rate of employment ("full employment") is defined as 5 percent, and that the government is committed to a goal of full employment. Initially, suppose that the unemployment rate is at the natural rate of 6 percent with prices increasing at 5 percent per year, as shown by point A in Figure 12.

To get the unemployment rate down to 5 percent, which it has defined as full employment, the government undertakes expansionary monetary and fiscal policies to stimulate aggregate demand. The short-term effect of the expansionary policies is to reduce the unemployment rate to 5 percent and to raise the rate of inflation to 8 percent along SPC_1. The acceleration of the rate of inflation, however, will soon lead consumers, producers, and workers to adjust their expectations. As the expected rate of inflation increases, the short-run Phillips curve shifts upward to SPC_2. If no further monetary or fiscal actions were taken, and if the expected rate of inflation didn't change, the unemployment rate would return to the natural rate of 6 percent, with a rate of inflation of 9.5 percent.

If the government were committed to an unemployment rate below the natural rate at any cost, the net result of discretionary monetary and fiscal policies to achieve this objective would be hyperinflation. However, hyperinflation is a highly unlikely result because society and the government are concerned about the rate of inflation as well as the unemployment rate. Suppose that the 9.5 percent annual rate of price increase at C in Figure 12 is considered excessive. The government's economic policy turns to monetary and fiscal restraint to dampen inflation. The short-run effect is to move from C to D on SPC_2. The rate of price increase falls to 7 percent per year and the unemployment rate increases 7.5 percent. But now the actual rate of inflation is *below* the expected rate, so firms and households will adjust their expectations downward, shifting the short-run Phillips curve to SPC_3. If no further actions are taken, the unemployment rate falls back to the natural rate at E with prices increasing at 6 percent per year.

Having succeeded in lowering the rate of inflation, the government now turns its attention to unemployment, since the unemployment rate has stopped falling before reaching the desired "full employment" rate of 5 percent. If expansionary monetary and fiscal policies are undertaken to push the unemployment rate down to 5 percent from point E, the process starts over, and a second "loop" begins. As the government deals alternately with unemployment and inflation, and expectations constantly adjust to changes, unemployment and inflation rates trace a series of clockwise loops, or a **price spiral** around the natural unemployment rate.

This analysis enables us to make some sense out of the behavior of unemployment and inflation in the 1960s and 1970s. The path $ABCDEFG$ in Figure 12 bears a striking resemblance to the spiral traced out by unemployment rates and rates of inflation for the United States in the 1960s and 1970s in Figure 8. Figure 8 suggests a spiral around an unemployment rate in the neighborhood of 5.5 percent, which is consistent with most estimates of the natural unemployment rate for the United States.

What does all of this suggest for policies to deal with unemployment and inflation? One possible conclusion is that no discretionary monetary and fiscal policies will be successful in keeping unemployment rates below the natural rate without excessive rates of inflation because the policies themselves will alter expectations in a way that offsets the effects of the policies. Another, not much more reassuring, implication is that monetary and fiscal policies will work only as long as people are fooled—i.e., until their expectations adjust to what's actually happening. Yet another implication is that traditional monetary and fiscal policies that are directed at the demand side of the problem of unemployment and inflation must *at the very least* be accompanied by other policies that affect unemployment and inflation from the aggregate supply side and by policies that reduce the natural unemployment rate. The problem, then, is not that economists don't know anything about the problem of unemployment and inflation or how to deal with it, but that what we do know isn't very pleasant or appealing. Some policy strategies to deal with unemployment and inflation are discussed in the next chapter.

Applying the Tools

Rational Expectations

Abraham Lincoln once asserted that "You can fool all of the people some of the time, and some of the people all of the time, but you can't fool all of the people all of the time." In the 1970s, a major innovation in macroeconomics by Professors Robert E. Lucas, Thomas J. Sargent, and Neil Wallace carries Lincoln's argument one step further by arguing in effect that "You can't fool anybody anytime"—at least as far as monetary and fiscal policies are concerned.

The **theory of rational expectations** derived by Lucas, Sargent, and Wallace argues that individuals and firms know what to expect from monetary and fiscal policies and adjust their expectations to announced or predicted changes in monetary and fiscal policies before the changes actually take place. For example, if workers and employers know that the government always increases the money supply and enacts expansionary fiscal measures if the unemployment exceeds 5.5 percent, they will expect these measures whenever the unemployment rate exceeds 5.5 percent, and will alter their economic expectations to take into account the forthcoming changes in monetary and fiscal policy. When the expected monetary and fiscal measures actually occur, according to this line of argument, they will have no effect because expectations have already anticipated them!

Figure A is a simplified sketch of the way that rational expectations offset the effect of discretionary monetary and fiscal policies on aggregate demand, output, and the unemployment rate. Initially, suppose that aggregate output is at $\hat{Y}$ and that the unemployment rate is at $\hat{UR}$. The government feels that the unemployment rate is too high, and announces that it will act to reduce the unemployment rate to UR^*. From previous experience, firms and households know that this means expansionary monetary and fiscal policies are on the way, and they expect a higher rate of inflation as a result. When the government expresses its concern with the unemployment rate and its commitment to reduce it, then, the expected rate of inflation increases from IR_e to IR_e', shifting the aggregate supply curve upward to YS' and the Phillips curve to PC'.

When the expansionary monetary and fiscal policies actually take place, aggregate demand increases to YD'. However, because the aggregate supply curve has already shifted to YS', the expansionary policies and the increase in aggregate demand have *no effect* on the aggregate output or the unemployment rate. They simply increase the rate of inflation at the same level of aggregate output and at the same unemployment rate. Since expectations had taken account of the effects of the policies, they don't even have any short-run effect on aggregate output or the unemployment rate.

The implications of the rational expectations hypothesis for discretionary monetary and fiscal policies are even stronger than the implications of the natural rate hypothesis. According to the natural rate hypothesis, discretionary monetary and fiscal policies have no effect on output or employment in the long run because they will move to their natural levels as expectations adapt to economic conditions. The implication of the rational expectations hypothesis is that, unless they come as a total surprise to the public, discretionary monetary and fiscal policies will have no effect *at all* on aggregate output or the employment rate.

Figure A

What types of monetary and fiscal policies are consistent with the rational expectations hypothesis? Since discretionary policies are defeated by changing expectations, monetary and fiscal policies should not attempt to regulate aggregate demand or alter output and unemployment. A constant rate of growth of the money supply should replace discretionary monetary policies. Fiscal policy should provide necessary services through the public sector, and pay for them with tax revenue—i.e., balanced government budgets should replace discretionary fiscal policy.

The rational expectations hypothesis is a highly controversial proposition. It is anathema to those who see an active role for discretionary monetary and fiscal policy in achieving acceptable unemployment rates and rates of inflation. Even monetarists, who tend to be highly critical of discretionary monetary and fiscal policies, have serious reservations about carrying the argument as far as the rational expectations hypothesis does.

Summary

1. Aggregate demand and aggregate supply will determine an equilibrium aggregate output and an equilibrium rate of inflation. Since aggregate output determines the level of employment and the unemployment rate, aggregate demand and aggregate supply will also determine the **unemployment rate**.
2. **Phillips curves** show the relationship between the unemployment rate and the rate of inflation. Through the 1960s, the most commonly held view of the Phillips curve was an inverse relationship, or trade-off, between unemployment and inflation.

3. In the long run, expectations define a **natural unemployment rate** where the actual and expected rates of inflation are equal. If the actual rate of inflation deviates from the expected rate, expectations will adjust to move the unemployment to the natural rate.
4. According to the **natural rate hypothesis,** the long-run supply curve is vertical at the natural level of aggregate output and the **long-run Phillips curve** is vertical at the natural unemployment rate.
5. If economic policy is committed to an unemployment goal below the natural rate of unemployment and to minimizing the rate of inflation, discretionary monetary and fiscal policies will alternate between stimulating aggregate demand to lower the unemployment rate and reducing aggregate demand to lower the rate of inflation, leading to a **price spiral** around the natural rate of unemployment.

Concepts for Review

rate of inflation
aggregate output per worker
productivity of labor
unemployment rate
Phillips curve

natural level of aggregate output
natural level of employment
natural rate of unemployment
natural rate hypothesis

long-run aggregate supply curve
long-run Phillips curve
price spiral
theory of rational expectations

Questions

1. Explain how increases and decreases in aggregate output would affect each of the following. Where possible, explain the long-run effects as well as the short-run effects.
   a. Aggregate employment.
   b. Output per worker.
   c. Demand for labor.
   d. Wage per worker.
   e. Costs incurred by producers.
   f. The rate of inflation.
2. Would you expect the aggregate output demanded this year to be greater if the price level had risen 10 percent since last year or if the price level had risen 20 percent since last year? Why?
3. How does the level of aggregate output affect the rate of inflation? What relationship do you expect between the level of aggregate output and the rate of inflation?
4. What is a Phillips curve? How is the Phillips curve related to aggregate demand and aggregate supply? How well does the Phillips curve explain the relationship between the unemployment rate and the rate of inflation in the United States in the 1960s? How well does it do for the relationship between unemployment and inflation in the 1970s? How can you explain the difference?
5. "The notion of a trade-off between unemployment and inflation is pure bunk, promoted by reactionary economists. During the past year, the unemployment rate fell and the rate of inflation slowed. Therefore, the way to deal with unemployment and inflation is to do whatever is

necessary to lower the unemployment rate, and the rate of inflation will fall along with it" (Senator A. Gass Bagg).

Analyze and evaluate the above statement on unemployment and inflation. If you think the senator is incorrect, how do you explain the fact that unemployment and inflation both fell? What would be the most likely consequences of following the senator's proposed policies to deal with unemployment and inflation?

6. Most estimates of the natural unemployment rate for the United States place it in the neighborhood of 5.5 to 6.0 percent.
    a. What would happen if society and the government were committed to a single goal of achieving and maintaining an unemployment rate of 5.0 percent through traditional discretionary monetary and fiscal measures?
    b. How would your answer to part (a) be different if society and the government set their goals for monetary and fiscal policy as maintaining an unemployment rate of 5.0 percent without excessive inflationary pressure?
    c. What would be some of the effects of accepting the natural rate of unemployment as the unemployment goal? How would monetary and fiscal policies be affected? What would be the implications for policy if we accepted the natural unemployment rate as our unemployment goal and we also accepted the rational expectations hypothesis?
    d. Would accepting a current natural unemployment rate of 5.5 percent necessarily mean that we could never achieve and maintain an unemployment rate of 5.0 percent without accelerating rates of inflation? Explain.

31

Inflation and Unemployment: Attacking the Problem

Preview: We have seen that unemployment and inflation may result from disturbances on either the demand side or the supply side of the economy. Not surprisingly, policies to deal with these problems may also be directed toward either demand or supply. Traditional Keynesian macroeconomics has tended to focus on aggregate demand management through discretionary fiscal and monetary policies as the key to the problems. In earlier chapters, we've looked closely at such policies to deal with inflation and unemployment through the manipulation of taxes, government spending, and the money supply. In this chapter, we turn our attention to a number of alternative strategies.

Monetarism and the Market Solution

The proper role of markets and government in the economy is one of the longest-running controversies in economics. Adam Smith's *Wealth of Nations*, the work that marks the birth of modern economics, was in large part a laissez-faire attack on 18th-century economic orthodoxy that stressed the importance of policy (economic "statesmanship") and economic controls. Contemporary laissez-faire critics of government policy argue that reducing the microeconomic and macroeconomic role of government to a minimum would contribute to lower unemployment rates and greater price stability.

The basic argument is that because of the absence of incentives to reduce costs or improve productivity in providing public services, the government is an inefficiently large and complex bureaucracy. Expanding the role of government shifts more of society's resources from the efficient private sector to the inefficient public sector, creating both unemployment and inflationary pressure. By reducing the scope of government in the economy, the proponents of laissez-faire assert, we'll make more efficient use of our resources, market forces will operate freely, and unemployment and inflation will diminish.

Further, according to advocates of laissez-faire and monetarism, government policies seldom achieve their objectives and tend to be destabilizing. If fiscal policies were limited to providing and financing only the services that the public needs, and not aimed at managing aggregate demand, the destabilizing effects of fiscal policy would be eliminated or at least minimized. Likewise, tying the change in the money supply to a *constant-growth-rate rule* would stabilize monetary policy and expectations.

On the microeconomic side, *laissez-faire* critics advocate the removal or drastic reduction of government regulations that reduce wage and price flexibility and competition. The specific targets are government regulation of particular industries or occupations, regulated prices, minimum wage laws that keep wages from adjusting to levels that would clear the market, and unemployment compensation laws that encourage workers to remain unemployed or keep searching for employment rather than accept their best wage offer. The underlying assertions in this strategy are that public regulations are the cause of unemployment and inflation, and that removing the regulations would allow competitive market forces and prices to clear markets of unsold goods and unemployed workers.

In the long run, real GNP and the unemployment rate would move to their natural levels, and prices would change at a constant rate. Disturbances due to exogenous shocks could cause the unemployment rate to fall below the natural level, accelerating the rise in prices, or to exceed the natural unemployment rate in which case inflation would slow down. However, the free operation of market forces and flexible wages and prices would restore the natural unemployment rate and a constant rate of price change more quickly and smoothly than would discretionary monetary and fiscal policies.

Is the laissez-faire prescription correct? Frankly, at the present state of our knowledge, there isn't a clear-cut answer to this question. The monetarists' predictions depend heavily on the assumption of flexible wages and prices, and such flexibility, particularly in a downward direction, is limited by a number of economic and institutional variables in the real world.

Modern corporations, like government agencies, are managed by large and complex bureaucracies, and contain some of the same sources of bureaucratic inefficiency that the proponents of laissez-faire attribute to the public sector. Most key industries in our economy are controlled by small numbers of large firms who share a common interest in avoiding vigorous price competition (or *price wars*), which contributes to downward inflexibility of prices in these industries. Most trade unions try to keep their members' wages from falling in periods of slack demand, and this contributes to downward rigidity of wages in organized industries.

If wages and prices were completely rigid downward, the classical adjustment mechanism to maintain full employment wouldn't work. If wages and prices are flexible but *sticky*, market adjustments will tend to be slow—perhaps too slow to be very appealing as a solution to the problems of unemployment and inflation. Even if wages and prices were totally flexible, the natural rate of unemployment and a constant rate of price change are *long-run* results. Short-run disequilibria and movements toward the long-run equilibrium may involve fairly long periods of calendar time with unacceptable levels of unemployment, inflation, and instability.

Proponents of laissez-faire, monetarists in particular, argue that eliminating the errors inherent in discretionary monetary and fiscal policy is desirable because monetary and fiscal policies won't amplify the effects of exogenous shocks. However, the activist reply to this argument is that discretionary monetary and fiscal policies are necessary for the simple reason that exogenous shocks *do* exist and discretionary policies can soften their impact on real GNP, unemployment, and inflation.

Managing Aggregate Demand: Fine Tuning

In periods of unacceptably high unemployment, the traditional activist prescription has been to stimulate aggregate demand through expansionary monetary and fiscal policies. In periods of high inflation, activists urge tight monetary and fiscal policies to dampen aggregate demand and inflationary pressures. Such discretionary stabilization policies have seemed quite successful in dealing with massive disturbances of aggregate demand—the Great Depression or World War II, for example.

The past two decades have witnessed dramatic developments in quantitative economics, or *econometrics*, and in the technology of gathering, synthesizing, and processing economic data. Sophisticated *econometric models* of the economy express economic relationships as statistically estimated equations. By feeding actual or projected data into the model, econometric models yield predictions of GNP, employment, interest rates, prices, and other key economic variables.

The development of such sophisticated econometric modeling techniques and the apparent success of demand management policies in dealing with major disturbances in aggregate demand led a substantial number of economists during the 1960s to argue that the impact of much less dramatic fluctuations could be smoothed out by relatively small changes in spending and the money supply—i.e., that the economy could be *fine tuned*.

- **Fine tuning** refers to discretionary monetary and fiscal policies to reduce the impact of relatively minor fluctuations in aggregate demand, employment, and prices.

The success of fine tuning, or the lack of it, depends on the ability of forecasting models to make accurate and specific economic predictions. The models must be sensitive enough to identify the kind and magnitude of fine tuning needed to achieve acceptable unemployment and inflation rates. Not surprisingly, fine tuning was most widely accepted in the 1960s, when the track record of economic forecasters was good, discretionary monetary and fiscal policies apparently were successful in achieving their objectives, and unemployment rates and rates of inflation were relatively modest. Unfortunately, the success of fine tuning didn't carry over into the 1970s. The relationship between unemployment rates and the rate of increase of the price level was less stable and predictable in the 1970s, and the track record of the economic forecasters wasn't nearly as strong.

Why were the forecasting models that were successful in the 1960s less so in the 1970s? One reason is that econometrics and econometric models can't foresee exogenous economic shocks. Econometric models are based on data from the recent past and work best when economic conditions and relationships aren't dramatically different from those of the recent past. The models tend to do worse when conditions and relationships are different from those in the recent past, and ironically this is when economic forecasts and policy prescriptions are most important.

No econometric model, for example, could estimate and predict the political tensions in the Middle East that produced the export embargo on oil shipments by the Arab members of the Organization of Petroleum Exporting Countries (OPEC) in 1973–1974. Furthermore, instead of a one-shot price hike on oil exports, OPEC raised prices on exported oil continually through the 1970s, generating and intensifying cost-push inflationary pressures—another variable even the best model couldn't foresee.

Second, economic policies are shaped ultimately by political forces as well as economic forces, and it is difficult if not impossible to incorporate political variables in empirical models. The Vietnam War was escalated and then ended in 1973, direct controls were instituted then removed during Nixon's New Economic Plan, and numerous shifts occurred in monetary and fiscal policies.

In addition to these problems with the forecasts on which the fine tuners relied, fine tuning in the 1970s suffered from many of the same problems as other demand management policies—lags in implementation and effect, uncertainty about timing and results, and expectations. Also, fine tuning may require more flexibility in monetary and fiscal policies than political institutions permit. There is no guarantee that better models would have resulted in better economic policies during the 1970s; politicians are often unwilling or politically unable to undertake the policies prescribed by the forecasters and fine tuners.

If econometric models, forecasts, and fine tuning took too much credit for the economic successes of the 1960s, they also took too much of the blame for the serious problems of unemployment and inflation of the middle and late 1970s. Few economists seriously argue that econometric models should be ignored or that econometrics should be relegated to the status of a black art. The only alternative to systematic quantitative forecasting is playing hunches, based on individuals' subjective feel for economic conditions. Improving quantitative methods and forecasting tools should remain a high priority item in the fight against unemployment and inflation.

Managing Aggregate Supply: Incomes Policies

The mixed record of traditional stabilization policies in maintaining acceptable levels of unemployment and inflation has led some economists and policymakers to take a closer look at *incomes policies*.

- **Incomes policies** aim to reduce inflation by restraining the ability of wages and prices to rise.

Incomes policies attack cost-push inflation by regulating aggregate supply. To the extent that they keep wages and prices from rising, they hold the aggregate supply curve down. Since they attack the supply side of the unemployment-inflation problem, incomes policies are *supply management* policies. Incomes policies range from persuasion and voluntary guidelines to mandatory controls of wages, prices, rents, profits, and interest income.

Voluntary Guideposts and Guidelines

In 1962, President John Kennedy's Council of Economic Advisers proposed the use of voluntary wage and price guideposts as a means of controlling inflation. The guideposts tried to eliminate cost-push inflation by tying the average rate of increase in compensation per worker-hour to the average rate of increase of output per worker hour. This would stabilize the *average unit labor cost* (ULC) of goods and services produced. Unit labor cost is

$$ULC = \frac{WR}{(Q/H)}, \tag{1}$$

where WR is the wage rate per worker hour and (Q/H) is output per worker hour. If the wage rate rose at the same rate over time as output per worker, ULC would remain constant, and one of the cost-push pressures would be eliminated.

Voluntary wage-price standards rely heavily on persuasion, moral suasion, and the force of public opinion for compliance. When firms and unions deliberately ignore or violate guidelines, government officials (typically the President) use the force of their offices to turn public pressure against the violators. The haggling and persuasive effort by the President to promote compliance with voluntary standards is called **jawboning**—presumably referring to the dialogue between the President, unions, and firms, although critics have been quick to point to the Old Testament account of Samson's slaying of a thousand Philistines with ". . . a fresh jawbone of an ass."

Bringing the weight and influence of the Presidency against wage and price actions of unions and firms can be a potent force. Perhaps the most dramatic example of that force was John Kennedy's famous 1962 showdown with the steel industry in which the companies finally backed off and rescinded their price increases. It seems naive, however, to expect moral suasion and voluntary compliance alone to keep powerful unions and firms from exercising their market power, especially in periods where there are strong demand-pull forces. By and large, Presidents haven't been as effective in jawboning unions and corporations as Samson apparently was in jawboning the Philistines.

Close-up

The Carter Wage-Price Guidelines

The voluntary guidelines–jawboning strategy emerged again in 1978, as the Carter administration turned its attention from unemployment to inflation. The 1978–1979 guidelines simply stated targets for wage and price increases.

> The voluntary wage and price standards call for an average rate of pay increase of 7 percent or less (in 1979). I also have asked businesses to hold their average rate of price increase to at least one-half percentage point below the average rate of increase in 1976–77. Where such price deceleration is not possible, the standards provide for limitations on profit margins.[1]

President Carter appointed a special chief inflation fighter, Alfred E. Kahn (who had been a Professor of Economics at Cornell, head of the New York State Public Utilities Commission, and Chairman of the Civil Aeronautics Board). In his public acceptance of his position, Kahn asserted that the only alternative to voluntary compliance with the wage and price standards was a massive recession, or a "deep, deep depression." When the White House expressed concern that Kahn's strong language would be alarmist, he agreed to substitute the word "banana" for recession and depression.

Some firms and unions agreed to comply with the standards, but the rate of inflation continued to accelerate in the first quarter of 1979. The du Pont Co., which had agreed to comply with the price guideline, announced in April 1979 that it might not be able to comply if inflation continued to accelerate.

The reaction of organized labor to the standards ranged from cool to frigid. George Meany and other key leaders in the AFL-CIO rejected the guidelines as unfair to labor, and large increases in corporate profits in early 1979 didn't make the AFL-CIO any more receptive to the guidelines. A Teamsters' strike in April of 1979 produced tragicomic episodes of Teamsters officials rejecting the guidelines and government officials attempting to show that the Teamsters' wage demands really were consistent with the guidelines. The Rubber Workers' Union opened its contract negotiations in the spring of 1979 with a demand for a 40 percent wage increase over the three-year term of the new contract, and the massive United Auto Workers Union also announced its intention to bargain very hard on wages.

By the spring of 1979, there was growing public admission that the most likely means of restraining inflation would be monetary and fiscal restraint which would produce a recession (or "banana"). Although the guideline program had had

---

1. *Economic Report of the President* (Washington: Government Printing Office, 1979), p. 9.

some success (most notably when Sears was convinced to cancel a scheduled price increase), and although the Supreme Court in June of 1979 had upheld the President's right to enforce his program by denying government contracts to violators, inflation continued at a rate well above ten percent.

Mandatory Wage and Price Controls

Some critics of guidelines and voluntary compliance advocate tougher measures to restrain wage and price increases and mandatory compliance with standards. Usually, these proposals for mandatory controls extend them to cover increases in all types of income—profits, interest, and rents as well as wages.

It isn't reasonable to expect unions to keep wage demands within wage guidelines if they can't be confident that price increases also will stay within price guidelines. Similarly, firms won't be likely to keep price increases within guidelines if workers demand excessive wage increases. The advocates of wage and price controls argue that making noncompliance with standards more difficult would lower the inflationary expectations and uncertainty of workers and employers and would thus weaken inflationary pressures without excessive unemployment.

Unless something is done that gets at the causes of inflationary pressure, however, wage and price controls may end up merely suppressing inflation. Wages and prices would remain stable or increase slowly, while inflationary pressure took such forms as empty shelves, waiting lists, and non-price rationing (formal or informal).

Mandatory wage and price standards have to be enforced to be effective, and enforcement isn't free. Manpower and other resources have to be allocated to enforce the controls, and these resources have alternative uses. Even during World War II, when the country faced very real external threats and there was almost unprecedented unity of purpose, enforcing of the price controls set by the Office of Price Administration (OPA) required a massive bureaucracy, plus thousands of volunteers who worked in the enforcement effort without pay. Enforcement of stringent controls certainly wouldn't be any easier in the political and economic climate of the 1980s.

Very stringent controls on wages and prices—such as a wage-price "freeze"—is like pinching a hose with the water turned on. Price increases slow down during the freeze, but inflationary pressures continue to build. When the freeze is lifted, the general pattern is for prices to take a sudden jump and then follow a more moderate rate of increase. There is very little evidence that temporary price and wage freezes have any long-term effect on inflation, so the only reasonable result to expect is a temporary slowing of price increases, followed by a short burst of rapid inflation and a return to the long-term price trend.

Can Incomes Policies Work?

To be effective, an incomes policy would have to reduce inflationary expectations. Households, workers, firms, and financial institutions have to be convinced that the policies will reduce the expected rate of inflation. If this happens, then the natural rate could be maintained with a lower rate of inflation. In Figure 1, for example, if the actual rate of inflation equals the expected rate of 10 percent per year at the natural unemployment rate of 6 percent, lowering the expected rate to 5 percent will result eventually in the natural rate of unemployment being maintained with a constant 5 percent per year rise in the price level.

Of course, if attempts at limiting inflation through incomes policies have a poor success record, a new incomes policy may not generate very widespread confidence, in which case it would have little if any effect on expectations. It's even possible that very stringent controls could raise inflationary expectations if people and institutions expect the typical pattern of rapid price increases after the controls are relaxed.

The final consideration in assessing the probable effectiveness of incomes policies is more political than economic. Well-heeled special interests will lobby hard for exceptions to the standards, and the interest groups and industries with the most economic and political clout will be the most successful in getting exceptions. This means that the standards will be enforced unevenly, with enforcement being the most stringent in the industries with the least influence.

Figure 1 Lowering the Expected Rate of Inflation

Managing Aggregate Supply: Indexing

Inflation erodes the purchasing power of money, and can create unforeseen windfall gains and losses. A worker whose money wage increases by less than the rate of inflation incurs an unexpected loss in real income. Lenders will suffer losses if the real value of the repayments of interest and principal are less than the real value of the original loan. Savers suffer losses of real wealth if the interest on their accounts is below the inflation rate. Since income taxes are based on money wages and money profits, inflation tends to produce unexpected increases in taxes—especially with progressive taxes. Further, efforts by those affected to anticipate future inflation through higher wage demands and interest rates only worsen the problem.

One way to eliminate unforeseen effects of inflation on purchasing power and real income is to tie money payments to the Consumer Price Index or some other measure of changes in the price level.

- **Indexing** of money payments would tie the value of money payments to an index of prices.

Proposals for comprehensive indexing of money payments aren't new. Alfred Marshall proposed indexing in the late 19th century. However, indexing remains a nontraditional approach to inflation. It has been tried in countries suffering chronic inflation (such as Brazil) with some success, but it doesn't have much of a record on which to base its likelihood of success.

Escalator Clauses

One form of indexing is relatively familiar, namely, the *escalator clause*.

- **Escalator clauses** adjust money payments automatically to changes in the price level.

Escalator clauses in collective bargaining agreements provide for adjustments to money wage rates to compensate for changes in the Consumer Price Index. For example, suppose that a contract provides for an initial wage of $10 per hour, and a three percent annual wage increase, with an escalator clause that adjusts money wages for changes in the Consumer Price Index. If there were no change in the Consumer Price Index after the first year of the contract, the wage would be $10.30 per hour in the second year—i.e., ($10 × 1.03 = $10.30). However, if the CPI increased ten percent during the first year of the contract, the money wage for the second year would have to be increased by ten percent as well. Thus the wage escalator would result in a three percent increase in the real wage, but the money wage for the second year would be ($10 × $1.13 = $11.30). Escalator clauses could thus reduce the tendency to push for large increases in money wages by guaranteeing the rate of increase in real wages.

A number of money payments in our economy are tied to the Consumer Price Index by escalator clauses. Social Security payments are adjusted for changes in the Consumer Price Index. Most public pension payments—military and civilian employees' pensions—provide for cost-of-living adjustments that index them to the Consumer Price Index. Many collective bargaining contracts provide for escalation of money wages if prices rise during the term of the contract.

Indexing Taxes

Because of the progressive structure of the Federal Income Tax, the American government is the biggest winner from inflation. Every rise in the price level means a huge increase in tax revenues. Some critics have even charged that the government has a vested interest in maintaining an inflationary economy.

Milton Friedman and other advocates of indexing have argued that indexing taxes would reduce the government's windfall revenues and would eliminate the false tax cuts that reduce tax rates but not total tax payments or revenue. One way to do this would be by indexing dependents' allowances, standard deductions, and tax brackets to compensate for changes in the Consumer Price Index. If prices rose by ten percent, for example, the dependents' allowance would be increased from $800 to $880, the standard deduction for a joint return would be increased from $1500 to $1650, and the $20,000 to $20,050 bracket which specifies a tax of $2536 would become the $22,000 to $22,050 bracket with a tax of $2790 for a family of four.

Indexing Interest Rates

Indexing proposals generally include indexing principal and interest payments to guarantee a real rate of interest. Suppose, for example, that a saver could buy a **purchasing power bond** for $10,000 that paid three percent yearly interest, adjustable to changes in prices. If, at the end of one year, the price level had risen by ten percent, the value of the interest and principal and interest would be $10,000 \times 1.03 \times 1.10 = \$11,330$, which is the equivalent of $10,300 at the original prices. In other words, indexing guarantees a *real interest rate of three percent a year*. Obviously, the incentive to save in periods of inflation will be greater if savers can be guaranteed a positive real interest rate.

The real value of interest payments and principal on loans could be guaranteed by issuing **purchasing power loans** indexed to the Consumer Price Index. If a bank loaned $20,000 for a year at four percent interest, and the Consumer Price Index rose by ten percent, the borrower would repay $20,000 \times 1.04 \times 1.10 = \$22,880$ after one year. The borrower would pay and the lender would receive a *real interest rate* of four percent a year. If loans were indexed, proponents of indexing argue, there would be no need for lenders to guess at the inflation premium component of nominal interest rates.

Control of Inflation or Surrender to It?

Critics of indexing argue that it would, in effect, strengthen inflationary pressures. Every buyer, seller, worker, employer, saver, borrower, and lender would be compensated for changes in prices. This, it is argued, would reduce the public pressure on government to fight inflationary pressure through monetary and fiscal restraint and other politically unpopular means.

Advocates assert that indexing would reduce cost-push inflationary pressures by stabilizing inflationary expectations. Uncertainty about future real income would be reduced by indexing money payments to changes in the piece level. Indexing would also reduce the unexpected windfall gains and losses, redistribution, and tax increases that accompany inflation.

Close-up

TIPs

One form of indexing that has received considerable attention in recent years is TIPs. *Tax-based incomes policies* (TIPs) attempt to limit the rate of increase of wages and costs through the tax system. There are two basic versions of TIPs —the "carrot" and the "stick."

Arthur Okun, formerly Professor of Economics at Yale and a Chairman of the Council of Economic Advisers under President Johnson, is the best-known proponent of the "carrot" approach. This approach seeks to limit wage increases by providing tax incentives to employees who keep wage increases below a specified rate. Workers who receive wage increases below the target rate would receive tax credits to bring their wage increases up to the target rate. President Carter's ill-fated "wage insurance" program was a variant of this approach. The logic is that workers will accept smaller wage increases as a result of the tax credits, and that this will slow the increases in labor costs and dampen cost-push pressures.

Henry Wallich is a widely respected economist and a Governor of the Federal Reserve. He is a proponent of the "stick" approach to TIPs which would impose tax penalties on corporations that paid wage increases above a targeted rate. The logic of the stick approach is that excessive wage increases and cost-push pressures would be lessened as employers try to avoid tax penalties by keeping wage offers down.

TIPs haven't been implemented on a meaningful scale, so we don't know how effective they would be against cost-push inflation. However, there are some potential problems. Workers who could get wage increases above the target rate would have no incentive to accept wage increases below the target rate and a tax credit that would bring their wage increases up to the target rate. At the same time, those who would receive wage increases below the target rate anyway could gain by receiving tax credits that bring their wage increases up to the targeted rate. The "stick" approach could add to cost-push pressures by levying tax penalties on firms. Tax penalties are added to the cost-push pressures of excessive wage increases, and higher costs have a habit of getting passed on as higher prices.

Won't Anything Work?

Where does our understanding of macroeconomics leave us on the problem of unemployment and inflation? Do we conclude that nothing we try will work? Can the analytical tools tell us anything about the problem and policies to deal with it or does macroeconomics simply lead us astray?

These are fair questions, and competent people have come up with different answers to each of them. However, one thing does seem clear—no simplistic solution will serve as a cure-all for the problem of unemployment and inflation. Also, the course of action we choose to attack the problem will not be without cost, and many measures that could be effective will be unacceptable on political or normative grounds. What follows is a brief sketch of the elements of what seems necessary to deal with unemployment and inflation. An effective policy has to attack the microeconomic and macroeconomic roots of unemployment and inflation, and must convince society that the policies will be effective against unemployment and inflation. This is a tall order, and no single policy will be effective by itself.

Monetary and Fiscal Policy

Discretionary monetary and fiscal policies can be effective shock absorbers to soften the effect of sudden economic changes on output, employment, and prices. However, these policies by themselves won't be effective against unemployment and inflation.

Fiscal policies should provide and finance society's needs that can't be met effectively through the public sector. Expenditures and revenues should aim at maintaining a balanced *full-employment budget*. Time lags, political controversy, and numerous mandated expenditures reduce the effectiveness and flexibility of fiscal policy as a means of fine tuning the economy.

Wide swings in monetary and fiscal policy should be avoided. Monetary policy should follow a stable course over time, although not necessarily a fixed rate of growth of the money supply. Rapid acceleration followed by hard braking in monetary policy has produced inflationary "booms" alternating with high unemployment "busts." This leads to unstable economic expectations which reduce the effectiveness of any monetary and fiscal measures. Also, the costs of wide swings in economic activity and employment usually impose the greatest human costs on the poor and those in chronically high-unemployment groups.

The Unemployment Target

If the unemployment rate is kept below the natural rate, prices will accelerate over time. If this acceleration is slow, we may well decide that the lower unemployment rate is worth the cost of slightly accelerating prices. However, if the rate of inflation continues to accelerate over time it will eventually reach a rate that society finds excessive and will have to be dealt with.

Setting the unemployment rate target at the natural rate of unemployment is one way of stabilizing the rate of inflation, and there may be some movement in this direction. Most estimates of the natural unemployment rate place it in the neighborhood of 5.5 percent. Since 1973, the Council of Economic Advisers has raised its "benchmark" unemployment rate for estimating potential GNP from 4.9 percent to 5.1 percent. Maintaining an unemployment rate of 5.5 percent doesn't relegate the same 5.5 percent of the population to perpetual unemployment, though, since persons move among labor force categories over time.

Reducing the Natural Unemployment Rate

The natural unemployment rate isn't determined by nature or etched in stone. If society decides that the natural rate of 5.5 percent is excessive, it is possible to lower the natural rate. Some means of lowering the natural rate will be popular and have broad appeal, but others will be controversial and unpopular. Also, programs that will be effective in lowering the natural rate are likely to be expensive.

Training and retraining programs can provide unemployed workers with employable skills and enhance their chances of finding employment. Increasing the mobility of labor out of economically depressed areas or encouraging employers to locate in these areas could reduce some chronic unemployment that contributes to the natural unemployment rate. Equal employment opportunity and affirmative action legislation and programs can reduce unemployment related to discrimination. Improved public employment services can improve the flow of labor market information and make job searches shorter and more effective. Some of these measures are controversial (affirmative action in particular) and all are expensive to implement and enforce. Society would have to decide whether the effectiveness of such programs is worth the cost.

The most controversial proposals for lowering the natural unemployment rate are those that would reform minimum wage legislation and unemployment compensation programs. Critics of minimum wages have argued for years that they restrict the employment opportunities of the young, the unskilled, and the untrained, and this argument has some empirical support. The implication is that the natural rate would fall if minimum wage laws were revised to exempt some groups and thus improve their prospects for employment.

Similar criticisms have been directed at unemployment compensation, which provides workers with income during periods of unemployment. Critics argue that the current unemployment compensation programs give the worker a strong incentive to keep searching and keep his or her reservation wage high until the benefits run out. Some have suggested that the natural unemployment rate would fall if unemployment compensation programs were modified in a way that shortened job searches and encouraged workers to accept employment —for example, by shortening the benefit period, lowering benefits, or including the benefits as taxable income.

Modifications of minimum wage legislation and unemployment compensation to reduce the natural unemployment rate carry obvious normative questions. In all but the most conservative constituencies, these measures would be politically treacherous.

Wage and Price Standards

Incomes policies have had a sorry record in controlling inflation, but publication of wage and price standards and of the firms and unions that choose to ignore the standards may have some effect on wages and prices through the force of public opinion. Standby authority to intervene in wage and price decisions may have a moderating effect if the workers and the firms want to avoid government intervention. However, it's not reasonable to expect such measures to have a dramatic effect on inflation.

Reducing Inflationary Expectations

Whatever combination of policies is chosen, its success in reducing unemployment without unacceptable increases in unemployment depends on its effectiveness in reducing inflationary expectations. If the expected rate of price increase falls, the rate of inflation at the natural rate of unemployment should also fall.

A long period of recession and high unemployment might reduce inflationary expectations, but the costs are high. It takes time for expectations to adjust to a declining rate of price increase, and in the meantime high unemployment imposes high costs on the unemployed and on the community in the form of lost output.

Selective indexing could reduce some of the inflationary expectations that contribute to cost-push inflation. Escalator clauses could reduce the incentive to push aggressively for high money wage increases, high nominal interest rates, etc. The escalators would guarantee the purchasing power of future money payments.

The success in reducing inflationary expectations may raise a "Catch 22" situation. To reduce inflation without high unemployment, inflationary expectations must be lowered. However, the most effective means of lowering inflationary expectations is to have a past record of success in reducing inflation without excessively high unemployment.

Summary

1. Monetarists assign a minimal role to discretionary monetary and fiscal policies as a means of achieving and maintaining full employment and stable prices. The monetarist strategy centers on the importance of market forces and flexible prices to achieve the objectives of full employment without unacceptable rates of inflation.
2. The traditional Keynesian approach to macroeconomic policies to achieve and maintain full employment or stabilize prices is *demand management*—i.e., regulating aggregate demand via discretionary monetary and fiscal policies.
3. **Fine tuning** refers to demand management policies that stabilize aggregate demand, output, and inflation through small changes in discretionary monetary and fiscal policies to minimize the instability of the economy over time. The success of fine tuning efforts depends heavily on the quality of information and the accuracy of economic forecasts.
4. **Supply management** policies attack unemployment, inflation, and instability that can be explained by instability of aggregate supply.
5. **Incomes policies** attempt to regulate aggregate supply by restraining increases in wages, prices, and costs. Incomes policies range from volun-

tary guidelines to compulsory controls.
6. **Indexing** would tie all wages, interest, and other payments to the Consumer Price Index. The object is to guarantee purchasing power and to reduce the incentive for workers, banks, and others to push for high nominal incomes to compensate for the effects of inflation. Since it attacks the cost-push forces, it is a supply management policy.
7. Any successful macroeconomic strategy must attack *all* of the forces that contribute to unemployment and inflation.

Concepts for Review

market solution
econometrics
fine tuning
incomes policies

supply management
tax-based incomes
 policies
jawboning

indexing
escalator clauses
purchasing power bond
purchasing power loan

Questions

1. Which of the following are demand management policies, and which are supply management policies? Explain how each could affect aggregate demand or aggregate supply.
   a. government subsidies of research and development activities to stimulate technological change;
   b. restrictive monetary and fiscal policies;
   c. compulsory wage and price controls;
   d. tax cuts;
   e. retraining and relocation programs for unemployed workers.
2. According to Professor Friedman and many other monetarists, cost-push inflation from aggressive wage demands of unions is impossible unless the monetary authorities go along.
   a. What implications does this argument have for the probable success of wage and price controls as a means of reducing inflation?
   b. What type of macroeconomic strategy follows from this argument?
3. "Our tools of economic policy are much better tools than existed a generation ago. We are able to proceed with much greater confidence and flexibility in seeking effective answers to the changing problems of our changing economy." (President Lyndon B. Johnson, *Economic Report of the President*, January 28, 1965)
   a. What type of macroeconomic strategy is implied in this quote? Why was this strategy so appealing in 1965?
   b. Would the strategy implied in Johnson's statement be as likely to succeed now as it was in 1965? Why?
4. Suppose that the natural unemployment rate is 5.5 percent, and that the unemployment rate would remain at 5.5 percent with prices rising at a constant rate of 8 percent per year. The government has established goals of lowering the unemployment rate to 5 percent and the annual rate of price increase to 5 percent.
   Is there *any* way that these unemployment and inflation goals could be achieved? Explain, and put together a "package" of policies that would be necessary to achieve the unemployment and inflation goals.

PART ELEVEN
The World Economy

The OPEC oil embargo of 1973 opened many people's eyes to the fact that the economies of the world have in recent years grown increasingly dependent upon one another. Gone are the days when a nation could close its doors to the rest of the world and hope to solve the problem of scarcity on its own. With the opening of relations with China, the decline of Cold War tensions between East and West, and the growth of multinational firms, trade today probably plays a more important role internationally than at any other time in history.

In this section, we'll explore the meaning and significance of **international trade**. The first two chapters lay the theoretical groundwork. We begin by asking the fundamental questions of *why* nations wish to trade with each other. What benefits do they derive from trade? We then move to the question of *how* nations trade, examining the role of national currencies in the international setting.

International trade is strongly influenced by *national* governments, through the **trade policies** they choose to enact. Increasingly in recent years, trade has been used as much more than merely a source of mutual benefit among nations. Import and export policies, for example, have been suggested and used as tools for achieving domestic goals—for controlling inflation and raising employment. Trade has also been employed more and more as a political weapon—a way of rewarding "friends" and punishing "enemies." In the last chapter of the section, we'll explore the effects and implications of various uses and abuses of trade policy.

32

The Gains from Trade

Preview: We live in an economically interdependent world, and international trade is increasingly important economically. We import nearly half of the oil we consume. Some goods—bananas and coffee, for example—wouldn't be available at all in the absence of international trade. The agricultural sector and some industries (such as machinery, aircraft, and transportation) are large-scale exporters. Foreign trade is a fact of life, but *why* do countries trade with each other?

The roots of international trade are about the same as the roots of trade within a country. Trade exists because it makes the traders better off than they could be without trade. In this chapter, we'll explore the motivation, terms, and impact of international trade in order to get a basic understanding of the gains from trade.

Specialization, Trade, and Efficiency

A few rather simple propositions lie at the heart of international trade theory.

- Specialization leads to greater efficiency in production.
- Specialization requires the ability to trade.
- Trade encourages greater specialization and greater efficiency.

These propositions comprise the *classical* case for free trade, which was stated first by Adam Smith in *The Wealth of Nations* two hundred years ago.

Smith built his free trade case on his famous pin factory example. In the example, initially each worker produced a complete pin—drew the wire, cut it, polished it, sharpened the point, attached the head, and put the pins in a box or on a card. Then production was reorganized so that each worker performed only one operation. With this **specialization**, each worker became better at his particular task, and the pin factory became more efficient. Smith used this example to show that specialization, or *division of labour*, leads to greater efficiency in production.

THE GAINS FROM TRADE 669

Specialization makes no sense without trade, and Smith argued that specialization is encouraged by trade, or by "the extent of the market." Since efficiency depends on specialization, and specialization depends on the ability to trade, it follows that expanding the ability to trade encourages greater efficiency.[1]

The classical case for free trade follows from this notion. Removing barriers to international trade will increase the "extent of the market," encourage greater specialization, and lead to greater efficiency.

Comparative Advantage

David Ricardo, and later John Stuart Mill, laid the groundwork for the modern theory of international trade in the nineteenth century with the **principle of comparative advantage.** Suppose that a renowned brain surgeon is a hunt-and-peck typist. Clearly, he should devote his time and energy to brain surgery and hire a secretary to do his typing.

But what if the brain surgeon can type 150 words per minute with no errors? Should he hire a secretary, or should he do his own typing? He still should hire a secretary, because he has a **comparative advantage** in brain surgery. He is a better typist than the typical secretary, but he is a *much* better brain surgeon than the typical secretary. Imagine what would happen if the doctor hired a secretary and they divided all duties equally. The doctor would do a good job on the letters and bills, but imagine the brain surgery performed by the secretary! This illustration of comparative advantage can be applied to the production of goods to show the gains from specialization on the basis of comparative advantage.

Comparative Advantage and Specialization

Oranges can be grown in Maine—with heated greenhouses, artificial fertilizers, and artificial sunlight. Very few oranges are grown in Maine, of course, because it is much cheaper and more efficient to grow them in California and Florida where the climate makes the artificial sunlight and heated greenhouses unnecessary. The crops that can be grown commercially in Maine, potatoes for example, don't require the sunlight and warm weather that oranges do, and Maine is more suited to potato production than orange growing.

Comparative advantage is easy to identify if the cost of producing oranges is lower in Florida and the cost of producing potatoes is lower in Maine. Clearly, Florida has a comparative advantage over Maine in oranges and Maine has a comparative advantage over Florida in potatoes. Florida should specialize in oranges and buy its potatoes from Maine, and Maine should specialize in potatoes and buy its oranges from Florida. Potatoes and oranges will be produced more efficiently

---

1. See Adam Smith, *An Inquiry into the Nature and Causes of the Wealth of Nations,* Book I, Chapter 3.

with specialization and trade than they would be if both states tried to be self-sufficient.

But what if both goods could be produced more cheaply in Florida than in Maine? In Table 1, oranges and potatoes can be grown at a lower cost per bushel in Florida than in Maine. It appears that there would be no gains from specialization because Florida is a more efficient producer of both goods, but this is not the case.

Assume initially that some oranges and some potatoes are grown in both states. Now suppose that orange production is reduced by one bushel in Maine and increased by one bushel in Florida. The change in combined orange production in the two states is

$$\begin{array}{r}\text{1 bushel increase in Florida}\\ -\text{1 bushel decrease in Maine}\\ \hline \text{0 change in combined orange production.}\end{array}$$

Reducing orange production by one bushel in Maine frees $100 that could be used for potato production. The cost of producing a bushel of potatoes in Maine is $4, so Maine could increase its potato production by $100/$4 per bu. = 25 bushels by reducing its orange production by one bushel.

In Florida, producing an additional bushel of oranges requires that $2 be diverted from potato production. The cost of producing a bushel of potatoes in Florida is $2, so increasing orange production by one bushel would cause potato production to fall by $2/$2 per bu. = 1 bushel.

The change in combined potato production in Maine and Florida is the difference between the increase in Maine and the reduction in Florida, or

$$\begin{array}{r}\text{25 bushel increase in Maine}\\ -\text{1 bushel decrease in Florida}\\ \hline \text{24 bushel change in combined potato production.}\end{array}$$

In other words, with the same resources, combined potato production increased by 24 bushels with *no* reduction in combined orange production.

Clearly, Maine should specialize in potatoes and Florida should specialize in oranges. Maine has a *comparative advantage* over Florida in

Table 1 Comparative Advantage

	Cost per bushel	
	Maine	Florida
Oranges	$100	$2
Potatoes	$ 4	$2

THE GAINS FROM TRADE   671

potatoes, and Florida has a *comparative advantage* over Maine in oranges. Florida is a better potato producer than Maine, but a *much* better orange producer than Maine.

Comparative Advantage and International Trade

Comparative advantage in international trade is the same as it is in the simple examples above. There will be gains in efficiency if countries specialize on the basis of comparative advantage and trade with each other, compared to efficiency in a world of economically self-sufficient countries.

To illustrate the effects of comparative advantage in international trade, consider two countries—call them America (A) and Japan (J). Assume that they produce and trade two goods—our old friends food (F) and clothing (C). Table 2 shows the cost per unit of food and clothing in the two countries. Could America and/or Japan benefit from specialization and trade? The first reaction might be that American producers couldn't compete with the Japanese in either good because the cost per unit is lower for both goods in Japan than in America, but a closer look will show potential gains from specialization and trade.

Comparative advantage depends on the *relative* costs in the two countries, or the ratio of the costs per unit. According to the table below, the cost per unit of clothing in the United States is 10 times as great as the cost per unit of food. This means that the **internal marginal rate of transformation** (MRT) in America is

$$MRT_A = -\frac{10\ F}{1\ C}.$$

By reallocating its own resources without trade, America could get 10 units of food for every 1 unit reduction in clothing, or 1/10 unit of clothing for every 1 unit reduction in food.

In Japan, the cost of producing a unit of clothing is three times as great as the cost per unit of food. The Japanese without trade, would have to give up 3 units of food for every additional unit of clothing, and 1/3 unit of clothing for every additional unit of food produced. The Japanese marginal rate of transformation without trade (MRT_J), then, is

$$MRT_J = -\frac{3\ F}{1\ C}.$$

Table 2   Comparative Advantage and International Trade

	Cost per unit		Opportunity cost per unit	
	America	Japan	America	Japan
Clothing	$50	$12	10 F	3 F*
Food	$ 5	$ 4	1/10 C*	1/3 C

*Comparative advantage

Relative costs and MRT define the **opportunity cost** of increasing production of one good in terms of the amount of the other good that has to be given up in a fully employed economy.

In America, the opportunity cost of an additional unit of clothing is the 10 units of food that have to be given up, and the opportunity cost of an additional unit of food is the 1/10 unit of clothing that has to be given up. In Japan, the opportunity cost of an additional unit of clothing is 3 units of food and the opportunity cost of an additional unit of food is 1/3 unit of clothing. The *opportunity costs* of producing the two goods in the absence of trade are also shown in Table 2.

In Table 2, the opportunity cost of a unit of clothing is less than the opportunity cost of a unit of clothing in America, but the opportunity cost of a unit of food is less in America than in Japan. In other words, *America has a comparative advantage over Japan in food*, and *Japan has a comparative advantage over America in clothing*. This means that there are potential gains in efficiency and economic welfare in both countries from specialization and trade. America should specialize in food, and Japan should specialize in clothing. America should export food and import clothing, and Japan should export clothing and import food.

Terms of Trade

Comparative advantage shows *potential* gains from trade between two countries. However, the actual gains from trade, the distribution of the gains from trade between the two countries, and whether the countries would trade with each other at all depend on the *terms of trade*.

- The **terms of trade** define the rate at which goods will exchange for each other in international trade.

In the above examples, the terms of trade would be the rate at which food and clothing exchange for each other in international trade.

Terms of Trade and Gains from Trade

For trade between America and Japan, or between any two countries, to take place, the terms of trade have to lie between the countries' internal MRTs. In Table 2, for trade to take place between America and Japan, the international terms of trade would have to lie between $3F:1C$ (MRT_J) and $10F:1C$ (MRT_A).

The terms of international trade are determined by world prices of goods. America and Japan aren't the only trading countries in the world, and world prices are determined by the demand for goods by all buyers and the supply of goods by all sellers in world markets. Suppose that the world price of clothing (P_C) is $30 and the world price of food (P_F) is $5. Since the price of clothing is six times as great as the price of food, it takes 6 units of food to buy 1 unit of clothing in international trade, or the terms of trade are $6F:1C$.

Table 3 Comparative Advantage and the Terms of Trade

	Opportunity cost with (without) trade			
	6F : 1C		2F : 1C	
	America	Japan	America	Japan
Clothing	6F (10F)*	6F (3F)	2F (10F)**	2F (3F)**
Food	1/6C (1/10 C)	1/6C (1/3 C)*	1/2C (1/10 C)	1/2C (1/3 C)

*Commodity country should import
**Commodity country should export

The terms of trade are determined by the ratio of prices. In the example, the terms of trade for food and clothing are

$$\text{Terms of Trade} = \frac{\Delta C}{\Delta F} = \frac{P_F}{P_C}.$$

The terms of trade define the opportunity cost of each good in international trade in terms of the amount of the other good that must be given up. With the given prices of food and clothing, the opportunity cost of an additional unit of clothing with trade is $6F$, and the opportunity cost of an additional unit of food with trade is $1/6C$. Table 3 shows the opportunity costs of food and clothing in America and Japan with trade at the given prices and without trade.

In the situation shown in Table 3, America should export food and import clothing because the opportunity cost per unit of clothing is lower with trade than the opportunity cost of producing it at home. Likewise, Japan should export clothing and import food because the opportunity cost of a unit of food with trade is less than the opportunity cost of producing it at home. In this situation, trade between America and Japan would be mutually beneficial.

Terms of Trade and Trade Between Countries

The terms of trade determine countries' gains from trade and whether or not any pair of countries will trade with each other at all.

- A country will not gain from trade if the international terms of trade are equal to the internal MRT without trade.

Suppose that the American MRT is $10F:1C$ and the Japanese MRT is $3F:1C$, as in Table 2, and that the world prices are $P_F = \$6$ and $P_C = \$60$. The international terms of trade are $P_F/P_C = 1C/10F$—the same as the American MRT without trade. In this case America would not gain from trading at all.

Japan's gains from trade with the international terms of trade = $10F:1C$ would be greater than they were with the international terms of trade = $6F:1C$. At the new prices, Japan would have to give up $1/10$ F per unit of C by trading—clearly more advantageous than $1/3F$ per unit of C without trade or $1/6F$ per unit of C at the old terms of trade.

If the international terms of trade were equal to Japan's internal MRT, this would eliminate Japan's gains from trade. The American gains from trade, on the other hand, would be greater if the international terms of trade were $3F:1C$ than with the international terms of trade = $6F:1C$.

These examples illustrate a very important point concerning the gains from trade.

- A country's gains from trade will be greater the greater the difference between the international terms of trade and the country's internal MRT.

If the international terms of trade lie outside the range between the American and Japanese internal MRTs, the Americans and Japanese would not trade with each other because they would gain by exporting or importing the same goods, as in the second part of Table 3 which shows the opportunity costs with and without trade with the international terms of trade = $2F:1C$. At these terms of international trade, both countries will gain by specializing in and exporting food and importing clothing. Obviously, America and Japan wouldn't trade with each other at these international terms of trade.

Trade and Welfare

Gains from trade make it possible for countries to reach higher levels of economic welfare with trade than they can reach without trade. Trade does not expand the country's *production possibilities*, but it expands the number of goods that a country can *consume*.

Production Possibilities in a Closed Economy

As you may recall from Chapter 2, the production possibilities curve (PPC) defines feasible combinations of goods than can be produced in a closed economy (no international trade) with given resources and technology. The PPC in Figure 1 defines feasible combinations of wheat (W) and steel (S) in a hypothetical closed economy. The slope of the PPC, $\Delta S/\Delta W$, is the economy's internal MRT, which shows the rate at which output of one good must be reduced to increase output of the other by reallocating the economy's resources internally.

Suppose that the best combination of wheat and steel for the country is combination A on the PPC, with 5 million tons of steel and 17 million bushels of wheat. The means by which the community decides that this is "best" is not important at this point. The main point is that combination A is the best the economy can do without trade. The slope of the line tangent to the PPC at A is the economy's internal MRT at A.

The Impact of Trade

If the country could trade at given world prices, how would this affect the community economic welfare, compared to the situation without trade? Without making value judgments, it is possible to say that the economy is doing "better" if it can increase its production of one good without reducing the output of other goods, or increase its output of both goods.

Suppose that the world wheat price is $P_W = \$5$ per bushel, and that the world price of steel is $P_S = \$10$ per ton. These aren't accurate approximations of actual world prices, but are only illustrative. The value of combination A at these prices is

$$V_1 = P_W W + P_S S$$
$$= \$5 \times 17 \text{ million} + \$10 \times 5 \text{ million} = \$135 \text{ million}.$$

Other combinations of wheat and steel that have the same value as combination A lie on the negatively sloped line, $V_1 = \$135$ million through A. The slope of V_1 is the ratio $-(P_W/P_S)$.

Combinations of wheat and steel outside the V_1 line have a value greater than $135 million at prevailing world prices, and will lie on other value lines that are parallel to V_1.

- The greatest value of wheat and steel the economy can produce with trade is the combination for which the internal MRT equals the international price ratio.

In Figure 1, the combination on the PPC with the greatest value at prevailing prices is combination B with 9 million tons of wheat and 13 million tons of steel. Combination B lies on the line $V_2 = \$175$ million which is tangent to the PPC at point B.

Figure 1 Trade and Economic Welfare

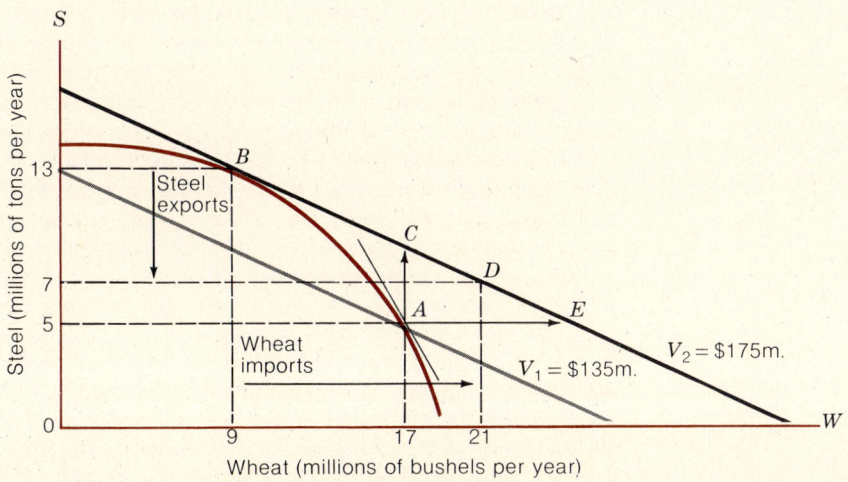

We cannot say that combination B on the PPC is better economically than combination A without making some kind of value judgment. However, with trade, the country can trade and consume any combination of goods on the line V_2. This line lies outside the PPC at all points except point B.

From point B, the country could export steel and use the revenue from the exports to import wheat. Any combination between C and E on V_2 is better than A economically because all combinations in this range have more of one good and no less of the other than combination A. If the community found that combination D were the best combination on V_2 with trade, it would be better off than at A (the best combination without trade) because it would have more wheat and more steel. To reach D, the country would export 6 million tons of steel and import 12 million bushels of wheat.

Figure 1 shows a theoretical result that has very important implications. First of all, the results show the gains from trade, the relationship between the international terms of trade and the gains from trade, and the degree to which the country will specialize in the good in which it has a comparative advantage at prevailing terms of trade. The results are more realistic because they portray one of many countries in world trade, while the earlier examples dealt primarily with bilateral trade between a pair of countries.

Applying the Tools

"The Importance of Being Unimportant"

The eighteenth and nineteenth centuries were a period in which the strong industrialized countries colonized and exploited the economies of the pre-industrial world. This development is described by the summary term *imperialism*. The imperialist epoch led many to the logical conclusion that the big gainers from international trade would be large, powerful economies with extensive resources, and that these gains would come at the expense of the smaller, weaker economies. This conclusion confuses the gains from trade with the political and military domination of small countries by large countries. In fact, the big gainers from trade are small countries without extensive and diverse resources.

To illustrate, classify goods as *farm products* (F) and *manufactures* (M). Figure A(i) shows the PPC for a large agricultural and manufacturing country, such as the United States or the Soviet Union. Figure A(ii) shows the PPC for a country, such as Japan, that has a substantial manufacturing capacity, but a small agricultural capacity. Combination A in Figure A(i) is the best combination of goods without trade for the large country, and combination A' in Figure A(ii) is the best combination of goods without trade for the smaller country.

Now, suppose that the countries can buy and sell farm products and manufactures at given prices, P_M and P_F. With trade, the large country would maximize the value of the goods it produces at point B on its PPC. From point B it moves to its preferred combination (C) on V_2. There are gains from trade, but they are fairly small compared to the best no-trade position for the large country.

Figure A

(i) Large Country

(ii) Small Country

By trading at given world prices, the small country would produce combination B' in Figure A(ii). By importing farm products and exporting manufactures, the small country moves to its best position (C') on V_2'. The gains from trade are much greater for the small country because the ratio of world prices and the international terms of trade are much different than the internal MRT at the small country's best no-trade position. Another factor contributing to the ability of small countries to realize large gains from trade is their inability to affect world prices. If the large country in Figure A(i) tried to specialize heavily in one good, it would lower the world price of the good, and its gains from trade would fall.

Because the smaller country gains more by trading over the best it could do without trade than the larger country, trade accounts for a larger share of the smaller country's national income than it does in the larger country. There is, of course, another side of the coin. Although small countries without diverse resources can gain the most from trade, fluctuations in international markets and international prices will have the greatest economic impact in these countries. This is especially true for countries that rely heavily on a single export to generate income.

Summary

1. International trade extends a country's markets, encourages international specialization, and raises the efficiency of the use of the world's economic resources.
2. The **principle of comparative advantage** identifies potential gains from specialization and trade, and the possibility of mutually beneficial trade between countries.
3. World prices determine the international **terms of trade,** or the rate at which goods will exchange for each other in international markets.
4. Countries will gain from trade if their **internal MRT** is different from the international terms of trade.
5. The potential gains from trade are greatest for relatively small countries without diverse resources, and international economic fluctuations have the greatest impact in these countries.

Concepts for Review

specialization
principle of comparative advantage
comparative advantage
internal marginal rate of transformation
terms of trade

Questions

1. Try to list some of the specific ways that international trade affects your economic welfare. What would be the effects of a complete abolition of the barriers to trade on your welfare? How would a complete cessation of international trade affect your economic welfare? Do you think that either more liberal foreign trade or cessation of trade would have the same impact on the economic welfare of all segments of society?
2. Suppose that Japan could produce all industrial goods at a lower average cost than the United States. Does it follow that the United States should import all industrial goods from Japan? Explain.
3. Some people argue that international trade is a means by which large countries exploit small countries because the small countries always lose in their trade with large countries. Is this notion consistent with the law of comparative advantage? Explain.
4. Countries with very narrow resource bases may have to specialize in the production of a single product for export. These countries stand to realize the greatest gains from trade, but trade also may lead to some serious economic problems in these countries. How could you explain this statement?

Problems

1. Never-Never Land and Almost-Never Land produce Bibles and rum. In Never-Never Land the cost of producing a Bible is $15 and the cost of producing a barrel of rum is $10. In Almost-Never Land, the cost of producing a Bible is $10 and the cost of producing a barrel of rum is $5.

a. In which good (if any) does each country have a comparative advantage over the other? Explain.
b. If the world price of Bibles were $18 and the world price of rum were $10, would it pay these countries to specialize and trade on the basis of comparative advantage?
If so, in which good should each country specialize? Would they trade with each other?
c. Would your answers to part b be the same if the world price of Bibles were $25 and the world price of rum were $10? Explain.

33

International Exchange

Preview: In international trade as in any other trade, goods go one way and money expenditure goes the other way. If we import goods from abroad, goods flow into our country and money flows out to pay for the goods. If we export goods to another country, the goods flow out of and money flows into our economy. The first requirement for any trade is the ability of traders to make exchanges. But since different countries use different currencies, international trade requires some means to enable buyers and sellers to deal with each other.

Exchange Rates and International Currency

Until 1973, the international monetary system was based on gold. Gold was universally acceptable as money in international trade. **Convertible currencies,** such as the British pound and the American dollar, could be converted to gold by purchasing gold at guaranteed prices. Currencies were convertible for each other because they could be converted to gold at guaranteed prices, and this made it possible for buyers and sellers in different countries to deal with each other. Although the international gold standard no longer exists, the international economy still uses convertible currencies.

To see how convertible currency works, suppose that you buy a British sports car from a British seller. The price of the car will be expressed in pounds (£). Your money, of course, is dollars. To buy the British car, there must be some means for either the buyer or the dealer to convert dollars into pounds. The conversion of one currency for another is accomplished by the sale and purchase of currency in international currency markets.

Purchasing the sports car from Britain will have the following effects:

1. The car will be imported into the United States, and represents a *U.S. commodity import.*

2. The car represents a *British commodity export*.
3. *Pounds must be purchased* in international currency markets to pay for the car.
4. *Dollars must be sold* in international currency markets to buy the pounds to pay for the car.

The number of dollars sold and the number of pounds purchased depend on the *exchange rate* between the pound and the dollar.

- The **exchange rate** between currencies is the rate at which one currency exchanges for another in international markets, or *the price of one currency in terms of another*.

With an international gold standard, exchange rates were defined by the official prices of gold in various currencies. Governments no longer guarantee the purchase and sale of gold at official prices, and exchange rates are determined by the market forces of supply and demand in international markets. The financial sections of some newspapers and the *Wall Street Journal* publish the exchange rates between the dollar and other currencies, expressed as the prices of other currencies in dollars.

Exchange Rates and the Prices of Exports and Imports

Exchange rates determine the prices that American buyers pay for imports and the prices that foreign buyers have to pay for U.S. exports. If the price of the British sports car in the previous example is £3000, how much will it cost in dollars? If the exchange rate of dollars per pound is \$2.00/£, the dollar price of the car is

$$\$2.00/£ \times £3000 = \$6000.$$

If a British firm imported a piece of machinery from the United States, the price of the machinery in pounds would be the exchange rate of pounds per dollar, multiplied by dollar price. If the price of the dollar in pounds is \$2.00/£, the price of the pound in dollars is £0.5/\$. If the price of the machine is \$2000, its price in pounds is

$$£0.5/\$ \times \$2000 = £1000.$$

Currency Appreciation and Depreciation

Changes in exchange rates affect the prices of imported goods to domestic buyers and exported goods to foreign buyers. If the dollar *appreciates* relative to another currency, the price of the dollar in that currency rises.

- **Appreciation** of a country's currency makes imported goods cheaper and exported goods more expensive.

Suppose that the price of the dollar rose from £0.5/\$ to £0.8/\$. The price of the pound would fall to \$1.25/£ as a result of the appreciation of the dollar. The dollar price of the £3000 British car would be

$$\$1.25/£ \times £3000 = \$3750.$$

The price of the exported U.S. machine in pounds would rise to

$$£0.8/\$ \times \$2000 = £1600.$$

Depreciation of a currency refers to a fall in the price of the currency in international markets.

- **Depreciation** of a country's currency makes its imports more expensive and its exports cheaper.

Suppose that the price of the dollar in pounds falls from £0.5/$ to £0.25/$, and therefore that the price of the dollar in pounds rises from $2.00/£ to $4.00/£. As a result of the depreciation, the price of the British sports car in dollars rises to

$$\$4.00/£ \times £3000 = \$12,000.$$

The price of the exported American machinery in pounds falls to

$$£0.25/\$ \times \$2000 = £500.$$

How Exchange Rates Are Determined

Exchange rates are currency prices, and like other prices they are determined by supply and demand forces in international currency markets. The supply and demand of currencies, in turn, depends on countries' imports and exports.

Foreign buyers must purchase dollars in international markets to pay for U.S. exports.

- The *demand* for a country's currency in international markets varies directly with its exports.

The demand curve for dollars in Figure 1a ($D_\$$) is negatively sloped, indicating an inverse relationship between the price of the dollar and the quantity of dollars demanded. As the exchange rate rises, U.S. exports become more expensive, and exports tend to fall. As exports fall, so does the quantity of dollars demanded to pay for them. If the price of the dollar falls, exports become cheaper, exports tend to increase, and the quantity of dollars demanded increases.

To pay for imports into the U.S., dollars have to be sold to purchase foreign currencies.

- The *supply* of a country's currency in international markets varies directly with its imports.

The supply curve for dollars in Figure 1b ($S_\$$) is positively sloped, indicating a direct relationship between the exchange rate (£/$) and the quantity of dollars supplied. As the exchange rate rises, imported goods become cheaper in the United States, and U.S. imports will tend to rise. As more goods are imported, more dollars must be sold to pay for them. If the dollar depreciated relative to the pound, the results would be just the opposite.

Figure 1 Determination of Equilibrium Exchange Rates

In the absence of restrictions, flexible exchange rates tend toward equilibrium, just as other flexible prices do. The equilibrium exchange rate is reached when the quantity of the currency supplied just equals the quantity demanded in international markets. The equilibrium exchange rate in Figure 1c reflects the U.S. demand for imports (in the $S_\$$ curve) and the foreign demand for U.S. exports (in the $D_\$$ curve).

If the exchange rate were below the equilibrium (for example, at £0.3/$ in Figure 1c) the dollar is **undervalued** relative to the pound, and there is an excess demand of dollars, or a *dollar shortage*. If the exchange rate were above equilibrium (at £0.7/$ in Figure 1c) the dollar is **overvalued,** and there is excess supply of dollars, or a *dollar glut*, in international markets.

The Balance of International Payments

The **balance of payments accounts** summarize the payments a country makes to the rest of the world and payments it receives from the rest of the world. A detailed look at the 1977 U.S. balance of payments accounts will be found in the appendix to this chapter. The following discussion uses a very simplified set of balance of payments accounts, containing only three accounts—a **merchandise** account, a **capital** account, and an **international settlements** account.

The Merchandise Account

The merchandise account shows the exports of goods to other countries and imports of goods from other countries. Exports are a *credit* item in the merchandise account.

- **Credits** are transactions that add to a country's assets or reduce its liabilities.

If the exports are paid for with convertible currencies, the exporting country's holdings of convertible currencies (an asset) increase. If the foreign buyers borrow to purchase exports, this increases the foreign obligations to the exporting country (also an asset).

Merchandise imports are *debits* in the merchandise account.

- **Debits** are transactions that reduce a country's assets or increase its liabilities.

When goods are imported, foreign sellers have to be paid, and paying them reduces the importing country's holdings of convertible currencies (an asset). If the imports are financed by borrowing, this increases the importing country's liabilities to foreign governments.

The **balance on the merchandise account** is the sum of the values of merchandise exports (+) and merchandise imports (−), or

$$\text{Balance on Merchandise Account} = \text{Merchandise Exports} - \text{Merchandise Imports}.$$

This is sometimes called **net exports** (as in the aggregate demand function) or the **balance of trade.**

The Capital Account

The capital account summarizes the capital flows between the United States and the rest of the world. An American firm's investment of capital abroad is a *capital export*. Foreign capital invested in the United States is a *capital import*.

There is a difference between entries in the capital account and the merchandise account.

- *Exports of capital* are debits (−) in the capital account.
- *Imports of capital* are credits (+) in the capital account.

If an American investor invests funds in another country, the funds have to be converted into the other country's currency, so dollars will be sold in international markets as a result of the capital export, and this sale will reduce U.S. holdings of convertible currencies (an asset). When foreign funds are invested in the U.S., the investment would have to be made in dollars, thus requiring purchases of dollars in international markets.

The balance on the capital account is the sum of capital exports and imports—i.e.,

$$\text{Balance on Capital Account} = \text{Capital imports} - \text{Capital exports}.$$

If capital imports exceed capital exports, the capital account will show a positive balance or surplus. If capital exports exceed capital imports, on the other hand, the capital account will show a negative balance or a deficit.

The International Settlements Account

Although the merchandise and capital accounts can show surpluses or deficits, the balance of *all* international payments must equal zero. The corollary of *There ain't no such thing as a free lunch* is *Everything bought or sold must be paid for.* Any difference between credits and debits in the merchandise and capital accounts must be made up for by some form of **international settlement.** With the international gold standard, imports and exports of gold and convertible currencies were important international settlements. Since the U.S. suspended gold payments in 1973, however, changes in the U.S. gold stock have been quite small, and other settlements (changes in reserves of convertible currencies, borrowing, and lending) have become the primary means of making international settlements.

The **settlement account** simply shows the amount that has to be settled with the rest of the world, and how these international settlements are made. Suppose, for example, that the United States exports goods and services worth $300 million, and that we import goods and services worth $250 million. The balance on the merchandise account in this case is

$$\text{Merchandise Exports} - \text{Merchandise Imports} =$$
$$\$300 \text{ million} - \$250 \text{ million} = \$50 \text{ million}.$$

In addition, suppose that capital imports are $100 million, and capital exports are $75 million. The balance on the capital account is

$$\text{Capital Imports} - \text{Capital Exports} = \$100 \text{ million} - \$75 \text{ million} =$$
$$\$25 \text{ million}.$$

The sum of the balances on the merchandise and capital accounts is the balance to be settled with the rest of the world, or the amount of international settlements to be made. In this example, international settlements are

$$\text{Balance on Merchandise Account} + \text{Balance on Capital Account} =$$
$$\$50 \text{ million} + \$25 \text{ million} = \$75 \text{ million}.$$

The surplus of $75 million means that the United States will receive payments or obligations from foreigners to make up for the surplus. To keep things simple, assume that imports and exports of convertible currencies are the only international settlements. The United States would import $75 million in convertible currencies from abroad. Imports of convertible currencies are debits, so the balance of all international payments in this example is $75 million (surplus on merchandise and capital accounts) − $75 million (currency imports) = 0.

It's a fairly common view that deficits in the merchandise and capital accounts are bad economically and surpluses good. In one sense, this is correct. Deficits in the merchandise and capital accounts must be settled by exporting convertible currencies, and convertible currency holdings are a precautionary asset for the country. When there are surpluses on the merchandise and capital account, convertible currency holdings rise, increasing a precautionary asset.

However, the effects of deficits in the merchandise and capital accounts on aggregate demand aren't necessarily bad, and the effects of surpluses aren't necessarily good. During periods of demand-pull inflation, deficits in the merchandise and capital accounts tend to dampen aggregate demand and inflationary pressure. Surpluses may stimulate aggregate demand and amplify inflationary pressures related to demand.

Capital flows create a potential conflict between the balance of payments position and domestic economic problems. Unemployment may suggest increases in the money supply and lower interest rates. However, lower interest rates discourage capital inflows into the country and encourage capital exports to countries where capital earns a higher return. Either of these results would reduce a surplus or increase a deficit in the capital account.

Exchange Rates and the Balance of Payments

Since exchange rates determine the prices of imports and exports, they will affect the country's balance of payments position by affecting merchandise imports and exports. With flexible exchange rates, changes in imports and exports will cause changes in the exchange rate. With fixed, or *pegged* exchange rates, changes in imports and exports will not affect the exchange rate, but will have other effects on the economy.

Pegged Exchange Rates

At a conference at Bretton Woods, New Hampshire, in 1944 the basic shape of the postwar international monetary system was established. One of the features of the Bretton Woods Agreement was fixed or *pegged* international exchange rates. The architects of the agreement, including John Maynard Keynes, saw flexible exchange rates and international currency speculation as one of the causes of the economic disasters of the 1930s, and fixed exchange rates were established to stabilize the international economy.

Exchange rates were pegged by pegging the dollar price of gold at $35 per ounce. The United States guaranteed foreign banks the conversion of dollars for gold at this price. The dollar prices of other currencies were also pegged. In short, exchange rates among currencies were pegged by pegged dollar prices of currencies and the exchange rates between currencies and gold were pegged by the pegged dollar price of gold.

Pegged exchange rates are not free to adjust to changes in currency demand and supply in international markets. Suppose that the price of the dollar is pegged at its equilibrium price $\bar{P}_\$$, in Figure 2a. Now suppose that the demand for U.S. exports increases, increasing the demand for dollars to $D_\$'$. With flexible exchange rates, the dollar would *appreciate*, and the price of the dollar would rise to $\bar{P}_\$'$. However, since the exchange rate is pegged at $P_\$^*$, the dollar is **undervalued** at $P_\$^*$.

Figure 2 Effects of *Pegged* Exchange Rates

(a) Rise in demand for dollars
(b) Decline in supply of dollars
(c) Decline in demand for dollars
(d) Rise in supply of dollars

The dollar would likewise appreciate as a result of a decline in the U.S. demand for imports. As imports fall, the supply of dollars would shift to the left to $S_\$'$ in Figure 2b. With the smaller supply of dollars and the pegged exchange rate, $P_\$^*$, the dollar would again be undervalued.

Reduced demand for a country's exports or increased demand for imports will cause its currency to depreciate with flexible exchange rates. In Figure 2c, reduced demand for U.S. exports would shift the demand for dollars from $D_\$$ to $D_\$'$ and lower the equilibrium price of the dollar to $\bar{P}_\$'$. At the pegged exchange rate, $P_\$^*$, the fall in U.S.

exports makes the dollar an **overvalued** currency. In Figure 2d, increased demand for imports in the United States increases the supply of dollars in international markets to $S_\$'$, and the equilibrium price of the dollar falls to $\bar{P}_\$'$. Again, with the exchange rate pegged at $P_\$^*$, the dollar is *overvalued*.

How can exchange rates be kept above or below equilibrium? One way is the purchase and sale of currency by the government. If there were excess demand for dollars, for example, the U.S. government could sell dollars in international markets to eliminate the excess demand. With an overvalued currency, the government could sell other currencies to buy up the excess supply of its currency.

What if a country's reserves of convertible currencies aren't sufficient to allow it to maintain a rate that overvalues its currency? It can borrow convertible currencies from other countries or from the International Monetary Fund to enable it to buy enough of its currency to maintain the exchange rate. Every country also has a predetermined quota of **special drawing rights** (SDRs) which serve as reserves to allow it to purchase other currencies to maintain exchange rates.

Overvalued currency in international markets may contribute to domestic unemployment problems. An overvalued currency makes imports a bargain for domestic buyers, and makes exports expensive to foreign buyers in export markets. This will tend to depress the level of domestic employment.

Pegging the exchange rate *below* the equilibrium level, or undervaluing the currency, has the opposite effects. It gives the sellers of underpriced exports an advantage in world markets and makes imports relatively expensive to domestic buyers. In periods of brisk aggregate demand, this may add to inflationary pressures.

In short, something has to give to keep the exchange rate above or below its equilibrium level. If the currency is overvalued, a country's reserves of convertible currencies will be depleted or it will have to incur a foreign debt by borrowing foreign currencies to buy up the excess supply of its own currency. An overvalued currency may be maintained at the expense of domestic employment. Keeping the exchange rate pegged below equilibrium will eventually contribute to inflationary pressure in the economy.

Further, there is no guarantee that even the most heroic efforts to maintain a pegged exchange rate will work. In the mid 1960s, the British government went to great lengths to maintain the value of the pound in international markets. At \$2.80/£, the pound was seriously overvalued. The British instituted incomes policies, bought surplus pounds in international markets, and borrowed heavily from the International Monetary Fund and the U.S. to buy pounds. All of these actions were to no avail, however, and eventually the pound was devalued anyway.

Applying the Tools

Pegged Exchanged Rates and the U.S. Balance of Payments, 1946–1972

The period 1946–1972 was one of massive changes in the international economy. Though decimated by World War II, the European and Japanese economies had by the 1960s been through a dramatic reconstruction and become major international economic powers. These changes had dramatic effects on U.S. exports and imports and on the demand for and supply of dollars in international markets, but the exchange rate between the dollar and other currencies was pegged for the entire period.

In 1946, the United States was the only major economy that had come through the war intact. The decimated economies of Europe and Japan were able to produce very little, so U.S. exports and U.S. dollars were in great demand. The supply of dollars in international markets was fairly low because of the low U.S. demand for imports.

With flexible exchange rates in 1946, the dollar would have appreciated dramatically. In Figure A, the demand for dollars (D_{46}) and the supply of dollars (S_{46}) would have determined a high price of the dollar (gold per dollar) at $\overline{P}_{46}$. However, the price of the dollar was pegged at $P^*_\$ = 1/35$ ounce of gold per dollar. This undervalued the dollar, and resulted in a *dollar shortage* in international markets. Foreign buyers settled with the United States by shipping gold and convertible currencies to the United States.

The U.S. gold stock increased during World War II and continued to increase after the war. Between 1946 and 1949, U.S. gold reserves increased from about $21 billion to about $24.5 billion. After 1949, a *gold drain* began. The U.S. gold stock was $17.8 billion in 1960, $13.8 billion in 1965, and $10.5 billion in 1972. Some blamed the gold drain on greedy American workers and unions that were "pricing our goods out of world markets." Others blamed greedy, shortsighted

Figure A

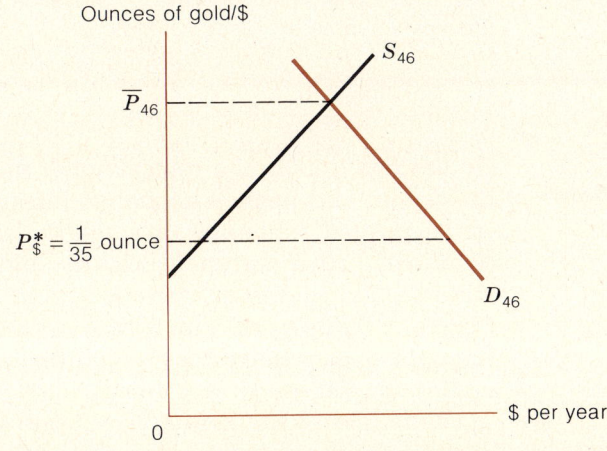

industrialists. Others blamed government deficits that were alleged to raise prices and "price our goods out of international markets." In fact, none of the popular explanations was sufficient to explain the gold drain.

As the European and Japanese economies recovered and grew in strength, their need for U.S. exports fell. By the 1960s competition from Japanese and European exports reduced world demand for U.S. exports, and U.S. producers faced increasing competition in domestic markets from imports.

The effect of the European and Japanese *economic miracle* on the demand for, and supply of, dollars is shown in Figure B. Falling demand for U.S. exports reduced the demand for dollars to D_{72} by 1972. Increased U.S. imports increased the supply of dollars to S_{72}. If the exchange rates had been flexible, the price of the dollar would have fallen to $\overline{P}_{72}$ by 1972.

Figure B

At the pegged exchange rate, however, there was excess supply of dollars or *dollar glut*, because the pegged exchange rate overvalued the dollar relative to other currencies. The United States settled with the rest of the world by exporting gold and convertible currencies. Thus, the gold drain was caused at least in part by the pegged exchange rate that overvalued the dollar. The overvalued dollar may also have contributed to domestic problems of sagging aggregate demand and unemployment in the United States.

Floating Exchange Rates

By the late 1960s, the international monetary system based on gold, the dollar, and pegged exchange rates had come under severe strain. At its pegged exchange rate, the dollar was an overvalued currency (its price in other currencies was too high to clear the market of dollars), and U.S. gold reserves were declining. Capital flows from the United States to Europe and Japan increased the number of dollars held by foreigners, and these foreign dollar holdings represented increased claims against the United States.

The failure of the British to support the overvalued pound through austerity and controls in the domestic economy and intervention in

Figure 3 Results of the 1973 Dollar Float

international monetary markets wasn't reassuring to those who supported fixed exchange rates. In January of 1973, the Italians allowed the value of the lira to float in international markets. The float of the lira was followed quickly by the float of the Swiss franc. In March, 1973, the Japanese allowed the value of the yen to float upward. The dollar was depreciated in 1973, and finally allowed to float. The international monetary system that had prevailed since the Bretton Woods Agreement in 1941 had collapsed.

When the dollar was allowed to float in 1973, it actually sank—i.e., its exchange rate fell against most convertible currencies. The reason is easy to understand in terms of simple supply and demand analysis. In Figure 3, the pegged exchange rate (or price of the dollar) is $P_\$^*$, above the equilibrium price P. Fixing a price above equilibrium created an excess supply of dollars, or a dollar glut, and removing the fixed price caused the price of the dollar to drop in international markets.

Although exchange rates aren't officially fixed or pegged, they aren't completely free to fluctuate either. The current exchange rate system is a **dirty float.** Governments and central banks intervene periodically in international currency markets to avoid what they see as excessive fluctuations in exchange rates. For example, when the United States floated the dollar, Germany and Japan bought large quantities of dollars in an attempt to keep the dollar from depreciating too rapidly or too far. In late 1978 and early 1979, the United States took a number of actions to bolster the value of the dollar in world currency markets—most notably raising interest rates and borrowing foreign currencies to buy dollars. The rationale behind the dirty float is that wide fluctuations in exchange rates will be destabilizing in international markets and will disrupt international trade.

A New International Monetary System?

The international monetary arrangements that had been established at Bretton Woods in 1941 were largely demolished by 1973. The current system is a mixture. Exchange rates aren't pegged, but they aren't completely flexible either. A stable monetary system and some form of international currency is essential for trade, but we only have clues concerning the shape of the international monetary system of the future.

Special Drawing Rights (SDRs)

In 1969, the International Monetary Fund (IMF) introduced Special Drawing Rights (SDRs) for making international settlements. Member countries are allocated SDR units on the basis of their share of international trade. The value of an SDR unit is based on the average value of the leading international currencies and therefore doesn't depend on the value of a money commodity (gold) or a single national currency (the dollar). The original purpose of the SDRs was to economize on gold as an international currency and to increase international liquidity. In a world in which the basic reserve currency (the dollar) floats, however, the SDRs have become increasingly important as a form of international currency.

The decline of the value of the dollar since the float in 1973 has caused concern about the stability of an international economy in which the dollar is the basic currency. This concern has been particularly strong among the oil-exporting countries. To understand this concern, suppose that an OPEC country agrees to sell oil to the United States at a specified dollar price—say, $20 a barrel. However, suppose that between the time of the agreement and payment by the U.S. importer the value of the dollar in international markets falls by 10 percent. In real terms, the exporter will receive 10 percent less than the agreed price for the oil. If the exporter and importer had agreed on a price in SDRs, depreciation of the dollar against other currencies wouldn't reduce the purchasing power received by the exporter for a barrel of oil, and this could reduce the incentive of oil exporters to increase the dollar price per barrel of oil to compensate for expected depreciation of the dollar. Of course, SDR prices would make oil more expensive for U.S. buyers because the SDR payments would be worth more dollars as the dollar depreciated.

The European Monetary System

On January 1, 1979, another clue concerning the shape of the future international monetary system appeared with the European Monetary System (EMS) and the European Currency Unit (ECU). The members of the EMS agreed to allow their currencies to float against the dollar, but set narrow limits within which the values of their currencies could fluctuate against each other.

The value of the ECU is a weighted average of the values of the currencies of EMS members, similar to the SDRs. The ECU floats against the dollar, and the range of fluctuations of EMS currencies against each other is defined by their values in ECU. If the exchange rate of, say, the French franc depreciated against the ECU and the German mark appreciated in ECUs so that the exchange rate between marks and francs went beyond the specified limits, the Germans and the French would agree to take appropriate policies to raise or lower the value of their currencies. The goal is to stabilize exchange rates within limits among EMS members.

What Next? The increasing importance of SDRs in world trade and the introduction of the ECU seem to indicate a trend toward an international currency whose value is a composite of the values of all convertible currencies. This would reduce the importance of the dollar or any other single national currency as an international reserve currency.

Even if there were a new international currency for making international settlements and setting the exchange rates among countries, there is still the question of the degree of flexibility of these exchange rates. Critics of flexible exchange rates argue that some regulation or limits are necessary to prevent the destabilizing effects of fluctuations in exchange rates on international commerce. The proponents of flexible exchange rates argue that they would in fact be stabilizing in the long run, since currencies wouldn't become so overvalued that they encouraged massive speculation on their inevitable depreciation (as was the case with the dollar in the 1960s).

The choice of fixed or flexible exchange rates involves yet another issue—the independence of countries in their own monetary policies. With fixed exchange rates, or with limits on changes in exchange rates, countries with large trade deficits or surpluses would have to alter their domestic monetary policies to support the fixed rate or to keep the rate within prescribed limits. For example, if a large trade deficit put downward pressure on a country's currency, the country would have to follow a restrictive monetary policy to reduce its deficit and support the international value of its currency, and this may well lead to greater domestic unemployment. If trade surpluses caused the currency to appreciate beyond the prescribed limits, expansionary monetary policies (for example, lowering interest rates) would be needed to bring the exchange rate down, and this could lead to domestic inflation.

Summary
1. International trade requires an internationally acceptable currency. Historically, gold has been a basic international currency, but recently convertible currencies have been the basic international currency.
2. The exchange rate between currencies is the price of one currency in terms of the other.
3. Flexible exchange rates will tend toward equilibrium where the quantity of the currency demanded equals the quantity supplied in international

markets. From World War II, the exchange rates between the world's major currencies were not flexible, but fixed by international agreement.
4. The balance of payments accounts summarize payments between a country and the rest of the world. The balance of all of a country's international payments must equal zero.
5. Flexible exchange rates will tend to reduce surpluses and deficits in a country's balance of trade.

Concepts for Review

convertible currency
exchange rate
appreciation
depreciation
overvaluation
undervaluation
currency glut

merchandise account
balance of trade
capital account
international settlement
settlement account
pegged exchange rate
special drawing right (SDR)

floating exchange rate
dirty float
European Monetary System (EMS)
European Currency Unit (ECU)

Questions

1. When the exchange rate between the dollar and other currencies was allowed to float, the price of the dollar fell in international currency markets.
   a. What does this tell you about the previously pegged exchange rate between the dollar and other currencies?
   b. Can you explain why the Japanese bought a large quantity of dollars to keep it from depreciating?
   c. What would you normally expect to happen to the balance of trade as a result of the depreciation of the dollar in international markets?
   d. A harder question: Under what conditions could the actual effect of depreciation of the dollar on the balance of trade be the opposite of the effects one would normally expect?
2. An article in the *Washington Post* in October 1978 contained the following statement: "Bad news for the dollar could not, in fact, be better news for the European market potential of the Detroit automobile industry."
   a. Explain how "bad news for the dollar" could affect the European sales of American cars.
   b. Could this same "bad news" affect the domestic sales of American cars? If so, how?
3. In June of 1979, Mr. Rene Ortiz of Ecuador—the Secretary General of OPEC—said that the OPEC *benchmark price* of crude oil should be raised from $14.55 to at least $20.00 a barrel. He asserted that "we (OPEC) still aren't at all fully compensated for our losses" as a result of the depreciation of the dollar in world markets and U.S. inflation. Explain carefully how U.S. inflation and the depreciation of the dollar would impose "losses" on OPEC.
4. The annual report of the Bank for International Settlements in Switzerland asserted that a U.S. recession would reduce worldwide inflationary pressure, reduce the U.S. trade deficit, and restore stability to international exchange markets. Specifically, the report

called for tighter monetary and fiscal policies and higher interest rates for the United States.
   a. Explain carefully how tight monetary and fiscal policies and a recession in the United States could affect worldwide inflation, the U.S. balance of payments, the strength of the dollar in international markets, and the stability of international exchange markets.
   b. Would monetary and fiscal restraint and a recession in France or Belgium have the same effect on worldwide inflation and the stability of international exchange markets? Why?
   c. Would the measures be necessary if international exchange rates were completely free to float? Why?
5. Although gold no longer serves as an international reserve currency, the price of gold in world markets remains important. When a currency *weakens* against gold, it means that the price of gold in that currency has gone up.
   a. When OPEC announced another price increase in 1979 on its oil exports, the dollar *weakened* against gold. How could higher OPEC oil prices cause the dollar to weaken against gold in international currency markets?
   b. Sometimes the price of gold in all major currencies will rise or fall. How would you interpret and explain a rise in the price of gold in all currencies? How would you interpret and explain a fall in the price of gold in all currencies?

Problems

1. The small country of Sokituya made the following international transactions in 1980. All figures are millions of cronies (the local currency).

Travel by foreigners to Sokituya	200
Private and public purchases of bonds in foreign companies	250
Foreign purchases of Sokituian bonds	100
Sales of military goods abroad	125
Pensions and unilateral transfers to foreigners	50
Purchases of corporate bonds in Sokituya by foreigners	500
Foreign travel by Sokituyans	150
Merchandise imports	750
Misc. services, net	−100
Income from foreign investments	100
Income paid to foreign investors	150

   a. Identify the credits and debits above, and put the appropriate sign (+ or −) before each.
   b. Find the balances for the merchandise, goods and services, current, and capital accounts.
   c. Sokituya makes all international settlements in dollars. Will it import dollars, export dollars, or neither? What value of dollars (if any) will it import or export?
   d. What is the balance of *all* international payments for Sokituya in 1980? Is this unusual?

APPENDIX

U.S. International Transactions, 1977

Most references to the balance of payments in the media and in political debate refer to the balance on the *merchandise account*, the *goods and services account*, or the entire *current account*. These are convenient summary figures, but they represent only a part of our transactions with the rest of the world.

Table A-1 is a summary of U.S. international transactions for 1977.

Table A-1 Summary of U.S. International Transactions, 1977 (millions of $)

Merchandise exports (+) and imports (−), net	−$31,130
Investment income, net	17,507
Net military transactions	1,334
Net travel and transportation	−3,044
Other services	4,749
BALANCE ON GOODS AND SERVICES	−$10,585
Remittances, pensions, and other unilateral transfers	−4,708
BALANCE ON CURRENT ACCOUNT	−$15,292
Change in U.S. assets abroad	−$34,419
Change in foreign assets in the U.S.	50,869
Errors, omissions, discrepancies	−927
BALANCE ON CAPITAL ACCOUNT	$15,523
COMBINED BALANCE, CURRENT AND CAPITAL ACCOUNTS	231
Official Reserve Assets	−231

Source: *Economic Report of the President, 1979.*

The Current Account

The *merchandise account* is fairly straightforward, and needs little explanation—it simply shows the difference between merchandise exports and merchandise imports. The United States showed a deficit in the merchandise account in 1977 of $31,130 million. This means that the value of our merchandise imports from other countries exceeded our merchandise exports to other countries by about $31 billion. The merchandise account showed surpluses (exports greater than imports) in every year between 1946 and 1970, and deficits in five of the years between 1971 and 1977. We don't have to look far for an explanation of this shift. In 1977, we imported nearly $45 billion worth of petroleum and petroleum products—$33 billion from the OPEC countries alone. By comparison, in 1972, our petroleum imports amounted to $4.7 billion, about $3 billion of which came from OPEC. If we excluded petroleum (or even excluded OPEC) imports, the remainder of the merchandise account would show a surplus.

Military transactions include the sales of military goods to other countries and direct military expenditures in other countries. Military sales (for example, international sales of arms and military hardware) are credits in the balance of payments, like any other commodity export. Direct military expenditures, on the other hand, are deficits in the balance of payments accounts. Direct military expenditures include such items as direct military assistance to other countries, maintaining troops abroad, etc. Direct military expenditures, in contrast to sales, involve the sale of dollars in international markets, and are therefore debit items. The military transactions account showed deficits every year from 1946 through 1975, and surpluses in 1976 and 1977.

The *travel and transportation* account is another one that consistently shows deficits—1951 and 1952 were the only postwar years in which this account showed a surplus. When an American travels abroad, he or she must exchange dollars for other currencies, and this increases the supply of dollars in international markets. When a foreign tourist visits the United States, on the other hand, he or she must purchase dollars. In short, Americans' travel expenditures abroad are debits and foreigners' travel expenditures are credits. Places like Athens, Greece, are apparently more attractive to American tourists than are Athens, Georgia, or Athens, Michigan, to foreign tourists.

Remittances, pensions, and other unilateral transfers are, like direct military transactions, unilateral payments abroad. Dollars are sent abroad, sold for other convertible currencies, and no payments flow back to the United States. Nonmilitary foreign economic aid is included in this account. Pension payments to American retirees who live in Ireland or other garden spots abroad also represent unilateral transfers.

Investment income (but not the investments themselves) are included in the current account. Payments of income to foreign investors on their investments in the United States are debits (−) because the dollars paid to foreign investors must be sold for the investors' own currencies. Similarly, income to U.S. investors on their investments abroad is a credit (+), because the foreign currencies must be sold for dollars by U.S. investors.

The sum of the balances on the merchandise, military transactions, investment income, travel, and unilateral transfers accounts is the *balance on the current account.*

The Capital Account

The *capital account* summarizes the international capital flows between the United States and the rest of the world. Actually, since all international payments except international settlements are either current or capital expenditures, the capital account basically includes the items that aren't included in the current account.

Capital flows are summarized as U.S. assets abroad and foreign assets in the United States. Just remember that *capital imports* are credits (+) and *capital exports* are debits (−). If a U.S. company builds a plant in Europe, this is a capital export, and it requires the sale of dollars at some point. On the other hand, if a Japanese company builds a plant in the United States, this is a capital import and it will require a purchase of dollars. The sum of the balances for capital flows and errors and omissions gives us the *balance on the capital account.*

International Settlements

Deficits and surpluses in the current and capital accounts are settled by changes in *official reserves*—government holdings of gold, convertible currencies, special drawing rights, and reserves with the International Monetary Fund. If the combined current and capital account balance shows a deficit (−), this is settled by exporting official reserves. Exports of official reserves are credits (+) and offset the deficit in the current and capital accounts. If the combined current and capital account balance shows a surplus (+), this is settled by importing official reserves (a debit) to make up for the surplus.

In 1977, the combined current and capital account balance showed a surplus ($231 million) due to the large surplus in the capital account. This was settled by importing official reserves from foreign governments (−$231 million). The balance of *all* international transactions and payments in 1977, as in any year, was zero.

34

Trade Policy: Mechanics, Problems, and Issues

Preview: The extent to which our trade with the rest of the world is "free" depends to a large extent on the **trade policies** enacted by the federal government. The government has the power to encourage imports and exports through subsidies, or to discourage them through tariffs and quotas. It may use this power for a variety of reasons: to achieve domestic economic goals, to gain political ends, to maintain national security. In this chapter, we'll examine the most important trade policy tools and assess the arguments for and against various trade policies.

Trade policy problems are nearly as old as international trade itself. International rivalries among emerging nation-states led to a basic economic strategy called **mercantilism** that stressed national economic, political, and military power. In international trade, mercantilist policies emphasized restriction of imports, encouragement of exports, and national economic self-sufficiency. Much of the classical economics of Smith, Ricardo, and Mill was an attack on mercantilist economic policy.

In U.S. history, too, trade policy has been important. The American colonies were restricted to trading almost entirely with England. A British tax on tea shipped to America was one of the catalysts that led to the American Revolution. In the nineteenth century, the United States imposed tariffs to encourage domestic economic development, protect domestic producers, and become as independent as possible economically.

Many of the old trade policy questions are still debated today. Can we reduce unemployment by imposing trade restrictions? Can our workers compete with cheaper foreign labor? Does national security demand economic self-sufficiency? Can we dampen inflationary pressures by restricting exports?

Tariffs and Import Quotas

A country may follow policies that restrict imports for a number of reasons. Some people believe that restricting imports will reduce domestic unemployment. Others advocate import restrictions in the interests of national self-sufficiency and national security. The merits of these and other arguments for restricted imports cannot be evaluated without some understanding of the effects of import restrictions on the economy.

The two basic ways to restrict imports are the imposition of **import quotas** that set maximum quantities of goods that can be imported and the imposition of a *tariff* on imported goods.

- A **tariff** is an excise tax on imported goods. It may be a tax per unit of a good imported or a percentage of the value of a good imported (*ad valorem*).

Tariffs and Efficiency

A British tariff on agricultural imports in the nineteenth century (the Corn Laws) was one of the critical issues that led to the development of classical free-trade arguments. Consider two countries—America (A) and Britain (B). Both countries can produce wheat, but the cost and therefore the supply price of any quantity of wheat produced in America is lower than in Britain because America has superior resources for growing wheat. In Figure 1, the American supply function (S_A) lies below the British supply function (S_B) at every quantity of wheat. Figures 2a and b show the equilibrium prices of wheat in America and Britain without trade. The price is higher in Britain because the inferior land makes wheat scarcer relative to the demand than in America.

Figure 1 Supply Curves for Wheat, Britain and America

Figure 2 Equilibrium Prices Without Trade

(a) America

(b) Britain

Suppose that American wheat growers are free to deal with British buyers.[1] With trade, there will be a single supply curve for the combined wheat produced in America and Britain—$S_W = S_A + S_B$ in Figure 3. Similarly, with trade, there will be a combined demand curve for America and Britain that shows the combined quantity demanded by American and British buyers at every price—$D_W = D_A + D_B$ in Figure 3. The combined demand and supply curves with trade determine an equilibrium price, $\bar{P}_W$, in Figure 3. This is the price at which British and American growers can sell wheat, and the price for which British and American buyers can buy wheat with trade.

In America, the wheat trade raises the price of wheat from $\bar{P}_A$ (without trade) to $\bar{P}_W$ in Figure 4a. The higher price of wheat reduces the American quantity of wheat demanded and increases American wheat production. The wheat in excess of the domestic quantity demanded is exported to Britain. In Britain, the effects are the opposite of those in America. Trade lowers the British price from $\bar{P}_B$ (without trade) to $\bar{P}_W$ in Figure 4b. At the lower price, British buyers will demand a larger quantity of wheat than at the higher price, but British growers will reduce the quantity of wheat supplied. The excess demand for wheat in Britain at $\bar{P}_W$ is filled by importing American wheat.

The wheat trade between America and Britain thus had the following effects:

---

1. To keep things simple, ignore the costs of shipping wheat between America and Britain.

Figure 3 Equilibrium Price with Trade

1. Wheat production became more efficient. Trade encouraged higher levels of output from the superior American resources and lower levels of output from the inferior British resources.
2. The price of wheat rose in America as a result of the export demand.
3. The price of wheat fell in Britain as a result of wheat imports from America.

In terms of efficiency of wheat production, the wheat trade was a good thing, but efficiency isn't the only thing involved in assessing the effect of trade on the community's welfare.

The wheat trade benefited American farmers, suppliers of resources needed in American wheat production, and British consumers. American growers received higher prices, produced more wheat, and purchased more resource inputs than without trade. British consumers paid lower prices as a result of the trade.

However, trade didn't make everybody in Britain and America better off. In fact, it made some people in each country *worse* off than they were without trade. American consumers paid higher prices for wheat products. British wheat growers suffered as a result of lower prices, and the suppliers of resource inputs to British wheat production were worse off as production fell.

In short, since trade made some people better off and others worse off in each country, value judgements are required to say that trade is good or bad. The inability to resolve normative questions analytically accounts, in large part, for the durability of controversies concerning trade policy.

Now suppose that the British impose a tariff that protects all of the wheat farmers who were growing wheat prior to trade. This tariff would make imported wheat just as expensive as wheat grown in Britain. The tariff would reduce British wheat imports to zero, increase the quantity of wheat supplied by British farmers, and return Britain to the same position it was in without trade in Figure 2b.

The tariff also returns America to its no-trade position in Figure 2a. With the export demand gone, American producers will face the American demand curve only. The price of wheat in America falls, and the quantity of wheat produced in America declines as a result of the British tariff.

Effective tariffs tend to reduce efficiency. By shutting off the wheat trade, less wheat is produced with the superior American resources, and more wheat is produced with the inferior British resources. However, a value judgement is needed to say that the tariff is a good thing or a bad thing. The British farmers, the suppliers of inputs to British farmers, and American consumers are better off as a result of the tariff. American wheat farmers, the suppliers of inputs to American wheat farmers, and the British consumers of wheat products are worse off as a result of the tariff.

Tariffs and Gains from Trade

Tariffs tend to reduce the volume of a country's trade, the efficiency of production of affected goods, and the country's gains from trade. Without trade, the country in Figure 5a can consume any combination of wheat (W) and steel (S) on or inside its production possibilities curve. Suppose that combination A (11 million tons of wheat and

Figure 4 Effects of Trade

(a) America

(b) Britain

17 million tons of steel) achieves the highest possible level of economic welfare for the country without trade.

Given world prices of wheat ($P_w = \$40$ per ton) and steel ($P_S = \$20$ per ton), the maximum value of wheat and steel the country can produce is combination B (19 million tons of wheat and 12 million tons of steel). The value of combination B is $V_1 = \$1,000$ million. All combinations on the line V_1 also have this value at the given prices, so the country can use trade to move to any position along V_1. We'll assume that the country chooses to move to combination C by exporting 5 million tons of wheat and importing 10 million tons of steel.

Now, suppose that the steel producers' lobby convinces the government to impose a tariff of \$20 per ton on imported steel. The tariff raises the price of imported steel to domestic buyers from \$20 per ton to \$40 per ton (\$20 world price + tariff of \$20), and makes imported steel more expensive relative to wheat. The terms of trade shift from

$$\frac{\Delta S}{\Delta W} = \frac{P_W}{P_S} = \frac{\$40 \text{ per ton wheat}}{\$20 \text{ per ton steel}} = \frac{2S}{1W}$$

without the tariff to

$$\frac{\Delta S}{\Delta W} = \frac{P_W}{P_S + \text{tariff}} = \frac{\$40 \text{ per ton wheat}}{\$40 \text{ per ton steel}} = \frac{1S}{1W}$$

with the tariff.

With the new terms of trade in Figure 5b, the economy moves from point B on the production possibilities curve to point D as a result of

Figure 5 Tariffs and the Gains from Trade

(a) Without Tariff

(b) With Tariff

the tariff. At point D, the domestic marginal rate of transformation (MRT) equals the terms of trade with the tariff (the slope of the line segment tangent to the production possibilities curve is the terms of trade with the tariff. In world prices, the value of combination D (15 million tons of wheat and 16 million tons of steel) is $V_2 = \$92$ million. By exporting wheat and importing steel along V_2 to point E (the best combination for the community on V_2), steel imports fall by 2 million tons (from 22 million to 20 million), and domestic steel production increases from 12 million tons without the tariff to 16 million tons as a result of the tariff. This is a desirable result for the steel industry, but it is not the only effect of the tariff.

The tariff lowers the total value in world prices of wheat and steel produced from $100 million to $92 million, reducing the country's gains from trade. If the community chooses combination E on V_2, it will consume less steel and less wheat than with free trade. A reduction in both goods represents a loss of economic welfare to the community.

The tariff thus reduces but does not eliminate trade and the gains from trade. Combination E is better than combination A (the best for the community without trade), but not as desirable as combination C.

Import Quotas

Import quotas reduce imports by setting maximum quantities of goods that may be imported. Obviously, effective import quotas must be set below the level of imports with free trade.

The results of import quotas are the same as those of tariffs. Quotas restrict the supply of imported goods and thus tend to raise the prices of imported goods to domestic consumers. The increase in import prices reduces import competition for domestic producers.

Quotas also reduce the gains from trade. Suppose that, instead of a tariff, the country in Figure 5 limits steel imports to 4 million tons per year by a quota. The quota reduces steel imports by the same amount as the tariff in the previous example. Reducing steel imports raises domestic steel prices, and moves the economy along its production possibilities curve to point D. The terms of trade are altered by the higher prices of steel, just as they were by the tariff. However, at world prices, the value of combination D is only $V_2 = \$92$ million in Figure 5b. The effect of the reduction of imports by 2 million tons with a quota is the same as the effect of the tariff that reduced imports by 2 million tons.

The Case for Import Restriction

Most of the common arguments for policies to restrict imports sound plausible at first, but break down on closer examination. Import restrictions create winners who benefit from them and losers who are worse off, so most arguments for restricting imports involve value judgements at some point. Some arguments for restricting imports are valid in special circumstances but must be examined closely.

Protecting American Workers from Cheap Foreign Labor

Perhaps the most common argument for restricting imports asserts that imports force American labor to compete with foreign workers whose wages and living standards are much lower than those of American workers. The argument asserts that competition with "cheap foreign labor" from Japan, Taiwan, Hong Kong, or Singapore will force American workers out of work. A point usually not stated explicitly is that restricting imports would protect the managers and owners in affected industries as well as the workers.

Although the claim seems plausible, it is one of the weakest arguments for restricting imports. In the first place, one reason wages are comparatively high in the United States is that labor is scarce in the United States relative to other resources. American workers have more land and capital to work with, and thus output per worker-hour of labor will be higher than in the countries where labor is very abundant.

Generally, the workers and industries in the United States that have suffered as imports increased are *labor-intensive*—i.e., production uses large labor inputs relative to other resources. In such industries—for example, cameras, radios, stereo equipment, and textiles—the high wages of U.S. workers make it difficult to compete with imported goods from countries where labor is much cheaper.

On the other hand, the United States has a comparative advantage over countries with abundant labor in the production of goods that require large inputs of land and capital relative to the labor input. For example, the United States can produce most agricultural products more efficiently than Japan because of the abundance of land and capital in the United States. Agriculture and *capital-intensive industries* that use large capital inputs per unit of output would be hurt by import restrictions because their output would decline.

What if most of the goods we consumed could be produced more cheaply abroad and imported than they could be produced at home? Even in this case, the cheap foreign labor argument for import restrictions breaks down on closer examination. First of all, as we saw in the discussion of comparative advantage, it is possible (even likely) that the United States would have a comparative advantage in some products. But what if differences in costs were such that we imported much more from Japan than we exported to Japan? As this continued, the exchange rate between dollars and yen would change—the dollar would depreciate relative to the yen, and the yen would appreciate relative to the dollar. As the yen appreciates relative to the dollar, Japanese goods become more expensive to American buyers. Appreciation of the yen would thus offset the effects of low wages on the cost of imported goods from Japan.

Fair Competition

As a variation of the cheap foreign labor argument, some people advocate import restrictions to put domestic producers on equal footing with foreign producers, or to ensure fair competition between domestic products and competing imports. As in the cheap foreign labor argument, one of the most glaring omissions is the effect of cost advantages on exchange rates. If a country had a distinct cost advantage over the United States in the production of goods, and U.S. imports increased, the dollar would depreciate in international markets and make the imports more expensive to U.S. buyers.

If a tariff were enacted to equalize the cost of imports and domestically produced goods—consistent with the notion of fair competition—there would be no gains from trade. With no gains from trade, there would be no trade, and domestic producers would face no import competition.

Tariffs and Full Employment: "Beggar-My-Neighbor"

Tariffs are often argued for as possible solutions to sagging aggregate demand and unemployment in the domestic economy. This is an appealing argument intuitively and makes some sense in the context of the basic Keynesian model. Aggregate demand, you will recall, is $AD = C + I + G + X - M$. Aggregate demand varies directly with exports (X) and inversely with imports (M). It appears that reducing imports would raise aggregate demand and equilibrium income and reduce unemployment. What could be wrong with the *beggar-my-neighbor* approach to the unemployment problem?

In the first place, there is the important qualification so frequently left out—*other things must remain unchanged*. For the beggar-my-neighbor policy to work, exports must not fall as a result of the policies that reduce imports. If the United States restricts imports to raise aggregate demand, other countries are likely to respond by restricting their imports from the United States, reducing U.S. exports.

Even in the absence of retaliatory policies abroad, our import restrictions may cause aggregate demand to fall. For foreign countries, U.S. imports are their exports. If U.S. imports fall, exports and aggregate demand will fall in other countries. As aggregate demand falls in other countries, their demand for our exports will fall too. The decline in foreign demand for our exports would at least partially offset the effect of reduced imports on aggregate demand.

The fatal flaw in the beggar-my-neighbor approach is that import restrictions tend to reduce the export flow as well. Also, it is difficult to export unemployment if unemployment is a common problem in other countries—as it was in the 1930s when this argument for import restriction was most popular.

Tariffs as a Source of Tax Revenue

Tariffs are excise taxes on imports. Why not use tariffs to raise government revenue, and get foreign producers to help us pay our taxes? First, tariffs are excise taxes, and at least part of an excise tax is passed on to buyers as a higher price. So domestic consumers end up paying at least a share of the tax. Also, there is an obvious conflict between the effectiveness of a tariff as a means of protecting domestic producers and as a source of tax revenue. If the tariff effectively excluded imports, tax revenue from the tariff would be zero.

Infant Industries

A country may have the resources to develop an industry that could compete against import competition and compete successfully in world export markets, but the industry is so poorly developed that it may not even be able to compete against imports at home. If such an *infant industry* were protected by a tariff, it could develop and mature. As the infant matures under the protection of the tariff and becomes more efficient, the tariff would become unnecessary because imports would not be any cheaper than domestically produced goods. Also, once it matured, the industry could compete successfully in international markets.

As a temporary measure to stimulate development of an infant industry, import restrictions may be beneficial, especially in underdeveloped countries. There are some potential problems, however. The most obvious is to identify an infant industry that has a chance of maturing successfully with the country's resources. Also, the gains to the community in the future after the industry matures must be weighed against the cost to the community of protecting it temporarily from import competition. Finally, of course, there is the problem of deciding when the infant has grown up enough to be on its own. There is a danger that an overprotected infant industry may not mature at all.

National Security

Import restrictions have been advocated for some industries in the interest of national security. For industries that *are* critical for national security, protecting them to allow us to meet our minimal needs makes some sense, but there is a catch. What industries really *are* critical for national security? No self-respecting lobbyist would miss a chance to argue that his industry is essential to the national security, and that it should be protected from foreign competition.

Further, what are our minimal needs of critical materials and products? Industries seeking protection on the grounds of national security generally seek exclusion of import competition. In fact, it may be possible to provide for national security without import restrictions by stockpiling critical materials and products.

National security arguments for import restrictions have to be analyzed as closely as others. All import restrictions involve losses of both efficiency and gains from trade. Are the gains in national security worth the cost to the community? Is the industry really essential to the national security? Can minimal needs of critical products be met without import restrictions?

Export Policies

Trade policies don't deal exclusively with imports. Governments may enact policies that affect the level of a country's exports, in order to stimulate aggregate demand or dampen inflationary pressures.

Export Subsidies

A subsidy is just the opposite of an excise tax on producers. By paying producers a subsidy per unit of output, firms may be able to sell at a lower price. Figure 6 shows hypothetical demand and supply curves for wheat *exports*. With no subsidy, the equilibrium price of wheat exports is $\bar{P}$, and wheat exports are $\bar{W}$. Subsidizing wheat exports drives the supply curve downward by the amount of the subsidy, and the price falls to $\bar{P}'$, where the subsidized supply curve intersects the demand curve. Wheat exports increase from $\bar{W}$ to $\bar{W}'$ as a result.

The logic behind such subsidies is that lower prices on exports will increase exports and increase aggregate demand. There are, however, a number of questions and potential problems involved in export subsidies. First of all, it is possible that the entire subsidy will not be passed on as lower prices. In Figure 6, for example, the equilibrium price does not fall by the amount of the subsidy. The difference between $(\bar{P}' + s)$ and $\bar{P}$ is retained by sellers as a higher price than they received without the subsidy.

Secondly, lower prices for exports may not increase the country's revenue from exports. If the volume of our exports rises by a smaller percentage than the percentage decline in the price of exports, lower

Figure 6 Effects of Export Subsidy

prices will reduce export revenue. Only if a given percentage reduction in export prices leads to a greater percentage increase in exports would lower prices raise export income, other things constant.

A third potential problem is international retaliation in response to our export subsidies. Countries that are affected adversely by a U.S. export subsidy may impose higher tariffs on their imports from the United States or subsidize their exports that compete with U.S. exports in world markets. These reactions would reduce the demand for the subsidized exports and at least partially offset the effect of the subsidy on U.S. exports and export income.

Most arguments for export subsidy overlook the important question of the source of the funds to pay the subsidy. Subsidy payments will increase government spending. If they are covered by additional taxes, the additional taxes tend to offset any effect the export subsidy would have on aggregate demand. If taxes are not increased, the subsidy may have to come at the expense of spending on other public sector projects with a fixed budget. If the additional spending simply increases the deficit in the government budget, it may contribute to inflationary pressures, and domestic inflation may offset the effect of the subsidy on the price of the exports subsidized.

Like tariffs, export subsidies cause the prices and terms of trade to diverge from the world prices and terms of trade. They tend to reduce the value of goods produced by the economy (in world prices), and to reduce the country's gains from trade. Finally, like tariffs, export subsidies benefit those associated with the subsidized industries at the expense of others in the community. This, of course, means that value judgements concerning gains to winners vs. losses to losers are implicit in arguments that export subsidies are good or bad for the community.

Restricting Exports

In recent years, a number of export restrictions have been imposed on certain goods (wheat, logs, and soybeans for example) to dampen inflationary pressures in the domestic economy. The logic behind arguments for export controls is fairly clear. On the macroeconomic side, if demand-pull inflationary pressures can be traced to export demand, reducing exports and export income will dampen aggregate demand and demand-pull inflation. On the microeconomic side, heavy export demand in specific industries may contribute to rising domestic prices in these industries and to cost-push inflation in related industries and an export quota may reduce this pressure. Unfortunately, such results may be a matter of wishful thinking.

Consider, for example, the possible effects of an imposition of export quotas on wheat. Figure 7 shows the demand for U.S. wheat exports, the supply of U.S. wheat exports, the price of wheat exports, and the equilibrium level of wheat exports. Now, suppose that exports are restricted to W* in order to dampen inflationary pressures. The effect of the restriction on aggregate demand and demand-pull

Figure 7 Effects of Export Quota

inflationary pressures depends upon its effect on world wheat prices, and upon the responsiveness of world demand for American wheat exports to changes in price. The U.S. is a major wheat exporter, and restricting American wheat exports would tend to raise prices of wheat in world markets. Note in Figure 7 that restricting wheat exports to W^* raises wheat export prices from $\overline{P}$ to $\overline{P}'$. If wheat exports fall by a smaller percentage than price rises, then U.S. income from wheat exports would rise as a result of the export restriction and higher price, increasing inflationary pressures. Also, of course, effective export restrictions reduce the country's gains from trade.

The effectiveness of export controls in reducing cost-push inflationary pressures depends on their effects on domestic production and on international reaction to the export controls. Export controls on wheat, for example, would encourage farmers to divert their land to other crops—or conceivably to nonagricultural uses. These actions would reduce the supply of wheat to domestic consumers and raise wheat prices.

Like import restrictions, export controls may have unfavorable international repercussions. Suppose, for example, that the OPEC countries responded to reductions of United States wheat exports with an embargo on oil exports to the United States. This would drive oil prices and the prices of all oil products upward and generate cost-push inflation in the United States. The same thing would happen if the

OPEC nations raised the price of oil exported to other countries to compensate for the higher prices of wheat in world markets as a result of U.S. export restrictions.

Finally, of course, there are value judgements implicit in arguments for export controls to fight inflation. Export controls shift the burden of fighting inflation to the industries whose exports are restricted and the suppliers of inputs to those industries. This doesn't mean that export controls are bad for the community, but it does require a value judgement concerning the losses in the affected industries vs. gains to the rest of the community.

Trade Policy Problems and Issues of the 1980s

Trends in trade policy in the 1970s were schizophrenic. On the one hand, the trend toward liberalization of trade that had begun in the 1960s continued in the 1970s, culminating in a new multilateral trade agreement in 1979 that lowered tariff and nontariff barriers to trade. On the other hand, slowing economic growth and recessions in the industrialized countries led to growing sentiment for protectionism to deal with domestic unemployment. These conflicting forces of liberalization and protection will continue to shape trade policy in this decade, and perhaps for the remainder of the century. Within this framework, there are a number of key issues and problems facing trade policy.

Dealing with OPEC

When Iran, Iraq, Kuwait, Saudi Arabia, and Venezuela formed the *Organization of Petroleum Exporting Countries* in 1960 to protect the interests of the oil producing countries against those of the multinational corporations who extracted and refined the oil, almost no attention was paid to it. Certainly, there was no alarm that OPEC could affect economic conditions in the United States. In 1970, OPEC (which had grown to 13 countries) agreed on a unified pricing system for oil exports, marking the birth of OPEC as a *cartel*.

- **Cartels** are groups of sellers who agree formally on common prices and terms of sale for their product.

During the 1970s a series of events pushed the OPEC benchmark price from $1.80 per barrel in 1970 to a maximum of $23 a barrel by mid 1979. Although it had been largely unnoticed in the 1960s, OPEC has emerged as the most important force in the international economy, and OPEC decisions are important determinants of prosperity or recession in the industrialized countries that depend on imported oil.

Anger and frustration have led many to propose "trade war" responses to OPEC actions—embargoes on exports to OPEC, boycotting OPEC oil imports, an international cartel of oil importers, etc.—to counter the power of OPEC as a seller of oil. None of these stand much chance of success in breaking the power of OPEC in world markets, and each would impose great costs on the oil importing countries. Countries that have no domestic oil sources can't become self-sufficient, and the costs of self-sufficiency in countries like the United States that can provide a substantial part of their own oil would be very great. Shutting off exports of agricultural and manufactured goods to OPEC countries isn't a realistic alternative because it would depress employment and income in the industrial countries. Cartels are only as strong as their weakest link, and a cartel of oil importers would be only as strong as the willingness of the countries with the greatest need for imported oil to hold out.

What then is the best way of dealing with the high prices of imported oil? It's easy to blame OPEC for our energy problems, but OPEC couldn't command such high prices for their oil if the demand by oil importing countries weren't so great. We have to recognize that the only way to respond effectively to high oil prices is to economize on the use of oil, a solution that is both obvious and unpleasant. At the Tokyo economic summit in 1979, the major industrial importers of oil—the United States, Japan, France, Germany, Britain, and Canada—agreed to put ceilings on future oil imports as a response to the decision of OPEC in June, 1979, to raise the price of oil exports for the second time during that year. What does this imply for the economies of these countries?

It would be nice if the demand for oil could be replaced easily by alternative sources of energy that are safe and clean, but this isn't likely. Alternatives to oil are in an early stage of development and are expensive. Extracting oil from shale, for example, wouldn't be economical unless the price of OPEC oil rose another fifty percent or so. Increased use of coal is an economically feasible solution, if we ignore or undervalue the environmental costs of extracting and burning more coal. The social costs and risks of nuclear power became painfully obvious in the Three-Mile Island "incident" in 1979. Massive use of solar and wind power and the development of clean and safe synthetic fuels has great potential as a source of energy in the twenty-first century, but not now.

For the majority of the population in the industrialized countries, oil conservation will take the forms of slow economic growth, changes in living standards and lifestyles, and more modest economic expectations. Smaller cars, smaller and more energy-efficient houses, less heat in the winter, less air conditioning in the summer, more mass transit, and less recreational automobile travel are some of the less appealing forms that energy conservation will take for most of us.

Dumping

Dumping is a rather uncomplimentary term for exporting goods at "unfair" prices. The criteria for identifying dumping vary somewhat from case to case, but the most typical criteria are charging prices for exports below the cost of production and charging lower prices for exports than the prices of the goods in the exporting country's domestic market. Legislation allows the President and the Congress to take specific actions against the dumping of exports in the United States. If dumping is confirmed, anti-dumping penalties are assessed equal to the difference between the price of the good in the exporters' home market and the price paid by American importers.

Why would exporters dump their goods at a low price? If they face greater competition in export markets than in domestic markets, and if the domestic and export markets can be separated, it may be more profitable to sell at a lower price in the export market than in the domestic market. Producers who overestimate demand for their goods and over produce may temporarily dump the goods by charging a low price to reduce inventories—in the same way that department stores "dump" goods by holding sales to reduce inventories.

Most anti-dumping arguments are standard protectionist fare—specifically, variations of the unfair competition arguments for protection. The standard argument against dumping is that the American economy is injured as a result of losing employment and income to unfairly priced imports. This argument fails to answer two basic questions that are central to its validity. First, what is the line that divides unfair dumping and vigorous price competition in export markets, and who is to decide what's fair? Secondly, what is so harmful to the economy about a form of price discrimination that benefits consumers in the United States?

There is one reasonable case that can be made for anti-dumping actions. Even though foreign firms may dump goods with no other purpose than reducing inventories by lowering price, this can create temporary disruptions for American producers who compete with the imports for sales. Anti-dumping penalties reduce the ability of the foreign seller to do this and reduce the disruptions of employment in import-competing industries in the United States. There is a cost, of course. American consumers won't be able to take advantage of temporary bargains offered by importers.

Routine anti-dumping complaints by import-competing industries, however, stem from basically protectionist motives. If the anti-dumping actions are successful, exporters will be hesitant to offer lower prices for the goods they ship to the United States. Even if anti-dumping suits aren't successful, however, they can create a negative public image of the imported goods as harmful of American economic welfare and can be relatively effective means of harassing foreign exporters and domestic importers from cutting prices on imports.

Trade Policy and International Politics

International trade, trade policy, and international politics have been intertwined for centuries. In some cases, trade policies are enacted to bring pressure and hardship on politically hostile regimes, such as the United States embargo on trade with Cuba since the late 1950s. In other cases, trade policies are used to protest policies of other governments and to bring pressure on these governments to alter policies—for example, the Arab embargo on oil exports to the United States in 1973 and the United States trade sanctions against Rhodesia to protest racial and human rights policies.

The relationship between trade policy and international political relationships is a vast subject. Without getting into the merits of protesting another country's government, human rights policies, etc., through trade policy, the important economic consequence is that these actions generally impose costs on the country imposing the sanctions as well as the sanctioned country. Imposing an export embargo reduces aggregate demand, aggregate output, and employment in the country that imposes the embargo. Barring imports from a sanctioned country reduces the gains from trade for the country imposing the sanctions by reducing the availability of lower-priced imports—as for example, the Rhodesian sanctions eliminated United States imports of chrome from Rhodesia.

The Tokyo Round and Future Trade Policy

In April, 1979, 99 countries signed a multilateral trade agreement that culminated the Tokyo Round of Multilateral Trade Negotiations. The agreement sets the rules for foreign trade policy for at least the next decade, and perhaps for the remainder of the twentieth century. Despite growing protectionist sentiments in many of the industrialized countries, the new trade agreement sets rules that would liberalize trade considerably over a period of years.

Tariffs are to be reduced by an average of one-third in the next eight to ten years. Some "sensitive" industries—such as the steel industry in the United States—would be given the most time over which tariffs would be cut.

Lowering tariffs is a step toward freer trade, but not as important as restricting the use of nontariff barriers. In recent years, nontariff barriers to free trade—subsidizing exports, subsidizing domestic producers to exclude imports, product safety requirements designed to exclude foreign products, import quotas, "orderly marketing arrangements" that reduce imports, barring foreign bidders from government procurement contracts, etc.—have become increasingly important as methods of restricting trade. The 1979 agreement sets specific limits on the use of nontariff restrictions as well as lowering tariffs. This is the first trade agreement that has restricted nontariff barriers.

How Free Foreign Trade?

If free trade or more restrictions on trade were good for everybody, or at least made nobody worse off, there would be no controversy over trade policy. However, controversies persist because greater restriction of trade or greater liberalization of trade would make some members of the community better off, others worse off, and affect the efficiency of world production.

On the grounds of efficiency alone, the case for free trade is compelling. All trade restrictions—regardless of their professed objectives—involve some loss of efficiency. If trade restrictions were lifted everywhere in the world, the long-run trend would be toward greater efficiency of utilization of the world's resources.

Adjusting to Freer Trade

Even the strongest advocates of free trade have to recognize that lowering trade barriers won't be good for everybody, and that the liberalization of trade restrictions will create economic problems for industries that face increased competition from imports. The industries that face stiffer import competition may have to cut back on production and employment, creating obvious problems for workers employed in these industries and for the communities in which these industries are large employers. At the same time, however, lower trade barriers internationally will increase world demand for the products of industries that enjoy a comparative advantage and had been excluded from world markets by import restrictions in other countries. If resources are mobile, higher demand in the expanding export industries will attract workers from the declining import-competing industries. Of course, the reallocation of resources can't be done overnight or without costs. If trade barriers were eliminated abruptly, and no additional measures were taken to aid affected industries and communities, the long-run gains from trade may be overshadowed by short-run disruptions and costs.

This does not mean that protection and the inefficiency and costs that result from protection have to be continued indefinitely to avoid the short-run costs of liberalization of trade. It does suggest that liberalization of trade restrictions should lower barriers over a period of time to minimize the short-run disruptive effects on protected industries. It also suggests that assistance should be provided to compensate workers and communities affected adversely by imports and to facilitate the reallocation of resources to the expanding export industries.

Trade policy and legislation in the United States since the 1960s has provided assistance for industries and communities who bear economic hardships as a result of liberalization of trade. Adjustment assistance has been in the forms of retraining and relocation programs for workers and public works programs for adversely affected communities. Over the years, the requirements for adjustment assistance have been liberalized, and the assistance is more accessible now than it has been in the past.

It's impossible to compensate individuals and communities fully for the costs of adjusting to economic changes that result from liberalized trade. Communities are disrupted, and many communities lose a vital part of their population as young workers are retrained and leave the community for employment elsewhere. Community ties, friendships, and family relationships may be disrupted. Individuals leave familiar communities to take advantage of employment opportunities in unfamiliar cities and different industries. However, the only way to avoid these psychological costs would be to continue protection indefinitely, in which case society bears the costs of inefficiency, higher costs and prices, and loss of employment opportunities in exporting industries.

Close-up

"On Sudden Changes in the Channels of Trade"

Trade policy was a central issue—perhaps *the* central issue—in the development of classical economics. Adam Smith's *Wealth of Nations* is an eloquent critique of eighteenth-century British mercantilism. The issue that prodded David Ricardo to formulate the backbone of classical economics in his *Principles of Political Economy and Taxation* was the protection of British landowners by the *Corn Laws*, a tariff against imports of low-priced foreign wheat.

Ricardo was unswerving in his opposition to the Corn Laws and other forms of protection, but conceded that there would be short-run disruptions if trade barriers were eliminated abruptly. In fact, he devoted a chapter of his *Principles* to this problem—On Sudden Changes in the Channels of Trade. With uncharacteristic clarity, Ricardo recognized the need for temporary measures to minimize the disruption from liberalizing trade.

> Notwithstanding, then, that it would be more productive of wealth to the country, at whatever the sacrifice of capital it might be done, to allow the importation of cheap corn [wheat], it would, perhaps, be advisable to charge it with a duty for a few years.[1]

Of those who advocated permanent protection for domestic wheat producers, however, Ricardo remained critical.

> They do not see that the end of all commerce is to increase production, and that, by increasing production, though you may occasion partial loss, you increase the general happiness.

A more recent example of the short-term costs of "sudden changes in the channels of trade" can be seen by leaping from England in the 1820s to Greece in 1979. Greece should become a member of the European Economic Community (or *Common Market*) on January 1, 1981. This will increase import competition for some Greek industries and will expand the export opportunities for others. Some industries are attempting to minimize the short-term costs of chang-

---

1. David Ricardo, *Principles of Political Economy and Taxation*, Third Edition. London: 1821, Chapter 19.

ing trade relationships with the Common Market countries by preparing for it rather than adjusting to it after it comes.

Greek appliance producers are preparing for import competition from the more efficient producers in the Common Market by undertaking a major drive to increase efficiency: laying off workers, consolidating operations, closing down plants, and other measures. The consensus in Greece is that employment in many manufacturing industries will decline with entry into the Common Market. However, in other industries—textiles, for example—firms will enjoy a wider export market in Europe, and employment in these industries will increase as a result of Common Market membership.[2]

2. Facts on the Greek appliance industry are from Philip Revzin, "Greek Companies Try to Shape Up to Enter the Common Market in '81," *Wall Street Journal*, May 18, 1979, p. 1.

The Future of Free Trade

It seems likely that the long-term trend will be toward freer international trade rather than more trade restrictions. Growing world population, rising expectations, and a growing realization that the planet's resources are finite make efficiency considerations increasingly important. This strengthens the case for international specialization and trade. However, in the short run, this will require efforts to minimize the costs of trade liberalization through retraining and even relocation.

It may be tempting, recognizing the limitations of monetary and fiscal policies, to look to the international sector to control domestic unemployment and inflation. This can be a dangerous course, however, and would probably create more domestic economic problems than it would solve.

Summary

1. Import restrictions generally raise the price of imports to consumers, reduce international efficiency, and reduce the gains from trade. They benefit the protected sectors of the economy.
2. The most common arguments for import restrictions are to protect domestic wages, promote full employment, and allow fair competition. Most are only partially correct and contain serious flaws. National security and infant industry arguments for import restrictions may be valid but must be examined closely.
3. Export subsidies try to increase exports by making them cheaper in international markets. The benefits go largely to the subsidized industries, and the costs of the subsidy are borne by the community.
4. Export restrictions may reduce excess demand and dampen cost-push inflationary pressures, but their effectiveness depends on many variables.
5. The persistent trade policy problems for the 1980s and beyond will be the high prices of oil imports, dumping, export subsidies, and moving toward a world with lower trade barriers.

6. Liberalization of world trade will improve efficiency in the utilization of the world's resources, but won't be beneficial to everybody, particularly in the short run. Some of the short-run disruptions and costs of liberalized trade can be reduced by assistance to industries, communities, and individuals who are injured economically as a result of lower trade barriers.

Concepts for Review

mercantilism
tariff
import quota
fair competition
infant industry
export subsidy
cartel
dumping
Tokyo Round

Questions

1. Textile workers, textile firms, and congressional representatives from textile producing states have protested imports of textiles from such countries as Hong Kong, Singapore, Korea, and Taiwan. The general complaint is that U.S. workers can't compete with the cheap foreign labor, and that textile imports contribute to domestic unemployment.
   a. To what extent is this a valid argument?
   b. Would a tariff on textile imports reduce domestic unemployment?
   c. Would you expect U.S. farmers to join in the demand for tariffs on textile imports?
2. "Self-sufficiency in energy" and "independence from foreign oil producers" were frequently stated as policy goals by the Nixon, Ford, and Carter administrations.
   a. What kinds of policies would achieve these objectives? What would be the costs and the benefits of these policies? Who would realize the benefits, and who would bear the costs?
   b. How many (if any) of the arguments for import restrictions would apply to restriction of oil imports?
   c. How would policies to ensure energy independence affect the domestic economic goals of full employment and stable prices?
3. Suppose that you are the first witness before a congressional committee to testify against a proposed program of import restrictions and export subsidies to reduce unemployment. You have been preceded by a number of witnesses testifying in favor of the proposal—union leaders, automobile producers, textile firms, the city of Detroit, etc. Construct your economic argument against the proposed program. You should point out the economic, and political consequences of the program, as well as the value judgments involved.
4. "Free trade is a joke and a myth... The answer is fair trade, do unto others as they do unto us—barrier for barrier—closed door for closed door." (George Meany, President AFL-CIO, December, 1977).
   a. How would you interpret the term *fair trade*?
   b. What are the implications of Mr. Meany's proposal for trade policy, for efficiency in production, for consumers, for import-competing industries, and for industries dependent on exports? Would Mr. Meany's proposed trade policy be good for the economy?
5. *Trigger prices* have been established on imports by the Treasury Department, based on the cost of production in the country that

produces the good most efficiently, plus costs of transportation. If prices of an imported good fall below its trigger price, importers are charged the difference between the import price and the trigger price.
   a. What practice is the trigger price designed to discourage?
   b. What are the implications of trigger prices for import-competing producers and domestic consumers?
6. "The way to achieve full employment is to promote our exports in world markets while restricting the imports that take jobs away from our workers." (Congressman I. M. Phogbound, Whig, Vermont).
Evaluate the merits of this strategy for trade policy.

Problems

1. Suppose that America produces two goods, steel (S) and wheat (W). With no trade, America produces on its production-possibilities curve where $MRT = 2S/1W$, and the prices of wheat in America without trade are $50 per ton of wheat and $100 per ton of steel. In international markets, the price of wheat is $80 per ton and the price of steel is $80 per ton.
   a. Would America benefit from trading at world prices? What should America export and what should she import? What would be the nature of the gains from trade?
   b. Would everybody in America benefit from trade? Who would benefit and who would be hurt by free trade?
   c. American steel producers argue that a $20 per ton tariff on steel is needed to protect American producers from unfair import competition. Would America benefit from trading if such a tariff were imposed? What happens to the gains from trade? What other consequences might follow the imposition of the tariff?
   d. Evaluate the desirability of the tariff from the points of view of American steelworkers, wheat farmers, steel stockholders, manufacturers of fabricated steel products, and consumers.
2. Foreign governments are often accused of unfair competition by subsidizing exports to allow exporters to sell at lower prices in world markets.
   a. Why would a foreign government subsidize exports?
   b. How effective would export subsidies be in maintaining high levels of aggregate demand, output, and employment in the exporting country? Explain analytically.

PART TWELVE
The Economic Future

In his October 1979 speech before the General Assembly of the United Nations, Cuban Premier Fidel Castro called for a "new economic order," a redistribution of the world's wealth from the richer countries to the poorer ones. The demand for fundamental changes in the economic relationships among nations is a growing one which no responsible person can ignore. In this final section of the text, we will explore the economic outlook for the future.

We begin with the issue of **economic growth**. Much of this nation's success has stemmed from its ability to enlarge the economic "pie" faster than the increase in the number of eaters. Today, however, many people are asking some fundamental questions about the desirability of further economic growth. Have the costs begun to outweigh the benefits? Can environmental concerns be reconciled with sustained growth? Can and should growth continue? Answers to such questions depend ultimately on value judgments, but close study of the issues involved can help make your own judgments informed ones.

The second chapter of the section focuses on the problem of **world poverty**. With thousands of people the world over starving to death every day, and *billions* more barely subsisting, the problem is not one that can be easily solved. Combatting poverty through **economic development** will impose major costs on all nations, rich and poor alike, but failure to pay those costs could lead eventually to world catastrophe.

The final chapter of the text explores some alternatives to the market economy, focusing in particular on the **centrally planned economy**, in which the key economic decisions of *what*, *how*, and *for whom* are made by individuals rather than impersonal market forces. Our examination of the economic future closes with a look at the so-called **convergence hypothesis** that all the world's economies are in fact evolving toward a single model.

35

Economic Growth: Boon or Bane?

Preview: Living standards in the industrialized countries have changed more in the two centuries since the beginning of the industrial revolution than they had in the previous millennia since the dawn of human civilization. At the same time, the current populations of societies untouched by industrialization and growth enjoy living standards similar to those of their distant ancestors. Do the past benefits of economic growth mean that we can rely on economic growth to raise living standards and solve economic problems in the future? In this chapter, we'll explore some of the basic concepts necessary to approach intelligently the brewing controversy over economic growth.

What Is Economic Growth?

In popular terminology, economic growth means changes in GNP. All changes in GNP do not constitute economic growth in the sense that economists use the term, however. Increases in GNP during a recovery from an economic recession are quite different from those which occur as a result of expanding productive capacity.

- **Economic growth** refers to changes over time in a country's potential or full-employment GNP.

Output and Capacity

Suppose that goods are classified as consumer goods (C) and capital goods (K). The economy's production possibilities curve (PPC), labeled K^*C^* in Figure 1, defines its capacity to produce consumer and capital goods. Any combination on the PPC represents full employment of capacity, and any combination inside the PPC indicates underemployment of capacity.

Given the prices of consumer goods (P_c) and capital goods (P_k), any combination of goods will generate a GNP (Y) of

Figure 1 Growth and Production Possibilities

$$Y = P_c C + P_k K. \tag{1}$$

In Figure 1, combination A, with C_a units of consumer goods and K_a units of capital goods per year, yields a GNP of $Y_a = P_c C_a + P_k K_a$. Other outputs that yield the same GNP lie on the line Y_a in Figure 1. Y_a does not employ the economy's capacity fully, since combinations on the PPC lie outside Y_a.

The maximum GNP that can be produced at the given prices in Figure 1 is $Y_b = P_c C_b + P_k K_b$. Increasing GNP from Y_a to Y_b represents a rise in real GNP, but there is no change in capacity or potential GNP. This change in real GNP represents *increased utilization of capacity*, and not economic growth.

To increase GNP beyond Y_b, capacity would have to expand. Suppose that an expansion of capacity moves the PPC to $K^{**}C^{**}$, and GNP increases to $Y_d = P_c C_d + P_k K_d$. This represents an increase in the country's potential GNP at the given prices, or economic growth.

Changes in Potential and Real GNP

Distinguishing a change in productive capacity from an increased utilization of capacity is easy in the simplified example above, but actually measuring growth of potential GNP empirically is not so easy. One common measure of economic growth in the U.S. is the growth of the *estimated potential GNP*. The President's Council of Economic Advisors (CEA) estimates the U.S. potential GNP as the GNP that would be reached with a measured unemployment rate of 5.1 percent of the labor force.

Since the CEA defines *full employment* as a measured rate of 5.1 percent of the labor force, potential GNP is in fact an estimate of the country's *full-employment GNP*. Increases in the estimated potential GNP due to higher labor productivity, growth of the labor force, etc., approximate changes in capacity and economic growth.

The most common year-to-year indicators of economic growth are changes in *real GNP* and changes in *per capita real GNP*. These are more meaningful indicators of growth than changes in nominal GNP or nominal GNP per capita. For example, the nominal GNP of the United States increased by about 5 percent between 1969 and 1970 (from $930.3 billion to $977.1 billion). In constant prices, however, real GNP fell by about 0.4 percent (from $752.6 billion to $722.5 billion).

Since economic growth is promoted as a means of raising living standards, changes in per capita real GNP are important indicators of growth. If GNP rises more slowly than the rate of population growth, per capita output of goods and services and living standards will decline over time—even though real GNP is rising.

Annual changes in real GNP and per capita real GNP do not measure economic growth alone. Generally, they reflect a mixture of expansion of capacity and increased utilization of capacity.

Sources of Growth

A number of important variables determine capacity and potential GNP. These *sources of growth*, however, also define *limits* on economic growth.

Quantity and Quality of Resources

Expansion of the resource base and improvements in the quality of resources represented a major source of economic growth in the United States and in the industrialized economies of Europe through the end of the 19th century. As the American frontier pushed westward, new industrial and agricultural resources were added to the economy's resource base, and in many instances the quality of the new resources was superior to that of existing resources.

Scarcity of labor throughout the 19th century led to liberal immigration policies, which expanded productive capacity by increasing the labor force. At the same time, the new imperialism gave industrialized nations both the means (by providing an expanded base of resources) and the motive (by providing a growing market for the growing output of goods) to expand productive capacity.

As long as resources could be increased by expanding frontiers or tapping external sources, scarcities of resources were not very obvious. *Unlimited* was a term used well into the 20th century to describe supplies of vital resources. As external sources were developed and frontiers closed, however, the scarcity of resources became increasingly apparent.

Wasting resources—such as oil, metallic ores, and coal—cannot be replenished as they are used up. It takes nature millions of years to make coal, iron ore, and oil. Once the reserves of wasting resources are known and developed, sustaining growth depends heavily on improved utilization and more thorough extraction. The current energy crisis is a long-term problem that has increased awareness of the scarcity of resources to the point that some people predict that growth and even production will eventually grind to a halt as resources are depleted. However, the quantity and quality of resources are not the only sources of economic growth.

Technology

Technological change comes from new scientific discoveries that can be applied to production and from the discovery of new applications of existing knowledge to production. Technological change makes it possible to produce greater outputs from given resource inputs and has been the major source of economic growth in the industrialized countries since the early 20th century.

Although many people have a nearly unlimited faith in the ability of technology to sustain economic growth, in truth even this seeming "sure-cure" is not without its problems. First, modern agricultural and industrial technology is relatively *energy intensive*, using relatively large amounts of energy per unit of output. The replacement of human, animal, wind, and water power with machines powered by electricity, coal, gas, and oil is one of the dominant themes in the evolution of modern technology. Unless future technological changes are energy saving, however, there will be a race between energy-intensive technology and diminishing reserves of energy resources.

- To sustain economic growth, technological change must expand productive capacity more rapidly than the depletion of basic inputs contracts it.

The technological changes most likely to sustain growth in a world of finite resources are those that reduce the drain on fossil fuel reserves without imposing prohibitive environmental and social costs. New technologies that would produce a larger share of energy needs from the wind, water, and sun would reduce the depletion of resources.

Second, most technological changes that increase capacity also impose costs on the community. The costs and benefits of nuclear generation of electric power provide a good case in point. Nuclear power plants reduce the drain on fossil fuels to produce electric power. At the same time, however, they impose substantial costs on the community in the forms of the risk of accidents or environmental damage and the costs of safe and effective disposal of wastes.

Investment and Capital Formation

Expansion of the capital stock expands capacity, so investment and capital formation are important sources of economic growth.

- The greater the current level of investment, the greater will be the future growth of capacity and output.

Of course, investment requires saving, and increasing current investment for future growth thus requires reductions in current levels of consumption. If voluntary saving is insufficient to generate desired levels of investment and growth, it may be necessary to restrict consumption and force saving. The problems of generating sufficient saving and investment are most difficult in countries where current incomes and living standards are very low—as in the Soviet Union in the 1930s and in many underdeveloped countries today.

Education and Human Capital

The stock of productive skills and abilities—or the stock of *human capital*—is a determinant of capacity and potential GNP. A well educated and trained labor force will be more productive and adaptable than an illiterate and unskilled labor force of the same size.

Education and training programs that improve the quality and productivity of the labor force represent investments in human capital, and they can be an important source of economic growth. Like other types of investment and capital formation, investments in human capital require current costs to generate future growth.

Close-up

Resources, Productivity, and U.S. Economic Growth

Growth of capacity and output requires increasing inputs of productive resources or increasing the productivity of resources. Increasing resource inputs by 10 percent with no change in productivity of resources will cause a 10 percent rise in aggregate output. However, if the productivity of resources doubles—for example, due to a technological change—output will rise by 20 percent if resource inputs increase by 10 percent. As our resource base has become fully developed, increasing resource inputs have made a decreasing contribution to economic growth, while the importance of rising productivity has become increasingly important. The table below tells the story clearly.

Future economic growth will depend even more heavily on productivity than has past economic growth. A generation of steadily declining birth rates and the depletion of critical natural resources—oil and fossil fuels in particular—mean that future economic growth will depend more and more heavily on our ability to increase the output per unit of resource input. This would indicate a rising priority for research and development in such areas as energy-efficient production methods and equipment, development of energy sources that don't depend heavily on fossil fuels, more efficient forms of economic organization, and of course raising educational and training levels of the labor force.

Contributions of factor inputs and productivity to the growth of net national product, 1840–1960

Contributions of	1840–1960	1840–1900	1900–1960
Panel 1: Average Annual Rates of Growth			
(1) Labor force	1.52%	1.88%	1.12%
(2) Land supply	.21	.38	.08
(3) Capital stock	.81	1.03	.60
(4) Productivity	1.02	.69	1.32
(5) Totals (growth of NNP)	3.56%	3.98%	3.12%
Panel 2: Percentage Distributions			
(1) Labor force	42.7%	47.2%	34.8%
(2) Land supply	5.9	9.6	2.5
(3) Capital stock	22.8	25.9	18.6
(4) Productivity	28.6	17.3	44.1
(5) Totals	100.0%	100.0%	100.0%

Source: Table 2.12, p. 39, in "The Pace and Pattern of American Economic Growth," from *American Economic Growth*, by Lance E. Davis, et al. Copyright © 1972 by Harper & Row Publishers, Inc. Reprinted by permission of the publisher.

Growth and Welfare

Advocates of economic growth from Adam Smith to the present have argued that growth is essential to improve the economic welfare of the community. However, the impact of economic growth on welfare depends on both the benefits *and* the costs of growth. If the benefits and costs are unevenly distributed among members of the community, moreover, value judgements are implicit in conclusions that growth is good or bad.

Growth and Living Standards

If *everybody* is to have a larger piece of pie than he or she now has, a larger pie obviously is required. This simple fact illustrates an important point concerning growth and living standards: if everybody is to have more goods and services, capacity and output must grow.

However, the *possibility* of raising everybody's standard of living through economic growth does not mean that growth necessarily *will* raise living standards for everybody. The effect of growth on living standards depends on the types of goods that account for the growth, and the distribution of the growing output among members of the community.

If real GNP is growing due to rising output of heavy industrial equipment and military hardware, for example, the living standards of the current population may not improve at all. It is also quite possible that the segments of the community that benefit most from growth are those with relatively high incomes and living standards. Those without the necessary education, training, and employable skills may benefit relatively little—or even be worse off.

Growth, Employment, and Inflation

The relatively high unemployment rates in the U.S. in the mid 1970s have been due in part to the fact that aggregate demand and real GNP have not grown fast enough to employ a growing labor force. The labor force has been growing largely as a result of greater labor force participation by women and others who generally had low participation rates in the past.

With unemployed capacity, basically Keynesian fiscal policies and discretionary monetary policies may stimulate aggregate demand and raise real GNP and employment. However, eventually, increasing aggregate demand to employ a growing labor force requires expansion of capacity.

Growth, the Environment, and Social Costs

One of the most dramatic costs of economic growth is environmental damage. A growth-at-any-cost strategy could involve massive environmental destruction due to such things as strip mining of coal and oil-bearing shale, proliferation of nuclear power plants, greater use of chemical fertilizers and pesticides, etc.

Many environmental pressure groups tend to emphasize a number of intangible environmental costs of growth—such as loss of wildlife, aesthetic damage, and blight. These *are* important costs of growth, but in addition *the environment is a resource.* Massive destruction of the environment to foster growth in the immediate future may be self-defeating over the long haul if environmental damage reduces the potential to expand production.

Some of the means of increasing capacity and output increase the risk of physical harm to consumers of the products. Steroids, for example, made it possible to increase meat output by speeding weight gain in cattle. Insecticides, herbicides, and chemical fertilizers contributed to growing output of many field crops. Research has shown, however, that residues of some steroids, insecticides, herbicides, and other agricultural chemicals remain in food products and are related to cancer.

Simply consuming a growing output of goods also imposes environmental and social costs. The growth of automobile production and the increasing numbers of cars on the road has had a devastating effect on the quality of the air—especially in areas with heavy automobile use. Consuming more goods creates more garbage and waste as well. Growing communities often find themselves hard pressed to dispose of their wastes. Traffic jams, air pollution, litter, and garbage are just as much the products of economic growth as are higher levels of output and consumption. The unpleasant or harmful externalities of growth reduce the community's benefits from the increased output.

Distribution of Benefits and Costs

Finding the proper balance of costs and benefits of growth is complicated by the fact that these costs and benefits are unevenly distributed. Many of those who bear heavy costs of growth get few of the benefits, and many of those that benefit bear relatively little cost.

Technological change, for example, makes some products and occupations obsolete. Unless the workers who are displaced by technological change move into jobs created by growth, they will bear costs but gain no benefits from growth. Workers already employed in industries and occupations that experience rising demand due to economic growth will bear relatively little cost to enjoy the benefits of growth.

If future growth comes at the expense of current consumption and living standards, some of those who bear the current costs may not live long enough to enjoy future benefits proportional to their costs. Future generations will enjoy the benefits of growth, but none of the current costs. During the ruthless Stalinist growth strategy in the U.S.S.R. between 1928 and 1953, an entire generation bore enormous costs and reaped meager benefits from Soviet economic growth.

The uneven incidence of costs and benefits of growth requires value judgments to be made concerning the importance of the benefits to the winners and the costs to the losers from any particular growth strategy. It may also require taxation of the winners to compensate the losers for their costs.

Can Growth Continue?

A surprising number of great economists have predicted that economic growth must and will come to an end eventually. The *stationary state* (an economy with no growth) is a common theme in classical economics. Karl Marx predicted that certain features of capitalist development would bring growth to a halt. In the 20th century, similar conclusions have been reached by *secular stagnationists* and others that growth can't continue indefinitely. On the other side of the issue are those who argue that expansion of knowledge, technological change, and expanding investment opportunities will sustain growth in the future.

The Classical Prognosis: The Stationary State

The classical prediction of an eventual stationary state with no economic growth rests on three basic propositions.

1. Investment is the source of growth of employment and real output.

2. Profits are the source of investment.
3. With fixed land and given technology, goods will be produced under diminishing returns.

To understand the classical argument, suppose that real GNP (Y) is divided between wages (W) and profits (π), or

$$Y = W + \pi. \tag{2}$$

Real GNP and wages vary directly with the level of employment (N). With diminishing returns, GNP will increase at a diminishing rate as employment increases, as in Figure 2. Assuming a constant wage rate, wages rise at a constant rate with increases in employment, as shown in Figure 2.

Aggregate profits (π) are the difference between GNP and wages, or

$$\pi = Y - W. \tag{3}$$

In an initial period (1), employment is N_1, GNP is Y_1, and wages are N_1. Profits in period 1 are $\pi_1 = Y_1 - W_1$, or the vertical distance between W_1 and Y_1.

The profits in period 1 provide investment funds to expand the capital stock and raise the level of employment to N_2 in period 2. In period 2, GNP rises to Y_2, and profits are: π_2. Profits in period 2 allow employment and income to rise to N_3 and Y_3 in period 3, and so on.

Figure 2 The Classical Stationary State

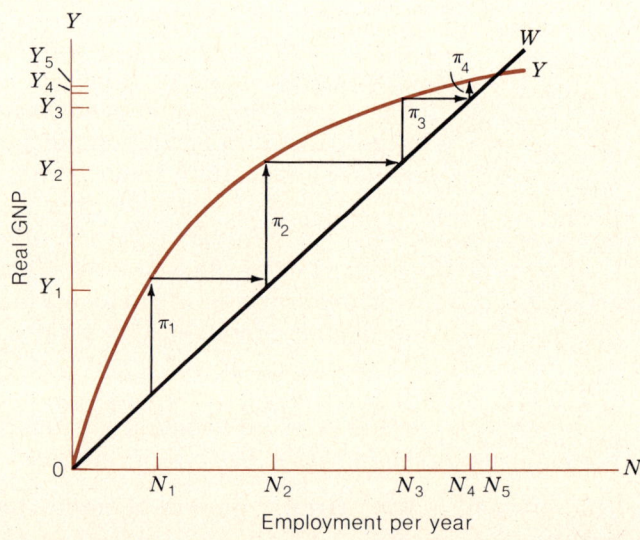

Diminishing returns eventually cause profits to fall as employment and GNP increase, as shown in Figure 2. Eventually, profits reach zero—at N_5 and Y_5 in Figure 2—and the stationary state is reached.

- In the classical **stationary state,** profits are zero, and there is no economic growth.

The Marxian Prognosis: "Fetters on Production"

Karl Marx, the great critic of capitalist society and bourgeois political economy, also predicted falling profits and an end to growth in capitalist economies. His analysis and its implications are different from those of his classical contemporaries, however. Marx argued that the drive of capitalists for profit (surplus value) encourages them to mechanize production to make labor more productive. A firm that mechanizes and thus lowers its costs, according to Marx, has an advantage over its competitors. It can sell at a lower price and earn more profit as sales increase, or it can maintain the same price as its competitors and earn greater profit as a result of lower costs. The advantage is temporary, however, and it hides another important effect of mechanization in the Marxian analysis.

Marx held that the source of surplus value is labor, not machinery. When competition drives all firms in the industry to mechanize, product prices fall and firms have lower profits than they had before mechanization. The lower rate of profit drives the weakest firms out of the market.

In the Marxian scenario, competition and the drive for profit force the remaining firms to continue mechanization of production, but competition and falling prices continue to drive the rate of profit down. As the process continues, more and more firms are driven out, and production is increasingly concentrated in a diminishing number of large firms. The monopoly power of the large firms, according to Marx, leads them to restrict output, to place "fetters on production" that cause growth to stop.

Meanwhile, displaced workers and capitalists swell the ranks of the working class (proletariat) and create a growing industrial reserve army of unemployed workers which keeps wages down. The working class becomes increasingly miserable in the Marxian model and doesn't provide expanding demand for the goods that could be produced with the growing capacity created by mechanization.

In short, according to Marx, capitalism can generate great expansion of capacity, but not a corresponding growth of demand and output. Eventually, the fetters on production by monopoly firms and the class warfare between the capitalists and the proletariat lead not only to an end to growth, but a revolutionary overthrow of the capitalist system by the proletariat.

Technological Change

The classical prediction of a stationary state assumes constant technology. Technological change may offset the effects of diminishing returns on output, profits, and growth.

Figure 3 Technological Change and the Stationary State

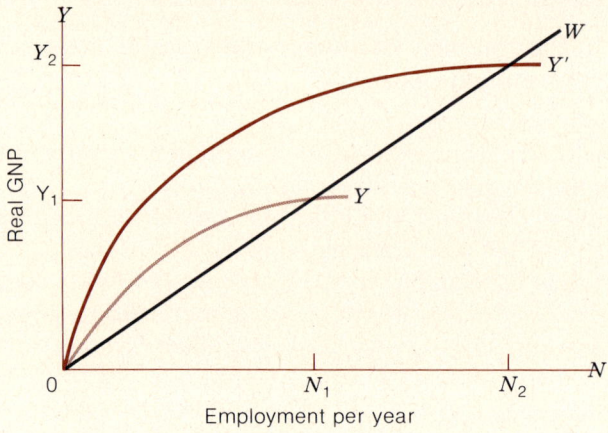

In Figure 3, the lower curve (Y) shows the relationship between employment (N) and real GNP with given technology. With no technological change, the stationary state would be reached at N_1 and Y_1 where profits are zero. Technological change shifts the curve upward to Y', and results in a higher level of output and GNP with any given level of employment. This allows employment and output to grow to N_2 and Y_2 before the stationary state is reached. Further technological changes would continue to postpone the stationary state.

The ability of technological change to sustain growth is not unlimited. Some basic resources are permanently fixed and become depleted. Also, the costs of technological change and growth may become prohibitive.

Investment Opportunities

In the 1930s, Professor Alvin Hansen of Harvard formulated a theory of **secular stagnation** that predicted declining economic growth as investment opportunities decline and the rate of return on investment falls. With no new investment opportunities, increasing investment lowers the marginal efficiency of investment (MEI), as shown by the movement along the MEI curve in Figure 4 as investment increases from I per year to I' per year. Eventually, as the rate of return on investment falls, there would be inadequate inducement to save and invest enough to sustain growth.

With the secular stagnationists' prediction of declining investment opportunities, the decline in the rate of return or the marginal efficiency of investment would be more rapid than with stable investment opportunities. In Figure 4, diminishing investment opportunities shift the marginal efficiency of investment curve to the left to MEI'. At any level of investment, the rate of return is lower on MEI' than on MEI.

Figure 4 Secular Stagnation and Investment

More optimistic contemporary assessments of our potential to sustain growth assert that ours is a world of expanding investment opportunities that will keep returns on investment high enough to sustain future economic growth. Expanding investment opportunities would shift the MEI curve to the right, as in Figure 4, and this could slow or even reverse the decline in the inducement to invest as investment increased over time. For example, if investment increased from I to I', and investment opportunities expanded at the same time and shifted MEI to MEI″, the rate of return is higher and the inducement to invest greater at I' than at I.

Changing problems and changing technology may indeed create new investment opportunities over time. The development of efficient solar energy equipment, the revitalization and reconstruction of the cities, and the improvement of public transportation technology and facilities are a few examples of areas in which investment opportunities are likely to expand in the future.

Must Growth Continue?

Simplistic growth-is-good arguments associate less or no economic growth with the end of the world. Economic growth is not an unmixed blessing, however, and a decline in growth or even zero economic growth need not be disastrous. Consider the following statement by the great classical economist, John Stuart Mill.

> I cannot . . . regard the stationary state . . . with the unaffected aversion so generally manifested by political economists of the old school. I am inclined

to believe that it would be, on the whole, a very considerable improvement on our present condition. I confess I am not charmed with the ideal of life held out by those who think that the normal state of human beings is struggling to get on. . . .[1]

The Pressure to Continue Growth

Increasing population is one source of the pressure to continue economic growth in the future. With a growing population, capacity and output must grow to keep per capita income from falling. If population growth slows down, as it has in most industrialized countries, it will exert diminishing pressure to continue economic growth.

Rising wants and expectations also exert pressure on a society to continue economic growth. As more and more people expect a rising material standard of living, economic growth becomes the only means of fulfilling the rising expectations of the poor without disappointing the rising expectations of middle and upper income groups through redistribution of wealth and income.

Declining rates of population growth, dampening material wants and expectations, and redistribution to alleviate poverty would weaken the pressures to sustain economic growth. Obviously, such goals are easier said than achieved. Population growth exerts overwhelming pressures for growth in the underdeveloped countries. Dampening expectations and changing traditional notions of the "good life" cannot be accomplished easily or quickly.

Zero Economic Growth (ZEG)

Recognition that the earth's resources are finite and that some basic resources may be depleted in a century or so at current rates of use has spawned a *zero economic growth* (ZEG) school of thought. The ZEG arguments are based on two basic propositions.

- The world's resources are insufficient to continue economic growth indefinitely, so economic growth must ultimately cease.

- The costs—pollution, environmental destruction, etc.—outweigh the benefits from continued economic growth.

The ZEG school differs from others who predict an end to economic growth in their advocacy of policies that would speed that end. Advocates of growth paint a grim picture of a world without economic growth, but the spokespersons for ZEG argue that the benefits of future growth are overwhelmed by the prohibitive costs of policies to continue economic growth and of the growth itself.

Stable real GNP with a growing population would reduce per capita GNP and eventually would depress standards of living. Therefore, the ZEG strategy is tied closely to a *zero population growth* (ZPG) strategy. If

---

1. John Stuart Mill, *Principles of Political Economy*, Book IV, Chapter VI.

population and real GNP are stable, per capita real GNP will be stable also.

ZEG and ZPG have been criticized because together they would doom the poor to poverty indefinitely. However, ZEG strategies generally include redistribution of wealth and income to raise the incomes of the poor in a world without economic growth. With adequate redistribution, ZEG need not mean abandoning efforts to alleviate poverty.

Close-up

"Bigger and Better" vs. "Small Is Beautiful"

Of the critics of modern industrial society and economic growth, none has been more critical or put forth more sweeping arguments than the late E. F. Schumacher. In a controversial book, *Small Is Beautiful*, Schumacher castigated modern industrial societies and modern economics for placing too much emphasis on the benefits from more material goods (*materialism*) and the economic advantages of large-scale production as an engine of economic progress (*giantism*). Schumacher argued that materialism and giantism lead people and society to ignore or understate the importance of social costs associated with modern industrial growth, and that they promoted forms of economic organization that are dehumanizing and lead to concentration of economic and political power.

Schumacher called for a technological revolution to improve the quality of life, but one quite different from the technological changes we have seen in our lifetimes.

> We need methods and equipment which are
> —cheap enough so that they are accessible to virtually everyone;
> —suitable for small-scale application; and
> —compatible with man's need for creativity.[1]

One of the most dramatic effects of modern technology has been the ability to produce ever greater outputs of goods and services. What if Schumacher's small-scale enterprises weren't so adept at producing as large factories are? Would this mean a decline in living standards? Schumacher admitted the possibility of producing smaller aggregate outputs of goods and services in his ideal society, but also argued that this wouldn't necessarily mean a decline in the qualitative standard of living, since the small producing units would be less destructive of the environment and would produce fewer pollutants.

Would people be happy in Schumacher's small and beautiful world with fewer goods and services than they enjoy as a result of modern large-scale production? For Schumacher, the key is to reduce the greed and envy that the modern economy has instilled in us, and to reduce and simplify our material wants—in other words, change "economic man." This is a tall order indeed!

1. E. F. Schumacher, *Small Is Beautiful: A Study of Economics as if People Mattered*. London: Blond & Briggs, 1973, pp. 29–30.

Dealing with Poverty: Growth or Redistribution?

The gap between haves and have-nots is a complex problem with serious political and social implications. Poverty tends to breed political and social instability, and these problems tend to grow with the income gap between the rich and the poor. There are two basic ways to attack poverty—by stimulating the growth of capacity and output and by redistributing wealth and income.

Growth makes it *possible* to raise the living standards of the poor and the nonpoor at the same time. However, economic growth also imposes substantial costs on the community. Many of the sources of past economic growth—such as abundant and cheap energy and unexploited sources of raw materials—are becoming exhausted. As the potential for continued growth dwindles or the costs of growth become prohibitive, dealing with poverty may require redistribution of wealth and income, and this is not accomplished easily.

Individuals tend to view their economic welfare in terms of their incomes and material standards of living. Few people would be willing to reduce their incomes voluntarily to raise the incomes and welfare of others. Contemporary hostility to welfare programs at home and foreign aid abroad, and the growing political chasm between the industrialized countries and the Third World are previews of the conflicts that might emerge with attempts to deal with poverty by large-scale redistribution of wealth and income domestically or internationally.

No effective solution to such long-range problems as poverty, unemployment, inflation, and environmental decay is easy or costless—with or without growth. Hard choices and informed and intelligent value judgements must be made on the basis of theory, facts, and political and social realities.

Summary

1. **Economic growth** refers to changes in potential, or full-employment, real GNP. Economic growth requires expansion of productive capacity.
2. Economic growth depends on increased quantity and quality of resources, technological change, and investment. These variables also impose limits on growth.
3. The effect of economic growth on economic welfare depends on the costs and benefits of growth and on the distribution of these costs and benefits among members of the community.
4. Sustaining growth in the future depends on the strength of forces that promote growth and the strength of the forces that retard growth.
5. The **zero economic growth** strategy advocates an end to policies that try to sustain growth because they see the costs of future growth as prohibitive. They also advocate a goal of **zero population growth** and redistribution to alleviate poverty in the absence of growth.

Concepts for Review

economic growth
potential GNP
stationary state

secular stagnation
fetters on production

zero economic growth (ZEG)
zero population growth (ZPG)

Questions

1. In the 1976 presidential campaign, Jimmy Carter based many of his economic policy statements and predictions on restoring and sustaining the "rates of economic growth" that had been experienced under Presidents Kennedy and Johnson between 1960 and 1968. Gerald Ford consistently referred to sustaining the trend of economic growth between 1975 and 1976.
   a. Were Carter and Ford using the term *economic growth* accurately? Explain.
   b. Do you think the candidates were realistic in predicting a continuation of the growth rate of real GNP between real GNP between 1975 and 1976 or a restoration and continuation of the rate of growth of real GNP between 1960 and 1968 in the future? Explain.

2. What are the implications of each of the following projections for the need for economic growth, the desirability of economic growth, and the potential for economic growth?
   a. a long-term decline in the birth rate and rate of population growth;
   b. aging of the population (rising average age);
   c. growing participation of women in the labor force;
   d. rising expectations of income and material standard of living.

3. Until the 1970s, most economists viewed economic growth as a major economic objective for society. During the 1970s, however, arguments critical of economic growth and even advocating a slowing or halt to economic growth became more common.
   Can you explain why historically we have tended to see economic growth as an important goal, and why attitudes have been changing on the merits of economic growth in recent years?

5. Economic growth strategies range from *growth-at-any-cost* to *zero economic growth*.
   a. Of these two extremes, which do you feel is the more appropriate? What considerations went into your answer?
   b. Combined growth strategies combine aspects of the two extremes. What do you think is the appropriate combination of strategies for growth? What considerations went into this answer?
   c. Would your answers to parts a and b be the same if you were much poorer and less educated than you are?
   d. Would your answer to parts a and b be the same if you were much richer than you are?

36

Economic Development and World Poverty

Preview: For the inhabitants of many of the world's underdeveloped countries, the problem of poverty is a matter of biological survival. The depth of poverty in these countries exerts overwhelming pressure for economic growth and development in the face of great obstacles and costs. **Economic development** involves more than the costs of growth discussed in the last chapter. Often, it requires the transformation of the entire society—economic organization and institutions, the family structure, traditional agriculture, the labor force, and the basic social and political structure. Economic analysis provides some insight into the nature of the problems and the general strategies for development, but the analysis of development is not as neat and concise as it is for most economic problems. The problems of development are complex, the solutions are seldom obvious and always difficult and painful, and most effective solutions face formidable political and social obstacles.

It is hard for most Americans to grasp the problem of world poverty because our own economic situation is so atypical.

Table 1 shows national income per capita in the various regions of the world. Per capita income in North America is high compared to Europe, let alone compared to the underdeveloped regions of Asia, Africa, and Latin America. Table 2 indicates the income gap between the underdeveloped countries and the industrialized developed countries.

The dollar figures in Tables 1 and 2 are not a completely accurate picture of the income gap between the developed and underdeveloped countries. All national income data are estimates, and there is a wide margin of error in the data for the underdeveloped countries. A great deal of production in the underdeveloped countries is by households for their own use and does not enter the national income figures.

Table 1 Per Capita Income by Region

Region	Per Capita National Income, 1975
North America	$7150
Ocear	5190
Europe	4950
Middle East	1560
Caribbean & Latin America	1160
East & Southeast Asia	590
Africa	430

Source: *United Nations Statistical Yearbook, 1977.*

Likewise the value of goods that are bartered is not included in the national income figures. The official exchange rates that express national income in the underdeveloped countries in dollars are very imperfect measures of the purchasing power of incomes earned in the underdeveloped countries. In short, the poverty in the underdeveloped countries probably is not as serious as implied by trying to live on $500 or so per year. However, the income gap is too wide to be explained away as a statistical quirk.

Table 2 Per Capita Income, Developed vs. Developing Economies

	Per Capita National Income		
	1960	1970	1975
All Market Economies	$ 520	$ 920	$1850
Developed Market Economies	1360	2670	5470
Developing Market Economies	130	210	470
Developed Economies as % of Developing Economies	1046%	1271%	1064%

Source: *United Nations Statistical Yearbook, 1972, 1977.*

The Roots of World Poverty

There is no single cause of poverty in the Third World, but a number of interrelated causes. The explanations of poverty in one country won't necessarily apply to all underdeveloped countries. The following discussion of the roots of poverty in the Third World, then, simply points out some of the general causes of poverty in these countries.

Resources

Productive capacity depends in part on the quantity and quality of resources available. Many underdeveloped countries have only modest resources, while in others the underdevelopment or underutilization of resources is a more important problem than the size of the resource base.

The quality of resources is also a problem. In many countries, the general health and literacy of the labor force is very low, so labor is not very productive. Many of the underdeveloped countries try to squeeze subsistence food output from deserts and tropical rain forests.

The underdeveloped countries have not been able to follow the pattern of countries such as Britain and Japan that developed with relatively limited resources through specialization and trade. In the first place, the resources in most underdeveloped countries are much more modest than those of Britain or Japan. The potential for specialization and trade has not been developed because many of the underdeveloped countries have been dominated economically and politically by the industrialized countries. The underdeveloped countries are developing late, and competition from the industrialized countries in export markets—and even in their domestic markets—has retarded the development of *infant industries*.

Imperialism

Imperialism—the economic and political domination of one country by another—is a frequently cited historical cause of poverty in the underdeveloped countries. The industrialized countries dominated the underdeveloped countries through the early twentieth century. Most of the European countries were colonial powers and controlled the economic development of their colonies. The economic and political interests of the United States dominated the economies of Latin America, and the United States held some "territories" (such as Hawaii, Alaska, and the Philippines) that were in fact colonies.

The imperialism of the nineteenth century was motivated by the economic interests of the industrialized countries—expanding markets for the growing output of the industrialized countries, controlling new sources of raw materials and cheap labor, and earning high rates of return on capital. The economic interests of the underdeveloped countries were seldom an important consideration.

Imperialism affected the economic development of the underdeveloped countries adversely in several ways—wastefully exploiting resources and gearing economic development to the needs of the industrialized countries. The struggles for independence following World War II retarded economic development further with great social, political, and economic disruptions. Economic problems in many of the underdeveloped countries worsened with independence, as many colonial powers simply abandoned their former colonies and left them with no effective means of ensuring sufficient political and social stability to promote economic development.

Imperialism is an emotionally charged issue, but it is not the only historical root of poverty in the underdeveloped countries. In fact, it had some positive effects on economic development that are frequently overlooked in anti-imperialist arguments. Imperialism broke down many traditional barriers to economic progress in many underdeveloped countries. Health and sanitation programs instituted by the colonial powers reduced the toll of chronic diseases and epidemics and contributed to a healthier and more productive labor force. Transportation, communication, and other types of social overhead investment promoted future development in many countries. Subsequent evidence has shown that many colonial and imperialistic ventures were unprofitable, thus contradicting the blanket explanation of the income gap in terms of the industrialized countries' earning great profits at the expense of the poorer countries in the past.

Tradition and Institutions

Traditional cultural values and institutions in many underdeveloped nations have hampered economic progress. Some traditional religions are geared more to an afterlife than to material progress and living standards, or hold basic views that hinder economic development. In many traditional societies, a person's estate is divided equally among all his heirs when he dies. This has fragmented landholdings into uneconomically small units. Extended families have hindered the mobility of labor out of the traditional agricultural sector. In some societies, traditional signs of wealth and status (such as gold jewelry or gold hoards) add nothing to productive capacity or output.

Traditional educational systems have been geared more to educating a few people for traditionally high-status positions (such as lawyers in Latin America) rather than preparing them for positions that contribute more to economic progress. Also, the traditional educational systems have not been effective in raising the level of literacy of the general population.

Population

The U.N. estimates that world population is about four billion people, and growing about two percent per year. This means that about eighty million people are added to the world's population every year, or an additional population equal to that of the United States every three years. At this rate, population grows about 219,000 persons per day, or enough additional population to populate a city about the size of Baltimore every four days.

Malthus: Population and Misery. In 1798, a British economist and clergyman named Thomas Robert Malthus wrote *An Essay on the Principle of Population*. Malthus predicted a losing race between food production and the growth of population. He asserted that the world's population grows geometrically, doubling each generation—1, 2, 4, 8, 16, . . . —while food production grows arithmetically—1, 2, 3, 4, 5, ... Thus, he predicted that food output would lag behind population growth, and that the amount of food per capita would fall over time.

According to Malthus, the growth of population would be checked only by what he called **positive checks** or **preventive checks**. Positive checks included misery, vice, war, pestilence, and famine. Preventive checks were late marriage and sexual abstinence.

Was Malthus Right? Technological change and investment in the United States and other industrialized countries have raised the output from any given labor input, offsetting the effect of population growth on living standards. As long as the effect of technological change on food output is stronger than the effect of diminishing returns with additional labor, food output may grow as fast as or faster than population.

In the underdeveloped countries, however, Malthus' grim forecast is being borne out. As shown in Table 3, birth rates, death rates, and population growth are higher in the underdeveloped countries than in the developed countries. Farming methods are primitive, farms tend to be too small to produce efficiently and are getting smaller as land is divided among a growing agricultural population. Subsistence living standards make saving for investment and technological change virtually impossible.

Table 3 Population Growth: Developed vs. Developing Countries

Country	Birth Rate per 1,000	Death Rate per 1,000	National Increase in Population per 1,000	Per Capita National Income
Kenya	48.7	16.0	32.7	$ 209
El Salvador	39.9	7.9	32.0	503
Iran	45.3	15.6	29.7	1,529
Brazil	37.1	8.8	28.3	1,239
Egypt	37.7	12.3	25.4	263
Guinea	46.6	22.9	23.7	—
India	34.5	14.4	20.1	136
Gambia	43.3	24.1	19.2	—
USSR	18.5	9.5	9.2	—
Canada	15.8	7.2	8.2	7,340
United States	14.7	8.9	5.8	6,995
Italy	14.0	9.7	4.3	2,758
France	13.6	10.5	3.1	5,860
Sweden	11.9	11.0	0.9	8,044
West Germany	9.8	11.9	−2.1	6,451

Source: *United Nations Statistical Yearbook, 1977.*

Reducing Population Growth. The faster population grows, obviously, the faster real GNP must grow to achieve a given increase in per capita income. If population grows at three percent per year, for example, real GNP would have to grow at about six percent per year to double per capita GNP in a generation (about 25 years). If population remained stable, per capita GNP would double in a generation with a three percent annual rate of growth of real GNP.

If reducing population growth is an obvious course of action, it is not easy to accomplish. Societies tend to go through several stages of transition from high birth and death rates to low birth and death rates, as sketched in Figure 1. Note that time itself is not the independent variable in Figure 1. Birth and death rates are determined by other variables that tend to vary over time—such as per capita income, education, preferences, and expected living standards.

The high death rates in Stage I are caused by epidemics, high infant mortality, local famines, and in some cases tribal warfare. Birth rates are high in this stage because people tend to have many children, expecting only a few to survive to adulthood. In agrarian societies, children are a source of farm labor and an economic asset. With extended families, a large family is a form of "social security" for the parents' old age. Traditional attitudes tend to keep birth rates high. Traditional views may see children as a sign of masculinity (*machismo*), as a source of good luck, or as gifts from heaven. With high birth and death rates, the rate of population growth (birth rate − death rate) tends to be low in Stage I, as shown by the distance between *BR* and *DR* in Figure 1.

In Stage II, the typical pattern is falling death rates and stable or rising birth rates, and an increasing rate of population growth. Note the distance between *BR* and *DR* in Stage II in Figure 1.

Reducing death rates and preserving human life are acceptable in virtually every religion and social ethic. Also, it is fairly inexpensive

Figure 1 Changes in Birth and Death Rates over Time

to improve public health and sanitation, and to reduce the toll of epidemic diseases by such means as mass vaccinations and spraying swamps. Economic and institutional changes also may reduce death rates in Stage II. Improvements in transportation tend to reduce the death toll from localized famines by shipping food to stricken areas or moving people out of them. Stable central governments and improvements in communication and transportation tend to reduce the toll of tribal or civil warfare.

Usually, the declining death rate is not matched by a concurrent decline in the birth rate in Stage II. Traditional views on children and family size do not change very rapidly. Preventing births is not as universally acceptable as the prevention of death and preservation of life. Many traditional religions, most notably Catholicism, are vehemently opposed to contraception and especially to abortion. Some Third World nationalists view birth-control programs in the underdeveloped countries as a subtle form of genocide by white European societies.

If the underdeveloped countries develop economically, their birth rates probably will fall—as shown by Stage III in Figure 1. In Stage III, birth rates fall as a result of education (general literacy and educational programs on the importance of population limitation), improved birth-control techniques, and the desire of people to substitute higher living standards for more children. In Stage IV—where most of the economically developed countries seem to be—population grows slowly with low birth and death rates.

Limiting population growth by simply allowing death rates to remain high in the underdeveloped countries would be unacceptable on normative grounds to many people (including the author). Limiting population with high death rates is the wrong course economically as well. High death rates in underdeveloped countries reflect high infant and child mortality. Many people live long enough to consume, but not long enough to produce anything. Many who survive chronic diseases and epidemics, which also contribute to high death rates, are left disabled and not very productive.

World Poverty: Is There a Way Out?

Economic development is a complex and difficult problem that does not lend itself to simple solutions. Economics can identify the general directions that effective development policies must take, but no set of specific policies is appropriate for all underdeveloped countries. Also, economics does not deal with the critical social and political barriers to development very well.

Investment and Capital Formation

The pressures to generate economic growth to raise living standards in the underdeveloped countries is overwhelming. Higher rates of growth, of course, require investment and capital formation to expand

Figure 2 Investment and Third World Production Possibilities

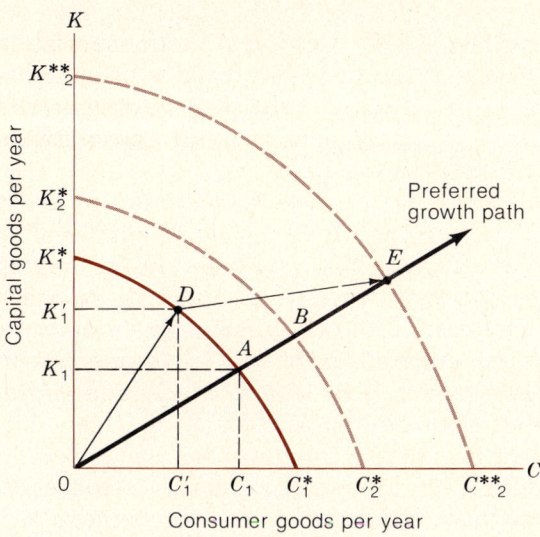

the economy's capacity to produce. The higher the rate of investment now, the greater the growth of capacity and income in the future.

To illustrate, assume that the economy's capacity to produce consumer goods (C) and capital goods (K) is given, and represented by the production possibilities curve $K^*_1 C^*_1$ in Figure 2. Suppose that the community prefers combination A on the production possibilities curve to maintain living standards. Producing K_1 capital goods per year in period 1 expands productive capacity to $K^*_2 C^*_2$ in period 2 and allows the community to move to point B on its **preferred growth path**. By increasing investment and the output of capital goods to K_1' in period 1 and moving to point D, however, it would be possible to expand capacity in period 2 to $K^{**}_2 C^{**}_2$, and to move further along the growth path to point E.

With a fully employed capacity, however, producing more capital goods to generate greater growth requires a reduction of consumer goods output—from C_1 to C_1' in Figure 2. This means even lower standards for the current generation and bodes ill for economic, social, and political stability.

Social Overhead A substantial portion of the investment undertaken to promote economic development should be **social overhead investments**, that lay the foundations necessary for improved utilization of resources and economic growth. In most underdeveloped countries, the success of programs to foster growth will require such social overhead projects as improved and expanded transportation and communication facilities, as well as the development of power networks and other public utilities.

Most of the social overhead investment will have to come from the public sector, since social overhead projects typically pay low returns (if any) in the distant future and would not attract private capital. Also, many forms of social overhead are public goods that cannot be provided by private markets.

Land Reform and Agricultural Investment

In most underdeveloped countries, improving agricultural efficiency and output should receive the highest priority. Unless the agricultural sector can produce a surplus above the subsistence needs of the agricultural population, it will be impossible to feed a nonagricultural labor force. Also, without a surplus above subsistence, saving and investment are impossible.

Land reform and reorganization of agricultural production may make agricultural production more efficient. One possibility is to form **producer cooperatives** in which individuals would pool their land and other resources to form an economically efficient size of farm and share in the proceeds from the farm. Raising agricultural productivity also generally involves increased agricultural investment and thus conflicts with the goal of increasing investment in industry.

In many agrarian areas of underdeveloped countries, there is actually *surplus labor* where population growth and diminishing returns have led to *zero returns* from labor—i.e., the additional labor doesn't add any output. Moving surplus labor from the land would make it possible to produce other goods with the labor without reducing agricultural production. However, unless the demand for nonagricultural labor increases, there will not be any place to employ the surplus labor that leaves agriculture. One possibility is to use the surplus labor to produce the social overhead projects that would promote development.

Some of the bloodiest conflicts and worst social and economic disasters in modern times have resulted from attempts to restructure traditional agriculture. In peasant societies, traditional attachments to the land make it difficult to get people to leave the land, sell it, or share control of it with others.

Foreign Assistance

Foreign economic assistance may make the development process somewhat less painful. In Figure 3, suppose that the economy must produce C_1 consumer goods per year to maintain living standards, and a capital goods output of K_2 to produce sufficient economic growth. The production-possibilities curve makes it impossible to produce C_1 and K_2 with the country's own resources.

Figure 3 Foreign Assistance and Third World Production Possibilities

With foreign assistance—grants or loans from foreign governments, loans from private lenders in foreign countries, or direct foreign investment in the underdeveloped countries—the country in Figure 3 could purchase the capital goods it needs in excess of K_1 while maintaining living standards. It could use the assistance to purchase the consumer goods it needs in excess of C_2 while increasing capital goods output to K_2. However, foreign assistance may not be the solution of many countries' development problems.

Countries with critical resources (such as oil) or strategic international positions tend to be most successful in getting assistance from the industrialized countries. Other underdeveloped countries tend to be ignored. Even the countries that can get assistance often get it with strings attached. Underdeveloped countries that depend heavily on aid from the major military powers risk involvement in international political and military conflicts. Private investment by foreigners may give them excessive economic and political influence. These are not attractive possibilities for the underdeveloped countries that have had long and unhappy relationships with the industrialized countries in the past.

Finally, foreign assistance may not be dependable. In the United States, the favorite targets for cutting government spending are "welfare" programs at home and foreign aid abroad. In 1978, U.S. nonmilitary assistance to underdeveloped countries was about $5.2 billion —less than one-fourth of one percent of GNP, and only about one percent of federal budget expenditures. Nonetheless, opinion surveys consistently show that popular opinion views our foreign aid as excessive.

Specialization and Trade

Many underdeveloped countries have the potential to realize gains from specialization and trade which could aid in their development efforts. In many instances, however, this potential has not been realized because of competition from the industrialized countries.

Infant industry tariffs may allow underdeveloped countries to develop their potential to realize gains from specialization in the long run. There is, however, a potential danger in specialization if it involves heavy dependence on a single export. With dependence on a single export, a country's development efforts rest on fluctuations in world markets for that export.

Economic and Political Control

Most effective development policies are likely to be painful and unpopular. Leaving development to individual decisions and market forces will probably be unsuccessful, at least in the early stages of development. Economic development generally requires stringent economic and political controls.

One of the most important uses of economic control is to force the saving required for investment and capital formation. In Japan, for example, forced saving was accomplished largely through taxes. In the Soviet Union, forced saving was accomplished by such drastic efforts as collectivization of agriculture, central control over wages and prices, central control over consumer goods production, and taxes that squeezed the consumer and the agricultural sector.

Direct controls may be required to ensure that the sectors of the economy that contribute most to future growth and development receive adequate resources. This generally means allocating more resources to heavy industry and capital goods production.

While economic development may alleviate the social and political tensions in the underdeveloped countries once it has been achieved, development *efforts* tend to increase tensions and strengthen the pressure for tight political controls. The prospects for economic development with anything resembling political democracy and decentralized market decision making are remote.

Although economic controls may be necessary to promote development, there are some potential problems (in addition to all of the normative questions involved in political and economic dictatorship). First of all, effective control requires considerable technical expertise and communication facilities that many underdeveloped countries lack. Also, controls can be self-defeating if they are imposed too long. As the economy grows and develops, the task of central control becomes more complex and maintaining central controls may be a source of inefficiency. Maintaining controls may dampen incentive to the point that the development effort will be stalled.

Limiting Population Growth

The necessity of limiting population growth and the difficulties of accomplishing lower rates of population growth in the underdeveloped countries have been discussed earlier in this chapter. It is mentioned again as part of the development strategy because the effectiveness of all of the other development efforts can easily be eaten up by rapid population growth.

Economic Development: Mission Impossible?

The prospects for substantial and quick improvements in living standards in the underdeveloped countries are bleak. In the absence of dramatic technological revolutions in production and massive redistribution of income from the rich countries to the poor, it will be impossible in the near future to raise living standards in the underdeveloped countries to a level that would be minimally acceptable in most industrialized countries. The continuing population growth in the underdeveloped countries casts a further pall on their prospects for higher living standards.

It is tempting to ignore difficult problems in the hope that somebody else will take care of them or that they will simply go away. The problems of the underdeveloped nations won't go away on their own, however, and could produce disastrous consequences for all nations. Desperation, political and social instability, and tensions in the Third World may lead the poor countries to strain their resources to fight each other, and in an increasingly interdependent world with nuclear overkill lurking in the background, this is hardly a cause for complacency.

Summary

1. The income gap between the developed and underdeveloped countries is wide and has widened since the 1960s.
2. The causes of poverty in the underdeveloped countries include resources, history, institutions, traditions that are hostile to economic progress, and population growth.
3. No single set of policies will work in all underdeveloped countries, but effective development strategies must increase investment and capital formation, restructure agriculture to make it more productive, move resources from agriculture to industry, and take advantage (where possible) of potential gains from specialization and trade.
4. Effective economic development efforts generally require political and economic controls.
5. All other development efforts may fail without adequate reductions in the rate of population growth.

Questions

1. To what extent do you think each of the following explains the income gap between the rich and poor countries?
   a. Climate and geography
   b. Natural selection
   c. Traditional attitudes toward wealth
   d. Different attitudes toward work
   e. Imperialistic exploitation
   f. Resources
   g. History and traditions
   h. Population pressure
2. How can you explain the ability of persons in the underdeveloped countries to live on incomes of $200 per year?
3. Suppose that you have the responsibility of designing a program to limit population growth in the underdeveloped countries. What would be the main features of your program? How would you convince the people of the desirability of limiting population growth? How successful do you think you'd be?
4. You have been asked to testify before Congress on the value of U.S. assistance to developing countries, and to international agencies that assist developing countries.
   a. How would you justify expenditures on foreign assistance, in light of the benefits from the funds if they were allocated to domestic programs?
   b. What would be the main features of an assistance program that would have a reasonably good chance of success in promoting economic development?
5. Outline and explain the main features of a program for economic development of an underdeveloped country. You should justify the elements of your program analytically, and in terms of their practical reality. Also, you should identify the potential problems that your program would be likely to face.

37

Alternative Economic Systems

Preview: The analytical tools we have studied up to this point have been useful in exploring the economic relationships, problems, and issues in our own economic system. Ours is not the only type of system, however, and many people believe that our system has in fact failed to deal effectively with the basic economic problem of unlimited wants and limited resources. In this chapter, we will take a general analytical look at how some other major kinds of economic systems would approach that basic economic problem, focusing particular attention upon two important features that play a role in a number of different economic systems: public ownership and central economic planning.

Socialism

Socialism is a widely misunderstood and misused word. Some people characterize all government actions in the economy—fiscal and monetary policies that alter aggregate demand, expansion of public programs, antitrust and consumer protection laws that limit the discretion of firms—as *socialism*. Because the Soviet, Chinese, and Eastern European economies call themselves *socialist* economies, there is a natural but mistaken tendency to associate socialism with tight economic and political controls. The actual definition of *socialism* is considerably more benign.

- **Socialism** is public ownership of the means of production.

In a completely socialized economy, all land and capital would be owned by the community, and all production would be carried out in publicly owned firms. However, even complete socialism generally leaves the individual with private property rights in his personal possessions and in the use of his labor.

Socialism and Democracy

In theory, socialism need not be associated with a loss of political freedom. In most European democracies—such as Britain, France, and Sweden—basic industries (such as coal and steel) are publicly owned and operated. Even where entire industries are not socialized, some firms in the industry may be—Renault automobile company in France, for example. In most European countries, public utilities (electric power, telephone, gas, and in some cases railroads) are publicly owned and operated. The Western European countries are not political dictatorships in the Soviet, Eastern European, or Chinese molds.

The key determinant of political freedom is the relationship between governmental authority and individual rights—not socialism, *per se*. It is quite possible to have socialism in a political democracy, just as it's possible to have private ownership of the means of production in a dictatorship (as in Chile today and Nazi Germany during the 1930s and 1940s).

Market Socialism

Another misconception concerning socialism is that the market mechanism must be replaced by a powerful economic planning authority that makes all economic decisions for the community.

- **Market socialism** is an economic system in which the means of production are publicly owned, but markets and prices play active roles in the community's economic decisions.

Market socialism is possible with or without central economic planning. With enough information, central planners could set product and resource prices so that the actions of firms and households would produce the outputs that the planners see as best for the community.

The Lange-Lerner Model of Market Socialism

The basic model of market socialism was developed by the late Polish economist Oskar Lange and Professor Abba P. Lerner of the United States. In this model, a **central planning board** (CPB) sets product and resource prices, but does not otherwise control the actions of firms or households. In setting prices, however, the CPB would try to ensure that community economic needs (as it perceives them) are met.

The Lange-Lerner model combines public ownership of resources, central planning, and most of the elements of perfect competition. Through trial and error, the CPB arrives at prices that are equivalent to long-run equilibrium prices with perfect competition, and the firms and households "take" the prices set by the CPB.

Equilibrium prices for resources in the market socialist model give producers signals to economize on the scarcest resources to minimize costs, just as in the competitive capitalist model. Workers are free to choose occupations in the Lange-Lerner model, and occupational wage differentials in the long run will equalize the total advantages in all occupations.

Nonlabor income—rent, interest, and profits—accrue to the community, not to individuals. This income, or the **national dividend**, is distributed among members of the community in a way that doesn't influence one's choice of occupation—in Lerner's model, every person receives an equal share of the national dividend.

The firm in Figure 1 takes the price P^* as set by the CPB. Resource prices (also set by the CPB) and the firm's production function determine its cost curves (MC and AC in Figure 1). If the firm is free to maximize profit, or labor and management incentives are tied to profit, it will produce where $P^* = MR = MC$. The CPB would adjust prices so that the price would cover minimum AC. This is the same result that is reached in perfect competition—$P^* = MC$, $P^* = AC$, and AC = minimum.

If the CPB achieves results similar to the competitive result, why bother with the CPB at all? According to Lange, the CPB would have a better view of community welfare than would individual firms and households—particularly in such areas as determining the mix between current consumption and future growth. Also, the CPB may have a better perception of externalities and social costs and would incorporate that perception into its product and resource prices. Finally, Lange argued that a CPB would find accurate scarcity prices and adjust to economic changes more quickly and efficiently than decentralized markets.

In practice, markets play a role in all economic systems—even the centrally planned Soviet-type economies. Soviet planners, for example, have relied on labor market incentives to induce labor into high-priority occupations and geographical areas. Private markets for agricultural products from the personal plots of collective farmers have been an

Figure 1 Firm Under Market Socialism

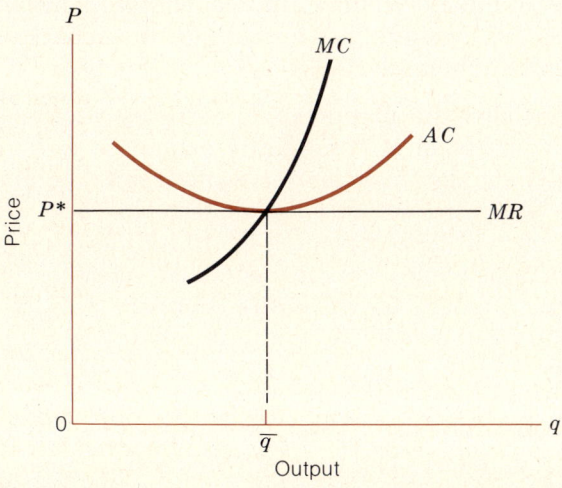

important source of many agricultural products in the Soviet Union. Soviet economic reforms since the late 1950s have increased the role of markets and market incentives in determining the mix of goods produced in the economy.

Central Economic Planning

Just as markets play a role in even the centrally planned economies of the world, so economic planning exists in every modern economy—even those that are thought of as "market" economies. The United States is almost unique among industrialized countries in the small role we give to central economic planning. Even in the United States, however, planning by large corporations and *ad hoc* planning by government agencies plays a significant role in economic decisions.

To some extent, the issue of central planning is independent of the issues of public ownership and political controls. The economies in which planning plays the most important role today are socialist economies, but central planning doesn't require public ownership of the means of production.

Planning and Economic Welfare

The goal of economic planning is to maximize the community economic welfare, subject to the constraints imposed by resources and technology. However, it is the *planners'* view of community economic welfare that determines the allocation of resources and the outputs that are produced.

Assume that the planners have a well-defined notion of the relationship between the outputs of goods and the community economic welfare, or a *planners' welfare function*.

- The **planners' welfare function** is the planners' view of *community* economic welfare, not necessarily the economic welfare of the planners themselves.

Assume that the planners can associate any combination of outputs with some level of community economic welfare, and that they can identify changes in economic welfare and combinations of outputs that yield the same community welfare. In short, the planners' welfare function will be represented by an indifference map similar to households' indifference maps, except that it refers to community welfare, and outputs of goods for the entire economy.

Figure 2 shows an economy producing two goods—machinery (M) and bread (B). The curve M^*B^* is the economy's production possibilities curve, introduced in Chapter 2. The indifference curves—WP_1, WP_2, etc.—represent levels of community economic welfare as seen by the planners. The best combination of goods, given the planners' welfare function, is $\bar{B}$ and $\bar{M}$.

Figure 2 Planners' vs. Households' Welfare Functions

Now, assume that the households have a consensus on community economic welfare and a community economic welfare function that reflects this consensus. In Figure 2, the broken indifference curves CW_1, CW_2, etc., represent economic welfare as seen by the households. There are some theoretical difficulties with the notion of community indifference curves, but they illustrate some important aspects of economic planning.[1]

In Figure 2, the combination of goods chosen by the planners does not yield the highest community economic welfare as perceived by the households. This does not make economic planning or planners' sovereignty "wrong"—if it is assumed that the planners have the best perception of community welfare. If this weren't assumed, or if planners and households had the same view of economic welfare, there would be no need for planning. The greater the divergence between the two views of community economic welfare, however, the more likely that central economic planning will be accompanied by political and economic controls.

1. The community indifference curves are illustrative. In reality, defining community economic welfare is difficult if households have different preferences. The subjective ordinal utilities of individuals can't be added to get community economic welfare. With consumer sovereignty, the community's preferences are defined by "dollar votes" and depend on the distribution of income. Even if every household had an equal vote, there are difficulties in defining community economic welfare and preferences clearly.

Figure 3 Planners' vs. Households' Growth Paths

One possible reason for accepting the planners' view of community welfare is that individual households may overemphasize the importance of current consumption and understate the importance of externalities, social costs, and growth of future output. In Figure 3, the planners would call for production of B_1 units of bread and M_1 units of machinery per year in period 1, and consumers' preferences would call for more bread (B_1') and less machinery (M_1') in the same period. However, the greater machinery output chosen by planners in period 1 would generate greater expansion of capacity than would the outputs chosen by consumers. Producing B_1 and M_1 per year shifts production possibilities to $M^{**}_2 B^{**}_2$ in period 2, while producing B_1' and M_1' in period 1 would expand production possibilities only to $M^*_2 B^*_2$. Even if outputs expanded along the planners' growth path, there would be a higher level of community welfare as seen by *consumers* in period 2 than could be reached on $M^*_2 B^*_2$.

The question that must be dealt with, of course, is the degree to which consumers will sacrifice their view of economic welfare to be better off in the future, and the number of years it takes to make up for their current sacrifice of welfare.

The Planners' Task: Feasibility

The most obvious task of planners is to formulate an economic plan that is feasible.

- A **feasible economic plan** is one that can be produced with the economy's resources and technology.

Feasible plans are those on or inside the production possibilities curve. Since maximizing economic welfare requires full employment of capacity, the planners must choose a plan on the production possibilities curve.

The Planners' Task: Consistency

Modern economies are made up of many interrelated sectors and industries. Every industry is related to others that supply inputs to it and to those that use its outputs. Industries are related, also, because they use the same basic resources to produce. This means that economic plans must be *consistent*.

- A **consistent economic plan** is one in which the planned output of each product equals its planned uses.

If the planned output of a good is either greater or less than the output required for the planned uses of the good, the plan is inconsistent, and this causes problems. If the planned uses of coal, for example, exceeded the planned output of coal, the users of coal could not meet their plans because there would not be enough coal. Output plans would have to be altered or the amount of coal produced for use as fuel by households would have to be reduced. If the planned output of coal exceeded the planned uses, resources would be wasted in producing the excess coal.

An anecdote concerning Soviet planning in the Stalin era asserts that in one year the planned output of boxcar doors exceeded the number required for the planned output of boxcars. To make matters worse, according to the story, the plan for boxcar doors was exceeded while the output of boxcars fell short of the planned output.

Material Balances Planning. One method of achieving consistency is by trial and error. The formal name for this is *material balances planning*. Material balances planning starts with a highly aggregated plan that reflects the planners' preferences, and their estimate of the economy's capacity to produce. As the initial plan passes through the planning bureaucracy, it becomes more specific, and finally firms receive initial output quotas. The firms estimate their resource requirements to meet the plan, and send them back to the planners.

The planners then compare the resources required to meet the plan with the resources available. If the planners are doing their job, trying to get the maximum output from the economy's resources and technology, the initial plan probably will not be feasible. Also, internal inconsistencies will show up. The planners alter the plan to eliminate inconsistencies and to reduce resource requirements to the resources available.

Revised plans are sent through the planning bureaucracy, and firms receive revised output quotas. The firms revise their resource requirements and send them back to the planners. The process continues until resource requirements equal the resources available.

Planners have considerable flexibility with material balances planning and can alter plans to take account of such developments as the discovery of new resources, depletion of resources, or technological change. This flexibility can be a disadvantage as well, however, because it leaves room for arbitrary actions by the planners.

Accuracy of information may be a problem because firms have an obvious incentive to understate their capacity to produce or overstate their resource requirements to meet their quotas. The planners have to cut as much fat as possible from the resource requirements sent in by the firms. This usually involves some guessing and arbitrary actions.

Planners have to work with a vast amount of information, even if they draw up material balances for the most critical goods. This makes material balances planning a slow process. In the Soviet Union, for example, it is not uncommon for firms to begin their production year without a specified output plan.

Even if the planners worked with information that was 100 percent accurate (which, of course, it isn't), they would have time to come up with only one consistent plan and one point on the production-possibilities curve. There could be other consistent, feasible plans that would yield a higher level of planners' welfare.

Input-Output Analysis. *Input-output analysis* is a mathematical technique that can formulate an internally consistent plan mathematically.

- **Input-output analysis** shows interrelationships between industries and gives internally consistent plans by simultaneous solution of output equations.

The formal mechanics of input-output are fairly complex, but the complexity isn't necessary to get a good idea of how it works and its potential for economic planning. Input-output analysis starts with equations that represent the output of each industry and the uses to which the output will be put. The output of each industry is made up of the amounts that will be used as inputs by other industry (*interindustry flows*) and the amount that will be used by the households and by the government (*final demand*). In very simplified form, the output equation for the oil industry would be

Output of oil = Interindustry flows + Final demand.

More specifically, the equation would include

Output of oil = Oil used for electric power + oil used for plastic +
        oil used for transport + . . . + Final demand.

Obviously, the planned output of oil is related to the planned outputs of electric power, plastic, and other products that use oil as an input, as well as the planned amount of oil for final use. There is an equation for each industry, and the system of equations is solved to yield an internally consistent plan. Solving very large sets of equations takes a matter of minutes with modern computers.

The speed of input-output allows planners to formulate a number of internally consistent plans. They can eliminate those that obviously could not be produced with the economy's resources and technology and those that obviously would not employ productive capacity fully. This leaves a number of consistent plans that employ capacity fully. The chance of finding the best plan is greater with several variants to choose from than with a single consistent plan.

The overwhelming advantage of speed over material balances, however, has to be balanced against some problems with input-output. The information required for a detailed plan for a large economy is immense. Planners have to know *technical coefficients* that show the amount of one good necessary per unit of another—the amount of coal per ton of steel, the amount of oil per ton of plastic, etc. In an economy with three interrelated industries there would be $3 \times 3 = 3^2 = 9$ technical coefficients. With only 20 interrelated industries, the number of technical coefficients jumps to $20^2 = 400$, and with 100 industries (still a small economy or a high level of aggregation) there are $100^2 = 10,000$ technical coefficients. Planners also would have to know the amount of each resource required per unit of each good, and the amount of each resource available.

Gathering the information necessary for the plan takes a great deal of time, and the information is likely to be inaccurate by the time it is in usable form for input-output. With inaccurate information, the input-output solution will be an inaccurate picture of economic reality. Computers are wondrous machines, but they only do what they are told to on the basis of the information fed in.

Input-output solutions may become inaccurate because of technological and other changes that make the coefficients inaccurate. Also, input-output operates with constant technical coefficients, thus assuming that every unit of steel requires the same inputs of coal, electricity, labor, etc., regardless of the level of steel output. There is no room for increasing or diminishing returns in the short run, nor for economies or diseconomies of scale in the long run. At best, the technical coefficients are approximations of actual economic relationships.

For the immediate future at least, planners will have to combine material balances and input-output in deriving consistent plans. Input-output can give planners several consistent plans to consider at once, and the planners could work out material balances for several variants of the plan at once rather than one at a time. This would combine the speed of input-output with the flexibility of material balances.

The Planners' Task: Optimality

To make the community as well off as possible with its technology and resources, the planners have to arrive at the *optimal plan*.

- The **optimal plan** is the feasible and consistent plan that maximizes the community's economic welfare.

The first requirement of optimality is full employment of the economy's productive capacity. All resources must be used and must be combined as efficiently as possible.

The optimal plan is the combination of goods on the production possibilities curve that the planners view as best for the community, as shown in Figure 2 earlier in this chapter. This sounds simple enough, but the information required to find one point on the production possibilities curve in a large economy is immense. Many critics of economic planning argue that information and organizational problems prohibit planners from reaching an optimal plan, although most admit that it is theoretically possible for economic planning to achieve optimality.

Indicative Planning

Economic planning doesn't always take the form of a central authority dictating its view of community economic welfare and determining an output plan for the economy. In some countries, France for example, economic plans are *indicative plans*.

- **Indicative planning** simply projects major economic developments for the next year and the basic directions of economic policy.

Indicative planning does not bind firms to output goals set by planners, nor is the government the only authority in drawing up the plans with indicative planning. In France, for example, the plans are formulated jointly by representatives of industry, agriculture, labor, finance, and government.

Some Long-Range Considerations: The Convergence Hypothesis

No economic system stands still over time; all economic systems change to deal with changing problems. Some observers and students of economic systems have noted that the world's economies are becoming more alike, or *converging*. The most common comparison is between changes in American mixed capitalism and Soviet planned socialism. In the American economy, the role of the government and of the public sector in the economy has increased in the past four decades. In the Soviet Union, the trend since the middle 1950s has been toward an increasingly active role for market forces and decentralized decision making.

Optimists suggest that economic convergence will lead to political convergence and improved international relations. Such optimism may be unfounded, however. Similar economic systems need not lead to cordial international relations. Certainly, the economic similarities between the Soviet Union and the People's Republic of China have not led to international friendship in the past decade or so.

The convergence hypothesis usually does not predict the type of economic system toward which the world's economies are converging or elaborate on the forces that promote convergence. In the past decade, however, at least two quite different points of convergence have been suggested.

The "New Industrial State"

In 1967, Professor John Kenneth Galbraith of Harvard published a popular but controversial book, *The New Industrial State*,[2] in which he identified some of the forces behind the tendency of economic systems to converge. The analysis in the *New Industrial State* is directed at the common characteristics of what Galbraith calls the **industrial system.**

Production in the industrial system is carried out with large capital inputs and a complex technology. The large amounts of capital and the complex technology mean an increasing role for economic planning and for technical experts (technocrats) in "capitalist" economies like the United States. Firms in the New Industrial State depend heavily on a stable economic environment, and this means an increasing role for government policies to stabilize economic conditions.

Galbraith argues that the industrial system is a common characteristic of all modern industrial economies, and that the industrial system in the Soviet Union is not drastically different from the industrial system in the United States. As in the United States, Galbraith predicts that the imperatives of the large amounts of capital, complex technology, and technical expertise involved in modern industrial production will alter the nature and operation of the planned socialist countries.

In the planned economies, however, Galbraith predicts that the nature of the industrial system will dictate more autonomy for firms and decentralization of decision making. The specialization and technical knowledge will make it impossible for central planners to dictate decisions to firms without great losses of efficiency. As in the U.S., he predicts an increasing role for technocrats in the planned economies.

Galbraith's view of the future is convergence of economic systems as a result of their common industrial system. It will mean an increasing role for planning and the public sector in the capitalist countries and greater decentralization and autonomy in decision making in the planned economies.

The Participatory Economy

A second vision of the future of economic systems is convergence toward something quite different from American-style "mixed capitalism," Soviet-style planned socialism, and Galbraith's "New Industrial

---

2. John Kenneth Galbraith. *The New Industrial State.* Boston: Houghton Mifflin, 1967.

State." It goes by several names—the **participatory economy**, the **labor-managed economy**, and the **cooperative economy**.

In the participatory economy, there is no distinction between labor and management. Firms are *producer cooperatives,* in which workers manage the firm and share in the profits. The employees, acting as a community, make all of the basic decisions for the firm—such as the level of output, the composition of output, the number of workers in the firm, and the persons who will manage the firm on a day-to-day basis.

Professor Jaroslav Vanek of Cornell University, who has done the most exhaustive analysis of the participatory economy, predicts a trend of convergence toward this type of economy. In the planned economies, he argues, the difficulties of formulating and enforcing plans for firms will make the participatory economy an attractive alternative. In industrial societies, giving employees more control of the management of the firm will reduce the alienation of workers from their jobs and will encourage greater efficiency and higher quality of work as the workers bear more managerial responsibility. In the underdeveloped countries, a participatory economy will be less foreign to workers who are used to communal village economies than a Soviet-style or American-style economy in which management is divorced from the workers.

It may seem odd to predict convergence toward an economic system that is so different from the major contemporary economies. However, the Yugoslav economy has established labor management as the norm, and many Western European and American firms are experimenting with new work arrangements—such as production teams and flexible work schedules—that are consistent with the notion of an increasing role for workers in decisions that were the sole domain of management in the past.

There are, of course, many possible types of economies that may emerge in addition to the ones discussed. As the basic problems facing the world's economies become more similar and interrelated, some convergence of economic systems can be expected. However, the existence of a strong trend toward covergence, the exact point of convergence, and the broader implications of convergence are not clear at this point.

What Is the Best Economic System?

Ignoring practical considerations, the best economic system is easy to identify—one that employs productive capacity fully, doesn't make mistakes or create inefficiency, yields the proper mix of current consumption and future growth, minimizes instability and economic uncertainty, fulfills normative standards of equity and social justice, and is consistent with desired social and political institutions. If such an economy existed, it would be accepted as the best kind of economy. However, no such system exists, and no economic system can accomplish all of these goals.

All economic systems have sources of inefficiency. Planners must work with incomplete and inaccurate information. The market power of firms and unions in many economies affects their efficiency. Planning bureaucracies in centrally planned economies and managerial bureaucracies in large private corporations are sources of inefficiency in planned and market economies alike. Environmental decay, pollution, and other social costs are also common in all types of modern economic systems.

Many of the considerations involved in deciding on the best type of economic system are normative. How much decision making should be taken from individuals and delegated to planners? Who should decide what is best for the community? The list of normative considerations could go on indefinitely. Although the tools of economic analysis can identify some of the costs and benefits of alternative economic arrangements, they provide (at best) only partial answers to the normative questions.

Summary

1. There are a number of alternative types of economic systems, and different economic systems represent alternative ways of dealing with the fundamental economic problems of scarcity and choice.
2. **Socialism** refers to public ownership of the means of production. The relationship between socialism and political freedom depends on the basic relationship between government and the individual, not on socialism itself.
3. **Market socialism** is an economic system in which the means of production are publicly owned, but prices and markets play active rationing and allocation roles. In fact, markets and market incentives play some role even in centrally planned economies.
4. In a **centrally planned economy**, the economic planners determine the mix of outputs which maximizes the community economic welfare, *as perceived by the planners*. This is generally different than economic welfare as perceived by individual firms and households. The goal of the planner is to arrive at a plan that is both **consistent** and **optimal**.
5. All economic systems change over time, and some people argue that the world's economies are converging, or becoming more alike.
6. Identifying an economic system as *best* involves efficiency considerations, balancing the advantages and disadvantages of alternative systems, and a number of normative questions. No system is *best* by all criteria.

Concepts for Review

socialism
market socialism
Lange-Lerner model
central planning board
national dividend
planners' welfare function

households' welfare function
feasibility
consistency
optimality
material balance planning

input-output analysis
indicative planning
industrial system
participatory economy

Questions

1. What are the basic goals and problems that all economic systems have in common?
2. All national economies are mixtures of different basic types of economic systems. How would you characterize the mixture of economic systems that comprise the United States economy? What changes can you identify in the United States economy that alter this mixture?
3. Some critics of an active role for government intervention in the economy—especially nationalization—portray this as a step toward a socialist economic and political dictatorship.
   a. To what extent does government intervention in the operation of the economy affect individual economic freedom?
   b. Do you agree that a growing role of the public sector in the economy and nationalization of public utilities would ultimately lead to a completely socialized economy?
   c. Do you think that public ownership and control of the means of production other than individual labor—i.e., socialism—is possible with democratic institutions?
4. The Lange-Lerner market socialist model has some important similarities with, and differences from, the perfectly competitive model developed in Chapters 10 and 11.
   a. Compare the Lange-Lerner and perfectly competitive models.
   b. What do you see as the major strengths and weaknesses of the two types of economy?
   c. What are the functions of the Central Planning Board (CPB) in the Lange-Lerner model?
5. Some critics of Soviet-type central economic planning assert that it can't maximize community economic welfare because consumer sovereignty is replaced by planners' preferences and planners' choices.
   a. Is this a valid *analytical* criticism of centralized economic planning?
   b. What are some of the practical barriers to maximizing community economic welfare through central planning?
   c. Could an active role for markets improve the efficiency of centralized planning? If not, why not? If so, in what ways?
6. Can you identify any long-term economic forces that could cause the world's economies to converge? Toward what type of economy do you see the world's economies converging, if any? What do you predict as the international economic and political consequences of the convergence of economic systems?

Index

Accelerator effect, 477, 579
Accounting cost, 138, 140, 189
Accounting profit, 139
Action lag, 506, 507, 572
Advertising, 109, 301–3
Aggregate demand, 386, 389, 399–93, 450–57, 612, 627
    fluctuations in, 465–84
    function, 441, 452, 460, 475
    as function of price level, 613–18
    and GNP, 465–83
    and inflation rate, 636–37
    management of, 654–56
    and output, 423–29
    and simple Keynesian model, 422, 440–45, 449–54
Aggregate demand-aggregate supply model, 388–92, 614–28
Aggregate demand (YD) curve, 389, 614–18, 62
    shifts in, 616–18
    slope of, 615–18
Aggregate output, 389–92, 400, 423, 425, 532–34, 626–28, 637, 643. *See also* Gross national product; Equilibrium GNP; National income
Aggregate price level, 389
Aggregate production function, 618–19
Aggregate supply, 386, 389–92
    determination in labor market, 620–24
    and employment, 621
    as a function of price level, 618–28
    and inflation rate, 634–36
    management of, income policies, 656–59
    management of, indexing, 656–62
    output and price level, 618–26, 627–28

Aggregate supply (YS) curve, 389, 623–28
    long-run, 645–47
    shape of, 623–24
    shifts in, 624–26
Agriculture, 200–5
Allocation of resources, 59, 236–37, 240, 248
American Economic Association, 580
Antitrust policy, 310–14
Appreciation of currency, 681
Arc approximation of slope, 18–19, 67, 75
Assets, 521–22, 542, 543
Automobile travel, demand for, 114–17
Autonomous consumption, 432–34
Autonomous expenditure, 427, 428
Autonomous expenditure multiplier, 458
Autonomous investment, 437, 440
Average fixed cost, 147
Average fixed cost curve, 147
Average product, 129–30
Average product curve, 129, 131
Average revenue, 184
Average variable cost, 148–49
Average variable cost curve, 148

Balance of international payments
    capital account, 683–84
    and exchange rates, 686–91
    international settlements account, 685–86
    merchandise account, 683, 696–97
Balance on merchandise account, 684
Balance of trade, 404, 684
Balance sheet, 542
Balanced budget, 492–93
Balanced-budget multiplier, 495–97
Banking system multiplier, 545–47

Barter exchange, 512–13
Becker, Gary, 376
Behavior, economic assumptions about, 4
Benchmark unemployment rate, 606
Benefit-cost analysis
   defining objectives, 253–54
   identifying benefits and costs, 254
   quantifying benefits and costs, 254–55
   ratios, 256–57
   usefulness of, 257–58
Black markets, 387
Blacks, economic problems of, 219, 339–40, 371–72, 605
Bretton Woods Agreement, 686, 691, 692
Budget, balanced. *See* Balanced budget
Budget deficit, 492
Budget, full employment, 493–95, 663
Budget surplus, 492
Built-in stabilizers, 480–83
Bureau of Labor Statistics, 370, 600
Business cycles, 466–69; political, 562

Cagan, Philip, 598
Capacity, 722–23, 724, 725–26, 739–40
Capital, 25, 125, 163–64
   formation, 726, 744–45
   human, 376–77, 726
   substitution for labor, 163–64
   supply, 40, 57, 221–22
Capital goods, 33
Capital-output ratio, 477
Cartel, 296–97, 326, 350, 712. *See also* Labor unions; Organization of Petroleum Exporting Countries
Central economic planning, 754–60
Ceteris paribus, 4
Chicago-school monetarism, 394
Christensen, Laurits R., 172
Circular flow, 399, 405, 423–30, 449
Civil Aeronautics Board, 316, 318–19
Clayton Antitrust Act, 310, 311
Collusion, 296, 298–99
Commercial banks, 541–47
Commodity export, 681; import, 680
Commodity money, 513–14, 547
Common sense, 6
Comparative advantage, 669–72, 673
   and international trade, 671
   and specialization, 669–71

Compensation, 405
Competition
   atomistic, 181, 209, 249
   impact of regulation on, 317
   and innovation, 304–5
   workable, 311
   See also Imperfect competition; Perfect competition
Complementary goods, 101, 113
Concentration, 314
   of market power, 285, 309, 312
   ratio, 255, 308, 356
Conglomerate merger, 309, 312
Constant-cost industries, 196–97
Constant returns, 132
Consumer durables, 470; nondurables, 403, 470
Consumer goods, 33
Consumer Price Index, 411–12, 594
Consumer sovereignty, 40, 41
Consumerism, 303–4
Consumption, 33–34, 429–37
   and instability, 470–74
   personal, 403
   ratchet effect in, 472
   and saving, 436–37
Consumption behavior, 433–34
Consumption expenditure flow, 400
Consumption function, 430, 432, 440; estimates of, 434–36
Convergence hypothesis, 760–62
Convertible currencies, 680
Corn Laws, 700, 717
Cost
   accounting vs. economic, 138, 139, 140
   analysis of, 138–51
   average, 147–48
   average fixed, 147
   of changing prices, 295
   economic, 138, 139, 140
   of economic growth, 728–29
   external social, 243–44, 414–15
   fixed, 142–43
   long-run analysis of, 155–75
   long-run average, 168
   long-run total, 167
   marginal, 143–45
   marginal factor, 211–12
   opportunity, 138, 139, 140, 672
   and output, 138–51
   short-run, changes in, 150–51

short-run, relationships, 149–50
social, 725
total, 143–44
of unemployment, 606–7
variable, 143
Cost-push inflation, 391
Council of Economic Advisors, 723
Credit crunch, 563–64
Crowding out, 574, 589–91
Crude quantity theory of money, 535
Currency
appreciation and depreciation of, 681–82
convertible, 680
demand for, 682
international, 680–83
overvaluation of, 683
supply of, 551, 682–83
undervaluation of, 683
Current account, 696–97
Curves, 17–20

Data lag, 572
Deadweight loss, 270
Decision lag, 506, 572
Decreasing-cost industries, 198–99
Deflationary gap, 444, 487, 491, 561
Demand
changes in, 43–45, 98–102
cross-elasticity of, 113–14
curve, 43, 62–63, 73, 96–98
excess, 50, 393
income elasticity of, 111–12
kinked demand curve, 193–95, 299–300
law of, 42–43
and price, 42–45
price elasticity of, 66–75, 79, 111–12
for resources, 210–17
schedule, 43
Demand curve, money, 615
Demand-deficiency unemployment, 444
Demand deposits, 517, 547
Demand management policies, 618
Demand-pull inflation, 390, 422, 492
Department of Commerce, 285
Dependent variable, 11–12
Depreciation, 142, 405, 407; of currency, 682
Diminishing returns, 131–33, 158, 214, 619; point of, 132
Dirty float, 691

Discount rate, 255, 555–56
Discretionary fiscal policies, 486–508, 663
and balanced budgets, 492
and government spending vs. taxes, 488–90
monetarist attitude toward, 578
and monetary policies, 572–76
multiplier effect in, 490–92
and national debt, 497–500
normative aspects of, 500–505
political problems, 505–6
Discretionary monetary policies, 486, 663
effectiveness of, 564–72
coordination with fiscal policies, 572–76
mechanics of, 560–64
monetarist approach to, 577–78
Discrimination
defined, 338–39
and disadvantaged, 340–41
and equal employment opportunity, 340–41, 378
in pay, 339, 340, 341–46
Diseconomies of scale, 165–66
Disequilibrium, 392
Disposable income, 409
Dissaving, 434
Distribution of income, 27, 208, 414, 434, 596, 736
functional, 227–28
marginal productivity theory of, 228
in perfect competition, 227–30
size, 228–29
wage differences, 229–30
Distribution of wealth, 27, 208, 228–29, 249, 736
Dividends, 405, 408
Double counting, 401
Duesenberry, James, 471
Dumping, 713–14
Duopoly, 292

Econometrics, 654
Economic analysis, 26
Economic behavior, 4
Economic development, Third World, 738–49. *See also* World poverty
Economic efficiency, 26, 27
Economic growth, 722–36
continuation of, 729–35
measure of, 723
and poverty, 736
sources of, 724–26

and stationary state, 719–31
Economic loss, 141–42
Economic models, 3–4
Economic profit, 139–40
Economic system, 36
   and economic welfare, 727–29
   in United States, 726–27
Economics
   classical, 392
   goal of, 3, 4–5
   theories of, 3, 4–7, 40
   three basic questions of, 26–28
Economies of scale, 165–66, 172
Effective maximum price, 53; minimum price, 55
Efficiency, 27, 28
   in allocation of resources, 236–37, 240
   economic, 161–63
   and economic profit, 267–68
   external social benefits of, 245
   impact of tariffs on, 700–703
   of information, 240–41
   marginal-cost pricing and, 236
   and minimizing cost of output, 235
   of perfect competition, 237–41
   in pricing and output, 238
   in production, 668, 669
   and optimum firm size and output, 235, 239
Elasticity coefficient, 66–67, 75; of resource demand, 216–17
Elasticity of demand
   cross, 111, 113–14
   income, 111–12
   price, 66–75
   and total revenue, 70–72
Elasticity of supply, 75–79
Empirical evidence, 5–6
Employment, natural level of, 643
Energy
   alternative sources of, 359–60
   cheap, 351–52
   conservation of, 713
   consumption of, U.S., 351
   crisis, 350
   depletion of reserves, 352
   economic concerns of, 350–63
   environmental effects of, 358–59
   nationalization of, 360–62
   price deregulation of, 354–58
   reducing demand for, 358
Equal pay, 340. *See also* Wage discrimination

Equation, solving, 12–13
Equation of exchange, 537–41
Equilibrium GNP, 450, 583
   and aggregate demand, 453–54
   balanced-budget multiplier effect, 496
   changes in, 454–58
   multiplier effect in, 458–62
   and supply of money, 432–58
Equilibrium, in imperfect competition, 288–91
Equilibrium output, 186–87, 264
Equilibrium price, 48, 264
   changes in, 51–53
   of resources, 210
Equity, 27–28, 248–49, 542, 543
Escalator clauses, 660
An Essay on the Principle of Population, 741
European Currency Unit, 692–93
European Economic Community (Common Market), 717–18
European Monetary System, 692–93
Exchange rates, 680–83
   determination of, 682
   floating, 690–91
   pegged, 686–90
Expansion path, 166–67
Expansionary fiscal policies, 487, 560, 617, 618
Expansionary monetary policies, 560–61
Expectations, 433, 474, 478–79, 570–71, 642–44, 648–49, 665, 734
Expenditure approach to GNP, 403–5
Expenditure flows, 399
Export policies
   restrictions, 710–12
   subsidies, 709–10
Exports, 683
External social benefits, 245; costs, 414–15
Externalities, 243; and government policy, 246–47, 315–16
Externally held public debt, 499

Factor payments, 400
Factor-payments approach to GNP, 403–4, 405–7
Factors of production, 399
Fair competition, 707
Fallacies
   of composition, 7, 387
   of division, 7, 387
   post hoc, 7
Farm price supports, 55

INDEX 769

Federal Aviation Agency, 316
Federal Maritime Commission, 316
Federal Open Market Committee, 550
Federal Reserve Act, 547
Federal Reserve System, 541, 547–56, 576–77
   control over money supply, 550–56
   structure of, 548–50
Federal Trade Commission, 311, 312
Federal Trade Commission Act, 310–11
Feldstein, Martin, 490
Fiat money, 515
Fine tuning, 654–56
Firm
   behavioral theories of, 122–23
   concentration in industry, 193
   cost of production in, 142–52
   defined, 39
   demand for resources of, 214–16
   entry into industry, 193–94
   equilibrium output of, 185–87
   expansion path of, 166–67
   flexibility of, 155, 156
   goal of, 40, 210–11
   in imperfect competition, 285–91
   marginalist theories of, 123–24
   in oligopoly, 292–300
   optimum output of, 169, 170, 235, 239
   optimum size of, 169, 170, 235, 239
   in participatory economy, 726
   price-taking, 180
   production function of, 126–27, 133–34
   production process in, 125–31
   profit of, 124, 187–88
   regulation of, 316–18
   returns of, 131–33
   revenue of, 184–85
   short-run supply curve of, 188–90
   shut-down point of, 188–90
   size decisions of, 165–66, 168–69
   size option of, 155, 164–71
   substitution option of, 155, 156–64
Fiscal policies, 394, 487, 572–76, 586–92, 653.
   See also Discretionary fiscal policy
Fixed cost, 142–43
Flat demand curve, 62–63
Flat supply curve, 62–63
Floating exchange rates, 590–91
Flows, 399
Food and Drug Administration, 302
Food production, Third World, 134–36. *See also*
Economic development, Third World;
   World poverty
Food stamps, 102–4
Foreign economic assistance, 746–47. *See also*
   World poverty
Fractional reserve banking, 541
Free silver movement, 539
Free trade, 700, 715–17, 718
Frictional unemployment, 602
Friedman, Milton, 380, 394, 472, 577, 578, 579, 580, 661
Full employment, 608, 724
   budget, 493–95, 663
   equilibrium, 392–93, 394
   and tariffs, 707
Full-employment GNP, 444, 724
Fully backed currency, 514
Functions, 12

Galbraith, John Kenneth, 304, 305, 392, 761
General equilibrium analysis, 56–59
General Theory of Employment, Interest, and Money, 393, 394, 431, 434, 507
Geographic immobility, 336; mobility, 377–78
George, Henry, 225
Gini index, 368
Government, economic role of, 308–24, 652–53, 748
   antitrust policies, 310–14
   demand management policies, 483–84
   discretionary fiscal policies, 486–508
   and instability, 479–80
   in Keynesian model, 448–49
   nationalization, 321–23
   political control, 748
   public regulation, 315–20
   spending, 448–49, 479–80, 488–92, 587
   workable competition, 311–14
Graphs, 14–21
Great Depression, 35, 455, 457, 564–65, 654
Great Society, 497, 508
Green Revolutions, 135–36
Greene, William H., 172
Gresham's Law, 514
Gross investment, 403, 477
Gross national product, 401–2
   basic measures of, 403–7
   composition of, 414
   fluctuations in, 465–84

gap, 607
and gross national cost, 414
growth indexes for, 418–20
as measure of social welfare, 413–14
nominal vs. real, 410
per capita, 413
Growth indexes, 418–20

Hansen, Alvin, 732
Hartwell, R. M., 366
Hayek, F. A., 321
Health and safety regulations, 315. *See also* Occupational Health and Safety Act
Heller, Walter, 507
Hicks, Sir John, 583
Hispanics, economic problems of, 371–72
Homer, Michigan, 224
Household
aggregate income of, 408
budgeting, 95, 96
defined, 39
demand curve of, 96–102
disposable income of, 409
expenditures of, 403
function in market, 40, 57
income constraint of, 90–92
indifference map of, 89–90
and market demand curves, 107–9
maximizing utility, 40, 84, 92–94, 101–2, 219
permanent income of, 408
personal income of, 408
preference of, 87–90
supply of labor, 620–21
Housing, demand for, 53–54, 110–11
Howard Johnson's, 261
Hume, David, 535
Hume's Fable, 535
Humphrey-Hawkins bill, 374, 488–89
Hyperinflation, 388, 598–600
Hypothesis, 11

Imperfect competition, in product market
defined, 284–85
demand curves of, 286–88
equilibrium in, 288–91
and industry, 289–91
oligopoly, 292–99
nonprice competition in, 300–305

Imperialism, 676–77, 740–41
Implicit Price Deflator, 412, 594
Imports, 684; quotas for, 700, 705
Income constraint, 90–92
Income distribution. *See* Distribution of income
Income elasticity of demand, 111–12
Income flow, 400
Income policies, 656, 659
Income subsidies, 102–4
Income transfers, 378–82
Increasing-cost industries, 197
Increasing returns, 131, 214
Independent variable, 11
Index numbers, 409
Indexing, 660
Independent variable, 11
Indicative planning, 760
Indifference analysis, 84, 87–104; and household budgeting, 95–96
Indifference curve, 88–89, 94, 97–98
Indifference map, 89–90, 219
Induced consumption, 431
Induced expenditure, 431
Induced investment, 474–77
Industrial system, 761
Industry
in imperfect competition, 285–91
infant, 708, 740, 748
in the long run, 193, 290–91
regulation of, 316–18
in the short run, 191–93, 289
Inferior goods, 98, 112
Inflation, 387–92
cost-push, 391
demand-management policies for, 391–92
demand-pull, 390
and paradox of thrift, 457–58
rate of, 634, 636
and restrictive monetary policies, 561
significance of, 594–600
and trade-off with unemployment, 639–47
and unemployment, 633–38, 652–65
YD-YS model, 389–92, 633–47
Inflationary gap, 444, 445, 487, 492
Information lags, 506
Innovation, 304–5
Input-output analysis, 758–60
Inside lag, 506
Interest, 221–22; net, 405
Interest rate, 486

equilibrium, 526–27
  indexing of, 661
  target of, 563
Intermediate goods, 401
Internal marginal rate of transformation, 671
Internally held public debt, 500
International currency, 680–83
International exchange, 680–93
International Monetary Fund, 692, 693
International monetary system, 692, 693
International settlements account, 683, 685–86, 698
International transactions, U.S., 696–98
Interstate Commerce Commission, 316, 317, 318
Investment, 403, 437–40, 726, 732–33, 742
  autonomous, 437, 440
  in economic development, 744–45
  induced, 437
  and instability, 474–79
  intended, 429
  investor expectations about, 474, 478–79
Invisible Hand, 233
IS curve, 583
IS-LM model, 583–85
Isocost-isoquant model, 155, 161–63
Isocost line, 159–61
Isoquant, 156–58
Isoquant map, 158

Jevons, William Stanley, 466–67
Job search unemployment, 603–4
Justice department, 312

Kahn, Alfred E., 318
Kemp-Roth bill, 489–90
Keynes, John Maynard, 155, 393, 394, 431, 432, 488, 565, 580
Keynesian economics, 393–94, 395, 507, 565, 612, 618
Keynesian model
  aggregate demand in, 440–45, 451–54
  changes in equilibrium income, 454–55
  equilibrium in, 449–54
  international sector in, 449
  multiplier effect in, 458–62
  and paradox of thrift, 457–58
Keynesians, 488, 559
Kinked demand curve, 293–95, 299–300

Korean War, economic impact of, 480

Labor, 25, 27, 125
  division of, 668
  effect of imports on, 706
  exploitation of, 278–79
  force, 600
  impact of monopsony on, 330–34
  marginal revenue product of, 620
  and minimum wage, 218–19
  and poverty, 374–76
  productivity of, 635
  supply of, 40, 57, 219, 220–21
Labor market
  discrimination in, 338–41
  equilibrium of, 620–21
  impact of monopoly on, 278–80
  imperfections in, 335–38
  monopsony in, 332–38
  union monopoly in, 326–32
Labor unions, 599
  bargaining power of 329, 330–32
  craft, 327–29
  function of, 327
  industrial, 329–30
  legal status of, 326–27
  weapons of, 331–32
Lags, 506, 507, 571–72
  fiscal policy, 184–85
  monetary policy, 249–50
Laissez-faire, 40–41, 395
Land, 25; supply of, 40, 57, 222–23
Land reform, 746
Lange-Lerner model, 752–54
Lange, Oskar, 752, 753
Law of demand, 42–43
Law of large numbers, 109
Leading economic indicators, 469
Leisure, 219, 220
Lerner, Abba P., 752
Liabilities, 542, 543
Life-cycle hypothesis, 473
Linear relationships, 17
Liquid assets, 521, 523
Liquidity, 521–23
  preference function, 524
  trap, 564–65
Living standards, 414, 436, 727–28
LM curve, 585

Loanable funds, 222, 573
Long-run average cost, 168
Long-run average cost curve, 168
Long-run equilibrium, 93–95
Long-run supply, 196–99; changes in, 199
Long-run supply cost curve, 197, 199
Long-run total cost, 167
Long-run total cost curve, 167
Lorenz curve, 367–68
Lucas, Robert E., 648
Luddites, 175

Macroeconomics, 386–87, 618, 662–63
   classical, 392–93
   Keynesian, 393–94
   monetarism, 394–95
   in next decade, 395–96
Malthus, Thomas Robert, 741, 742
Marginal analysis, 6
Marginal cost, 143–45
Marginal cost curve, 145
Marginal cost pricing, 202, 236
Marginal efficiency of investment, 438–40;
   curve, 615
Marginal factor cost, 211–12
Marginal product, 127–29
Marginal product curve, 131
Marginal propensity to consume, 430, 431–32
Marginal propensity to invest, 474
Marginal propensity to save, 436
Marginal rate of technical substitution, 89, 158, 237
Marginal revenue
   and elasticity of demand, 263–64
   in monopoly, 263
   in perfect competition, 184–85
   product, 178, 212–13
Marginal tax rate, 481
Marginal unit, 6
Market
   defined, 39
   and democracy, 40
   information, 181, 209, 240–41, 336
   period, 191
   power, 308–9
   regulation, 316–18
   structures, 39
Market demand
   changes in, 109–10

   cross-elasticity of, 113–14
   curves, 108–9
   income elasticity of, 11–12
   price elasticity of, 111
Market failure
   external social benefits of, 245
   external social costs of, 243–45
   and government policy, 246–47
   sources of, 241–43
Market socialism, 752
Marshall, Alfred, 366, 660
Marx, Karl, 249, 466, 729, 731
Marxian analysis, 731
Material balances planning, 757–58
Mathematical review, 11–23
Medicaid, 102, 379
Medicare, 379
MEI curve. *See* Marginal efficiency of investment
Mercantilism, 699
Merchandise account, 683, 696–97
Microeconomics, 386–87, 618, 653
Mill, John Stuart, 366, 376, 669, 733
Mine Safety and Health Administration, 317
Minimum wage, 55–56, 218–19
Mitchell, Wesley Clair, 468
Modern quantity theory of money, 535
Modigliani, Franco, 473, 489, 580
Monetarism, 394–95, 577–81
Monetarists, 395, 488, 559, 579
Monetary policies, 394, 572–76, 586–88, 654.
   See also Discretionary monetary policies
Money
   as an asset, 521–23
   basic functions of, 516
   commodity, 513–14
   and credit cards, 519–20
   defining aggregates of, 516
   demand for, 517, 520, 523–26
   demand curve for, 524
   fiat, 515
   and gold standard, 514–15
   history of, 512–16
   motives for holding, 520–21
   real balances, 520
   supply of, 517, 518, 532–56
Money markets, 526–28, 583–85; equilibrium
   in, 526–28, 539–41, 585–86
Money supply, 486
   changes in, 588
   and commercial banks, 541–47

and Federal Reserve, 547–56
   growth target of, 563
   quantity theory of, 534–41
Monopoly, 260–80, 284
   and competition, 266–70
   consumer surplus in, 268–70
   deadweight loss in, 270
   demand and revenue of, 261–64
   efficiency and economic profit of, 267–68
   equilibrium in, 264–66
   goal of, 264
   impact on labor market of, 278–80
   impact on social welfare, 270
   of labor unions, 326–27
   price discrimination in, 271–74
   price and marginal cost in, 266–67
   in telephone companies, 262
Monopoly, natural. *See* Natural monopoly
Monopsony
   and labor, 330–34
   and professional sports, 335
Multiplier effect, 368–71
   of government spending, taxes, 490–92
   in Keynesian model, 460–61
   size of, 461–62

National Bureau of Economic Research, 468
National debt, 497–500
National dividend, 753
National income, 407–8, 423
   flow of, 399–400
   measuring, 400–409
   See also Aggregate output; Gross national product
National income accounts, 403, 406–7
National Labor Relations (Wagner) Act, 326
National Monetary Commission, 547
National output, flow of, 399–400; measuring, 400–409
National product, 400. *See also* Aggregate output
National security, 708
Nationalization. *See* Energy; Government, economic role of
Natural Gas Act of 1978, 354–55
Natural monopoly, 313–14; in public utilities, 274–78
Natural unemployment rate, 664; hypothesis, 645
Near monies, 518

Negative income tax, 379–80
Negative returns, 132
Negative slope, 15–16
Negotiated order of withdrawal accounts, 290, 517
Net exports, 449; *See also* Balance of trade
Net investment, 477–78
Net national product, 407
Net taxes, 348
The New Industrial State, 761
Nominal GNP, 410, 412
Nonlinear relationships, 18
Normal goods, 98
Norris-LaGuardia Act, 326
NOW accounts. *See* Negotiated order of withdrawal accounts
Nuclear power, 359, 360, 713

Occupational Health and Safety Act, 317
Occupational immobility, 337
Office of Price Administration, 658
Okun, Arthur, 489, 662
Oligopoly, 284–85
   cartels, 296–97
   changing prices in, 295
   collusion in, 296–97, 298–99
   interdependence and decision making in, 292–93
   kinked demand curve in, 293–95, 299–300
Open market operations, 553–55
Opportunity cost, 30–31, 672
Organization of Petroleum Exporting Countries (OPEC), 297–98, 350, 655, 711–12, 712–13
Outside lag, 506, 507, 572

Paradox of thrift, 457–58
Partial equilibrium analysis, 56
Partially backed currency, 515
Participatory economy, 761–62
Peak, of economic cycle, 467, 468
Pegged exchange rates, 686–90
People's Republic of China, 751, 752, 761. *See also* Socialism
Per capita income, 413–14
Perfect competition, 264
   effectiveness of, 233–50
   and welfare, 248–49

Perfect competition, in product market, 180–205
  changes in long-run supply of, 149
  characteristics of, 180–81
  constant-cost industries in, 196–97
  decreasing-cost industries in, 198–99
  equilibrium price in, 182–84
  increasing-cost industries in, 197
  long-run equilibrium in, 193–99
  loss in, 187–90
  profit in, 185–88
  revenue in, 184–85
  short-run equilibrium in, 191–93
Perfect competition, in resource market, 208–31
  characteristics of, 109
  equilibrium price in, 210
  and income distribution, 227–30
  resource demand in, 210–19
  resource supply in, 219–27
Permanent income hypothesis, 472–73
Personal income, 408; disposable, 409
Phillips, A. W., 633, 639
Phillips curve, 638–41; long run, 645–47
Political business cycle, 562
Pollution, 243, 315–16, 359, 415, 728
Population, 741–44, 749
Portfolio of assets, 521–22
Positive slope, 15
Potential GNP, 606–7, 723
Poverty, 366–83
  absolute standards of, 370–71
  defined, 367–70
  demographics of, 371–73
  economic roots of, 373–74
  possible solutions for, 374–83
  and transfers of income, 378–82
  See also World poverty
Prices and pricing
  and aggregate demand, 614–18
  and aggregate supply, 618–26
  block, 273–74
  as common denominator, 401
  constant, 410
  controls, 53–56
  and demand, 42–45
  discrimination, 271–74
  elasticity, 66, 111
  impact of money supply on, 534
  in oil industry, 354–58
  leadership, 299
  and marginal cost, 266–67
  in market economy, 41–42
  market splitting, 271
  measuring change in, 409–12
  peak-load, 271–72
  predatory, 311
  and quantity, 43
  regulated, 353–54
  of resources, 210
  and supply, 45–48
  supports, 55, 202–5
  transfer, 337
  wars, in banking, 290
Price indexes, 410, 520–21
Price spiral, 647
Price takers, 180, 209; in stock market, 181–82
Principle of comparative advantage, 669
Principle of diminishing marginal utility, 86
Principle of diminishing returns, 131–33, 619
Principle of substitution, 162, 181
Principles of Political Economy and Taxation, 366, 717
Producer cooperatives, 746, 762
Product differentiation, 301, 302
Production
  and growth, 33–34
  limits on, 24–25
  long-run analysis of, 155–75
  possibilities, 28–34, 674
  in short-run, 122–36
  and technology, 31–32
Production function, 126, 158, 618; changes in, 133–34
Production-possibilities curve, 28–30, 31, 32
Production, Third World, 33–34, 134–36. *See also* Economic development, Third World; World poverty
Productive capacity, 26, 388, 392
Productivity, 30, 130, 726–27
Profit
  accounting, 139
  corporate, 405, 408
  economic, 139
  and economic cost, 138–42
  in Marxian analysis, 731
  monopoly, 265
  zero economic, 239
Profit maximization, 4–5, 40, 123, 125, 211, 288, 300
Progress and Poverty, 225
Proprietors' income, 405

Psychic costs, 141–42
Psychic income, 141–42
Public broadcasting, 242–43
Public goods, 241–42
Public ownership, 321–23, 752
Public regulation, 315–20
Public utilities, 274–78

Quantity, 43, 44, 45, 47–48
Quantity theory of money, 535

Rate of return, 521–22
Rational expectations theory, 648–49
Real balances, 520–21
Real GNP, 410–11, 412, 465, 723
Real income, 90, 101, 410
Recession, 467, 468
Recognition lag, 506, 572
Reference cycle, 468
Regulation. See Public regulation; Government, economic role of
Relative income hypothesis, 471–72
Rent
  controls, 53–55
  differential, 223
  economic, 222–24
  for special abilities, 225–26, 337–38
  as wages, 337–38, 376
Rental income, 405
Replacement investment, 477
Required reserves, 541, 542, 543
Reservation price, 225; wage, 603
Reserve ratio, 545, 551–53
Resource, 726–27, 739–40
  combination, 156–61
  demand, 210–16, 217
  environment as, 728
  equilibrium price of, 210
  homogeneous, 209
  limitations of, 25
  mobility, 209
  quantity and quality of, 724–25
  substitution, 158, 161–63, 181
  supply, 219–27, 724–25
Restrictive fiscal policies, 487, 561, 618
Returns to scale, 165–66
Revenue, 184–85, 261–64
Revenue Act of 1964, 717

Ricardo, David, 370, 669, 717
Risk, 521, 522, 523

Samuelson, Paul A., 507
Sargent, Thomas J., 648
Satisficing behavior, 123
Saving function, 436–37
Savings, under inflation, 597
Say's Law, 392
Scarcity, 24, 28, 41–42, 724
Schumacher, E. F., 735
Schumpeter, Joseph A., 304
Secular stagnation, 732–33
Settlements account. See International settlements account
Sherman Antitrust Act, 310, 311, 326
Short-run cost relationships, 149–50
Short-run costs, changes in, 150–51
Short-run equilibrium, 193
Short-run shut-down point, 189, 266
Short-run supply, 190–93
Short-run supply curve, 190, 191, 192
Shortages, 50; in housing, 53–54, 110–11
Simon, Herbert A., 123
Slope, 14–17, 62–66, 92
Small Is Beautiful, 735
Smith, Adam, 233, 565, 652, 668, 669, 717, 727
Social cost, 728
Social insurance, 408
Social overhead investment, 745–46
Socialism, 751–54
Soviet industrialization, 34
Soviet Union, 748, 751–53, 757, 760, 761
Special drawing rights, 688, 692
Specialization, 668–69, 748. See also Comparative advantage
Standard of living, expected, 434
Stationary state, 729–31
Statistical estimation, 21–23
Steep demand curve, 62–63
Steep supply curve, 62–63
Stein, Herbert, 490
Stigler, George, 299, 490
Stocks, 399
Store of value, money, 516
Structural unemployment, 604
Supply
  changes in, 47–48
  curve, 46–47, 62–63

elasticity of, 66, 75–79
excess, 50, 392–93
schedule, 45–46
Supply-management policies, 656
Supply shocks, 624
Surplus, 50–51
Sweezy, Paul, 293

Tariffs
and efficiency, 700–703
and gains from trade, 703–5
and import quotas, 700–705
and import restrictions, 705–8
Tax function, 481
Tax revolt, 488. *See also* Taxation, Proposition 13
Tax-based incomes policies (TIPs), 662
Taxes
on corporate profits, 405–6
direct, 409
excise, 78–79, 707–8
on farm land, 141
and government spending, 448–49, 488–92
indexing, 661
induced, 481–83
and inflation, 597–98
loopholes and reform, 504–5
net, 448–49
net tax flow, 449
on polluters, 246–48
progressive, 483, 502, 503, 597
proportional, 502
and Proposition 13, 490, 493, 505
regressive, 112–13, 502
sales, 112–13
and single tax movement, 225
tax cut of 1964, 507–8
value added, 402
and Vietnam surcharge, 497
Technical coefficients, 759
Technological change, 31–32, 304–5, 625, 725, 729, 731–32, 742
in agriculture, 32
and computer revolution, 173–74
impact on captial, 174
impact on labor, 172–73
impact on production, 171
social costs of, 174–75
Technology, 25, 28, 31–32, 125–26, 171, 725–26

Tennessee Valley Authority, 321
Three-Mile Island, 360, 713. *See also* Nuclear power
Time deposits, 517, 556
Tobin, James, 489
Tokyo Round of Multilateral Trade Negotiations, 715
Total cost, 142–44
Total cost curve, 144
Total expenditures, 70–71
Total product, 127–28
Total product curve, 127
Total revenue, 184
Trade, 668–77
between countries, 673–74
gains from, 672–73
impact of, 657–77
import restrictions on, 705–8
policy problems of, 699–718
terms of, 672–74
and economic welfare, 674–76
Transfer income, 225
Transfer payments, 404, 408, 448, 449
Transfer price, 337
Trough, of economic cycle, 468

Underdeveloped countries. *See* Economic development, Third World; World poverty
Underemployment, 605
Unemployment, 56, 367, 372–73, 387–92
benchmark rate for, 663–64
costs of, 606–7
demand-deficiency, 444
demand-management policies for, 391–92
and expansionary monetary policies, 560–61
and growth, 728
and inflation, 633–37, 652–65
kinds of, 602–6
measurement of, 600–601
and monetarism, 578–79
natural rate of, 643
rate of, 638
setting goals for lowering, 608
significance of, 600–606
and trade-off with inflation, 639–47
Unemployment insurance, 483
Unemployment target, 663–64
Unintended disinvestment, 425
Unintended investment, 424–25

Unions. *See* Labor unions
Unit of account and exchange, money as, 516
United Mine Workers, 163
Urban housing markets, 110–11
U.S. vs. The New York Great Atlantic & Pacific Tea Co., 313
Utility, 4, 40, 90
   cardinal, 85
   diminishing marginal, 86
   marginal, 85–86, 93–94, 96–97
   maximizing, 93–96
   ordinal, 85
   total, 85

Value added, 401
Value of the marginal product, 278
Vanek, Jaroslav, 762
Variable cost, 143
Variable cost curve, 143
Variables, 11–13
Velocity of money, 536–37
Vietnam War, economic impact of, 480, 497, 508, 563

Wage
   competitive, 328, 329
   differentials in labor market, 335–36
   discrimination, 339–40, 341–46
   impact of unions on, 327–30
   minimum, 55–56, 218–19
   rachet effect in, 330
   reservation, 603
   subsistance, 370
   transfer, 225
   under monopoly, 279–80
Wage bill, 334
Wage-price policies
   controls, 658–59
   guidelines, 657–58
   standards, 665
Wallace, Neil, 648
Wallich, Henry, 662
Wealth of Nations, 233, 652, 668, 717
Welfare, 381, 736; fraud, 382
Welfare, economic, 413–15, 674–77, 727–29, 736, 754–56
Women, economic problems of, 341–46, 371–72, 605
World poverty
   relief of, 744–49
   roots of, 739–44
World War II, aggregate demand during and after, 455–57
World War II, economic impact of, 35–36, 341, 435, 455–57, 654, 658, 689

Zero economic growth, 734–35
Zero population growth, 734